LORD LIVERPOOL
AND LIBERAL TORYISM

1820 to 1827

Robert, 2nd Earl of Liverpool

BY SIR THOMAS LAWRENCE

National Portrait Gallery

LORD LIVERPOOL
AND LIBERAL TORYISM
1820 to 1827

by

W. R. BROCK

Fellow of Selwyn College, Cambridge
Sometime Fellow of Trinity College, Cambridge

FRANK CASS & CO. LTD.

1967

Published by
FRANK CASS AND COMPANY LIMITED
67 Great Russell Street, London W.C.1
by arrangement with Cambridge University Press.

Thirlwall Prize Essay 1939

First edition   1941
Second edition   1967

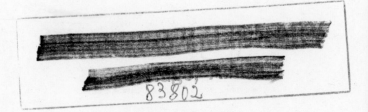

Printed in Great Britain by
Thomas Nelson (Printers) Ltd., London and Edinburgh

PREFACE TO THE SECOND EDITION

This book was written between 1937 and 1939, it was prepared for the press under the conditions described in the earlier preface, and it was published in a very small edition in the dark days of 1941. If I were to write the book again I should consult more sources and qualify some of my judgments, but it is difficult to retrace paths which were trod so many years ago and it may be best to leave the enthusiasm of youth undiluted by the caution of middle age. For these reasons I have left the original text untouched except to correct a number of minor errors. More than any other part of the book the scholarly apparatus suffered from the haste with which it was prepared, and I have taken this opportunity of making the footnotes more intelligible and of replacing a valueless bibliography by a list of sources.

Selwyn College, Cambridge.   W. R. BROCK
1965

CONTENTS

ILLUSTRATIONS

Robert, 2nd Earl of Liverpool, K.G.   *frontispiece*
  Painting by Sir Thomas Lawrence, P.R.A. (detail)

George Canning   *facing page* 230
  Painting by Sir Thomas Lawrence, P.R.A. (detail)

TO MY MOTHER

PREFACE TO THE FIRST EDITION

THIS ESSAY formed the Thirlwall Prize for 1939; but, in the months which followed the award of the prize, it has been rewritten and some new material has been added. I must hope that the reader will not bear too hardly upon any minor errata which he may notice, for the final stages of rewriting were carried out during the anxieties of autumn 1939, the revision has been unduly hurried owing to the imminence of military service, and the proofs have been read in a barrack room. I would not, however, claim any indulgence for the views expressed, and I hope sincerely that they may at least occasion some thought upon a period of English history which has not always been considered with sympathy and understanding, and that, in particular, they may rouse some interest in a Prime Minister who, though his talents were not brilliant, has suffered an undeserved eclipse, and who had a considerable though not an ostentatious influence upon the course of nineteenth-century English history.

I should like to express my thanks to Professor G. M. Trevelyan, Mr J. R. M. Butler, and Mr G. Kitson Clark for their advice and encouragement, and my profound regret that the illness and death of Professor H. W. V. Temperley prevented me from gaining the full benefit of his advice. Mr K. Scott of St John's College has given me valuable assistance in reading the proofs and in verifying some references.

W. R. BROCK

1941

CHAPTER I

INTRODUCTION. THE EARLY CAREER OF LORD LIVERPOOL

IF there is a dark age in nineteenth-century England it is the period of five years following the battle of Waterloo. It was a period dominated by the fears of the upper classes and the discontents of the working classes; it was a time in which national glory had grown stale, in which the propertied classes were conscious of fighting a rearguard action, and in which a bitter populace lacking education and understanding of political affairs was ready to follow any inspiring leader. In retrospect it may be seen that the working class had not the sustained vigour to make a revolution, and that the upper classes were not brutal tyrants. Yet it remains the one period during the nineteenth century in which a revolution could have taken place, and the significant and sinister figure is that of "Orator" Hunt, a born demagogue and a born autocrat. With a little more luck, with a little more cleverness, and with a phalanx of devoted and desperate followers, Hunt might have been the leader of the English revolution.

Very different is the change which did take place. With the return of prosperity there was also a change in the whole tone of Government; within a few years the very suspicion of revolution had vanished, and the broad outlines of Victorian England had been sketched by a Government which has some claim to be called the first of the great improving ministries of the nineteenth century and one of the mainsprings of later political thought and action. Approbation took the place of execration, ministers who had gone in fear of their lives found themselves objects of national respect, and the Prime Minister of a Government which had been accused of truckling to continental despots was threatening to "play the whole game of liberal institutions". Parliament was still unreformed, the Catholics still went under galling and outworn restrictions, but, in its foreign and economic policy, the Government was winning the approval of thinking men and has retained the admiration of posterity. This is the period which may be called that of Liberal Toryism. The name is artificial—that is to say it is not found in the mouths of contemporaries—but because the High Tories accused the Government of "liberalism", then a suspect and dangerous thing, because the "liberals" who dominated the Cabinet felt acutely their estrangement from the "ultras", and because the meaning of the phrase is readily intelligible to a later age, it is not inappropriate to speak of "Liberal Toryism".

Liberal Toryism is usually associated with the name of Canning, and Canning certainly struck the public eye more than any other minister. Yet Canning was primarily a Foreign Secretary, he stuck fairly closely to his own department, and Liberal Toryism must mean a good deal more than Canning's foreign policy. Canning's peculiar contribution was his use of public opinion as a political weapon; but in that age politicians could not live by public opinion alone, and Canning himself could not have remained in power a day had he not had the unswerving support of the Prime Minister, Lord Liverpool. The view taken in the following pages is that Liverpool as much as Canning was responsible for the experiment of Liberal Toryism. Within the Cabinet Liverpool was the mainstay of "liberal" opinion, he was perhaps the only man who could persuade the Tory party as a whole to sanction such opinions, and he was certainly the only man who could hold together the Cabinet between 1822 and 1827.

A modern estimate of Liverpool's services as a statesman is long overdue, and this work deals only with his work as Prime Minister during the last few years of his Government. Nevertheless, there is some excuse for this limited treatment in that Liverpool's main claim upon the gratitude of posterity must derive from these last few years. Before 1820 Liverpool had fulfilled useful and important duties, but they were duties which would not earn him more praise than many another administrative statesman; he had held the premiership under conditions which any moderately capable politician could have fulfilled; after 1820 he performed services which no one else, at that time, could perform. Before 1820 the Tory Government had been the only possible Government, after 1820 Liverpool alone made possible the Government he desired.

Lord Liverpool was born, as Robert Banks Jenkinson, on 6 June 1770. His life thus covered the whole period of the Tory ascendancy; his earliest memories were those of Lord North and the American war; he had grown to maturity and entered public life under the mighty shadow of Pitt; his own administration carried England to the eve of Catholic Emancipation, Parliamentary Reform, and the breaking of the old Tory party. His father was Charles Jenkinson, sometime the private secretary of Bute, who rose to sinister eminence as the leader of the "King's Friends", acquired respectable fame as Pitt's President of the Board of Trade, became a peer and lived to write an authoritative work upon the currency. The spiritual descendant of Charles Jenkinson is the modern civil servant, and his son, though fifteen years Prime Minister, has often more in common with the permanent head of a department than with a modern democratic statesman.

From the first Charles Jenkinson destined his son for high political office, and to his father the son's character owed much. Years afterwards it was said of him that "he always quotes his father"[1], and it seemed indeed that the lives of father and son had blended together to form an unrivalled experience of fifty years in high politics. The early years of his life were completely dominated by his father. If Liverpool lacked imagination, he lost it following his father's precepts; if he compensated for this deficiency by perseverance and industry, it was his father who instilled in him these virtues. Young Jenkinson was sent to Charterhouse, and a letter written to him in 1784 survives.[2] It deserves quotation, for, in the paragon which Charles Jenkinson wished his son to be, may be seen the lineaments of the future Prime Minister: "You should not be satisfied in doing your exercises just so as to pass without censure, but always aim at perfection; and be assured that in doing so you will by degrees approach to it. I hope also you will

1 Add. MSS. 38743, f. 266, Arbuthnot to Huskisson.
2 Yonge, *Life of Lord Liverpool*, i, 7. (Hereafter cited as 'Yonge').

avail yourself of every leisure moment to apply yourself to algebra and the mathematics: you will thereby attain not only a knowledge of those sciences, but by an early acquaintance with them you will acquire a habit of reasoning closely and correctly on every subject, which will on all occasions be of infinite use to you. The hours which are not employed in the manner before mentioned you will give to the reading of history and books of criticism, and here the knowledge you have of the French language will furnish you with many excellent books." And, lest the fourteen-year-old schoolboy should become frivolous even in his reading, his father adds: "I would wish you for the present not to read any novels, as they will only waste your time, which you will find not more than sufficient for the pursuit of more useful and important studies." By the time he reached Oxford in 1786, Jenkinson was an exceptionally well-educated young man; it is in fact surprising to find that he retained any youthful spirits at all. The impression he made at Christ Church is told by one with whom he was intimate:[1] "When at the University he was not only a first-rate scholar, but he had confessedly acquired a greater share of general knowledge than perhaps any undergraduate of that day. He was an excellent historian and his attention had been directed so early by his father to the contending interests of the European nations, that intricate political questions were already familiar to his mind."

It is interesting to contrast the impressions which he made at this age with those made in the last fifteen years of

[1] J. F. Newton, *Early Days of the Right Honble George Canning*, London, 1828.

his life. As a Prime Minister he is praised for kindness, for amiability, for fairness, and for consideration; as an undergraduate the impression is that of a pushful and self-important young man. Lady Stafford, who saw him in his father's house during 1787, found him "well educated, well informed, and sensible", but she found him too ready, in the presence of Pitt and Thurlow, to put forward his own ideas rather than attending to theirs.[1] His tutor also seems to have found him too opinionative,[2] and at all times he was ready to put his ideas into a flood of language. He himself realised this fault: "Though I had contracted a habit of disputing in company during the first two or three terms I was here, I have been long since convinced of the bad effects arising from that habit, and I have prevented these bad effects in the most particular manner by avoiding as much as possible all mixed companies and living as much as possible with a few particular people."[3] Even so Leveson Gower found his "excessive importance" had become "very disgusting", spoke slightingly of his abilities, but thought that "a wonderful fluency of words and no share of mauvaise honte may cause his making some figure in the House of Commons".[4]

But there was also something in Liverpool's character which prevented him from becoming a mere prig. A Christ Church contemporary speaks of the "benignity of his personal intercourse", and remarks that his "temper was extremely conciliatory".[5] There was also a habitual dis-

1 Leveson Gower, *Private Correspondence of Lord Granville*, 1, 8.
2 Yonge, 1, 9: "My tutor has frequently thought that I have been too much run away with by general ideas."   3 *Ibid.*
4 Leveson Gower, 1, 35.   5 Newton, *op. cit.*

regard of his own dignity which contrasted strangely with his self-conscious importance. His father had told him while at school that he should pay proper attention to his person, for "every failing in this respect creates disgust or exposes a man to ridicule in such a manner as to defeat the advantages which he could otherwise derive from his parts or learning".[1] The fault, if it can be called a fault, remained with him through life, and years afterwards Mme Lieven found him "the oddest figure imaginable, full of the most amusing blunders". And when he was a rising star in the political horizon, one who had known him well said: "It is very odd that in all the time I have known him I never observed what a very plain and awkward man he is."[2] This did perhaps lose him some of the respect he might have enjoyed, and Leveson Gower, from whose bitter remarks jealousy was not absent, said that those who had known him well at Oxford "cannot certainly look up to him with any great admiration".[3] But it was this combination of amiability and gaucherie which won him the friendship of George Canning, whom he met for the first time at Oxford.

Canning could well appreciate the solid qualities of Jenkinson, and he looked upon him as a future rival. Both belonged to a select "speaking society", where "looking forward to some distant period when we might be ranged against one another on a larger field, we were perhaps neither of us without the vanity of wishing to obtain an early ascendancy over the other".[4] But the pleasant temper of both converted the possible rivalry into a close, though

1 Yonge, I, 7.   2 Leveson Gower, I, 345.   3 Ibid. I, 217.
4 Newton, op. cit., quoting a letter received later from Canning.

not always an easy, friendship. Canning was always ready
to exploit his brilliant and slightly malicious wit, Jenkinson was always apt to turn suddenly from a genial companion to an offended and pompous young man, and, in the
words of the Dean of Christ Church, they were "quarrelling
and making it up all day long".[1] Still they made it up and
the intimacy endured even though its most frequent incidents were the injuries of one at the apparent unkindness of
the other. The irritation which both felt at times was born
of affection, and Jenkinson retained a sincere admiration
for Canning. In the future there was to be a serious
estrangement which was not completely healed for nine
years, but the permanent result of this friendship was seen
in 1821 and after, when Liverpool looked to Canning,
though his fellow-Tories would gladly have seen Canning
consigned to the outer darkness.

Oxford was followed by foreign travel. Here perhaps the
rigour of his education was relaxed, though even the
beauties of Italy did not prevent him from studying
Blackstone. But naturally it was the Roman poets, and
Virgil above all, who commanded attention in such a place.
"I have travelled with Aeneas through the grotto of the
Sybill and the lake of Avernus; I have passed with him from
Tartarus to Cocytus and from Cocytus to Elysium. I have
drunk Falernian wine in the villa of Hortensius, contemplating from the same spot the Temple of Venus, the
houses of Cicero and Caesar, and the reputed (though
falsely so) tomb of Agrippina. I have visited the baths of
Marius and the famous ruin of the temple of Jupiter.

1 Dorothy Marshall, *The Rise of George Canning*, p. 18.

Virgil has been my constant companion; I have found him not inferior in geography to poetry, and I shall in a few days pay my homage at the tomb of the divine poet, remembering with a grateful heart the luxurious moments his verses have so lately afforded me."[1] Did Liverpool turn in later years from affairs of state to the "divine poet"? Perhaps he did, but the classics were not for him the constant solace that they were for Canning or for Gladstone. He who has had to turn the long folios of Liverpool's official correspondence may also wish that he had retained the vigorous style of this early letter, but the parenthetic "though falsely so" is symptomatic of the cautious phrasing which was to rob his writing of all force and character.

In the summer of 1789 his travels led him to Paris, and there he stood as a spectator at the first scene of the Revolutionary Epic, the taking of the Bastille. It was not an experience which inspired him with any respect for the wisdom of the mob. In the years which followed the war it was not without importance that the Prime Minister had seen the infuriated men and women marching upon the Bastille.

In 1790, while still under age, he was returned for the borough of Appleby by Sir John Lowther. But it was another year before his voice was heard at Westminster. When the time came for him to speak it was not necessary for him to force his way forward, for he was chosen by Pitt to defend the Government against a vote of censure on what was known as the Russian armament question. Russia had embarked upon war with Turkey, and Pitt had announced

1 Yonge, I, 12.

an increase in the navy with the avowed object of opposing Russia if necessary. Jenkinson drew attention to the designs of Russia, which threatened not only the neighbouring states but the whole balance of power in Europe; he made a long and careful examination of the situation, and his conclusion was voiced in the fine phrase, "Great Britain is constitutionally the foe of all wars of ambition and wanton aggression, and a stable peace is equally her interest and her inclination". The speech was more successful than its author could possibly have hoped. "I cannot resist", wrote Dundas to Charles Jenkinson, "the impulse I find to inform you that your son has just made one of the finest speeches I have ever heard. Mr Pitt thinks exactly as I do with regard to it." And Pitt praised it publicly as "not only a more able first speech than had ever been heard from a young member, but one so full of philosophy and science, strong and perspicuous language, and sound and convincing arguments, that it would have done credit to the most practised debater and most experienced statesman that ever existed". It cannot be said that Liverpool fulfilled entirely the promise of this maiden speech, but it is usually forgotten that he remained a Parliamentary speaker of a very high order. In later years, in the House of Lords, he was equal to the task of bearing almost the full burden of debate upon the Government side. As a speaker Wellington placed him alone with Pitt, and, even if it be granted that Wellington probably shut his ears when Canning spoke, it is still high praise from one whose Parliamentary experience extended over so many years.

In the years which followed, Jenkinson did not take a

frequent part in debate, but when he did speak it was upon
important questions. His reputation grew steadily and was
confirmed in 1793 by a seat at the India Board. In 1796 he
obtained election for Rye, so freeing himself of a patron
and establishing a connection with the Cinque Ports which
was to last until his death. His frequent absences from
Parliament can be accounted for by two things: he was a
conscientious colonel of the Kentish Militia, and he had
become a lover. The Kentish Militia was employed upon
garrison duty, and was stationed for a considerable time in
Scotland, where, he told his father, "the style of living is
rather gross, though very hospitable. The servants are few,
and very dirty; but there is a great quantity of meat put
upon the table, and after dinner the bottle passes rather
quicker than I like." The story of his courtship is told in
Dorothy Marshall's *Rise of George Canning*, and in Canning's own words.[1] The object of his choice was Lady
Louisa Hervey, daughter of the Earl of Bristol, and the affair
went smoothly to the declaration and acceptance, but in
obtaining the consent of the two fathers unexpected hazards
arose. The Earl of Bristol acquiesced and promised a dowry
of £10,000, but Hawkesbury[2] raised difficulties. He thought
the match "imprudent and ineligible in many respects",
and would have his son unmarried until he was thirty
unless "he should marry a fortune indeed"; the Herveys
were Whigs and a young Tory would not profit by marrying
one. Canning busied himself on Jenkinson's behalf, but it
was Jenkinson himself who discovered the right form of

1 Pp. 135 ff.
2 Charles Jenkinson had become Lord Hawkesbury in 1786.

pressure. Hawkesbury valued his son's career before all
things, and Jenkinson now gave out that he was so broken
in spirit that he must absent himself from Parliament.
Before this threat Hawkesbury gave way, consent was given,
and the marriage took place on 17 March 1794 ("Jenkinson in such spirits and such fidgetts that it was quite un-
comfortable to sit near him"). In spite of the help which he
had given, Canning found the marriage not entirely to his
liking; Lady Louisa was something of a prude, she imposed upon the buoyant spirits of Canning an uncom-
fortable restraint, and Jenkinson's house ceased to be a
centre of Canningite society. It is from the time of his
marriage that the warmth of Jenkinson's intimacy with
Canning began to cool. Jenkinson, however, was extremely
happy with his wife, she suited exactly that solemn side of
his character which Canning was so fond of ridiculing, and
she was an admirable if not a very interesting young
woman.

In 1796 two events occurred to advance the fortunes of
the Jenkinson family. Hawkesbury became Earl of Liverpool, Jenkinson assuming the courtesy title of Hawkesbury; and the latter was made Master of the Mint. He was
now definitely on the road to Cabinet office, occupying one
of the chief subordinate offices; but his further promotion
might have been delayed for some years. He was young
and could afford to wait; his seniors were but in middle age
and were not likely to move. But all prospects were put
out of joint, and Hawkesbury's were immensely improved,
when Pitt resigned over the Catholic question. The Jenkin-
sons had both been opponents of the Catholic claims, and

both were prepared to serve under Addington, who, faced with a dearth of experienced ministers, made Hawkesbury, just thirty years of age, his Foreign Secretary.

It is not here intended to refer more than briefly to the twelve years which now elapsed before Liverpool became Prime Minister. As Foreign Secretary under Addington it was his duty to negotiate the Peace of Amiens, and his career at this time belongs to the controversies which surround that peace. By his period as Foreign Secretary it cannot be said that he added greatly to his reputation, but he did not, on the other hand, lose, and, by occupying such an important position, he established a claim which would entitle him to consideration in any future Government. Thus, when Pitt succeeded Addington, he became Home Secretary; there was perhaps a slight lessening of the esteem in which he was held, but there was nothing tangible, nothing which would retard seriously his future career. In addition, he had, under Addington, taken up that position which he was to hold until his retirement, Tory leader in the House of Lords.[1] Addington, weak in both Houses, had found himself especially weak in the Lords where no speaker of merit could oppose the Whigs, Grenvilles, and Pittites; he had, then, raised Hawkesbury to the House of Lords, and Pitt had continued him as Government leader in that House.

It was during Pitt's second ministry that there occurred a serious quarrel between Hawkesbury and Canning; and Canning, with the bitter frankness of an injured friend,

[1] Portland was Prime Minister over Liverpool, but he is said never to have spoken in the House of Lords.

told Pitt that Hawkesbury "is not either a Ninny or a great and able man. He has useful powers of mind, great industry, and much information." Pitt was more kind: "With his information...and the habits of reflection which he has acquired, he is by no means a contemptible adviser"; he confessed that he could not do without him in the Lords; but he added that he was not a man "to whose decisions, singly, I would commit a great question of policy".[1] These were not perhaps the warmest of recommendations for a man who was to take up the burden of Pitt, and under whom Canning was to serve for eleven years. But to compensate for this he had grown into great favour with the King who, on the death of Pitt, offered him the premiership. To a man of thirty-five it was a tempting bait; to refuse might mean long years of waiting, until he was too old to enjoy the great heritage, or until some other young man had risen in the political firmament. It says much for the calm judgment of Hawkesbury that he read the omens aright—and the omens said that no man save Pitt could succeed where Pitt had almost failed—that he did refuse, and that he advised the King to waive his objection to Fox. This advice the King followed, and the ministry of All Talents was formed, but not before he had forced Hawkesbury to accept another legacy of Pitt, the splendid and profitable Lord Wardenship of the Cinque Ports. This ensured him a sufficient income until his death and gave him a pleasant house at Walmer Castle.

Hawkesbury led the Opposition to the Talents, and, upon their fall, the King hoped once more that he would

1 Marshall, *op. cit.*, p. 290.

take the Treasury. But it had been decided previously that the best way of reconciling the factions and jealousies within the Tory party was to entrust the lead to the Duke of Portland, who had not the ability to raise a faction, and whose part in politics had, of late years, been too obscure to arouse any jealousies. Under Portland the Government was virtually that of a committee, with Liverpool, Canning, Castlereagh, and Spencer Perceval as its members. It was a system which could not endure for long, particularly when one of the members was possessed of Canning's restless ambition. The quarrel between Canning and Castlereagh brought about the fall of Portland and placed the premiership once more within Liverpool's reach. Portland had become deeply involved in the quarrel; he had promised Canning that Castlereagh should be replaced by Wellesley, but he had concealed this promise from most of his colleagues. At the beginning of September Canning called upon Portland to fulfil his promise, and it was not Portland's honour alone which was involved, for Portland had backed his promise with a promise which he had— "most unfairly", says Liverpool—extracted from the King. With Canning's demand the whole transaction came to light and the rest of the Cabinet objected to a step upon which they had not been consulted and of which they did not approve. A complete dissolution of the Government seemed imminent, and Liverpool decided that the best course would be to hasten the dissolution in such a way as to relieve them of some of their difficulties. "The promise, however, was absolute," he wrote, "and, having been made in the King's name, must necessarily be fulfilled. The state of the Duke of Portland's health had become more critical every day; and it occurred to me that the best means of obviating the various difficulties with which we were surrounded, was by persuading the Duke of Portland to retire, and by making, in consequence, an entire new arrangement of the administration."[1] In a new administration there would be an initial difficulty to be overcome in the House of Commons: the lead would be disputed between Canning and Perceval. Canning had held the key position of Foreign Secretary and he had a longer administrative experience than Perceval, but the latter had been "entrusted with the general direction of business in the House of Commons" and was not prepared to serve under Canning. Perceval proposed a sensible solution: that both should serve under a peer. Liverpool was implied though not mentioned by name, but Canning replied that he would resign if Portland resigned, that the Prime Minister must be in the Commons, that he was willing to serve as Premier, but in no other situation. When this deadlock became apparent Liverpool and Perceval obtained the King's permission to negotiate with Grey and Grenville.

What this offer to the Whigs might have been is not known, for the mere proposal to negotiate was met by Grey with an instantaneous refusal. The Whigs were, in the severe words of their most recent historian,[2] "well content to leave Perceval to flounder on in office—to allow him to carry on the Government of the country at a very critical moment of the war, with the assistance of such incompetents as Ryder, Westmorland, and Mulgrave—and to

1 Yonge, 1, 287.   2 Michael Roberts, *The Whig Party*, 1807–12.

supplement purely destructive criticism by a stiff intracta-
bility in negotiation". The duel between Canning and
Castlereagh put both out of the question so far as office was
concerned, and Perceval was left to face the future with only
a sad rump of the great Pitt party to support him.

Nevertheless, this ministry endured for three troubled
years; it was able to carry on the war, to resist a strong
Parliamentary Opposition, and to stop the rot which seemed
to be eating its way into the Tory party. It cannot be said
that it was a good Government, but it was a useful one and
might have led on to greater things. It refused the Bullion
Report, it imposed the Orders in Council which caused
great domestic distress and brought the United States into
the war, and the irritation with which the Foreign Secretary, Wellesley, regarded the pedestrian methods of his
colleagues was not entirely unwarranted. But, at this time,
vigorous government was almost a fair substitute for good
government; and vigorous government Perceval supplied.
He was a lawyer and a High Tory, which was not perhaps a
combination likely to recommend him for popularity, but
he was also a man of spirit and determination, and, in a
House of Commons which saw little spirit or determination
on either front bench, he commanded respect and support.
"Perceval's character", Liverpool told Wellington, "is
completely established in the House of Commons; he has
acquired an authority there beyond any minister within my
recollection except Mr Pitt."[1] Had the Tories found, in
fact, another Pitt, and would Perceval rise phoenix-like
from the ruins of 1809 as the great man had risen from the

1 Yonge, I, 372.

ruins of Empire and Coalition? Prophecies and prognostications were cut short with the life of their subject, for, on 11 May 1812, Perceval was shot dead in the lobby of the House of Commons by the lunatic Bellingham.

The confused period of negotiation which followed has been recently examined with accuracy and detail;[1] this fact and the scope of the present work make unnecessary more than a brief résumé. The circumstances of the time seemed to point directly to the formation of a "mixed administration", and the Regent would probably have welcomed such a result provided that the formula "Tory bloc plus independent supporters" could be maintained, and that he would not have to accept a predominantly Whig administration. The Prince had thrown over the friends of his youth too recently to allow one to approach the other without bitterness; he was convinced that Whig rule would mean ruin to the country, the Whigs were convinced that they could not accept office save on their own terms and as a single united party. He first hoped that the remaining Tory ministers would be able to carry on, and he employed Eldon to discover their sentiments. The consensus of opinion was that the prospects of the Government as it stood were doubtful but not desperate "if the administration is known to possess the entire confidence of the Prince Regent". Consequently the ministers chose Liverpool as their head, and he was entrusted with the Government by the Prince Regent.

Liverpool had now entered upon the situation which he was to hold for nearly fifteen years; he had been placed in

1 Michael Roberts, *op. cit.*, pp. 382–405.

that position by the unanimous vote of his colleagues—in
itself something of a novelty—and with the approval of the
Prince. But it seemed at first that his premiership would
be short and inglorious. Liverpool sought the support
of Canning and Wellesley; he offered them good offices and
upon the Catholic question a compromise—rendered necessary even without their participation by the number of
Catholic sympathisers among the ministerial Tories—that
this question should remain "open", all Government supporters being free to speak and to vote upon it as they
wished. There was certainly considerable difference between leaving the question to its fate in a House of Commons where anti-Catholics could command a small
majority, and making it a Government measure and placing
all the resources of ministerial management at the service
of the "Catholics"; and this compromise did not satisfy
Canning and Wellesley. Canning hinted that a larger
arrangement was necessary, entertained "a most anxious
hope that His Royal Highness would send for Lord
Moira",[1] and thought that Wellesley ought "to receive
authority to make some specific proposal to the Opposition
which might bring over to us some of the best of that
body".[2] The fact was that Canning would not come in as
an ally to an established Government, and he required a
Government in which he and his friends would have the
central and controlling interest. On these vague grounds
the negotiation was broken off, and Liverpool determined
to stand alone; but optimism was not enough and on 21 May
Stuart Wortley carried a motion in the House of Commons

1 *Letters of George IV*. I. 75. C. Arbuthnot to Colonel McMahon (18
May 1812).   2 *Ibid.*

praying the Regent to form an efficient administration. Wortley was a Tory, an admirer of Perceval, and member for Yorkshire; a number of his supporters upon this motion were country gentlemen of the same type. The significance of the vote of 21 May was that it was not a party victory, and so far as the country could speak it had spoken against the continuance of the weak Tory ministry. The resignation of the ministers followed as a matter of course, but they continued with their departmental business until successors could be found.

The Prince had now to fulfil his constitutional function of finding a Government capable of governing. It is possible to blame him for not applying directly to the Whigs, but it is also fair to remember that the Whigs could not command a majority in the Commons, that only the most unscrupulous use of patronage could have procured them a majority from the electorate, and that the chief objection to them was not their ideas of reform but their defeatist attitude to the war. There were, on the other hand, influential members of both Houses attached to neither party, and it was to Wellesley that the Prince now entrusted the formation of a "mixed administration". Here an unexpected obstacle arose: Wellesley had just sanctioned the publication of an explanation of his resignation in February, which reflected bitterly upon Perceval; the colleagues of the late minister now refused, in duty bound, to serve under Wellesley. Wellesley then hoped to coalesce with the Whigs, but the Prince urged the ministers to reconsider their decision. They replied adhering to their refusal, and from the explanations which the Prince demanded there emerges an interesting fact. The majority of the ministers were in favour of negotiation with Wellesley and Canning, but they concurred with the minority, headed by Liverpool, in order not to split the party. There are hints that Liverpool himself felt that his withdrawal from politics for a few months—until the Catholic question had passed—would be the best solution of everybody's problem; but his colleagues stood by him, and thus early the position of Liverpool was made the cardinal point in the composition of a Tory ministry.

Wellesley now pressed to be allowed to make an approach to the Whigs, and at last, on 1 June, the Regent gave him full powers and he immediately made the Whigs an offer. They were to have four or five places in a cabinet of twelve or thirteen; Canning, Moira, Erskine, and Wellesley himself would fill four more places; and the remaining four might be filled from among the old ministers. The Whigs would secure the passage of Catholic Emancipation, their favourite measure, and, with two sympathisers in Erskine and Moira, they would be able to dominate the Cabinet. But the Whigs refused Wellesley's offer outright: they would come in as a party and in sole control, or they would not come in at all; it was to the principle of disunion and jealousy that they objected; to the supposed balance of contending interests in a Cabinet so measured out by preliminary stipulation. The Whigs had been asked to come forward as individuals and to unlearn the lessons of party government; their refusal may be justified in principle but it was impolitic in practice.

Wellesley had failed, and the Prince now turned to his

friend Moira who might make a ministry from the moderate men of all parties. Moira was convinced that nothing could be expected from the Whigs, but in order "to take from them the last shadow of excuse which they might attempt in saying that I had made no overture to them", he made them an offer. He sought an interview with Grey and Grenville, at which both sought a convenient excuse for the termination of the negotiations. The excuse was found in Moira's attitude to the household officers, for he refused to allow the Whigs to exercise their right of dismissing these officers, insisting, not that it was beyond their powers, but that such an action would constitute an insulting and unnecessary triumph at the Prince's expense. On the refusal of the Whigs, Moira began to plan a ministry with the Canningites. By 7 June he had a Cabinet outlined and had obtained a promise of support from Liverpool; at this seemingly favourable juncture he suddenly resigned his commission, and Liverpool succeeded quietly to that situation which he had seemed to lose irretrievably on 21 May.

Moira's sudden relinquishment of his chances remains something of a mystery. To his cousin, Sir Charles Hastings, he explained that it was necessary to have a ministry ready immediately as the Treasury was almost empty, that Erskine and the Duke of Norfolk had suddenly drawn back, that this would have meant bringing in two more of the old ministers, and that this in turn would have "appeared to compromise my principles for the sake of being at the head of a ministry". It is also probable that the Prince played upon Moira's doubts and fears, and persuaded him to withdraw in favour of Liverpool. Moira was certainly de-

voted to the Prince; he believed that he "had just done the
good of proving that the Prince has bent himself fairly and
frankly to the wishes of the Commons"; and a little later he
was complaining that "my attachment to the Prince has
barred the field of fame against me". It seems, moreover,
that Moira had some arrangement with the ministers before
he withdrew. In 1815 Liverpool reminded Vansittart of
the time when "Lord Moira assisted us so *materially* in
1812", and the fact that he also mentions Colonel Doyle as
"one of the only two for whom he seriously pressed"
seems to point to some hurried arrangement.[1] The facts
seem to be that Moira would have wished to launch a
ministry, but that, at the last moment, he encountered new
difficulties; that the Prince encouraged his timidity, emphasising the absolute necessity of having a ministry in
power immediately; and that Moira agreed to see Liverpool, and to connive at the resurrection of the old ministry
as a stopgap. He continued to hope for a further change,
and was soon advising Wellesley not to associate with the
Whigs as he might soon be called upon by the Prince. But
he misread the motives of the Prince, whose chief wish was
for a "safe" ministry commanding a Parliamentary majority.
The House of Commons having asked for a stronger
ministry was now convinced that no better ministry could
be found, and a steady majority supported Liverpool.

So, as an admitted second best, the ministry, which was to
rule for almost fifteen years, entered upon its heritage. Liverpool was shortly to make a bid for the support of Canning,
but the negotiation broke down upon Canning's inveterate
jealousy of Castlereagh. In 1814, however, Canning made

1 Add. MSS. 31231, f. 214.

peace with the Government and was definitely reconciled to Liverpool; in that year his followers accepted subordinate office and he himself went on a mission to Lisbon; in 1816 he consented to enter the Cabinet by the back door and succeeded Buckinghamshire at the Board of Control on the latter's death. In 1818 the Duke of Wellington was persuaded to enter the Cabinet, and these were the sole changes during the next eight years, and, in all its essentials, the Government which had been considered hardly strong enough to rule for a day remained without alteration for that period.

A general election in the autumn of 1812 strengthened the Government slightly, but more important to its situation were the victories of Wellington which silenced criticism of war policy and turned the attention of the public from domestic complaints to military success. When the Government reached the period of the peace treaties it was as strong as any Government of the century. After the war, however, a reaction set in and the country began to demand a return to pre-war conditions which could not be accomplished; the expenses of Government had risen during the war, and it was never possible to bring them back to anywhere near the figures of the 1790's. Caught between the upper and nether millstones of public demand and expenditure which could not be reduced, the Government nearly perished; it just survived, and the radical agitation rallied independent Tories around the Government once more. At the very time, however, that it was possible to look forward to a new and happier era in domestic politics, the melancholy business of the Queen cut across political affairs and reduced the Government to impotency. Once more the Government just managed to survive, but it was clear that if it was to survive for any length of time it must be transformed in personnel and, far more important, in spirit. It is with that transformation, with its effects upon the course of government, and with the pre-eminent part played by Liverpool both in that transformation and in the new policy which resulted, that this work is principally concerned. First, however, it is necessary to examine the character of Liverpool, his methods as Prime Minister, and the state of politics which produced the phenomenon known as Liberal Toryism.

CHAPTER II

THE CHARACTER AND OPINIONS OF
LORD LIVERPOOL

"HIMSELF immovable in his hostility to the demands of the Catholics, it was still he who had introduced into office Mr Canning.... The alterations in the Silk Trade, the Navigation Laws, the Corn Laws, in the whole system, in short, of the duties and prohibitions had taken place under Lord Liverpool's authority and with his approval. His character at the same time was to the public a sufficient pledge that love of novelty and theory would not be allowed to run into extravagance—for seldom has a minister, not distinguished by any striking brilliancy of genius, and greatly inferior to more than one of his colleagues in popular oratory, gained so much weight and conciliated so much universal favour by the mere force of his personal character. He possessed a sound, cautious mind; a long political life had stored it with all the political knowledge that a minister requires.... Above all the country trusted his pure and unquestioned integrity." In these words, and without undue bias, the writer of Liverpool's obituary in the *Annual Register* summed up his character. A combination of pure Tory and Liberal opinions, long experience in Government, and a high moral character which had helped to convince people that the politician was not dishonest by definition, were the principal features which impressed his contemporaries; they were also the qualities which fitted him for the premiership.

His many years as Prime Minister had merged the man into the trained administrator. He had become an institution, and with his seizure it seemed as though some pillar of the constitution had fallen, but he had acquired also much of the impersonality which belongs to an institution. His private life contained no scandal and few anecdotes which might endear him to the public mind, his virtues were not those upon which men would lavish extravagant praise, his failings were not those which would be attacked with violence. It is these things which account for the slight hold which Liverpool has had upon the memory of posterity. Other ministers, with far less service to recommend them, are remembered if only for some particular action or some particular mistake; Liverpool, with fifteen years as Premier to his credit, gives his name to a ministry and nothing more.

Something has already been said of Liverpool's early career; he had gained a wider experience of Government than any other statesman, and he had proved himself an effective speaker. But able men have not always shown the qualities required of a Premier; in Liverpool's case the asset of his own character, which fitted him for the business of managing a Cabinet, far outweighed his abilities as an executive statesman. To begin with a negative quality: the frankness and amiability of his character made him a man whom others forbore from hurting if they could. He was extremely sensitive to the opinions of others, and, when accused of harshness or injustice, he suffered the greatest anguish of mind, and this might in turn precipitate periods of gloom and depression. His friends, who were accus-

tomed to his behaviour when at ease with life, refrained
from harassing him unduly, and those who met him only in
an official way were still struck with his straightforward and
honest manner. Those who worked with him display a
respect which amounted to affection. In 1822 Huskisson,
contemplating resignation, wrote: "I could not conclude
this letter without entreating you to believe that however
much that connection by creating opportunities of frequent
intercourse has strengthened the personal sentiments which
I entertain towards you, they could not be impaired by its
interruption, and I shall at all times set the same high value
on your friendly regard and retain the same feelings of
esteem and respect for your character both public and
private."[1] And the sincerity of this is shown by a letter
to Canning: "In respect to the personal feelings which
I shall retain towards Lord Liverpool it is more easy to
state them to you than to himself. My sense of his
kindness during the last seven years as well as of his
individual good will and friendship at all times will remain
unabated."[2] Arbuthnot, who worked for many years under
Liverpool at the Treasury, became almost extravagant in
his expressions of devotion: Lord Liverpool could have
commanded his very life.[3] Others who knew him less
intimately also paid their tributes of respect: W. H. Fremantle, for instance, entertained for him the "highest
personal respect and warmest feeling", and would have
been pleased to work under him at the Treasury.[4] This
respect and his "kindness" could play an important part

1 Huskisson, *Papers*, p. 137.   2 *Ibid.* p. 120.   3 *Ibid.* p. 159.
4 Buckingham, *Memoirs of the Court of George IV*, I, 257. (Hereafter
   cited as 'Buckingham').

in the running of a Government. Thus in 1822 Arbuthnot, after talking with Canning of the ways in which Wallace, Vice-President of the Board of Trade and a man with a grudge, could be soothed, wrote to Liverpool: "We both thought that a communication to him from yourself would gratify the most, and would give us the best chance.... We, either of us, should be ready to lend you all our aid for the purpose; but, as I have said, we strongly feel that kindness expressed by yourself would carry far more weight."[1]

Publicly Liverpool enjoyed a respect which few disputed; some might disparage his abilities, none doubted the integrity and honesty of his character. At no time is this more noticeable than in the months immediately after the Queen's "trial", when ministers were not likely to be lightly praised even by their friends. Lord Dacre, who had presented the Queen's petition in the Lords, said that Liverpool was "very able and the honestest man that could be dealt with. You may always trust him...and though he may be going to answer you after a speech, you may go out and leave your words in his hands and he will never misrepresent you."[2] From the west country a Tory clergyman wrote that even political enemies "very generally agreed to praise the great good conduct and talent of Lord Liverpool in a situation of peculiar difficulty".[3] Greville thought him "a model of fairness, impartiality, and candour";[4] while a Tory who complained of the ministry as a whole wrote that Liverpool's conduct was "quite unexceptionable, and be-

1 Add. MSS. 38191, f. 233.   2 Phipps, *Memoir of R. P. Ward.*
3 Add. MSS. 31232, f. 255, Dean of Bristol to Vansittart.
4 *The Greville Memoirs* (ed. L. Strachey and R. Fulford). I, 108. (Hereafter cited as 'Greville').

coming a judge as well as a statesman".[1] This respect was an important qualification for his office, and it gave to the ministry a prestige which usually escapes comment in accounts of the period. When Liverpool told Stuart Wortley that he would resign if the Queen's name was not excluded from the Liturgy, Wortley replied: "Upon this ground I applaud your determination of giving up your office rather than give way. Retirement upon such grounds will only add to the weight of your character, which now stands so high that I will venture to say this, even if you do retire, you will not remain out of office."[2] In Liverpool's personal reputation Canning saw the chief hopes of the ministry at this time: "Nothing but plain management, or rather absence of all management, will suit the crisis; and happily Liverpool stands in a situation in which *his own* word will carry him through."[3] During the long premiership of Liverpool an imperceptible change took place in one aspect of English manners: at the end of the eighteenth century, and in spite of Pitt's great name, the average Englishman endorsed Adam Smith's verdict upon that "insidious and crafty animal, vulgarly called a statesman or politician"; by the time of the great Reform Bill there is already found the alliance between politicians and the respectable middle class. Victorian Governments would have been utterly different in character had not politics become the profession for honest men as well as the recreation of landed aristocrats. In the eighteenth century an honest politician had been, in the public eye, an extraordinary and praiseworthy

1 Colchester, *Diary*. III, 181, F. Burton to Colchester.
2 Yonge, III, 117.   3 *Ibid*. p. 181.

exception to a general rule; in the nineteenth century the corrupt time server was singled out for reprobation because he was an isolated case and not the symbol of a class. In accounting for this change something must be allowed to the hold which Liverpool established in the esteem of the respectable middle class, and to the honesty with which his Government was administered.

Liverpool was never a social success. He "had no habits of any but official employment", and it was impossible to imagine him being happy in retirement.[1] To Madame Lieven he appeared gauche, and at Brighton Pavilion he was "the oddest figure imaginable", making "the most amusing blunders".[2] He had been a great favourite at the simple court of George III, he was out of place amid the splendours and frivolities of his son. In spite of this Madame Lieven seems to have liked him, and he, in his turn, provided a rare breath of scandal by his liking for her—"It is a common joke in this circle of society that he takes a very great interest in me; I quite like Prime Ministers"—and one evening, after a "long and solemn dinner, he amused us by the odd fancy of jumping over the back of a big sofa, on which I was seated, and establishing himself on a little footstool in front of me. The great Liverpool hovered and then settled on the ground, looking very comic."[3]

If Liverpool lacked social graces, he was a very different man in the company of those who understood him. There he could shake off his reserve and delight them with "the benignity of his personal intercourse". No trace of humour

1 Buckingham, II, 85. Wynn found Coombe Wood "unquestionably the dullest house in which I have ever passed a day". *Ibid.* p. 33.
2 *Private Letters of Princess Lieven to Metternich*, p. 160.
3 *Ibid.* p. 195.

appears in his correspondence, and, indeed, private and intimate correspondence did not come easily to him ("Jenkinson never writes when he can possibly help it"[1]), but in conversation he does not seem to have been without the art of amusing. Thus at a visit to Dropmore "he was chatty, full of anecdote, and evidently anxious to please".[2] He was one of those whose chance actions have the knack of becoming grotesque—whether it was vaulting over a sofa to alight at the feet of Madame Lieven, or meeting Canning at Bath in "a huge pair of jack-boots, of the size and colour of fire buckets"—and, without certain real abilities, he would certainly have become buffoon or butt in ordinary to Canning and his friends.

The figure which emerges from the scanty references to his private life is that of a likeable man, modest, shy, and sometimes awkward, not easy to know, but repaying the effort of making his acquaintance with the pleasantness of his personality. He was honest and he was conscientious, but this last virtue was apt to run to excess and bring on a terrible and wearing anxiety. His pain at the thought of offending others and his troubled thoughts for the morrow produced depression or irritation which seriously affected his health and temper. At fifty he was already an old man with many of the failings of old age; and Huskisson in his letters to his wife made frequent mention of Liverpool's fidgets—"Liverpool is in one of his grand fidgetts"—"Liverpool beats Binning at figitatis. He ought to be the Grand Cross of the Order"—"I am so worried with the

1 Dorothy Marshall, *The Rise of George Canning*, p. 135.
2 Buckingham, II, 19.

grand figitatis at Fife House"[1]—and the King thought him "in the highest degree irritable without having any feeling".[2] In 1824 Eldon found him "damned ill and damned cross",[3] and in 1826 he had become more than usually peevish and was careless of the opinions of others when things were left to his decision.[4] This irritability became more common as the years went on, as his mind was more and more distracted with the dissensions of his colleagues, but, fortunately, it was an acquired, not an inherent characteristic, and his periods of irritability contrasted strongly with his normal equanimity.

Men will not suffer for long the leadership of a man who is no more than an amiable party manager, and the backing for authority must be sound principles and solid ideas. Again his correspondence gives little clue to the man, for his deviations from the strict path of administrative business are rare. But, particularly in his early life, there are references to his "habits of reflection", and the man who, at Oxford, impressed his contemporaries with the wealth of his general knowledge must have had thought and reason behind his actions. Sound judgment was one of his principal qualifications for high office, it was this which could take him out of the politician and make him a statesman. He was slow, but not afraid, to decide, and he adhered to a decision once made; "I have been long enough in life", he told Arbuthnot, "to know the advantages of a straight course on the one hand, and all the inconveniences

1 Add. MSS. 39949, fs. 38, 42, 50.
2 Croker, *Diaries*, I, 199. (Hereafter cited as 'Croker').
3 Buckingham, II, 31.
4 *Ibid*, II, 126. Not a first-hand opinion, being that of Lord Lonsdale.

which arise out of contrivencies on the other."[1] He considered each question fully, but his mind was not clogged, as were those of so many Tories, by outworn sentiment; he attempted to consider each question on its merits, and the result was that he was neither "liberal" nor "ultra", but remained in an intermediary position. He was representative of his age in a way that few statesmen have been, for he reflected both its prejudices and its enlightenment in exact proportions, and, like the early nineteenth-century world around him, his mind was a curious mixture of High Toryism and the new ideas of "economists" and "philosophers". He seems, at one moment, to be looking back to the eighteenth century, at another to have set his face towards the prosperous commercial world of the high nineteenth century. In his mind these ideas were reconciled, and he succeeded in reconciling those ideas within his ministry; there is no sign that he saw the deep antagonism between the spirit of Canning and the spirit of Eldon, to him both were true within their limits; at this blend of ideas within Liverpool's mind it is possible to rejoice, for it made possible the brilliant last period of his ministry.

The Tories acknowledged two masters, Burke and Pitt. Yet there was, in this ancestry, an inherent conflict, and two renegade Whigs could hardly provide a consistent body of doctrine for the flamboyant creed of "Church and King". The old Pitt went ill with the young Pitt, the Burke of the *Reflections* was hard to reconcile with the Burke of the Rockinghams. To these cross strains in their ancestry most Tories were impervious, but they were nevertheless prolific

1 Yonge, III, 147.

of conflicts and misunderstandings within the party. All Tories were united in their opposition to Parliamentary Reform; the majority of Tories were opposed to the Catholic claims, but some of the most eminent were not; the majority despised the notions of political economists without a foot of land to their names, but a few were converts to the new doctrines. All were united once more in the basic sentiment of Toryism, which was a sense of the harmony of society. Neither King, Lords, Commons, nor people should govern, but each had an allotted sphere, and each could disturb the balance by venturing beyond that sphere; but these spheres were, of course, quite without definition, and attempts to define might once more set Tory against Tory. Generally speaking the Tories fell into two divisions, between which the line of demarcation became clearer after 1822: there were first the old or High Tories, who resisted reform wherever it appeared, who supported the old penal code, the old commercial system, and the old representative system; against them were the "liberals" who wished generally for administrative and legal reform, for Catholic Emancipation and for Free Trade, but who would still join in a defence of the Unreformed Parliament. Liverpool was able to keep both High and Liberal Tories within his Cabinet because he belonged completely to neither party, he shared important opinions with both, and between the two he was prepared to mediate.

The Radical disturbances of 1816 to 1819 retarded rather than advanced the cause of Parliamentary Reform. The Tories were more convinced than ever of the wickedness of reformers, and the Whigs became lukewarm in a cause which they saw so supported. After 1820 the question of Reform was quiescent, and the Tories were allowed to retain, without responsible criticism, their time-honoured objections to Reform just as the Whigs retained their traditional adherence to it. It is, however, interesting to turn back to one of Liverpool's earliest speeches, and to see in it a defence of the representative system couched in moderate, reasonable, and philosophic language. "The effects of government on the people do not so much depend on general principles and general theories as on little accidental circumstances which are frequently not even perceptible; and consequently, if plausible theories ought never to be an objection to Reform when practical grievances are felt, so defective theories ought not to be a ground for Reform, when not only no practical grievance, but every political advantage, is felt. . . . In the first place. . . every person would agree that the landed interest ought to have the predominant weight. The landed interest is in fact the stamina of the country. In the second place, in a commercial country like this, the manufacturing and commercial interest ought to have a considerable weight, secondary to the landed interest but secondary to the landed interest alone. But is this all that is necessary? There are other descriptions of people, which, to distinguish them from those already mentioned I would style professional people, and whom I consider as absolutely necessary to the composition of the House of Commons." Among these professional people he included those eminent in the army, navy, and law, and those "who wished to raise themselves to the great offices of the state", for the representatives of the landed and commercial interests were not usually by experience fitted or by temperament inclined towards the business of government. These persons could find their way into Parliament by way of the rotten boroughs, and to say that the rotten boroughs had brought into Parliament many hard-working administrators is a far better justification than the traditional excuse that they had brought in a few brilliant young men. "The House of Commons, as the democratic part of the constitution, as the virtual representatives of the people, certainly to a degree, ought to be affected by public opinions in their operations. It must, however, never be forgotten that the first quality of the House of Commons is that of being a deliberative assembly. If public opinion is necessarily to affect their decisions on every occasion, it will cease to be a deliberative assembly, and the members of it would have nothing to do but to go to their constituents, and desire to be directed by them in the votes they are to give on every important subject. Public opinion ought then to have certain weight in the conduct of that House; but public opinion ought never to have so great a weight as to prevent their exercising their deliberative functions." And finally the reformers attributed to the representative system effects which must be part of every system: "Form a House of Commons as you please—assemble the people on Salisbury Plain—you cannot prevent their having improper attachments and improper aversions. The defect is not in the representation; it is in human nature, and our eyes had better be turned to the improvement of that."[1]

During the whole of Liverpool's Government—in spite

1 *Parliamentary History*, xxx, 810ff.

of the expressed willingness of Tories to reform in specific instances where corruption was proved—there was but one change in the detail of the representative system; and that was the disenfranchisement of Grampound in 1821 when the patron, Sir Manasseh Lopez, was imprisoned for gross corruption. To the Tories the smallest change—the extension of the franchise to the neighbouring hundreds—would have been most acceptable; but this was rendered impossible by local conditions. The Whigs then suggested that the franchise should be transferred to Leeds, and in this form the disenfranchisement bill passed the Commons. In the Lords Liverpool succeeded in amending the measure to transfer the two members to the county of Yorkshire instead of to the town of Leeds. His reasons for doing so are interesting: "I should say that the giving of the right of election to the populous manufacturing towns was the worst remedy which could be applied. In the first place, it would be the greatest evil conferred upon these towns, it would subject the population to a perpetual factious canvass, which would divert more or less the people from their industrious habits, and keep alive a permanent spirit of turbulence and disaffection amongst them. Against such a measure the most respectable inhabitants of those towns would, I am convinced, protest. . . . I do not wish to see more of such boroughs as Westminster, Southwark, and Nottingham. I believe them to be more corrupt than any other places when seriously contested. . . and the persons who find their way into Parliament from such places are generally those. . . who are least likely to be steadily attached to the good order of society." He added that he would prefer a project of borough reform to any other provided that it should substitute a "pure and well-conditioned borough for a corrupt one".[1]

Parliament was supposed to provide a virtual representation of the people, in other words it represented interests if it did not represent numbers. The support for which the Tories hoped was that of the educated classes, of the Church, of the Universities, of the gentry, and of respectable tradesmen or men of commerce. Most Tories affected to despise public opinion, but they were not consistent, for, at times, they were frankly opportunist: in 1827 Croker wrote, "You know how I despise popularity, and I set no store upon so hollow and fugacious a support, but it will in this instance probably last long enough to enable Mr Canning to form a Government strong enough to forfeit it with impunity", and in 1825 Wellington wanted Liverpool to dissolve Parliament while advantage might be taken of a wave of anti-Catholic feeling. The Tories thought popularity an odious thing—when the Whigs were popular—but they were ready to use it when the occasion arose.

This was the first article of Liverpool's Tory orthodoxy; during the years of his ministry the second was to be of far more immediate importance. The fact that Liverpool opposed the Catholic claims not only postponed Catholic Emancipation until after his death, but also enabled him to keep the precarious allegiance of the "ultras". A "Catholic" alliance to carry the question had been a possibility in 1812, and that it was still a possibility was shown in 1822

1 Yonge, III, 137-44.

when a meeting of the sponsors of the relief bill was attended by Tierney, Newport, Parnell, Canning, Grant, Phillimore, Plunket, and Wynn.[1] Because the Catholic question remained open the Tory "Catholics" could join without injuring their consciences, but it was only because Liverpool held also some liberal views that they were ready to do so. On the other hand, after 1822, the High Tories, growing loud in their complaints against Canning and Huskisson, remained in office only because Liverpool was the surest safeguard against Catholic Emancipation. No Government which did not contain both elements could man its front bench effectively or gain sufficient support in the House of Commons. The movement for Catholic Emancipation was carried on in England by a part of the upper class—it was unpopular in the country, and "No popery" could still win elections—in Ireland by the whole nation save the Protestant minority. The question was really an Irish one and, when it is so considered, the reason behind the apparent unreason of the Tories can be seen; behind the stereotyped arguments of dual allegiance was the very real fear of Irish demagogues at Westminster, of Ireland ruled at the dictation of the priests, and of the English power in Ireland broken for ever. The Tories claimed that the English rule in Ireland was based upon Protestantism, and that no securities could safeguard that power once the Irish peasants could elect their natural leaders; in that simple argument history has proved them right, and the present age is still too obsessed with the

1 Buckingham, 1, 314. Similar meetings were held at other times as the occasion demanded it.

problems of nationality to say whether or not they were right in reason and in justice. Characteristically Liverpool based his opposition on expediency rather than principle, he "expressly stated that circumstances might arise in which in his judgment some alteration in those laws might be advisable", but at the present time he said "I will fairly own that in the present state of the opinions and feelings of the Roman Catholics, I do not believe such a project to be practicable, consistently with the attainment of the avowed objects of really satisfying the Roman Catholics and of affording an adequate security to the Established Church and Constitution".[1]

If Liverpool followed the old and not the young Pitt on the question of Parliamentary Reform, if he deserted his master entirely upon the Catholic question, he went farther than Pitt had ever gone in his allegiance to the economic ideas of Adam Smith. Questions of commercial policy he found most congenial to his mind, and upon them he spoke always with the authority born of long study. He recognised the ability of Huskisson and he invited his close co-operation; how close this co-operation became may be judged from a note which Liverpool sent with the draft of a speech in 1822: "...as there may be a chance of your being able to look it over early tomorrow and I beg you will *cut* and *slash* it as much as you please."[2]

Liverpool was a convinced free trader. In 1812 it is interesting to find him saying: "It has been well said in a foreign country, when it was asked what should be done to make commerce prosper, the answer was *laissez-faire*; and

1 Parker, *Sir Robert Peel*, I, 68. (Hereafter cited as 'Parker').
2 Add. MSS. 39948, f. 53.

it was undoubtedly true that the less commerce and manufacturers were meddled with the more they were likely to
prosper."[1] In the concluding years of the war, and during
the post-war troubles, there was little opportunity for
putting these ideas into practice—save a little done by
Wallace at the Board of Trade towards freeing commerce
from its restrictions—but in 1820 Liverpool was able to
tell a free-trade deputation that he had long been convinced
of the truth of their principles. There were, of course,
difficulties; there were many interests dependent upon
the protective system, and he could promise no immediate legislative improvement; but in spite of this he
delivered, a few days later, one of the first thoroughgoing
free-trade speeches delivered in an English Parliament. He
attacked the principle of agricultural protection; "Some
suppose that we have risen because of that system. Others,
of whom I am one, believe that we have risen in spite of
that system." He brought out remarks, which, coming
from an English Prime Minister, seemed novel to his
hearers, but which were to be the platitudes of the nineteenth century: "If the people of the world are poor, no
legislative interposition can make them do that which they
would do if they were rich", and "our manufacturers must
wait with patience until the supply and demand adjust
themselves"; "he was for leaving capitalists to find out the
way in which their capital could be best employed, being
perfectly convinced that, under such circumstances, the
interests of the public were not distinct from the interests of
the individual"; "on all commercial subjects the fewer

1 Hansard, XXIII, 1249.

laws the better. He was sorry to see so many on our statute book."[1]

Beside the immediate difficulties of putting any free trade ideas into practice, his views were modified by two other considerations. He held strongly that view of the solid and comprehensive nature of the national economy which has been one of the most persistent and most reasonable tenets of conservative economic thought: free development was good, but the balance of economic interests within the community must be preserved, and the whole economic organisation of the nation was a unity within which there should be no conflict. In May 1820 he accused Earl Stanhope of having made "a most dangerous distinction between the manufacturing and the agricultural interests; and by stating the policy of the British Government, which in reality afforded equal protection to both, had hitherto led it to support the former at the expense of the latter interest".[2] On another occasion he returned to this point: "The great interests of the country, the agricultural, the manufacturing, and the commercial interests... must stand or fall together.... As on the one hand the agriculture of the country is the basis of its power and wealth, so, on the other hand, agriculture would not be what it now is had agriculture been fostered by manufacture and commerce." This led him, as it led all but the most doctrinaire of economists, to support some measure of agricultural protection, even though, as a general principle, "the thing must be left

1 Hansard, I (1820), 576ff.
2 Hansard, I, 1119. Note that the Government is accused of favouring the commercial interest.

to right itself". The other consideration which he allowed
to modify his *laissez-faire* views was an honourable one;
it is unfortunate only that he did not allow it to influence
him more generally than it did. In 1818 a bill was introduced to regulate the hours of children in cotton factories;
when this bill was opposed in the House of Lords Liverpool said, "Free labour ought not to be interfered with,
however unwholesome or deleterious might be the nature of
the business or manufacture; but to have free labour there
must be free agents; and he contended that children were
not free agents", no medical evidence would convince him
that the children were unharmed by the excessive labour,
and "it was therefore necessary to resort to some legislative
enactments to prevent them from being exposed to the
excessive labour to which they were at present exposed in
cotton factories".[1]

The "liberal" trait in Liverpool's mind was almost as
pronounced upon questions of foreign policy as it was upon
economic questions. He trusted Castlereagh implicitly,
but he never wholly reconciled himself to Castlereagh's
close association with Metternich; in 1812 he would have
preferred Canning, and after 1822 he fell immediately into
line with Canning's policy. Upon foreign questions he had
a great store of information, but it cannot be denied that he
had no breadth of vision and no guiding principles for the
future—it was perhaps the example of his foreign secretaryship which led Pitt to say, in 1804, that he was a wise
councillor but not the man to decide a great question of
policy—he never comprehended Castlereagh's European

1 Hansard, XXXVIII, 548.

ideals, and he had Canning's insularity without Canning's sense of what was new and powerful and inevitable in the world. His arguments were sound and painstaking, he often arrived at the same conclusions as his two great foreign secretaries without having any of their larger inspiration. But it was perhaps this pedestrian method which made him invaluable to Canning, for the "ultras" might be roused to unreasoning antagonism by Canning's intuitive methods, but they could not help being shaken in their resistance by Liverpool's careful arguments. If all else failed it was finally the simple and self-evident strategic superiority of Liverpool and Canning which won the day; others would have been glad enough to see Canning go, but Liverpool would go with him, and they were "architects enough to know how much the removing a main wall shakes a house, and how little anyone could tell where such alterations might lead".

Liverpool was indeed the keystone of his ministry, and only he could hold together the different elements of his ministry as they gradually diverged in the years which followed. One-half of the ministry remained ultra to the core, the other half were the masters of Melbourne, Palmerston, Gladstone, and Disraeli. Within the Cabinet one member was himself undergoing a slow course of political education, and when Peel came to office in 1841 it was at the head of a government which he had impregnated with the traditions of Liverpool's ministry. The last period of Liverpool's ministry was, in fact, one of the main-springs of nineteenth-century legislation and policy; and this ministry owed not only its existence but also its character to the Prime Minister. No man could be less of a charlatan, no man could veil solid abilities more successfully in a habitual reserve; Canning was a far more striking and brilliant figure, Wellington was a greater man; neither could have done Liverpool's work. The amiable figure of Lord Liverpool does not fill the early nineteenth-century scene, but that scene would have been very different without him.

CHAPTER III

LORD LIVERPOOL AS PRIME MINISTER

UPON the office of Prime Minister there can be but one final judgment: that it is what its holder makes it. To this the most recent writer upon the Cabinet adds a rider, that the function of the Prime Minister is primarily one of giving advice when it is asked.[1] Liverpool has suffered by comparison with Pitt, the most autocratic of Prime Ministers, and with Peel, the model of all Prime Ministers. With those who followed after Peel he compares more favourably; his control over the general policy of the Government and his influence upon the departments was probably as great as that of Lord Salisbury, of Mr Asquith, or of Mr Baldwin, to name three who have since held office for periods comparable with his own. To the outside world, and to many subsequent historians, he appeared as a dim and elusive figure, as a phantom Prime Minister; for this belief the real foundation is the fact that he did not speak in the House of Commons, and that his influence can only be gauged from ministerial correspondence and from a surmise of private conversations.

"The misfortune of this government is that it is a government of departments," wrote George IV in 1823, and, writing to Liverpool himself, drew the inevitable comparison with Pitt.[2] Liverpool never attempted to exercise a commanding influence over all the departments, and he was

1 I. Jennings, *Cabinet Government*.
2 A. A. Aspinall (ed.), *The Letters of George IV*, No. 1110. (Hereafter cited as '*George IV*').

often content with a general approval of the policy pursued by the departmental chief; in the great offices of state he was fortunate to have strong and tolerably efficient colleagues. Neither Castlereagh nor Canning required much guidance; Melville[1] at the Admiralty and Bathurst[2] at the Department for Colonies and War were both experienced administrators; Eldon and Wellington were both strong men; Sidmouth as Home Secretary has found few defenders but, as an ex-Prime Minister, he occupied a unique place in the Cabinet, and his deficiencies have been more apparent in retrospect than they were to his contemporaries. These departmental chiefs would not come to the Prime Minister for advice save when some peculiarly difficult question arose, or when the policy of their particular departments seemed to become a matter of national interest.

1 Melville's chief part in Government was the administration of Scotland, where he ruled as virtual dictator, but with fairness and ability. Cf. Cockburn, *Memorials of his Time*, p. 386 (ed. of 1872): "The retirement of Lord Melville from the government of Scotland was not an event for which, *in itself*, any candid Scotch Whig could rejoice; because no man, individually, could have conducted the affairs of the country with greater good sense and fairness, or with less of party prejudice or bitterness."

2 For an estimate of Bathurst see *Exposition and Defence of Earl Bathurst's administration of the affairs of Canada*, by R. Wilmot-Horton, who worked under him for eight years: "The character of Lord Bathurst as an efficient public servant...is very imperfectly appreciated by the English public. Undoubtedly his general politics did not respond to the movement of the latter days in which he lived; yet in all cases where first rate practical good sense, and a rapid yet discreet view of intricate subjects was essentially required, Lord Bathurst possessed a mind far more able to grapple with difficulties than many of those persons who underrated his political efficiency. Lord Bathurst had no affection for political economy *by name*, but to the results of a wise combination of Colonial measures, which in their character might more or less belong to the science of political economy, no man was more alive."

A great mass of detailed administration lies, and must lie, outside the immediate ken of the Prime Minister; for advice on such matters the Under-Secretaries in the various departments will be responsible, and, as Castlereagh once remarked to Croker, "No government was ever better manned in the subordinate departments than ours".[1] Croker himself had an unrivalled knowledge of naval matters, Palmerston was a tower of strength at the War Department, Huskisson had few parliamentary duties as First Commissioner of Woods and Forests, but he acted as an auxiliary upon all economic matters. At the Board of Control the perennial secretary was T. P. Courtenay, a member of Parliament, of whom Canning said that "no office ever had an individual more completely conversant with every detail belonging to it".[2] In every department the Prime Minister had a reserve of power to be exercised at his discretion or invoked at the discretion of the departmental head; but when there was general agreement upon the principles and methods of government, there was little need to use that discretionary power.

If Liverpool was one of the least dictatorial of Prime Ministers, he was, nevertheless, one of the most experienced. He had held each of the three secretaryships and had also been connected with the India Board. No man would scorn his advice, and, during his premiership, he was always cognisant of even the details of the various departmental business; indeed he had frequently to pilot the various departmental measures through the House of Lords. There his speeches never displayed ignorance of his

1 Croker, I, 251.   2 Add. MSS. 38288, f. 386.

subject, and frequently showed a great wealth of accurate information. It would be necessary for him to go through the various measures with the greatest care and to discuss many points with the ministers concerned; in such discussions it can hardly be doubted that his suggestions would have great weight, but intimate conversations, often the most important part of the business of government, leave few traces upon the records of the time. To estimate the exact influence of Liverpool upon the departments would be impossible; it would be a rash man who declared it to be negligible, and few would care to say with his biographer, C. D. Yonge, that he was "the presiding genius of the Ministry both in its foreign and domestic policy". Such a verdict should be carefully tested even when dealing with the greatest of Prime Ministers, of Gladstone even and of Disraeli it would require qualification.

The three great departments in the state were those of Finance, of Foreign Affairs, and of Home Affairs. The Prime Minister was expected to have most influence in the two former, for current practice demanded that the Home Secretary should be allowed an almost free hand in a department which was, in normal times, concerned entirely with routine business. When the secretaryship had been divided into the Northern and Southern Departments, the Prime Minister had acted as a co-ordinating link between two jealous ministers; but their duties at home were of small importance compared to their duties abroad, where it was necessary to present to the outside world a uniform foreign policy, and it followed that the Prime Minister's work of co-ordination was exercised primarily in foreign affairs.

When the secretaryship became divided into Foreign and Home Departments, the Prime Minister continued to be in the closest contact with foreign affairs, but the Home Secretary succeeded to a heritage of detailed routine business in which the Prime Minister was not accustomed to interfere. Sidmouth conducted the Home Office after his own fashion, and the Prime Minister was called in only when the business of that department faced a crisis, when counter-revolution became a national policy. Peel, when carrying out his reform of the penal code, sent to Liverpool a general outline of the policy he would follow, but for the details of the measure he sought the advice of Henry Hobhouse, the permanent head of the department. But the Prime Minister did exercise a closer control over one sphere of the Home Secretary's duties; that sphere was the government of Ireland. Divided responsibility was not the least of the evils which afflicted the English rule in Ireland: within the Cabinet the Prime Minister, the Home Secretary, and the Lord Chancellor might all have something to say upon the affairs of Ireland; at Dublin it was difficult to fix the division of responsibility between Lord Lieutenant, Chief Secretary, and Assistant Secretary, who, as an Irishman with long experience of Irish government, was often the real director of Irish affairs.

The relationship between Prime Minister and Foreign Secretary was of the closest possible nature. In nearly all modern English Governments the core of the ministry has been the alliance of these two ministers. As effective head of the state, the Prime Minister must accept a full share of responsibility for its foreign policy, and the Foreign Secretary must be one whom he can trust implicitly. The arduous duties of diplomacy must necessarily occupy the whole attention of one man and they must also be considered the exclusive prerogative of one man; if the history of modern nations taught nothing else, it would teach the folly of dual foreign policies. A Prime Minister with a Foreign Secretary whom he cannot trust is in the most lamentable situation, he must either venture out of his proper sphere and attempt the disastrous experiment of going behind the back of his Foreign Secretary to conduct his own foreign policy, or he must precipitate a Cabinet crisis by dismissing the offending minister. Liverpool was fortunate in his generation, for, not only was he given two Foreign Secretaries of first-rate ability, but he was also given two whom he trusted implicitly. With both Castlereagh and with Canning he was on the most intimate and cordial terms, with both he entered into frank and detailed discussions of future policy, and to both he gave an almost free hand in the execution of that policy. He acted as a brake upon what may be called the "oecumenical" aspect of Castlereagh's policy, and upon the rasher moves of Canning. To both he was, as might be expected, the counsel of caution; but, and this too was characteristic, he did not shrink from great risks when he was convinced of a policy's rightness. With Castlereagh the whole Cabinet was in substantial agreement, and Liverpool's task—that of acting as a link between Castlereagh and the Cabinet, particularly during the Congresses—was not an arduous one. But Canning did not find favour with the majority of the Cabinet, and Liverpool had, of necessity, to become a partisan. With Castlereagh the influence of the

Prime Minister lay principally in his criticism of details, with Canning it lay in the support of principles. It has been shown that, towards the end of his life, Castlereagh was moving slowly along the path which Canning subsequently followed, and that the difference between the two men was one of method rather than of measures; it is strange that those who argue for this continuity should not have stressed the fact that both worked in close and cordial co-operation with Liverpool.

Different again was the relationship of the Prime Minister with the Finance Department, which comprised the Exchequer and the Treasury. The Prime Minister was First Lord of the Treasury, and in Liverpool's day the duties of this office were not nominal but real. Of the Treasury Board he was, according to his own definition, "primus-inter pares".[1] In 1826 Peel referred to Liverpool as "the Minister who presides over the finances of the country".[2] In 1822 Wellington gave as a reason for not making Canning Chancellor of the Exchequer, that "it would be impossible to place two leading men in the Treasury".[3] And in 1821 W. H. Fremantle, referring to a possible choice between the Treasury and the Board of Control, wrote, "I should certainly prefer acting under Lord Liverpool, for whom I entertain the highest personal respect and warmest feeling".[4] It is clear that the First Lord filled some important place in the financial administration of the country; what that place was is not so clear. In 1813 Liverpool wrote: "If any person were to ask me to

1 Add. MSS. 38576, f. 37.   2 Parker, I, 397.
3 Wellington, Supplementary Despatches (New Series), I, 277.
4 Buckingham, I, 257.

define the duties and powers of the First Lord of the Treasury and Chancellor of the Exchequer in this country, I could not do it. This very circumstance may have led to the union of these two offices, much oftener than to their separation. They have however, at times, been separated, and the Government has gone on with perfect harmony and concord."[1] In 1823 C. W. W. Wynn said: "Robinson will be a decided improvement on poor Van... but as to measures Liverpool must of course give the orders and he obey."[2] This is probably an overstatement, but it is at least certain that the Chancellor of the Exchequer was looked upon more as the First Lord's assistant than as an independent minister; the position of the Chancellor was still much inferior to that of a Secretary of State.[3] In theory the Chancellor of the Exchequer was concerned with supply, the First Lord with the regulation of expenditure; in practice the Chancellor was probably concerned with the details of raising money, while the First Lord exercised a general supervision over financial policy. Contemporaries were right in attributing to Vansittart the "expedients and ingenious devices" of post-war finance, but to Liverpool is probably due the general outlines of the policy, maintenance of a Sinking Fund and a return to gold when circumstances should allow it.

Beyond the actual direction of financial policy the Prime Minister performed another important function in connec-

1 Parker, I, 109.
2 Buckingham, I, 411.
3 Cf. Croker, I, 364: "The Foreign Office would be a severe test, and perhaps too high a step for Robinson." Robinson had been four years Chancellor of the Exchequer when this was written.

tion with economic matters, he acted as a link between the Exchequer and the general economic policy of the nation. After 1822 it is possible to trace the existence of a small "economic cabinet" consisting of Liverpool, Robinson, Huskisson, and Bexley (Vansittart);[1] at such a meeting would be discussed all matters of fiscal and commercial policy. From 1814 onwards Liverpool always had Huskisson at his side, and this intimacy does not seem to have been interrupted by a momentary coolness over Huskisson's position in the Government during 1821 and 1822. At Liverpool's invitation Huskisson criticised drafts of his speeches, and submitted long plain-spoken memoranda on economic questions.[2] It has usually been assumed that Huskisson was the inspiration of those parts of Robinson's budgets which introduced free trade measures;[3] but no one has explained how it was that Huskisson came to exert this influence. Robinson and Huskisson were not particularly intimate—indeed Robinson had been the follower and protégé of Castlereagh, Huskisson the devoted friend of Canning—and there is no obvious reason why Robinson should have invited the assistance of a man in another office whom he might well suspect of personal jealousy. The problem is solved when it is remembered that both ministers stood in very similar relationships to Liverpool, and that finance was not the exclusive concern of the Chancellor of the Exchequer.

1 Cf. pp. 192-3 below.
2 Add. MSS. 39948, f. 53. Cf. p. 41 above, and p. 180 below.
3 Greville, I, 157 "Everybody knows that Huskisson is the real author of the finance measures of the Government."

It is then in matters of finance and economic policy that the direct and personal influence of Liverpool is most likely to be found. Robinson was an able man, but he was also a lazy one, and frequent solicitation for his wife's health concealed inadequately his own decided preference for the fields of Lincolnshire over the labours of Whitehall. In consequence Liverpool and Huskisson are frequently found acting alone when Robinson might at least have been expected to be present. During the crisis of 1825 the famous banker, Alexander Baring, was called into consultation by Liverpool and Huskisson, but Robinson does not seem to have been at this emergency meeting.[1] His absence on this occasion may have been accidental, but it is certain that, in the following year Liverpool and Huskisson prepared a new Corn Law, and that the plan was communicated to Robinson only when it was complete. Strictly speaking a new Corn Law was not within the province of the Chancellor of the Exchequer, but one would expect him to take part in the preliminary discussions of such an important item of economic policy. It is a safe generalisation to say that, as on foreign affairs the deciding factor was the alliance between Liverpool and Canning, so on economic affairs it was the alliance between Liverpool and Huskisson. But in economic affairs Liverpool played a commanding part which he never assumed in foreign affairs.

However great were the powers of the Prime Minister in practice, however small they might be in theory, he still exercised them at the King's command and with the King's

1 *The Financial and Commercial Crisis Considered,* by Lord Ashburton (A. Baring), London, 1847.

permission. All the ministers were the King's servants, the Prime Minister was the servant who possessed the confidence of the King; it was this which distinguished the Prime Minister from the other ministers, it was this which allowed him to make a ministry, and the loss of this precious confidence would be the death-blow to the power of any Prime Minister. In the years before 1812 the Whigs had based their hopes upon the confidence of the Prince; in 1812 the weak remnant of the Tory ministry thought their position precarious but not hopeless "if the administration is known to possess the entire confidence of the Prince Regent"; in 1821 the real point at issue was whether the Government was the real government, whether it possessed the confidence of the King. The King's confidence was a symbol of stability, and, once it was certain that the Government possessed it, then timid men, independent men, careful men, and Grenvilles would rally to the support of the ministers. George III had made the bestowal of his confidence a real expression of the royal wishes; under a fully-fledged constitutional monarchy it was to be merely a confirmation of the strongest party's title to power; during the Regency and reign of George IV it was neither one thing nor the other. In launching a ministry the King's choice was still the deciding factor, but it was also becoming evident that no ministry would willingly be dependent upon the whim of the King, and that the King's confidence, once given, must be given until death or adverse divisions did them part. In 1821 Liverpool suspected "a secret scheme, not to destroy the Government at present, but to have the means of destroying it whenever the opportunity may be more convenient".[1] Upon such terms no ministry would continue in office, and, at the end of 1821, the King was forced to choose whether he would dismiss his ministers or whether he would let it be known publicly that they possessed his full confidence.

Into this dilemma the circumstances of party conflict were forcing the King. Like his father he had hankered after a "mixed administration": on the one hand it might be said that a government freed from party would be in the best interests of the country, on the other it was certain that such a government would be a royal government, for the King would be called upon to mediate between the various parties represented in the Cabinet. The Patriot King still lingered in the background, but in practice the Patriot King found his action hampered by the existence of two parties, each of which were bound together by strong ties of loyalty, from neither of which was it possible to detach individual members, and one of which was quite out of the question. Forced to make the unwelcome choice between Whig and Tory, the King would always choose the Tories. He might dally with the Whigs in the days of his youth, he might flirt with their leaders when Tory ministers tried his patience, but in the day of trial he must choose that party which maintained a traditional respect for the crown, which did not promise to weaken the power of the crown in favour of oligarchs or radicals, which would not emancipate the Catholics, and which would not betray the interests of the country in a vain search after the Holy Grail of Liberalism. The political nightmare which haunted the

1 Yonge. III, 146.

King was the "day when I may be shut out on all sides from any set of men, as servants, that could make my life tolerable".[1] The Tories might not always give full satisfaction, but, so far as the essential interests of the King and the country were concerned, they were safe. Faced with this situation the King had, at times, to make great concessions to his Tory ministers; and, in a way which was not altogether pleasing to them, the Whigs helped to formulate the modern relationship of a constitutional King and his government.

Liverpool showed that, when the occasion demanded it, he was ready to stand up for the rights and powers of a Prime Minister; he was prepared to press the King far, but his Toryism would not allow him to make the fullest use of his advantage. Toward the King the Tories maintained, through whatever difficulties they might encounter, a kind of impersonal loyalty: a loyalty expressed in the maxim, "The King's government must go on". They might be embarrassed by the King, they might demand concessions from him, but in the last resort they had a higher duty which could not be gainsaid. In this resolution they were fortified by the belief that Whig government would be a disaster for the country. The exact expression of Tory feeling was found, as it was so often found, by the Duke of Wellington: "The question for us is not, whether we shall bear with the many inconveniencies and evils resulting from the King's habits and character, and which none of our predecessors ever bore, or make way for others equally capable with ourselves of carrying on the public service? But, whether

1 *George IV*, No. 880.

we shall bear all that we have to endure, or give up the government to the Whigs and Radicals, or, in other words, the country in all its relations to irretrievable ruin? I believe if it were not for this consideration there are few of us who would stay where we are."[1]

Under Pitt had been consummated the ideal of George III: government by a close working partnership of King and Prime Minister. But if bestowal of his confidence and the ultimate control of patronage gave the King the last word, Pitt had been able to demand and to win the right to control the personnel of his Cabinet. The Prime Minister claimed, and most men felt that he was right in claiming, that the Cabinet must be his and his alone; he must choose whom he liked, he must exclude whom he disliked, and no other minister should claim to interpret the royal policy. The final settlement of these points in the Prime Minister's favour was still in the distant future; under George IV the relationship of King and Prime Minister remained anomalous and ill-defined. Briefly, the King could not choose but he could refuse, the Prime Minister could choose but it was difficult for him to insist. In 1821 George IV warned Castlereagh that he must not deceive himself by supposing "that any expediency shall ever induce me to give up the sacred privilege of naming the personal servants of the crown".[2] In 1821 he was able to sustain his objection to Canning, in 1822 he was forced to yield. From 1821 to 1824 he was able to keep Sidmouth in the Cabinet, but to this arrangement Liverpool had raised no objection. In 1812 there had been no call for royal choice, for the ministry

1 Wellington. i, 195.   2 George IV, No. 958.

had been ready-made. In 1823 he objected to the large size of the Cabinet—possibly with the conscious aim of excluding Huskisson—but the question was compromised. On the other hand, Liverpool never found reason to object to the presence in the Cabinet of any minister; always unwilling to treat old friends and faithful colleagues with anything which savoured of ingratitude, he never dismissed a minister from the Cabinet. His request for the resignation of Lord Maryborough (Wellesley Pole) in 1823 was almost a dismissal, but this was avowedly for the necessities of Cabinet making and not for any political offence. It was necessary to treat any wish of the King with respect, and even his prejudices had to be tactfully circumvented rather than overborne or ignored; on the other hand, the strength of the Prime Minister lay largely in the strategic position of the moment and in the loyalty of his colleagues. For this reason the relative shares of King and Prime Minister in choosing the servants of the crown defy definition, the Prime Minister had by far the larger share, but the King maintained the right of crying "I object", and, given favourable circumstances, he could sustain that objection.

Upon the same plane was the influence of the King upon policy: he had lost the power to initiate, but retained the power to obstruct. The secret of George III's great personal influence upon policy had been his own unremitting industry; George III had been prepared to spend long hours in the consideration, not only of the general principles of national policy, but also of the minute details of patronage and administration. This energy and this in-

dustry George IV was not prepared to expend. In 1821
Croker, usually a shrewd observer of men and manners,
confessed that "whether it be the King's own popular
manners, or the habits into which the Regency has led his
Minister, or the levelling temper of the times, the Royal
authority and the King's person are treated with a striking
degree of levity, and no reformers, if they knew the whole
secret, would wish to reduce the monarch lower in real and
effective state and power than his ministers place him".[1]
Croker overstated his case, but his remarks are some indication of the impression formed by those who had heard
tell of George III in his prime. George IV was generally
content with the expression of a general satisfaction or a
general disapproval of ministerial policy; his excursions into
the field of detailed and positive politics were sporadic and
were never long sustained; his interference in the workings
of the patronage system were infrequent and always to
gratify some personal wish.

The ministers consciously disavowed the wish to make
the King the prisoner of any party, but, at the same time
they viewed with the greatest suspicion any attempt by the
King to provide himself with an inner circle of intimate
advisers. It was fortunate for the smooth working of
politics and for the ease of all concerned that the Carlton
House party was dissipated after 1812, and that its members
became assimilated to one or other of the two great parties.
The party went, but its organiser, the Regent's private
secretary, remained, and in the situation of this individual
the ministers saw a constitutional menace. The private

1 Croker, I, 211.

secretary had unique opportunities for misusing his position: it was the nature of George IV that he sought always for a confidant; when doubtful he wished for reassurance, when he knew he was right he wished for someone to tell him that he was not wrong; the private secretaries came, in this way, not only to be cognisant of the most important state secrets, but also to exercise a great influence over the decisions of the King. As the channel of communication between the King and the outside world, as the man whose commands would be obeyed by a small number of influential men and whose favour would be sought by a great many more, the possibilities before the private secretary were almost limitless. Fortunately McMahon was hardworking, honest, and not particularly ambitious; Bloomfield was tactless and never enjoyed the King's favour to the full; and Knighton, who enjoyed greater power than either of the others though without the title of the office, was watched jealously by the ministers—who refused to him the rank of Privy Councillor even when it was asked by the King—and, though he was not above intrigue, he does not seem to have aimed at higher things for himself. The private secretary already enjoyed power and privilege far above the usual expectation of men of his rank; and in an age which preserved many of the social ideas of the eighteenth century this was enough for most men.

The private secretary was a threat to the Prime Minister's situation as the sole possessor of the royal confidence, but it was a threat which did not develop; another threat, and one which had been defeated by Pitt when in 1792 he dismissed Thurlow, still raised its head during Liverpool's premiership. Could the King restrain the Prime Minister's freedom by making one of the other ministers his friend and confidant? The answer, according to the relatively new convention, was that he could not; but the further question is whether this convention would prove strong enough to defeat the attempts of the King. Three ministers were, at various times, singled out for especial favour by George IV; they were Eldon, Sidmouth, and Wellington. There was a persistent rumour that Eldon was a second Thurlow, a rumour voiced in Brougham's jeer, "As to Lord Liverpool being Prime Minister, he is no more Prime Minister than I am. . . . Lord Liverpool may have collateral influence, but Lord Eldon has all the direct influence of Prime Minister." This was ironic nonsense, but still the suspicion lingered. In 1821 Croker thought that the King had been intriguing with the Lord Chancellor in order to exclude Canning,[1] but, at the end of August, Eldon told Bathurst that he had heard nothing of the trouble between King and Prime Minister until a few days previously.[2] In September of the same year the King saw Eldon and refused to see Liverpool, but as he also saw Castlereagh and Bathurst it was not evidence of sinister influence in the Closet, but an example of the King's constitutional right to consult with whom he pleased in a time of crisis combined with a deliberate insult to the Prime Minister. After Castlereagh's death the King again saw Eldon privately, but again it was a time of crisis and the King was entitled to all the advice which he could gather. Eldon was the revered sage of the Tory party, he was also not above intrigue; but, and especially after 1822,

1 Croker, I, 191: 11 June 1821.
2 Historical MSS. Commission, *Papers of Earl Bathurst*, p. 512. (Hereafter cited as 'Bathurst').

he counted for very little in the determination of policy. Indeed, in the changing world of the 1820's he was a pathetic rather than a powerful figure: he had grown to maturity in an age of leisurely and remunerative politics, in that world he had made his own career, but now there crowded in upon him new ideas which he scorned to understand and new men who appreciated not his worth. "I cannot conceive why it should signify whether the person who has threatened to resign executes that threat or not,"[1] wrote C. W. Wynn in 1824; and even the Prime Minister, who might have been expected to understand how a gentleman should conduct politics, thought his administration of Church patronage a scandal,[2] and told him that his delay in preparing the report of a Commission upon the Court of Chancery was of the greatest inconvenience to the Government.[3]

Sidmouth, though he had been the close friend of Pitt and a Prime Minister, was a lesser man than Eldon. Almost the last shreds of his energy had been expended in defeating the designs of the villain Hunt and the assassin Thistlewood, in 1824 he protested against the recognition of the South American republics and his protest was ignored; he resigned, and his resignation passed almost without notice. On one or two occasions he was consulted independently by the King, but he never occupied the position of King's confidant. His chief influence derived from the fact that he led a small family "connection" to which Vansittart, Bragge Bathurst, and Hiley Addington

1 Buckingham, ii, 66.   2 Add. MSS. 38298, f. 279.
3 Add. MSS. 38301, f. 1.

belonged, and which was the repository of political wisdom
for an exclusive band of correspondents—clergymen and
respectable magistrates[1]—throughout the country. All the
Sidmouths were notable for the purity of their lives rather
than for the brilliance of their talents, and all were ageing
men: Hiley Addington died in 1814, Brother Bragge was
tactfully ousted from the Cabinet in 1822, Vansittart withdrew from the front rank of the battle to the labours of the
Chancellorship of the Duchy of Lancaster, Sidmouth himself went out in 1824. This was hardly promising material
with which the King might build a secret camarilla, and it
must be said for the Sidmouths that not one of them could
have been drawn into anything which had the suspicion of
dishonesty or disloyalty.

Wellington was in a different position. Bound by a rigid
sense of duty he was the last to fail in this respect; but
he was guided by the idea that, in view of his national
and European position, he was bound to act above mere
partisan considerations and sometimes to act as a mediator
between King and ministers. Always he was unwilling to
sink the saviour of Europe in the minister of state, and, impressed with a sincere desire for European peace, he was
betrayed into a position which was hardly in accord with
men's ideas of constitutional rectitude. The story of his
temptation and fall may be traced in the pages of Madame
Lieven's letters to Metternich. In the spring of 1823 the
King spoke to her of Canning: "I do not like him any
better than I did," he said, "I recognise his talent, and

1 Beeke, Dean of Bristol and a financial expert of some standing, was
one of the most eminent.

I believe we need him in the House of Commons; but he is no more capable of conducting foreign affairs than your baby."[1] And on 19 March he ordered the Duke "not to let a day pass without seeing Canning, and finding out what he is up to in his office".[2] This Wellington was bound to refuse; but during 1824 he did drift into confidential relationship with the King and with the ambassadors of Austria and Russia, and the object of this—the famous "Cottage Coterie"—was to circumvent the foreign policy of Canning, which was also the policy of the Prime Minister, and, whatever the ultras might suspect, of the Cabinet majority.

This attempt to influence policy from outside the Cabinet failed, and it failed in spite of the fact that the King, the two most powerful ambassadors, a woman diplomat with a flair for intrigue, and the greatest living Englishman were all drawn into the meshes of the plot. It failed because the Prime Minister stood behind the Foreign Secretary, and because both were prepared to resign if that policy was not carried out. The convention of collective responsibility and Cabinet loyalty stood the test; and Wellington found that, instead of his close association with the King strengthening his hand, his opinions in the Cabinet were set at a discount. He seems to have been dropped from the most intimate councils of state—"I see the Duke of Wellington every day," Madame Lieven told Metternich in June 1823, "and every day I am more and more convinced that he counts for nothing in affairs"[3]—and his fellow ministers regarded his actions with a suspicion which would never have occurred

1 Lieven, p. 241.   2 *Ibid.* p. 243.   3 *Ibid.* p. 268.

to them but for his unfortunate association with the Cottage Coterie. In 1824 Arbuthnot, who was by this time fully in the Duke's confidence, wrote to Bathurst: "I wish to observe that the only way to keep the Duke right will be to support him in the Cabinet when he delivers an opinion in accordance with your own. I know he thinks he is deserted; and that some of his colleagues, who agree with him, are afraid of saying so lest they should be supposed to be giving support to the *King's favourite*."[1] In 1825 the King and the Duke had to choose between accepting the recognition of the South American republics or breaking the Government; neither was likely to choose the latter alternative. The firm stand of the Prime Minister and the newly founded doctrine of collective responsibility had broken the attempt of the King to control foreign policy; it was an experiment which no one cared to repeat, but Wellington did not forgive Canning and barely forgave Liverpool.

Liverpool ended his long career as Prime Minister in a position as strong as any holder of that office: he had fought for the dignity of his position and, though his victories had not always been swift, they had been sure. For eight years the constitutional difficulties which surrounded the relationships of Prime Minister, King, and fellow ministers came little to the fore; after that time the most important questions for the future of the constitution were agitated and were finally decided in the Prime Minister's favour. The right of the Prime Minister to select his colleagues was not fully settled, and far into the nineteenth

1 Bathurst, p. 565.

century Queen Victoria was to object to ministers and to carry her point; but at least it might be said that, after the happenings of 1821 and 1822 no sovereign would dare to make personal dislike the ground for objection. The King's right to object to measures was still maintained—indeed many would regard that right as a fundamental of the constitution—but his attempt to initiate a personal policy had been decisively defeated. The King's attempt to make Wellington his agent in the Cabinet had failed. Under Liverpool the Cabinet was a more solid body than it had been at any time previously, but this solidarity depended almost entirely upon the Prime Minister; by all he was acknowledged to be indispensable, and all, ultras and liberals alike, feared the day when his shattered health should force him out of public life. Even in the times of greatest disagreement between the various ministers the working of the Cabinet had been relatively smooth and according to accepted constitutional machinery; there had been no open disagreement, and, save for Sidmouth, there had been no resignations. To have kept the Government in being, and to have done so without ostentation and without dictatorial methods, was perhaps Liverpool's greatest achievement; for this reason, and because the smooth working of the machine must be one of the first concerns of every Prime Minister, it is now necessary to examine briefly the methods by which Liverpool obtained and maintained his quiet control.

The Prime Minister was adviser to the departmental chiefs, he was confidential minister to the King, he was also chairman of the Board of Directors known as the Cabinet.

Here the Prime Minister had to preside over the meeting of fourteen gentlemen, most of whom had some departmental axe to grind, and whose collective assent was necessary before any policy could be put into execution; here the Prime Minister had to exercise whatever qualities of tact and management he possessed; and here, in the approval or disapproval of his colleagues, the power of a Prime Minister would be made or broken. It was the business of the Prime Minister to see that the policy he favoured was approved, and to do so without offending any minister beyond hope of reconciliation.

In 1821 Wellington said that "ours is not, nor ever has been, a controversial cabinet upon any subject".[1] Indeed, during the first eight years of Liverpool's ministry there is no record of any serious disagreement within the Cabinet, and certain admirers of Canning have striven in vain to show that he disapproved of any measure of government during these years. The ministers were all men well acquainted with one another, they had all been bred in the same school of official business, and none of them displayed disturbing inspiration or alarming inefficiency. But for the even tenor of the Government's way Liverpool must be given some credit. It was he who first welded the followers of Perceval, the Sidmouths, and the Canningites into one ministry; and it was he who finally accomplished his favourite project—the reunion of the old Pitt party—by drawing in Wellesley and the Grenvilles. With characteristic modesty he outlined his feelings upon succeeding to the premiership: "I have had no resource but to bring

1 Buckingham, I, 237.

forward the most promising young men, on whose exertions the fate of the Government in the House of Commons will very much depend. I should be most happy to see another Pitt amongst them, I would willingly resign the Government into his hands, for I am fully aware of the importance of the minister being, if possible, in the House of Commons. I can assure you I never sought the situation in which I find myself now placed; but having accepted it from a sense of public duty, I am determined to do my utmost for the service of the Prince Regent as long as I have reason to believe that I possess his confidence."[1] These sentiments were generally known to his friends and colleagues, and it is no small tribute to Liverpool that, in spite of his constant readiness to efface himself, there never was any serious attempt to remove him. They knew he would go, and bade him go not; they knew he stayed from his sense of duty, and they were ever ready to emphasise that duty.

After 1822 the harmony of the Cabinet was dissipated. Upon foreign policy, and, to a lesser extent upon economic matters, meetings of the Cabinet degenerated into furious debates and into angry personal altercations. Years afterwards Wellington gave to Greville a description of Canning in the Cabinet: "he prided himself extremely upon his compositions" but he would "patiently endure any criticisms upon such papers as he submitted to the Cabinet, and would allow them to be altered in any way that was suggested". The Duke himself had "often cut and hacked his papers, and Canning never made the least objection,

1 Parker, I, 32.

but was always ready to adopt the suggestions of his colleagues. It was not so, however, in conversation and discussion. Any difference of opinion or dissent from his
views threw him into an ungovernable rage, and on such
occasions he flew out with a violence which, the Duke said,
had often compelled him to be silent that he might not be
involved in a bitter personal altercation.... Canning was
usually silent in the Cabinet, seldom spoke at all, but when
he did he maintained his opinions with extraordinary
tenacity."[1] When Cabinet meetings became a duel between
Wellington and Canning, or when, which annoyed Canning
even more, Westmorland, "le Sot Prive", obstructed business for hours with persistent opposition to unimportant
details, then the work of the Prime Minister became
vastly complicated. Liverpool was heart and soul behind
Canning, but he had also to think of the Government;
resignation of the ultras would have meant the end of the
ministry, and Liverpool knew that the end of his ministry
would mean the coming of the Whigs. Only Liverpool
prevented the split of 1827 from happening in 1824; he was
successful, but the attempt ruined his health and ruined his
temper.

To some extent Liverpool was helped by his strategic
position: the intense distrust of the Whigs and the fear of
Catholic Emancipation kept the High Tories from pressing
their opposition to its logical limits. But their forbearance
would not last for ever; the future was to see the great
secession of 1827, and behind the seceders were the legions
of Dr Humbug "who had proved Mr Canning to be The

1 Greville, I, 184.

Beast in St John's Revelation". When all is taken into consideration it is still extraordinary that the crucial decision upon foreign policy—"that it is the opinion of the Cabinet that the question of any further step to be taken towards the South American States should be decided without reference to the opinions and wishes of the Continental Allied powers"—should have been made with but one dissentient voice.

The success of Liverpool in overcoming the opposition within the Cabinet is largely explained by the fact that the Cabinet frequently did little more than ratify decisions which had already been taken, and that these decisions were really taken in private and less formal meetings. "We all know", wrote Charles Wynn when he was himself a Cabinet minister, "that business can never really be settled in the meeting of so numerous a Cabinet, but that it must be in fact arranged at more private meetings and dinners."[1] Cabinet dinners were an important institution; to them it was not necessary to ask every minister, and in intimate conversation over the dinner table the policy of the country could be freely discussed. But the Cabinet dinner was not the heart of the Cabinet. Wynn gave it as his belief "that the only real and efficient cabinet upon all matters consists of Lords Liverpool and Bathurst, the Duke of Wellington and Canning, and that the others are only more or less consulted upon different business by these four".[2] These were the four ministers who received all

1 Buckingham, I, 398. In this letter Wynn was complaining that he was not invited to the Cabinet dinners, (though he may have meant private dinners given by Cabinet ministers).
2 Ibid. p. 494.

state documents as a matter of course, but to their intimate discussions the Prime Minister could invite, or not invite, whom he pleased. There are signs that, when the Duke of Wellington was moving heaven and earth to defeat Canning's policy he was not invited to the "inner cabinet".[1] Behind the Cabinet, behind informal discussions, behind even the "inner cabinet", there was a still more select council when two or three were gathered together. To his country houses—Coombe Wood, Kingston, or Walmer Castle—Liverpool would invite the minister with whom he wished to talk; there, in the relative seclusion and during the parliamentary recess, the first plan of the policy to be pursued was mapped out. Canning was a frequent visitor, Huskisson another, the remaining ministers came on occasions. The importance of these meetings was that, before the matter even reached the stage of discussion by the inner Cabinet, Liverpool's mind was made up, and he was ready to support the minister concerned against any opposition. It was the unity of aim between Liverpool and Canning which finally defeated all opposition within the Cabinet, and Huskisson's free trade measures were forced through in the same way. Another use of the invitations to Coombe Wood or Walmer was the conciliation of the discontented; in 1823 Wynn's complaints of neglect had risen in volume and in bitterness, the sequel was an invitation to Coombe Wood where he passed two days and was "much pleased".[2] Every measure required these extensive and private preliminaries before it came finally before the Cabinet; if the preliminaries were completely successful

1 Pp. 67–68 above.   2 Buckingham, II, 34.

the formal Cabinet could do no more than agree, but upon some questions—notably the great questions of foreign policy—it was not possible to satisfy all objections before the Cabinet meetings, and it was then that Cabinet meetings became long, tiresome, and angry. But even upon these great questions, which divided the Cabinet into two mutually suspicious parties, much was done, and successfully done, before the measure reached the Cabinet stage. Wellington led the opposition in the Cabinet, but, save for some guerilla attacks by Westmorland, he usually found himself without support; those on whom he counted sat in uneasy silence, for they had already been persuaded and had already committed themselves to Liverpool and Canning. They wished Wellington well, but "the leaders of the two Houses thought otherwise", and they must perforce acquiesce.

These were Liverpool's methods of government, and, of their type, they were successful. They were methods which could have been rendered successful only by a man of great tact and great persuasion, and these were qualities which Liverpool possessed to the utmost. He will never be numbered among the most brilliant of Prime Ministers, but, for his party and for his time, he was a good Prime Minister. His party was bound by loose ties and his time was one of disintegration and new ideas; nothing is more certain than that the rule of an inspired and autocratic Prime Minister would have shattered the party, which suffered already from the malaise of the times. For this reason Canning, though he was the most striking personality in the ministry during the latter years of Liverpool's premiership, was quite out of the question as Prime Minister. The final split was, perhaps, inevitable; it might have been postponed had Liverpool been able to arrange, as he meant to arrange, for the quiet succession of Canning; but this was, perhaps, a task which would have overtaxed even his powers of conciliation. The dissolution of the Tory party could not be long averted, but in averting it for the few years after 1822, Liverpool made possible five years of useful legislation, of legislation which left a great heritage to the succeeding years. The ministry of 1822 to 1827 was the first of those nineteenth-century governments which, without being called "reforming", may certainly be called "improving". It was Liverpool's leadership which made this ministry possible, and, for this reason, it is not altogether fantastic to call this most cautious and least inspired of Prime Ministers one of the architects of the nineteenth century.

CHAPTER IV

GOVERNMENT, PARTY AND PUBLIC OPINION IN 1820

WHIG publicists of the early nineteenth century were fond of alluding to contemporary politics in the same terms as the historical conflicts of the past. English history was seen as a long struggle between the people and the despotic power, whether a King or a Government wielded despotic powers: the picture which they delighted to draw was that of a ministerial party loaded with places and privileges ruling by means of corruption with a total disregard of public opinion. Modern historians would, of course, modify this over-simplified picture, but this view still colours most accounts of the period. It is, however, a view which will hardly bear investigation, and a most cursory reading of political correspondence will show that the patronage system was on the decline and ceasing to be an effective means of party organisation; that the Government was frequently at the mercy of public opinion expressed through a large independent section of Parliament; and that the ministers themselves were professional administrators who inclined in their opinions to the commercial rather than to the landed interest. The great social and economic changes of the time do not go without reflection in the higher walks of politics, and, with Parliament still unreformed, there is the spectacle of a Tory Government implementing a liberal foreign policy, reforming the criminal code, and acting upon the principles of *laissez-faire*. This last phase of the Tory Government was largely dictated by the state of public opinion in the country, and it is usually supposed to begin in the year 1822. It is here intended to examine the state of the Tory party, of public opinion, and the relation of both to the Government on the eve of this change.

First it may be asked: Who actually governed? The answer is that England was governed by professional politicians. It is the measure of George III's work that, after 1761, the great landed aristocrats never regained control of the state; during his reign there grew up a very large Tory aristocracy, but it was never a governing aristocracy. In the early nineteenth century the road to political power did not lie through great landed possessions or great borough influence, it lay through sheer hard work and an apprenticeship in the lower ranks of Government. Of the ministers in Liverpool's Cabinet eight were peers, but of these only two had titles which went back for more than a generation, and only these two, Westmorland and Bathurst, belonged to the old landed aristocracy. Eldon, Wellington, Sidmouth, and Bexley had raised themselves to the peerage by their own efforts, and the fathers of Liverpool, Melville, and Harrowby had been the first peers in their respective families. The distinguishing characteristic of these ministers was not birth but training and environment; they lived in their own circle of society, and this was the circle of neither Whig nor Tory aristocrats.

To this generalisation there was one exception: that of the Grenvilles, for they did form an aristocratic family "connection", and attained office as a "connection". But the attitude of contemporaries to the Grenvilles shows how much the idea of government by connection belonged to the past. After Grenville's retirement the group was led by the Marquis of Buckingham who controlled six boroughs and some fifteen members of the House of Commons. Other peers had equal influence, but only Buckingham tried to use this influence as a qualification for political office. In 1821 the Grenvilles joined the Government and Buckingham expected office; but Liverpool and the King were both agreed that he was quite unqualified for such a position. Of the Grenvilles only Wynn, who had a certain parliamentary reputation, was given cabinet office, and Wellington refused to see in this a concession to the idea of "connection". "As well as I recollect what passed when Mr Wynn was appointed," he wrote to Buckingham, "you expressed a wish that Mr Wynn should have an office which would...give him a seat in the Cabinet; and Lord Liverpool, Lord Castlereagh and others who were at that time H.M. Ministers considered Mr Wynn's talents, character and station such as to render him an acquisition to the Cabinet. This I believe to be the real state of the transaction; and I don't think it ever was admitted that it was necessary that a connection of yours should as such be a member of the Cabinet."[1] Buckingham continued to complain of his exclusion, and to demand office as of right, not of grace. The usual channel for his complaints was Wellington, and Wellington always replied in the same vein. "I am certain that if Lord Sidmouth was to relinquish his seat...you would experience insurmountable difficulties in

1 Aspinall, *The Formation of Canning's Ministry*, p. 46.

being called to fill it," and "it is impossible for any man to force himself into that situation".[1] While the whole notion that this sort of influence could be exerted within a Government was erroneous: "There is another point...in which I think you are mistaken, that is the expediency or desirableness of having two members of the same family or party in the Cabinet. Whether it is a fault or otherwise, I assure you that such confederacy in the existing Cabinet does not exist, and if it did it would be useless. I have never known two members of the existing Cabinet go into the Council determined to be of the same opinion, and it is a mistake to suppose that the relationship which existed between Lord Sidmouth and others, or between the late Lord Londonderry and Robinson, gave either more weight or more facility in the Cabinet than they would have had otherwise. I do not think that my position in the Cabinet is altered by the relinquishment by my brother of his seat there."[2]

These remarks are emphasised by a calculation which Croker made in 1827.[3] He found, to his surprise, that of the 116 members returned to Parliament by the great Tory borough owners, only eighteen held office, and of this eighteen no less than twelve had been given their seats at the request of the Government. Beyond this 116 thirty peers returned one member each, two commoners returned four each, sixteen two each, and seventeen two each. Some

1 Wellington, I, 132 and 145.   2 *Ibid*. p. 132.
3 Croker, I, 371. Other principal sources for the composition of the House of Commons are: Oldfield, *History of Representation*; *Biographical Guide to the House of Commons* (1808); *The Assembled Commons* (1838); *The Black Book of* 1820; *The Pamphleteer* (1822); H. S. Smith, *Register of Contested Elections*.

of the borough owners among the commoners belonged to the commercial rather than the landed interest, but, with these exceptions, it may be said that about two hundred Tory members represented the interest of the great land-owners, and on the Whig side there were some seventy more. Yet it is a paradox of the time that the Government was not dominated by this interest, and that it chose to pursue a foreign and an economic policy which was little to the liking of the Tory landowners. Lord Redesdale, an acute High Tory lawyer, lamented that "If landed pro-perty had not a predominant influence, the British consti-tution which is founded on the predominance of landed property, cannot stand. We are rapidly becoming—if we are not become—a nation of shopkeepers";[1] and "Trade, manufacturers, and money are everything. The landed proprietors are mere ciphers, they are of no consequence, either with ministers or with Opposition."[2]

The country gentlemen—most of them members for English counties—were always considered the most in-dependent men in the House. Their temper was the barometer of the House, it was necessary at all times for the Government to pay particular attention to their de-mands, and the stoutest Tory amongst them might turn against the Government on some particular question. In 1816 T. S. Gooch, the member for Suffolk, who could certainly be described as a stout Tory, declared that the ministers could no longer enjoy his support unless they embarked upon a policy of retrenchment and economy;[3]

1 Pellew, *Life of Sidmouth*. 2 Colchester, *Diary*, III, 401.
3 Hansard, XXXIII, 461.

and in the same year many country gentlemen joined with the Whigs to defeat the Property Tax. The next spate of opposition by the country gentlemen came between 1820 and 1822, when the distresses of agriculture led them on to attack the measures of the Government, particularly the resumption of Cash Payments. "The country gentlemen treat the Government exceedingly ill;" wrote Wellington, "what I complain of is their acting in concert, and as a party independent of, and without consultation with, the Government."[1] The recognised leader of the agricultural interest was not a Tory but C. C. Western, the Whig member for Essex; and Tory gentlemen were quite capable of joining hands across the House with their Whig brethren when agriculture was threatened. During 1822 thirty were consistent supporters of the Government, twenty-eight voted against on certain questions, and ten voted for on certain questions. The opposition of the country gentlemen was dangerous because they could claim, with some show of reason, that their demands were "completely free from party feeling and had nothing in view but the good of the country".[2] Yet the Government was saved by the fact that Tory rule was the first essential for the good of the country, and, as Thomas Grenville wrote to the Duke of Buckingham, "these blockheads all profess that they do not wish to change the Government, though they are doing all they can to annihilate them".[3]

After the aristocratic and landed interests the most im-

1 Buckingham, *George IV*, I, 292.
2 T. S. Gooch during the debate on Western's motion for a Committee of Enquiry into Agriculture, 7 March 1816.
3 Buckingham, *George IV*, I, 291.

portant section of Parliament was the commercial, under which vague term can be included all those engaged in banking, commerce, and manufacture. This "interest" had not the solidity of the agriculturalists, and their various demands frequently conflicted; it is, nevertheless, of great importance that there were nearly one hundred members of the House of Commons intimately connected with commerce.[1] Their numbers in the unreformed House of Commons are not generally realised: of bankers and financiers there were thirty-three, of general merchants twenty-two, the great and often hostile interests of the East and West Indies claimed nine each; finally there were six brewers and six manufacturers. Innumerable difficulties confront anyone who attempts to make an exact classification, for complex blending of classes has always been a characteristic of English social life. Two mercantile families had entered the ranks of the political aristocracy: two Alexanders, cousins of the Earl of Caledon, sat for Old Sarum, while the banking house of Smith, Payne, and Smith, whose head was the Earl of Carrington, owned two boroughs. At Bridgnorth a Whitmore had filled one seat with very few breaks since 1621; in 1820 two Whitmores sat for this borough, and they might certainly be counted as landed gentry, yet one, T. Whitmore, was a Governor of the Bank of England, and the other, W. W. Whitmore, was a director of the East India Company and a free trader. A large number of the "merchants" had bought their way into Parliament; once there they could make exactly the same claims to independence and to freedom from influence. So perplexed was Southey

1 Appendix A.

by this species of corruption, which gave the House some of the "most independent men...as the mob representatives are undoubtedly the least so", that he proposed a novel piece of parliamentary reform; why should not "the illegality be done away with; and the purchase of a certain number of seats authorised and regulated, and the money appropriated to a fund for public works of local and general utility"?[1]

To the party manager it was more important that these men could not be controlled. About forty-five of them were professed Tories, but twenty of these might be considered as doubtful and a number of them did in fact desert over the Property Tax. The standard of information and argument on commercial questions was certainly higher than it had ever been before, and on certain questions, such as the defence of cash resumption, the Government could enlist the support of men who were Radical rather than Whig. Such a one was the great Ricardo, whose defence of the Government came with an authority more in accordance with the Treasury Bench than with the Radical back benches. The Government could gain as much as it lost from the independence of mercantile men, and, after 1820, it began to play for their support.

From these two sections of Parliament which exercised the largest measure of independence, the Tory party managers could estimate a possible maximum of something over a hundred, but they had to allow for a possible defection of about fifty. In addition there was the possibility of some great magnate deserting on some question or re-

1 Essays on the State of Public Opinion and the Political Reformers (1816). R. Southey, *Essays, Moral and Political*. London 1832. p. 388.

leasing his members from their party allegiance. There were also members who might be called away on military or naval business, members who showed a reluctance ever to appear at Westminster, and members who were liable to grow tired as the night advanced and to slip off for late supper before the vital division had been taken. It is these difficulties which account for the frequent weakness of the Government in the House, and for Treasury miscalculations such as the estimate that the Property Tax, defeated by thirty-seven, would pass by forty.

The greatest source of Government weakness was that there was not a ministerial group sufficiently large to guarantee safe divisions. In 1822 a Committee of the House of Commons reported that eighty-nine members of the House of Commons were in places of profit under the crown. This figure and the list compiled was seized upon by Radical writers as the "Treasury Phalanx". It seems incredible that the list can have passed the most casual scrutiny of those who were seeking the sinister hand of corruption, for it included such "places of profit" as King's Counsel, and one of these was a consistent Whig! On the other hand the list does contain the names of a fair number of those belonging to the ministerial "interest". The word "interest" is used advisedly, for the "official men" in the House of Commons may be said to form an interest as distinct as those of the landed and commercial classes. The solid core of this interest was composed of those who held active office under the Government; these were regular in attendance and could be relied upon for departmental business. The Household Officers were expected to vote with the Government, but their attendance was less regular. The sinecurists were now few in number, most of them were superannuated servants of the crown, and few were prepared to play an active part in the day-to-day work of the session. The ministerial interest was recruited by a number of men whose family connections bound them to the ministry, or who owed their seats solely to Government influence, and there were, of course, a number of hangers-on and careerists who were looking for particular favours or political employment. But these were fewer than there have been in many Parliaments; the Liverpool ministry was in office for nearly fifteen years and during that time there were remarkably few changes even in the subordinate Government offices; it followed that the young man looking for quick advance found the opportunities meagre and the competition severe. Particularly noticeable is the absence of lawyers making their way quickly to the front; the careers of Thurlow, Dundas, and Wedderburn did not find counterparts in Tory politics of the early nineteenth century.

The Government could count on the unconditional support of about a hundred, and the regular attendance of rather less. This was useful, but it was not enough, and, to be safe, the Government had to rely on the support of a hundred or even a hundred and fifty more members. There were certainly enough Tories to fill this need, but many of them laid claims to an independence which they were not afraid to exercise. The time of trial came when the Government felt bound to press measures which it deemed necessary but which public opinion found distasteful.

Besides the uncertainty of divisions upon such topics, the decline of the patronage system left the Government very weak in debate. Most Government officials were immersed in the business of their departments, and there were no great sinecurists ready to defend the Government on any question. In 1826 Canning wrote to Liverpool: "I think it due to myself and to the Government to represent to you the state in which we are left in the House in respect of official support. The offices of Treasurer of the Navy, and Master of the Mint, can never henceforth be looked to as other than accessory situations to be held by persons whose hands are otherwise full of business—they never again can stand alone as available for the general business of the Government. The second Paymastership is already absorbed in the same manner. The remaining Paymastership is the single office of rank now remaining from which any aid, beyond departmental duty, can be derived. In this state of things it behoves us to take care that other offices—usually Parliamentary—are not lost to us by our own fault. There are three to which I particularly allude, which have for the first time been allowed to go out of Parliament by the present Government.... I mean the Master of the Rolls, the Judge Advocate, and the King's Advocate: all important, in the highest degree to the well carrying on of the King's business in the House of Commons; all within my memory, and till of very late years, useful and efficient supporters of the Administration."[1]

The Government of Lord Liverpool was working in some respects under the conditions of a modern Govern-

1 Add. MSS. 38193, f. 239.

ment, for there was not enough patronage to provide a certain majority. But a modern Government has the advantage of a strict and efficient party machine, and this advantage Liverpool's Government did not possess. It got the worst of both worlds, the importance of the independent member was greater than it had been or has been in later years, and public opinion, once it had passed through the narrow doors of the representative system into the open forum of Parliament, could have a considerable effect upon the course of policy. The character of Lord Liverpool did not make the problem any easier, though his failure in this respect was entirely honourable to himself and, in the long run, probably established the personal esteem with which he was regarded. For Liverpool's honesty always precluded him from promising that which he could not give; "I believe", he wrote to an applicant, "that there is no individual in a public situation who has been more cautious on the subject of making promises than I have. In most cases in which I have made one either directly or implicated I have desired the individual to write to me in order that he might have an answer which should state beyond the power of future misconceptions what the nature of the promise was and what qualifications or exceptions were connected with it."[1] How this strictness might affect the business of party management may be gathered from another letter: "I do not see how it is possible for me to hold out the expectation suggested to Lord Charleville. I could have had *four seats* from Sir L. Holmes and *three* from Sir W. Manners if I could have promised them that they should

1 Add. MSS. 38572, f. 141.

have been made peers upon the first creation, I have *lost* them and I would rather lose them than make an engagement, and though it has been intimated to me that, without making an engagement, I might have held out the expectation...I have always felt that such a course of proceeding was either a virtual engagement or an act of deception."[1] Liverpool believed that these principles would ultimately strengthen rather than weaken the Government; to Peel he wrote: "Do not suppose me too Romantic...but (independent of my indifference to office unless I can hold it creditably) I am satisfied that a disposition to contract engagements of this description will in the end rather weaken than strengthen any government."[2] In the long run he was probably right, but he shut off from the party managers some of their time-honoured devices, and the immediate effect was inevitably to lose support in the House of Commons.

This strict attitude towards the administration of patronage was dictated in part by the diminishing resources of the spoils system. Burke's Economic Reform and subsequent Acts of the same type had abolished large numbers of ancient offices; yet still the House of Commons clamoured against sinecures, it was necessary to administer patronage with the utmost discrimination, and finally, in 1817, to pass an Act which abolished further offices. Some idea of these difficulties may be gained from a correspondence between Liverpool and Masterton Ure, the Parliamentary manager for Weymouth and Melcombe

1 Add. MSS. 40181, f. 23. The names are omitted from Parker, I, 43.
2 Parker, I, 43.

Regis: Ure pointed out that in the past few years he had returned nine loyal Government supporters, including himself, and that he was now anxious for some office tenable with a seat in Parliament, "the duties of which can be performed in London, or, if a situation elsewhere, which does not require personal attendance".[1] Liverpool replied that "situations tenable with a seat in Parliament having official duties annexed to them are few in point of number and are subjected to so many strong claims of an official as well as a political nature, that I must confess I see no prospect of any opportunity being afforded of me having the pleasure of promoting your views in this respect. In regard to situations of another description alluded to in your letter—viz. such as are tenable with Parl^t and have no official duties to require personal attendance—there are scarcely any of that nature now existing and such as may exist are subject by late acts of Parliament to regulations in the event of their becoming vacant as will dispense them hereafter of the character of sinecures."[2] It was indeed becoming difficult to find suitable rewards for faithful servants, and Liverpool said in the House of Lords that "there was no country where the salaries of great offices are so small, or have been so little augmented as in this country. Let anyone look at the last fifty years, and compare the increase of salary with the increase in price of every article, and he will be convinced that the rise in official salaries had been less than any other rise. There had been many instances of persons totally ruined in fortune by the public service; and indeed such must be the case, unless the officer

1 Add. MSS. 38262, f. 352.   2 Add. MSS. 38283, f. 121.

had a reasonable private fortune."[1] On another occasion he was writing, "The Pension Fund is so limited, as to be scarcely able to meet the just claims which are daily made upon it for the distressed nobility, and for the persons and families of those who have long laboured in the public service", and he replied to solicitations for a pension by saying, "I could on no account make such a grant to a connection of my own, who has been some years in a similar situation, and is the father of a numerous family."[2]

Nor could the deficiencies of the pension fund be supplemented by the provision of posts in the civil service. These required constant attendance and undivided attention, which hardly fitted them for the gentlemanly friends of "friends". To one applicant Liverpool wrote: "The prospects of a young man in an official department in this country are very limited. There are few persons who have ever risen in this way to any distinction, and even in the higher situations in the Office to which they may expect to come in very slow succession, the emoluments . . . are barely sufficient to cover the expenses of a Gentleman."[3] Moreover about 1820 Liverpool initiated some reforms in the most important of civil service departments, the Treasury, which on the one hand removed it entirely from the political sphere, and on the other hand increased the chances within the service for a really able man. This reform has been little noticed by constitutional historians, but it seems to mark the definite acceptance of the civil service as a non-political

1 Hansard, xxxiv, 812.
2 Add. MSS. 37310, f. 233: Liverpool to Wellesley, who had applied for a pension to his Private Secretary.
3 Add. MSS. 38275, f. 173.

sphere in which rewards were given to ability alone.[1] There
were some valuable appointments in India, but here again
the Government could offer very little, and Liverpool had
to confess to an applicant that "the influence of Government at this time over the East India Company as a body is
positively none. So far from the Court as a body having
any disposition to comply with our wishes on any point,
which is within their own discretion, I really believe, and in
more instances than one I have found, that they have a
satisfaction in mortifying the Government by opposing
what they desire."[2]

In the past the Church had often been used as an aid to
parliamentary management; but in the early nineteenth
century the Church was receding from politics. This was
due in no small measure to the conscientious manner in
which Liverpool administered his Church patronage. The
improvement in the manners of the clergy was much remarked upon, and Liverpool, when writing to Wilberforce,

1 *Report upon Re-organisation of the Civil Service*, 1854-5. P. 406–evidence
of G. Arbuthnot, Auditor of the Civil List, explains that about 1820
"Lord Liverpool, with a patriotism for which he has never received
due credit, voluntarily surrendered the influence obtained by the
power of making direct appointments to the superior offices of the
Customs Department...from that time all collectorships and other
offices of importance were filled by the advancement of officers
already in the service, instead of by the appointment of strangers to it
on a political recommendation". See also the Treasury Minute of
10 August 1821. The salaries of all officers were regulated and every
office was restored to its condition in 1797 unless adequate cause
could be shown for acting otherwise. Useless offices were abolished;
promotions were to be by merit at the discretion of the departmental
head, and there was to be a regular superannuation scheme consisting
of a 5 per cent charge on all salaries and an additional charge on
salaries which had been excessive.
2 Add. MSS. 38474, f. 69.

could not forbear from laying some claim to a share in this
improvement: "It is never pleasant to speak of oneself, but
I must begin by setting myself so far right, that I believe
I can safely say that no minister ever made so little use of
the patronage of the Church for political or family purposes, as myself, nor ever given so much preferment solely
on the score of merit without any connection with, or
personal knowledge of many of the individuals to whom it
has been given."[1] Insistence upon the necessity for preserving or improving the purity of the Church was a
constantly recurring theme in his correspondence. At the
very beginning of his premiership he wrote to the Lord
Lieutenant of Ireland that "it is a lamentable circumstance
to reflect how little eminence there is on the Bench of either
country—and I am satisfied that unless this can be corrected
the Church will not long be able to hold up its head against
the Dissenters and Sectaries which are opposed to it. I am
far from thinking that all bishops should be learned men,
or that it does not often happen that those who are not are
as decent and correct in the exercise of their Episcopal
duties as the most eminent members of the Church. But it
is indispensibly necessary that there should be a proportion
of learned men upon the Bench in both countries. When
I say learned men, I mean of men who are known to be
learned by their works, and by their zeal and activity in
propagating thro' their works the Doctrines of Religion.
We have in England lost within these few years Morley,
Markham, Douglas, Porteus, and their places, I must say,
have been most miserably supplied."[2] In the same letter

1 Add. MSS. 38287, f. 272.   2 Add. MSS. 38252, f. 310.

he set the tone of his policy towards the Church by recommending Dr Magee for an Irish bishopric, in spite of objections as to his political opinions. He was anxious that men appointed by him should perform their duties efficiently: to a prospective Dean of St Paul's he wrote: "I feel it however an imperious duty upon me to offer it conditionally. I know of no situation in the Church where residence is of more importance and I have long determined therefore if this preferment should be vacant whilst I was minister not to recommend any person for it who would not promise to reside six months in the year at least at the Deanery."[1] And when his own family was honoured by the appointment of John Jenkinson to the See of St David's, he wrote to another brother: "It only remains that you impress upon him not to be singular in anything, and where he is in doubt, to take the advice of those of his Brethren on the Bench whose characters stand highest for Piety, learning, combined with a due proportion of Prudence and Moderation. His proceedings will be more watched than those of an ordinary bishop."[2] Nor did he cease to criticise Eldon for what he conceived to be a scandalous misuse of his patronage: "The Chancellor", he complained to Peel, "has nine livings to the Minister's one. With respect to these he does occasionally attend to local claims, but he has besides four Cathedrals, and to no one of these Cathedrals has any man of distinguished learning or intellect been promoted."[3]

Modern party discipline depends largely upon a rigid

1 Add. MSS. 38286, f. 120.   2 Add. MSS. 38300, f. 55.
3 Add. MSS. 38298, f. 279.

control over the electoral machine; in the early nineteenth century this control could only be exerted through the local government patronage. In a few boroughs only was the Government patronage so considerable that it could decide elections alone, and even those which were considered the safest ministerial seats might give trouble at times. Such a one was Harwich, where the Customs House, the Port Administration, the Mail Pacquet, and the Revenue cutter had long been considered the deciding factors in elections; yet in 1822 Vansittart, who had been ten years member for this borough, wrote to Liverpool that "Harwich will require some attention. I have acquired some weight there and should probably have no difficulty in a re-election unless there is time for a previous cabal: but the second seat is not at all secure. If Canning went down there, the Corporation would be flattered and I believe there would be no difficulty, but they must have a man either of patronage, éclat, or else a man who resides near enough to pay them a good deal of personal attention."[1] "Patronage, éclat, or personal attention": these might well be taken as the key-words of the old representative system. In a borough such as Harwich patronage might suffice, but even there a "previous cabal" might succeed. Elsewhere patronage might play a very subsidiary part.

In 1820 Lord John Russell wrote: "A class of offices which is more important perhaps than all the rest, is that of persons employed in the collection of the revenue; upwards of four millions a year are spent in this necessary service.... The offices of the excise are generally given by

1 Add. MSS. 38191, f. 214.

the commissioners of excise appointed by the government, a few being reserved for the patronage of the Treasury; i.e. in other words for members of the House of Commons. The offices of the customs are entirely at the disposal of the Treasury; the offices of the stamp and post-offices are given by the Treasury at the recommendation of members of Parliament voting with the government. The receivers general of the land-tax, whose poundage alone amounts to about 78,000*l*. a year, and whose balances give as much more, are appointed at the recommendation of county members voting with the government. In the instance of one county, this office was lately divided into two, to increase the patronage. Where the members for the county both vote with the opposition, the appointment is given to the person whom the First Lord of the Treasury thinks ought to be the member for the county. Thus it is that the influence of the crown has not only been augmented, but organised, and directed in a manner never before known."[1] The accuracy of the last statement may be doubted, so may the general assumption that all this was corrupt; given a system in which these large number of offices were to be filled by nomination, they had to be filled at the recommendation of somebody, and the Government could hardly be blamed if it favoured a friend. The whole matter was argued out by Liverpool and Canning during the latter's period of Opposition in 1812–13. Canning, after his election for Liverpool, approached Lord Liverpool on the subject of local patronage: "The revenue offices, and other places at Liver-

[1] *Essays and Sketches of Life and Character*. By a Gentleman who has left his Lodgings [Lord John Russell]. London, 1820, p. 148.

pool in the gift of the Treasury and of its subordinate boards, have, so I understand, uniformly been given to applications from the principal individuals and interests of the town: and such applications have been uniformly made through the Members. I have of course received and expect to receive, in common with my colleague, many such applications to forward. In forwarding them, I wish you to understand two things: the first that I can have no personal wish to gratify, and no personal interest of my own to consult, on such occasions; my only concern will be to endeavour to decide between rival claims...with impartiality:—the second, that as I shall never make such applications with any personal views of my own, so I shall not consider the compliance with them in any degree as a personal obligation....Should you choose to point out another channel through which you would prefer to receive such applications for Liverpool patronage...I should not take such a declaration amiss....But if you do not think it necessary to do this, then I hope and trust I may rely upon you, that my relation to the Government will never be allowed to weigh with you in deciding upon any applications from Liverpool of which I may happen to be the channel."[1] Canning was trying to have it both ways, and Liverpool replied that "in far the greater number of instances which will arise the considerations which will govern my decision must be of a mixed nature, as there will be few offices in any such place to which there will not be several and in most cases many claimants, whose pretensions may be equal, or nearly equal, and the individual who

1 Add. MSS. 38568, f. 33.

obtains it will receive it therefore as a mark of personal
favour as well as of public confidence. I have only to add
that you will find me at all times ready to attend to your
recommendations but I shall often think it right to communicate with your colleague, or with other persons before
I decide upon the different applications."[1]

Nor can the Tories be accused of a rigid adherence to
political qualifications, for, in the highest prizes of local
patronage they admitted exceptions. A letter of Lord
Liverpool respecting the Lord Lieutenancies may be quoted
here: "The rules respecting Lords Lieutenant of Counties
have been, of course, always to give them to the friends of
Government where there could be anything like fair competition. The Whigs never, I believe, would have made an
exception. The Tories have." And he cited the instances of
the Duke of Devonshire and the Marquis of Buckingham,
made Lords Lieutenant in Derbyshire and Buckinghamshire while in opposition.[2] Great honours were also occasionally conferred outside the party bounds; in 1826 the
Duke of Devonshire was given the Garter in spite of
Wellington's complaint "that many of our great Tory supporters had been of late out of sorts with the Government,
and he should have wished not to give them this cause of
dissatisfaction".[3]

But the crucial point about the patronage system was that
nothing save a salaried office could ensure the votes of a
member, and such offices were relatively few in number.
A Tory country gentleman might vote against a measure

1 Add. MSS. 38568, f. 34.   2 Add. MSS. 40311, f. 64.
3 Add. MSS. 38302, f. 117.

which the Government believed to be of the greatest importance, but should the Government take from him the administration of local patronage the outcry would have shamed the Government into weakness far more serious than the one lost vote. When Fitzwilliam was dismissed from the Lord Lieutenancy of the West Riding for an offence which many believed to be almost revolutionary, the Whigs raised a loud and popular cry; louder and more damaging would have been the cries of a loyal country gentleman deprived of his just rights for exercising that independence which was his prerogative. In the election of 1826 Liverpool did, indeed, refuse to give Government aid to Holme Sumner, the peculiarly difficult member for Surrey; but this was largely the outcome of local quarrels in the county, and of the fact that Liverpool himself was, to some extent, involved in these local matters. "The real cause of the contest is not political," Liverpool told Peel, "the cause of it is Sumner's personal unpopularity, he is hated by all parties except his own immediate friends, his temper and his manners are considered as offensive and overbearing."[1]

Government influence might sometimes turn the scale, but only in alliance with some powerful local interest. In rivalries between squires and territorial magnates, between corporations and local landowners, between rival parties in the boroughs, the spirit of party was kept alive; the Government profited somewhat from the spirit and vigour which these local animosities breathed into the mouldering frame of ancient political differences, but it was also at the mercy

1 Add. MSS. 40305, f. 187.

of these many small conflicts when it tackled the problem
of party organisation. The Government found itself compelled to tread a tortuous path amid the contending forces
of local politics, but it could seldom, after the fashion of
modern party machines, reconcile all differences by providing a stranger and a safe man. The weakness of the
central organisation meant that it had to combine with
those who were already on the field; and the simplest and
most direct form of control was precluded by the operation
of Curwen's Act. This Act, passed in 1809, prohibited the
purchase of parliamentary seats; it was practically a dead
letter so far as private persons were concerned, but the
Government was forced to observe it rather than risk
scrutiny and exposure. In 1812 Liverpool instructed Peel
that it "will be absolutely necessary that we should so
conduct ourselves...as to be able distinctly to state that
we have been no parties to any money transactions whatever between those who may have influence in boroughs
and persons who may be elected to represent them".[1] To
Sir William Scott, brother of the Lord Chancellor, he
wrote: "You will, perhaps, be surprised when I tell you
that the Treasury have only one seat free of expense, for
which our friend Vansittart will be elected. I have two
more which personal friends have put at my disposal; and
this is the sum total of my powers free of expense. Mr Curwen's bill has put an end to all money transactions between
the Government and the supposed proprietors of boroughs.
Our friends, therefore, who look for the assistance of
Government must be ready to start for open boroughs

1 Parker, 1, 38.

where the general influence of government, combined with a reasonable expense on their own part, may afford them a fair chance of success."[1] When the Government had so little to offer, it is not surprising that its terms had to be easy, and Liverpool is found writing: "I only expect from my friends a generally favourable disposition, and I shall never attempt to interfere with his right to vote as he may think consistent with his duty upon any particular question."[2]

It will be seen that the Government was severely limited in the control which it could exert over members, yet, to a majority of members the continuance of the Tory Government was of the first importance. It is by an exploitation of this same feeling that a modern party relies for much of its discipline; a disposition to criticise is restrained by the knowledge that the Government may feel bound to resign if it is defeated even upon a snap vote; and the independent member has to rely more upon his arguments outside Parliament than upon the use of his vote within it. In the early nineteenth century there was a very strong sentiment of Toryism and this played its part in perpetuating the Tory rule even when the ministers appeared to be weakest; but there was hardly any attempt to exploit this sentiment on the part of the Tory politicians. In 1820 Castlereagh did inform office holders that their support was vital to the Government,[3] but this is exceptional and an example of the general laxity of party control rather than a sign of strict party management. On the contrary, the

1 Yonge, I, 372. 2 Parker, I, 41.
3 A. Aspinall in *E.H.R.* 1926, p. 395, quoting from Hatherton MSS.

Government seemed as a rule more anxious to pander to the independent judgment of members than to request that they should curb their criticisms for the good of the party.

There was no established convention by which the Government should resign when defeated, and on the great question of the income tax, the defeat of which altered the whole financial policy of the Government, there was no idea of resignation. The precise moment at which a Government should resign was left to the discretion of the Prime Minister, and his discretion was guided by the capacity of the Ministers to carry on the King's Government, not by the occurrence of isolated defeats. The complete difference in tone between modern and early nineteenth-century party management may be gathered from a letter written by Arbuthnot, who conducted a great deal of party business; he was asking for the vote of a member upon the Army Estimates in 1816, and he added: "I would particularly notice to you the strong line of distinction between the question of those establishments and the Property Tax; as many of our friends seem to imagine (most erroneously) that they are committing themselves upon the latter by giving a previous vote in favour of the former."[1] Nothing illustrates more clearly than this letter the plight of the Government which had to connive at the frequent adverse votes of those from whom it hoped to obtain a general support.

If the Government forbore from putting pressure upon its supporters, it might be expected that it would take steps

1 Add. MSS. 19242, f. 288, Arbuthnot to Gooch.

to see that they were well informed of the Government's intentions. But party meetings were few, and were usually held only when the Government had particularly unpopular measures to propose. Such meetings were held in 1817 and 1818, the one to disclose the Government's plans for sinecures and the other to inform members of proposals to make marriage allowances for the royal Dukes. Even at such meetings little more was said than a bald statement of fact, and Peel, who probably had a clearer idea than any other Tory of the problems of party management, declared that he was never more surprised in his life than to hear Liverpool "intimate to a very numerous assembly of the supporters of this administration its intention of proposing to Parliament allowances to the royal Dukes which there could not be a hope of Parliament acceding to...a man must be really infatuated who could flatter himself that this House of Commons, now perhaps on the eve of dissolution, which was prevailed upon with the utmost difficulty and after the most unpleasant discussions to grant 60,000 *l.* a year to the Duke of Cumberland, could now be induced to grant him...12,000 *l.* more."[1] This particular attempt at party management seems to have been singularly maladroit, for, after announcing its intentions the Government heard no statement of views, and went on to suffer an irritating defeat in the Commons.

Members frequently received letters from the party managers—Holmes,[2] Arbuthnot, or the leader of the House —but these were no more explicit than the ministerial

1 Parker, I, 263.
2 W. Holmes, Treasurer of the Ordnance and Tory "whip".

statements at party meetings.[1] Liverpool, in requesting the
attendance of members controlled by Rutland and Lonsdale, was more explanatory;[2] but this was an exceptional
case. The summonses, indeed, were illustrative of the
Government's difficulty in obtaining the attendance of
supporters, not of efficient "management".

Very different would have been the result if party
meetings had been the regular rule; many independent men
could have been induced to vote with the Government;
and, what is hardly less important, the Government supporters would have gone down to the House with a clear
notion of the arguments for a motion instead of hearing it
for the first time from the Treasury Bench. In this way the
Government could have gained the initiative in debate and
a safe majority. At times Liverpool held meetings of one
particular "interest". Thus in 1815 he called a "very full
meeting of the landed interest" to discuss the proposed
Corn Law; this meeting included Whigs as well as Tories,
and the Government took the extraordinary course of
leaving to the meeting the decision upon the measure. The
Government would have preferred a sliding scale but the
meeting "almost unanimously and particularly Mr Western"
preferred the prohibition of import when the price fell
below 80s.[3] Occasionally meetings seem to have been used
to recruit fresh support; in 1818 the Grenvilles were beginning that dalliance with the ministers which was to

1 Cf. Add. MSS. 19242, f. 269, for a typical example. Castlereagh to
   T. S. Gooch: "No questions of the greatest importance will come
   under discussion.... I trust you will excuse my expressing to you the
   anxious wish that I feel for as full an attendance as possible at the
   opening of the session."   2 Add. MSS. 38262, fs. 323 ff.
3 Add. MSS. 38742, f. 4.

lead them finally to office in 1821, and one of their number, J. H. Stanhope, received a note from Liverpool asking him to call; he went and found, to his surprise, that he was in the midst of a party meeting. The use of party meetings seems to have been sporadic, and inspired by no consistent plan of party leadership.

The impression left by an examination of these details of party management is certainly not that of an efficient machine. Rather it is that of men often at their wits' end to know how to carry on the day-to-day business in the House of Commons, frequently at the mercy of a capricious independent vote, and realising but slowly that their methods were ill adapted to the needs of the time. Liverpool is found writing with pained surprise that the Government was "exposed to the most acrimonious, systematic and persevering opposition that I can ever recollect to have seen in Parliament",[1] and again that the Government "certainly hangs by a thread", for neither defeats nor concessions had had the "least effect in conciliating those who have deserted us".[2] Liverpool complained that the "spirit of the House of Commons" was worse than it ever had been; and this spirit reflected the tone of public opinion in the country at large. There was a very large body of Tory opinion in the country, but, just as it failed to instruct their parliamentary supporters, so the ministers failed to inform or encourage their supporters in the country at large.

Against the Government the Whigs ranged all the modern apparatus of propaganda and popular appeal. In 1816

1 Yonge, II, 270.   2 *Ibid.*

Brougham organised county and parish meetings against
the Property Tax, and, for many nights, the House of
Commons was monopolised by the Whigs as they poured
forth furious eulogies of the petitions presented by these
meetings. For country gentlemen the extravagance of the
ministers was stressed, for commercial men the inquisi-
torial nature of the tax, and for everyone the shocking behaviour of the tax collectors. The result was one of the
greatest victories for public opinion and one of the greatest
blows to sound finance in the history of Parliament. The
Whigs followed up this success with a wholesale attack
upon the various items of a supposedly extravagant administration. Again they had public opinion on their side,
and a motion to reduce the salary of the Secretary to the
Admiralty—which Liverpool considered a direct vote of
censure upon the Government—was defeated only because
Brougham overstepped the mark with a personal attack
upon the Prince Regent. From this Opposition offensive
there resulted various measures for the reduction of expenditure and, in 1817, for the abolition of those sinecures
which still remained.

The riots and agitation of 1817 had the effect of frighten-
ing the independent members, and in that year the Government becomes somewhat stronger and the direct influence
of public opinion upon legislation becomes less marked.
Public opinion had, however, one further victory to score
in these post-war years. In 1819 the Government announced its intention of postponing cash payment for one
more year, but when the irritation of the Commons and the
public at this became apparent the Government changed

its mind and consented to a Committee of Enquiry. Both parties were agreed that a return to the Gold Standard was desirable, but the Tories said that it was impossible to restore it until the Bank had accumulated sufficient bullion, while the Whigs insisted that it could be restored at any time if the Government and the Bank would observe the principles of the Bullion Report of 1810. The findings of the committee amounted to a complete vindication of the Whig view, the Government yielded gracefully, and even implemented its recommendations with enthusiasm. Yet this, as much as the Property Tax, was a victory for public opinion and in a far worthier cause. The adoption by the Government of Peel's committee had one important result: it meant that the Government had espoused a commercial rather than an agricultural policy. Resumption of cash payments meant a restriction in the circulation and a fall in prices, and the class which felt this most was the agricultural class with its fixed rents and long-term contracts arranged under a depreciated currency and to be paid under an appreciated currency. During 1821 and 1822 the Government faced a persistent and angry attack from the agriculturalists and this meant that, in searching for the approval of public opinion, the Government sought consciously for commercial support.

When Radical disturbance had subsided and with the great achievement of resuming cash payment to their credit it seemed that the ministers might look forward more happily to the future, but all their hopes were dissipated when George IV insisted that penal measures must be taken against his Queen. "Now that the circulation is settled on a fixed foundation, and that the annual loans are beginning to be no longer wanted," wrote Liverpool, "the Country appears, for the first time, to be settling itself into a state of peace. It is provoking under such circumstances to have such a business as that now depending before the House of Lords to keep the country in a ferment and to give so strong a handle to the disaffected of all classes and descriptions."[1] Once again it may be said that public opinion was the Queen's salvation; indeed had the Queen been a little less disreputable nothing could have saved the Government. Public enthusiasm could not clear the Queen of guilt, nor could it replace her name in the Liturgy from which it had been excluded, but it could convince a very large number of men that, whatever the Queen's crimes, it was impolitic to punish her for them. When the majority in the House of Lords on the third reading of the Bill of Pains and Penalties fell to nine, the Government took the line that the Queen's guilt had been proved and that it was inexpedient to carry the matter any further. It was another victory won by public opinion over a Government which commanded the King's favour, a majority in both Houses, and all the resources of the spoils system.

So, in the five years which followed the greatest victory in the annals of British history, the Government which had presided over that victory was repeatedly forced to bow to public opinion. At the end of these five years it was so weakened in personnel and in prestige that some change in its composition was essential; it will be seen hereafter that public opinion had its part to play in the transformation of the Government, but first it will be as well to ask on what

1 Add. MSS. 38742, f. 26.

opinion the Government could depend, what opinion had supported it through these difficult years, and what steps it took to organise and foster this opinion.

The Tory party was far stronger in sentiment than it was in organisation. The old traditions of "Church and King" were enshrined with the new administrative efficiency in the memory of Pitt. Throughout the country Pitt clubs performed for the Tories the service which Holland House and the great country mansions performed for the Whigs, and with long after-dinner speeches, well-drunk toasts, and execrable verses the Tories saluted their idol. The ministers, most of whom had been the friends or protégés of Pitt, caught some of the reflected glory; and in them the power of sentiment was substantiated by honesty and ability which did not descend to the vulgar arts of popularity. But, as strong as any sentiment and far stronger than any reasoned belief, was the simple feeling of dislike for the Whigs. In the Whigs were united aristocratic insolence and the unseemly violence of democracy; they were the men who would have surrendered weakly to Napoleon; they would even now let in Popery; and no man could trust them not to lay sacrilegious hands upon the constitution. The strength of the Tory party lay in the Church and in the smaller landed proprietors, but there was also a very considerable Tory following in the commercial classes of the large towns. There was, it is true, a Tory aristocracy; but the Tory aristocrats did not lead their party as the Whig aristocrats led theirs. The typical Tory was still the squire, and the party reflected in equal proportions his good and his bad qualities.

The ordinary Tory was not an enthusiastic politician

unless he was stirred, and, above all things, the Tories required encouragement similar to that which the Whigs gave to their country supporters. But this encouragement was not forthcoming: throughout the country Tories were hissed upon the hustings, their arguments went unheard, and even when they were accorded a hearing, they had little original to say, for their leaders did not provide them with a programme. Members of the Government seldom spoke out of Parliament, and most of them, as peers, had not even the necessity of composing election addresses. Only Canning showed any eagerness to speak outside Parliament, and he, when he persuaded Liverpool to speak in public at Bristol in 1824, wondered whether he would be accused of seducing the Prime Minister into the base courses of popularity.[1]

Nor could the Tories look for much inspiration in the press. The Tory *Courier* was a pedestrian journal to place beside *The Times* and the *Morning Chronicle*, while other Tory newspapers such as the *Sun*, were mere time-serving rags whose editors were playing for pensions.[2] For the most part the Tories had to fall back upon their own inspiration when they wished to rebut Whig arguments and upon their own initiative when they wished to call counter meetings or carry counter petitions. Their weakness is revealed by a speech of George Rose during the Property Tax agitation of 1816: "If people were told that by petitioning they would get relief, they would naturally take

1 E. J. Stapleton, I, 234.
2 Cf. Castlereagh, *Mem. and Corr.* XI, 17, Liverpool to Castlereagh: "No paper that has any character, and consequently an established sale, will accept money from Government."

the advice given to them. He recollected a meeting which
he attended when it was proposed to petition against the
tax. Every hand was held up in favour of the proposition,
which was seconded by a friend of his who paid nearly
£3000 per annum property tax. If any person had then
stated that, if the tax were removed, the sum would
probably then fall on individuals not so wealthy as he was,
he had no doubt that some difference of opinion would have
been excited."[1] The trouble was that no one did say this,
the Tories were cowed, and their leaders either ignored or
deplored such popular manœuvres. From 1816 to 1821 the
impression formed by a study of popular agitation and of
popular petitions presented in the House of Commons is
that the country was solidly Whig and Radical; in truth
this is testimony not so much to the strength of Whig
opinion but to the weakness of Tory party organisation.

For this neglect of public opinion the Tories reaped their
reward during the Radical agitation. The ministers were
extremely loath to take legislative action against the Radicals, and they felt very keenly that Tory magistrates
throughout the country were not doing their duty. In
1817 Sidmouth told the Nottinghamshire magistrates that
"The prevailing impression certainly was that there was a
want of vigilance and activity in the magistracy. Government could do no more than give the impulse, and all the
aid that could be afforded, to the execution of the laws."[2]
And Liverpool told a Yorkshire Tory that "The Property
of the country must be taught to protect itself. The active
disaffected in any quarter are not numerous. The majority

1 Hansard, XXXII.   2 Pellew, *Life of Sidmouth*, III, 152.

go with the tide, and if they see all the zeal and activity on one side, and only apathy on the other, their choice cannot be expected to be doubtful."[1] This was written in 1819, and it shows that by this time the ministers were aware of the true state of affairs; indeed, throughout the debatable events which followed Peterloo, the dominating motive of the Government was the necessity of encouraging Tories throughout the country.

To Canning the rights or wrongs of the magistrates' action at Peterloo was almost irrelevant. "To let down the magistrates", he wrote, "would be to invite their resignation, and to lose all gratuitous service in the counties liable to disturbance for ever. It is, to be sure, very provoking that the magistrates, right as they were in principle, and nearly right in practice, should have spoilt the completeness of their case by half an hour's precipitation."[2] In the months which followed Peterloo the Whigs tried to repeat the tactics which had proved so successful against the Property Tax: they called large county meetings and petitioned for enquiry. Lawrence Dundas appeared and spoke at a meeting in York, and shortly afterwards Earl Fitzwilliam signed a requisition for a county meeting in Yorkshire and spoke at it in favour of petition. Earl Fitzwilliam was Lord Lieutenant of the West Riding, and the reaction of the Government was to dismiss him from his post. This was not a mere manifestation of party spite but a sign that the Government did not intend to repeat the mistake of 1816. Liverpool was convinced that strong measures would have the desired moral effect: "Our forbearance", he

1 Add. MSS. 38280, f. 205.   2 Add. MSS. 38741, f. 314.

wrote, "would be ascribed to nothing but timidity, and would discourage our best friends."[1] The decided line taken by the ministers had its effect in heartening the sadly perplexed Tories. The Bishop of Lincoln had heard from a friend with connections in Lancashire and Yorkshire that "everybody rejoices in the dismissal of Lord Fitzwilliam and in the vigour of ministers".[2] The action of the magistrates at Peterloo, whether justified or not, had given the Whigs a great opening; left to themselves, as they had been left in previous years, they would probably have been able to bring the whole force of a well-directed stream of public opinion to play upon the Government; but the action of the Government turned the tables and robbed them of their advantage. From York the President of the "King and Constitution Club" reported that many of the respectable Whigs were against the meeting;[3] the Grenvilles condemned the meeting for "childish folly and imbecility"; Sir Robert Heron was unable to call meetings in Lincolnshire and Northants "such were the fears of some and the apathy of others.";[4] and the ministers found, to their surprise, that they were able to pass all their remedial measures with relative ease before Christmas. Success came to them now because they had at last realised the necessity for leading and encouraging Tory opinion.

The same idea determined the principle of the new laws, the notorious gag acts. "The encouragement which has been given to the seditions and blasphemies by meetings in other counties...has aggravated all the evils ten fold,

1 Bathurst, pp. 479-80.   2 Add. MSS. 38280, f. 80.
3 Add. MSS. 38280, f. 80.   4 Sir R. Heron, *Notes*, p. 107.

and makes me seriously doubt whether in some parts of Lancashire and Cheshire we should soon find magistrates to execute their duty unless the law is in some degree strengthened," [1] wrote Liverpool, and he thought that "the alarm in the country is now considerable and we ought to take advantage of it". [2]

The Government encouraged its followers by its example, but the Government was far from initiating a "publicity campaign". It saw that Tories must be given a lead, and that the very large reserve of Tory sentiment should be utilised; but Canning was the first Tory to view public opinion in the way that Brougham or the other Whig organisers did, and Canning did not make conscious use of public opinion as an instrument of policy until after 1822. The characteristic attitude of the Tories can be judged from the remarks which usually preceded the presentation of a petition in the House of Commons: the highest recommendation was that the petitioners were "numerous and respectable", failing that respectability was a far higher recommendation than mere numbers, and the enemies of a petition would usually attempt to prove that it was signed by a numerous rabble. In Tory eyes the political part of the nation began with the educated middle class, below that people had, or ought to have, no politics but merely loyalty and industry. Nor was this view merely reactionary, for it was reinforced by the most modern and most humane theories alike. The new doctrines of *laissez-faire*, to which the Prime Minister was a convert, taught that economic ills had nothing to do with political grievances and could be

1 Add. MSS. 38280, f. 121.   2 Add. MSS. 38280, f. 146.

remedied only by the free interaction of economic causes; while the Evangelicals, under whose influence most of the ministers had fallen, taught the duty of obedience to Christian governors. The deduction which the ministers were not slow to make was that the whole alliance of distress with political agitation was not only foolish but also immoral.

It followed that the principal aim of the Government was to break the alliance between politics and social distress, and the last method to which they would resort was that of counter agitation among the working classes. In defending the suspension of the Habeas Corpus Act in 1817 Liverpool said that in 1812 "the manufacturing parts of the country were in a disturbed and dangerous state, in consequences of which certain papers were laid before both Houses of Parliament. Those papers were referred to a secret committee and upon the report of that committee some new laws were formed to meet the evil; but it never was in contemplation of Government to adopt any measures similar to the present, because it was the firm conviction of that committee that political opinions were not the foundation of the evils that then existed. There might indeed have been some remote connection but it was so remote as not to call for the kind of proceeding which it was now proposed to adopt."[1] During the Radical agitation the most frequent phrases in Tory mouths was "the deluded people", and it was the aim of Tory legislators to prevent the access to the people of those who deluded them. It was this theory and not mere panic which dictated the much

1 Hansard, xxxv, 568.

criticised acts limiting the right of public meeting and the freedom of the press.[1] The first restriction manifested what may be called the "parochial" element in Tory thought. Liverpool could conceive "nothing more outrageous than that bodies of men at a distance should take upon themselves to exercise this judgment upon the conduct of magistrates placed in a critical and difficult situation".[2] Every man was concerned with the affairs of his own parish and might meet with others to discuss local affairs, but men had not the right to assemble in large congregate meetings to discuss things which did not directly concern them. The Tories did not wish to interfere with county meetings legally convened by the constituted authorities, though they might deplore the use which Whigs might make of these meetings, but the mass meeting convened at the discretion of a Radical orator was ruled out by the new restriction of meetings other than county meetings to the inhabitants of the parish in which it was held, or, in certain large parishes, to specified districts containing a population of 10,000. In the same way they took from the agitators the weapon of the press. "An effectual and permanent remedy for these monstrous evils is the thing to be found if possible," wrote Canning, "the root of them is the Press; and who is prepared to go to that root directly"?[3] and the press was, in

1 The correspondence of the Whig leaders shows that they too were disturbed by the phenomenon of large mass meetings. Lambton, who expressed also Grey's opinion, wrote to Wilson: "The only thing we did not quite approve of was your welcome of Hunt.... Keep clear of him as you would of infection": Add. MSS. 30109, f. 78. Brougham and Erskine both expressed their doubts of the legality of such meetings, and Mackintosh, Scarlett, and the two Lambs condemned them even while they censured the magistrates.
2 Add. MSS. 38277, f. 363.   3 Add. MSS. 38741, f. 314.

Liverpool's opinion, the "real source of the evil—but one more subject to embarrassment as a source of legislation, than any of the other evils of the day".[1] The result of these considerations was two Acts, one punishing blasphemous and seditious libels, the other bringing political pamphlets under the same licensing and stamping regulations as newspapers.

In judging the reaction of the Government to the great Radical agitation of 1819 it is necessary to remember that it acted under the immediate apprehension of revolution, and that its remedies certainly did achieve their object in divorcing political agitation from social evils. Bootle Wilbraham, a Tory magistrate and member of Parliament, wrote of the disaffection in Lancashire which had become "open hostility, not only to the Government but to all the higher classes, whose landed property is in this County (I understand) actually parcelled out for future distribution".[2] Lambton wrote that "The Tories in Yorkshire are greatly alarmed at the state of things. They fully expect a revolution, and in my opinion nothing can prevent its taking place but the removal of the ministers";[3] and Grey, in rebuking Wilson for his dalliance with the Radicals, wrote: "Look at the men themselves who lead in this cause. Is there one among them with whom you would trust yourself in the dark? Can you have, I will not say, any confidence in their opinions and principles, but any doubt of the wickedness of their intentions? Look at them, at their characters, at their conduct. What is there more base, and more detestable, more at variance with all tact and decency, as well as all

1 Add. MSS. 38741, f. 314. 2 Add. MSS. 38280, f. 19.
3 Add. MSS. 30109, f. 79.

morality, truth, and honour? A cause so supported cannot be a good cause. They may use Burdett as an instrument for a time, and you also if you place yourself in their trammels, but depend upon it, if a convulsion follows their attempt to work upon the minds of the people, inflamed as they now are by distress, for which your reform will afford a very inadequate remedy, I shall not precede you many months on the scaffold, which you will have assisted in preparing for us both."[1] It requires an effort to realise that the writer of this passage was the Whig leader, and, when men were writing openly in this vein, it is hard to censure the ministers for measures which, with all their faults, were successful. The Radicals were not able to make the Queen's trial the occasion for a rebellion, and, what is more striking, in 1825 the great distress of that year was not accompanied by any political agitation.

The Government had, with some reluctance, taken strong measures and encouraged the Tories by example. By the beginning of 1820 Tory opinion had rallied after the threat to its very existence as an articulate force in 1816; with the Queen's "trial" Tory opinion was once more eclipsed, but general belief that the Queen had been more sinful than sinned against, the operation of the Six Acts, and the fact that the ministers did not push the case to a decision, enabled the Tories to revive in the following year. During 1821 the Tories still demanded signs and portents

1 Add. MSS. 30109, fs. 56 ff. Other examples of the predominant fear are found in Dropmore MSS. x, e.g. p. 449: "If the history of all ages did not shew how constantly the moderates have in all revolutions been made first the tools and then the victims of the most furious agitators." And in Add. MSS. 38280, f. 168, Bootle Wilbraham to Liverpool. There was enough evidence to "satisfy anybody but a Whig that a plot of the most serious nature exists".

that their cause was good. The Government was deplorably weak in the House of Commons and, to add to its other difficulties, there was a revolt of the landed interest against the operation of Peel's Act. Liverpool responded to the obvious need of his party for stimulus, and initiated a considerable change in the personnel and the tone of his Government. During the next two years Sidmouth was replaced by Peel, the Grenvilles and Wellesley joined the Government, Canning took Castlereagh's place, Robinson succeeded Vansittart, and Huskisson entered the Cabinet. These changes meant not only a strengthening of the Government's debating power, but they meant that the Government had consciously begun to cultivate the good opinion of the commercial classes. In 1825 Liverpool, speaking at Bristol, said: "If there be any merit on my part in the course of the administration of public affairs, with which I have been trusted, that merit consists in good intentions. I certainly have used my best endeavours to further the good of the country, but neither those good intentions nor those best endeavours would have been successful, if they had not received the valuable support, and been aided by the talents, of my excellent and able colleagues, and, above all if they had not received the support of the great commercial interests of the country."[1] It was this conscious union of the Government with commercial opinion which produced the brilliant last period of Liverpool's administration, the period of Canning, of Huskisson, and of young Peel, the period which may be called that of Liberal Toryism.

1 Speech transcribed in the *Morning Chronicle*, 16 January 1825, from the *Bristol Gazette*.

CHAPTER V

THE TRANSFORMATION OF
THE GOVERNMENT

In December 1820 Huskisson told Canning that he still thought the ministers would "break down, or be broken down before Easter".[1] He thought so notwithstanding "all the reliance which may be placed on the blunders, the intemperance and the dissensions of their opponents and on the alarms and fears of the squirearchy". These prophecies were echoed by Croker—"a government cannot go on without the gift of the gab"[2]—and Peel looked upon their obvious weakness as the outward and visible sign of an inward failing: "Do you not think", he asked Croker, "that the tone of England—of that great compound of folly, weakness, prejudice, wrong feeling, right feeling, obstinacy, and newspaper paragraphs, which is called public opinion —is more liberal—to use an odious but intelligible phrase —than the policy of the Government?...Will the Government act on the principles on which, without being very certain, I suppose they have hitherto professed to act? Or will they carry into execution moderate Whig measures of reform? Or will they give up the government to the Whigs, and let them carry those measures into effect? Or will they coalesce with the Whigs, and oppose the united phalanx to the Hobhouses, and Burdetts, and Radicalism?"[3] At the end of 1820 men were sure of one thing: the Government must gain new strength or it must fall. It was one of those

1 Add. MSS. 38742, f. 156.   2 Croker, I, 184.   3 *Ibid.*

rare times at which men feel that they have seen the end of an epoch and that the future will demand new men and new ideas.

The immediate threat to the existence of the Government came from the King. On 16 November he had prepared, though he had not sent, a paper stating to the Cabinet that "he considers himself under the necessity of taking measures for the formation of a new administration".[1] At the same time he set in motion the whole machinery of backstairs negotiation in order to discover the dispositions of the various political groups. He had resolved "to proceed upon the road of negotiation if possible with Lord Grey",[2] but Grey, as was his wont, had retired to Howick so soon as parliamentary business was over.[3] The King's intimate adviser throughout was Sir William Knighton, who now first enjoyed the full light of the King's favour, and the first emissary was Lord Dacre, who had to discover whether the Opposition had "any settled plan of conduct for future difficulties",[4] in other words whether they had any plan for dealing with the Queen. Dacre saw Tierney, but his report was not very encouraging.[5] Lauderdale, now hovering between his former Whig allegiance and a Tory conversion, was also consulted; he advised against the expediency of changing the Government before the Queen's business was settled, and told the King that "a middle government" would be hard to find.[6] For Knighton the King summed up his

1 *George IV*, No. 867. 2 *Ibid.* No. 878.
3 *Ibid.* 4 *Ibid.*
5 *Ibid.* 6 *Ibid.* No. 877.

views: the Queen would have to agree to anything proposed by the Opposition, since she could not have recourse to the old ministers and the Radicals were too few; and by a change of Government "the publick mind would probably be diverted", and proposals coming from new ministers would "be more likely to suit the temper of the times, than anything coming from the old government". On the other hand the known principles of the Opposition "may be designated under the term Liberaux", suppose they wished to release Bonaparte, to change the system and spirit of foreign policy, to emancipate the Catholics, and to reduce the army; the Government had frequently failed to consult his feelings, but "they have been a good government for the country"; and above all was the fear of the day when he might "be shut out on all sides from any set of men, as servants, that could make my life tolerable".[1] Other friends of the King made enquiries among the Opposition leaders. Lord Donoughmore saw Lansdowne, who was sympathetic but thought that no government could be formed under the circumstances. Lord Hutchinson saw Tierney, who gave the same advice and added: "Let them proceed taking full responsibility upon themselves, and if beat it would be very fortunate"; the Whigs were naturally unwilling to come in as the King's nominees, but should the Government be beaten in the House of Commons, then it would be a very different matter. Leach, the Vice-Chancellor, saw Holland, who would say or do nothing without Grey. Bloomfield saw Buckingham, who condemned the Government, "but thought it would be complete ruin to me were

1 *George IV*, Nos. 879, 880.

I reduced to hold any communication, or to throw myself in any shape upon Holland House". Faced with the results of this unofficial negotiation, the King decided that he must "continue without yielding and with trust in providence".[1]

The Tories were still in possession of the field but rumours of the King's negotiations had been widely circulated, and it was known that the Government did not possess the confidence of the King. This made the position of the Government peculiarly awkward; they were weak, but without the promise of stability implied in the King's confidence none would join them. No one realised this more clearly than Liverpool. In December 1820 he requested Bragge Bathurst, Chancellor of the Duchy of Lancaster, to undertake the duties of the Board of Control, which Canning had relinquished: "In the state in which the business now stands," he wrote, "it cannot be surprising that persons not connected with the Government should be unwilling to take responsible offices"; if Bathurst would take temporary charge of the Board of Control it would avoid encountering any refusals, and would give an opportunity of strengthening the Government at a future date, for "if the Government is to remain, something must be done sooner or later to strengthen it, and it appeared to be inexpedient to put out of our power so important an office as that now vacant".[2] Nor was Liverpool entirely unaware of that change in the tone of the country upon which Peel had commented, though he attributed it to that natural recovery from post-war troubles which he always foretold. In September 1820 he had seen the country "for

1 *George IV*, No. 881.   2 Add. MSS. 38288, f. 386.

the first time to be settling itself into a state of peace".[1]
The Queen's business had prevented him taking any advantage of this during the closing months of 1820, but
during 1821 his course was plain, he would attempt to
strengthen his Government, and he would attempt to give
the country a Government suitable to a "state of peace".

The first to whom Liverpool looked was Canning; he
had not seen the necessity of Canning's resignation over
the Queen's trial, and he took the first opportunity to negotiate for his return. There was no political difference which
might hinder this object, but, on the other hand, the Tories
if they accepted Canning did not accept him gladly; they
recognised his abilities and they realised that their Prime
Minister had set his heart upon restoring Canning to the
Cabinet, but they still harboured a suspicion that his
talents were not balanced by honour, that his ambition was
not countered by loyalty, and that he was a charlatan without an acre of land in the country. For this reputation
Canning had himself to blame, and a Tory unable to
appreciate the greatness of the man might look with justi-
fiable reprobation upon his past record.

The apparent turning point in Canning's career was the
year 1812. Before that he had made many enemies, but
Brother Bragge and Brother Hiley might forgive and Castlereagh showed himself ready to forget. In the negotiations
which led to the formation of Liverpool's ministry he had
played a part to which not much exception could be taken,
and it was after the establishment of that ministry that he
made his fatal error. In August Liverpool made to Canning

1 Add. MSS. 38742, f. 26.

an offer which Canning himself described as "perhaps the handsomest that ever was made to an individual". Canning was to have the Foreign Office, Wellesley was to have Ireland, and most of the Canningites were to have subordinate office. There was but one condition: that Castlereagh was to retain the leadership of the House. In an evil hour some of Canning's friends suggested that he should demand this too, and in an evil hour Canning agreed to do so. Of all demands it was the most unwise to make and the most impossible to concede. Castlereagh was already acting as leader of the House, and he had already made a great concession to Canning by yielding the Foreign Office and contenting himself with the Chancellorship of the Exchequer. Nor would the leadership give Canning much more real power than he would possess as Secretary of State; as leader Castlereagh would have to arrange the business of the House, speak for the Government when the minister concerned was in the House of Lords, and share in the distribution of Government patronage, though his influence so acquired would scarcely recompense him for the great patronage of the Foreign Office which he relinquished voluntarily. Castlereagh was, in fact, acting a disinterested and generous part; it was Canning who was being arrogant and unreasonable. Canning soon realised his mistake: "With regard to what is called the lead in the House of Commons," he told Liverpool, "I heartily wish that it had never been mentioned at all." But the trouble was that, once the subject had been mentioned, neither could yield without a sense of self-humiliation, and Liverpool was certainly not going to put pressure upon Castle-

reagh in order to make him yield to an unjust demand.
Canning, on the other hand, stated his case as: "While
I beg, on the one hand, that I may be considered as not
claiming it for myself, I cannot, on the other hand, submit
to the claim of it for Lord Castlereagh."[1] There was, however, no suitable person under whom both could serve, and
on that note the negotiation ended.

Canning had put himself thoroughly in the wrong. He
had put personal jealousies before national advantage, he
had tried to dictate terms to a Government which was
already treating him with extraordinary generosity, and,
from an entirely selfish point of view, he had allowed a
momentary consideration to hinder his political advance.
Throughout the Canningite correspondence of the next
ten years there hangs an air of melancholy and a sense of
lost opportunity. In 1815 Canning was writing, "My
'abdication' took place in 1812. I felt it so then and never
for a moment since...have altered that opinion."[2] Huskisson was "as fully convinced as Canning himself that the
decision of 1812 was irretrievable by any subsequent negotiation";[3] and in 1821 Canning wrote in gloomy retrospect,
"Wellesley is now just where he might have been—by my
doing—in 1812. No other person...is ever likely to regain
what they then lost."[4]

To Liverpool it was due that Canning did not ruin his
career by the decision of 1812, and but for Liverpool the
career of Canning would be simply one of disappointed
ambition. In 1814 Canning, with a somewhat specious

1 Yonge, 1, 405–6.   2 Add. MSS. 38740, f. 109.
3 Add. MSS. 38740, f. 198.   4 Add. MSS. 38743, f. 129.

gesture, disbanded his "party", or, in other words, told his friends that they might fend for themselves. The result was that Huskisson, Sturges Bourne, and Ellis took office, and Canning himself accepted a splendid and pointless embassy to Lisbon. Canning was peculiarly gratified with Liverpool's action at this time—probably on account of the generous provision made for his friends—and this year marks the resumption of really intimate relations between the two men. "I cannot wait", wrote Canning to Liverpool, "to express to you, not from politician to politician, but with the genuine warmth of old Christ Church feelings, the exceeding satisfaction which I have derived from the fairness and friendliness of your whole conduct in these discussions."[1] The result of the arrangement of 1814 was that the Canningites had shyed off any flirtation with the Whigs,[2] that they had identified themselves with the Government, and that Liverpool would bring Canning into the Cabinet when the occasion arose.

Canning professed no great anxiety to get back into office: the succession of a Whig Government was perhaps the only circumstance "in which I should ever *wish* to resume my place in the House of Commons",[3] and in 1816 "nothing is further from my wish than that *any* opening should occur at this moment and I would not on any account have one *made*".[4] These professions may, however, be

1 Add. MSS. 38193, f. 25.
2 Add. MSS. 38739, f. 271, Canning to Huskisson: "It is a satisfaction to me that those most inclined to them among my friends must now see...that the hatred of the Whigs to me is tenfold greater than that of any part of the Opposition to the Government or than any part of the Government to us."　　　3 Add. MSS. 38739, f. 271.
4 Add. MSS. 38739, f. 278.

attributed to the grapes which were sour; Canning had been assured of Liverpool's "friendly and cordial feeling", Huskisson held a watching brief on his behalf,[1] and, on the death of Buckinghamshire, Canning immediately accepted Liverpool's offer of the Board of Control.

Canning had now humbled himself and had taken an office not of the first rank in the ministry which he had aspired to dominate. In this situation he continued for four years, not without looking to the prospect of promotion when one of the older ministers should retire, yet doing so without ostentation. In August 1819 he had an interview with Liverpool, which, he told Huskisson, "was an intimation in the most amicable tone that on *any* opening I should expect to be consulted as to the whole. Not however seeking or wishing for any; but not thinking that any could arise which must not affect me far otherwise than the only one which had arisen since my succession.[2] ... The answer was 'Certainly'—accompanied with an assurance that nothing of any sort was at present in contemplation or in prospect—except as to what Ld Sidmouth might meditate for himself, and he appeared now to have given up entirely the notion of retreat which he occasionally professed to entertain. I said not one word as to his particular situation —or as to any other, except incidentally as to my own, to which I reminded L. that your wishes, and mine for you, were entirely directed. The whole conversation did not

1 Immediately the death of Buckinghamshire was announced Huskisson wrote to Liverpool with a specific reminder that Canning would expect the offer. Add. MSS. 38741, f. 4.
2 Lord Mulgrave had retired from the Mastership of the Ordnance to give Wellington a Cabinet office. Mulgrave was, however, still attending the Cabinet in 1820.

take up more time than it will cost you to read this account of it. The acquiescence was so prompt, that I had nothing to combat or to stimulate, and I wished to say what I had to say with as little emphasis as possible, lest the exposition of my expectation as to an eventual contingency might be misconstrued into a design to hasten the event." [1]

So, in 1819, Liverpool was looking forward to a reconstruction of his ministry, and in that reconstruction Canning would have played an important part. The retirement of Sidmouth was the anticipated occasion for Cabinet changes, but Liverpool was also thinking of a junction with the Grenvilles [2] and Peel was an obvious candidate for Cabinet office; so it may be assumed, with some show of probability, that the changes which were finally completed in 1823 were being considered by Liverpool four years earlier. But whatever plans he was forming at this time were rendered void by the insistence of George IV to be rid of his Queen. Canning had been a friend of the Queen, and he felt that he could not now be party to proceedings against her. [3] Nor, at the end of the year,

1 Add. MSS. 38741, f. 314.
2 Add. MSS. 38272, f. 104: R. P. Ward to Liverpool, 9 June 1818, shows how the Grenvilles and the Government were sending out feelers to ascertain views as to a possible alliance. Ward reported that Buckingham was "clearly and distinctly satisfied...as to your Lordship's conduct...of the Government at large", and he elicited the important fact that "the Catholic question might not produce so vital a difference as to be fatal to a connection with the Grenvilles".
3 Liverpool did not think that Canning's scruples need have taken him to the step of resignation. The inference is that Canning may have known the Queen better than is usually imagined—there is a hint in Dorothy Marshall's *Rise of George Canning* which seems to point that way—but there is no need to draw from that the inference drawn by George IV, that the Queen had been Canning's mistress.

could Peel be persuaded to join, and any attempt to recon-
struct the ministry had to be postponed until the last
echoes of that dismal affair had died away.

Liverpool had, however, taken such steps as he could
to leave open the way for Canning's restoration to the
Cabinet as soon as the Queen's business was over. The
editor of a volume of Canning's papers[1] went to some
lengths to show that Canning's real reason for resignation
was his disapproval of the Government's social and foreign
policy. But Canning had been looking for promotion in the
previous year, and nothing had happened since to change
the Government's policy; he had been a convinced supporter of the ministerial policy after Peterloo, and Foreign
Policy was now nearer to his views than it had been at any
other time since the war. The true state of the case seems
to be quite the contrary, for Canning was at pains to show
that the Queen's business alone necessitated his retirement,
and, at Liverpool's suggestion, he took the unusual course
of circulating an explanatory memorandum to the Cabinet
stating that he "separates from them with unfeigned reluctance, that he bears them collectively and individually the
sincerest good-will; and that it is a deep mortification to
him that one unfortunate question should, from circumstances over which he has no control, prevent him at a
moment like the present from continuing to take his full
share in upholding in conjunction with them those principles of policy external and internal, upon which they have
been acting cordially together". One of the replies which
he received was from his old enemy Sidmouth, which

1 E. J. Stapleton, *Some Official Correspondence of George Canning.*

shows how very much Canning had been on his best
behaviour during the past four years: "Your kind, cordial,
and honourable conduct has made a strong and lasting
impression on my mind."[1] These things point not to a deep
dissatisfaction with the course of Government, but, on the
contrary, to a desire for early reunion with it. There is also
the attitude of his friends towards his resignation. At the
end of 1820 one of them wrote: "Had I resigned at the
same time, and if I do not, I can assure you that it is from
no strong attachment to my office, I should have been
acting very unfairly by Mr Canning in giving to his retirement a character which does not belong to it."[2]

1 A. G. Stapleton, *Life and Times of Canning*, p. 318.
2 Add. MSS. 38742, f. 159. This letter, which is found among the
Huskisson papers, is signed G. W. The author may be Sir George
Warrender. Stapleton also asserted that Canning hung back from
office in 1821 for the same reasons; in support of this he uses an
argument which is largely hypothetical, but produces as proof a letter
from Canning to Chateaubriand explaining why he had not joined
the Cabinet during the year: "Le Roi a bien voulu s'opposer à
outrance à ma rentrée dans le ministère. . . . Ce que je sais bien, c'est
que si j'avais risquer cette question, quoiqu'il est possible que
j'aurais été la cause de la chute du Ministère ou, au moins, de la
démission de Lord Liverpool." Stapleton comments: "Why should
Canning's acceptance have upset the ministry, or at least the dismissal
of Lord Liverpool? The only explanation is that Canning himself
would feel bound, once in the ministry, to protest against and obstruct
High Tory policy." But it is obvious that Canning refers only to the
question of his admission, not to the consequences of that admission.
In any case Canning would be unlikely to give to a foreign statesman
an impression which he carefully avoided giving to anyone at home.
In view of his expressed opinions in Parliament, in private letters,
and in the circular to the Cabinet, this attempt to plant in Canning's
mind the Liberal disapproval of Liverpool's Government before
1822 would make him out to be the most consummate of charlatans.
Canning suffered enough in his lifetime from suspicions of disloyalty
and insincerity; enough is now known of his character to say that,
had this been the real motive for his actions, he would have said so;
at least he would not have denied it.

Canning was Liverpool's first object, but beyond that he looked to Peel, to Wellesley, and to the Grenvilles; in short to his favourite plan, the reunion of the old Pitt party. Peel was a "Protestant", and the favourite of the older High Tories; he had also been one of Liverpool's most successful promotions in 1812. But in 1821 Liverpool was less well disposed towards him than he had been in former years; in 1818 he had resigned from the Chief Secretaryship of Ireland for private reasons, at the end of 1820 he had refused the Board of Control for private and public reasons. Either he had a genuine desire to retire from politics, or he was playing some deep game; in neither case were his actions likely to recommend themselves to a Prime Minister sorely pressed by weakness in the House of Commons; in no case would Liverpool consider Peel an equal rival with Canning. No two men had displayed more personal bitterness than Liverpool and Wellesley in 1812, but Liverpool was always ready to forgive, and Wellesley was mellowed by near ten years without power and without friends. But past history would still preclude him from joining in a cabinet with the ministers whom he had formerly offended; on the other hand he required some place of dignity and authority. Ireland seemed to answer these necessities. Wellesley was a "Catholic", and his appointment to Ireland would raise many qualms in High Tory hearts; but it would quiet the scruples of the Grenvilles, who had, for the past two years, been hovering between Whig and Tory, and whose only real difference with the Government was upon the Catholic question. Any attempt to strengthen the Government would mean a strengthening of the "Catholic" element, but this Liverpool was quite prepared to do. More Catholic sympathisers might be found in high places, but this would not alter the voting strength of the two parties, and, so long as the Catholic question could be kept "open", the opinions of individual ministers would count for no more, perhaps for less, than their opinions as independent members. But whatever the claims of other aspirants to office, Liverpool would consider those of Canning first; Canning was Liverpool's friend, he was the greatest orator in the House of Commons, and he must be given a good office—he was not above sinecures, but he would not re-enter the Government unless he was given a post of influence. Liverpool looked for the first opportunity to bring in Canning, and that opportunity seemed to occur immediately; for, at the beginning of 1821, Sidmouth signified his wish to retire from the Home Office.

On 23 April Liverpool saw Canning, and the latter wrote to Huskisson: "I had a long talk with Liverpool...in the course of which we opened our minds fully to each other and I touched upon every point which I had reserved in our first conference. I should not like to *write* all that passed: and I am persuaded it will be more satisfactory to us both, that we should be able to say that we have not repeated anything personal to anyone." Canning went on to ask what changes other than the most desirable—Huskisson's known aim was the Board of Control—would be welcome: "Would Treasurership of the Navy?—I suppose it would. Would Mint?—I doubt it. Would Ireland?—I doubt it still more. Is there anything else?"[1] The plan of campaign arranged by Liverpool and Canning had no out-

1 Add. MSS. 38742, f. 202.

ward effect until far on in May; on the 31st Croker noted
that "Lord Melville tells me that he is about to be kicked
upstairs (his expression) from the Admiralty to the Home
Office".[1] It was expected that the King might object to
Canning at the Home Office, for the Home Secretary was
the minister, apart from the Prime Minister, who saw most
of the King; he was also the minister who would have to
carry through any arrangement for the Queen. Melville
therefore would be put in Sidmouth's place, Canning
would take the Admiralty, and something would be done
for the other Canningites.

The High Tory objection and alternative was obvious:
if the Queen's business was sufficiently a matter of the past
to allow Canning to rejoin the ministry, surely it would no
longer be considered a bar to office by Peel; why should not
Peel have the Home Office, and Lord Melville remain
where he was most useful and most satisfied? Accordingly
Liverpool approached Peel, but his desire to bring in Canning made him less straightforward than was his usual
custom. On 2 June he offered Peel Cabinet office "in a
strange shuffling hesitating sort of way", and from expressions used Peel understood that he meant the Board of
Control. On 6 June Peel gave an explicit refusal to the
Board of Control; "Lord Liverpool said hastily, 'And anything else I should offer?' Peel begged to say that, when
anything else was offered it would be time enough to
decide on it." Peel would probably have given a general
refusal had he not suspected that Liverpool wanted one,
which "piqued him a little". Croker's explanation of these

1 Croker, I, 186.

manœuvres is plausible; Liverpool wished to be able to tell Melville that Peel would not enter the Cabinet and that he alone could succeed Sidmouth.[1] In spite of this small rebuff—or rebuff not large enough—Liverpool proceeded with his plan and persuaded Melville to concur.

But while this negotiation was being pushed forward behind the scenes, Liverpool was shocked to find the extent of the King's objection to Canning. Brooding over the fiasco of the Bill of Pains and Penalties the King had magnified Canning's retirement into a great betrayal; he lent a ready ear to a rumour that the Queen had been Canning's mistress, and the action of Canning's friends in the House of Lords, in voting against the bill, confirmed his suspicions. "Canning has been misused by his friends in the Lords," Arbuthnot told Huskisson, "they have followed precisely that conduct which is calculated to do Canning harm."[2] But it was not dislike of Canning alone which influenced the King; in addition to his other complaints against the Government, he now had a personal grudge against Liverpool. Early in April the King had requested that Sumner, the tutor of the Conyngham children, might be given a vacant canonry at Windsor. Sumner was young and obscure, the canonries of Windsor were among the most prized positions in the Church, and Liverpool refused to comply with the King's wishes. After sending a protest which enumerated all the misdeeds of the Government, the King gave way; but he did not forgive. Later in the year Wellington told Liverpool that "the King has never forgiven your opposition to his wishes in the case

1 Croker, I, 188.   2 *Ibid.* p. 187.

of Mr Sumner. This feeling has influenced every action of his life in relation to his government from that moment; and I believe to more than one of us he avowed that his objection to Mr Canning was that his accession to the government was peculiarly desirable to you."[1] These embittered feelings were hardly auspicious beginnings to a difficult political negotiation.

On 10 June Liverpool laid his arrangements before the King; Canning was to go to the Admiralty, and Wynn, the most prominent parliamentarian of the Grenvilles, was to have the Board of Control. The King replied with indignant objections to Canning, and on 16 June Liverpool, his spirits dragged down by this unexpected vehemence and by the death of his wife four days before, unburdened himself to Arbuthnot: "It is idle to say that the question respecting Canning is not one of *proscription*. What King or what individual can ever say that he *proscribes another* for *ever*? Excluding a man at the time his services are wanted, and when there is an opening for him, is to all intents and purposes *proscription*—and upon such a principle I cannot agree to remain at the head of the Government. Recollect the question is not whether Canning should be forced into an office of constant personal intercourse with the Sovereign. Such a step I should never press, but the office which I have proposed is one of those in the whole Government in which there is least necessity even for personal communication between the Sovereign and the individual who holds it. The considerations I have already stated are sufficient, but you know as well as I do,

1 Wellington, I, 195.

what has been passing behind the scenes. The Objection to Canning, if it really exists, is one of *personal* pique and *resentment*. These qualities unfortunately existing where they do exist have been the source of all our past Errors and Calamities. I doubt however whether on the present occasion they would have led to what appears now to be the determination if there had not been a secret scheme, not to destroy the government at present, but to have the means of destroying it whenever the opportunity may be more convenient. I look upon the principle of the present arrangement as the test whether we are or are not the government."[1]

Politics were becoming exceedingly intricate. Liverpool would have Canning, looked upon this as a test whether the Government was to continue or whether it waited only upon the King's whim, and was prepared to go if his point was not granted. The King would not have Canning and he would be pleased to see Liverpool go; but on the other hand his experiments in November 1820 had proved to him that he could form no government to his liking, so he wished to keep the Tory Government, if possible without Liverpool. To Croker "he began to complain of Lord Liverpool. He says he cannot go on with him and will not; that he likes all the rest of his cabinet, nobody for instance better than Castlereagh; that if the Cabinet chose to stand or fall with Lord Liverpool, they must fall; if not he does not wish for any further change.... He asked how it could be suspected that he wished to get rid of his Ministers, he who had made them himself. But Lord Liverpool was

1 Yonge, III, 146.

captious, jealous, and impracticable; he objects to everything, and even when he does give way, which is nine times
in ten, he does it with so bad a grace that it is worse than an
absolute refusal.... He is rex Dei gratia, and Dei gratia rex
he would be."[1] Between these two were the other ministers,
who now found themselves in a peculiarly difficult position;
torn between loyalty to their leader, the traditional respect
of Tories for the Sovereign, and their personal indifference
to Canning, their only hope was for a compromise. All
knew the disruption which the resignation of Liverpool
would bring about, and all looked upon the Whigs as
irresponsible and impossible; it is not, then, surprising
that every member of the Cabinet who was aware of the
serious nature of the crisis, and every subordinate minister
with a taste for intrigue, should have begun to conciliate,
to argue, and to hope that one or other of the two contestants would find himself able to yield with honour. All
were with Liverpool when he complained that the King
was not giving the Government his full confidence, but
when he made Canning the test of the King's intentions
they were less happy. "The refusal of the King to allow
the Government to be strengthened would occasion a
necessity to break it up," Wellington wrote to Bathurst,
"but the refusal of the King to receive Mr Canning into his
Government at this moment does not amount to a refusal
to strengthen the Government, particularly as such a refusal
is accompanied by an offer to allow Lord Liverpool to
make any other arrangement he pleases."[2]

In spite of this Liverpool, on 21 June, deliberately re-

1 Croker, i, 199.　　　　　　2 Wellington, i, 176.

jected an easy way out which was offered to him. Canning wrote: "I entreat you not to let any consideration for me endanger the stability of the Administration, and least of all your own situation in it. If I have myself felt (as you know I have) the impossibility of my succeeding to the office of Home Secretary of State, so long as the recollections and perhaps some of the practical difficulties belonging to the conflict with the Queen should be still alive, I have no right to be surprised if the same considerations should appear to the King to extend further."[1] Liverpool communicated the substance of this letter to the King, but he added that it "could make no difference to the advice he must humbly submit". Liverpool wished to strengthen his Government, but he wanted Canning for himself alone, and he believed that no Government would be possible in which the "personal pique and resentment" of the King was allowed to determine the composition of the cabinet. "A King should be most cautious of acting upon such a principle, for the effect of it will generally be to exalt the individual and lower the King. . . . I was the person in 1806 to advise the late King to waive his exclusion to Mr Fox."[2]

Wellington had his doubts, but no one can accuse him of failing in loyalty to Liverpool; he could, perhaps, see both points of view, but he inclined to Liverpool's view of the constitution, and was prepared, in private, to use much the same arguments as Liverpool. In an interview with Bloomfield, at which Arbuthnot was also present, he endeavoured

1 E. J. Stapleton, *Some Official Correspondence of George Canning*, I, 24.
2 Hist. MSS. Comm. Bathurst, p. 449.

to put the Prime Minister's case in a reasonable and acceptable way: "What I lament is this: the King is proving by
various of his acts that we have not His confidence, and is
proving it also by the unwillingness he has manifested to
allow us to strengthen ourselves. His Majesty cannot suppose that we are not sensible that Mr Canning's conduct
was not very advantageous to us. But viewing the state of
the Government, we were convinced that he was the person
most likely from his Parliamentary talents to assist the
Government if in office, and on the other hand to be
elevated to a situation in which he would have the power of
being most mischievous if *left out*. That *being left out* he
would immediately be surrounded by the discontented of
all descriptions, and by the young Philosophers who would
look to him as their rallying point; and that in short he
would have the means of collecting round him such members as would put the Government really in his hands. The
only mode therefore of preventing him from attaining this
power, and of rendering him really useful was to bring him
into the Cabinet."[1]

For four months, from July to November, affairs remained in a state of suspended crisis. At the King's
request Sidmouth remained in office during the coronation
and the state visit to Ireland, but he was old and tired and
his retirement could not be long postponed. A further delay
was caused by the King's visit to Hanover; in spite of
efforts by the ministers to settle matters one way or the

1 From the "Substance of a conversation between the Duke of Wellington, Sir Benjamin Bloomfield, and Mr Arbuthnot". This was
   sent to Liverpool by Arbuthnot on 21 July: Add. MSS. 38370,
   f. 25.

other, the King sailed for Germany and left his Government to await his pleasure when he should have done with his progresses. During this long delay two minor matters added to the general bad feeling between King and Prime Minister. After the coronation Lord Hertford wished to retire from the office of Lord Chamberlain, and the question of his successor became a problem. Liverpool professed that he had "no personal or political wishes on the subject, and he is earnestly desirous upon this occasion, as upon all others of a similar nature, to meet the personal feelings of the King as far as he can do so consistently with the responsibility which necessarily belongs to his situation as His Majesty's First Minister".[1] The King replied that he wished Lord Liverpool "distinctly to understand that whatever appointments the King may think proper to make in his own family are to be considered as quite independent of the controul of any minister whatever",[2] and further, it was his pleasure that the new chamberlain should be Lord Conyngham. But Liverpool suspected that Lady Conyngham was largely responsible for the "secret scheme", and the appointment of her husband to the head of the Household would be a public humiliation for the ministers. And in any case, if the Prime Minister could not advance his friend who was a distinguished statesman, why should the King be allowed to advance the husband of his mistress who was a nonentity? The other event which kept bad feeling alive was the funeral of the Queen, who died on 7 August. The funeral was mismanaged and caused some rioting, and a few weeks later Liverpool was complaining

1 *George IV*, No. 945.   2 *Ibid*. No. 946.

that this was "the *great sin* of which the King now accused
the ministers".[1]

The King was employing his favourite strategy, a waiting
game. He knew that Liverpool's colleagues were not so
friendly towards Canning that they would risk all for him.
He hoped that either Liverpool would weaken or that there
would be a revolt against his authority; and of the two he
would prefer the latter. Nor did the King fail to drop
broad hints in private conversation; Croker, by his own
account, received a large share of these hints, and Croker,
who was a gossip and easily flattered, passed on the con-
fidences of the King to those who would think most deeply
upon them. To Sidmouth the King hinted that political
worry might induce in him his father's madness.[2]

Slowly the seeds of compromise grew. On 9 September
Croker "hinted that Lord Liverpool had perhaps some
personal excuses to make on one or two points", and tried
to persuade him to meet the King "not argumentatively,
but kindly and frankly". Liverpool compared himself to
the lamb and the King to the wolf in the fable, but seems to
have decided to make a conciliatory move. On 16 September he called at Carlton House, but found himself subjected to the astounding insult of being refused an audience.
At the same time the King saw Eldon, Londonderry, and
Bathurst. It was, said Croker, "a mortification to which
I wonder Lord Liverpool can submit". It may be hazarded
that it was the King's object to make Liverpool come to
the same decision; if Liverpool could be impelled into
offering his resignation, the other ministers could hardly

1 Croker, I, 209.   2 Add. MSS. 38370, f. 57.

go with him on such a personal question. On 24 September the King sailed for Hanover, and during the next month it would be necessary for him to make up his mind.

Meanwhile another prospect had opened before Canning. Moira, become the Marquis of Hastings, might retire from the Indian Vice-Royalty, and Canning, discouraged by the prejudices against him at home, flattered with the approaches which the Court of Directors made to him, and sorely embarrassed in his finances, might take the splendid exile. This seemed to settle every man's problem: the King would not have to accept him as a Cabinet minister, the ministers would be relieved from the fear of Canning at large in the House of Commons, and the way would be open for an honourable retreat by Liverpool. The idea was sufficiently attractive to the King to allow him to make the barren concession, in a letter to Londonderry during his Hanover visit, that he would admit Canning to the Cabinet were he in a position far removed from personal intercourse and if he would take India when vacant.[1] Londonderry had gone to Hanover with the King, and he now began to use his influence to soften the King's prejudice against Liverpool. To his brother he described the fruit of his labours: the King put the whole matter in his hands, "and he sent me to Liverpool to hold confidential intercourse before matters came into formal discussion. After much negotiation I brought matters to bear."[2]

Londonderry's way had been made smooth by the advice

1 *George IV*, No. 958.
2 Quoted by Aspinall, *George IV*, II, 471, note 1.

of Liverpool's friends and colleagues at home. "I implored him", said Arbuthnot, "not to take any decision in consequence of the King's persevering repugnance to admit Mr Canning into the Cabinet, and...told him that those of his colleagues with whom I had conversed considered him as the Pivot upon which the whole machine turned. That were he to abandon the Government the whole country would be thrown into confusion, and that without him the other members of the Cabinet would not under such circumstances have a hope of remaining together."[1] This advice was reinforced by a long and important letter from Wellington: he began by saying that he was still anxious for Canning to be brought into the Cabinet, but he went on: "I don't believe you will find your colleagues ready to incur all risks for this object, although I believe they were all sincerely desirous of having Mr Canning in the Cabinet; some, like myself, thinking it desirable on the ground of the services he can render to the Government and on his own account, and others out of deference to you. But I don't think that you will find many of them disposed to resign the government from their hands if they should not attain that object. Neither...do I believe you will find the party in general disposed to approve your resignation on this ground. There is no doubt that Mr Canning is not very popular with them....I would recommend you to propose him to the King, then, not in the spirit of hostility, not as an alternative to be taken between Mr Canning and us, or anything else the King can find as a government, but...as an arrangement calculated for the strength of the Govern-

1 Add. MSS. 38370, f. 57.

ment, the benefit of the country, and the honour of the King."[1] As to the new Lord Chamberlain, Wellington said: "Why should *we* look for a quarrel? Is it not rather our duty to settle this petty question?...I don't mean to depreciate the importance of a point of honour to a government; but I would observe that the prevention of this particular appointment became a point of honour after the rejection of Canning in June, the question of the Irish peerages, and of the Green Ribands, and all the follies of the Coronation." The Duke went on to say that the Government could not resign with a clear conscience for in doing so it would hand over the country to Whigs, Radicals, and irretrievable ruin. "The result may be that we shall break down; but we shall have the satisfaction of reflecting that this misfortune is the effect of the circumstances in which we are placed, and of the character of the person with whom we have to deal, and not our own act."

The result of this pressure upon the two chief disputants made both ready for some compromise at the end of the Hanover visit. "One thing seems certain," wrote Croker on 12 November, "that the King and Lord Liverpool will come to an understanding."[2] The formal reconciliation took place on the following day, and by the 21st London-derry was able to tell his brother that "Liverpool is now very well received", and on the 24th that "complete harmony has been restored between the King and his Government, and he has received Liverpool with cordiality".[3] By the beginning of the new year the King was asking Liver-

1 Wellington, I, 192.　　　　2 Croker, I, 127.
3 Londonderry MSS. Quoted by Aspinall, *George IV*, II, 471, note 1.

pool for personal advice and underlining the words "as my friend".[1]

The terms of the reconciliation appeared as a victory for the royal right to exclude, but they were also a victory for the idea that the King must give his confidence to a government supported by Parliamentary majorities. Canning was to remain out of the Cabinet and to be offered India when the vacancy occurred, but, on the other hand, there were to be no more "flirtations with the Whigs". Had the ministers, other than Liverpool, been whole-hearted in their advocacy of Canning, compromise would have been impossible; but, even beyond the indifference or dislike which some of them felt towards Canning, there was the traditional Tory dislike of forcing the King's hand. Wellington knew well the deficiencies of their royal master, but his loyalty and his theory of the constitution made him regard a certain freedom of action by the King as an essential; the King might do wrong but the ministers must be able to show that they had treated him fairly. In the long run it was probably of more importance that the King was forced to give his confidence to ministers whom he had wished to turn out than that he maintained his right to exclude undesirable ministers; henceforth backstairs intrigue and communications with the Opposition would be not only wrongheaded but also unconstitutional.

Canning took his exclusion with philosophic resignation; he too was a Tory, and he too had shown his unwillingness to force the hand of the King. He looked back upon his political career, upon his great mistake of 1812, upon the

1 *George IV*, No. 982.

thwarting of his ambitions, upon his subordination in a ministry which he had hoped to command, which he had at first despised, and whose continuance he now thought to be of more importance than his own ambitions. To Huskisson he wrote: "Enough of retrospect which can now do no good—not even as experience so far as I am concerned— since I foresee no imaginable combination of things through which I can ever again be engaged upon a political negotiation."[1] Moreover, with all his disappointments, there was still India, with its opportunities for putting large ideas into practice and for recouping a shattered fortune. But, in spite of his protestation to Huskisson, he still cast his eyes longingly upon office at home, and there remains one curious letter written to Liverpool in January 1822, and when Liverpool had already offered the Home Office to Peel: "Here are a few remarks with which I threatened you yesterday. When you say that 'it would be easier to persuade P. to remain *out of office altogether for the present* than to induce him to change the one office for the other':—do you mean to use *that* expression only as an illustration of great difficulty as when one says 'I would rather cut off my right hand than do so and so'? Or does it imply that there would be a chance of obtaining the decision which you speak of as 'easier'? The words 'for the present' seem to countenance the latter construction; and the proposition so construed tallies with rumours which have been current (I understand) for the last two or three months of a delay in P.'s acceptance of office.

"Now, supposing Peel (for *any* reason) inclined to post-

1 Add. MSS. 38743, f. 129.

pone his accession to the Government, and supposing the Home Office vacant, I confess I do not see the difficulty relating to that office in the light which it appears to strike you—though you know how little I like it. I think the natural course would be to propose me for *that* office to the King. I think if H.M. consented at all it would be in a spirit of grace and oblivion, and I have a strong feeling that a month's intercourse in business would do more to efface unpleasant retrospects and recollections, than years of occasional and unwilling communication. I would not therefore that, in such case, Melville should be troubled with any proposition on your part or wish on mine. If the *King* insisted upon the one great arrangement, it would be for H.M. to press it, not for you.

"But, as on my part, the death of the Queen has removed all publick and stateable objection to the Home Office— so, on the other hand, I can hardly believe that (the getting rid of me in the H. of C. once out of the question) the King would think it right, or expedient, to make me the single exception to that general amnesty which (if I am not mis- informed) he is proclaiming or allowing to be proclaimed.

"You say that the entire relinquishment of India must necessarily precede office. Be it so. You say that 'time' is requisite for the subsiding of what has passed upon this subject. To that proposition there is one objection—that, if during that 'time', P. becomes Sec. of State—the door is closed against me for ever. The question is, therefore, would a declaration of the final relinquishment of India on my part enable you to re-cast this part of your arrange- ment? Whether now, or some time hence, matters not;

provided no insuperable impediment grows up during the interval."[1]

This letter is interesting only as proof that Canning still hankered after office, that Liverpool was still looking forward to a time when Canning might be brought in, and as a clue to the hesitations and changes of mind in which Canning was indulging over India; nothing was done upon the lines suggested by Canning, and it was but a few days later that Peel received the seals of the Home Office. The door seemed to close against Canning for ever.

At the end of November Liverpool was able to state that "there was now no question of the government's continuance or of the King's confidence". This new-found stability enabled him to turn his mind to those other changes, which he had contemplated formerly, but which he had considered as secondary to the accession of Canning. On 28 November he offered the Home Office to Peel, who promptly accepted. With no further difficulty Wellesley was offered and accepted Ireland; his appointment was valuable in itself and it would facilitate the next move— negotiations with the Grenvilles—by satisfying some of their scruples over the Catholic question. This idea, of a union with the Grenvilles, had been in the air for some time; Liverpool had mentioned it to the King in June, and the Grenvilles, with their final separation from the Whigs and the attempt to form—for bargaining purposes—a "third party", had shown themselves ready to treat.[2] Within the ministry the idea was strongly favoured by

1 Add. MSS. 38568, f. 112.
2 Hist. MSS. Comm. Dropmore, vol. X *passim*.

Londonderry, "I attach so much importance to the Grenville connection not being left loose in the House of Commons for obvious reasons," he had written to Liverpool,
"that, although ready to try our strength without them,
I cannot too strongly urge their acquisition."[1] Throughout
1821 the Board of Control—with its valuable patronage—
had been kept open as a bait to the Grenvilles, and, at the
end of the year, negotiations began. In the early nineteenth-century world the Grenvilles retained the ideas and
methods of an eighteenth-century connection; they had a
certain uniformity of political creed, but this creed was of
sufficient flexibility to allow them, in normal times, to work
with either political party; upon their Whig allies they had
acted as a dead weight, combating every proposal which
savoured of Radicalism, and emphasising always the division between the patrician Whigs and their plebeian associates; they had broken with the Whigs over the social
questions and supported the coercive measures of the
Government; they now found nothing, save a few doubts
upon the Catholic question, to divide them from the
Government, and, whatever other consideration should
arise, they were heartily sick of opposition. But they were
prepared to exact a pound of flesh as the price of their
adherence, and it seemed at first that Liverpool's extra-
ordinarily generous terms—a dukedom for the Marquis of
Buckingham, the Board of Control for Wynn, a post at the
embassy in Switzerland for H. Wynn, a seat at one of the
principal Boards for Fremantle, and possibly the Attorney
Generalship of Ireland for Plunket—would not satisfy

1 Yonge, III, 162.

them. The aim of the Marquis of Buckingham was Cabinet office, but he had no political experience, he was personally unpopular, his appointment would bring the odium of a "job" upon a Government which had preserved a relatively high standard of political morality, and the days were past when the hereditary leader of a "connection" could claim office as a matter of right. Fortunately Lord Grenville, still the sage and the most able member of the group though living in retirement, approved of the ministerial terms— "there was *no possible objection* to the proposed arrangement"[1]—and faced with this emphatic approval Buckingham was bound to accede to Liverpool's proposals, and to accept the Dukedom of Buckingham and Chandos as a sufficient share of the spoils.

The accession of the Grenvilles meant more than the addition of some dozen votes, of one great orator in Plunket, and of one somewhat ineffective President of the Board of Control in Wynn; by crossing the floor of the House this small group passed an emphatic vote of confidence in the Government, and their crossing signified that the Government's difficulties from the King and from doubtful supporters, were at an end. There was still more: the Grenvilles had been members of Pitt's party, and their reunion with the parent stem completed the last stage in that project which Liverpool had accepted as a chief part of his political mission, the restoration of the old Pitt party. But the winning of the Grenvilles had undoubtedly been expensive, and it could hardly be accomplished without the mortification of some junior members of the ministry, who now saw

1 Buckingham, I, 241.

the Grenvillites stepping easily into positions for which those in the lower ranks of government had striven long and faithfully. No man was more bitterly offended than William Huskisson.

Huskisson's ambition was the Board of Control, and already, in June of 1821, he had shown his chagrin at the prospect of being left out in a possible rearrangement. Now, with Wynn appointed to the coveted office, his resentment boiled over; he spoke of his "mortification", he thought he had been "most unfairly and unkindly used", he lamented "the injury and injustice with which his zealous and unrelenting exertions to make himself useful to the Government had been requited".[1] Liverpool offered Huskisson a place in Ireland, or to make Palmerston an English peer if he would vacate the Secretaryship at War in Huskisson's favour. Huskisson refused the one, Palmerston refused the other, and Huskisson had perforce to remain First Commissioner of Woods and Forests—an office of which he was heartily sick—and to continue his complaints of injustice. His letter to Binning explaining why he did not resign is interesting, for it shows the feelings of a Tory upon the reunion of the Pitt party, the feelings of a Canningite upon the relationship between his leader and the Prime Minister, and the feelings of a typical member of the "official" class toward the Grenville ideas of an aristocratic right to rule: "The considerations on which they lay so much stress are these—that I could not go out now without appearing to invite a comparison of personal pretensions, a thing in itself too invidious not to be avoided if

1 Add. MSS. 38742, f. 255.

possible—that it is an arrangement which brings together so many of Mr Pitt's friends and followers, it will not be pleasant to be held out as detracting either from its harmony or its value as an accession of strength—and further I could not go out now (when S[turges] B[ourne] is also retiring) without creating a surmise that there existed or was likely to exist a want of cordiality between L[iverpool] and C[anning]. This I own has most weight with me....If the arrangement was of more worth I might the less repine: but I own I cannot bring myself to believe that the numbers of the Grenvilles in our House, backed by all their talents, are sufficient to outweigh their want of popularity, their sinecures, their lofty and greedy pretensions, and the sore feelings at the expense of which their pretensions are to be gratified in other and more faithful friends of the present Government."[1]

The result of the negotiations of 1821 was to give the ministry, which, at the beginning of the year, had seemed ready to die of weakness, a new lease of life. It was now certain that there would be no change of government so long as a party split could be averted. Taken with the more settled and prosperous state of the country, this seemed to be a fair augury for the future, and such men as Peel—perhaps Liverpool himself—would not be content to ride passively upon the crest of the wave, they would take the opportunity to effect some long-needed improvements. Peel made clear that he would treat the question of penal reform as one to be decided upon its merits, not as an attack on the constitution to be resisted to the last;[2] Liver-

1 Add. MSS. 38743, f. 59.   2 Yonge, III, 216.

pool had already told a Free Trade deputation that he had long been convinced of the truth of their theories,[1] and, with great and characteristic caution, he was considering the whole question of economic reform; at the Board of Trade the Vice-President, Wallace, was earning much praise for the first tentative steps in the same direction. The Bank had found itself able to renew cash payments before the prescribed time, and Government spokesmen were already being forced into some solid economic thought and argument in order to resist the attacks of the agriculturalists upon Peel's Act; and it is an omen of no small significance that, in this resistance, they were backed at every point by Ricardo. The great nineteenth-century alliance of theorists and practical politicians was already at hand. On the other hand there were still disadvantages: Vansittart pursued his amiable and incompetent way at the Exchequer, Huskisson was still a disappointed man, the spirit of Eldon and Sidmouth was still strong, especially when it could enlist the support of a man such as Wellington, and two members of the Cabinet—Bragge Bathurst and Maryborough—did little to justify their positions. But after the changes of 1821 little could be done; should Liverpool attempt further changes he would risk another battle with the King, which might mean the end of his ministry, or he would offend faithful supporters, and whatever happened he would seem to be in a hurry to get rid of old friends. To a Prime Minister such as Liverpool these were weighty considerations, nor was it entirely weak good nature and a wish to avoid difficulties, for his

1 Tooke, *History of Prices*, vol. VI, Appendix.

hold upon his ministry depended largely on a reputation for fairness and integrity, and such things would be challenged by a charge of ingratitude. So matters rested, in tranquillity and without further change, until 12 August 1822.

The exultation of Liberals at the succession of Canning has obscured the fact that the suicide of Castlereagh was one of the major tragedies of the nineteenth century. In the same way his quarrel with Canning has lent colour to the illusion that he was the blindest of reactionaries. In truth the difference between the two men was one of temperament and of method rather than of policy. Castlereagh was already moving slowly, perhaps reluctantly, along the road which Canning was to follow with spirit and enthusiasm; both realised the impossible folly of binding England unconditionally to the Allied Powers and to the existing order in Europe. But the work of Castlereagh was not confined to the business of the Foreign Office, he was also leader in the House of Commons, and commanded the respect of the whole Tory party. He spoke badly, but his stumbling sentences were dearer to Tory gentlemen than all the oratory of a Canning or a Whig. "He goes on as usual," wrote Croker in December 1821, "and like Mont Blanc continues to gather all the sunshine upon his icy head. He is *better* than ever; that is colder, steadier, more 'pocurante', and withal more amiable and respected."[1] Here was a man of business and a gentleman, far more to be trusted than any of those "damned men of genius"; yet Castlereagh knew his own deficiencies, he could command the stout Tories, but his speeches lacked the power to draw

1 Croker, I, 219.

over the doubtful or the independent votes; for this reason he had been anxious to see Canning on the Treasury bench. Canning could not be brought in, and in 1822 Castlereagh prepared himself once more for a task which was over-taxing his physical and mental strength; a task which was now rendered more difficult by the attacks of the agricul-turalists upon the Government and by the doubts which began to gather around the policy of the Concert of Europe. Few suspected that his powerful mind and his unruffled temper were breaking under the strain: according to Pro-fessor Webster he betrayed signs of strain in May when, normally an introvert, he became temporarily an extravert and burdened comparative strangers with unexpected con-fidences; but on 1 August Madame de Lieven found him in excellent spirits.[1] On 9 August he called upon the King and betrayed every symptom of mental disorder—he was a fugitive from justice, he was accused of a terrible crime, he had ordered his saddle horses and would fly to Portsmouth and from there to the ends of the earth—the King at-tempted to calm him, a doctor was sent for, and he was got away safely to his home at Cray Farm.[2] There, in the early hours of 12 August, he cut his throat, and died crying, "It is all over".

By this time the King was in Scotland, where he was making a ceremonial visit. Peel was with the King; Liver-pool, Wellington, and Bathurst were in or near London; the other ministers were out of town.[3] Liverpool imme-diately sent the news to the King and to Peel. "What a sad

1 *Letters of Princess Lieven to Metternich*, p. 187.
2 *Ibid.* p. 189.   3 Parker, I, 334 (from Diary of H. Hobhouse).

catastrophe this is, Publick and Private," he wrote, "What a conclusion to such a life. Pray God have mercy on his soul."

All discussion upon his successor was deferred until the King should return from Scotland. But the King foresaw the danger of Canning, and wrote that the arrangements for India must remain unchanged, and tried to enlist Peel's support by telling him what he had done. Peel, with exemplary constitutional propriety, refused to express an opinion and sent to Liverpool an account of the interview. Whoever might be qualified to take over the Foreign Office, only Canning could succeed Castlereagh in the House of Commons; this was something upon which nearly every one connected with politics was agreed. "It would be worse than nothing to attempt a Government without Canning" was the opinion of Lord Grenville, and "such seems to be the opinion of everybody, such was the language of all official men". The consequence was that Buckingham wrote to Wellington intimating that, if an offer was not made to Canning, the Grenvilles would feel themselves at liberty to withdraw from the Government. Liverpool's mind was already made up, but the action of the Grenvilles was a useful card to play against any objections from the older ministers and subsequently against the King. Liverpool "had locked himself up and declined talking to those whom he wished to avoid", but he was said to be "very cast down and depressed in the extreme"; he hinted that he expected more than simply a new secretary.

Certainly the attitude of the King did not promise an easy victory for those who favoured Canning. Croker found him "evidently averse from Canning" when he returned on 2 September, he had "made up *his* mind on that point".[1] Liverpool saw the King and recommended Canning, adding that the Cabinet majority was with him; but Sidmouth and Eldon both advised against Canning, the latter saying that he would "get rid of all his Majesty's old servants".[2] The King's immediate reaction was to express himself as "much surprised" by Liverpool's proposition, he had hoped that Liverpool would make no approach on this subject, as he had particularly desired that the arrangements regarding India should remain undisturbed. "The King cannot but regret that Lord Liverpool and those members of the Cabinet who agree with him should not have thought it due to the King's feelings to have submitted a double project; they would thus have fulfilled what they might have considered a duty to *themselves* without setting aside all delicacy towards the King, of which the King feels he has just reason to complain. The King now waits for Lord Liverpool's second project before the King will come to any decision on that already proposed. If there be no alternative the King takes for granted that Lord Liverpool and the other members of the Cabinet are prepared to break up the Government."[3] It seemed that, between the King and his Prime Minister, matters had reached a breaking point; but Liverpool was now in a far stronger position—in spite of the defection of Eldon and Sidmouth—than he had been in 1821, and the sequel to

1 Croker, I, 222.
2 Parker, I, 325 (Diary of H. Hobhouse).
3 *George IV*, No. 1042.

the King's answer was a letter from Wellington, which probably decided the King.[1] Wellington wrote that Canning's "talents and abilities are much considered, and the continuance of his presence in the House of Commons is anxiously desired by many of the best friends of the government, whose support would probably be lost if advantage were not taken of this opportunity.... I am convinced that he will serve your Majesty in that situation with ability, zeal, and fidelity, and will give your Majesty satisfaction, that his principles and opinions are in all points of your Majesty's policy, domestic as well as foreign, the same as those of your other servants; and that there is no other arrangement which will not leave the government in a state of inefficiency in one or more departments.... There is no difference of principle or opinion between the Lord Chancellor and Mr Canning, which does not exist between the Lord Chancellor and others of your Majesty's servants.... The honour of your Majesty consists in acts of mercy and grace, and I am convinced that your Majesty's honour is most safe in extending your grace and favour to Mr Canning upon this occasion."[2] This, coming from the most respected man in Europe and the man whom the King wished to see at the Foreign Office, was powerful advocacy. On 8 September the King at last brought himself to swallow the "bitter pill".

An offer was to be made to Canning, and that offer could be one thing only. Huskisson had told Arbuthnot, and Arbuthnot would have told Liverpool, that "If it should be

[1] According to Greville it was Bathurst who finally decided the King. Greville, I, 130.
[2] Wellington, I, 274.

thought right to call for his services in the House of Commons, I cannot too strongly impress on your mind, that the offer must be unaccompanied with anything which could look like a contrivance to curtail the situation now vacant".[1] In other words Canning must have the whole heritage of Castlereagh, he must be both Foreign Secretary and Leader of the House. Yet on 9 September Canning received a letter from Liverpool which Mrs Canning later described as "vague and unexplanatory and confirming a general impression that the offer would not be acceptable".[2] Canning was then at Birmingham; he arrived in London on the 11th. He was still very doubtful of the wisdom of sacrificing India; "by far the greater number of considerations public and private were against acceptance, and to the last day I hoped that the proposal made to me might be one that I could refuse".[3] But when he saw Liverpool he learnt that "the Proposal *was* that which... I could alone have accepted".[4] Even so he did not give an immediate reply, and Liverpool, seeing his hesitation, wrote to him the same evening: "I cannot refrain from declaring to you that after the severe calamity which the King and the Country have sustained and under all the circumstances of the present Crisis, a Sense of Public Duty must preclude you from making any difficulty as to taking your part in the

1 Melville, *Huskisson Papers*, p. 143. Huskisson said much the same thing to Croker (Croker, I, 227). And on 7 September Wellington prepared a memorandum for Lady Londonderry in which he said, "He must be leader of the House", and went on to show that he must be Foreign Secretary as well (Wellington, I, 277).
2 Temperley, "Some Letters of Joan Canning", *E.H.R.* 1930.
3 Bagot, II, 137, Canning to Bagot.
4 *Ibid.* p. 133, to Bootle Wilbraham.

Councils of the King's Government at this time."[1] Canning was certainly disposed to make difficulties, for he objected to the terms of the King's letter. The King had said that he was aware that "the brightest ornament of his crown is the power of extending grace and favour to a subject who may have incurred his displeasure". Canning saw here lavish expressions of forgiveness, where he recognised no offence; it was, he said, like being given a ticket for Almack's and finding "Admit the rogue" written on the back. For three days Canning hesitated, and Greville heard from Lady Bathurst that the ministers were "greatly surprised at the delay". But by the 14th his friends had prevailed upon him to sink these scruples, and he accepted the Foreign Secretaryship and the Leadership of the House of Commons.

A tragic accident had brought into the ministry the man for whom Liverpool had striven in 1821; it remained to be seen whether Liverpool would press on further changes in the ministry. Eldon had warned the King that Canning would get rid of all his old servants, and Arbuthnot told Huskisson that "having had a good deal to do with the discussions which preceded the offer to Canning, I am able to tell you that had not his question been an isolated one, all our efforts with the King would have failed. He expressed great fear and jealousy lest there should be a secret intention to extend the arrangements; and he most positively declared that should there be a secret intention to extend the proposal made to him to introduce into the Cabinet any other person, he would not consent to have an offer made to Canning."[2] In spite of this Canning

1 Yonge, III, 201.   2 Add. MSS. 38743, f. 200.

began to use his influence on Huskisson's behalf, and Liverpool was prepared to promote him if possible. The first chance was that the vacancy in India might be used to give Huskisson the object of his ambition, the Board of Control. Manners Sutton, the Speaker, might be made Viceroy, and Wynn might be moved to the Speaker's chair. But Liverpool had in mind a more extensive arrangement, and on 3 October Canning discovered that he was thinking of displacing Vansittart.

"I have had", he wrote to Huskisson, "a long talk with L, a much fuller and in some respects more satisfactory than any former one...the satisfactory part...is that Van is not immovable. He would take the Board of Control, if proposed to him. But what is satisfactory or unsatisfactory to me, according as you may feel on the subject, [is that] L is confident that Robinson would not only take the Ch. of the Ex. if offered to him; but that he would feel himself passed over if the offer were not made. This course of arrangement would open to you Robinson's office." Canning gave an account of his conversation, "I asked him whether he was as much wedded to Van, and Van to his seals as ever? The answer, to my infinite surprise was, Oh no! I could get him out, and would if I saw my way to an arrangement that I was sure would satisfy all parties; but I could not get him out for Huskisson to succeed him, and the India Board which is H's object would be the surest lure to Van.... The trouble is, I believe, he *still likes* Van better than anything which could be put in his room; I believe that he would like *you* better in V's room (if he is to have anyone) than a politician; but he thinks he could not carry that change with

Van, with the King, or his colleagues; and he would therefore perhaps have been as little inclined to make any change
now as last year, if he had not received some intimation
from Robinson of his willingness to be put forward....
I think it right to tell you, that you would do right to
acquiesce in this arrangement. The grounds of that opinion
are shortly these. First, the getting Van out of the Exchequer is so great an object, for the Publick, for the House
of Commons, and for the Government, that if it were
known or suspected that that object had been frustrated
by your adherence to the succession to Wynn instead of
Robinson, the best friends of Government and of our own
friends too (Littleton for example) would never forgive you.
...Secondly the bringing forward of Robinson would be
scarcely less popular in the H of C than the getting out
poor Van." Finally, Canning added a sentence which was
to give Huskisson much pain: "L asked me whether you
would insist upon Cabinet with the I. Bd...there would
be great objection to it. I asked if on the part of the K?
He said 'Yes and elsewhere too'."[1]

The King would see, in any attempt to place Huskisson
in the Cabinet, the first step in a plan to replace the
existing ministers by Canningites; he was prepared to
resist this, and other members of the Government would
regard it with scarcely less jealousy. The King was already
insisting that the Cabinet was too large and must be reduced; he was perhaps looking forward to the inevitable
retirements of the older ministers within a few years, and
was safeguarding himself against the promotion of an over-

1 Add. MSS. 38743, fs. 217ff.

whelming number of Canningites; but the size of the
Cabinet was then, as it has been so often, a frequent cause
of complaint. It was unfortunate that the attempt to reduce
the Cabinet—or to exclude Canningites—should involve
Huskisson; for Huskisson felt that he had been neglected,
and this feeling was made the more bitter by his over-
sensitive realisation of his own social obscurity. He was
quite ready to take the Board of Trade and to forgo the
patronage of the Board of Control, and he agreed that the
Cabinet might, with advantage, be reduced in size, "but
when the attempt is made, it should be made with a
younger man...and, if I may fairly state all my feelings
with someone in a different (I mean a higher) sphere of life
from myself...I cannot be what Robinson now is in office
and remain excluded from the Cabinet".[1]

The prospects of this negotiation were blighted at the
outset by the attitude of the Grenvilles. Canning succeeded
in winning the support of Lord Grenville, who agreed to
press Wynn to take the Speakership.[2] But Wynn was very
unwilling to leave the Cabinet, and Buckingham delivered
an ultimatum: if Wynn left the Cabinet, the Grenvilles
would leave the Government, unless Buckingham himself
was given office. This was typical "connection" politics,
but for the moment they seemed to promise success, and
Liverpool even proposed Buckingham to the King as a
minister without portfolio. Showing sound political sense
the King refused to consider this, and, even Huskisson,
who would have benefited immediately, admitted that the

1 Add. MSS. 38743, f. 223.
2 Add. MSS. 38743, f. 215: "Nothing could be fairer or kinder than
L⁴ G. He wrote to C. W., and I brought the letter back to town."

admission of Buckingham would be against the public interest. All attempts to move Wynn, without losing the lately won allegiance of the Grenvilles, having failed, Huskisson wrote bitterly: "I must make up my mind to remain as I am till that chance which Liverpool pointed out before Londonderry's death—the millennium when Bragge Bathurst will discover that his retirement might be an accommodation to the Government."[1]

It was precisely this possibility, the hastening of this millennium, which now occupied Liverpool's mind. If Bathurst could be persuaded to retire, Vansittart might consent to take his office, the Chancellorship of the Duchy of Lancaster; Robinson could then succeed Vansittart, and Huskisson take Robinson's place. The first condition was that Huskisson should withdraw his claim to Cabinet rank before the negotiations commenced, since Canning was sure that Liverpool would not begin if he felt that it would entail a battle with the King.[2] Huskisson does not seem to have abandoned his claim, and he certainly returned to it later with added force and resentment; but Liverpool decided to go forward nevertheless.

Bragge Bathurst had been Chancellor of the Duchy of Lancaster since 1812, and during the year 1821 he had taken charge of the Board of Control; apart from this service he had played little active part in the business of Government. But he was related both to Sidmouth and to Bathurst, and beyond these useful connections he seems to have had certain real qualities; his speeches in the Commons were infrequent, but Liverpool paid tribute to his disinterestedness and to his accommodating temper, and

1 Add. MSS. 38743, f. 230.   2 Add. MSS. 38743, f. 248.

Wellington to his usefulness at the Council table; but whatever qualities might have originally supported his claim to Cabinet rank, he was now grown old and was no longer able to fulfil even those small duties which had been demanded of him. It now seemed time to hint that his retirement might be more useful than his services; and it is interesting to note that it was to Sidmouth that Liverpool saw fit to make his explanations. "Connection" was no longer a vital force in politics, but men still observed some of its conventions. Liverpool's letter to Sidmouth is an excellent example of his tactful approach to such difficult personal matters: "You well know my sincere regard for Mr Bathurst and that there is no man living whom I should be more unwilling to wound or distress in any matter.... I should never therefore have thought of saying what I did say... to you, if I had not understood that his health had been on various occasions much affected, and tho' it improved always in the country, he had for some time invariably suffered by a continued residence in London. If I could hope that for any reasonable period he could continue to go thro' the fatigue of the House of Commons in an official situation, and at times like the present, I never could have contemplated that which actually did present itself to my mind. But if circumstances should arise to make him wish to retire at no distant period it might happen at a moment when the vacancy of his office, so far from being any convenience or advantage to Govt in other respects, might on the contrary be the cause of considerable embarrassment."[1]

On 14 December Liverpool wrote "a letter of dismissal"

1 Add. MSS. 38291, f. 150.

to Vansittart, which, in spite of rumours to the contrary,[1] was expressed in the kindest terms and written in his own hand. Whatever were Vansittart's private feelings he showed no resentment in his reply: "I shall consider your proposal in the same spirit of kindness in which I am convinced it has been made....In what you suggest with respect to Robinson and Huskisson, I see much prospect of public advantage and nothing could be more satisfactory to me than to have Robinson for my successor in respect of private feeling. I have long felt myself growing unequal to the labor of the House of Commons, and, as I told Arbuthnot lately, I think nothing could reconcile me to enter upon another Parliament. My inclination would rather lean to a total retreat, if it could be managed without the appearance of public or private difference; but this might not be easy to avoid."[2] This seemed very satisfactory, but the reference to the "labor of the House of Commons" contained an obvious hint, which Liverpool either ignored or failed to perceive; it was not until Arbuthnot pointed out the obvious recompense which Vansittart expected, that Liverpool recommended him for a peerage.[3] He retired to obscurity and the Upper House as Lord Bexley.

With Bathurst out of the Cabinet, and Vansittart out of the Exchequer, there remained only the question of Huskisson and Cabinet rank. At the end of December he was still protesting that exclusion from the Cabinet was a positive dishonour and an insuperable objection to his succeeding Robinson.[4] Canning and Arbuthnot both used their

1 Colchester, III, 300.
3 Cf. Add. MSS. 38291, f. 237.
2 Add. MSS. 38291, f. 220.
4 Add. MSS. 38291, f. 285.

influence to persuade him to relinquish his claims. The King, on the other hand, consented to waive his objection, and to sacrifice temporarily his object of reducing the Cabinet. It was now urged upon Huskisson that it would be graceful in him to yield, and not to force himself into a situation where the King, in spite of his concession, would resent his presence; such an action would avoid offending the King, and would make "all the difference in the world as to the tone of his future connection" with Liverpool.[1] A compromise was finally suggested: Huskisson should enter the Cabinet after twelve months' service at the Board of Trade; to this he consented, though with a bad grace.

One more difficulty arose. Wallace, the able and energetic Vice-President of the Board of Trade, was offended at Huskisson's promotion over his head. He would have been ready to see a peer placed over him, but he was not prepared to see himself effaced by Huskisson. No other office could be opened for him, and, in spite of a kind and conciliatory letter from Liverpool, he insisted upon resigning.

In January 1823, in an effort to find some office for Wallace, Liverpool suggested to Lord Maryborough that his resignation from the Cabinet in favour of a House of Commons man might be a great convenience to the Government. Maryborough, formerly Wellesley Pole, was a brother of the Duke of Wellington; since 1814 he had been Master of the Mint with Cabinet rank, and had, if anything, played even less part in the active business of government than Bragge Bathurst; but he was tenacious of his rank, and refused to resign. It was not until August that he at last gave up the struggle for his position, and

1 Add. MSS. 38291, f. 299.

allowed himself to be "sent to the dogs"; in other words accepted the Mastership of the Buckhounds. This enabled Liverpool to offer the Mint to Wallace—"This is the greatest relief to my mind...you know how I felt for his disappointment last year, and how deeply I was impressed with the opinion that he had the strongest claims, public and personal, upon me and upon the government"[1]—and to give his place in the Cabinet to Huskisson, some months before he would otherwise have gained that honour. This occasioned one last protest from the King: he had supposed that Maryborough had been removed "for the purpose of lessening the numbers of the Cabinet this might have been, perhaps a reason, altho' a very questionable one, especially as that individual had been sitting in the same Cabinet, with the same members, for the last nine years. But there was a graver consideration, as it appears to the King, namely, the delicacy and propriety of feeling which should have been observed in relation to the Duke of Wellington. Can it be supposed that the Duke of Wellington can view with indifference and without silently feeling what must, indeed, be considered ungracious conduct towards his brother?...Mr Huskisson may be a very clever man, but he is not always a prudent one."[2] Fortunately the Duke seems to have raised no objection to the removal of his brother, and to have made no complaint, public or private.

So was completed the transformation of the Government; and already, in the spring of 1823, the effect had been felt in political life. Members of the House of Commons listened attentively while the pleasant voice of Robinson made the mysteries of finance appear as lucid as a

1 Add. MSS. 38296, f. 168.   2 *George IV*, No. 1110.

lesson in elementary mathematics. At the Foreign Office Canning had almost completed the break with the Continental Allies, and was taking the independence of nations as the key-note of English policy. At the Home Office young Peel was increasing the reputation which he had already won as Chief Secretary of Ireland; it was his good fortune to increase his experience in a happier field, to appear as an angel of reform not a demon of coercion. At the Board of Trade Huskisson and his chief assistant, Deacon Hume, had embarked upon that laborious task, the consolidation of the Customs Laws.

This reconstruction of the Cabinet had been the work of Liverpool and of no other; it was he who had had to bear the wrath of the King; it was he who had had to quell the doubts of recalcitrant colleagues; it was he who had had to bear all the personal difficulties, the reproaches of old friends, the insistent resentment of the disappointed. The letters which survive present no more than a façade, behind which the real struggle took place; every move had its pitfalls, every move might see a cry raised against the ingratitude or the rashness of the Prime Minister, and every move might raise an alarm at the direction which the changes were taking. Liverpool was a man peculiarly sensitive to the feelings of others; thus in a matter which might appear of comparatively small importance—the resignation of Wallace—he wrote: "I can assure you most sincerely that since I received your answer to my first letter, I have suffered more than I can recollect to have done on any occasion of the same nature in the course of my life." He was all anxiety to avoid offending Bragge Bathurst or Vansittart, and it is possible to detect the mental anguish which he underwent. Those nearest to him were able to realise how much these personal questions preyed upon his mind; in January 1823 Canning wrote that "Liverpool's agitation has, in some stages of this business, amounted to illness, and to him every successive stage has been an effort such as when I came into the Government. I thought it utterly hopeless that he should find nerves to undertake it."[1] Others were less sympathetic or less ready to appreciate his difficulties: "I really pity Lord Liverpool from the bottom of my heart," wrote Arbuthnot to Huskisson, "but in truth he has brought the whole upon himself by his gaucherie. He has wounded *you*, and me, and Wallace, and he contrived at first to mortify poor Van."[2] But those offended were few in comparison with those affected by the changes of these two years; in common with many men who depend upon tact and reason to accomplish their ends, he had sometimes overestimated the power of these weapons; but, on the whole, they had served him well. In the verdict upon his conduct during these lengthy and tiresome negotiations Canning may be allowed, not inappropriately, the last word; and to Huskisson Canning wrote: "I will not deny myself the opportunity of saying that I am quite satisfied with L's conduct; that he has worked honestly, perseveringly, and sincerely, with great dexterity, and (what was essential) without alarm.... I am perfectly confident that with less management or with more brusqueness the thing *could not have been done*."[3]

1 Add. MSS. 38291, f. 299.   2 Add. MSS. 38744, f. 57.
3 Add. MSS. 38743, f. 277.

CHAPTER VI

ECONOMIC LIBERALISM

THE economic condition of England in 1820 was the despair of all clear-thinking men. The finances of the country had, for eight years, been under the care of the well-meaning Nicholas Vansittart; possessed of a very wide knowledge of financial affairs, he was more adept at demonstrating the curiosities of financial history than at deducing any coherent system of finance; not entirely ignorant of the principles of liberal economics, he was quite incapable of explaining in a lucid manner even the few praiseworthy points in his policy; himself greatly impressed with the intricacy of his task, he asked no more of the House of Commons than a blind faith in the mystic rites of which he was the attendant priest. Yet from post-war finance it was possible, for those with sufficient patience, to discover a system not altogether unsound; the commercial legislation of the country presented, on the contrary, the picturesque confusion of a garden, once well ordered, now overgrown with weeds. The ideas of Adam Smith had been for some time familiar to the upper classes—he was quoted in Parliament more than any other author, and to prove every conceivable case—but vested interest and the diversion of public attention to other matters had left the commercial system of the country unattended for the first twenty years of the century. The one positive task of economic regulation which had been undertaken since the war was the Corn

Law, and this was open to attack from the free traders, formed a staple item of working-class agitation, and had not proved satisfactory even to the agriculturalists.

In the realm of finance the Government considered that it had followed a consistent policy, and the measures taken after 1822 were looked upon as a natural continuation of that policy. The change from Vansittart to Robinson was particularly noticeable because Robinson could talk and Vansittart could not, but it is a fact that Liverpool and Vansittart had already agreed upon the scheme of finance which was to win much praise for Robinson in his first two years as Chancellor. In commercial legislation, on the other hand, there was a complete breakaway from earlier practice: Liverpool's Government began, with all due caution though not without considerable results, that free trade policy which was to be one of the main themes of nineteenth-century history, and the beginnings of free trade legislation in England can be dated definitely in 1820. With respect to the Corn Law there was an attempt to emend its workings in 1822, but this attempt proved abortive, and it was not until 1826 that a radical change was proposed; then Liverpool undertook a measure which would have gone far to settle the vexed question by a blend of protection and free trade, but this measure was also abortive, for Liverpool's seizure wrecked its chances in the House of Lords.

The chief problem of the Government after the war was an enormous increase in public expenditure. In 1800 the Government had asked for a supply of £39,500,000, in 1813 it asked for £68,686,000, and, though the men of 1815 knew it not, it would never again be possible to reduce expenditure below £50,000,000. But increased taxation had not been able to cover the full expense of the war, and in 1815 the National Debt stood at £860,000,000. Was this debt to be a permanent feature of the financial system? The statesmen of 1815 had their answer in that most famous legacy of Pitt, the Sinking Fund. This Fund was an annual payment of £1,000,000 towards Debt redemption, but the Debt redeemed was not cancelled and its yearly interest was paid into the Sinking Fund, so the yearly interest charge of the Debt remained constant, but each year a larger proportion of the charge was available for Debt redemption. When the payment of the Sinking Fund reached one forty-fifth part of the total Debt, it would cease to accumulate, and would pay off the whole Debt in forty-five years, while stock purchased could be cancelled or its interest treated as a surplus on the Sinking Fund applicable to current expenditure. Fool-proof in operation, this scheme encountered only one difficulty: when there was no surplus of revenue over expenditure it meant that a certain sum was raised by loan and used to pay off old Debt. The Sinking Fund as originally planned contained no provision for its suspension when there was no surplus, and, though Fox added a clause authorising loans to be taken from the Sinking Fund, no Tory financier would agree either to suspend the Fund or to treat it temporarily as current supply. On the other hand the Sinking Fund was a constant temptation to hard-pressed financiers, and Vansittart, while insisting upon the sanctity of the Fund, resorted, in 1813 and 1819, to complicated accountancy and even more complicated excuses in order to take a limited sum from the Sinking Fund. The explanation of the Tory devotion to the Sinking Fund lies in its psychological effect: "This is not a mere question of profit and loss," said Liverpool in 1822, "we must look at the moral effect produced. We must look at the effect which the Sinking Fund produces on public credit. We must look at the way it multiplies and augments our resources; and enables us in any war, as it enabled us in the last war, to raise money with facility by way of loan, instead of being compelled to have recourse to the more burdensome, and at times scarcely practicable operation of raising the supplies within the year."[1] The Sinking Fund was considered as the pledge of national good faith; as long as it was so considered there was a justification for it.

The other great expedient of the war years was the Bank restriction. First passed in 1797 as an emergency measure to save the Bank in a time of panic, it had been continued when the value of a flexible paper currency was understood. By freeing the currency from gold the Government made possible that great expansion in credit which had taken place; without it there would have been no possibility of carrying out the financial operations—quite without precedent in point of size—which had been necessary in order to provide the sinews of war for England and her allies. But, whatever these advantages, no one doubted that they were outweighed by those of a stable currency based upon gold, or that the return to cash payments was an essential part of the return to conditions of peace. The debate until 1819 lay between those who stressed the evil and those who

1 *Speech upon Agricultural Distress* (Pamphlet), London, 1822.

pleaded the necessity. Before the Bank could pay in gold, it would be essential that it should have a sufficient gold reserve; the mistake of the Bank and of the Government lay in assuming that such a reserve would accumulate in the natural course of things. In 1810 a famous committee of the House of Commons was appointed to enquire into the apparent discrepancy between the Mint price of bullion and the market price. The question was whether gold had gone up in price owing to scarcity or demand, or whether the paper currency was depreciated. The committee decided that the currency had depreciated, and that this depreciation had arisen because, in regulating their issues, the Bank paid no attention to the state of foreign exchanges or the market price of bullion. "There is at present an excess in the paper circulation of this country, of which the most unequivocal symptom is the very high price of bullion, and, next to that, the low state of the continental exchanges; that this excess is to be ascribed to the want of sufficient check and control in the issue of paper from the Bank of England, and originally, to the suspension of cash payments which removed the true and natural control."

The Government sprang to the defence of the Bank, taking as their text, "The Bank notes are equivalent to money for every common and legitimate transaction in life except for foreign exchanges". Vansittart, not yet a member of the Government but their spokesman on this question, proposed a set of counter resolutions. He went through an elaborate and well-informed survey of the other causes which might raise the price of bullion, he admitted the desirability of returning to cash payments, but thought it inexpedient to do so immediately, and, as his third resolution, moved that "the promissory notes of the Bank of England have hitherto been and are, at this time, held in public estimation to be equivalent to the legal coin of the realm, and are generally accepted as such in all pecuniary transactions to which such coin is lawfully applicable". Subsequently, with an irony which Government speakers failed to appreciate, it was necessary to pass laws forbidding the sale of guineas at more than their face value. By its rejection of the Bullion Report the Government did not, as has sometimes been implied, commit itself to an indefinite prolongation of the Bank Restriction, but they did refuse to take measures to facilitate its repeal. So long as bullion fetched a higher price in the market than at the Mint, men would not bring their gold to the Bank and they would withdraw gold from the Bank were the restriction removed. So far the argument against cash payment was sound; but this state of affairs could be remedied if the Bank restricted its issues, and this the Bank would not do, nor would the Government compel it to do so.

The Government emerged from the war with a clear plan of finance, which Liverpool outlined in a memorandum drawn up for the Committee on Cash Resumption.[1] The object of this policy was a return to normal finance and the return to cash payments in particular. Liverpool and Vansittart were quite aware that the finance of the war would not stand the test of peace-time criticism;[2] and they now

1 Add. MSS. 38741, f. 271: House of Lords Report upon Cash Resumption, Appendix A.
2 Add. MSS. 31231, f. 56, Vansittart to Castlereagh: "I need not remind you of the difficulties which we have had to struggle with,

hoped to reduce the funded and unfunded debt held by the Bank and so enable the Bank to buy up bullion in order to return to the gold standard. To pay off nearly £20,000,000 of Exchequer Bills held by the Bank the Government proposed to continue certain war-time taxes—the Property Tax chief among them—and this would also relieve them of the necessity of peace-time loans. The cardinal point was the retention of the Property Tax, and, as Liverpool informed a Tory deputation, "he felt the continuance of the tax as proposed to be of such essential importance to the country and that so much public inconvenience must result from the loss of it, that he was determined if the tax could not be continued that it should be the act of the House of Commons and that the Government should have nothing to reproach itself with upon that subject".[1] But the tax was wildly unpopular in the country, and the Government's plan of finance was thrown out of joint by its rejection in the House of Commons. The Government was thrown back upon the undesirable policy of peace-time loans, but it still maintained the Sinking Fund intact and it still hoped to resume cash payment by "natural" means.

In 1819 came the important change in the cash resumption policy, and at the same time there was a clarification of the Government's financial aims. Peel's committee recom-

---

but when I look back upon them, and particularly upon the enormous expense of the Spanish war, I cannot but feel astonished that they have been in any way surmounted. It has indeed sometimes been by expedients which only the necessity of the case could justify, but which it is now possible to supercede by more advantageous arrangements."

1 Add. MSS. 38741, f. 271. Omitted from House of Lords Report, Appendix A.

mended the return to cash payments, and, in order to achieve this, recommended the principles of the Bullion Report. It was necessary to recognise the depreciation of the paper currency and to start payment at a rate above the Mint price. At the same time issues would have to be contracted, and the currency brought back to its face value. The Government hardly looked upon these recommendations as a reversal of its former policy: it had consistently aimed at cash resumption, it had consistently claimed that immediate resumption was impossible, and the committee had now discovered the only means which would make the gradual resumption possible. Since 1814 Huskisson had been the intimate economic adviser of the Prime Minister, and early in 1819 Huskisson addressed a memorandum to Liverpool which may be considered as the result of previous consultations; in this memorandum the findings of the committee were foreshadowed and the Government's part in the great work was stressed. The memorandum recommended a gradual diminution of the circulation in order to bring the foreign exchanges to par, a large provision of bullion by the Bank by the purchases of gold at the market price, and a great reduction of the funded and unfunded debt to enable the Bank to buy bullion and contract issues without contracting mercantile discounts. If these measures had already been under discussion it is easy to see why the Government was prepared to accept the findings of Peel's committee with enthusiasm. In the House of Lords Liverpool explained the report at great length, and with great accuracy; in the years which followed he claimed cash resumption as one of the proudest achievements of his

Government. These facts show how far wide of the mark is the conventional view of cash resumption as a measure forced upon an unwilling Government; the Government did not suffer a great defeat, but in the years which followed some of its supporters among the landed gentry were to feel that, on this question, the Government had cruelly deserted them.

The other great alteration of 1819 was in the operation of the Sinking Fund. In the memorandum already quoted, Huskisson maintained that "the mystery of our financial system no longer deceives anyone in the money market; selling exchequer bills daily to redeem funded debt daily, then funding those exchequer bills once a year, or once in two years, in order to go over the same ground again; whilst the very air of mystery, and the anomaly of large annual or biennial loans in times of profound peace, create uneasiness out of the market, and in foreign countries an impression unfavourable with respect to the solidity of our resources. ...In finance, expedients and ingenious devices may answer to meet temporary difficulties; but for a permanent and peace system, the only wise course either in policy or for impression is a policy of simplicity and truth."[1] The effect of these criticisms was seen in Vansittart's budget, in which the principle that the only real Sinking Fund was a surplus of revenue over expenditure was explicitly stated, and three millions of new taxes were imposed in order to create a real Sinking Fund of £5,000,000. The taxes of 1819 were not a success, and Vansittart had one more "expedient and ingenious device" in the Dead Weight

1 Yonge, II, 383-4.

Annuity Scheme of 1822, but it may be said that from the year 1819 the Government was aiming at a sound and simple financial system. After 1820 there was a progressive improvement in the revenue, which helped forward this policy, and Robinson was able to step into the heritage of a sound financial system. How much he owed to the earlier efforts of Liverpool and Vansittart may be seen from a letter written by Liverpool to Vansittart on the eve of the latter's departure from the Exchequer. After commenting on the favourable state of the revenue, Liverpool went on: "If you are a bold man you will perhaps think me a bolder, in submitting for your consideration what I would not at present hint to anyone, whether we could not go still further than you suggest. I set out with assuming that we should go to the utmost point to which we can go, as our own act, and then make our stand. I am further impressed with the opinion that the best chance of saving our five millions surplus is giving up whatever may exceed it."[1] It was precisely this principle—the retention of a five millions Sinking Fund and the use of any further surplus for the remission of taxation—which formed the main proposal in Robinson's "Financial Statement", delivered to the House of Commons a month after his accession to the Exchequer.

The new Chancellor of the Exchequer "had always expressed a great dread of the labor and confinement of the situation",[2] and a candid friend, in congratulating him upon his appointment, added: "Though your promotion in the present instance will continually impose considerable additional labour upon you, I am not sure that it will not

1 Yonge, III, 249.   2 Add. MSS. 38291, f. 219.

be to your advantage to be placed in an office where you will be *compelled* to labour. No one is more *capable* of application than yourself, and you deserve more credit for this, as perhaps no one has a stronger *Penchant* for indolence—I am not at all sorry therefore to see you placed in a situation where *work* you must and *speak* you must."[1] But he had genuine abilities, he was attached to "liberal" principles, and no one was more popular in the Commons.[2] The Duke of Wellington indeed thought his appointment very bad indeed, he was totally unfit and would change his mind twenty times a day.[3] Not until 1828 was the truth of Wellington's estimate proven, in 1823 it seemed that the appointment had been amply justified.

Before considering the inauguration of the new commercial policy, it will be useful to digress for a moment to see what were the main currents of opinion which would influence the Government in its economic legislation. For the most striking feature of this period is the virtual abandonment of the agriculturalists by the Government and its conscious seeking after commercial support. At times during 1820, 1821 and 1822 it seemed that a new party—a "country" party—had been born. It was recruited from all parties, but its fighting strength came from the Radicals

1 Add. MSS. 40862, f. 87.
2 Add. MSS. 38743, f. 218: "The bringing forward Robinson would be scarcely less popular in the House of Commons than getting out poor Van."; Canning to Huskisson. At the end of his life it was possible to say, and to say justly, "He is a person of very delicate sensibility, accompanied with some warmth of temper; yet, in six and thirty years of political controversy he never wounded the feelings of an opponent or lost the regard of a friend." Ryall, *Portraits of Eminent Conservatives*.   3 Add. MSS. 38291, f. 244.

and the Tory country gentlemen. The Tories had something in common with Cobbett, they had nothing in common with Hume; but for a short time the independent Tories found common cause with Hume and his Radical phalanx in a demand for tax reduction and retrenchment. The Radicals demanded this on principle as a part of their political creed; the Tories demanded it because taxes and administrative extravagance seemed to be responsible for agricultural distress. Agriculture was admittedly in a shocking state, but Liverpool gave the agriculturalists cold comfort by telling them to wait for the natural self-adjustment of economic conditions. The country gentlemen cast about for their own remedies, and in 1822 the voice of rural England spoke at a county meeting in Norfolk which "consisted of persons of all parties, and many who were of no party whatever; and yet, in a meeting thus constituted, the call for retrenchment and reduction of taxation was unanimous. Both the members of the county were there, and one of them, a gentleman who had always supported the Government (Mr Wodehouse) concurred in opinion with the meeting, that a reduction of taxation was the only remedy for the existing distress."[1] Wodehouse's Whig colleague, Coke of Holkam, told the House of Commons that "unless there should be a union of both Whigs and Tories, unless the country gentlemen on both sides of the House should combine their efforts, the total destruction of the agricultural interest must ensue".[2] Country gentlemen, faced on the one side by falling rents and on the other by an unsympathetic Government, even dallied with

1 Hansard, VI, 430.　　　　2 Ibid.

Parliamentary Reform; when a Reform proposal was put forward it was again the all too independent Wodehouse[1] who substituted for the usual uncompromising negative the conciliatory statement that "he did not know what was the nature of the reform asked for. Before he could give any opinion on the question, he must wait till it came before the House in definite shape."[2]

The agricultural revolt was a great opportunity for the Whigs. A vote-catching speech in 1822 by Brougham failed to bring over the country gentlemen, but a few days later the Salt Tax was saved by only four votes, and the Government failed to convince the House that the services of one Lord of the Admiralty and of one assistant Postmaster-General were necessary parts of the administration. One Whig exclaimed triumphantly that "it was a consolation to him that gentlemen were now shaking off the dust which had been so profusely thrown in their eyes, and that the hon. members for Suffolk, Cheshire and Norfolk were beginning to take a correct view of the conduct of minis-

1 "Wodehouse is always queerish...and does not choose to commit himself till he knows what others think": Arbuthnot to Liverpool, December 1820, Add. MSS. 38574, f. 232.
2 In 1823 Cobbett carried a Reform Petition at a County Meeting in Norwich which, said the Whig Michael Angelo Taylor, "went to direct revolution in Church and State". But an amusing account by Hudson Gurney, the Norwich banker, shows that this was a freak result: "When I entered the Hall, Mr Cobbett appeared to be speaking with the most violent gesticulations from one end of the hustings; a reverend gentleman was speaking with apparently equal energy from the other; and the under-sheriff was reading a large paper in the middle; whilst from the unintermitted clamour of the circle that surrounded them, it appeared to me that not one of them knew that the others were also holding forth.... It was however a very good humoured meeting, everybody was laughing." Hansard, N.S. VIII, 1257.

ters". Ministerialists lamented that "some of the country gentlemen, who represent agricultural counties, literally seemed to have run wild"; and Wellington complained that they acted as an independent party.

The Government was not broken, for the Tory country gentlemen disliked the Whigs, disliked the Radicals even more, and disliked Brougham, who led the Whigs in these matters, most of all. But in the course of their revolt the agriculturalists raised two important points: agricultural protection and the effects of cash resumption. The Corn Law of 1815 had failed, though its form had been largely dictated by the agriculturalists themselves. It did not prevent prices falling to levels which ruined the farmer, it did not prevent them from rising to levels which starved the consumer, it did not prevent a sudden inrush of foreign corn and a consequent glut on the market so soon as the price reached 80s. On 7 March 1821 at four o'clock in the morning the agriculturalists won a great victory when T. S. Gooch's motion for a committee of enquiry into the state of agriculture was carried by four votes. But the capabilities of the agriculturalists were not sufficient to lend argument to their sentiments; the hard-won committee became, in the hands of Huskisson and Ricardo, an occasion for a free trade manifesto.[1]

The agricultural discontents were aggravated by the resumption of cash payments. Contracts had been made,

---

1 "Huskisson drew it [the report of the committee] up, and it is but justice to him to say that he is for establishing the trade on the most free and liberal foundation": Ricardo, *Letters to McCulloch*, p. 109. "When the Committee broke up there were very few points on which Mr. Huskisson and I did not agree": Ricardo, *Letters to Trower*, p. 155.

money had been borrowed, and taxes assessed under the paper regime; with the return to the gold standard the value of money would rise, prices would fall, and debts contracted would have to be paid in currency of an enhanced value. Throughout 1820 gold poured into the Bank, its note issue was diminished, and a considerable rise in the value of money followed. Cobbett roused the people against fundholders who were to receive full interest in an appreciated currency; while landlords had to adjust their rents, though they lagged behind prices with consequent distress. The agriculturalists asked for a reduction in the interest and principal of the National Debt. Here, however, the country gentlemen parted company from the parliamentary Radicals and from the main body of the Whigs. The Government was resolved to stand firm; and events vindicated this determination. In 1825 Liverpool was able to say that cash resumption had been accomplished "without violating a single previous engagement which they had made with the public creditor. The task had been a Herculean one; but we had accomplished it and were now enjoying our reward—England had reached a state of prosperity greater than any other country enjoyed, nay, greater than she herself, at any antecedent period, had ever attained."[1] One concession was, however, made to the agriculturalists. The time during which £1 notes should be legal tender was extended from 1826 to 1833. This meant that some of the bullion collected by the banks was of no immediate use, and the country banks were encouraged to make very large issues of notes. For this concession, for

1 Hansard, XII, 24.

excessive optimism, for over easy advances upon credit, the country was to suffer severely in 1825 when confidence changed suddenly to panic.

The influence of the agriculturalists upon policy was negative rather than positive, but there were some whose criticism the Government would not only fear but also respect. Better informed than the country gentlemen, though often equally biased by particular interests, was the mercantile class. In political opinions they ranged from Tories to Radicals, but all alike spoke with the authority of practical men, and many were also converts to the new political economy. There was indeed one among them who might be called the High Priest of political economy; David Ricardo was in Parliament five years only, but few have built up so wholesome a reputation in so short a time. In politics he was a professed Radical, but on questions of political economy he was but seldom actuated by political feeling.[1] He was free in his criticism of Government finance, but he gave useful help in the resistance to the agriculturalists. With the country gentlemen he was indeed most unpopular; "If we were once in a position to export and import corn without restriction," he told the House, "this country, possessing the greatest skill, the best machinery, the most strenuous and enlightened industry, and every other advantage in the greatest degree, would attain to an almost inconceivable degree of prosperity and happiness."[2] This in no way convinced the country

1 One exception is his attitude to the Sinking Fund. He criticised it not upon principle, but because the ministers could not be trusted with it.

2 During the debate on Agricultural Distress, 30 May 1820.

gentlemen, for, as T. S. Gooch said, "the doctrine that we should buy our corn where we could get it cheapest could not be listened to; for if the manufacturer bought his bread in the foreign market, the farmer at home could not purchase his manufactures, and finally, both would suffer". Ricardo's premature death in 1823 robbed the House of one of its most useful members. The general feeling was expressed by Lord Grenville in a letter which he wrote to Liverpool: "Radical as he was I consider Ricardo's death a great loss both to the country and to Government. The extreme caution of his mind and conduct contrasted very strikingly with the extravagance of his political opinions."[1]

In the "mercantile interest" a few other names are worthy of mention. Alexander Baring, the most famous banker of his day, the "cock of the funded and paper interest", was one of the most influential men in Parliament. He was a Whig, had been untiring in his opposition to the Property Tax yet had been employed by the Government in negotiating a financial settlement with France. His ideas were not always orthodox—he advocated bimetallism as a solution of the difficulties arising from cash resumption —but he spoke frequently and with great authority. In 1825 he was called into consultation by Liverpool and Huskisson and so had considerable influence over Government decisions in the great crisis of that year. Hudson Gurney, a Norwich banker, and Pascoe Grenfell, yet another banker, were both men of influence; the former had a panacea for all ills in the reduction of the standard. W. Manning, a West India merchant and a Bank director, had taken a

1 Add. MSS. 38297, f. 63.

prominent part against the abolition of the slave trade, he was now the chief spokesman for the Bank of England. J. Marryat and A. Robertson were the acknowledged representatives of the shipping interest; Nicholas Calvert was the most forward of the brewers in the House. W. Smith was the champion of the Methodists, and represented their interests in Parliament. Except upon a few questions the names of these and other merchants appear far more frequently in Hansard than those of any agriculturalist; their presence gave to the House of Commons a leaven of practical information upon commercial topics which it had lacked in earlier times. The Government, with the exception of Huskisson, did not represent the commercial classes; but it was peculiarly sensitive to the criticism of those classes. When such criticism was made the Government tried to meet it and it was in this imperceptible modification of policy, not in spectacular revolts against the ministers, that the influence of the mercantile class lay.

The wish of the Government for commercial support was manifested in 1820 when the well-known Merchants' Petition was presented to the House of Commons. This petition had been prepared by Tooke, an economic theorist convinced of the benefits of free trade, and the petition constituted an elaborate plea for the release of commerce from the restrictions imposed upon it. In order to test the ground before presenting his petition Tooke presented it privately to Liverpool, and was agreeably surprised to find the Prime Minister as convinced a free trader as himself. "There was not a principle, not a sentiment in which he did not entirely and most cordially concur," and, though he added that "in this country, which is burthened with so heavy a debt; in which so many vested interests had grown up, and are so connected and complicated with the existing commercial system, the case is very different; and the question of any change in that system ought not to be approached but with the utmost caution," it was still, as Tooke remarked, a great step forward for the free traders to have received this authoritative blessing.[1] Liverpool followed this up with speeches in the House of Lords which embodied theoretical expositions of free trade doctrines and enunciation of those utilitarian truisms which were to be the economic dogmas of the nineteenth century.

Liverpool was unable "to hold out the prospect of any great or immediate alteration"; but during 1821 Wallace, the Vice-President of the Board of Trade, was winning golden opinions with the commercial reforms which he in-augurated. His only material legacy was the reform of the Timber Duties, but, as Chairman of the Foreign Trade Committee, he constituted a link between the Government and mercantile opinion. His considered verdict was that "we were labouring under burdens which pressed on the industry of no other country in Europe", and the remedy lay in "a full and complete revision of our commercial system. We must also get rid of that feeling of appropriation which exhibited itself in a disposition to produce everything necessary for our own consumption and to render ourselves independent of the world—no notion could be more absurd or mischievous". The influence of

1 The account of this interview with Liverpool is given in Tooke, *History of Prices*, VI, 340.

Adam Smith—with his "sneaking arts of underling tradesmen...erected into the political maxims for the conduct of
a great empire"—is obvious. Liverpool had already implied the same thing—"if the people of the world are poor,
no legislative interposition can make them do that which
they would do if they were rich"—and there is no doubt
that he approved the actions and statements of Wallace, for
two years later he was saying that Wallace had "the strongest
claim, public and personal, upon me and upon the government".[1]

With the changes of 1821–3 Liverpool was able to gather
round him a group of liberal-minded men ready to take
whatever opportunities were offered for economic reform.
Huskisson had been his confidential adviser since 1814 and
was now President of the Board of Trade; Robinson became Chancellor of the Exchequer; Wallace eventually
became Master of the Mint, but he does not seem to have
been consulted upon commercial measures; Vansittart,
become Lord Bexley, was prepared to make available his
tried wisdom;[2] Peel played a small part in the formulation
of economic policy when he could spare time from the
Home Office. As Prime Minister and as First Lord of the
Treasury Liverpool was the head and the co-ordinating

1 Add. MSS. 88296, f. 168. So much did Wallace efface Robinson at
the Board of Trade that the Annual Register of 1823 makes an under-
standable error in referring to him as the President.
2 The inclusion of Vansittart as a liberal-minded man may seem to be
merely ironic; but Vansittart, with all his incompetency, was not
entirely in the outer darkness. In 1824 Robinson said: "He could
confidently state that no individual in the country was more impressed with the principles of Free Trade than the late Chancellor of
the Exchequer": Hansard, x, 1227.

agent in his "economic cabinet"; by inclination he was not likely to shirk any of the duties and the responsibilities which belonged to such a situation.

The next two years were of the greatest importance in the history of economic policy. They saw the application of the principles of free trade, the consolidation of the Customs Laws, the repeal and subsequent re-enactment in a modified form of the Combination Laws, and the launching of a new colonial policy. It is not here intended to give a history of these events, but only to trace, so far as is possible, the part which Liverpool played in them.

Liverpool did not initiate any of these policies; that was, indeed, the function of the departmental ministers concerned; but he did have to advise, to assent, and to co-ordinate. Huskisson had a great influence upon Robinson's budgets, but this influence must have been transmitted through Liverpool. A good example of the way in which the "economic cabinet" worked, and of the encouragement which Liverpool gave to every measure of commercial liberalism, is provided in a memorandum by Huskisson on the Reciprocity of Shipping Dues Bill: 1823. "On May 2 I requested a meeting at the Board of Trade of the following members of the Cabinet:—Lord Liverpool, Lord Bexley, Mr Canning, Mr Peel, Mr Robinson; Mr Canning, being prevented by other business, did not attend. I submitted to the other members, who did attend, three measures, which had been prepared for the consideration of this Board, and upon which it became necessary to obtain their decision." One of these measures was the Spitalfields Bill which was opposed in the House of Lords by some members of the Cabinet and lost, though Huskisson "distinctly stated to the meeting that each of the three measures...would meet with more or less of opposition, and that the fitness of moving them at all must depend not so much upon their abstract merits, of which the Board of Trade might be competent to judge, as upon other considerations not to be decided by that Board but by the King's Government". The bills had been approved by the "economic cabinet", but the question was now whether that decision bound the Government or "whether I must consider that decision as nothing more than the expression of their individual opinions". Dissentient members of the Cabinet certainly had a right to protest that they had not been consulted, and no view of the constitution could support Huskisson's contention that a decision of a few ministers could be equally binding as the decision of the whole Cabinet; but, in the existing balance of political forces, it was virtually binding.[1] Huskisson's memorandum was endorsed by Liverpool: "I think this measure of great importance in the present state of commerce, to this country," and the bill eventually passed.

The budget of 1824 was the first to contain proposals of avowed free trade. Robinson had at his disposal a surplus of £2,762,000, which he proposed to use "as a means of commencing a system of alteration in the fiscal and commercial regulations of this country". The bounties upon whale fishery, herring curing and linen export would not be

[1] The misunderstanding probably arose because Huskisson was not yet a member of the Cabinet, and so had no idea of what had passed after the decision by the "economic cabinet": E. J. Stapleton, *Correspondence*, I, 88 ff.

renewed, the duties on rum, coal, wool, and silk would be reduced. It was the proposal to touch the silk trade which aroused the most severe opposition, led by Baring, who deserted his free trade principles in this instance. The duties upon raw silk were to be reduced, the prohibition upon the import of manufactured silk was to be abolished and it was to be subject to a duty of 30 per cent. The boldness of this project lay in the fact that of all industry, silk manufacture had been most pampered by the Government, and as an exotic trade it was thought to require extreme measures of protection. Robinson and Huskisson stuck to their points, the bill was passed and, in spite of some subsequent complaints, was eminently successful in the long run.[1]

In the following year Robinson was able to report a surplus of nearly £1,000,000 more than he had estimated. The duty upon iron ore was reduced from a prohibitory level to 30s. a ton, and Robinson pointed out that England should feed her foundries and workshops with iron from whatever source. The duties upon hemp, coffee, cocoa, wines and British spirits were also reduced, and a few vexatious items among the assessed taxes were taken off.

That Liverpool continued to exercise a close supervision over the finances is shown in a letter of 19 October 1824 to Canning, which shows also the soundness of his financial ideas. Canning had written: "Are you forward in your financial plans? and can you remit us any more taxes? If so, I am for direct ones this season."[2] Liverpool replied: "The

1 Tooke, *History of Prices*, v, 414–17. But the mid-nineteenth-century prosperity of the silk trade was also proof of a proposition which no nineteenth-century economist would admit, the wisdom of fostering the trade in the first place.   2 E. J. Stapleton, I, 179.

state of the revenue is very satisfactory, and all the papers respecting it shall be ready for consideration, when we meet at the beginning of September. It is important however that you should know that we *must* make a reduction in the spirit duties of England, and we *ought* to make a reduction in those on tobacco. We shall have, I fear, no margin for any further reduction; and there really is not a pretence for any reduction in our direct taxation, except the facility which it might give us in getting through the business of the session in the House of Commons, which I do not mean to undervalue. Since our last reduction of the assessed taxes, the whole of our direct taxation does not exceed four millions per annum; less in proportion to our whole revenue than is paid by the subjects of any other country in Europe. When we made the reduction in the assessed taxes, two years ago, the distresses of the country, and particularly of the landed interest, were grounds for it; these distresses have now, in a great measure, disappeared. If we *could* do what we *ought* to do (do not be alarmed, I am not going to propose it), we should make an augmentation in our direct taxes of at least two millions; and, as a compensation, take off indirect taxes to the amount of four or five millions. By such an arrangement we should not materially reduce our revenue, and we should considerably increase the wealth and resources of the country, by the relief which might be afforded to commerce. We are already experiencing advantages from the measures adopted last session. Having said all this, I quite agree in the propriety of a careful review of the assessed taxes, particularly the house and window tax. That we should yield nothing to clamour, and that if there is anything which we cannot maintain we should make it a matter of voluntary concession as early in the session as possible."[1] The budget as eventually presented followed very closely upon these lines, save that the surplus seems to have been a little larger than the first estimate.

Huskisson may have inspired the free trade proposals in the budgets, but he had not, meanwhile, been idle in his own department. His first attempt to remove ancient restrictions had suffered a severe set-back when the House of Lords threw out the Spitalfields Bill in 1823. The history of the Spitalfields Acts "remains a curious and untimely record of the difficulties which beset trade agreements, wage boards, and compulsory arbitration in times of rapid economic change".[2] The London silk manufacture was regulated in a way peculiar to itself, but in a way which was also the last relic of that spirit which had animated the old labour code. Wages and the minutest details of manufacture were settled by magistrates, masters could not employ weavers from other districts or employ their capital elsewhere, the same wages were paid for work well and ill done, the same rates were paid for machine and for handwork. The result was that the Spitalfield weavers had an unusually high standard of life—they played a great part in the intellectual life of London, and many famous societies originated among them—but the regulations had driven manufacturers to leave London, and large works were set up in the provinces. The most usual argument

1 Yonge, III, 311.
2 J. H. Clapham, *Economic Journal*, vol. XXVI.

against the repeal was that it would impoverish the weavers
—the philanthropist Fowell Buxton argued this very
strongly—but Huskisson's reply was that under existing
conditions there would soon be no manufacture to support
them. He succeeded in passing the measure through the
House of Commons against all manner of interested and
disinterested opposition, but in the Lords it had a rough
passage. Liverpool supported it, but Eldon and Harrowby,
the dissentient ministers who infuriated Huskisson, were
against. It remained indeed for Harrowby to find the most
ingenious argument, an argument dictated neither by
philanthropy nor by political economy but by a considerable
measure of good sense: "He considered that the residence
of a large manufacturing body in the metropolis was prima
facie a great evil. . . but the best description of manufacture
was that which was domestic. In plans from which domestic
machinery had been banished, the mischievous effects had
been strikingly manifest. If the present bill should pass,
thousands of weavers who now lived with their families
would be taken away from them, and stowed into enormous
buildings, where they would be exposed to every evil, and
where their excellent moral habits would be destroyed,
while half a dozen great manufacturers would amass large
fortunes."[1] Liverpool, speaking with the tongue of many a
future philosophic radical or poor-law commissioner, said:
"Whether the bill was or was not against the wishes of the
operative manufacturers, it was for their interest that it
should pass."[2] The bill was defeated in 1823, but a similar
bill introduced in 1824 by Lauderdale passed both Houses

1 Hansard, IX, 1530.　　　2 *Ibid.*

with little opposition; an anticlimax to a question which had threatened to become a great battle-ground of the new and the old principles.

Other bills coming from the Board of Trade had been the important Trade Duties Reciprocity Bill, authorising the King in Council to reduce duties in order to carry out reciprocal commercial negotiations with other countries; and the consolidation of the Customs. This had been carried out, under Huskisson's supervision, by a hard-working civil servant, J. D. Hume, and the Act which resulted repealed no less than three hundred ancient and obsolete statutes. A new colonial policy was launched which broke in upon the sacred terrain of the navigation laws. Henceforth the intercourse between the colonies and foreign countries would be free, but trade between the colonies and England was still confined to British ships. One innovation, which might well have aroused agricultural alarms but which passed without much comment, was the admission of Canadian wheat at a fixed duty of 5s. No one of these steps towards free trade was in itself considerable, taken together they formed an important advance in that direction; at the same time protection was limited by restricting all protective duties to 30 per cent.

The last measure of economic reform was not the work of the ministers, indeed it passed without their serious consideration. Hume, acting upon the report of a committee which he had obtained, introduced bills repealing the Combination Laws; these passed so quietly that they escaped the notice of Hansard's reporter. But the boom of 1824 brought with it labour troubles which were accentuated by the repeal of the Acts; and in 1825 a committee was appointed, with Wallace as its chairman, to reconsider the Acts. The Act which resulted made all combinations illegal except those to fix wages and hours, and magistrates were given summary powers to punish any man using force to compel membership of an association or participation in a strike.

In estimating the influence of Liverpool upon the course of legislation in these two years the scanty nature of his papers forms a considerable obstacle. It would not be fair to assume from this that he played an insignificant part, indeed the reverse would rather be true. Every measure would require the Prime Minister's sanction, and the absence of written communications leads to the assumption that all was done verbally. It is not, therefore, unreasonable to suppose that Liverpool with his "economic cabinet" passed the proposed measures under review and that correspondence was rendered unnecessary by intimate personal discussion. In two measures only is it possible to trace Liverpool's own initiative; neither of them is unimportant, but both are off the main stream of legislation. In the budget of 1824 Robinson was able to announce, in consequence of the repayment of the Austrian Loan,[1] two special grants, one of £500,000 towards the building of churches, the other of £60,000 towards the purchase of pictures for a National Gallery. Church reform and church improvement had always been a special object of Liver-

1 This was a loan made early in the war; repayment was hardly expected; but Austria offered to do so at the Congress of Verona, and negotiations were completed during 1823.

pool's ambition, and he was sympathetic to the Evangelical movement (though by Evangelical clergy he understood those who were attentive to their duties, not those who adopted the manners of a distinct sect).[1] In 1818 he had been able to make a grant of £1,000,000 towards the building of new churches in the Government's only constructive remedy for social troubles, and in 1824 it was said that these churches were all full. Liverpool was anxious that a part of the Austrian Loan repayment should be allotted to church building, and carried his point; for what better employment could be found for a godsend than a work of God? The second measure is interesting, for, in the official portrait of Liverpool by Lawrence now in the National Portrait Gallery, he is shown holding the charter of the National Gallery. Beyond this he has received little recognition for a work in which he bore the chief responsibility. The occasion was the sale of the collection of J. J. Angerstein in 1823. In that year Liverpool wrote to Baring: "In expectation of the final success of the negotiations relative to the Austrian Loan, I more than five weeks ago authorised Sir C. Long to open a negotiation with Mr Angerstein for the purchase of his collection of pictures. I had determined upon going thus far whatever was the ultimate result of the Austrian negotiation."[2]

During the year 1824 prosperity had never stood so high; in every enterprise fortune seemed to smile, the more so by contrast with what had gone before; while, in South America, a new field was opened for the employment of

1 Add. MSS. 38289, f. 117.　　　2 Add. MSS. 38297, f. 71.

British capital. Nothing, men felt, could hinder the success of their enterprises and 1825 opened in a mood of extravagant optimism. Every form of speculation was undertaken, money was very plentiful, and credit was given upon the slenderest securities. In the period which followed the war Liverpool might have been criticised for confident faith in a recovery which took place only after long delay, but in 1825 he was alive to danger which few men foresaw. In March 1825 "he would not say he took, he created almost an occasion of stating...what, sooner or later, would be the effect of this rash spirit of speculation",[1] and delivered this warning: "In a country like this, where extensive commercial interests are constantly at work, a great degree of speculation is unavoidable, and, if kept within certain limits, this spirit of speculation is attended with much advantage to the country. In a moment like the present, in a time of profound peace, and when the interest of money is low, it is to be expected that speculation should exist in a very considerable degree. To this I have no objection, but I wish that the public should be set to rights as to the situation in which they stand. I never knew a moment when there was a greater prospect of lasting peace than the present; but still, no man can say how long that peace may last. Now, I would ask every man to reflect what would be the situation of the public if (not to speak of actual war) any thing short of a war—any embarrassing event—were to occur?...When commercial embarrassments occurred during the late war, banks and merchants came forward and applied to Parliament for aid, which they obtained by

1 Hansard, XIV, 15.

issues of Exchequer Bills; I wish it, however, to be clearly understood, that those persons now engaged in Joint Stock Companies, or other enterprises, enter on those speculations at their own peril and risk. I think it my duty to declare, that I never will advise the introduction of any bill for their relief; on the contrary if such a measure were to be proposed, I would oppose it and I hope that parliament will resist any measure of this kind. I think that this determination cannot be too well understood at the present moment, nor made too publicly known. I have felt myself particularly called on to make this declaration, because I understand that the speculations are not confined to the metropolis, where people may have a better opportunity of judging for themselves, but that endeavours are being made, by means of country bankers, to engage people in the country to embark in speculation, the object of which they cannot know. I am one of the last men ever to interfere, by legislative provisions, with the property of individuals, or to endeavour by any means, to prevent men from spending their own money as they please. But as the consequences of the present extensive speculations might be serious, I thought, filling the situation which I do, that I should be bound to declare that I am determined not to give relief, or to listen to any claims made on account of distress, arising from such sort of speculation. In stating my opinion, it is in reference to no particular measure, but to that general spirit of speculation which is going beyond all bounds, and is likely to bring the greatest mischief on numerous individuals."[1]

[1] Hansard, XII, 1194.

Mention has already been made of the concession in 1822 to the agriculturalists whereby £1 notes continued in circulation until 1833. But by 1822 the banks had already accumulated large stores of bullion, and this encouraged them to increase their issues of notes. Under these circumstances prices rose, the value of money fell, and there was a steady drain of bullion from the country. During 1824 the Bank's reserve sank from £14,000,000 to £10,721,190; by May 1825 it had fallen to £6,131,300. At this the Bank took alarm and began to call in its notes; but at the same period the folly of many speculative ventures was being realised, and the effect of the Bank's change in policy was to increase this disquiet. Nothing could stop the drain of bullion from the Bank, and in the autumn the reserve stood at about £3,500,000. In the country depression and lack of confidence descended upon those who had taken advantage of rising prices to launch enterprises with money borrowed upon insufficient securities; many, faced with falling prices and a glutted market, could look forward only to bankruptcy.

In spite of his earlier fears Liverpool remained fairly calm. "The state of the money market has for some time occupied my attention", he wrote on 3 September, "I have no doubt it has been affected by the measures taken by the Bank (with our approbation and connivance) for reducing their circulation, in consequence of the state of the Exchanges. I am not in any alarm as to the result; provided no false step is taken, I am convinced that in a short time things will set themselves right." It is interesting to note that the Government and the Bank had been following the principles of the Bullion Report in regulating the currency

with reference to the Exchanges, but in doing this insufficient attention had been paid to the psychological effects in
the country. As a remedy for "the embarrassments in which
we may be shortly placed" Liverpool suggested raising the
interest on Exchequer Bills—"it is the plain, obvious and I
may add the *honest* remedy"—which would succeed better
than increasing the circulation and keeping up funds.[1]

All optimism was, however, shattered by the failure of
Elford's Bank at Plymouth on 29 November. The Bank had
already refused to discount bills for Payne and Smith, the
Barings, Rothschild, and Harman;[2] and the news from the
West Country was sufficient to spread panic in the City.
On 3 December the Bank heard that the great London
house of Pole, Thornton & Co. was in serious difficulties,
and decided to place £300,000 at its disposal. In spite of
this Pole, Thornton & Co. fought a losing battle for a week
and failed on 12 December, carrying down with them many
country concerns. This failure brought on the worst period
of the crisis.

At the end of November Liverpool had written to Bexley:
"I foresee considerable distress and commercial embarrassment, but this is the natural result of the over-speculation
of the last two years, and any attempt to interfere by the
authority of Government would only aggravate the evil
instead of remedying it."[3] But the Government kept a
close watch upon events. It was to be most intimately
concerned, for, as the Bank reserve dwindled away to
nothing, there came the inevitable demand for a stop upon

1 Add. MSS. 38300, f. 172. 2 Add. MSS. 38301, f. 37.
3 Add. MSS. 31232, f. 343.

cash payments. This the Government was resolved to avoid at all costs.

The two days following the failure of Pole, Thornton & Co. were the worst of the crisis; almost all the bullion had gone from the Bank, every house in the City trembled upon the brink of disaster, money could not be obtained even upon the best of securities, and men of sound fortune wandered disconsolate in the streets wondering whether the next hour would see them ruined. Liverpool called Huskisson, the Governor of the Bank, and Alexander Baring into conference;[1] the result of their deliberations was a very bold decision. There was no gold to be had, but Bank of England notes were still as good as gold; it was now decided to stem the panic by reversing the Bank's policy and putting into circulation as many notes as possible. This was on 14 December and £5,000,000 of notes were immediately printed and lent "by every possible means, and in modes never adopted before".[2] This policy was completely successful, panic was allayed in London, and on Saturday, the 17th, Richards, the Deputy Governor of the Bank, was able to go to the Cabinet, reeling with fatigue and with just sufficient strength to call out to Lord Liverpool that all was well.[3]

1 *The Financial and Commercial Crisis Considered*, by Lord Ashburton (A. Baring), London, 1847. This compares the crisis of 1847 with that of 1825. Cf. also Huskisson in the House of Commons: "The Bank throughout their prompt, efficacious and public spirited conduct, had the countenance, advice and particular recommendation of the First Lord of the Treasury and his Right Hon. friend (Robinson) to assist them" (Hansard, XIV, 231).

2 MacLeod, *Theory and Practice of Central Banking*, II, 5th Ed., 117. Quoting Harman, a bank director.

3 *Ibid.* p. 116.

The crisis was at an end in the City, but in the provinces, where it had begun earlier, it was to run in all for nearly four weeks. It was not until 24 December that conditions were once more normal, and further bank failures had only been averted by a happy accident. After the 17th there were neither notes nor gold which could be sent out to the country—or so it seemed until one of the directors remembered a case of £1,000,000 old unused notes in one of the Bank cellars—these were immediately despatched and stopped the panic.

So ended the great crisis of 1825, and there remained only the work of repair and restoration. There were many who clamoured for immediate relief, but Liverpool, adhering to his earlier resolution, was resolved against this. The first cause of the crisis had been over-confidence and ignorant speculation, but there had been contributory causes: the over-issue of paper and the irresponsibility of the country banks. By charter the Bank of England had the exclusive right of conducting a joint-stock bank in England; and the country banks were frequently in the hands of single capitalists. Liverpool disapproved wholeheartedly of this system, it was "one of the most absurd ever invented. It was in the teeth of all sound policy or common sense. It had grown up gradually and was not the result of any original plan or system."[1] And, in one of his few sentences which is frequently quoted, "any small tradesman, a cheesemonger, a butcher, or a shoemaker, might open a country bank; but a set of persons with a fortune sufficient

1 Hansard, XIV, 17 February 1826. Not perhaps a typical Tory argument.

to carry on the concern with security were not permitted to
do so".[1] In this respect Scotland differed from England;
there, joint-stock banking was legal and very few failures
had occurred in the past fifty years. Accordingly Liverpool and Robinson entered into correspondence with the
Bank directors to persuade them to forgo their privileges.
The Bank gave way with a bad grace, and on conditions;
the privilege was still to be operative for a distance of fifty
miles round London, and the Bank was empowered to set
up branch banks in the principal cities. This last proposal
was particularly pressed by Liverpool, but it cannot be
said that it had the effects which he hoped, and Huskisson,
who criticised the proposal, was justified.[2] The door was
now open for the formation of great joint-stock banks,
though it was but slowly that the country banks took
advantage of these facilities.

The second remedy was to put an end to the indiscrimi-
nate issue of paper. In 1821, 1822 and 1823 the average
annual value of country notes issued was £4,200,000, in
1824 it was £6,000,000, in 1825 over £8,000,000. Under
the original provisions of Peel's Act £1 notes would have
ceased to be currency on 1 February 1826, but in 1822, in
response to pressure from the agriculturalists, the time

1 Hansard, XIV, 15.
2 *Report of Committee on Banks of Issue*, 1841, evidence of Vincent
Stuckey: "Mr Huskisson said to me: 'Lord Liverpool is extremely
keen upon having branch Banks of England, and I do not see any
objection to them; but I very much doubt whether it will answer in
the long run; it appears to me that the Bank Directors have now as
much or more than they can do in London, if you throw them upon
the country circulation they will soon get into considerable difficulties;
therefore I should rather confine their business to London.'"

limit had been postponed to 1833. It was now necessary to reverse this decision, and it was this proposal which was likely to meet with most opposition in the Commons. "We expect great difficulties...from a combination of country bankers and city merchants, with no small sprinkling of country gentlemen connected with the former class, which threatens to run very hard Robinson's one pound note proposition."[1] The measure survived this ordeal in the Commons, but only because the Opposition supported the Government. "It is but just to the opposition," wrote Canning, "to Brougham especially, as well as to Tierney, Wilson, and others, to say that their cordial support helped very much to discourage a combination of our *friends*; which, if formed upon the basis of an adverse attack from our usual opponents, might, in the present state of suffering and consequent discontent, have been very formidable."[2] Unpopular as this measure was in England, in Scotland it was completely unacceptable. The Scots, with their stable banking system, had long been attached to their £1 notes and fully realised the advantages, when security was assured, of a paper currency. That wholehearted Tory Sir Walter Scott made his first and last appearance upon the political stage as an anti-Government pamphleteer, and his friend Croker took up the Government's defence; but in spite of Croker, and in spite of the Government's determination, the Scots won the day, and Scotland was excluded from the measure.

1 Wellington, *Supplementary Despatches* (*N.S.*), III, 97. Canning to Wellington, who was at this time on a mission to Petersburg; from Canning, Peel and Croker he received letters upon happenings at home.
2 *Ibid.*

There was, however, one measure demanded by the country; this was the issue of Exchequer Bills upon the security of goods to distressed merchants. Canning doubted "whether we should get through the crisis without an issue of exchequer bills, which, objectionable as it may be, and is, in principle, appears to be the only remedy to which the moneyed world will look with confidence".[1] In March Liverpool had given his specific warning that the Government would give no relief to speculators; but the general opinion was that "as soon as the whole mercantile body, as soon as Tierney at the head of the opposition, as soon as every man of the old Pitt party expressed a unanimous concurrence in that measure, we all thought it would do us no great harm to adopt it as a special remedy in a special case".[2] Every man of the old Pitt party counted without their leader's adherence to the principles of *laissez-faire*. Throughout the year he had deprecated any proposals for Government interference, now he refused completely to concur in any measure which would teach men the habit of relying upon Government when their own efforts failed. "I know that if I studied my own ease or popularity, I could not do so more effectively than by coming down to Parliament with such a proposition. If I have not adopted that course, I trust the House will give me credit for abstaining from it, from a thorough conviction that it was not likely to be attended with beneficial results. I have always thought that the precedent of 1793, in that respect, was not a favourable one and therefore ought not to be followed. But there is a great difference between that period and the

1 Wellington, III, 116.   2 Croker, I, 314.

present; for it cannot now be pretended that the commercial distress which now existed has any connection with political events.... What would be the effects of such a measure? Not to leave the people to rely upon themselves. What is that but the very evil I have deprecated; namely, looking to government for aid, to relieve them from the consequence of their own extravagance. It is now three or four years since the landed interest was suffering great distress: and not a month passed at that time, that I was not beset with the most urgent applications for relief by the issue of Exchequer Bills...the applications, however, were rejected."[1] Accordingly, when a petition for the issue of Exchequer Bills was about to be presented in the House, Liverpool sent for Canning and told him that he would resign if such a measure was forced upon the Administration, and authorised Canning to say this in the House. Canning felt he could not "leave Lord Liverpool in the lurch" and announced to the House "in a very bold and uncompromising tone, that if the House chose to adopt the proposed measure they must also be prepared to find Ministers to execute it, for that they *would not*; and this he repeated very steadily, and to the ears of some country gentlemen offensively".[2]

Liverpool felt keenly his personal responsibility, and even went so far as to suggest that "the best mode of solving the difficulty was for him to retire from office, the rest of the members of the Government retaining their offices". This stirred Peel to remonstrate: "I went to him when he was alone, and told him I thought him very wrong in using that

[1] Hansard, xv, 450.   [2] Croker, I, 324-5.

language, that if he resigned when the country was in a crisis of financial difficulty—he, the minister who presided over the finances of the country—he would lose all the credit he had gained by long and successful service; that the country would right itself in two or three months; that the man who might succeed him would get all the credit and he personally all the blame. I added also, that what he proposed to do, to retire singly, should not take place; that I should feel it dishonourable to allow one member of the Government—and that member the head of it—to make himself a sacrifice; and if he retired...I could not but consider that his retirement under such circumstances would be a dissolution of the government."[1] A compromise was then discovered which satisfied both Liverpool's scruples and the demands for relief; by a clause in the Bank's Charter it was empowered to issue notes upon the deposit of goods. The Government requested the Bank to do this, and also to purchase Exchequer Bills in the open market; this the Bank consented to do, but only when the Government agreed to repay some of the debt to the Bank. "If", said Liverpool, "the Bank chose to go into the market, and purchase a limited quantity of Exchequer Bills for the purpose of affording relief to the public, the government would pay them part of the six million which they owed them, to prevent them from experiencing any inconvenience in so doing." But this transaction was upon a different principle than that of direct relief by the Government.[2]

The incident had come near to causing a revolt in the

1 Peel to Wellington: Parker, I, 397.　　2 Hansard, xv, 450.

party, many had "whispered about that we were acting
quite in a different manner from that in which Mr Pitt did
act, and would have acted had he been alive";[1] and Croker
thought it "altogether the most ridiculous political intrigue,
if it may be so called, I ever saw". But Peel gave it as his
firm opinion "that we were right in refusing, and that had
we consented we should have defeated our other measures
and not impossibly have had to answer for another Bank
Restriction". Liverpool based his defence in the House of
Lords largely upon moral argument—that men should not
depend upon the Government—but Peel gives some account of the practical considerations as they were brought
forward in the Cabinet. "There are thirty million of
Exchequer Bills outstanding. The purchases lately made by
the Bank can hardly maintain them at par. If there were a
new issue to such an amount as contemplated—viz. five
million—there would be a great danger that the whole mass
of Exchequer Bills would be at a discount and would be
paid into the revenue. If the new Exchequer Bills were to
be issued at a different rate of interest from the outstanding ones—say bearing an interest of five per cent—
the old ones would be immediately at a great discount
unless the interest were raised. If the interest were raised
the charge on the revenue would be of course proportionate
to the increase of the rate of interest."[2]

From outside the Government the economist Tooke advanced more reasons in support, in a pamphlet which, said
Huskisson, would "check a great deal of nonsense which,
without some preliminary discussions to direct and guide

1 Wellington, III, 143 ff.   2 *Ibid.* p. 143.

the thoughts of those who do not think much for themselves, would probably find vent in the House of Commons".[1] Tooke argued that the characteristics of commercial distress were lack of lenders and lack of buyers,
since it is no profits and no loans which mean ruin for the
individual. The issue of Exchequer Bills would supply
neither of these wants. Since they went straight to persons
in distress, the number of lenders or buyers would not be
increased; an individual would, indeed, be able to exchange Exchequer Bills for cash, but, since the amount of
money had not been increased, some less fortunate person
would have to go without a loan. The issue of Exchequer
Bills would benefit certain people, it would direct capital
into certain channels, but it would not be a measure of
general relief. If the Bank bought up Exchequer Bills and
issued notes in excess of the natural limit imposed by the
state of the Exchanges, then, "the temporary relief would
be dearly bought at the expense of the alternative of suspension or of such a degree of subsequent contraction as
might renew the distress in an aggravated form".[2] In a
private letter to Huskisson, Tooke added another argument: the issue of Exchequer Bills might have the effect of
bringing out hoarded money, but the same argument—
that bills would not add to the amount of money available
—would still apply; for the Bank, seeing money to be more
abundant, would again reduce its note issue.[3]

From the great crisis England emerged sadder but saner;

[1] Add. MSS. 38747, f. 194.
[2] *Considerations on the State of the Currency*, 2nd ed. Postscript.
[3] Add. MSS. 38747, f. 217.

and henceforth caution would restrain the hands of the speculator. The real prosperity of the country, the progress of its industry and commerce, was touched only upon the surface, and soon returned to a healthy condition. One valuable result of the crisis was the reform of the country banking system, and a result which was welcomed by many was the substitution of gold coin for small notes. In England, though not in Scotland, the Government was able to carry all its measures; but in order to do so it had to rely upon Whig support. Thus one effect of the crisis was to strengthen the bonds of sympathy between Liberal Tories and Whigs, and to emphasise the division between the former and "those who do not think much for themselves".

During the session of 1825 W. W. Whitmore, the member for Bridgnorth and a persistent advocate of Corn Law reform, spoke in favour of a fixed corn duty of 10s. During the debate which followed Huskisson promised to consider the whole question during the next session. The agriculturalists had been loud in their complaints of the Corn Law, but now that a change was threatened by the suspect Huskisson they rallied to its defence. The change they desired was more adequate protection, the change they foresaw was some measure of free trade.

The corn question had been one of constant difficulty for the Liverpool Government, and the attempt to reconcile the persistent demand of the farmers for a closed market with the equally forcible demand of the consumers for cheap bread, had not so far proved very successful. The agitation of the question had begun as early as 1813 and it had continued—under changing circumstances—ever since. In 1808 the price of wheat was 80s. per quarter, it rose to over 100s. in 1810, and after a slight drop in 1811, to 126s. in 1812; it was still over 110s. in August 1813, but between August and December it dropped to 73s. The downward trend continued until it reached the abysmal depth of 48s. in February 1816. In 1816 the expectation of a bad harvest brought the price back to 103s., but it dropped in 1817 to 78s., and was at 80s. during the greater part of 1818 until it fell at the end of the year to 78s. From these figures it will be seen that both producers and consumers had much cause for complaint; the former suffered a great set-back in 1814 and never recovered their war-time position, the latter had to pay starvation prices before 1814, in 1817, and in 1818; both alike were victims of sudden fluctuations in price, both would gain from the Government's policy of ensuring a steady supply without fluctuations in price. Had the Government been successful in that policy it would have solved one of the perennial problems which face modern governments.

Under the Corn Law of 1804 a prohibitory duty of 24s. 3d. was imposed when the price was less than 63s., there was a duty of 2s. 6d. between 63s. and 65s., and of 6d. when over 65s.; there was also a bounty of 5s. upon export when the price was less than 48s. and a prohibition of export when it was over 54s. But since that date prices had been generally over 65s., foreign corn could come in at a nominal duty, and export was forbidden. Under these circumstances it might be asked why in March 1813 there began an agitation for a change in the law. The answer is that it began not with the English but with the Irish producers, and it was aimed not at altering the import regulations but at freeing the export trade. Ireland ate potatoes and exported wheat; the first aim of Irish landowners was to sell their wheat on the continent, and it was with this object that Sir Henry Parnell moved for a committee to enquire into the Corn Trade of Ireland. But a return had just been published showing that, in the last twenty-one years, £58,634,135 of foreign corn had been imported, even while prices had risen to famine level. Under the stimulus of this return the words "United Kingdom" were substituted for "Ireland", and a few English members were added to the committee as originally named by Parnell. The obvious comment was that home supply should be increased and that prices should be lowered; but during the discussion of the committee a very fair prospect opened before the Irish members. If foreign corn was subjected to a virtual prohibition, Irish corn would have the run of the English market. In presenting the committee's report Parnell argued that importation did not lower prices—he could point to the last few years as proof—it discouraged home farmers, and so restricted produce and raised the price. He recommended a duty of 24s. 3d. when the price was less than 105s. 2d., of 2s. 6d. between 105s. 2d. and 135s. 2d. and of 6d. over that price. Export should be free at all times.[1]

These were proposals which no Government could consider, and Parnell seemed to have failed. In 1814, however, the discussion was resumed under very different circumstances. Prices had fallen suddenly upon the prospect of peace, and "steady prices" had become the catch-

[1] Hansard, XXV, Appendix pv. ff.

word of the agriculturalists. Though prices were now 74*s*.
imports were still admitted under the old law, and the high
wages and rents of former years remained constant. Parnell
now proposed 84*s*. as the price at which the prohibitory
duty of 24*s*. 3*d*. was to apply, and 87*s*. was the price at
which the nominal duty should come into force.[1] These
proposals created great alarm among the commercial and
labouring classes; many petitions were presented, and it
was decided to postpone the discussion until 1815 while
setting up a committee to examine these petitions.

The attitude of the Government to this demand was one
of modified approval: it would not admit the propositions
of the extreme protectionists, but it would admit the necessity for some new measure. Liverpool gave to the question
his particular attention. "I have", he said, "for the last
three years been revolving the subject in my mind....I
have read with all the attention in my power, all the evidence
which has been given upon the question and all the publica-
tions which have been given to the world....If there ever
was a question on which my mind was free from all undue
bias towards one particular view of it rather than another,
that is this question....My decided opinion is that the
commercial interests of this country ought not to be sacrificed to the agricultural; but with all due regard to the
commercial interest—and I have been educated in a school
where I was taught highly to value the commercial interest
—I must also say that the agricultural interest ought not to
be sacrificed to the commercial....The general principle,
supposing all nations to act upon it, is that in these cases the

1 Hansard, XXVII, 663: 5 May 1814.

legislature ought not to interfere, but leave everything to find its own level. In such a state of the world it is perfectly clear that every nation ought to be left to prosecute without interference that particular species of industry for which by its nature and condition it was in all respect best adapted. But unfortunately the period is not yet arrived when nations would have the wisdom to act upon such a system."[1]

The measure which would have found most favour in the eyes of the Government would have been an adoption of the sliding scale principle of 1804. In 1814 Huskisson countered Parnell's proposals by a scheme which would make 63s. the price at which the prohibitory duty of 24s. 3d. should apply and diminish the duty by 1s. for every 1s. increase in price until at 86s. the duty would expire.[2] The committee appointed in 1814 ignored the many petitions against the measure and suggested 80s. as the lowest possible "regulating price". The Government would still have preferred Huskisson's proposals, but it was also anxious to produce a measure acceptable to the agriculturalists; to ascertain the feelings upon the measure Liverpool called "a very full meeting of the landed interest" which "almost unanimously and particularly Mr Western" preferred the alternative measure.[3] As there did not seem to be much to choose between the two measures, the Government accepted this ruling, and Robinson introduced a simple measure which prohibited import when the price was less than 80s. and allowed free import above that

1 Hansard, xxx, 175 ff.: 15 March 1815.
2 Hansard, xxvii, 663 ff.   3 Add. MSS. 38742, f. 4.

price. In spite of many protests from the manufacturing districts the bill passed by 245 to 77.

In supporting this measure the Government was extremely anxious to avoid any imputation of class legislation. "Were the measure one which stood upon the narrow ground of affording relief to a particular class", said Liverpool, "I would not support it...not from any want of feeling towards the sufferings of any particular body of men, nor from any indisposition to alleviate these sufferings but because from long experience I have come to the conclusion that you cannot relieve one class of people without injuring some other class more or less. Upon that subject there is a great deal of mistaken legislation in our statute books; but with regard to the present measure, it is so far from being one which looks only to the relief of a particular class, that it embraces the interests of all, and of the poor above all."[1] These arguments were expanded by Huskisson in a letter to his constituents at Chichester. "My sole object is to prevent...corn from ever again reaching the late extravagant prices. But if we wish to cure an evil of this alarming magnitude we must first trace it to its source. What is that source? Obviously this, that, until now, we did not, even in good years, grow enough corn for our own consumption...in order to ensure a continuance of cheapness and sufficiency, we must ensure to our own growers that protection against foreign import which has produced these blessings."[2] If corn were admitted free "the small farmer would be ruined, improvements would everywhere stand still, inferior land now producing corn could be given

1 Hansard, xxx, 147. 2 Add. MSS. 38739, f. 198.

up and return to a state of waste...to protect the small farmer is ultimately to protect the people". "Let the bread we eat be the produce of corn grown among ourselves, and I for one care not how cheap it is; the cheaper the better." And Liverpool proclaimed that "the great object is the interest of the consumer, and this, I contend, will be effectually promoted by the present measure the object of which will be to render grain cheaper instead of dearer. The important point to obtain is a steady and moderate price...it has been argued most fallaciously that this import price of 80s. would be a *minimum* price... instead of being a minimum the import price has been more generally the *maximum* in the market."[1]

The chief benefit of the law was psychological in that it did bolster up, to some extent, the confidence of the farmer. The Government was, for this reason, anxious to pass some measure without delay. "If the Bill is passed", said Liverpool, "and any inconvenience is found to arise from it, a remedy may be immediately applied, but if the measure is rejected, and capital in consequence withdrawn from agriculture, fifty years might be necessary to replace us in our present situation."[2] It might, on the other hand, be argued in retrospect that the hopes of the farmers were bound to be false hopes and that they would have done better to restrict their production immediately. The law probably did something to smooth over the brutal transition from war to peace, but nothing so important as its authors had foreseen, and whatever its merits they were largely negative. The depression of 1816 struck a blow at

1 Hansard, XXX, 175 ff.   2 *Ibid.*

English farming from which it would not recover for many years. Cultivation on the "new lands" ceased to be remunerative, the Banks pressed for repayment of loans made in order to open up these lands, the tithes pressed heavily upon the farmers, and as conditions became worse the burden of the Poor Rate became proportionately greater. In 1816 Agricultural Distress was a great item of debate in the House of Commons, and the agriculturalists demanded the reduction of taxation or, at least and with some show of justice, that a part of the burden of taxation should be transferred to the manufacturers.

The Corn Law proved very unsatisfactory in operation. It could not guarantee to the farmer a fair and steady price, and the market was liable to be flooded so soon as the price reached 80s. and large stores of foreign corn were released from bond. On the other hand prices could rise to starvation level in times of scarcity before distress could be alleviated by introduction of foreign corn. These considerations led to a revision of the law in 1822: 70s. was now taken as the price at which corn should be admitted, and above that price a graduated duty was imposed.[1] But this law was not to come into operation until the price reached 80s., and during the years which followed prices never reached this level. But though the price was low by the standard of the immediate post-war years it was steady, and, after the difficulties of transition, agriculture had been able to adjust itself and was, by 1825, in a most flourishing condition. Yet in these years there emerged another doubt:

[1] Between 70s. and 80s. the duty was 12s.; over 80s. and under 85s., 5s.; over 85s., 1s.

was there really enough corn in the country to feed the urban populations at all times? Complaints of scarcity were frequent, and in 1826 the artisans of the industrial districts attributed their distresses directly to the Corn Laws. The prosperity of agriculture was in itself an argument that something might be done to increase the supplies—by the admission of foreign corn at a duty—without injuring the interest of the farmer.

Huskisson's promise in 1825 was inconvenient to the Government, which was not anxious to agitate this difficult question in the last session of an expiring Parliament and before there seemed to be any pressing need to do so. In the summer, when Canning was pressing Liverpool to postpone the dissolution until 1826 when the heat of "No Popery" might have died away, Liverpool made it one of his conditions that the corn question should not be brought forward in the old Parliament. But, by the spring of 1826, the condition of England had changed very much for the worse, and it was Liverpool himself who first tampered with the Corn Law.

The financial crisis of 1825 was followed by severe distress in the manufacturing districts, and there were many complaints of the dearness of bread. Under these circumstances Liverpool proposed two measures of immediate relief and committed himself to some wholesale changes in the Corn Law. The two temporary measures— which Liverpool avowed were his own proposals and for which he was especially responsible—were the admission of warehoused corn at a reduced duty, and the grant to ministers of a discretionary power to admit more corn at a low duty.[1] He also announced that he would introduce a new Corn Law in the new Parliament, and that the choice would lie between the principle of the existing law with an alteration in the limiting price, and the imposition of protective duties.

For this proposed alteration in the law Liverpool was peculiarly responsible. He told Canning that "You and I ought to take the lead in the whole business both in Cabinet and Parliament. It will obviate much jealousy and prejudice, and will give an authority to our measure, which would not equally belong to it if it could be considered a Department question. God knows this is not a pleasant undertaking for either of us."[2] This was particularly so as the Department concerned was the Board of Trade, and Huskisson had been stirring a hornets' nest over this very question. During his election campaign at Liverpool a local paper reported Huskisson as saying that "the whole question was settled and the trade in corn is to be free, and that corn is hereafter to be admitted upon a duty to the great benefit of the ship owners and the trading part of the community in general".[3] Wellington immediately wrote a furious letter to Liverpool, and Canning told Huskisson that it was difficult to describe the *sensation* which the report had created among their colleagues.[4] Huskisson complained that he had been incorrectly reported, that

1 Yonge, III, 272: "They only desired to be prepared to use it if adverse circumstances should render the exercise of it necessary to preserve the country from famine. It was a power which ought to be entrusted to any ministry."
2 Add. MSS. 38748, f. 151.   3 Wellington, III, 342.
4 Add. MSS. 38748, f. 128.

"I studiously endeavoured not to go one tittle beyond what the head of the Government had gone in the House of Lords. I am very confident that I did not",[1] and wished that he had been given the opportunity of explaining. Indeed the Press was notoriously unreliable and any other minister would have been given the benefit of the doubt; it was simply "the unjust prejudice which prevailed respecting him".[2] This trivial incident was painful to Liverpool for it showed the spirit in which some of his colleagues would approach any discussion of the Corn Laws and, even if Liverpool took the lead himself, Huskisson would have to be the chief adviser of the policy.

In October Huskisson prepared a lengthy memorandum on the corn question, but Liverpool doubted "the prudence of circulating it amongst our colleagues". Writing from Walmer, "in the midst of agriculturalists with land of high farming and expensive living amongst the farmers", Liverpool had found the gentlemen "dreadfully alarmed; but would be satisfied with protection up to 60s.". He went on: "I do not anticipate any very material difficulty as to the duty not exceeding 5s. when wheat reaches 70s. the quarter, and expiring altogether (or becoming merely nominal) when the price reaches 75s. But I think the country gentlemen will expect a protection of 25s. up to 55s. the quarter, or even to 60s. If this however should be pressed there could, I conceive, be no difficulty in still adhering to your principle and only providing that between 60s. and 90s. the duty shall decrease at the rate of 1s. 6d. or even 2s. for every

1 Add. MSS. 38748, f. 131.
2 The phrase is Liverpool's. Yonge, III, 431.

ECONOMIC LIBERALISM   225

shilling addition in the price, instead of the reduction of one
shilling as proposed by you.... I think the *main points* are
these, that 60s. is, as matters now stand, a *remunerating
price*, and that beyond 60s. the monopoly ought to cease,
and foreign corn flow into the country with a moderate
duty."[1] The scale ultimately agreed upon conformed very
closely to these proposals: at 60s. the duty was 20s., it
decreased 2s. for every shilling increase in price, and
increased 2s. for every shilling decrease in price. At 70s.
the duty expired, at 55s. it reached the prohibitive figure
of 30s.

Liverpool devoted all the energy which he could command to forwarding the measure. The new Parliament met
in November, and, though there was no hope of bringing
the Corn Law before Parliament until the new year, Liverpool pressed forward a decision upon the principle of the
Corn Law. He wished the subject to be settled "for it will
be impossible...to avoid daily debates in which sentiments may be elicited which may prove very inconvenient
if the Cabinet are not agreed substantially upon the whole
question".[2] He laboured to impress upon his reluctant
colleagues that "it was as fair an arrangement between the
great interests as could be made",[3] and that it would render
any temporary measure or special expedient unnecessary
in the future.[4] When it is remembered that of the ministers
Wellington, Eldon, Bathurst, Melville and Westmorland

1 Yonge, III, 429ff.
2 Add. MSS. 38748, f. 151, Liverpool to Canning. Also Add. MSS.
  38302, f. 80, Liverpool to Bathurst.
3 Add. MSS. 38302, f. 105.
4 Add. MSS. 40305, f. 318.

voted, after Liverpool's retirement, for a crippling amendment in the House of Lords, the difficulties which faced
Liverpool can be imagined.[1] He could only overcome them,
he could only obtain a united cabinet, and he could only
ensure that the measure would pass in the House of Lords,
by an adroit exploitation of his own authority and reputation. He devoted himself "heart and soul" to the measure,
and "it was so understood by many who would have made
almost any sacrifice of their own opinions to have kept him
at the head of the Government".[2]

Every detail was arranged when Parliament met on
8 February; even the tactful intimation to Huskisson that,
though Canning was too ill to speak, it would be better for
Peel to conduct the question through the Commons, than
for Huskisson to attempt it. Above all there must be no
partial explanations, "we must expose our whole system at
once",[3] and so, on 8 February Liverpool announced that
on Monday se'nnight he would introduce the new Corn
Law. So, with interest, with alarm, or with hope, the
country awaited for Monday se'nnight; but before that
time an entirely unexpected misfortune had come upon
English political life. On 17 February Liverpool collapsed

1 The feeling among the Tories may be judged from a letter by the
Duke of Rutland to Lady Shelley. "Lord Liverpool feels convinced
he could never carry his projected measure of an alteration in the
Corn Laws during the last session of a Parliament, with the feelings
of the country strongly against him; and he therefore takes the
chance of being enabled to carry it with a Parliament just formed....
I trust the landed interest will not only show their teeth but *bite*, if
he proposes anything which is likely to disturb the prosperous breeze
under which the agricultural interests are at present gliding down a
smooth stream": *Diary of Frances, Lady Shelley*, II, 129.
2 Huskisson, *Papers*, p. 217.   3 Add. MSS. 40305, f. 318.

over the breakfast table, and was found lying unconscious and paralysed upon the floor.

Liverpool's stroke was to be of fatal consequence to the party which he had held together; it was of immediate consequence to the measure which should have crowned his career as an economic reformer. Huskisson was in despair; and Canning's only hope was to introduce it "under the shadow of Liverpool's authority though in abeyance".[1] But, with Canning still upon the sick bed, it was necessary to postpone discussion, and when it was finally introduced Robinson, become Viscount Goderich, had to steer it through the Lords. On 1 June, partly through a desire to limit the action of the bill, partly through misunderstanding, Wellington carried a hostile amendment to prevent the admission of warehoused corn until the price reached 66s. This robbed the bill of its effect as an immediate measure of relief, and the ministers gave up the bill. So, after Liverpool's fatal seizure, after a vain attempt to carry the bill intact, it was defeated by that section of the Tories whom his authority alone had kept in check.

1 Add. MSS. 38749, f. 99; Aspinall, *The Formation of Canning's Ministry*, p. 8.

CHAPTER VII

LIVERPOOL AND CANNING

FROM the moment of his re-entry into the ministry, from the moment that he became Foreign Secretary, the personality of George Canning dominated the Government. Whether in leading England on to some bold stroke of diplomacy, or whether in driving the "Ultras" to indiscreet fury, that domination was evident. But the least discriminating of Canning's panegyrists have not denied his debt to Liverpool, though they may have underestimated it. Without Liverpool Canning would not have entered the ministry; without Liverpool he could not have overcome the hostility of the King, of foreign powers, and of dissentient colleagues; without Liverpool he would have had no Government behind him. The events of 1821 and 1822 had certainly not diminished the affection, they had probably increased the respect with which Canning regarded Liverpool; and the two men entered immediately into the most intimate and cordial relationship. They differed upon the Catholic question, but by tacit consent they avoided dispute upon it; apart from this there was, in four and a half years, but one hint of a disagreement. Canning was certainly the senior partner in foreign policy, though Liverpool was by no means negligible as a consultant; in economic policy Canning played very little part; in the business of keeping the Government together, of closing the ragged gaps left in the administration by Canning's progress, the work was all Liverpool's. In that precarious balance upon which the fate of the Government depended—"liberalism" on the one side, "Protestantism" on the other—only Liverpool could hold the scales. As the life of the ministry lengthened, both parties among the ministers realised this fact even more clearly: and both sides were ready to forgo treasured objects of policy, both were ready to use every entreaty, in order to keep Liverpool at the head of affairs.

It will be well to ask here what was the real cause of the division in the Cabinet, and what were the great sins of Canning. The root of the conflict lay far back: perhaps in the fact that Pitt had changed his policy and Burke had changed his mind; perhaps, ultimately, in the endemic difference between two types of English mind. The party of Mr Pitt had been a coalition; subsequent events had never quite robbed it of that character, and it was to be once more evident in its last years. In a situation in which there were many elements of discord, yet in which remarkable harmony had been maintained, Canning was a catalyst. With a force which he himself hardly realised, Canning drove on events towards the dissolution of that party to which he owed allegiance. Yet who would deny that, in so doing, he gave to England a policy and a tradition which she would do ill without?

Whether the destruction of the Tory party was of God or of man, no better agent could have been chosen than Canning. Everything in his history, his method, and his manner was calculated to inspire distrust in those who could not realise that he might also be great. The duel with Castlereagh, the calculating refusal of 1812, the desertion

of 1820, were not things that honest, faithful supporters of
the Government would readily forget. Yet, until 1822, the
difference was personal rather than political; and in 1821
Wellington reminded Liverpool that "there is no doubt
that Mr Canning is not very popular" with the party in
general.[1] The Tories were prepared to overlook accidents
of social origin—was not Eldon the son of a Newcastle coal
merchant?—but Canning retained many of the characteristics of the parvenu. He was self-assured, he was not
slow to expose the failings of his seniors, and he could
seldom resist mixing a cruel wit with such criticism. Yet,
by 1822, the Tories were prepared to believe that Canning
had learnt wisdom and restraint; at this very time he
attained office, and embarked immediately upon the course
of "liberalism". It is hard indeed to define the meaning,
to Tory ears, of this terrible word. Peel called it "odious
but intelligible"; yet "liberal" had been a favourite word
of Burke, and there was no question of confounding
"liberal" with "jacobin". The word had acquired a new
significance from the appearance of "liberales" as the
popular party in Naples, in Spain, and in South America.
Liberalism had hardly become nationalism, but it had
become the policy of the people in defiance of established
systems. His opponents called Canning a liberal; yet it was
not his acceptance of any heterodox theory which made
them do so; it was not his approval of popular revolts, for
even they knew how guarded that approval was, nor was it
simply his break with the continental allies; primarily it
was because he brought in popular opinion as his ally, both

1 Wellington, I, 192.

George Canning

BY SIR THOMAS LAWRENCE

National Portrait Gallery

in the councils of England and the councils of Europe; it was his oratory, and his publication, when it suited him, of diplomatic correspondence which a more timid—or, his opponents would add, a more gentlemanly—minister would have regarded as secret.

The High Tories in the Cabinet were Wellington, Eldon, Sidmouth so long as he remained, Bathurst, Westmorland, and Melville in all but the Catholic question. The King was frequently behind them, the Duke of York was always behind them. Outside the immediate circle of government was the imponderable mass of the Tory aristocracy, surrounded with its honours and its boroughs, the Dukes of Rutland, Beaufort and Marlborough, the Marquis of Hertford, and the Earl of Lonsdale. It was a power which could not be gainsaid, and, though few of these great peers played much part in politics, their good-will could make or break a government. To all these Canning and his system was anathema: "political theorists without a foot of land of their own in the country", grumbled Rutland; and the lawyer Redesdale spoke for them all when he said: "I am persuaded it has become necessary to cry aloud and spare not. *Liberality* is the word of the day...it is seriously threatening the British Empire with the overthrow of all its ancient institutions by which it has been nourished."[1] The liberals were Canning, Robinson and Huskisson. If the High Tories could call up the support of the borough mongers, the liberals had the good opinion of many in the House, particularly of the commercial interest; their support in Parliament did not

1 Colchester, III, 300.

measure accurately the much larger body of support outside; and they had the Press. All sources of power suspect
to High Tories, but all very valuable in spite of that. In an
intermediate position was Peel; though he belonged by
choice to the party of Eldon and Wellington, he was always
open to conviction, and he always looked upon the continuance of the Government as a first essential. He had
studiously avoided setting himself up, or being set up, as
the High Tory trump to take Canning's ace, and though,
when the time of choice came, he chose Wellington rather
than Canning, his first desire was to avoid that choice.
Harrowby, Wynn and Bexley belonged to neither party,
and the position of each was analogous to that of Peel. The
High Tories could command six, the "liberals" three with
a probable three more, and the votes of Peel and Liverpool
were crucial. Liverpool was always with Canning, and the
authority of a Prime Minister, coupled with the impossibility of replacing him, provided the essential strategic
point, the point which produced a united Cabinet in place
of a deadlock.

The unalterable basis of England's foreign policy had
been stated by Castlereagh in his State Paper of 5 May
1820: "We shall be found in our place when actual danger
menaces the system of Europe, but this country cannot and
will not act upon abstract and speculative Principles of
Precaution." It was this principle which had gradually
emerged during the five years which followed the war, it
was accepted by Canning as the text for his policy. "I
found", he said, "in the records of my office a state paper,
laying down the principle of non-interference with all the

qualification properly belonging to it." The difference in policy, as distinct from difference in method, between the two men was, that Castlereagh wished to maintain the conference system for known and limited objects while Canning considered that England could do no good at such conferences, that she would be tricked into the acknowledgment of principles which she should not acknowledge, that her protests would be ignored, and that she would be dragged at the chariot wheels of the continental allies. When in the famous Troppau Protocol the sovereigns of Austria, Russia and Prussia demanded "the right of maintaining peace, of delivering Europe from the scourge of revolution, of diverting or checking, according to their means, the evils resulting from the violation of all principles of order and morality", it seemed that England could indeed go no more with them. But in October 1821 Castlereagh took the opportunity of the King's visit to Hanover to arrange a meeting with Metternich. The great matter in dispute was Turkey and the Greek revolt: on this specific question Castlereagh agreed to attend another Congress.[1]

The drift away from the continental powers was by no means unpleasing to Liverpool. He had been a loyal supporter of Castlereagh's policy because he saw it as a peace policy, and "I am convinced that, for all our interests, but especially for those of France, every effort must be made to prevent the sword being drawn in Europe under any pretence for a few years to come". Any war following upon

1 Professor Temperley believed that Canning objected to this decision, though not publicly: *Foreign Policy of Canning*, p. 47 and p. 48, note 1.

the recent war would mean that "the revolutionary spirit would break forth again in full force, and the continent would be plunged into all the evils under which it has groaned for the last twenty years". But he was as convinced as Canning that the interests of England in Europe should be strictly limited. In 1815 he was writing to Wellington criticising Castlereagh's conduct of the Polish dispute: "We are very much dissatisfied at the last accounts we received from Vienna. The course which the negotiation has taken is particularly embarrassing. Lord Castlereagh has been substantially right in all his points; but I wish we had not been made so much *principals* in the Polish question." And in 1818 he conveyed the views of the Cabinet to Castlereagh at Aix, after the latter had written that there might be "a protocol, or declaration, to be made public, in which any sentiments arising from the present conference might find their place, and in which the allied sovereigns might announce their indissoluble union, maintenance of engagements, etc., and proceed to declare their friendly sentiments towards France". Liverpool replied: "We cannot but express the great doubts we entertain whether it would in any way be advisable by any new act to proclaim to Europe that it was the intention of the four powers to hold continual meetings at stipulated periods. ... The notion of such meetings would create a great degree of jealousy amongst the other powers of Europe." Castlereagh was already moving towards the position of Canning, though he would not glory in flaunting the continental powers as Canning did. Liverpool was able to work with either Foreign Secretary at the period when both were most useful, but he had none of Castlereagh's "European" out-look, and, by the time of Castlereagh's death, he was very ready to fall in with the more "liberal" and more insular policy of Canning.

In particular he had an appreciation of the great change wrought by the war, the emergence of nationalism. The best he could do for Poland, after stating that the restoration of Polish independence would be a "measure most just in itself and most satisfactory to the people of this country", was to hope that "there should be...some record of our having expressed our opinion how desirable it would be to restore Poland"; but he was aware of the new force of nationalism which Castlereagh tended to ignore or to deplore. At the end of 1813 he was speaking of the war in a thoroughly "liberal" manner: "We have seen during the last twenty years coalitions whose size promised strength crushed by the power of the enemy. What then, we may ask, is this new life which has given an irresistible impulse to the present confederacy of northern nations? The feeling of national independence, that sentiment which impels all men to stand before the liberties of their countries! This feeling, which first arose in the nations of the Peninsula, gave the war a new character, and afforded grounds to hope not only for the deliverance of those nations, but also of the rest of Europe." The man who placed this faith in the principle of national independence would feel far more at ease with the policy of Canning than he had done with the policy of Castlereagh. Canning took the lead, but Liverpool was a most willing partner; between them there was the most perfect union of ideas.

When Canning came to the Foreign Office, Wellington had already received his instructions as Castlereagh's successor at the Congress. These instructions had been drawn up while Canning had no connection with the Government, but they could hardly be attacked save on the general ground of disapproving of all congresses. Greece and the South American colonies were two chief items, and Castlereagh thought that it might be necessary to recognise the Greeks as belligerents, while the recognition of the revolted Spanish colonies was a question of time, not principle. But the question which was to dominate the Congress was that of the Spanish revolution.

The rule of Ferdinand, the Bourbon King of Spain, had mixed the worst features of an inefficient despotism with the worst of a corrupt anarchy. In 1820 a revolution, with hardly more recommendation to the admiration of posterity, had forced the King to accept a constitution. It had been a military revolution and Spain now lived under a King who had no intention of observing his oath to the constitution, and a government which blended militarism and extreme democracy. Alexander, now in his last most mystical and most monarchical phase, had proposed joint intervention to restore the King to his former power. It was this proposal which had called forth the State Paper of 8 May 1820. By 1820 the situation had not eased: democratic revolution was still in command of Spain; but now France, not Russia, was most materially concerned. In the autumn of 1822 the French proposed to advance upon Madrid to deliver the King from his enemies, and to do so, if possible, with the sanction of the Holy Alliance. France did not ask for active help, indeed the policy she wished to pursue was avowedly French and French alone, but she would welcome the moral support of Europe signified by the withdrawal of ambassadors from Madrid. Under these circumstances Canning sent to Wellington a new set of instructions: should the allies project interference "by force or by menace", England would not join such interference "*come what may*". Wellington obeyed his instructions to the letter, declaring that "interference appeared to be an unnecessary assumption of responsibility". His action precluded any idea of a united Congress action against Spain, but there remained the question of France's intentions and France showed every intention of invading Spain in spite of England's attitude. Wellington remonstrated with the French, urged them to keep the peace, and returned to England under the impression that he had succeeded.

The English Parliament met on 4 February, and in the debate upon the Address Liverpool opened the new era of English foreign policy with a speech "intended to encourage the revolutionaries" which had a "very bad effect".[1] "The policy of the British Government is distinctly declared, and it rests on the principle of the law of nations, which allows every country to be judge of how it can be best governed, and what ought to be its institutions; and, if exceptions to that rule may arise out of self-defence, they are to be considered as exceptions, and are to stand on their own peculiar merits. His Majesty's Government, I have no hesitation in declaring, views the question of Spain as one clearly and purely Spanish."

1 Lieven, p. 247.

Wellington may have been sincerely desirous of peace, but it is certain that his indiscreet expressions, together with those of the King and other Cabinet ministers, encouraged France in the correct belief that she could undertake the invasion of Spain without interference.[1] On 28 January the French King had made a most famous and spectacular speech to his Parliament: a hundred thousand French were ready to march to the aid of a brother Bourbon, and the arguments were not merely those of expediency, for "let Ferdinand be free to give to his people the institutions they cannot hold but from him". This speech had a startling effect in England, and Liverpool omitted the word "neutrality" from those passages in the King's Speech dealing with France and Spain. But the Cabinet were, for once, united upon a question of foreign policy: no one thought of war as either desirable or practicable. In a Cabinet memorandum the well-known difficulties of conducting a defensive war in Spain, the uselessness of a naval war for achieving the present object, the possibility of a rupture with other European powers, were stressed. But a significant qualification was added; France, if successful, might "attempt to carry into execution, what she had already held out, the measure of putting at the command of Spain her fleets and armies to assist the Spanish operations in South America", but "we have the means of easily and effectually preventing any such projects".[2]

From Verona Wellington returned vaguely dissatisfied

1 Temperley, *Foreign Policy*, p. 82.
2 Yonge, III, 231–3; E. J. Stapleton, I, 35–8. The authorship of this memorandum is uncertain; it is unsigned and undated. Yonge claims it for Liverpool, but it is probably by Canning.

with the part he had played; he had broken with the allies, he had failed to preserve peace, and he attributed both developments to Canning. Immediately after his return began the complaints which were to be a constant theme of his politics until 1827; he "complained of the haste with which Canning formed his decisions...he does not think that Canning is to be depended upon...he has a less high opinion of him as an able statesman than he had before, and he thinks he often decides in haste and then writes in haste, and that what he does write has better sounding phrases than good solid sense".[1] The Duke now bethought himself of the part which he had played in placing Canning at the Foreign Office, and he remembered the King's admonition at the time, "Thus ends this last calamity; my reliance is upon you my friend".[2] Incomparably the greatest figure in England, the part he played upon the European stage was hardly less, and he himself was the last person to underestimate it; honoured by every sovereign, he was not prepared to sink the saviour of Europe in the minister of state, nor was he prepared to observe strictly the conventions which might regulate lesser men. He began to conceive that he had a mission, a mission to watch over the indiscretions of Canning and to bring back England into the allied fold. To Madame Lieven he said that "he quite understood that his visit to Verona had had worse results than those which had at first appeared; that every day the separation of England from the great Alliance became...

1 Add. MSS. 38291, fs. 241 ff., Arbuthnot to Liverpool, 23 December 1822.
2 Wellington, I, 284.

more noticeable; that it was certainly a misfortune for England; and that he did not know to what to ascribe it".[1]

Encouraged by this confidence, Madame Lieven began to tempt Wellington with that blend of personal attraction and political intrigue of which she alone was mistress. Wellington showed her some letters—"Damme, I'll show you what I wrote about Spain; and you'll see if M. de Metternich ever said anything stronger"—and Madame Lieven suggested that he should show them to her husband and Esterhazy, the ambassadors of Russia and Austria. This Wellington refused "without permission of my cabinet", but Madame Lieven proved too subtle in argument. "Do you approve", she asked, "of your Cabinet making itself out worse than it is? Frankly no one places any confidence in Mr Canning.... If personal relations with you were valuable, even at a time when our confidence in Lord Londonderry was everything we could desire, how much more precious those relations must be now with a minister who inspires mistrust? You can do good, a great deal of good; don't lose your chance!" In the middle of February she wrote again to Metternich: "It seems to me that they are paying very dearly for the satisfaction of seeing Mr Canning in an odour of sanctity among the Liberals.... The poor Duke does his best; he feels, both for the Government and for himself, the necessity of getting back in our good books—hence his confidences. He tries them first of all on me. When I point out to him that to do any good he must extend them to our two

[1] Mme. Lieven to Metternich, 26 January 1823 (Lieven, p. 227).

ambassadors, he begins by resisting; then lets himself be persuaded."[1]

But there was also a greater than Madame Lieven drawing Wellington from the paths of constitutional rectitude. To his intimates George IV was expressing himself very freely about Canning: "I do not like him any better than I did," he told Madame Lieven, "I recognise his talent, and I believe we need him in the House of Commons; but he is no more capable of conducting foreign affairs than your baby." On 19 March he ordered the Duke "not to let a day pass without seeing Canning, and finding out what he is up to in his office".[2] Wellington was bound to refuse this—there were some lengths to which no minister could go—but by the spring of 1823 Wellington was in close communication with the ambassadors, and he knew in his conscience that this was a breach of loyalty to his colleagues.

Against this conspiracy to circumvent Canning's policy, there was the close union between Liverpool and Canning, and there were also the constitutional conventions which had grown up in the last fifty years. The Duke found that his weight in the Cabinet was impaired by the suspicion that he spoke as the "King's favourite", and some who were with him in spirit told him that "as the leaders in the two houses had taken a different view, they had thought it best to acquiesce".[3] His confidant Arbuthnot knew him to be "so conscious of honourable intentions that this idea sours his mind, and may lead to the very worst conse-

1 Lieven, p. 237. She adds: "Now these documents are in complete contradiction to the official language of Mr. Canning, and above all to the Parliamentary language of Lord Liverpool." (15 February 1823).
2 Lieven, p. 243.   3 Cf. p. 68 above.

quences".[1] If the Duke found himself losing weight in the Cabinet, there are also signs that he was being excluded from those intimate discussions which were really more important than cabinets. In June 1823 Madame Lieven saw him every day, and was every day more convinced that "he counts for nothing in affairs. For some weeks he has known nothing about them. He feels it, though he tries to put a good face on it."[2]

The great occasion of dispute was to be the Spanish-American question. England's consistent attitude had been that these republics were either actually independent, or were likely to become so; if they were independent, English interests would be placed in an intolerable position if they had still to defer to the nominal authority of Spain; therefore, sooner or later, the South American states must be recognised. Two considerations retarded the final decision: the uncertain and precarious nature of the republican governments, and the desirability of avoiding all conflict by making Spain take the first step in recognition. The crisis was brought on by the French invasion of Spain, for there was the danger that France might recompense herself for her expenses and her slight material gains in Spain by taking over some of the Spanish colonies. The prospect of a French army, backed by all the moral support of the Holy Alliance, was not altogether remote. The continental powers tried to push forward the idea of a Congress on South America. Canning resolved to act separately with France; and, in conference with Polignac the French ambassador, he extracted an admission that the South American states

1 Bathurst, p. 565.   2 Lieven, p. 268.

were virtually independent and a renunciation of any desire on the part of France for territorial gains or for any exclusive advantages in South America. On England's part, she would recognise the colonies if any trade restrictions were enforced against her by Spain, she would not tolerate any French interference in America, and she would not attend a Congress unless the United States was also a member. On 30 January 1824, the United States having expressed their isolation by the Monroe Doctrine, Canning expressed his by refusing to join a Congress.

Canning had not been half-hearted in his attempt to mediate between Spain and the republics. He offered to guarantee Cuba if Spain would recognise the independence of her colonies; this offer was refused. At the same time Canning was gathering information on the state of the South American republics. In July 1824 the consul-general at Buenos Aires was empowered to make a commercial treaty with that state. Completion of such a treaty would amount to recognition, but the step was not made public, and the general question of recognition was undecided.

Meanwhile the storm against Canning had been blowing up in high places. The occasion for the first protest by the King was Canning's attendance at the Lord Mayor's banquet on Easter Monday, for the Lord Mayor on this occasion was Waithman, an extreme Whig and former protagonist of the Queen. The incident is also interesting in that it illustrates Canning's attitude to popularity. Personal and public motives were strangely mixed in the King's mind: "The public life of the individual filling the office of

Chief Magistrate of the City of London has been marked
by a continued series of insults to the Government, to the
monarchy and above all, personally to the king himself";
and "The king will never consent that his Government
shall be degraded by such attempts to acquire popularity".
He also thought that "Mr Canning could not be ignorant
of this, and has long known that his visit to the Mansion
House would in the highest degree be offensive and personally disagreeable".[1] Liverpool had now to find some
means of soothing the King's feelings.[2] From Canning he
received a long letter of explanation, and sent it to the King
with a letter composed by Wellington and himself. Liverpool recalled his own attendance at a similar dinner during
the impeachment of Melville in 1805, which certainly
prevented the expression of public sentiments "which
would indubitably have been manifested in the absence of
any of the king's ministers".[3] Canning offered the same
defence: his presence had curbed expressions which might
have been highly embarrassing to the Government and
very unfavourably received abroad. "I am, I own, decidedly of opinion that the Government should not, on
such occasions, leave a clear stage to their opponents. *The
City* may be a very inconvenient power in the state. But

1 Yonge, III, 280.
2 Canning had tried to persuade Liverpool himself to attend (E. J.
Stapleton, I, 147–8) and Liverpool told the King that "he should have
had no objection to have been present at the Mansion House if he
had happened to be in town that week" (Yonge, *ibid.*). That unexceptionable man Lord Bexley had also written to Liverpool:
"I really think it desirable that some members of the Government
should attend the Lord Mayor's dinner" (Add. MSS. 38298, f. 257).
3 Yonge, III, 282. The last and most humble part of the original draft
is in Wellington's handwriting.

there it is.... I flatter myself that I have as good right as any publick man of the present day not to be suspected of courting popularity by a compromise with Jacobinism. I have passed near thirty years in fighting the battle with it. I have incurred as much unpopularity at various times, in that contest, as any man, and have braved that unpopularity as fearlessly. But I think that the battle is now fought. I think we have gained the victory. And I think it would be something like a dereliction of publick duty not to reap the full advantages of the present position of the Government."[1] This argument was no mere afterthought, for he had written to Liverpool when announcing his intention of attending the dinner. "I think our business is to admit the extinction of party feeling, rather than show a determination to keep it alive."[2] That his attendance would be "in the highest degree offensive and personally disagreeable", he had no suspicion; and that the King's wishes had been intimated to him, as the King seemed to imagine, by Lord Francis Conyngham, he denied.[3] Those explanations sufficed to allay the storm, but the suspicion with which every step of the Foreign Secretary would be watched had been amply demonstrated.

The next occasion for disquiet was Canning's disposition to travel in the autumn of 1824. In September Canning proposed to visit Wellesley in Ireland, and the High Tories immediately scented a "Catholic" plot. Liverpool seems to have doubted Canning's discretion if faced with an enthusiastic Irish audience, and it was only with promises of

1 *George IV*, No. 1163.   2 E. J. Stapleton, II, 148.
3 *George IV*, No. 1163.

good behaviour that he was allowed to go. Canning seems to have accepted the doubts of his colleagues in good humour: "Depend upon my not getting into difficulties," he wrote to Liverpool, "I have inculcated privacy on Wellesley, and he has engaged for it; and I am determined not to go any where without him." A far more serious dispute arose when the King of France died, and Canning proposed to go himself upon a mission of condolence and respect.

The first objection came not from the King but from Liverpool. On 18 September Canning told Liverpool of a conversation which he had had with the King in expectation of this event: "For congratulation, whenever that might come, the mission of a grandee would probably be advisable ...that for condolence, I thought I might either send Granville to Paris...or, that as soon as we saw to what hands the new king entrusted his ministry, I might make it a pretext to go there myself, for the purpose of coming to an understanding with Villèle, supposing him to be the person...." The King's remark upon this suggestion was, "I think it would be your duty to do so."[1] Liverpool replied: "If the mission is to be in any degree political, I think it would be better that you should go than any other minister, but I doubt the policy of giving it this character. Diverging as our policy does on so many points, but more especially respecting South America, from that of the other great Powers, the arrival at Paris of any minister of ours, but particularly of a Secretary of State on such an occasion, would create alarm amongst all the other missions and their

1 E. J. Stapleton, II, 162.

respective Governments. And the very circumstance of the alarm might embarrass the French Government, and render them less disposed to be open and explicit with us than they might be through Granville or through any other ambassador in whom they knew you and the Government had implicit confidence."[1] Canning replied: "There may be all the objection which you state to the project, which I had meditated; and I am not quite sure that the purpose with which I conceived it may not be answered a short time hence in another way." He said that he did attach considerable importance to seeing Charles X and Villèle, but he admitted that the easiest solution of the present problem would be to send Granville, already destined for the Paris Embassy, on the dual mission of conveying condolence and succeeding Sir Charles Stuart.

Here it might seem that the matter would end. Canning's own version was that when he found Liverpool to be *"rather* against the measure I gave it up at once", but he had also hinted at some other means of accomplishing his purpose. On 4 October the Duke was astounded to hear from Lord Francis Conyngham that Canning intended to make a personal visit to Granville at Paris on the 15th or 16th; the announcement was made before some foreign ambassadors who "were put in a fever on hearing it, for they felt that he would make much confusion at Paris by his negotiations".[2] The revelation was not only indiscreet but also inaccurate, for Canning had named no date, but,

1 Yonge, III, 292 ff.
2 Add. MSS. 40340, f. 104, Arbuthnot to Peel, 3 November. It is here that Lord F. Conyngham is named as the informant.

according to his own profession, "when the novelty of the
new reign shall be a little worn off, I thought and still
think—that a visit to Granville there might be not only
pleasant but useful". He told Liverpool of this project,
and he mentioned it to the King. The King told Wellington, but saying that he had heard it not from Canning himself "but from some other quarter".[1] The King was, in
fact, abusing the confidence of his Foreign Secretary, but
did not reveal that it was a confidence. Wellington did
nothing until he heard the announcement on 4 October
naming a specific date less than two weeks ahead; this and
the obvious displeasure of the ambassadors induced him to
write to Canning on 5 October. Canning believed that this
letter was concocted with the King.[2] Wellington's letter
was not angry, and ended with the sentence, "I hope you
will excuse me for the frankness with which I write to you
on this subject, and will impute my doing so to the real
motive, my conviction of the inconvenience to the public
and annoyance to yourself which will result from it".[3]
Canning's temper was never of the most even, and he now
lost it; he saw in Wellington's letter not a private remon-
strance but an "Ultra" plot. He began in his reply by
practically doubting Wellington's account of the disclosure: "I recollect accurately the only persons to whom
I have ever said a word upon the subject...and none of
those persons *can* possibly have fallen into the blunder of

1 Bathurst, p. 574.
2 Wellington neither admitted nor denied this. The truth would seem
to be that he wrote it alone, but knowing that he expressed the
views of the King, with whom he had had conversations (cf. Bathurst, p. 574).   3 Wellington, II, 313.

the Equerrys' Room." A blunder there had certainly been, for Canning had never thought of the 16th as a possible date, but the scene in the Equerrys' Room is confirmed by Madame Lieven, who was there. Canning then brought out his strong point: Westmorland had recently had a conversation with Charles X in Paris, he had reported this to the King but not to Canning. Canning declared himself willing to forgo his visit to Paris if the King commanded him, but hoped that the King would lay "a similar interdiction" upon other ministers. He hinted also that the whole protest had been dictated by the influence of the Russian ambassador.[1] Wellington's two letters to Bathurst[2] practically clear Wellington of the accusation of acting in 'concert either with the King or with the ambassador, but he realised that his own dealings with the "Cottage Coterie" made it extremely difficult to offer any excuses which would be believed. The root of the whole unfortunate quarrel seems to have lain with the King, who offered no objection to Canning's proposal, but who tried to stimulate Wellington to object, and who allowed Wellington to believe that his information came from rumours, not from Canning's confidence. Even then the whole matter might have been settled verbally, but for Conyngham's foolish gossip in the Equerrys' Room.[3] After several exchanges of letters with Wellington, Canning laid his case before Liverpool. He would yield to "grave and substantial reasons", but he could not yield when he knew that

1 Wellington, II, 315.
2 *Ibid.* and Bathurst, p. 574.
3 His gossip carried some conviction because he was an Under Secretary at the Foreign Office.

the whole truth was not told to him. "I *know* that the first letter...was written after a long conference with the king, which took place on Saturday the 2nd, two days after my interview with his Majesty upon my return from Ireland. I *know* that in that conference the king repeated to the Duke of Wellington what passed in my interview, because the Duke of Wellington repeated it to a person who repeated it to my informant. I know that the letter of the 5th was shown to the king before it was sent to me. And yet neither in that letter nor in any subsequent part of the correspondence is there any admission that the king was privy to it. Now this I hold not to be fair. I have the highest respect for the Duke of Wellington, and I do not presume to limit the confidences of the king. But when one finds that all that passes between the king and one's self is repeated as a matter of course to a third person, and that third person one who thinks himself at liberty to repeat it to others, at the same time as he conceals the fact of his knowing it from one's self, it is high time to look about one, and to beware of what Burke calls 'traps and mines'."

Liverpool refused to take sides in the matter. He reiterated his former objections to the Paris visit—the French Government would not risk its popularity by an ostensible *rapprochement* with the English Foreign Secretary, though it might come to an understanding through the usual diplomatic channels, "a failure, or even *negative success* in a Secretary of State is very different from the same result in a minister or ambassador", and the visit would be unpopular in England—and he made no comment upon Wellington's letter. He would object naturally to "secret influence", but might suspect that the whole incident was exaggerated; he did, however, forward Canning's letter to Wellington.[1] The Duke attempted no defence, and the whole matter was at an end, for Canning did abandon his visit to Paris. His reason for doing so, as given to Granville, shows how Canning, even when angry, was still generous and balanced: Wellington, he said, was "entitled to every consideration—even when one's opinion is not exactly the same, nothing could be so agreeable to the Ultras or so inconvenient to me, as the divergence of our opinions on any question or action, of real or supposed importance". Canning was the most forgiving of men once the occasion of dispute had passed, but Wellington neither forgave nor forgot.

In all these matters Liverpool was called upon to act both as a mediator and as a partisan. It was his business, as Prime Minister, to see that the Government was not dissolved; it was his business, as a convinced supporter of Canning, to see that his policy was pushed through the Cabinet. Throughout 1824 the question of South America hung like a great cloud on the horizon. By both parties in the Cabinet it was accepted as the great test of Canning's policy: if England recognised the South American republics, in defiance of France, of Spain, and of the Continental Alliance, she set her feet for all time on a path separate from Europe; if she did not recognise those states, she might once more play that part in the Councils of Europe which she had played under Castlereagh. Canning was deter-

---

[1] It is in the Wellington papers, and can only have come there if Liverpool gave it to Wellington.

mined to read "England" for "Europe"; Liverpool, who had never been completely at ease with Castlereagh's policy, was resolved to support him. Throughout the year the division in the Cabinet became more and more marked. The language Canning used in speaking of "the opposing and superior party in the Cabinet is quite unmeasured. 'THEY' have done this, and '*they*' choose to do that, is the mildest sort of phraseology he uses. Neither he nor Lord Liverpool conceals their feeling as to the preponderance."[1] Liverpool was Canning's only support, for Robinson and Huskisson could hardly pull their weight in such discussions, and Canning fully realised how much his position depended upon the goodwill of the Prime Minister.[2] Liverpool became to doubt his ability to carry on in this heated atmosphere, and in July he was pushing forward certain matters in his office "because I possibly may not be the person to settle them if delayed".[3] Wynn stated accurately the balance of power within the Cabinet: "I think Canning with Liverpool's support too powerful to allow the introduction of a foe, and I think that power is viewed with too much jealousy to admit of its being further increased."[4] But all asked how long this could continue; Liverpool's health seemed to be breaking down, and the rate of his pulse became a matter of national importance.[5]

1 Buckingham, II, 126, R. P. Ward to Buckingham.
2 Buckingham, II, 126: "His greatest ally is Lord Liverpool, who, to use the expression used to me, is 'Ultra against the Ultras'."
3 Buckingham, II, 110, R. P. Ward to Buckingham, 31 July.
4 *Ibid.* p. 113.
5 *Ibid.* p. 91, Fremantle to Buckingham: "How we shall meet again I won't pretend to say: it all depends entirely on Lord Liverpool's health." Colchester, Diary, 4 June: "Lord Liverpool, who for some

In July the King protested against the decision to negotiate a commercial treaty with Buenos Aires; he feared that it carried with it "the appearance and promise of an early recognition to the different insurrectionary States of South America...it is impossible that the Great Allied Powers can view the policy of this country, as regards South America, with indifference; and sooner or later this policy will endanger the peace of Europe". In view of "what he supposes to be the unanimous opinion of his Cabinet" he would not oppose, but he delivered a solemn warning: "When the Prince of Wales undertook the Regency of this Kingdom...[he] abandoned all those friends with whom he had lived on terms of the most unqualified friendship during the best years of his life: because the Prince, as Regent, thought their liberal and anti-monarchical sentiments unfavourable to the good government of his father's dominions; but the king now finds that the opinions of the opposition and liberals are uniformly acted upon. The king cannot be supposed to be blind to this state of things."[1]

"The cabal against Canning grows in strength", wrote Madame Lieven on 2 September. The autumn of 1824 was indeed a trying time for the nerves of all in political circles. Wellington was furious with Canning, and did not speak to Liverpool save at Cabinet meetings. The King said Canning was a scoundrel, Canning complained bitterly of Westmorland, who "continues to agree in measures and to differ in words, and to labour to bring down the state-

months past has always favoured and laid up *one* leg, now puts *both* legs upon the bench where he sits, and is evidently in worse health. His pulse was forty in March fifty four when he returned from Bath, and is now forty again." 1 *George IV*, No. 1187.

ment of measures to his own standard—that is, to the standard of his own language at Crockford's and White's".[1]
Madame Lieven, in giving Canning a courtesy invitation to dinner, found herself in some difficulty; who was to be invited to meet him? "All the ministers have quarrelled with him. There is the same difficulty with members of the social world. I suggested it to several persons; they all begged me to excuse them from meeting him."[2] But for Liverpool Canning would have been isolated; even with Liverpool on his side it seemed that a split would be driven in the Government. "How this will all end I cannot guess," wrote Arbuthnot to Peel, "I do not mean this discussion with the Duke, for it is over, but I mean this general state of things. I feel sure that the Duke will never lose his temper. He will however watch Canning closely, and I am certain that he will agree to nothing which he thinks false policy and wrong."[3]

At the beginning of December Liverpool came in strongly on Canning's side, and circulated a memorandum urging immediate recognition of the South American states in the clearest and most forcible terms. The result was an offer of resignation by Wellington. "As for my part," he wrote, "I came into the Government to support yourself and the principles on which you had been acting, and for which we had struggled in the field for such length of time. I should wish to go on as I have done, and nothing makes me so unhappy as to differ in opinion from you. But as you know, I am not inclined to carry these differences further

1 E. J. Stapleton, I, 213.   2 Lieven, p. 339.
3 Add. MSS. 40340, f. 104.

than is necessary; and I have advised, and shall invariably advise, his Majesty to follow the advice of his cabinet. But I can easily conceive that it must be equally irksome to you to have a colleague whose opinion upon any subject is so undecidedly different from yours; and I can only assure you that I am ready whenever you wish to retire from your government."[1] It seemed that the dreaded moment had arrived, that Cabinet unity could no longer be preserved, that Wellington, and doubtless others with him, would break off from the Government; yet, on the other hand, Wellington's letter was definitely conciliatory in tone, he included a personal compliment to Liverpool, he hinted that he would not press matters to a final crisis, he promised to use his influence with the King to make him accept the Cabinet's advice, and he placed the decision in Liverpool's hands. Liverpool replied in similar vein; he could only assure Wellington "most truly that nothing could give me more sincere pain, *privately* or *publicly*, than your separation, from any cause, from the Government";[2] he lamented the difference over South America, but asserted his very reasonable conviction that "if we allow these new states to consolidate their system and policy with the United States of America, it will in a very few years prove fatal to our greatness, if not endanger our safety"; he lamented also the "strong prejudices" of the King, and thought that he should be made to feel "that the opinion which he sometimes avows on the subject of legitimacy would carry him to the

1 Wellington, II, 365–6.
2 Yonge, III, 305. It must not be imagined that Canning was in any way desirous for Wellington's resignation. See p. 251 above.

full length of the principle of the Emperor of Russia and Prince Metternich". If the Duke's letter had been conciliatory in tone, Liverpool's was masterly in the way that it threw back the onus of decision upon Wellington, while bringing forward the two arguments to which Wellington was likely to be most sensitive. This exchange of letters made it fairly certain that Wellington would not resign, and that Liverpool and Canning could bring the full weight of their authority to bear upon the Cabinet minority and the King.

A lengthy memorandum upon the South American question was circulated in the Cabinet. The memorandum went far back into historical origins, and proceeded to the present problem. "Is it possible to leave so large a part of the world for any length of time in a state of *outlawry*?" The United States of America had already acknowledged the republics, England's commercial interests could not long delay her acknowledgment; the objection of the legitimists would be exactly the same twenty years hence; Austria, Russia and Prussia have "positively no national interest, not the slightest in the matter"; France had an interest, namely "first to thwart our views, and secondly, to profit by them when accomplished". "Are we to sacrifice the advantage and prosperity of the people of this country to the extravagant principles or prejudices of governments which have proved to us that in their own concerns in Europe they are not disposed to sacrifice a tittle of their views and their policy to the views and policy of the British Government, when a difference of opinion arises between us?" The existence of a French army of occupation in

Spain made the question urgent, "we should prevent the American dependencies of this Power from being involved in that same objection". The commerce of the states would foster England's naval power, it would certainly foster that of the United States if allowed exclusive rights of commerce. The naval supremacy of England might one day be threatened by a combination of France and the United States, but "the disposition of the new states is at present highly favourable to England. If we take the advantage of that disposition, we may establish through our influence with them a fair counterpoise to that combined maritime power. Let us not, then, throw the present golden opportunity away, which, once lost, may never be recovered."[1] The Cabinet considered this memorandum on 6 December and the all-important resolution—"that the question should be decided without reference to the opinions of Continental Allied Powers"—was passed with Sidmouth alone dissenting. But this left unsettled the main question of recognition, and Canning determined to force the issue. Through Granville he enquired whether France would undertake to withdraw her troops from Spain; and Villèle would not give such an assurance. With this additional argument in their favour, Canning and Liverpool prepared to force immediate recognition upon the King and the Cabinet. Liver-

---

1 Yonge, III, 297–304. The authorship of the memorandum has been disputed. Yonge, whose discrimination is not to be relied upon, claims it for Liverpool. Professor Temperley thought (*Foreign Policy*, p. 498) that it was "technically at any rate, by Liverpool, with touches by Canning". But Canning sent it to Wellington and his covering note is quite clear: "The subject of the enclosed memorandum is that which I shall bring first before the Cabinet tomorrow. Lord L. only has seen it; but I will send another copy in circulation."

pool prepared a memorandum; Canning revised his.[1] Both
then faced the Cabinet and threatened to resign if their
advice was not taken. The plain alternative was offered—
recognition of the South American states or the end of
the Government—and Peel, the wisest of the Tories, reluctantly came round to their side. Sidmouth had resigned
after the Cabinet of 6 December, though not ostensibly for
that cause, and the "Ultras" were now in a minority.
Liverpool and Canning won the day, and the Cabinet
recommended that the King should recognise the South
American republics. "The fight has been hard", wrote
Canning triumphantly to Granville, "but it is won. The
deed is done. The nail is driven. Spanish America is free;
and if we do not mismanage our matters sadly, she is
English and 'Novus saeclorum nascitur ordo'. You will
see how nobly Liverpool fought with me on this occasion."[2]

After the Christmas holiday there came one last protest
from the King: "The Jacobins of the world, now calling
themselves the Liberals, saw the peace of Europe secured
by their great measure and have therefore never ceased to
vilify the Quadruple Alliance. The late policy of Great
Britain has loosened these beneficial ties, by demonstrating

1 Canning to Liverpool, 11 December: "I return your paper. I have
not changed the order of the topics, nor added any new one. The
object of my scratchings and interpolations is chiefly to make the
course of argument more clear by dividing into heads—of which
there is one more than Hydra had" (viz. ten). Same, 14 December:
"Your paper is very greatly improved by this alteration and addition.
I am recasting mine" (Stapleton, pp. 212–13). An official memorandum was sent to the King with the Cabinet's advice; another is
printed in Temperley's *Foreign Policy*, p. 550, from the Vansittart
papers in the British Museum; this he believed might be the work of
Canning.　　　　　　2 Stapleton, *Life and Times*, p. 411.

a restless desire of self-interest in direct opposition to those wise and comprehensive principles, by which the peace and general interest of Europe were bound together."[1] And "the king would wish to ask Lord Liverpool whether he supposes, the great abettors of this South American question (connected with the Opposition) give their support to a recognition of the Spanish Provinces in relation to the great mercantile advantages which this measure may offer to this country, or from their love of democracy, in opposition to a monarchical aristocracy".[2] But the King was abandoned, and he had to admit defeat; though he did so with a bad grace.

Since the summer of 1821, save for the interlude between December 1821 and August 1822, the King had been consistently on bad terms with his Government. He had fallen readily into the schemes of the foreign ambassadors, he had helped to seduce Wellington from constitutional integrity, he had used every means to support the Cabinet opposition to Canning and Liverpool. Matters had come to a head at the end of 1824 when "the intemperance or miscalculation of the king" led to a premature *dénouement*.[3] Canning said that he would have resigned over South America, declared that he had been driven from office by the Holy Alliance, and allowed public opinion to run its course.[4] But the King was now undergoing a change of heart; he had decided to endure what could not be cured. On 27 April he sent Sir William Knighton on a courtesy

1 Stapleton, *Life and Times*, p. 418.
2 *George IV*, No. 1139.
3 Canning to Granville (E. J. Stapleton, 1, 256). He may mean the controversy with Wellington.   4 *Ibid.*

visit to Canning who was ill; Knighton intimated that the King had changed his views, and had become reconciled to Canning. Before the end of the year Canning was freely and intimately enjoying the confidence of the King. At the same time the King was drawing closer to Liverpool in their common resistance to the Catholic claims. It is to those claims, and to their effect upon the course of Government, that it is now necessary to turn.

As England rejoiced in a new-found prosperity, as Canning wrote the name of England large upon the Liberal map, there remained the grim spectre of Ireland to haunt the minds of English statesmen. English rule was the rule of a Protestant minority, and the High Tories saw clearly something from which "liberals" always turned their faces, that, without the exclusion of Catholics from the Government, it could no longer be English. If the Irish masses—whom Pitt had indiscreetly enfranchised—returned the men of their choice, Westminster would be overrun with Irish demagogues, Dublin Castle would fall to the Catholics, and the separation of the two countries must finally ensue. This idea was the basis of Liverpool's resistance to Catholic Emancipation; it was not always possible to state the naked alternatives, and it was necessary to clothe them in the time-worn arguments of dual allegiance and the Pope's political power; but in insisting that the Irish question was not religious, that it was political and social, Liverpool had the root of the matter. The weakness of the Protestant argument lay in the necessity for suppressing social and religious tendencies in order to assert a political fact, the English hegemony. Liverpool was not an intolerant man, and his attitude to the Catholics is shown clearly by his support, in 1824, of two bills, one to enfranchise English Roman Catholics, the other to allow Roman Catholics to act as magistrates.[1] Concessions might be made to the Catholics in England, where they formed an upper class minority with little political influence; they must be resisted in Ireland, where the Catholics formed a popular majority with potential political power.

Since the House of Lords had thrown out Plunket's Relief Bill in 1821, much had happened to confirm the Protestants in their view. In 1823 all secret societies had been superseded by O'Connell's Catholic Association, a representative body of Irish Catholics which provided itself with funds by the "Catholic Rent", a subscription of one penny a month from all members. O'Connell succeeded in uniting all Irish Catholics, priests and laity, in the demand for unconditional Emancipation. Catholic Emancipation, from being the favourite project of liberal-minded Englishmen, became the popular demand of nationalist Ireland.

Friends of Ireland had hoped for happier days when Talbot, a narrow-minded High Tory, had been succeeded by Wellesley, and when Plunket went to Ireland as Attorney-General. But, in spite of Wellesley's continued optimism, matters went from bad to worse; it was necessary to apply the Insurrection Act to check the Catholic Association; bottles were thrown at the Lord Lieutenant in Dublin Theatre; Plunket failed in his prosecution of O'Connell,

1 In spite of Liverpool's support the bills were lost. Part of the second allowed the Duke of Norfolk to exercise his hereditary function of Earl Marshal, but even this was refused.

and only succeeded in embroiling himself with the Orange Association. These events embittered feelings on the Catholic Question: the "Protestants" cried all the louder for resistance, the "Catholics" pointed with ever-insistent logic to the need for concession.

On 19 November 1824 the King dropped a bombshell. "The king is apprehensive that a notion is gone abroad that the king himself is not unfavourable to the Catholic claims. It is high time for the king to protect himself against such an impression, and he has no hesitation in declaring that if the present proceedings continue, he will no longer consent to Catholic Emancipation being left as an open question in his Cabinet. This indulgence was originally granted on the ground of political expediency, but that expediency dissolves when threatened rebellion calls upon the king for that which the king never will grant."[1] This letter was sent to Peel, to be shown to Wellington and Eldon. Wellington first thought that it should be kept secret—"it would really create an alarm which it is not intended to create, and can do no good"—but upon consideration he thought it should be shown to Liverpool. "When it is shown to him it becomes of no importance; as long as it is concealed from him it is of importance, and the concealment gives an air of intrigue." Liverpool saw the King and heard from him "nothing which gave the slightest uneasiness or cause for complaint".[2] Nevertheless the incident was disturbing, for the man behind the King's protest was the Duke of York, the heir to the throne and the centre of the extreme High Tory group; it seemed that pressure might soon be exerted

1 Parker, I, 349.   2 Ibid. p. 351.

to drive the "Catholics" out of the Government. Fortunately the last people who desired this were the High Tories in the Cabinet; they knew that, so long as Liverpool was Prime Minister and the question was "open", Catholic Emancipation might not pass.

Something had, however, to be done with the Catholic Question; the King had threatened to break the Government if something were not done, and Wellington had written: "If we cannot get rid of the Catholic Association, we must look to Civil War in Ireland."[1] At the beginning of the session of 1825 a bill against all Associations—preserving a show of impartiality by banning the Orange Association as well—was introduced and supported by the "Catholic" ministers. Liverpool's speech is remarkable for its extreme forbearance: "I believe there are many innocent, many well-disposed members of that Association. I believe that the great majority of the Association do not see the dangers which they are bringing on their country. But my objection to the Association is, that no such body can exist in any nation, or under any state of things, without the production of the greatest evils. I impute no special blame to it, as distinguished from similar bodies. I well know what any men so associated could do and say; of how much intemperance they must necessarily be guilty, of what endless evils their combination must be productive. ...If the Catholics of Ireland are to be permitted to associate, who would say that the Protestants also would not unite? It is the natural course of things; combination necessarily leads to counter combination. Nor, however

1 Parker, I, 348.

superior in number the Catholics in Ireland may be, are the
Protestants so contemptible in point of numbers, wealth,
intelligence and character, as not to constitute a formidable
party; and under such circumstances, how is justice to be
administered in Ireland? What must be the result of permitting the existence of rival societies, each supported by
the whole strength of one religious party, and of necessity
full of animosity against every other? Nothing less...than
an aggravation of all the evils from which Ireland has
suffered; nothing less than to give additional strength and
vehemence to all those feelings, by which dissension will be
fomented and religious animosities increased."[1]

All the difficulties of the Government now gathered
around the Emancipation Bill introduced by Sir Francis
Burdett. It passed through all stages in the House of Commons by the end of April, and awaited its fate in the Lords.
Much would turn upon the line taken by the Prime
Minister; should he accept the verdict of the Commons,
Emancipation would not be delayed, and rumours had
been industriously circulated of his "supposed conversion
to popery". A denial of these rumours was inserted in the
Courier,[2] but some still thought the language of the denial
not very emphatic.

At this stage Peel intimated to Liverpool that, having
been beaten in the House of Commons, he could not remain in office. Liverpool replied that if Peel resigned, he
too must resign; he would resign in any case if Emancipation passed the Lords, and how could he fill Peel's office
when he did not expect to remain many weeks in office

1 Yonge, III, 321–5.　　　2 An unusual course of action.

himself? The simplest solution would be for Peel and himself, the two Protestant ministers, to retire and leave the
rest to settle the Catholic Question. The High Tories were
in great alarm, and they urgently pressed Liverpool and
Peel to reconsider. Liverpool showed himself full of
scruples: "How could I carry on the Government with
dignity or credit without some *organ* of my own sentiments,
and of the Protestant feeling in the House of Commons?"
he asked Bathurst, who took an unusually forward part in
this matter. "You would not wish me, I am sure, to close
a long political life with disgrace. This must inevitably be
the case if I appear now to be clinging to office when my
opinions have been overruled in the House of Commons
and when I cannot expect to be able to defend the Protestant cause much longer in the House of Lords."[1] Bathurst replied by speaking of the reliance which the Church
placed upon him, and concluded: "It is your duty to cling
to office, when by so doing you cling to your principles
and your friends."[2] And when it seemed that entreaty to
Liverpool failed, Bathurst and Wellington turned to Peel;
"I will not call to your recollection to what a personally
painful struggle you are exposing the king, by making a
change of councils necessary, nor what may be felt by the
University, who placed their confidence in you at so early
a period of your political life. But is it fair to the public,
who are doing you at this moment justice for the firmness
of temper with which you have singly as a minister in the
House of Commons maintained your opinions?...I am
aware of the popularity which is apt to follow any display

1 Bathurst, p. 580.　　　　　2 *Ibid.* p. 585.

of indifference to office; but you will find that public men, who have by their resignations exposed the country to great trouble and sudden convulsions, are not easily forgiven."[1] In response to these arguments Peel ultimately and reluctantly withdrew his resignation, but meanwhile the existence of the Government had been saved in the House of Lords.

When, on 17 May, the peers met to debate the Catholic Bill, those in the confidence of ministers knew that more was at stake than the acceptance or rejection of the measure. If it passed Liverpool would resign, for he had written to Wellington: "The more I reflect upon the question, the more impossible it appears to me that I should be a party to the *new system*, much less the instrument of carrying it into effect."[2] If Liverpool went, the Government could not continue. The Whigs were nearer than they knew to the brink of office on 17 May.

Feelings ran high. On 25 April the country had been startled by an unexpected and unprecedented event. The Duke of York, presenting a petition against Emancipation from the Canons of Windsor, reminded the House of his father's resistance to the Catholic claims, and hinted that he might soon be in his father's place, when he said that he would continue that resistance "to the latest moment of my life, whatever may be my situation in life. So Help me God!" Encouraged by this royal example, and little deterred by Whig complaints of unconstitutional interference,

---

1 Parker, I, 374–5.
2 Wellington, II, 435. Canning does not seem to have been aware of this consequence, at least he gave no hint of such knowledge. Liverpool studiously refrained from making his resolution public for that would have prejudiced the question unfairly.

Protestant fervour manifested itself in every part of the country. Copies of the Duke's speech emblazoned in gold were popular purchases, and the old cry of "No Popery" was heard once more in the streets. The 17th of May was such a night as is rarely seen in the House of Lords. The debate had already gone on for several hours when the Prime Minister rose to speak; Lord Colchester, the Speaker Abbot of Protestant glory, had moved the postponement of the bill for six months; the Church, personified by the Bishops of Llandaff and Chester, had supported him; Lord Anglesey, a former friend of the Catholics, had said: "Every concession that has been made to them had been followed by increased restlessness and sedition; their conduct and the language which they have adopted are such as to show that emancipation alone would not satisfy them, and that they would be content with nothing but Catholic ascendancy." The opinion of the House seemed slightly against the measure, but its fate, if not immediately at least in the near future, depended upon the tone of Liverpool's speech. His speech was an uncompromising rejection of the Catholic claims, phrased in language far more vehement than he had ever before used. "My peculiar objection to the Roman Catholic religion is that it penetrates into every domestic scene, and inculcates a system of tyranny never known elsewhere.... I say that, if this measure should pass, the Protestant succession would not be worth a farthing.... The House ought not to deceive the people. They ought at once to declare that, if the bill were to pass, Great Britain would no longer be a Protestant State. The evil I apprehend from the passing of such a bill will not be immediate, but it will be inevitable, and it will come upon the country in a manner little expected.... Can the House...not see that a great and powerful engine is at work to effect the object of re-establishing the Catholic religion throughout these kingdoms? And if once established, shall we not revert to a state of ignorance, with all its barbarous and direful consequences? For the last hundred and thirty years the country had enjoyed a state of religious peace, a blessing which has arisen from the wisdom of our laws. Those laws granted toleration to all religious creeds, at the same time that they maintained a just, reasonable and a moderate superiority in favour of the established Church. Your lordships are now called upon to put Protestants and Roman Catholics upon the same footing; and if you consent to do this, certain I am that the consequence will be religious dissension not religious peace."[1] The result of the debate was a magnificent majority of forty-eight for Protestantism.

"God be thanked", wrote the King to Liverpool. "I congratulate you most sincerely on your successful efforts of last night."[2] "Nobody", said Canning, "expected other than a defeat; but the vehemence of L's speech was an astounding disappointment."[3] It may now be asked what were Liverpool's real sentiments upon the Catholic question; not as a matter of principle, for he had shown himself opposed beyond all hope of compromise, but as a matter of political expediency. The surprising answer is that he was convinced it must pass, was prepared to facilitate its passing,

1 Yonge, III, 331 ff. 2 Wellington, II, 451.
3 E. J. Stapleton, I, 270.

and in particular to recommend Canning to the King as his successor; to Bathurst he wrote: "The *crisis* cannot be averted many months. I should be forced out, if not by any direct act of my colleagues, by the circumstances of the Government. Whenever the *crisis does come*, the *Protestants* must go to the wall."[1] He proposed to go while he could go honourably, and to the consternation of the Duke suggested Canning as his successor. Canning seems also to have contemplated resignation. Five days after the Lords' debate, Liverpool wrote to Bathurst: "I cannot, however, agree with you that it would be right for me to let Canning resign, if the majority of the Cabinet should still be for keeping the question in *abeyance*, and then give up the Government as incapable of forming one on the exclusive protestant principle. It appears to me to be my duty to inform the king of the actual state of his Government and let him know that the formation of a Government upon the principle of resisting the Catholic claims is *absolutely impracticable*, whereas the formation of a Government upon the opposite principle, even from amongst his present servants with some few additions, is within his power."[2] Peel's withdrawal of his resignation, the genuine alarm of his colleagues, and the prospect of the King's obstruction to any "Catholic" ministry, induced Liverpool to give up this resolution. He would stay in office, but he would do nothing further to postpone the ultimate and inevitable concession of the Catholic claims.

This resolution was put to the test immediately. The Parliament had been elected in 1820, it had still a year of

1 Bathurst, p. 580. 2 *Ibid.* p. 583.

statutory life, but it was without precedent to allow a
Parliament its full statutory life. The Protestant enthusiasm
aroused by the Duke of York's speech was still running
high, and, as Canning wrote to Granville, "a dissolution at
present would give us a 'No Popery' Parliament, and array
England against Ireland".[1] For precisely this reason Wellington urged a dissolution. "It is impossible", he wrote to
Liverpool, "that, constituted as the government is, you
should dissolve Parliament upon the declared principle of
an appeal to the people upon the Roman Catholic question
...but I should contend that, viewing the question as you
and Peel do, as one of principle, and seeing the difficulties
and dangers from which by tranquillity and good management alone we recently extricated ourselves, it is a point of
duty to decide upon the period of the dissolution in reference only to the effect which that decision might produce
eventually upon the Roman Catholic Question in the House
of Commons."[2] Liverpool deferred the decision until September, and in the middle of that month a minor Cabinet
battle took place. Canning wrote very fairly to Liverpool:
"As to the general reasons for or against [dissolution],
supposing the Catholic question out of the way, I think
there can be no doubt but that those for it greatly pre-
dominate";[3] but, whether avowedly so or not, dissolution
would appear as an appeal upon the Catholic Question.
Liverpool inclined to a dissolution now, but both he and
Canning were prepared to admit the arguments of the
other. On 12 September Canning, who had been making

1 E. J. Stapleton, I, 272.
2 Wellington, II, 463–4.   3 E. J. Stapleton, I, 289.

a tour of the country houses, was more definite; the friends whom he had seen and his correspondents were as one in urging "that there is a fury upon the Catholic question, ready to break forth, the instant that the now expected dissolution takes place".[1] Liverpool's own solution, which was the one finally adopted, was ingenious: "If we can *all* agree to keep the Catholic and the Corn question in abeyance during the next session, I am very indifferent as to immediate dissolution."[2] The Government and the House of Lords were saved from the inconvenience of another pro-Catholic vote in the Commons; and Canning loyally supported Liverpool by sending a circular letter impressing upon Catholic sympathisers the inexpediency of raising the question in the last session of an expiring Parliament.

Yet the doubts and dissensions of the ministers were not at rest, and a symptom of this is the number of small but irritating problems which began to gather around the harassed Prime Minister. An unfortunate division of opinion arose over the election to a vacancy in the representative peerage of Ireland. Clanricarde, Canning's son-in-law, put himself forward, and was opposed by the Orange Lord Farnham; at home Canning urged the claims of Clanricarde, Peel took up the battle for Lord Farnham.

1 E. J. Stapleton, I, 293.
2 Wellington, II, 499; Add. MSS. 40305, f. 86, Liverpool to Peel: If the Government supporters of Catholic Emancipation were "prepared to discourage its being brought on, and if brought on, to move a previous question or adjournment upon it...I have no desire to press the dissolution during the present autumn. I say *press the dissolution*, because I think the reasons for and against it are nearly balanced."

Liverpool had to reconcile the two and point objections to both candidates. Clanricarde had involved himself in the sedition of the Catholic Association by paying the Catholic Rent; Liverpool would overlook this youthful folly but thought his candidature would raise more problems than it would solve. Against Farnham there was a more serious objection, for he was cited as a stock example of the brutal Irish landlord; to support this there was a disgraceful incident in which, while sitting on the magistrates' bench, he had flogged a boy in person. "Indeed", Liverpool told Peel, "I do not know how I could consistently with the Principles on which I have invariably acted, press Lord Farnham upon the Lord Lieutenant."[1] The King too had his candidate in Lord Glengall, but Liverpool did not think that he would insist.[2] The Earl of Westmeath proposed himself and began to canvass. Liverpool put forward the Earl of Mount Cashell as the most unexceptionable candidate, but no sooner had he received Government support than he expressed himself violently in public against the Catholics. "Is there no other eligible person", asked Canning, "who at least has not shown himself to be such a goose? And such a violent goose too?"[3] Westmeath offered to retire and place the votes he had gained at Mount Cashell's disposal if the Government would support him in a future election; this Liverpool refused, for such a promise would tempt every Irish peer to make a similar bargain. Finally, in spite of letters written by Liverpool to promi-

1 Add. MSS. 38300, f. 194.
2 Add. MSS. 38300, f. 195: "His Majesty does not care about Lord Glengall, he was persuaded by others."
3 E. J. Stapleton, II, 300.

nent Irish peers, Protestant fury won the day for the odious
Lord Farnham.

The dissolution of Parliament brought forward another
host of problems. Wellington advised Liverpool to keep
Government influence in his own hands, "and not to allow
yourself to attend to the recommendation of anybody for a
seat in Parliament whom you should not have a hope that
he would oppose further concessions".[1] But Liverpool remained scrupulously fair; ten seats were placed at his disposal, and "Catholics" and "Protestants" were given five
each.[2] Throughout the country the division of the Tory
party was reflected upon the hustings. Canning's friend
Gladstone opposed the Beresfords at Berwick; Palmerston
with the help of Whig votes just defeated the Protestant
Goulbourn at Cambridge University; and Wellington became furiously angry when he heard reports, probably inaccurate, of free trade promises made by Huskisson at
Liverpool. To Peel's disgust Liverpool refused Government aid to Holme Sumner in Surrey, and the seat was lost
to Liverpool's Whiggish friend Pallmer. Elsewhere "No
Popery" defeated well-established Whigs; Lord John
Russell lost Huntingdonshire, Lord Howick lost Northum-
berland, Brougham failed to steal a Lowther seat in Westmorland, Taunton and Chippenham both went to High
Tories. The Tories gained in all forty-two seats in England,
Scotland and Wales, mostly won by Protestants; the Whigs
gained only twenty-three. In Ireland, however, the Whigs
gained twelve, and the Tories eight. The Government came

1 Wellington, III, 314.
2 Wellesley, II, 160.

back with an increased majority, but the division between
High and Liberal Tory, between Protestant and Catholic,
was more marked than it had ever been before. The position of a Prime Minister who was both Liberal and Protestant was becoming increasingly difficult; the great Tory
peers were "out of sorts with the Government",[1] and the
new Parliament was faced with the dangerous topic of Corn
and the inevitable Catholic question.

This unpleasing prospect was not relieved by any cessa-
tion of personal quarrels. The dissolution had occasioned a
fresh batch of peers; the King agreed to Liverpool's list
with more cordiality than he had ever shown on such questions, but the High Tories saw in it the dread hand of
Canning. "Everybody", wrote Greville, "cries out against
Charles Ellis's peerage; he has no property, and is of no
family and his son is already a peer.... Clanricarde, too,
being made a Marquis and an English peer is thought an
indirect exertion of Canning's influence."[2] The Duke of
Devonshire was given a Garter, in spite of a protest by
Wellington.[3] Canning's friend Morley insisted that he had
a claim to the Post Office, vacant by Lord Chichester's
death; Wellington demanded a bishopric for his brother
Gerald. Morley was the least able and most disliked of
Canning's friends, and Liverpool told Canning that Morley would be an unpopular and unsuitable appointment.
Morley was prepared to treat for a peerage, but Liverpool

1 Wellington's phrase: Add. MSS. 38302, f. 117.
2 Greville, I, 160–1. Ellis was an old friend of Canning, and Liverpool's nephew; his son was Lord Howard de Walden.
3 Add. MSS. 38302, f. 117.

saw danger ahead: "Our last batch of peers", he told Canning, "is so unpopular that I am not prepared to add to the number." A solution might be to put Robinson in the Lords, Palmerston in his place, and make Morley Secretary at War; but this would be "considered at this time as an admission of Robinson's failure". He concluded that "bad as the appointment will be, and nothing can be worse in itself, I think the *single evil* less than creating new ones"; he would propose Morley to the King, but "if His Majesty objects, I do not feel called upon to press it. I am no Whig, and though I have proved that I am prepared to *press* a point when I am convinced I am clearly right, I cannot press a point upon my Sovereign when I know that I am *wrong*."[1] Apparently the King did object, for Lord Frederick Montagu was appointed Postmaster-General.

The question of Wellington's brother was peculiarly unfortunate, for, though in most ways unexceptionable, Gerald Wellesley was separated from his wife. He did not institute divorce proceedings, so the assumption was that his wife could recriminate. Lord Wellesley first advanced his brother's claims, then appeared to recognise Liverpool's objections, but wrote to Wellington urging him to press their brother's case with all the means in his power. An extremely bitter correspondence ensued between Wellington and Liverpool. Liverpool was much hurt by Wellington's accusations: he could not accuse himself of having overlooked Wellington's fair pretensions, and for his family "I have done much more...than I have for my

[1] Add. MSS. 38301, fs. 262 ff.

own".[1] Liverpool carried his point, but the incident did not improve his relationship with Wellington.

Hints had been given in 1825, and perhaps Wellington suspected Liverpool's real intentions. Those intentions he confided to Canning during 1825, and to Arbuthnot at the beginning of 1827. Canning said later that Liverpool was anxious "to have the trial of strength on the Catholic question as early as possible in the new Parliament. If the issue should be in favour of the Catholics and he fully expected it to be so—he would (in my conscience I believe) have retired, recommending to the king to form a Government fit to manage the final adjustment of the question, and to the House of Lords to acquiesce in that adjustment."[2] To Arbuthnot he said that he was determined to retire at the end of the session in 1827; he said that "not only quiet and retirement were requisite for his much shattered health, but that the time had arrived when he felt it necessary to take into consideration the Catholic claims"; he himself had taken too prominent a part against the Catholics, and he could neither desert Peel nor carry Emancipation without him.[3] Liverpool anticipated the inevitable concession; he could not take an active part in granting it, but it would be facilitated by the passive act of resignation.

With this in his mind, the action taken by the Duke of York in November 1826 was peculiarly embarrassing. In the last few years York, as the heir to a sovereign who

1 Yonge, III, 383–96, for the whole correspondence.
2 Wellesley, II, 160. He was slightly more definite, but still reserved as to details in January 1827 (Temperley, *E.H.R.* 1930, quoting letters of Joan Canning). See Appendix B: "Canning's Supposed Negotiations with the Whigs."   3 Parker, III, 353.

was almost a chronic invalid, had gradually come to play a more prominent part in politics. He had viewed with increasing mistrust the trend of affairs, and his good humour had not been restored by Liverpool's refusal to engage the Government to pay his debts.[1] Then in November he realised that he would never be King, that his limbs were swollen with incurable dropsy, and that his splendid constitution had given out before his brother's rotten physique and astonishing vitality. It was with the awful solemnity of one who knows his days are short that he sought an interview with Liverpool to make a protest against the whole course of government—half-measures were leading to disaster, a firm stand must be taken, an exclusively Protestant ministry must be formed—and he spoke the general alarm of Churchmen and Tory squires. Fortunately all other High Tories and the King had abandoned the idea of an exclusive Protestant ministry as an ideal not to be found in an imperfect world. Tactfully ignored by the High Tory ministers, snubbed by the King, the Duke went back to die with the pathetic knowledge of having led a forlorn hope.

One other embarrassment was to come from the royal family. When the Duke of York died, the Commandership-in-Chief became vacant. There was only one possible choice for his successor, but for some reason the King hesitated.

---

1 Liverpool to Sir Herbert Taylor, the Duke's Secretary: " I am willing to deal liberally with respect to the house. It is an intelligible and a limited object. But with respect to the debts, not even the Duke himself knows what they are. I am satisfied that the Government by implicating themselves in them, might occasion a Revolution in the country": Add. MSS. 38302, f. 21.

Wellington was prepared to see the hand of Canning even in this, but Peel assured him that the extraordinary reason was an idea of the King that he himself might become Commander-in-Chief. Liverpool called the idea "preposterous", and Wellington was appointed. The result was more satisfactory than might have been expected, for it came near to effecting a reconciliation between Wellington and Liverpool.

But before this the Cabinet quarrel had returned to the familiar theme of foreign policy, and Liverpool was able to perform one last service for Canning by aiding him to his greatest triumph. On 10 March 1826 died John VI of Portugal. His heir was Dom Pedro, the Emperor of Brazil, but the security of the kingdom was threatened by the exiled younger son, Dom Miguel, and his mother the Queen. Before his death John had appointed a Council of Regency from which both were excluded. On 22 June came news from Brazil: Dom Pedro resigned the crown of Portugal to his eight-year-old daughter and appointed his sister, Infanta Isabel, as Regent; before abdicating he had performed one act of sovereignty, he had given Portugal a constitution. This was to unite the throne with the Portuguese liberals, but there was also a strong absolutist party which looked to Dom Miguel, to the Queen-Mother Carlotta, and to her brother, Ferdinand of Spain. Canning was "*little* pleased" to hear of the constitution—which was certainly a very bad one—but his sense of humour was delighted by the spectacle of Metternich trying to prove that even a king could not introduce fundamental change. On 11 July he sent a circular to Paris, Berlin and Vienna, which denied any English complicity in Dom Pedro's action, but warned the powers against interference in Portugal. On 24 July the Ambassadors' Conference at Paris took the hint and advised Spain not to interfere. But a new situation arose when Portuguese troops attached to Miguel deserted and crossed into Spain, and Spain lent countenance and succour to these deserters who began to muster for an invasion of Portugal.

On 19 September Canning arrived in Paris on that long-promised visit to Granville. In secret meetings he brought the French and the Russians round to his side, and, when news arrived of military preparations among the Portuguese deserters, he ordered Lamb, the ambassador at Madrid, to withdraw unless they were dispersed. On the 7th he cancelled this instruction as the Spanish seemed to be complying, but England had threatened once and the threat would be carried out if the same provocation arose.

On 10 October Liverpool wrote a long and particularly interesting letter to Canning. There are those who have believed that Liverpool was simply a puppet in Canning's hands, but this letter, written during Canning's absence, showed him to be more Canningite than Canning himself. He began by expressing the hope that joint Anglo-French action might bring Spain to reason, but "Suppose, however, Spain to become the *aggressor*, and Portugal *to call upon us* as her ally?" He would first issue an order "for seizing and detaining all ships under the Spanish flag in every part of the world", declaring that they would be restored "in case just satisfaction was given within a reasonable time". He would call upon the allied powers to use their influence with Spain, "upon the principle that as both Spain and Portugal were independent kingdoms, neither had a right to interfere in the internal concerns of the other". And "I would announce to the Allies that if they declined the proposed intervention, *or* if they should fail in compelling Spain to retrace her steps, we should be forced to play the whole game of liberal institutions in Spain as well as in Portugal; that we should send the Spanish patriots now in England or on the Continent to Gibraltar, and should spare no exertion to raise the Standard of the Constitution again in Spain".[1]

Canning returned home on 25 October and found a violent opposition in the Cabinet; Wellington complained that Canning, on his sole authority, had run the risk of war by recalling Lamb, and there was the accumulated bitterness of four years in his letter to Bathurst: "Canning certainly is the most extraordinary man. Either his mind does not seize a case accurately, or he forgets the impressions which ought to be received from what he reads, or is stated to him; or knowing or remembering the accurate state of the case, he distorts and misrepresents facts in his instructions to his ministers with a view to entrap the consent of the Cabinet to some principle on which he would found a new-fangled system."[2] Liverpool supported Canning; once more the opposite parties in the Cabinet were arrayed in the familiar way; once more the Ultras had to yield.

But Spain was not to be warned; her hostility towards

1 Yonge, III, 406–7.
2 Bathurst, p. 615. Omitted without indication from Wellington, III, 403.

Portugal became more open, the raids of the Spanish armed
deserters became more daring. The Portuguese Government appealed to England, and on 8 December a despatch
from Sir William A'Court convinced Canning of the
urgency of the matter. On the following day the Cabinet
decision was taken. Three days later troops were em-
barking for Portugal. The gesture was rewarded with complete success; by the end of the year Portugal was peaceful
within, and those who had threatened her frontiers were
disarmed and dispersed by the Government which had
fostered their attempt. It was Canning's greatest diplomatic triumph, it was also the occasion of his greatest
parliamentary triumph. "We go to Portugal, not to rule,
not to dictate, not to prescribe constitutions—but to
defend and preserve the independence of an ally. We go to
plant the Standard of England on the well-known heights
of Lisbon. Where that Standard is planted, foreign dominion shall not come!" And later, in his reply, he placed his
whole foreign policy under review and closed with that
most famous declaration: "Contemplating Spain, such as
her ancestors had known her, I resolved that if France had
Spain, it should not be Spain 'with the Indies'. I called
the New World into existence to redress the balance of the
Old."

Canning and the Government had never stood higher in
public estimation, yet the difficulties of that Government
were no less. Liverpool knew that his time was short,
perhaps in this life, certainly as head of the ministry. On
16 December he wrote to Robinson, who had found in his
wife's continual ill-health an honourable excuse to absent

himself from the labours of Westminster and to ask for removal to an easier office and the House of Lords:[1] "I must begin by telling you that I have been *very ill*. I am recovering, but this last illness I cannot but consider as a hint that I am better fitted now for repose than for the labours, and still more for the anxieties of the situation which I have held for so many years.... I cannot in a letter enter into all the particulars, but be assured the Government hangs by a thread. The Catholic question in its present state, combined with other circumstances, will, I have little doubt, lead to its dissolution in the course of this session; and any attempt to make a *move* now, in the more efficient offices, would infallibly hasten the crisis."[2] He had set himself two tasks—to carry the new Corn Law, and to facilitate the accession of Canning—neither was he destined to accomplish.

Upon the Corn Law "he was resolved to stake (more perhaps than any minister... has ever done upon any measure of such a nature), that eminent reputation, which was naturally most dear, as well as most honourable to an individual in his exalted station, and if necessary, that station itself".[3] After that he would recommend Canning as his successor, and he would perhaps use what remained of his authority in persuading others to accept Canning. These were anxieties enough for a man who already felt himself exhausted in body and mind.

On 16 February Joseph Planta had never seen Liverpool

1 Add. MSS. 38302, f. 113.   2 Yonge, III, 438–9.
3 Canning in the House of Commons, 1 March 1827; Hansard, XVI, 759.

"in higher force—or in more comfortable state", but that night the speaker who was never at a loss for a word, seemed to stumble and referred to the Duchess of Clarence as a "worthy and deserving object". At ten o'clock on the following morning he was found lying paralysed on the floor of his breakfast room. It was as though a pillar of the Constitution had fallen; everyone felt a loss, few a personal loss. Greville remarked how little anybody seemed to care about the man, Croker found "no grief, or even a decent pensiveness".[1] During a month of intense political speculation Liverpool lay unconscious. On 25 March he rallied sufficiently to answer a question; when Lady Liverpool hoped that he would soon be well enough to resume business, he murmured, "No, no, not I—too weak, too weak". It was his last appearance on the political stage, for his utterance "relieved the Ministers from the silence which delicacy had imposed upon them".[2] The ministry of Lord Liverpool was at an end.

Liverpool lingered for nearly two years in a semi-conscious condition before he died on 4 December 1828. On the 8th his body was taken to the family vault at Hawkesbury in Gloucestershire. His funeral was as unostentatious as his life, but "the absence of public splendour was amply supplied by the strongest exhibition of public feeling".[3] Of public men only his brother-in-law, the Marquis of Bristol, his Kingston friend Pallmer, Lord Sidmouth, and the Duke of Clarence followed the hearse; but the inhabitants of Kingston lined the road to pay a last

1 Greville, I, 168; Croker, I, 362. 2 Croker, I, 366.
3 This account is taken from the *Gentleman's Magazine* of 1828.

tribute. So "amid his good works and his charities and attended by the tears of the multitude, his lordship received the parting blessing of a community, to which for more than twenty-six years he had been an unceasing benefactor".

With Liverpool's funeral cortège went also the dead body of the old Tory party—the party of George III and of Mr Pitt, the party which inherited the flamboyant creed of "Church and King", the party whose honest unthinking supporters had stood behind two generations of able administrators. Canning was already dead and his followers were estranged from the party; Wellington and Peel were thinking of a strategic retreat upon the Catholic Question; Whigs had presumed to enter the Council Chamber and were hopefully awaiting the day when they might take full possession. The Tory Government had been identified with Liverpool, it was amply proved that no one could take his place.

The English party system in the 1820's did not represent a sociological division. The clash of opinions within the Cabinet did represent a clash of interest in the country at large, but it was of great value to England to have at the head of affairs a man who was an administrator rather than a partisan. Thereby England learnt a small part of the hardest political lesson, the separation of personal interests and political judgment. A bold man might have done more; he might have done much less. Nor, with all his caution, did Liverpool lack courage, and he was able, often against great difficulties, to give England the Government and the policy which he desired. Above all his great honesty made a deep impression in the country; it, as much as any other thing, helps to bar off the politics of the nineteenth century from those of the eighteenth. It was this integrity of character, combined with real but not striking abilities, which secured him at the head of the Government, and it was this, as much as the brilliance of Canning, which earned for the Government the respect of the middle classes. The greatest merit of the Government lies in the fact that it represented more than a single class, and more than a single interest; for this phenomenon Liverpool can claim as much credit as any man. If the historian feels, at times, tempted to sneer at his lack of brilliance, if his career seems pedestrian and uninspired, then the historian may call to mind Liverpool's own motto, "Palma non sine pulvere".

APPENDIX A

THE MERCANTILE INTEREST

This list includes all those who can be shown to have had immediate mercantile connections. Some, in spite of their connection, would undoubtedly have preferred to think of themselves as country gentlemen.[1] The most probable omission is of a number of West India proprietors.[2]

Alexander, J. Alexander, J. D. }	Old Sarum	Connected with the E. India trade.
Astell, W.	Bridgwater	Director, E. India Co.
Attwood, M.	Callington	Banker and London merchant.
Baillie, J.	Heydon	A "nabob".
Baring, Sir T.	Wycombe	} Sons of Sir Francis Baring, the financier.
Baring, Alexander	Taunton	
Baring, Henry	Colchester	
Beecher, W. W.	Mallow	
Bent, J.	Totnes	W. India planter.
Benyon, Ben	Stafford	
Bernal, R.	Rochester	Barrister, father a W. India planter.
Birch, J.	Nottingham	Liverpool merchant.
Blake, Sir F.	Berwick	Banker of Newcastle.
Bridges, Sir G.	London	A former Lord Mayor.
Bright, H.	Bristol	W. India merchant.
Brogden, J.	Launceston	Russia merchant. Chairman of the Committee of the House.
Butterworth, J.	Dover	A "Saint", a methodist, and a bookseller.
Buxton, T. F.	Weymouth	Brewer, philanthropist, and dissenter.
Calvert, N.	Hertford	Brewer.

1 Thus in 1826 W. W. Whitmore, a director of the East India Company, referred to himself as a member of the landed interest (Letter to the Electors of Bridgnorth). The Whitmores had been established in Shropshire for over two hundred years, so there was justice in his claim; the landed property of others was not more than a generation old.

2 Hansard, 22 May 1823. Mr Forbes "saw more clearly than ever that the West India interest in the House was paramount to every other".

Calvert, C.	Southwark	Brother to above.
Calvert, J.	Huntingdon	Cousin to above.
Carter, J.	Portsmouth	Brewer.
Chaloner, R.	York	York banker, brother-in-law to Lord Dundas.
Cherry, G. H.	Dunwich	A "nabob".
Cockerell, Sir C.	Evesham	Banker, E. India merchant.
Collett, E. J.	Cashell	Hop merchant of Southwark.
Cripps, J.	Cirencester	Banker of Cirencester.
Crompton, S.	Retford	Derby banker.
Curtis, Sir W.	London	Merchant (biscuits, fisheries, brewing).
Dent, J.	Poole	London banker.
Divett, T.	Gatton	
Ellison, C.	Newcastle	Banker of Newcastle.
Gaskell, B.	Maldon	Manufacturer.
Gordon, R.	Cricklade	London merchant.
Grossett, J. R.	Chippenham	
Gurney, Hudson	Newtown (I. of W.)	Bankers of Norwich.
Gurney, R. H.	Norwich	
Haldimand, W.	Ipswich	Bank director.
Heygate, W.	Sudbury	Alderman and banker of London.
Hodson, J.	Wigan	
Horrocks, S.	Preston	Manufacturer.
Houldsworth, T.	Pontefract	Manchester manufacturer.
Hume, J.	Aberdeen	
Huskisson, W.	Chichester	
Innis, J.	Grampound	London merchant.
Irving, J.	Bramber	London merchant.
Maberley, J.	Abingdon	Army contractor.
Maberley, W. L.	Northampton	Son of above.
Madocks, W. A.	Chippenham	
Manning, W.	Lymington	W. India merchant, Bank director.
Marryat, J.	Sandwich	London merchant.
Martin, J.	Tewkesbury	London banker.
Miles, P. J.	Westbury	W. India merchant, banker at Bristol.
Mitchell, J.	Hull	W. India planter.
Money, W. T.	St Michael's	E. India director.
Moore, P.	Coventry	A "nabob".
Morland, Sir S. B.	St Mawes	London banker.
Ommaney, Sir F.	Barnstaple	Navy agent.
Pares, T.	Leicester	Barrister, son of a Leicester banker.
Pease, J.	Devizes	Bank director.
Phillips, G. R.	Wootton Bassett	Lancashire manufacturer.
Phillips, G. R.	Steyning	Son of above.

Plumer, J.	Hindon	W. India merchant.
Pole, Sir P.	Yarmouth	London banker.
Ramsbottom, J.	Windsor	London banker.
Ricardo, D.	Portarlington	Financier.
Rickford, W.	Aylesbury	Banker of Aylesbury.
Ridley, Sir M. W.	Newcastle-on-Tyne	Banker of Newcastle.
Robarts, A. W.	Maidstone	London banker.
Robarts, G. R.	Wallingford	London banker.
Robertson, A.	Grampound	London merchant.
Rumbold, C.	Yarmouth	A "nabob".
Scott, S.	Whitchurch	Corn dealer.
Shaw, Sir R.	Dublin	Alderman of Dublin.
Smith, G.	Wendover	
Smith, S.	Wendover	Relatives of Lord Carrington, and
Smith, J.	Midhurst	members of the banking firm of
Smith, A.	Midhurst	Smith, Payne, and Smith.
Smith, Hon. R.	Berkshire	
Smith, C.	St Albans	Liquor merchant, London alderman.
Smith, W.	Norwich	London banker, a leading Methodist.
Taylor, C. W.	E. Looe	West India planter.
Thompson, W.	Callington	London alderman.
Tulk, C. A.	Sudbury	London merchant.
Walker, J.	Aldborough	Iron master of Rotherham.
Wall, C. Baring	Guildford	Related to the Barings.
Wells, J.	Maidstone	Shipbuilder.
Whitmore, T.	Bridgnorth	Bank director.
Whitmore, W. W.	Bridgnorth	Director, E. India Company.
Widman, J. B.	Colchester	W. India merchant.
Wigram, W.	Wexford	Banker.
Williams, R.	Dorchester	London banker.
Williams, W.	Weymouth	London banker.
Wilson, T.	London	Merchant.
Wood, M.	London	Alderman.

CANNING'S SUPPOSED NEGOTIATIONS
WITH THE WHIGS

In 1831 Arbuthnot told Greville (*Diary*, ii, 172) that Canning had negotiated with the Whigs before Liverpool's seizure, that Brougham took the initiative from the Whig side, and that Sir Robert Wilson acted as an intermediary between Brougham and Canning. The source of Arbuthnot's story has never been discovered. On 10 March 1827 he wrote to Peel that the Duke "cannot bring himself to put trust in Canning. He thinks that in his own department there is much trickery; he sees that the sons and relations of our most vehement opponents are taken into employ; and he cannot divest himself of the idea that, directly or indirectly, there has been an understanding with some of the leaders of the Opposition" (Parker, i, 452). So in March 1827 there was only a suspicion, and in the ensuing four years Arbuthnot acquired the circumstantial evidence. Among none of the papers of the period is there a shred of evidence in support of the story, and it can only be assumed that Arbuthnot put his knowledge of the negotiations after March 1827 and his suspicion of negotiations before February 1827 together and produced the story which he told to Greville. The question has been discussed by Professor Temperley (*Foreign Policy, etc.*, pp. 521–30) and Dr Aspinall (*The Formation of Canning's Ministry*, pp. xxix–xxxi) and both have come to this conclusion. The private letters of Princess Lieven to Metternich were not, however, available to Professor Temperley, and Dr Aspinall has made inadequate use of them. The Lieven letters have to be used carefully as she was liable to repeat gossip as substantiated fact. Her story of a meeting between Canning and Lansdowne at an Inn near Marlborough may be so dismissed. But on 2 May she used a conversation with Canning as proof of the rumours she had reported. Now a report of a conversation is a different matter to a rumour, and it may be assumed that Canning did use the words, or at least the sense, which she attributed to him. Canning said: "Sooner or later, we must join with Lord Lansdowne. He is a moderate man. Lord Grey is the difficulty; with him it will never be possible to come to an agreement." Having heard previous rumours of negotiations with the Whigs Princess Lieven assumed that this proved them. Actually it does nothing of the sort, but it does throw a valuable light upon the trend of Canning's ideas at this time. He believed that the Tory party had done its great work (cf. his letter to the King, p. 245), and in 1824 he had written to Liverpool, "I think our business is to admit the extinction of party feeling rather than to show a determination to keep it alive". The great obstacle to a fusion of parties was the Catholic question, that would inevitably separate those with whom the Whigs could unite from those with whom they could not. Loyalty to Liverpool prevented Canning from precipitating the question, but Liverpool's health was so bad that there was little prospect of his staying in office for more than a year, and Canning knew that he would retire if the new Parliament passed a measure of Catholic relief. It was then but natural that Canning's thoughts should anticipate the future and that he should look forward to a Catholic coalition when Liverpool retired. But there is no evidence to show that he took any steps towards facilitating that coalition, and when Liverpool did retire he tried honestly and sincerely to form a Tory Government. It seems that not only is Canning cleared, but that he must also be credited with a loyalty to his colleagues which bade him hold his hand, even when he realised that he would probably have to seek Whig aid after Liverpool's retirement.

LIST OF SOURCES

I. UNPUBLISHED MATERIALS.

Additional Manuscripts in the British Museum (cited as Add. Mss), viz:
The papers of Lord Liverpool, Huskisson, Lord Bexley (Vansittart).
Sir Robert Peel, the Marquess of Ripon (Robinson, the Marquess of Wellesley, Lord Aukland, and Sir Robert Wilson).

II. PRINTED SOURCES (including secondary authorities which include source material)

Ashburton, Alexander Baring, 1st Lord. *The Financial and Commercial Crisis Considered.* 2nd Ed. London 1847.

Aspinall, A. A. *The Formation of Canning's Ministry.* (Royal Historical Society, Camden 3rd Series). London 1937.

Aspinall, A. A. (ed.) *The Letters of George IV.* 3 Vols. Cambridge 1938.

Bagot, J. *George Canning and his friends.* 2 Vols. London 1909.

Bathurst (See Historical Manuscripts Commission).

The Black Book. London 1820.

Buckingham and Chandos, 2nd Duke of. *Memoirs of the Court of England during the Regency.* London 1856, and *Memoirs of the Court of George IV.* London 1859.

Buxton, S. C. 1st Earl of Buxton. *Finance and Politics: an historical study.* 1783-1885. London 1888.

Colchester, Charles Abbot, 1st Baron. *The Diary and Correspondence of Charles Abbot, Lord Colchester.* London 1861.

Commons, House of
　A biographical index to the present House of Commons
　London 1808
　The Pamphleteer Vol. XXI. No. XLII. London 1821.
　p. 293. *Alphabetical List of the Members of the Commons.*
　Ibid. Vol. XXII. No. XLIV London 1882. p. 451.
　Analysis of the British House of Commons.
　The Assembled Commons or Parliamentary Biographer.
　By a Member of the Middle Temple. London 1838.

Croker, Rt. Hon. J. W. *Correspondence and Diaries* 1809-
　1830, (ed. L. J. Jennings). London 1884.

Dropmore (See Historical Manuscripts Commission).

George IV. *Letters* (see A. A. Aspinall, ed.).

Greville, C. C. F. *A Journal of the Reigns of King George
　IV, King William IV, and Queen Victoria.* 8 Vols.
　(ed. L. Strachey and R. Fulford.) London 1938.

Hansard, T. C. *Parliamentary Debates*, 1st Series 1803-
　1820, 2nd Series 1820-1830.

Hastings (See Historical Manuscripts Commission).

Heron, Sir Robert. *Notes.* 2nd Ed. Grantham 1851.

Herries, J. C.

Historical Manuscripts Commission
　Report on the MSS of Earl Bathurst. 1913.
　Report on the MSS of J. B. Fortescue at Dropmore
　(cited as 'Dropmore'), Vol. X. 1915.
　Report on the MSS of R. R. Hastings. 1934.

Huskisson, Rt. Hon. William. *The Huskisson Papers*,
　1792-1830. (ed. L. Melville). London 1931.

——*Speeches* (*with a biographical memoir*). 3 Vols. London
　1831.

Leveson-Gower, G. (1st Earl Granville). *Private Corres-
　pondence*, 1781-1821. (ed. Castalia, Countess Gran-
　ville). London 1916.

Lieven, Princess. *The Private Letters of Princess Lieven*

to Prince Metternich, 1820-6 (ed. P. Quennell). London 1937.

MacLeod, Henry D. *The Theory and Practice of Banking*. 5th Ed. London 1893.

Memoir of Lord Liverpool. London 1827.

Newton, J. F. *Early Days of the Rt. Hon. George Canning*, London 1828.

Oldfield, T. H. B. *The Representative History of Great Britain and Ireland*. 6 Vols. London 1816.

Parker, C. S. (See Peel).

Parliamentary Papers:
  Report from the Select Committee . . . on the High Price of Gold Bullion. 1810 (349) III.1.
  Reports . . . on the Resumption of Cash Payments. 1819 (202, 282) III.1; 1819 (291) III.363.
  Report . . . on the circulation of the country by the various Banking Establishments issuing notes payable on demand. 1840 (602) IV.1; 1841 (366) V.1; 1841 (410) V.5.
  Report on the Reorganization of the Civil Service. 1854-5 XX.1.

Peel, Rt. Hon. Sir Robert. *Sir R. Peel . . . from his private correspondence* (ed. C. S. Parker). London 1891.

Pellew, Hon. George. *The Life and Correspondence of the Rt. Hon. Henry Addington, First Viscount Sidmouth.* 3 Vols. London 1847.

Phipps, E. *Memoirs of the political and literary life of R. P. Ward.* London 1850.

Ricardo, David. *Letters to J. R. McCulloch* (ed. J. R. Hollander). New York 1895.

——*Letters to T. R. Malthus* (ed. J. Bonar). Oxford 1887.

——*Letters to Hutches Trower* (ed. J. Bonar and J. R. Hollander). Oxford 1899.

[Russell, Lord John]. *Essays and Sketches of Life and Character.* By a gentleman who has left his lodgings. London 1820.

Smith, Henry Stooks. *The register of parliamentary contested elections.* London 1814.

Southey, Robert. *Essays, moral and political.* 2 Vols. London 1832.

Stapleton, A. G. *The Political Life of George Canning.* 2nd Ed. 3 Vols. London 1831.

——*George Canning and his times.* London 1859.

Stapleton, E. J. *Some official correspondence of George Canning.* London 1887.

Tooke, Thomas. *A letter to Lord Grenville on the effects ascribed to the resumption of cash payments on the value of the currency.* London 1829.

——*A History of prices and of the state of the circulation from 1793 to 1856.* 6 Vols. London 1838-57.

Twiss, H. *Life of Lord Chancellor Eldon.* 3 Vols. London 1844.

Wellesley, Marquess, *The Wellesley Papers.* 2 Vols. (ed. L. Melville). London 1914.

Wellington, Duke of, *Supplementary despatches, correspondence and memoranda, 1794-1818.* (ed. by his son). *New Series* begins 1819. London 1858-72.

Yonge, C. D., *Life and Administration of Robert Banks, Second Earl of Liverpool.* 3 Vols. London 1868.

INDEX

THE LOEB CLASSICAL LIBRARY

SAINT BASIL

THE LETTERS

SAINT BASIL

THE LETTERS

WITH AN ENGLISH TRANSLATION BY

ROY J. DEFERRARI, Ph.D.

OF THE CATHOLIC UNIVERSITY OF AMERICA

IN FOUR VOLUMES

II

LONDON : WILLIAM HEINEMANN
NEW YORK : G. P. PUTNAM'S SONS
MCMXXVIII

Printed in Great Britain

PREFATORY NOTE

ST. BASIL'S letters in the present volume include numbers LIX to CLXXXV, and in nearly every case are of great human interest. Highly technical letters, as, for example, on the Trinity or on the Canons, do not appear.

All of the letters included here, with the exception of numbers LXIV and CII, appear in the MS. known as Coislinianus 237 (sig.=E). No letter of this volume, however, appears in any of the other MSS. collated by the author, *i.e.* Parisinus 506 (A), Parisinus 763 S (B), Parisinus 967 (C), Parisinus 1021 S (D), and Parisinus 1020 S (F). The last-named MS. (F), noted in the Benedictine edition as Harlaeanus, has since the time of that edition been greatly curtailed, a large portion at the end having been destroyed. This accounts for the appearance of readings from that MS. as noted by the Benedictine editors, and not as my own collations. Other important or interesting readings from the edition of the Benedictines have also been included in the critical apparatus. One probably important fact has been noted in the process of this work : the Benedictine editors frequently quoted readings as found only in the earlier editions (*editi antiqui*), and apparently without any MS. authority, but our collation of E has shown most of these readings to exist also in that MS.

PREFATORY NOTE

I am greatly indebted to the members of my Greek seminar of the years 1925–26 and 1926–27, with whom many of these letters were made an object of special study, for much assistance in bringing this second volume to a completion. In a special manner, I wish to acknowledge my indebtedness also to Mr. Martin R. McGuire, Instructor in Greek and Latin of the Catholic University of America.

Roy J. Deferrari.

NOTE ON LETTER VIII

Although the question of the authenticity of Letter VIII had been raised at times, and Abbé Bessières had called attention to a rather weak manuscript tradition for it in the Basilian corpus, no one had given the matter any serious attention. It remained for Robert Melcher in an article entitled "Der 8 Brief des hl. Basilius, ein Werk des Evagrius Pontikus" (*Münsterische Beiträge zur Theologie*, Heft 1, 1923),[1] to treat the subject for the first time in a definitive manner. The Very Reverend Melcher not only demonstrates convincingly that the letter does not belong to St. Basil, but makes a strong case for assigning it to Evagrius and for dating it toward the end of the fourth century. He approaches his problem from the strictly philological and historical point of view, and especially from the view-point of theological content.

---

[1] I regret that this important monograph did not come to my attention until Vol. I was well through press.

CONTENTS

CONTENTS

CONTENTS

CONTENTS

CONTENTS

CONTENTS

CONTENTS

CONTENTS

COLLECTED LETTERS OF
SAINT BASIL

ΤΟΥ ΕΝ ΑΓΙΟΙΣ ΠΑΤΡΟΣ ΗΜΩΝ ΒΑΣΙΛΕΙΟΥ ΕΠΙΣΤΟΛΑΙ

LIX

Γρηγορίῳ θείῳ

Ἐσιώπησα. μὴ καὶ ἀεὶ σιωπήσομαι, καὶ ἀνέξομαι ἐπὶ πλεῖον τὴν δυσφορωτάτην ζημίαν τῆς
σιωπῆς κυρῶσαι κατ' ἐμαυτοῦ[1] μήτε αὐτὸς ἐπιστέλλων, μήτε ἀκούων προσφθεγγομένου; ἐγὼ
μὲν γὰρ μέχρι τοῦ παρόντος ἐγκαρτερήσας τῷ
σκυθρωπῷ τούτῳ δόγματι, ἡγοῦμαι πρέπειν
κἀμοὶ τὰ τοῦ προφήτου λέγειν· ὅτι Ἐκαρτέρησα
ὡς ἡ τίκτουσα, ἀεὶ μὲν ἐπιθυμῶν ἢ συντυχίας
ἢ λόγων,[2] ἀεὶ δὲ ἀποτυγχάνων διὰ τὰς ἁμαρτίας
τὰς ἐμαυτοῦ. οὐ γὰρ δὴ ἄλλην τινὰ αἰτίαν
ἔχω τοῖς γινομένοις ἐπινοεῖν,[3] πλήν γε δὴ τοῦ

---

[1] Paulo post Harl. τὰ αὐτὰ τῷ προφήτῃ.
[2] λόγου E.   [3] εἰπεῖν duo MSS.

---

[1] Written at about the same time as the preceding letter,
in 371. The subject matter is likewise the same as that of
Letter LVIII. Basil's uncle Gregory, bishop of an unknown
see, was in sympathy with the disaffected bishops of Basil's
province. Gregory of Nyssa, in an effort to bring about a
reconciliation between his uncle and brother, went so far
as to forge more than one letter in the name of the uncle.
This crude counterfeit, when discovered, naturally increased

2

COLLECTED LETTERS OF SAINT BASIL

LETTER LIX

To Gregory, his Uncle[1]

I HAVE kept silence. But shall I always keep
silence, and shall I endure[2] still longer to impose
upon myself the most unbearable punishment of
silence, by neither writing myself nor hearing the
greeting of another? For having up to the present
time persevered in this sullen resolution, I believe
that it is fitting to apply the words of the prophet[3]
to myself also: "I have been patient as a woman in
labour," always longing for an interview or a discussion with you, but always failing to obtain them
on account of my sins. For I certainly cannot
imagine any other reason for what is happening,
except that, as I am convinced, I am paying the

the bitter feeling between the two, which was overcome
later only with difficulties.

[2] Cf. Isa. 42. 14. The reading of the Septuagint according
to Swete (Cambridge, 1912) is: ἐσιώπησα, μὴ καὶ ἀεὶ σιωπήσομαι
καὶ ἀνέξομαι; ὡς ἡ τίκτουσα ἐκαρτέρησα, ἐκστήσω καὶ ξηρανῶ
ἅμα. The Douay Version, which is clearly based on a
different text, reads: "I have always held my peace, I have
kept silence, I have been patient, I will speak now as a
woman in labour: I will destroy, and swallow up at
once."

[3] Cf. note 2 above.

πεπεῖσθαι παλαιῶν ἁμαρτημάτων ἐκτιννύειν
δίκας, ἐν τῷ χωρισμῷ τῆς ἀγάπης σου· εἰ δὴ
καὶ ὀνομάζειν χωρισμὸν ὅσιον ἐπὶ σοῦ καὶ οὐτι-
νοσοῦν τῶν τυχόντων, μὴ ὅτι γε ἡμῶν, οἷς ἐξ
ἀρχῆς ἐν πατρὸς γέγονας χώρα.

Ἀλλ᾽ ἡ ἁμαρτία μου νῦν, οἷα νεφέλη βαθεῖά
τις ἐπισχοῦσα, πάντων ἐκείνων ἄγνοιαν ἐνεποίησεν. ὅταν γὰρ ἀπίδω, πλὴν τοῦ ἐμοὶ λύπην
τὸ γινόμενον φέρειν, μηδὲν ἕτερον ἐξ αὐτοῦ
κατορθούμενον,[1] πῶς οὐχὶ εἰκότως ταῖς ἐμαυτοῦ
κακίαις ἀνατίθημι τὰ παρόντα; ἀλλ᾽ εἴτε
ἁμαρτίαι τῶν συμβάντων αἴτιαι, τοῦτό μοι
πέρας ἔστω τῶν δυσχερῶν· εἴτε τι[2] οἰκονομούμενον ἦν, ἐξεπληρώθη πάντως τὸ σπουδαζόμενον.
οὐ γὰρ ὀλίγος ὁ τῆς ζημίας χρόνος. διό, μηκέτι
στέγων, πρῶτος ἔρρηξα φωνήν, παρακαλῶν ἡμῶν
τε αὐτῶν ἀναμνησθῆναι καὶ σεαυτοῦ, ὃς πλέον
ἢ κατὰ τὸ τῆς συγγενείας εἰκὸς παρὰ πάντα τὸν
βίον τὴν κηδεμονίαν ἡμῶν ἐπεδείξω, καὶ τὴν
πόλιν νῦν ἡμῶν ἕνεκεν ἀγαπᾶν, ἀλλὰ μὴ δι᾽
ἡμᾶς ἀλλοτριοῦν σαυτὸν τῆς πόλεως.

Εἴ τις οὖν παράκλησις ἐν Χριστῷ, εἴ τις
κοινωνία Πνεύματος, εἴ τινα[3] σπλάγχνα καὶ
οἰκτιρμοί, πλήρωσον ἡμῶν τὴν εὐχήν· ἐνταῦθα
στῆσον τὰ κατηφῆ, ἀρχήν τινα δὸς τοῖς φαιδρο-
τέροις πρὸς τὸ ἑξῆς, αὐτὸς τοῖς ἄλλοις καθη-
γούμενος[4] ἐπὶ τὰ βέλτιστα, ἀλλ᾽ οὐχὶ ἀκολουθῶν
ἑτέρῳ[4] ἐφ᾽ ἃ μὴ δεῖ. καὶ γὰρ οὐδὲ σώματος

[1] κατορθούμενον, πῶς οὐχί] κατορθούμενος, πῶς οὐκ editi antiqi.
[2] τό add. editi ; om. E.   [3] τινα] τις E.
[4] ἑτέροις Harl.

4

penalty for my old offences in this separation from your love—if indeed it is not sacrilege to use the word "separation" in connexion with you and anybody in the world, much less in connexion with ourself, for whom, from the first, you have taken a father's place.

But now my guilt, having spread over me like a heavy cloud, has caused me to be ignorant of all this. For when I consider that no other result of what is happening, except its bringing sorrow to me, is satisfactory, how can I in all reason help ascribing the present state of affairs to my own wickedness? But if sins are answerable for what has taken place, let this be the end of my difficulties; or if some sort of discipline was intended, the object has been completely fulfilled. For not short is the time of my punishment. Therefore, containing myself no longer, I have been the first to speak out, exhorting you to be mindful both of us and of yourself, who throughout our whole life have shown greater solicitude for us than the nature of our relationship requires, and also at this time to cherish the city for our sake, instead of alienating yourself from the city[1] on account of us.

If, then, there is any consolation in Christ, if there is any communion of the Spirit, if there is any compassion and pity, fulfil our prayer: Here and now put an end to our dejection, grant some beginning to greater cheerfulness for the future, yourself guiding the rest of us to the best course, but not following another to what is wrong. For indeed

---

[1] *i.e.* Caesarea. Basil, on being elevated to the metropolitan see of Caesarea, was very anxious to secure the support of the various bishops, among them his uncle Gregory, who was in sympathy with the bishops of the opposition.

COLLECTED LETTERS OF SAINT BASIL

χαρακτὴρ ἴδιος οὕτω τινὸς ἐνομίσθη, ὡς τῆς σῆς
ψυχῆς τὸ εἰρηνικόν τε καὶ ἥμερον. πρέποι[1] δ᾽
ἂν οὖν τῷ τοιούτῳ τοὺς ἄλλους ἕλκειν πρὸς
ἑαυτόν, καὶ παρέχειν πᾶσι τοῖς ἐγγίζουσί σοι,
ὥσπερ μύρου τινὸς εὐωδίας, τῆς τοῦ σοῦ τρόπου
χρηστότητος ἀναπίμπλασθαι. καὶ γὰρ εἴ τι
καὶ ἀντιτεῖνόν ἐστι νῦν, ἀλλὰ μικρὸν ὕστερον
καὶ αὐτὸ τὸ τῆς εἰρήνης ἀγαθὸν ἐπιγνώσεται.
ἕως δ᾽ ἂν ἐκ τῆς διαστάσεως αἱ διαβολαὶ χώραν
ἔχωσιν, ἀνάγκη ἀεὶ τὰς ὑποψίας ἐπὶ τὸ χεῖρον
συναύξεσθαι. ἔστι μὲν οὖν οὐδὲ ἐκείνοις πρέπον
ἀμελεῖν ἡμῶν, πάντων δὲ πλέον τῇ τιμιότητί
σου. καὶ γὰρ εἰ μὲν ἁμαρτάνομέν τι, βελτίους
ἐσόμεθα νουθετούμενοι. τοῦτο δὲ ἄνευ συντυχίας
ἀμήχανον. εἰ δὲ οὐδὲν ἀδικούμεν, ἀντὶ τίνος
μισούμεθα; ταῦτα μὲν δὴ οὖν[2] τὰ τῆς ἰδίας
ἐμαυτοῦ δικαιολογίας[3] προΐσχομαι.

Ἃ δ᾽ ἂν ὑπὲρ ἑαυτῶν αἱ ἐκκλησίαι εἴποιεν, οὐκ
εἰς καλὸν τῆς διαστάσεως ἡμῶν ἀπολαύουσαι,
βέλτιον μὲν[4] σιωπᾶν. οὐ γὰρ ἵνα λυπήσω τοῖς
λόγοις κέχρημαι τούτοις,[5] ἀλλ᾽ ἵνα παύσω τὰ
λυπηρά. τὴν δὲ σὴν σύνεσιν πάντως οὐδὲν δια-
πέφευγεν· ἀλλὰ πολλῷ μείζω καὶ τελειότερα
ὧν ἡμεῖς νοοῦμεν αὐτὸς ἂν ἐξεύροις τῇ διανοίᾳ,
καὶ ἄλλοις εἴποις, ὅς γε[6] καὶ εἶδες πρὸ ἡμῶν
τὰς βλάβας τῶν ἐκκλησιῶν[7] καὶ λυπῇ μᾶλλον
ἡμῶν πάλαι δεδιδαγμένος[8] παρὰ τοῦ Κυρίου

[1] πρέπει Ε.   [2] δὴ οὖν om. Ε.
[3] διστολογίας editi antiqi.   [4] με Ε.
[5] τούτοις add. Ε ; om. editi.   [6] ὅς γε] ὥστε Ε.
[7] τὰς βλάβας τῶν ἐκκλησιῶν] τῶν ἐκκλησιῶν τὴν ζημίαν
alii MSS.

6

no trait of any man's body has been considered so characteristic of him as peacefulness and gentleness are characteristic of your soul. It would be meet, therefore, for a man of your character to draw others to himself, and to afford to all who approach you an opportunity of being filled with the excellence of your character as with the fragrance of some perfume. For even if there is now a certain opposition, still, in a little while, the goodness of peace will of itself be recognized. But so long as, because of the present dissension, slanders are given room, suspicions will necessarily ever increase for the worse. It is accordingly not becoming even for the men I have in mind to ignore us, but still less for your Honour. For if we do anything sinful, we shall become better by being admonished. But this is impossible without an interview. And if we do no wrong, why are we hated? Such, then, are the statements which I submit in my own justification.

What the churches might say in their own defence for the advantage they are basely taking of our dissension, it is better to pass over in silence. For it is not to cause pain that I have employed these words, but to put an end to that which causes pain. Your sagacity is such that nothing has escaped it; but you might, by using your powers of discernment, discover for yourself and relate to others much greater and more serious instances than those which we know, seeing that you must have noticed, before we did, the harm being done to the churches, and by a distress greater than ours must long since have

---

8 προδεδιδαγμένος editi antiqi.

μηδενὸς τῶν ἐλαχίστων καταφρονεῖν. νυνὶ δὲ
ἡ βλάβη οὐκ εἰς ἕνα ἢ δεύτερον περιορίζεται,
ἀλλὰ πόλεις ὅλαι καὶ δῆμοι τῶν ἡμετέρων
παραπολαύουσι συμφορῶν. τὴν γὰρ ἐπὶ τῆς
ὑπερορίας φήμην τί χρὴ καὶ λέγειν ὁποία τις
ἔσται περὶ ἡμῶν; πρέπει οὖν ἂν[1] τῇ σῇ μεγα-
λοψυχίᾳ τὸ μὲν φιλόνεικον ἑτέροις παραχωρεῖν·
μᾶλλον δὲ κἀκείνων ἐξελεῖν τῆς ψυχῆς, εἴπερ
οἷόν τε· αὐτὸν δὲ δι’ ἀνεξικακίας νικῆσαι τὰ
λυπηρά. τὸ μὲν γὰρ ἀμύνεσθαι παντός ἐστι
τοῦ ὀργιζομένου, τὸ δὲ καὶ αὐτῆς τῆς ὀργῆς
ὑψηλότερον εἶναι, τοῦτο δὴ μόνου σοῦ, καὶ εἴ
τίς σοι τὴν ἀρετὴν παραπλήσιος. ἐκεῖνο δὲ οὐκ
ἐρῶ, ὅτι ὁ ἡμῖν χαλεπαίνων εἰς τοὺς μηδὲν
ἀδικήσαντας τὴν ὀργὴν ἐπαφίησιν.

Εἴτε οὖν παρουσίᾳ, εἴτε γράμματι, εἴτε κλήσει
τῇ πρὸς ἑαυτόν, εἴτε ᾧπερ ἂν ἐθέλοις τρόπῳ,
παραμύθησαι ἡμῶν τὴν ψυχήν.[2] ἡμῖν μὲν γὰρ
εὐχὴ ἐπὶ τῆς Ἐκκλησίας φανῆναι τὴν θεοσέβειάν
σου, καὶ ἡμᾶς τε ὁμοῦ καὶ τὸν λαὸν θεραπεῦσαι
αὐτῇ τε τῇ ὄψει καὶ τοῖς λόγοις τῆς χάριτός
σου. ἐὰν μὲν οὖν τοῦτο ᾖ δυνατόν, τοῦτο κρά-
τιστον· ἐὰν δέ τι ἕτερον δόξῃ, κἀκεῖνο δεξόμεθα.
μόνον παγίως γνωρίσαι ἡμῖν τὸ παριστάμενον
τῇ φρονήσει σου παρακλήθητι.

LETTER LIX

been taught by the Lord to despise not even the least.[1] Now, however, the harm is not confined to one or two men, but whole cities and peoples get the benefit, indirectly, of our misfortunes. For as to what the talk concerning us will be beyond our borders, why need I speak of it? Therefore it would be becoming in your Magnanimity to leave contentiousness to others; nay rather, to pluck it even from their hearts if it is at all possible, and yourself through your forbearance to vanquish this painful state of affairs. For whereas the taking of revenge is appropriate to anyone who is aroused to anger, yet to rise superior to anger itself belongs in truth to you alone or to any man who may be like you in virtue. This, however, I shall forbear to say—that he who is wroth with us is letting his rage fall on those who have done nothing wrong.

Accordingly, either by your presence, or by a letter, or by an invitation to visit you, or by whatever way you may wish, pray comfort our soul. For our prayer is that your Reverence may be seen in our Church, and that you may heal at once both ourselves and the people by your very presence and by the words of your grace. If this, then, is possible, it will be best; but if something else may seem best to you, we shall accept it also. Only yield to our request to inform us exactly as to what your prudence decides.

[1] Cf. Matt. 18. 10. ὁρᾶτε μὴ καταφρονήσητε ἑνὸς τῶν μικρῶν τούτων. "See that you despise not one of these little ones."

---

[1] ἄν om. E.

[2] παραμύθησαι ἡμῶν τὴν ψυχήν] παραμυθῆσαι ἡμῶν τὴν ψυχὴν καταξίωσον editi antiqi, Harl.

9

LX

Γρηγορίῳ θείῳ

Καὶ πρότερον ἡδέως εἶδον τὸν ἀδελφόν μου.
τί γὰρ οὐκ ἔμελλον, ἀδελφόν τε ὄντα ἐμαυτοῦ,
καὶ τοιοῦτον; καὶ νῦν[1] τῇ αὐτῇ διαθέσει προσε-
δεξάμην ἐπιδημήσαντα, μηδέν τι τῆς ἐμαυτοῦ
στοργῆς παρατρέψας. μηδὲ γὰρ γένοιτό τι
τοιοῦτο παθεῖν μηδέν, ὅ με τῆς φύσεως ἐπιλαθέσθαι καὶ ἐκπολεμωθῆναι πρὸς τοὺς οἰκείους
ποιήσει. ἀλλὰ καὶ τῶν τοῦ σώματος ἀρρωστημάτων, καὶ τῶν ἄλλων ἀλγεινῶν τῆς ψυχῆς,
παραμυθίαν ἡγησάμην[2] εἶναι τὴν τοῦ ἀνδρὸς
παρουσίαν· τοῖς τε παρὰ τῆς τιμιότητός[3] σου
δι᾽ αὐτοῦ κομισθεῖσι γράμμασιν ὑπερήσθην· ἃ
καὶ ἐκ πολλοῦ μοι ἐπεθύμουν ἐλθεῖν, οὐκ ἄλλου
τινὸς ἕνεκεν ἢ τοῦ μὴ καὶ ἡμᾶς τι[4] σκυθρωπὸν
διήγημα τῷ βίῳ προσθεῖναι, ὡς ἄρα τις εἴη
τοῖς οἰκειοτάτοις πρὸς ἀλλήλους διάστασις,
ἡδονὴν μὲν ἐχθροῖς παρασκευάζουσα, φίλοις δὲ
συμφοράν, ἀπαρέσκουσα δὲ Θεῷ, τῷ ἐν τῇ
τελείᾳ ἀγάπῃ τὸν χαρακτῆρα τῶν ἑαυτοῦ μα-
θητῶν θεμένῳ. διὸ καὶ ἀντιφθέγγομαι ἀναγκαίως
εὔχεσθαί σε ὑπὲρ ἡμῶν παρακαλῶν, καὶ τὰ
ἄλλα κήδεσθαι ἡμῶν ὡς οἰκείων.

Τὸν δὲ νοῦν τῶν γινομένων[5] ἐπειδὴ αὐτοὶ
ὑπὸ ἀμαθείας συνιέναι[6] οὐκ ἔχομεν, ἐκεῖνον ἐ-

---

[1] δέ editi et MSS., om. E.
[2] αὐταρκεστάτην add. Med. et Harl.
[3] κοσμιότητος E.   [4] τι om. E.
[5] τῶν γεγραμμένων alii MSS.   [6] ἀμαθίας συνεῖναι E.

LETTER LX

To Gregory, his Uncle[1]

In times past I have always been glad to see my brother. Why should I not have been, since he is not only my brother but such a man! And at the present time I have welcomed him on his visit in the same mind, having in no wise altered my affection for him. May no such misfortune ever befall me as would cause me to forget the ties of nature, and be set at enmity with my own kindred. On the contrary, I have considered the man's presence to be a consolation both for the ills of the body and for the afflictions of the soul as well; and I was exceedingly pleased with the letter from your Honour which he delivered, a letter which I had long been eager to receive, for one sole reason—that we might not, as others have done, attach to our lives a melancholy story of a quarrel which divided the nearest and dearest from one another, a quarrel which would afford pleasure to our enemies and be a calamity to our friends, and would also be displeasing to God, who has defined the distinguishing mark of His disciples as perfect love. Therefore I feel myself constrained to repeat my request that you pray for us, and that you in general care for us as your kinsman.

As for the significance of what has happened,[2] since we ourselves through our ignorance cannot

---

[1] Of the same date and on the same general topic as the preceding letter.

[2] Cf. Letter LIX, note 1.

κρίναμεν ἀληθῆ εἶναι νομίζειν, ὃν ἂν αὐτὸς ἡμῖν
ἐξηγήσασθαι καταξιώσῃς. ἀνάγκη δὲ καὶ τὰ
λειπόμενα παρὰ τῆς σῆς μεγαλονοίας ὁρισθῆναι,
τὴν συντυχίαν ἡμῶν τὴν πρὸς ἀλλήλους, καὶ καιρὸν τὸν πρέποντα, καὶ τόπον ἐπιτήδειον. εἴπερ οὖν
ὅλως ἀνέχεται καταβῆναι πρὸς τὴν ταπείνωσιν
ἡμῶν ἡ σεμνότης σου, καὶ λόγου τινὸς μεταδοῦναι
ἡμῖν, εἴτε[1] μετ' ἄλλων, εἴτε κατὰ σεαυτὸν βούλει
γενέσθαι τὴν συντυχίαν, ὑπακουσόμεθα, τοῦτο
ἅπαξ ἑαυτοῖς συμβουλεύσαντες, δουλεύειν[2] σοι
ἐν ἀγάπῃ καὶ ποιεῖν ἐκ παντὸς τρόπου τὰ εἰς
δόξαν Θεοῦ παρὰ τῆς εὐλαβείας σου ἡμῖν ἐπι-
τασσόμενα.[3]

Τὸν δὲ αἰδεσιμώτατον ἀδελφὸν οὐδὲν ἠναγκάσα-
μεν ἀπὸ γλώττης εἰπεῖν ἡμῖν· διότι οὔτε[4] πρότερον
μεμαρτυρημένον εἶχε τὸν λόγον ὑπὸ τῶν ἔργων.

LXI

Ἀθανασίῳ, ἐπισκόπῳ Ἀλεξανδρείας[5]

Ἐνέτυχον τοῖς γράμμασι τῆς σῆς ὁσιότητος, δι'
ὧν τοῦ ἡγεμόνος τῆς Λιβύης, τοῦ δυσωνύμου
ἀνδρός, κατεστέναξας. καὶ ὠδυράμεθα μὲν τὴν
ἡμετέραν[6] πατρίδα, ὅτι τοιούτων κακῶν μήτηρ
ἐστὶ καὶ τροφός· ὠδυράμεθα δὲ καὶ τὴν γείτονα

---

[1] καί add. E. [2] δουλεύειν editi antiqi.
[3] γραφόμενα E. [4] τό add. E.
[5] τῷ μεγάλῳ Ἀθανασίῳ editi antiqi.
[6] ἡμετέραν] ἑαυτοῦ editi antiqi.

---

[1] Written about the year 371. This is the first of six
extant letters written by St. Basil to the famous St.

comprehend it, we have decided to accept as true
whatever explanation you have deigned to give us.
But the matters which still remain must also be
determined by your Magnanimity—our interview
with each other, a suitable occasion, and a convenient place. So if your lofty dignity can at all
endure to descend to our lowliness and to grant us
some speech with you, then, whether you desire our
interview to be private or in the presence of others,
we shall answer the summons, inasmuch as we have
decided once and for all upon this course for ourself—
to serve you in love and in every way to do whatever,
to the glory of God, your Reverence enjoins upon us.

As to our most venerable brother, we have not
constrained him to tell us anything by word of
mouth; the reason is that his words on a former
occasion were not attested by the facts.

LETTER LXI

To Athanasius, Bishop of Alexandria [1]

I have read the letters of your Holiness, in which
you have expressed your grief at the conduct of the
governor of Libya, that man of evil name. We also
have mourned for our country [2] because she is the
mother and nurse of such evils; and we have

Athanasius. Basil is here answering a letter in which
Athanasius announced that he had excommunicated a vicious
governor of Libya, a native of Cappadocia. The remaining
five letters from Basil to Athanasius (LXVI, LXVII, LXIX,
LXXX, LXXXII) deal with the much more important
matter of the union of the churches.

[2] Cf. Homer, *Od.* 13. 219: ὁ δ' ὀδύρετο πατρίδα γαῖαν.

τῆς ἡμετέρας [1] Λιβύην, τῶν ἡμετέρων κακῶν
ἀπολαύουσαν,[2] καὶ θηριώδει ἤθει παραδοθεῖσαν
ἀνδρὸς ὠμότητί τε ὁμοῦ καὶ ἀκολασίᾳ συζῶντος.
τοῦτο ἦν ἄρα τοῦ Ἐκκλησιαστοῦ τὸ σοφόν· Οὐαί
σοι, πόλις, ἧς ὁ βασιλεύς σου νεώτερος (ἐνταῦθα
δέ ἐστί τι καὶ χαλεπώτερον), καὶ οἱ ἄρχοντές σου
οὐκ [3] ἀπὸ νυκτὸς ἐσθίουσιν, ἀλλὰ μεσούσης τῆς
ἡμέρας ἀκολασταίνουσι, βοσκημάτων ἀλογώτερον
ἀλλοτρίοις γάμοις ἐπιμαινόμενοι! ἐκεῖνον μὲν
οὖν αἱ μάστιγες μένουσι παρὰ τοῦ δικαίου κριτοῦ,
τῷ ἴσῳ μέτρῳ ἀντιμετρηθησόμεναι, ἃς αὐτὸς
προλαβὼν ἐπέθηκε τοῖς ἁγίοις αὐτοῦ.

Ἐγνωρίσθη δὲ καὶ τῇ ἐκκλησίᾳ ἡμῶν ἐκ τῶν
γραμμάτων τῆς σῆς θεοσεβείας, καὶ ἀποτρόπαιον
αὐτὸν πάντες ἡγήσονται,[4] μὴ πυρός, μὴ ὕδατος,
μὴ [5] σκέπης αὐτῷ κοινωνοῦντες, εἴπερ τι ὄφελος
τοῖς οὕτω κεκρατημένοις κοινῆς καὶ ὁμοψήφου
καταγνώσεως. ἀρκοῦσα δὲ αὐτῷ στήλη, καὶ
αὐτὰ τὰ γράμματα ἀναγινωσκόμενα πανταχοῦ.
οὐ γὰρ διαλείψομεν πᾶσιν αὐτοῦ καὶ οἰκείοις καὶ
φίλοις καὶ ξένοις ἐπιδεικνύντες· πάντως δέ, κἂν
μὴ ἅψωνται αὐτοῦ παραχρῆμα τὰ ἐπιτίμια, ὥσπερ
τοῦ Φαραώ, ἀλλ᾽ εἰς ὕστερόν ποτε βαρεῖαν αὐτῷ
καὶ ἀλγεινὴν τὴν ἀνάδοσιν [6] οἴσει.

---

[1] ὑμετέρας E.   [2] ἀπολαύσασαν E.
[3] οὐχί E.   [4] ἡγήσαντο E.
[5] δέ add. E (supra m [1a]).   [6] ἀντίδοσιν editi antiqi.

mourned, too, for our neighbouring land of Libya, which shares in these evils of ours, and has been delivered over to the brutal character of a man who spends his life equally in cruelty and licentiousness. This, then, it would seem, was the meaning of the wise saying of Ecclesiastes:[1] "Woe to thee, O land, when thy king is a child, and"—here is something even more severe—"when thy princes eat" not at night, but they revel licentiously at mid-day, being mad after the wives of others, more irrationally than cattle! Now as for him, the scourges of a just Judge await him, and they shall be meted out to him in an equal measure with those which he himself has already inflicted upon His saints.

He has become known to our Church also through the letter of your Reverence, and all men will account him abominable, sharing with him neither fire, nor water, nor shelter; if in truth anything can be of avail to those who have thus won for themselves a common and unanimous condemnation. But sufficient for him is a published bulletin, and your letter itself read everywhere. For we shall not cease to show it to everyone who has to do with him, to relatives or family or strangers. At all events, even if the penalties imposed do not lay hold upon him immediately, even as upon the Pharaoh,[2] nevertheless at some later time they will bring upon him a heavy and grievous increment.

---

[1] Ecclesiastes 10. 16. Basil greatly expands the last part of this quotation. οὐαί σοι, πόλις, ἧς ὁ βασιλεύς σου νεώτερος, καὶ οἱ ἄρχοντές σου πρωὶ ἐσθίουσιν. "Woe to thee, O land, when thy king is a child, and when the princes eat in the morning."

[2] An allusion to the plagues and the final destruction of the Pharaoh as described in Exodus.

LXII

Τῇ Ἐκκλησίᾳ Παρνασσοῦ παραμυθητική

Καὶ ἔθει ἑπόμενοι παλαιῷ ἐκ μακρᾶς τῆς ἀκολουθίας κεκρατηκότι, καὶ τὸν καρπὸν τοῦ Πνεύματος, τὴν κατὰ Θεὸν ἀγάπην, ὑμῖν ἐπιδεικνύμενοι,
διὰ τοῦ γράμματος τὴν εὐλάβειαν ὑμῶν ἐπισκεπ-
τόμεθα, κοινωνοῦντες ὑμῖν τῆς τε ἐπὶ τῷ συμβάντι
λύπης, καὶ τῆς φροντίδος τῶν ἐν χερσίν. ὑπὲρ
μὲν οὖν τῶν λυπηρῶν τοσοῦτον λέγομεν, ὅτι καιρὸς
ἡμῖν ἀποβλέψαι πρὸς τὰ τοῦ Ἀποστόλου παραγ-
γέλματα, καὶ μὴ λυπεῖσθαι Ὡς καὶ οἱ λοιποί, οἱ
μὴ ἔχοντες ἐλπίδα· οὐ μὴν οὐδ᾽ ἀπαθῶς ἔχειν
πρὸς τὸ συμβάν, ἀλλὰ τῆς μὲν ζημίας αἰσθάνεσθαι,
ὑπὸ δὲ τῆς λύπης μὴ καταπίπτειν, τὸν μὲν ποιμένα τοῦ τέλους μακαρίζοντας, ὡς ἐν γήρᾳ πίονι
τὴν ζωὴν καταλύσαντα, καὶ ταῖς μεγίσταις παρὰ
τοῦ Κυρίου τιμαῖς ἐναναπαυσάμενον.

Περὶ δὲ τῶν λοιπῶν ἐκεῖνα παραινεῖν ἔχομεν,
ὅτι προσήκει, πᾶσαν ἀποθεμένους κατήφειαν,
ἑαυτῶν γενέσθαι, καὶ πρὸς τὴν ἀναγκαίαν πρό-
νοιαν τῆς Ἐκκλησίας διαναστῆναι, ὅπως ἂν ὁ
ἅγιος Θεὸς ἐπιμεληθείη τοῦ ἰδίου ποιμνίου, καὶ
παράσχοιτο ὑμῖν ποιμένα κατὰ τὸ αὐτοῦ θέλημα,
ποιμαίνοντα ὑμᾶς μετ᾽ ἐπιστήμης.

---

[1] This letter, written ostensibly to console the people of
Parnassus on the loss of their bishop, was composed, according to Maran (*Vita S. Basilii*, xvi), before the visit of
Valens in 372, which gave the Arians of this church such
power. Parnassus was a town in Northern Cappadocia, on
the right bank of the Halys, at a ford a few miles higher up
than modern Tchikin Aghyl. The real purpose of this letter
was to urge the Parnassenes to elect an orthodox bishop.

LETTER LXII

CONSOLATION TO THE CHURCH OF PARNASSUS [1]

FOLLOWING an old custom which has become prevalent through a long observance, and also making
manifest to you the fruit of the Holy Ghost, which
is the divine love, we visit your Piety by letter,
sharing with you both your grief at what has
befallen and your anxiety concerning the matters
now at hand. In regard to these painful circumstances, then, we have only this to say—that it is
seasonable for us to fix our gaze upon the exhorta-
tions of the Apostle,[2] and not to be sorrowful "even
as others who have no hope"; we should not, however, be indifferent to what has occurred, but while
being sensible of our loss, we should not be overcome
by our grief, accounting our shepherd happy for his
end, as having left this life at a ripe old age,[3] and as
having gone to rest amid the highest honours the
Lord can give.

As for the rest, we must admonish you that, after
you have put away all sorrow, you should become
your own masters, and should rise up and face your
unavoidable duty of providing for the Church, to the
end that the holy God may assume charge over His
flock, and, in accordance with His will, may supply
you with a shepherd who will tend you wisely.

This they did in the person of Hypsis (or Hypsinus), whom
the Arians expelled in 375 in favour of a certain Ecdicius.
Cf. Letter CCXXXVII.
[2] Thess. 4. 13.
[3] Cf. Homer, *Odyssey*, 19. 367-8: ἀρώμενος εἶος ἵκοιο | γῆράς
τε λιπαρὸν θρέψαιό τε φαίδιμον υἱόν. "With prayer that thou
mightest reach a sleek old age and rear thy glorious son."

LXIII

Ἡγεμόνι Νεοκαισαρείας

Τὸν σοφὸν ἄνδρα, κἂν ἑκὰς ναίῃ χθονός, κἂν μήποτ' αὐτὸν ὄσσοις προσίδω, κρίνω φίλον· Εὐριπίδου ἐστὶ τοῦ τραγικοῦ λόγος. ὥστε, εἰ, μήπω τῆς κατ' ὀφθαλμοὺς ἡμῖν συντυχίας τὴν γνῶσίν σου τῆς μεγαλοφυΐας χαρισαμένης, φαμὲν εἶναι φίλοι σου καὶ συνήθεις, μὴ κολακείαν εἶναι[1] τὸν λόγον κρίνῃς. ἔχομεν γὰρ φήμην πρόξενον τῆς φιλίας, μεγαλοφώνως τὰ σὰ πᾶσιν[2] ἀνθρώποις συμβοῶσαν. ἀφ' οὗ μέντοι καὶ τῷ αἰδεσιμωτάτῳ Ἐλπιδίῳ[3] συνετύχομεν, τοσοῦτόν σε ἐγνωρίσαμεν, καὶ οὕτω κατ' ἄκρας ἑαλώκαμέν σου, ὡσανεὶ πολὺν χρόνον συγγεγονότες, καὶ διὰ μακρᾶς τῆς πείρας τῶν ἐν σοὶ καλῶν τὴν γνῶσιν ἔχοντες. οὐ γὰρ ἐπαύσατο ὁ ἀνὴρ ἕκαστα ἡμῖν τῶν περὶ σὲ διηγούμενος, τὸ μεγαλοπρεπὲς τῆς ψυχῆς, τοῦ φρονήματος τὸ ἀνάστημα, τῶν τρόπων τὴν ἡμερότητα, ἐμπειρίαν πραγμάτων, σύνεσιν γνώμης, σεμνότητα βίου φαιδρότητι[4] κεκραμένην, λόγου δύναμιν, τἄλλα ὅσα αὐτὸς μὲν διὰ πολλῆς τῆς πρὸς ἡμᾶς ὁμιλίας ἀπηριθμήσατο, ἡμῖν δὲ γράφειν οὐκ ἦν δυνατόν, ἵνα μὴ ἔξω τοῦ μέτρου τὴν

---

[1] εἶναι om. E.   [2] τὰ σὰ πᾶσιν] ἅπασιν E.
[3] Ἐλλαδίῳ E, Harl.   [4] φαιδρότητα E.

---

[1] Written about 371. Cf. Maran, *Vita S. Basilii*, xvi.
[2] From an unknown play of Euripides. Cf. Nauck, *Trag. Graec. Frag.*, No. 902: τὸν ἐσθλὸν ἄνδρα, κἂν ἑκὰς ναίῃ χθονός, κἂν μήποτ' ὄσσοις εἰσίδω, κρίνω φίλον. Note that Basil has σοφόν for ἐσθλόν For similar expressions, cf. Iamblichus,

LETTER LXIII

To the Governor of Neocaesarea [1]

"The wise man, e'en though he dwell in a distant
land, though I may never behold him with my eyes,
I account my friend," is a saying of the tragic poet
Euripides.[2]   If, therefore, in spite of the fact that
no face-to-face meeting has as yet given us the
pleasure of acquaintance with your Magnanimity,
we say that we are your friend and associate, do
not consider this assertion to be flattery.   For as
the promoter of our friendship we have Fame, who
with mighty voice proclaims your deeds to all mankind.   Ever since the day, moreover, on which we
met the most reverend Elpidius,[3] we have known you
to be so great a man, and we have been so utterly
captivated by you, as if we had been associated with
you for a long time, and had knowledge of your
noble qualities through long experience.   For Elpidius
did not cease recounting to us your every characteristic—your magnanimity, the loftiness of your spirit,
the gentleness of your manners, experience in affairs,[4]
sagacity of judgment, dignity of life mingled with
affability, ability as an orator, and the many other
qualities which he enumerated to us in the course
of a long conversation, but which we cannot mention
to you now without carrying the letter beyond its

de vita Pythag. 33. 237 ; Procop. Gaz., *Epist.*, 154 ; and Cicero,
de nat. deorum, 1. 44. 121.

[3] Note that some MSS. read Helladius.   In the following
letter, however, all MSS. agree on Elpidius.   Cf. also
Letters LXXVII and LXXVIII.   The Elpidii mentioned
herein may or may not be the same man.

[4] For the same expression, cf. Antiphon 5. 1 : τὴν ἐμπειρίαν
τῶν πραγμάτων.

ἐπιστολὴν προαγάγωμεν. πῶς οὖν οὐκ ἔμελλον
ἀγαπᾶν τὸν τοιοῦτον; πῶς γοῦν ἠδυνάμην
ἐμαυτοῦ κρατῆσαι, πρὸς τὸ μὴ οὐχὶ καὶ ἐκβοῶν
τὸ τῆς ψυχῆς ἐμαυτοῦ πάθος διασημαίνειν;

Δέχου τοίνυν τὴν προσηγορίαν, ὦ θαυμάσιε, ἐκ
φιλίας ἀληθινῆς καὶ ἀδόλου σοι προσαγομένην·
πόρρω γὰρ θωπείας δουλοπρεποῦς τὰ ἡμέτερα·
καὶ ἔχε ἡμᾶς τῷ καταλόγῳ τῶν σεαυτοῦ φίλων
ἐναριθμίους, γράμμασι συνεχέσι σαυτόν τε δεικνὺς
καὶ παραμυθούμενος τὴν ἀπόλειψιν.

LXIV

Ἡσυχίῳ

Ἐμὲ πολλὰ μὲν ἦν καὶ ἐξ ἀρχῆς τὰ συνάπτοντά
σου τῇ τιμιότητι, ὅ τε περὶ λόγους κοινὸς ἔρως,
πολλαχοῦ παρὰ τῶν πεπειραμένων περιφερόμενος,[1]
ἥ τε πρὸς τὸν θαυμάσιον ἄνδρα Τερέντιον[2] ἡμῖν
ἐκ παλαιοῦ φιλία. ἐπεὶ δὲ καὶ ὁ πάντα ἄριστος,
καὶ πάσης ἡμῖν οἰκειότητος ὄνομα ἐκπληρῶν, ὁ
αἰδεσιμώτατος ἀδελφὸς Ἐλπίδιος εἰς λόγους ἀφίκετο, καὶ ἕκαστα τῶν ἐν σοὶ καλῶν διηγήσατο
(δυνατώτατος δέ, εἴπερ τις ἄλλος, καὶ ἀρετὴν
ἀνθρώπου καταμαθεῖν, καὶ παραστῆσαι ταύτην

---

[1] συμπεριφερόμενος Codex Medicaeus.
[2] Τερεντῖνον editi antiqi.

---

[1] i.e. of "friend."
[2] i.e. for the lack of the Governor's personal presence.
[3] Dated with the preceding letter. Nothing is known of
this Hesychius, except such information as may be gathered
from the present letter and Letter LXXII.

proper limits. How, then, could I help loving such a man? How, at any rate, could I so far control myself as not with loud voice to make known my soul's emotion?

Accept, therefore, admirable sir, the appellation,[1] which is applied to you out of a friendship that is true and genuine; for our character is far removed from servile adulation; and do you keep us numbered in the roll of your friends, by frequent letters, both showing yourself to us and consoling us for the lack.[2]

LETTER LXIV

To Hesychius [3]

Even from the beginning there have been many things which have bound me to your Honour—your love of letters, common to me also, which is everywhere bruited abroad by men who have had experience of it, and our long-time friendship for that admirable man Terentius.[4] But when, too, that most excellent man, who satisfies the title of every intimate relationship with us,[5] our most venerated brother Elpidius,[6] conversed with us and described each of your noble qualities (and he, if any man, has superlative ability both to discern a man's virtues

[4] Terentius: a general and count of the orthodox faith. Cf. Letters XCIX, CCXIV, CCXVI. For a letter from Basil to the daughters of Terentius, deaconesses at Samosata, cf. Letter CV.

[5] Cf. *Iliad*, 6. 429–30: Ἕκτορ, ἀτὰρ σύ μοί ἐσσι πατὴρ καὶ πότνια μήτηρ | ἠδὲ κασίγνητος, σὺ δέ μοι θαλερὸς παρακοίτης. "Hector, truly thou art to me a father and revered mother, and brother, as thou art to me a goodly husband."

[6] Cf. Letter LXIII, note 3.

τῷ λόγῳ), τοσοῦτον ἡμῖν τὸν ἐπὶ σοὶ πόθον ἐξέ-
καυσεν, ὥστε εὔχεσθαι ἡμᾶς ἐπιστῆναί σέ ποτε
τῇ παλαιᾷ ἑστίᾳ ἡμῶν, ἵνα μὴ ἀκοῇ μόνον, ἀλλὰ
καὶ πείρᾳ τῶν ἐν σοὶ καλῶν ἀπολαύσωμεν.

LXV

Ἀταρβίῳ [1]

Καὶ τί πέρας ἔσται τῆς σιωπῆς, εἰ ἐγὼ μέν, τὰ ἐκ
τῆς ἡλικίας πρεσβεῖα ἀπαιτῶν, ἀναμένοιμι παρὰ
σοῦ γενέσθαι τὴν ἀρχὴν τῆς προσφωνήσεως, ἡ δὲ
σὴ ἀγάπη ἐπὶ πλεῖον βούλοιτο τῇ βλαβερᾷ κρίσει
τῆς ἡσυχίας [2] ἐγκαρτερεῖν; ἀλλ᾽ ὅμως ἐγώ, τὴν
ἐν τοῖς φιλικοῖς ἧτταν νίκης ἔχειν δύναμιν ἡγησάμενος, ὁμολογῶ σοι μὲν παραχωρεῖν τῆς ἐπὶ τῷ
δοκεῖν περιγενῆσθαι τῆς οἰκείας κρίσεως φιλοτι-
μίας. αὐτὸς δὲ πρῶτος ἐπὶ τὸ γράφειν ἦλθον,
εἰδὼς ὅτι ἡ ἀγάπη πάντα στέγει, πάντα ὑπομένει,
οὐδαμοῦ ζητεῖ τὸ ἑαυτῆς· διόπερ οὔτε [3] ἐκπίπτει
ποτέ. ἀταπείνωτος γὰρ ὁ κατὰ ἀγάπην τῷ πλη-

---

[1] Αὐταρκίῳ cod. Claromontanus.
[2] συκοφαντίας quinque MSS.   [3] οὐδέ E.

---

[1] Of the year 371, or, according to Maran, some time
before 373, when the enmity between Atarbius and Basil
became manifest. Atarbius was a bishop of Neocaesarea,
and probably related to Basil. Cf. Letter CCX. Letters
LXI, CXXVI, CCIV, CCVII, and CCX contain information
on this break, and subsequent effort on the part of Basil to
mend the breach and to rescue Atarbius from the errors of
Sabellianism. Tillemont wrongly makes Atarbius an Armenian bishop, but he belongs clearly to Neocaesarea, since
(1) he is so designated in some MSS. of St. Basil's letters;

and to make them known by speech), he enkindled in us such a longing for you, that we pray that you may some day visit this old fireside of ours, so that not only by report but by actual experience also we may derive pleasure from the noble qualities which reside in you.

LETTER LXV

To Atarbius[1]

WHAT end indeed would there be of our silence, if I should claim the prerogative of my age, and wait for you to take the initiative in salutation, but your Affection should wish to persevere still longer in its baneful resolution of keeping silent? However, since I consider that in matters of friendship defeat has the force of victory, I acknowledge that I am conceding to you what you make a point of—the appearance of having seemingly prevailed over my own judgment. But I myself have been the first to begin writing because I know well that "charity beareth all things, endureth all things, seeketh not her own," and so "never falleth away."[2] For he who subjects himself to his neigh-

(2) the character and circumstances of Atarbius, as depicted in Letters LXI and CXXVI, entirely agree with those of the unnamed bishop of Neocaesarea referred to in Letters CCIV, CCVII, and CCX; (3) in the Acts of the Council of Constantinople he represents the province of Pontus Polemoniacus, of which Neocaesarea was the Metropolis.

[2] A rather loose quotation of 1 Cor. 13. 5, 7, and 8: ἡ ἀγάπη . . . οὐ ζητεῖ τὰ ἑαυτῆς . . . πάντα στέγει, πάντα πιστεύει, πάντα ἐλπίζει, πάντα ὑπομένει. ἡ ἀγάπη οὐδέποτε ἐκπίπτει. "Charity . . . seeketh not her own . . . beareth all things, believeth all things, hopeth all things, endureth all things. Charity never falleth away."

σίον ὑποτασσόμενος. ὅπως οὖν καὶ αὐτὸς πρὸς
γοῦν τὸ ἑξῆς τὸν [1] πρῶτον καὶ μέγιστον καρπὸν
τοῦ Πνεύματος ἐπιδεικνύμενος,[2] τὴν ἀγάπην, ἀπορ-
ρίψῃς μὲν τὸ τῶν ὀργιζομένων σκυθρωπόν, ὅπερ
ἡμῖν διὰ τῆς σιωπῆς [3] ὑποφαίνεις, ἀναλάβῃς δὲ
χαρὰν ἐν τῇ καρδίᾳ, εἰρήνην πρὸς τοὺς ὁμοψύχους
τῶν ἀδελφῶν, σπουδὴν καὶ μέριμναν ὑπὲρ τῆς τῶν
ἐκκλησιῶν [4] τοῦ Κυρίου διαμονῆς. γίνωσκε γάρ,
ὅτι, εἰ μὴ τὸν ἴσον ἡμεῖς ἀγῶνα ὑπὲρ τῶν ἐκκλησιῶν ἀναλάβοιμεν, ὁπόσον ἔχουσιν οἱ ἀντικείμενοι
τῇ ὑγιαινούσῃ διδασκαλίᾳ εἰς καθαίρεσιν αὐτῶν καὶ
παντελῆ ἀφανισμόν, οὐδὲν τὸ κωλῦον οἴχεσθαι
μὲν παρασυρεῖσαν ὑπὸ τῶν ἐχθρῶν τὴν ἀλήθειαν,
παραπολαῦσαι δέ τι καὶ ἡμᾶς τοῦ κρίματος, μὴ
πάσῃ σπουδῇ καὶ προθυμίᾳ ἐν ὁμονοίᾳ τῇ πρὸς
ἀλλήλους καὶ συμπνοίᾳ τῇ κατὰ τὸν Θεὸν τὴν
ἐνδεχομένην μέριμναν ὑπὲρ τῆς ἑνώσεως τῶν ἐκκλησιῶν ἐπιδειξαμένους.[5]

Παρακαλῶ οὖν, ἔκβαλε τῆς σεαυτοῦ ψυχῆς τὸ
οἴεσθαι μηδενὸς ἑτέρου εἰς κοινωνίαν προσδεῖσθαι.
οὐ γὰρ κατὰ ἀγάπην περιπατοῦντος οὐδὲ πληροῦν-
τός ἐστι τὴν ἐντολὴν [6] τοῦ Χριστοῦ τῆς πρὸς τοὺς
ἀδελφοὺς συναφείας ἑαυτὸν ἀποτέμνειν. ἅμα δὲ
κἀκεῖνο λογίζεσθαι τὴν ἀγαθήν σου προαίρεσιν
βούλομαι, ὅτι τὸ τοῦ πολέμου κακὸν κύκλῳ
περιιὸν καὶ πρὸς ἡμᾶς εἰσέλθοι ποτέ, κἂν μετὰ
τῶν ἄλλων καὶ ἡμεῖς τῆς ἐπηρείας παραπολαύ-

[1] τόν om. E.   [2] ἐνδεικνύμενος E.
[3] ἀγάπης E.   [4] τοῦ Θεοῦ add. Harl.
[5] ἐπιδεξαμένους Med.   [6] τὸν νόμον editi antiqi.

[1] Cf. Gal. 5. 22 f. : ὁ δὲ καρπὸς τοῦ πνεύματός ἐστιν ἀγάπη,
χαρά, εἰρήνη, μακροθυμία, χρηστότης, ἀγαθωσύνη, πίστις, πραότης,
24

bour in a spirit of charity is not humbled. Therefore, for the future at any rate, see to it that
you too exhibit the first and greatest fruit of the
Spirit, charity,[1] and cast aside that sullen look of a
man in anger—which we can infer from the silence
you maintain—and once more take up joy into your
heart, peace toward brothers of kindred spirit, and
zeal and solicitude for the perpetuity of the churches
of the Lord. For be assured that, unless we assume
a labour in behalf of the churches equal to that
which the enemies of sound doctrine have taken
upon themselves for their ruin and total obliteration,
nothing will prevent truth from being swept away
to destruction by our enemies, and ourselves also
from sharing in the condemnation, unless with all
zeal and good will, in harmony with one another
and in unison with God, we show the greatest
possible solicitude for the unity of the churches.

I exhort you, therefore, to cast from your mind
the thought that you have no need of communion
with another. For it does not befit the character
of one who walks in charity, nor of one who fulfils
the command of Christ, to cut himself off from all
connexion with his brethren. At the same time
also I wish your good will to consider this—that
if the evil of the war [2] which now goes on all about
us should sometime come upon ourselves likewise,
and if we too along with the others shall receive

ἐγκράτεια· κατὰ τῶν τοιούτων οὐκ ἔστι νόμος. "But the fruit
of the Spirit is, charity, joy, peace, patience, benignity,
goodness [longanimity], mildness, faith, modesty, continency
[chastity]. Against such there is no law." The bracketed
words of the Douay version do not appear in the Greek.
The word order is also slightly changed.

[2] *i.e.* the persecutions of Valens.

COLLECTED LETTERS OF SAINT BASIL

σωμεν, οὐδὲ τοὺς συναλγοῦντας εὑρήσομεν, διὰ τὸ
ἐν καιρῷ τῆς εὐθυμίας[1] ἡμῶν μὴ προκαταβαλές-
θαι τοῖς ἠδικημένοις τὸν τῆς συμπαθείας ἔρανον.

LXVI

Ἀθανασίῳ, ἐπισκόπῳ Ἀλεξανδρείας

Οὐδένα τοσοῦτον ἡγοῦμαι λυπεῖν τὴν παροῦσαν
τῶν ἐκκλησιῶν κατάστασιν, μᾶλλον δὲ σύγχυσιν,
εἰπεῖν ἀληθέστερον, ὅσον τὴν σὴν τιμιότητα· συγ-
κρίνοντα μὲν τοῖς ἀρχαίοις τανῦν, καὶ παρὰ πόσον
ταῦτα ἐκείνων ἐξήλλακται λογιζόμενον, καὶ ὅτι εἰ
κατὰ τὴν αὐτὴν ὁρμὴν ὑπορρέοι ἐπὶ τὸ χεῖρον τὰ
πράγματα, οὐδὲν ἔσται[2] τὸ κωλῦον, εἴσω ὀλίγου
χρόνου πρὸς ἄλλο τι σχῆμα παντελῶς μεθαρμοσ-
θῆναι τὰς ἐκκλησίας. ταῦτα πολλάκις ἐπ᾽ ἐμαυτοῦ γενόμενος διενοήθην, ὅτι εἰ ἡμῖν οὕτως ἐλεεινὴ
τῶν ἐκκλησιῶν ἡ παρατροπὴ καταφαίνεται, ποίαν
τινὰ εἰκὸς ἐπὶ τούτοις ψυχὴν ἔχειν τὸν τῆς
ἀρχαίας εὐσταθείας καὶ ὁμονοίας περὶ τὴν πίστιν
τῶν ἐκκλησιῶν τοῦ Κυρίου[3] πεπειραμένον; ἀλλ᾽
ὥσπερ τὸ πολὺ τῆς λύπης τὴν σὴν τελειότητα περι-
ίσταται, οὕτως ἡγούμεθα προσήκειν καὶ τῆς ὑπὲρ
τῶν ἐκκλησιῶν μερίμνης τὸ πλέον τῇ σῇ διαφέρειν φρονήσει. πάλαι οἶδα καὶ αὐτός, κατὰ τὴν
ἐνυπάρχουσάν μοι μετρίως τῶν πραγμάτων κατά-
ληψιν, μίαν ἐπιγνοὺς ὁδὸν βοηθείας ταῖς καθ᾽

---

[1] εὐθηνίας editi antiqi.   [2] ἔστι E.
[3] Θεοῦ editi antiqi.

26

a share of its spitefulness, we shall find none to
sympathize with us, because in the season of our
tranquillity we failed to pay betimes our contribution
of sympathy to the victims of injustice.

LETTER LXVI

To Athanasius, Bishop of Alexandria [1]

I consider that no one is so pained as your
Honour at the present condition of the churches,
or rather, to speak more truthfully, at their utter
ruin ; for you can compare the present with the
past, and reflect on the extent of the change that
has taken place between them, and also on the
thought that, if our affairs should continue to ebb
for the worse at this same speed, there will be
nothing to prevent the churches from being completely changed into some other form within a brief
period of time. Many a time, while by myself, I
have reflected upon this thought, wondering what,
if to us the error of the churches appears so pitiable,
the emotion must be in regard to the present state
of affairs of a man who has experienced the pristine
tranquillity and concord of the churches of the Lord
touching the faith.[2] But just as greater sorrow
devolves upon your Excellency, so we hold that it
is proper for your prudence also to bear a greater
solicitude for the churches. I also have long since
been aware, from the moderate comprehension of
events which I possess, that I recognize but one

---

[1] Written in 371. Cf. Letter LXI, note 1.
[2] Athanasius, born about 25 years before Basil, could well
remember the peace of the Church preceding the outbreak of
Arianism.

27

COLLECTED LETTERS OF SAINT BASIL

ἡμᾶς ἐκκλησίαις, τὴν παρὰ τῶν δυτικῶν ἐπισκόπων σύμπνοιαν. εἰ γὰρ βουληθεῖεν, ὃν ἀνέλαβον
ὑπὲρ ἑνὸς ἢ δύο τῶν κατὰ τὴν δύσιν ἐπὶ κακοδοξίᾳ
φωραθέντων ζῆλον, τοῦτον καὶ ὑπὲρ τῆς παροικίας
τῶν καθ’ ἡμᾶς μερῶν ἐπιδείξασθαι, τάχα ἄν τι
γένοιτο τοῖς κοινοῖς ὄφελος, τῶν τε κρατούντων τὸ
ἀξιόπιστον τοῦ πλήθους δυσωπουμένων, καὶ τῶν
ἑκασταχοῦ λαῶν ἀκολουθούντων αὐτοῖς ἀναντιρρήτως.

Τίς οὖν ταῦτα διαπράξασθαι τῆς σῆς συνέσεως
δυνατώτερος; τίς συνιδεῖν τὸ δέον ὀξύτερος; τίς ἐνερ-
γῆσαι τὰ χρήσιμα πρακτικώτερος; τίς πρὸς τὴν
καταπόνησιν τῶν ἀδελφῶν συμπαθέστερος; τίς τῆς
σεμνοτάτης σου πολιᾶς[1] πάσῃ τῇ δύσει αἰδεσι-
μώτερος;[2] κατάλιπέ τι μνημόσυνον τῷ βίῳ τῆς
σῆς ἐπάξιον πολιτείας, τιμιώτατε πάτερ. τοὺς
μυρίους ἐκείνους ὑπὲρ τῆς εὐσεβείας ἄθλους ἑνὶ
τούτῳ κατακόσμησον[3] ἔργῳ. ἔκπεμψόν τινας ἐκ
τῆς ἁγίας τῆς ὑπὸ σὲ ἐκκλησίας ἄνδρας δυνατοὺς
ἐν τῇ ὑγιαινούσῃ διδασκαλίᾳ πρὸς τοὺς κατὰ τὴν
δύσιν ἐπισκόπους· διήγησαι αὐτοῖς τὰς κατασχού-
σας ἡμᾶς συμφοράς· ὑπόθου τρόπον ἀντιλήψεως·
γενοῦ Σαμουὴλ ταῖς ἐκκλησίαις· πολεμουμένοις
τοῖς λαοῖς συγκακοπάθησον· ἀνένεγκε εἰρηνικὰς

[1] πολιτείας tres MSS. et Medicaeus sec. man.
[2] αἰδεσιμώτατος E.
[3] κατάστησον editi antiqi.

---

[1] παροικία: primarily "a sojourn in a foreign land"; then
applied, as here, to groups of Christians in general, since
Christians regarded themselves merely as sojourners in this
world. From this arose the meaning of "an ecclesiastical
district," "a diocese," and later "a parish."

28

avenue of assistance to the churches in our part of
the world—agreement with the bishops of the West.
For if they should be willing to exhibit in the case
of the ecclesiastical districts [1] of our region that zeal
which they have assumed in behalf of one or two
persons [2] in the West who were discovered to be in
heterodoxy, perhaps some benefit would result to our
common interests, since our rulers are timid about
the fidelity of the masses, and the peoples everywhere follow their bishops [3] unquestionably.

Who, then, is more capable of accomplishing this
than a man of your wisdom? Who is keener to
perceive what is needed? Who is more successful
in working out useful projects? Who is more
sympathetic towards the suffering of his fellow-men?
What is more venerated in the entire West than
the white hair of your majestic head? Most
honoured father, bequeath to the living some
memorial worthy of your polity. By this one work
embellish those innumerable labours which you have
performed for the sake of the true faith. Send
forth from the holy church under your care to the
bishops of the West a number of men who are
mighty in the true doctrine. Describe to these
bishops the misfortunes which afflict us. Suggest
a method of assistance. Become a Samuel to the
churches. Share in the sufferings of our people
who are feeling the miseries of war. Offer prayers

[2] On the margin of the codex Regius Secundus is found
this scholion: περὶ τῶν κατὰ Ῥώμην ἐπισκόπων Αὐξεντίου, καὶ
τῶν περὶ αὐτόν. "Concerning the bishops at Rome, Auxentius,
and those with him."

[3] According to the Benedictine editors, Valens is meant
by τῶν κρατούντων, and the bishops, not the rulers, by αὐτοῖς.
I have so interpreted the passage.

προσευχάς· αἴτησον χάριν παρὰ τοῦ Κυρίου,
εἰρήνης τι μνημόσυνον ἐναφεῖναι ¹ ταῖς ἐκκλησίαις.
οἶδα ὅτι ἀσθενεῖς αἱ ἐπιστολαὶ πρὸς συμβουλὴν τοῦ
τοσούτου πράγματος. ἀλλ’ οὔτε αὐτὸς τῆς παρ’
ἑτέρων παρακλήσεως χρήζεις, οὐ μᾶλλόν γε ἢ
τῶν ἀγωνιστῶν οἱ γενναιότατοι τῆς παρὰ τῶν
παίδων ὑποφωνήσεως· οὔτε ἡμεῖς ἀγνοοῦντα δι-
δάσκομεν, ἀλλ’ ἐσπουδακότι τὴν ὁρμὴν ἐπιτείνο-
μεν.

Πρὸς μὲν οὖν τὰ λοιπὰ τῆς ἀνατολῆς ἴσως σοι
καὶ πλειόνων συνεργίας προσδεῖ, καὶ ἀνάγκη
ἀναμένειν τοὺς ἐκ τῆς δύσεως. ἡ μέντοι τῆς κατὰ τὴν
Ἀντιόχειαν ἐκκλησίας εὐταξία προδήλως τῆς σῆς
ἤρτηται θεοσεβείας· ὥστε τοὺς μὲν οἰκονομῆσαι,
τοὺς δὲ καθησυχάσαι, ἀποδοῦναι δὲ τὴν ἰσχὺν
τῇ ἐκκλησίᾳ διὰ τῆς συμφωνίας. καὶ γὰρ ὅτι
ὀφείλεις, κατὰ τοὺς σοφωτάτους τῶν ἰατρῶν, τῆς
ἐπιμελείας ἐκ τῶν καιριωτάτων ἄρχεσθαι, παντὸς
ἀκριβέστερον αὐτὸς ἐπίστασαι. τί δ’ ἂν γένοιτο
ταῖς κατὰ τὴν οἰκουμένην ἐκκλησίαις τῆς Ἀντιοχείας ἐπικαιριώτερον ; ² ἢν εἰ συνέβη πρὸς

¹ ἐναφεθῆναι editi antiqi.
² ἔτι καιριώτερον alii mss.   καιριώτερον editi antiqi.

---

¹ Combefisius observes the following scholion on the
margin of Codex Regius 25 : ὅτι τούτων τῶν εἰρηνικῶν προσευχῶν μέμνηται καὶ ἐν ταῖς μυστικαῖς εὐχαῖς τῆς θείας λειτουργίας ὁ
μέγας πατήρ. "The great father also recalls these prayers
for peace in the mystic prayers of the divine liturgy."
² Reference is made here to the schism caused by the
refusal of the Eustathian or Old Catholic party to recognize
Meletius as bishop of the whole orthodox party. After the
death of Eustathius himself, under whom the church of
Antioch had been a bulwark of orthodoxy, several bishops
entirely unequal to the task were elected to take his place,

for peace.[1] Ask as a grace from the Lord that He may send upon the churches some memories of peace. I know that letters are weak as regards giving advice in a matter of this character. Still, you yourself do not need exhortation from others any more than the best athletes require encouragement from boys, nor are we teaching one who is ignorant on these points, but, on the contrary, we are urging an additional effort on the part of one who is already earnestly at work.

Regarding the rest of the affairs of the East, you perhaps need the co-operation of a larger number also, and it is necessary to await those from the West. The good condition of the Church at Antioch, however, clearly depends upon your Piety, so that it is your duty to use forbearance toward some, to tranquillize others, and through concord to restore strength to the Church.[2] For you yourself understand more exactly than anyone else that, after the manner of the most learned physicians, you must give your first care to the most vital parts. Now what could be more vital to the churches of the world than the Church of Antioch? If it came to

and the church was rent with dissension. Finally, Meletius was elected as a compromise candidate. He seems to have been neither a thorough Nicene nor a decided Arian, although he was esteemed by such men as St. John Chrysostom, St. Gregory Nazianzen, St. Gregory of Nyssa, St. Basil, and even his adversary St. Epiphanius. The churches of the West and of Egypt for the most part supported Paulinus who had been ordained by Lucifer of Cagliari, bishop of the Old Catholics. The East supported Meletius. The Benedictine editors suppose the word οἰκονομῆσαι, which is rendered "control," to refer to Paulinus, and Basil may here be urging the dismissal of Paulinus as bishop. Cf. St. Ambrose, Letter XIII, which deals with this same general topic.

ὁμόνοιαν ἐπανελθεῖν, οὐδὲν ἐκώλυεν, ὥσπερ[1]
κεφαλὴν ἐρρωμένην, παντὶ τῷ σώματι ἐπιχορη-
γεῖν τὴν ὑγίειαν. τῷ ὄντι δὲ τῆς σῆς δεῖται
σοφίας καὶ εὐαγγελικῆς συμπαθείας τὰ ἐκείνης
τῆς πόλεως ἀρρωστήματα· ἥ γε οὐχ ὑπὸ τῶν
αἱρετικῶν διατέτμηται μόνον, ἀλλὰ καὶ ὑπὸ τῶν
τὰ αὐτὰ φρονεῖν ἀλλήλοις λεγόντων διασπᾶται.
ταῦτα δὲ ἑνῶσαι καὶ εἰς ἑνὸς[2] σώματος συναγα-
γεῖν ἁρμονίαν ἐκείνου μόνου ἐστί, τοῦ καὶ τοῖς
ξηροῖς ὀστέοις τὴν εἰς νεῦρα καὶ σάρκα πάλιν
ἐπάνοδον τῇ ἀφάτῳ αὐτοῦ δυνάμει χαριζομένου.
πάντως δὲ τὰ μεγάλα ὁ[3] Κύριος διὰ τῶν ἀξίων
αὐτοῦ ἐνεργεῖ. πάλιν οὖν καὶ ἐνταῦθα τῇ σῇ
μεγαλοφυΐᾳ πρέπειν τὴν τῶν τηλικούτων διακονίαν ἐλπίζομεν, ὥστε καταστορέσαι μὲν τοῦ λαοῦ
τὸν τάραχον, παῦσαι δὲ τὰς μερικὰς προστασίας,
ὑποτάξαι δὲ πάντας ἀλλήλοις ἐν ἀγάπῃ, καὶ τὴν
ἀρχαίαν ἰσχὺν ἀποδοῦναι τῇ Ἐκκλησίᾳ.

LXVII

Ἀθανασίῳ, ἐπισκόπῳ Ἀλεξανδρείας

Ἐμοὶ μὲν ἐξαρκοῦν ἐφάνη ἐν τοῖς προτέροις
γράμμασι πρὸς τὴν σὴν τιμιότητα τοσοῦτον ἐνδείξασθαι, ὅτι πᾶν τὸ[4] κατὰ τὴν πίστιν ἐρρωμένον
τοῦ κατὰ τὴν ἁγίαν ἐκκλησίαν Ἀντιοχείας λαοῦ
εἰς μίαν συμφωνίαν καὶ ἕνωσιν χρὴ ἐναχθῆναι,
πρὸς τὸ δηλῶσαι, ὅτι τῷ θεοφιλεστάτῳ ἐπισκόπῳ

---

[1] ὡσπερεί E.   [2] μίαν E.
[3] ὁ om. E.   [4] ὅτιπερ τό editi antiqi.

pass that this church returned to a state of concord, nothing would prevent its affording health, in the manner of a sound head, to the whole body. And verily the ills of that city stand in need of your wisdom and evangelical sympathy; for it has not only been completely divided by heretics, but it is also being torn asunder by those who affirm that they hold identical opinions with one another. But to unite these parts and to bring them together into the harmony of a single body belongs to Him alone, who by his ineffable power grants even to dry bones a return once more to flesh and muscles. Certainly, however, the Lord performs His mighty deeds through those who are worthy of Him. Again, therefore, on this occasion also we express the hope that the conduct of such important matters may seem fitting to the nobility of your nature, so that you may calm the confusion of the people, put an end to factional usurpations of authority, subject all men to one another in charity, and restore to the Church her pristine strength.

LETTER LXVII

To Athanasius, Bishop of Alexandria [1]

It seemed to me sufficient in my former letter to point out so much to your Honour—that all that section of the people of the holy church of Antioch which is strong in its faith ought to be brought into a single harmony and union, my purpose being to show clearly that those who are now divided into

---

[1] Written at about the same time as the preceding, and on the same general topic.

Μελετίῳ δέοι τὰ εἰς μέρη πλείονα νῦν διῃρημένα συνάψαι. ἐπεὶ δὲ ὁ αὐτὸς οὗτος ὁ ἀγαπητὸς συνδιάκονος ἡμῶν Δωρόθεος ἐναργεστέραν τὴν περὶ τούτων ἐπεζήτησε μνήμην, ἀναγκαίως ἐπισημαινόμεθα, ὅτι καὶ πάσῃ τῇ ἀνατολῇ δι᾽ εὐχῆς, καὶ ἡμῖν τοῖς παντοίως αὐτῷ συνημμένοις ἐπιθυμητόν, αὐτὸν ἰδεῖν τὴν ἐκκλησίαν διέποντα τοῦ[1] Κυρίου, τῇ τε πίστει ἀνεπίληπτον ὄντα, καὶ τῷ βίῳ οὐδεμίαν πρὸς τοὺς ἄλλους ἐπιδεχόμενον σύγκρισιν, καὶ τῷ[2] τοῦ παντός, ὡς εἰπεῖν, σώματος τῆς ἐκκλησίας αὐτὸν προεστάναι, τὰ δὲ λοιπὰ οἷον μερῶν ἀποτμήματα εἶναι.

Ὥστε πανταχόθεν ἀναγκαῖόν τε ὁμοῦ καὶ σύμφερον τῷ ἀνδρὶ τούτῳ συναφθῆναι τοὺς ἄλλους, ὥσπερ τοῖς μεγάλοις τῶν ποταμῶν τοὺς ἐλάττους· περὶ δὲ τοὺς ἄλλους γενέσθαι τινὰ οἰκονομίαν, τὴν κἀκείνοις πρέπουσαν, καὶ τὸν λαὸν εἰρηνεύουσαν, καὶ τῇ σῇ συνέσει καὶ περιβοήτῳ ἐντρεχείᾳ καὶ σπουδῇ ἐπιβάλλουσαν. πάντως δὲ οὐκ ἔλαθέ σου τὴν ἀνυπέρβλητον φρόνησιν, ὅτι ἤδη καὶ τοῖς ὁμοψύχοις σου τοῖς κατὰ τὴν δύσιν τὰ αὐτὰ ταῦτα συνήρεσεν,[3] ὡς δηλοῖ τὰ γράμματα τὰ διὰ τοῦ μακαρίου Σιλουανοῦ κομισθέντα ἡμῖν.

---

[1] τοῦ om. E.   [2] τό editi antiqi.
[3] συνήρεσκεν sex MSS. et editi antiqi.

several parties should unite with the bishop Meletius, dearly beloved of God. But since this same beloved deacon of ours, Dorotheus,[1] has requested that our memorial regarding these matters be made clearer, we perforce are now indicating to you that it is both the desire of the entire East in its prayers and our own also, who are completely in union with Meletius, to see the latter directing the Church of the Lord, since he is a man not open to censure as regards his faith, and in respect to his life admits no comparison with the rest, as also in this respect, that he stands at the head of the whole body of the Church, so to speak, while the residue are, as it were, segments of its limbs.

Accordingly it is for every reason necessary and at the same time expedient that all the rest should unite with this man, just as smaller streams unite with mighty rivers; and respecting these others also, that some sort of an arrangement should be adopted which will be proper to them, will reconcile the people, and will be in accord with your own wisdom, your far-famed industry and zeal. Moreover, it surely has not escaped the notice of your unsurpassed wisdom that this same course of action has already been pleasing to your co-religionists in the West, as is evident from the letter which was brought to us by the blessed Silvanus.[2]

---

[1] Dorotheus, a deacon of the church of Antioch, attached to the communion of Meletius, and employed on several occasions by Basil to carry letters. Cf. Letters XLVIII, L, LII, LXI, LXII, CCLXXIII.

[2] Silvanus: his identity here cannot be determined exactly.

LXVIII

Μελετίῳ, ἐπισκόπῳ Ἀντιοχείας

Τέως μὲν ἐβουλήθημεν[1] κατασχεῖν παρ' ἑαυτοῖς τὸν εὐλαβέστατον ἀδελφὸν Δωρόθεον τὸν συνδιάκονον, ὥστε, ἐπὶ τῷ τέλει τῶν πραγμάτων ἀποπεμψάμενοι, γνωρίσαι δι' αὐτοῦ ἕκαστα τῶν πεπραγμένων τῇ τιμιότητί σου. ἐπεὶ δὲ ἡμέραν ἐξ ἡμέρας ὑπερτιθέμενοι εἰς πολὺ τοῦ χρόνου παρετάθημεν, καὶ ἅμα, ὡς ἐν ἀπόροις, βουλή τις ἡμῖν ἐνέπεσε περὶ τῶν πρακτέων,[2] ἀπεστείλαμεν τὸν προειρημένον ἄνδρα καταλαβεῖν ὑμῶν τὴν ὁσιότητα, καὶ δι' ἑαυτοῦ τε ἀνενεγκεῖν ἕκαστα, καὶ τὸ ὑπομνηστικὸν ἡμῶν ἐπιδεῖξαι, ἵνα, εἰ φανείη χρησίμως ἔχειν τὰ παρ' ἡμῶν ἐννοηθέντα, εἰς ἔργον ἐλθεῖν παρὰ τῆς ὑμετέρας τελειότητος σπουδασθείη.

Ὡς δὲ συντόμως εἰπεῖν, γνώμη ἐκράτησεν ἐπὶ τὴν Ῥώμην διαβῆναι τὸν αὐτὸν τοῦτον ἀδελφὸν ἡμῶν Δωρόθεον, διαναστῆσαί[3] τινας τῶν ἀπὸ[4] τῆς Ἰταλίας, πρὸς τὴν ἐπίσκεψιν ἡμῶν θαλάσσῃ χρησαμένους, ἵνα τοὺς ἐμποδίζοντας διαφύγωσι. τοὺς γὰρ παραδυναστεύοντας τοῖς κρατοῦσιν εἶδον μηδὲν βουλομένους μήτε δυναμένους ὑπομιμνήσκειν αὐτὸν[5] περὶ τῶν ἐκβεβλημένων, ἀλλὰ τὸ μή τι χεῖρον ἰδεῖν ἐν ταῖς ἐκκλησίαις γινόμενον κέρδος τιθεμένους. εἰ οὖν καὶ τῇ σῇ φρονήσει χρήσιμον εἶναι τὸ βούλευμα παρασταίη, καταξιώσεις καὶ ἐπιστολὰς τυπῶσαι, καὶ ὑπομνηστικὰ

---

[1] ἐβουλήθημεν Ε, ἠβουλήθημεν editi antiqi.
[2] προκειμένων tres MSS.   [3] διαστῆσαι Ε.
[4] ἐκ Ε.   [5] αὐτούς editi antiqi.

LETTER LXVIII

To Meletius, Bishop of Antioch [1]

For a time we wished to keep with us the most reverend brother Dorotheus,[2] our deacon, so that, sending him back at the conclusion of our business, we might use him to inform your Honour of our transactions in detail. But when we kept putting off this conclusion from day to day and found ourselves delayed for a considerable period of time, and when, too, in our perplexity a plan occurred to us regarding the course of action to be adopted, we despatched the aforementioned deacon to meet your Holiness, to report all the facts in person, and to present our memorandum, in order that, if our ideas should appear expedient, they might speedily be put into effect by your Perfection.

To put it briefly, this view prevailed : that this same brother of ours, Dorotheus, should cross over to Rome, and should urge that some of our brethren in Italy should visit us, travelling by sea, so as to avoid any who might seek to hinder them. For I have noticed that those who are very powerful at court are neither willing nor able to bring to the Emperor's attention the question of the exiles, but rather count it as gain that they see nothing worse happening to the churches. If, therefore, the plan should also seem expedient to your wisdom, you will deign to have letters written, and to dictate memo-

---

[1] Of the same date as the preceding. For the identity of Meletius, cf. Letter LXVI, note 4. For a description of his character by Basil, see the previous letter.

[2] Cf. letter above.

COLLECTED LETTERS OF SAINT BASIL

ὑπαγορεῦσαι περὶ ὧν χρὴ διαλεχθῆναι αὐτὸν καὶ
πρὸς τίνας.[1] ὥστε δὲ ἔχειν ἀξιοπιστίαν τινὰ τὰ
γράμματα, συμπαραλήψῃ πάντως τοὺς ὁμογνώ-
μονας, κἂν μὴ παρῶσι. τὰ δ᾽ ἐνταῦθα ἔτι ἐστὶν
ἐν ἀδήλῳ, τοῦ Εὐΐππίου παραγενομένου μέν,
μηδὲν δὲ τέως ἐκφήναντος. ἀπειλοῦσι μέντοι καὶ
συνδρομήν τινα ὁμογνωμόνων αὐτοῖς ἔκ τε τῆς
Ἀρμενίας τῆς Τετραπόλεως, καὶ ἐκ τῆς Κιλι-
κίας.

LXIX

Ἀθανασίῳ, ἐπισκόπῳ Ἀλεξανδρείας

Ἢν ἐκ παλαιοῦ[2] περὶ τῆς σῆς τιμιότητος
ὑπόληψιν ἔσχομεν, ταύτην ὁ χρόνος προϊὼν ἀεὶ
βεβαιοῖ· μᾶλλον δὲ καὶ συναύξει ταῖς προσθήκαις τῶν κατὰ μέρος ἐπιγινομένων. ὅτι τῶν μὲν
ἄλλων τοῖς πλείστοις ἐξαρκεῖ τὸ καθ᾽ ἑαυτὸν
ἕκαστον περισκοπεῖν, σοὶ δὲ οὐχ ἱκανὸν τοῦτο,
ἀλλ᾽ ἡ μέριμνά σοι πασῶν τῶν ἐκκλησιῶν τοσαύτη, ὅση καὶ τῆς ἰδίως παρὰ τοῦ κοινοῦ
Δεσπότου ἡμῶν ἐμπιστευθείσης ἐπίκειται· ὅς γε
οὐδένα χρόνον διαλείπεις διαλεγόμενος, νουθετῶν,
ἐπιστέλλων, ἐκπέμπων τινὰς ἑκάστοτε τοὺς ὑπο-
τιθεμένους τὰ βέλτιστα. καὶ νῦν δὲ ἀπὸ τοῦ
ἱεροῦ πληρώματος τοῦ ὑπὸ σὲ κλήρου τὸν αἰδε-

[1] καὶ ὅτε (" and when ") add. editi antiqi.
[2] ἔκπαλαι tres MSS. recentiores.

---

[1] i.e., the deacon, Dorotheus.

38

randa regarding what matters he [1] must discuss and with what persons. In order, too, that your letters may possess a certain sanction, you will, of course, include the names of all those who are of like mind with yourself, even if they are not present. The state of affairs here is as yet not certain, for, although Euippius [2] is present, up to now he has made no disclosure. However, they are threatening to hold some sort of a meeting of those who are in sympathy with their views both from the Tetrapolis of Armenia and from Cilicia.

LETTER LXIX

To Athanasius, Bishop of Alexandria [3]

THE opinion of your Honour which we long ago conceived is being ever confirmed by the passage of time; or rather, it is even being enhanced by the new evidence of particular events. Athough most men deem it sufficient to look each to his own particular charge, this is not enough for you, but, on the contrary, you have as great solicitude for all the churches as for the one especially entrusted to you by our common Master; for at no time do you cease to discourse, to admonish, to write, and on each occasion to send out men who give the best advice. Even now we have received with great joy the most

[2] Euippius: a bishop with Arianizing tendencies, from whom in the cause of truth Basil felt obliged to separate. Cf. Letter CXXVIII. Eustathius of Sebaste, in 360, declaimed against Euippius as not worthy of the name of bishop, but in 376 he united with Euippius, and recognized the bishops and presbyters Euippius had ordained. Cf. Letters CCXXVI, CCXXXIX, CCXLIV, CCLI.

[3] Written at the same time as the preceding.

σιμώτατον ἀδελφὸν Πέτρον ἐκπεμφθέντα μετὰ
πολλῆς χαρᾶς ἐδεξάμεθα, καὶ τὸν ἀγαθὸν αὐτοῦ [1]
τῆς ἀποδημίας σκοπὸν [2] ἀπεδεξάμεθα, ὃν ἐπι-
δείκνυται κατ᾽ ἐντολὰς τῆς σῆς τιμιότητος, τὰ
ἀντιτείνοντα προσαγόμενος, καὶ τὰ διεσπασμένα
συνάπτων. ὅθεν τι καὶ ἡμεῖς συμβαλέσθαι τῇ
περὶ τοῦτο σπουδῇ βουληθέντες, ἐνομίσαμεν
ἐπιτηδειοτάτην ἀρχὴν τοῖς πράγμασι δώσειν, εἰ,
ὥσπερ ἐπὶ κορυφὴν τῶν ὅλων, ἐπὶ [3] τὴν σὴν
ἀναδράμοιμεν τελειότητα, καὶ σοὶ συμβούλῳ τε
χρησαίμεθα καὶ ἡγεμόνι τῶν πράξεων. ὅθεν
καὶ τὸν ἀδελφὸν Δωρόθεον, τὸν διάκονον τῆς
ὑπὸ τὸν τιμιώτατον ἐπίσκοπον Μελέτιον
ἐκκλησίας, ἀγαθῷ κεχρημένον περὶ τὴν τῆς
πίστεως ὀρθότητα ζήλῳ, καὶ ἐπιθυμοῦντα καὶ
αὐτὸν τὴν εἰρήνην τῶν ἐκκλησιῶν ἐπιδεῖν, πρὸς
τὴν σὴν θεοσέβειαν ἀνεπέμψαμεν,[4] ὥστε, ταῖς
σαῖς ὑποθήκαις ἀκολουθοῦντα (ἃς καὶ τῷ χρόνῳ
καὶ τῇ τῶν πραγμάτων πείρᾳ, καὶ τῷ ὑπὲρ τοὺς
ἄλλους ἔχειν τὴν ἐκ τοῦ Πνεύματος συμβουλίαν,
ἀσφαλεστέρας ποιεῖσθαι δύνασαι), οὕτως ἐγχειρεῖν
τοῖς σπουδαζομένοις.

Ὃν καὶ ὑποδέξῃ δηλονότι, καὶ προσβλέψεις
εἰρηνικοῖς ὀφθαλμοῖς, στηρίξας τε αὐτὸν τῇ διὰ
τῶν προσευχῶν βοηθείᾳ, καὶ ἐφοδιάσας γράμμασι,
μᾶλλον δὲ καὶ παραζεύξας τινὰς [5] τῶν αὐτόθεν
σπουδαίων, ἐπὶ τὰ προκείμενα ὁδηγήσεις. ἐφάνη
δὲ ἡμῖν ἀκόλουθον ἐπιστεῖλαι τῷ ἐπισκόπῳ
Ῥώμης, ἐπισκέψασθαι τὰ ἐνταῦθα, καὶ δοῦναι
γνώμην, ἵν᾽ ἐπειδὴ ἀπὸ κοινοῦ καὶ συνοδικοῦ

---

[1] αὐτοῦ om. E.   [2] κόπον E.   [3] ἐπί add. Capps.
[4] ἀνεπέμψαμεν Capps, ἀναπέμψαι MSS.   [5] τισί editi antiqi.

LETTER LXIX

reverend brother Peter, sent from the holy company
of the clergy under your care, and we have approved
the noble object of his journey, which he explains
according to the commands of your Honour, winning
over the recalcitrant and uniting what has been torn
asunder. Wherefore we also, wishing to make
some contribution to the general enthusiasm for
this matter, have thought we should be supplying a
most suitable initiative to our undertaking if we
should again have recourse to your Perfection, as to
the highest of all, and should make use of you as
both adviser and director of our actions. Wherefore
we have again sent to your Piety our brother
Dorotheus, the deacon of the church under the
jurisdiction of the most honoured bishop Meletius,
he being a man of good zeal regarding orthodoxy in
faith, and like yourself eager to see peace in the
churches, to the end that he, following your counsels
(which you, by reason of your years and your
experience in affairs, and of your possessing beyond
the rest of us the guidance of the Spirit, are able
to make more nearly unerring), may with such
help from you take in hand the matters which are
the objects of our zeal.

You will no doubt give him welcome, and you will
regard him with the eyes of peace; and when you
have buttressed him with the support of your prayers
and have furnished him with letters for his journey
—or better, have attached to him some competent
men from this region as companions—you will give
him directions for his mission. It has seemed to us
advisable in the circumstances, moreover, to write
to the bishop of Rome, that he may examine into
the state of affairs here, and give us his opinion, so

δόγματος ἀποσταλῆναί τινας δύσκολον τῶν
ἐκεῖθεν, αὐτὸν αὐθεντῆσαι περὶ τὸ πρᾶγμα,
ἐκλεξάμενον ἄνδρας ἱκανοὺς μὲν ὁδοιπορίας πόνους
ὑπενεγκεῖν,[1] ἱκανοὺς δὲ πραότητι καὶ εὐτονίᾳ
ἤθους τοὺς ἐνδιαστρόφους τῶν παρ' ἡμῖν νουθε-
τῆσαι, ἐπιτηδείως δὲ καὶ οἰκονομικῶς κεχρημένους
τῷ λόγῳ, καὶ πάντα ἔχοντας μεθ' ἑαυτῶν τὰ
μετὰ Ἀριμῖνον πεπραγμένα ἐπὶ λύσει τῶν κατ'
ἀνάγκην ἐκεῖ γενομένων· καὶ τοῦτο μηδενὸς
εἰδότος, ἀψοφητὶ διὰ θαλάσσης ἐπιστῆναι τοῖς
ὧδε, ὑπὲρ τοῦ φθάσαι τὴν αἴσθησιν τῶν ἐχθρῶν
τῆς εἰρήνης.

Ἐπιζητεῖται δὲ κἀκεῖνο παρά τινων τῶν ἐντεῦθεν, ἀναγκαίως, ὡς καὶ αὐτοῖς ἡμῖν κατα-

---

[1] διενεγκεῖν editi antiqi.

---

[1] On the Council of Ariminum or Rimini the Catholic
Encyclopaedia says: "The Council of Rimini was opened
early in July, 359, with over four hundred bishops. About
eighty Semi-Arians, including Ursacius, Germinius, and
Auxentius, withdrew from the orthodox bishops, the most
eminent of whom was Restitutus of Carthage; Liberius,
Eusebius, Dionysius, and others were still in exile. The
two parties sent separate deputations to the Emperor, the
orthodox asserting clearly their firm attachment to the faith
of Nicaea, while the Arian minority adhered to the Imperial
formula. But the inexperienced representatives of the
orthodox majority allowed themselves to be deceived, and
not only entered into communion with the heretical delegates,
but even subscribed, at Nice in Thrace, a formula to the
effect merely that the Son is like the Father according to the
Scriptures (the words 'in all things' being omitted). On
their return to Rimini, they were met with the unanimous
protests of their colleagues. But the threats of the consul
Taurus, the remonstrances of the Semi-Arians against hinder-
ing peace between East and West for a word not contained

that, as it is difficult to send men from Rome by a general synodical decree, he may himself exercise full authority in this matter, selecting men capable of enduring the hardships of a journey, and at the same time capable, by the gentleness and vigour of their character, of admonishing those among us who are perverted, men who possess the power of appropriate and effective speech and are fully cognizant of all that has been done since the Council of Ariminum[1] for the undoing of the actions taken there under compulsion; and when all this has been done without the knowledge of anyone, our thought is that the bishop of Rome shall quietly, through a mission sent by sea, assume charge of affairs here so as to escape the notice of the enemies of peace.

It is also demanded by certain people here—quite necessarily, as it seems to us as well—that they[2]

in Scripture, their privations and their home-sickness—all combined to weaken the constancy of the orthodox bishops. And the last twenty were induced to subscribe when Ursacius had an addition made to the formula of Nice, declaring that the Son is not a creature like other creatures. Pope Liberius, having regained his liberty, rejected this formula, which was thereupon repudiated by many who had signed it. In view of the hasty manner of its adoption and lack of approbation by the Holy See, it could have no authority."

[2] *i.e.* the Romans, particularly the proposed commissioners. Basil bore it ill that Marcellus, whom he regarded as a trimmer, was in the words of St. Jerome "fortified by communion with Julius and Athanasius, popes of Rome and Alexandria." Cf. *De Vir. Illust.* 86: " se communione Julii et Athanasii, Romanae et Alexandrinae urbis pontificum, esse munitum." St. Athanasius, however, according to Cardinal Newman, upheld him "to about A.D. 360," but attacked his tenets pointedly, though without naming him, in his fourth oration against the Arians.

φαίνεται, τὸν τὴν Μαρκέλλου αἵρεσιν αὐτοὺς[1]
ὡς χαλεπὴν καὶ βλαβερὰν καὶ τῆς ὑγιαινούσης
πίστεως[2] ἀλλοτρίως ἔχουσαν, ἐξορίσαι.[3] ἐπεὶ
μέχρι τοῦ νῦν ἐν πᾶσιν οἷς ἐπιστέλλουσι γράμμασι, τὸν μὲν δυσώνυμον Ἄρειον ἄνω καὶ κάτω
ἀναθεματίζοντες καὶ τῶν ἐκκλησιῶν ἐξορίζοντες
οὐ διαλείπουσι, Μαρκέλλῳ δέ, τῷ κατὰ διάμετρον
ἐκείνῳ τὴν ἀσέβειαν ἐπιδειξαμένῳ, καὶ εἰς αὐτὴν τὴν ὕπαρξιν τῆς τοῦ Μονογενοῦς θεότητος
ἀσεβήσαντι καὶ κακῶς τὴν τοῦ Λόγου προσηγορίαν ἐκδεξαμένῳ, οὐδεμίαν μέμψιν ἐπενεγκόντες
φαίνονται. ὃς Λόγον μὲν εἰρῆσθαι τὸν Μονογενῆ
δίδωσι, κατὰ χρείαν καὶ ἐπὶ καιροῦ προελθόντα,
πάλιν δὲ εἰς τὸν ὅθεν ἐξῆλθεν ἐπαναστρέψαντα,
οὔτε πρὸ τῆς ἐξόδου εἶναι, οὔτε μετὰ τὴν ἐπάνοδον
ὑφεστάναι. καὶ τούτου ἀπόδειξις[4] αἱ παρ᾽ ἡμῖν
ἀποκείμεναι βίβλοι τῆς ἀδίκου ἐκείνης συγγραφῆς
ὑπάρχουσιν. ἀλλ᾽ ὅμως τοῦτον οὐδαμοῦ διαβα-
λόντες[5] ἐφάνησαν, καὶ ταῦτα αἰτίαν ἔχοντες ὡς,
τὸ ἐξ ἀρχῆς κατ᾽ ἄγνοιαν τῆς ἀληθείας, καὶ εἰς
κοινωνίαν αὐτὸν ἐκκλησιαστικὴν παραδεξάμενοι.
ἐκείνου τε οὖν μνησθῆναι πρεπόντως ἀπαιτεῖ τὰ
παρόντα, ὥστε μὴ ἔχειν ἀφορμὴν τοὺς θέλοντας
ἀφορμήν, ἐκ τοῦ τῇ σῇ ὁσιότητι συνάπτειν τοὺς
ὑγιαίνοντας καὶ τοὺς πρὸς τὴν ἀληθῆ πίστιν

---

[1] αὐτοῖς E.　　　　　　　[2] διδασκαλίας ὡς E, Harl.
[3] ἐξορίζεσθαι editi antiqi.　　　　　　[4] ἀποδείξεις E.
[5] οὐδαμοῦ διαβαλόντες] οὐδαμῶς διαβάλλοντες editi antiqi.

---

[1] On Basil's opinion of the heretical doctrines of Marcellus
of Ancyra, cf. Letters CXXV and CCLXIII. Marcellus had
upheld the cause of orthodoxy at Nicaea. Later, however,
while attacking the errors of Asterius, he was supposed to

should themselves exterminate the heresy of Marcellus[1] as being both dangerous and harmful, and
foreign to the true faith. For up to the present, in
all the letters which they send, while they do not
cease anathematizing the abominable Arius up and
down and banishing him from the churches, yet
against Marcellus, who has exhibited an impiety
diametrically opposed to that of Arius, who has in
fact been impious concerning the very existence of
the Only-begotten Godhead, and has accepted a
false signification of "the Word," they have
manifestly brought no censure whatever. He gives
it as his opinion that the Only-begotten was called
"the Word," that He made His appearance in time
of need and in due season, but returned again whence
He came, and that neither before His coming did
He exist nor after His return does He still subsist.[2]
And as proofs of this there exist the documents in
our possession containing that wicked essay of his.
But nevertheless, they have nowhere come out with
a repudiation of this man, and that too although
they are open to the charge of having (at the
beginning in ignorance of the truth) even received
him into ecclesiastical communion. Of this man,
therefore, the present circumstances demand that
appropriate mention be made, so that those who
seek an opportunity[3] may have no opportunity,
in consequence of our uniting with your Holiness
all who are sound in the faith, and of our reveal-

have taught that the Son had no real personality, but was
merely an external manifestation of the Father.
    [2] ὑφεστάναι, i.e. does not exist in essence.
    [3] i.e. of following the heresy of Marcellus, as they could
safely do so long as he remained in good standing for
orthodoxy.

45

ὀκλάζοντας φανεροὺς πᾶσι ποιῆσαι· ὥστε τοῦ
λοιποῦ γνωρίζειν ἡμᾶς τοὺς ὁμόφρονας, καὶ μή,
ὡς ἐν νυκτομαχίᾳ, μηδεμίαν φίλων καὶ πολε-
μίων ἔχειν διάκρισιν. μόνον παρακαλοῦμεν
εὐθὺς ὑπὸ τὸν πρῶτον πλοῦν ἐκπεμφθῆναι τὸν
προειρημένον διάκονον, ἵνα δυνηθῇ κατὰ γοῦν τὸ
ἐφεξῆς ἔτος γενέσθαι τι, ὧν προσευχόμεθα.

Ἐκεῖνο δὲ καὶ πρὸ τῶν ἡμετέρων[1] λόγων
συνιεῖς τε αὐτὸς καὶ φροντιεῖς δηλονότι, ὅπως
ἐπιστάντες, ἐὰν ὁ Θεὸς θέλῃ, μὴ ἐναφῶσι ταῖς
ἐκκλησίαις[2] τὰ σχίσματα, ἀλλὰ τοὺς τὰ αὐτὰ
φρονοῦντας παντὶ τρόπῳ εἰς ἕνωσιν συνελάσωσι,
κἄν τινας ἰδίας τῶν πρὸς ἀλλήλους διαφορῶν
ἀφορμὰς εὕρωσιν[3] ἔχοντας, ὑπὲρ τοῦ μὴ τὸν
ὀρθοδοξοῦντα λαὸν εἰς πολλὰ κατατέμνεσθαι μέρη
τοῖς προεστῶσι συναφιστάμενον. πάντα γὰρ δεῖ
σπουδάσαι δεύτερα ἡγήσασθαι τῆς εἰρήνης, καὶ
πρὸ πάντων τῆς κατὰ Ἀντιόχειαν ἐκκλησίας
ἐπιμεληθῆναι, ὡς μὴ ἀσθενεῖν ἐν αὐτῇ τὴν ὀρθὴν
μερίδα περὶ τὰ πρόσωπα σχιζομένην. μᾶλλον
δέ, τούτων ἁπάντων καὶ αὐτὸς εἰς ὕστερον ἐπι-
μελήσῃ, ἐπειδάν, ὅπερ εὐχόμεθα, Θεοῦ συνεργοῦν-
τός σοι, πάντας λάβῃς τὰ τῆς καταστάσεως τῶν
ἐκκλησιῶν ἐπιτρέποντας.

---

[1] εἰρημένων editi antiqi. [2] τὰς ἐκκλησίας E.
[3] τύχωσιν Vat. Cod. ac Reg. secund. et Coisl. sec.

ing to all men those who are slack in the true faith. The result will be that henceforth we shall be able to recognize those who are of one mind with us, instead of being like those who fight a battle at night—unable to distinguish between friends and foes. We only urge now that the deacon whom we have spoken of be sent away immediately, by the first boat, in order that some of the objects for which we pray may possibly be realized next year at least.

Our next observation you will both understand of yourself even before we make it, and will doubtless see to it that these men assuming charge, it God wills it, do not let schisms loose among the churches, but that they by every means urge into unity those who hold identical doctrines with us, even though they find some who have private reasons for differing with one another, in order that the orthodox laity be not cut up into many factions, by following their leaders into revolt. For they must zealously endeavour to count all things secondary to peace, and above all they must be solicitous for the Church at Antioch, lest the orthodox section of it be weakened by being divided on the question of the persons.[1] Or rather, you yourself will henceforth assume care of all these things, as soon as, according to our prayers, God being your helper, you shall have everyone entrusting into your care whatever pertains to the restoration of peace among the churches.

---

[1] *i.e.* of the Godhead.

LXX

Ἀνεπίγραφος περὶ συνόδου

Ἀρχαίας ἀγάπης θεσμοὺς ἀνανεοῦσθαι, καὶ πατέρων εἰρήνην τὸ οὐράνιον δῶρον Χριστοῦ καὶ σωτήριον, ἀπομαρανθὲν τῷ χρόνῳ, πάλιν πρὸς τὴν ἀκμὴν ἐπαναγαγεῖν, ἀναγκαῖον μὲν ἡμῖν καὶ ὠφέλιμον, τερπνὸν δὲ εὖ οἶδα ὅτι καὶ τῇ σῇ φιλοχρίστῳ διαθέσει καταφανήσεται. τί γὰρ ἂν γένοιτο χαριέστερον, ἢ τοὺς τοσούτῳ τῷ πλήθει τῶν τόπων διῃρημένους [1] τῇ διὰ τῆς ἀγάπης ἑνώσει καθορᾶν εἰς μίαν μελῶν ἁρμονίαν ἐν σώματι Χριστοῦ δεδέσθαι; ἡ ἀνατολὴ πᾶσα σχεδόν, τιμιώτατε πάτερ (λέγω δὲ ἀνατολὴν τὰ ἀπὸ τοῦ Ἰλλυρικοῦ μέχρις Αἰγύπτου), μεγάλῳ χειμῶνι καὶ κλύδωνι κατασείεται, τῆς πάλαι μὲν σπαρείσης αἱρέσεως ὑπὸ τοῦ ἐχθροῦ τῆς ἀληθείας Ἀρείου, νῦν δὲ πρὸς τὸ ἀναίσχυντον ἀναφανείσης καὶ οἱονεὶ ῥίζης πικρᾶς καρπὸν ὀλέθριον ἀναδιδούσης, κατακρατούσης λοιπὸν διὰ τὸ τοὺς μὲν καθ᾽ ἑκάστην παροικίαν προεστῶτας τοῦ ὀρθοῦ λόγου ἐκ συκοφαντίας καὶ ἐπηρείας τῶν ἐκκλησιῶν ἐκπεσεῖν, παραδοθῆναι δὲ τοῖς αἰχμαλωτίζουσι τὰς ψυχὰς τῶν ἀκεραιοτέρων τὴν τῶν πραγμάτων ἰσχύν. τούτων μίαν προσεδοκήσαμεν λύσιν τὴν τῆς ὑμετέρας εὐσπλαγχνίας ἐπίσκεψιν· καὶ ἐψυχαγώγησεν ἡμᾶς ἀεὶ τὸ παράδοξον τῆς ὑμετέρας ἀγάπης ἐν τῷ παρελθόντι χρόνῳ, καὶ φήμη

---

[1] διειργμένους editi antiqi.

---

[1] Written in the autumn of 371. All, including Tillemont

48

LETTER LXX

To renew the ties of an old affection and to
restore into full bloom the peace of the Fathers,
that heavenly and salutary gift of Christ which has
become withered by time, is for us both necessary
and expedient, and I know well that it will seem
delightful to your Christ-loving disposition also. For
what could be more pleasant than to behold men
who are separated from one another by so vast a
diversity of places of residence, bound by the unity
of love into a single harmony of members in the body
of Christ? Almost the whole East, most honoured
Father (by " East " I mean everything from Illyricum
to Egypt),[2] is being shaken by a mighty storm and
flood, since the heresy, sown long ago by Arius, the
enemy of truth, and now already grown up into
shamelessness, and, like a bitter root, producing a
deadly fruit, at last prevails, because the champions
of orthodox teaching in every diocese have been
banished from their churches through slander and
insult, and the administration of affairs has been
surrendered to men who are making prisoners of
the souls of those more pure in faith. As the one
solution of these difficulties we have looked forward
to the visitation [3] of your sympathetic heart; for in
times gone by your marvellous affection has always
refreshed us, and we were strengthened in our souls

and the Benedictine editors, are agreed that this letter is
addressed to Pope Damasus.

[2] *i.e.* roughly, the two eastern prefectures of Diocletian
and his successors.

[3] *i.e.* an official visit of a bishop.

φαιδροτέρᾳ πρὸς βραχὺ τὰς ψυχὰς ἀνερρώσθημεν,
ὡς ἐσομένης ἡμῖν τινὸς ἐπισκέψεως παρ' ὑμῶν.
ὡς δὲ διημάρτομεν τῆς ἐλπίδος, μηκέτι στέγοντες
ἤλθομεν ἐπὶ τὴν διὰ τοῦ γράμματος [1] ἡμῶν
παράκλησιν, διαναστῆναι ὑμᾶς πρὸς τὴν ἀντίληψιν ἡμῶν, καὶ ἀποστεῖλαί τινας τῶν ὁμοψύχων,
ἢ τοὺς συμβιβάζοντας τοὺς διεστῶτας, ἢ εἰς
φιλίαν τὰς ἐκκλησίας τοῦ Θεοῦ ἐπανάγοντας, ἢ
τοὺς γοῦν αἰτίους τῆς ἀκαταστασίας φανερωτέρους [2]
ὑμῖν καθιστῶντας· ὥστε καὶ ὑμῖν φανερὸν εἶναι
τοῦ λοιποῦ, πρὸς τίνας ἔχειν τὴν κοινωνίαν
προσῆκε.

Πάντως δὲ οὐδὲν καινὸν [3] ἐπιζητοῦμεν, ἀλλὰ
τοῖς τε λοιποῖς τῶν πάλαι μακαρίων καὶ θεοφίλων
ἀνδρῶν σύνηθες, καὶ διαφερόντως ὑμῖν. οἴδαμεν
γὰρ μνήμης ἀκολουθίᾳ, παρὰ τῶν πατέρων ἡμῶν
αἰτηθέντων καὶ ἀπὸ γραμμάτων τῶν ἔτι καὶ νῦν
πεφυλαγμένων παρ' ἡμῖν, διδασκόμενοι, Διονύσιον
ἐκεῖνον, τὸν μακαριώτατον ἐπίσκοπον, παρ' ὑμῖν
ἐπί τε ὀρθότητι πίστεως καὶ τῇ λοιπῇ ἀρετῇ δια-
πρέψαντα, ἐπισκεπτόμενον διὰ γραμμάτων τὴν
ἡμετέραν ἐκκλησίαν τῶν Καισαρέων, καὶ παρα-
καλοῦντα τοὺς πατέρας ἡμῶν διὰ γραμμάτων,
καὶ πέμπειν τοὺς ἀπολυτρουμένους ἐκ τῆς αἰχ-
μαλωσίας τὴν ἀδελφότητα. ἐν χαλεπωτέρῳ

---

[1] τοῦ γράμματος] γραμμάτων editi antiqi.
[2] φανερώτερον editi antiqi.
[3] ἄκαιρον E, editi antiqi, δεινόν Clarom.

---

[1] i.e bishops of Rome. The Benedictine edition points out
that the kindness of the bishops of Rome, here mentioned
by Basil, is borne out by the evidence both of Dionysius,

for a brief space by the joyful report that we should receive a visitation from you. But since we have been cheated of our hope, unable to contain ourselves longer, we have had recourse to urging you by this letter to rouse yourself to our assistance, and to send us men of like mind with us, who will either reconcile the dissenters, or restore the churches of God to friendship, or will at least make more manifest to you those who are responsible for the confusion. It will thus be clear to you also for the future, with what men it is proper to have communion.

And the request we make is by no means a novel one, but, on the contrary, has been habitual not only with all the blessed and God-beloved men of the past, but also and especially with yourself.[1] For we know through a continuous tradition, by the teaching received from our Fathers in answer to our questions and from letters which even to this day are preserved among us, that Dionysius,[2] that most blessed bishop, who was pre-eminent among you both for the orthodoxy of his faith and for his virtue in general, was wont to visit our Church of Caesarea by letter, and to exhort our fathers by letter, and to send men to ransom the brethren from captivity. But our present state of affairs is

---

bishop of Corinth (cf. Eusebius, *Hist. Eccl.* 4, 23), of Dionysius of Alexandria (Dionysius to Sixtus II, in Euseb., *Hist. Eccl.* 7, 5), and of Eusebius himself in his history. The troubles referred to here took place in the time of Gallienus, when the Scythians plundered Cappadocia and the neighbouring countries (cf. Sozomen, *Eccl. Hist.* 2, 6).

[2] A Greek by birth, and consecrated July 22, A.D. 259, on the death of Sixtus II, during the persecution of Valerian. Nothing is recorded of him except his efforts against heresy.

δὲ νῦν καὶ σκυθρωποτέρῳ τὰ καθ᾽ ἡμᾶς, καὶ
πλείονος δεόμενα τῆς ἐπιμελείας. οὐ γὰρ οἰκοδο-
μημάτων γηΐνων καταστροφήν, ἀλλ᾽ ἐκκλησιῶν
ἅλωσιν ὀδυρόμεθα· οὐδὲ δουλείαν σωματικήν,
ἀλλ᾽ αἰχμαλωσίαν ψυχῶν καθ᾽ ἑκάστην ἡμέραν
ἐνεργουμένην παρὰ τῶν ὑπερμαχούντων τῆς
αἱρέσεως καθορῶμεν. ὥστε εἰ μὴ ἤδη διανα-
σταίητε πρὸς τὴν ἀντίληψιν, μικρὸν ὕστερον
οὐδὲ οἷς ὀρέξετε τὴν χεῖρα εὑρήσετε, πάντων
ὑπὸ τὴν ἐπικράτειαν τῆς αἱρέσεως γενομένων.

LXXI

Γρηγορίῳ Βασίλειος [1]

Ἐδεξάμην τὰ γράμματα τῆς σῆς εὐλαβείας [2]
διὰ τοῦ αἰδεσιμωτάτου ἀδελφοῦ Ἑλληνίου· καὶ
ὅσα ἐνέφηνας ἡμῖν, αὐτὸς ταῦτα γυμνῶς διηγήσατο. ἀκούσαντες δὲ ὅπως [3] διετέθημεν, οὐκ ἀμφι-
βάλλεις πάντως. πλὴν ἀλλ᾽ ἐπειδὴ ἐκρίναμεν
πάσης λύπης ἀνωτέραν ποιεῖσθαι τὴν πρὸς σὲ
ἀγάπην ἐδεξάμεθα καὶ ταῦτα ὡς ἦν προσῆκον,

---

[1] Γρηγορίῳ ἑταίρῳ alii MSS.
[2] τῆς σῆς εὐλαβείας] τῆς εὐλαβείας σου editi antiqi.
[3] αὐτὸς ταῦτα . . . ὅπως] καὶ ταῦτα διηγησαμένου ἀκούσαντες
ὅπως editi antiqi.

---

[1] Written in the year 371. Gregory Nazianzene had
already refused to aid in effecting the election of Basil as
Archbishop of Caesarea. He later refused to support him
in his throne, by refusing to accept any high responsibilities
such as τήνδε τῆς καθέδρας τιμήν (cf. Greg. Naz., Or. XLIII),
possibly the coadjutor-bishopric at Caesarea. Gregory's

more difficult and more gloomy, and requires greater solicitude. Indeed, it is not the destruction of earthly buildings that we mourn, but the seizure of churches; nor is it corporeal slavery that we behold, but the captivity of souls which is being brought about daily by the champions of the heresy. Accordingly, unless you immediately rouse yourself to our assistance, you will shortly not even find men to whom to stretch forth your hand, since all will have come under the dominion of the heresy.

LETTER LXXI

Basil to Gregory [1]

I received the letter of your Reverence through our most reverend brother Hellenius,[2] who in person related in plain language what you had intimated to us. How we were affected in hearing this, you certainly can be in no doubt. However, since we have decided to put our love for you above any grievance, we have received even these communications in a becoming manner, and we pray the holy

plea was that it was better for Basil's own sake that there be no suspicion of favour to personal friends, and he begged to be excused for staying at Nazianzus. Cf. Greg. Naz., Letter XLV. The present letter is partly an answer to the letter from Gregory which announced this stand, partly a plea that Gregory pay no attention to certain Nazianzene scandal-mongers who had charged Basil with heterodoxy.

[2] Hellenius: a surveyor of customs at Nazianzus, the confidential friend both of Basil and Gregory Nazianzene. Besides delivering to Basil the message here referred to, we find him in 372 conveying a message from the bishops of Lesser Armenia. Cf. Letter XCVIII.

καὶ εὐχόμεθα τῷ ἁγίῳ Θεῷ, τὰς λειπομένας
ἡμέρας ἢ ὥρας[1] οὕτω[2] διαφυλαχθῆναι ἐν τῇ
περὶ σὲ διαθέσει, ὡς καὶ ἐν τῷ κατόπιν χρόνῳ,
ἐν ᾧ οὐδὲν ἡμῖν αὐτοῖς οὔτε μικρὸν οὔτε μεῖζον
ἐλλελοιπόσι συνέγνωμεν.

Εἰ δὲ ὁ δεῖνα ἄρτι, παρακύψαι φιλοτιμούμενος
πρὸς τὸν βίον τῶν Χριστιανῶν, εἶτα οἰόμενος
αὐτῷ σεμνότητά τινα φέρειν τὸ ἡμῖν συνανατρί-
βεσθαι, ἅ τε οὐκ ἤκουσε κατασκευάζει, καὶ ἃ
μὴ ἐνόησεν ἐξηγεῖται, θαυμαστὸν οὐδέν. ἀλλ'
ἐκεῖνο θαυμαστὸν καὶ παράδοξον, ὅτι τούτων
ἀκροατὰς ἔχει τοὺς γνησιωτάτους μοι τῶν παρ'
ὑμῖν ἀδελφῶν, καὶ οὐκ ἀκροατὰς μόνον, ἀλλὰ
καὶ μαθητάς, ὡς ἔοικεν. εἴ γε[3] καὶ ἄλλως ἦν
παράδοξον τοιοῦτον μὲν εἶναι τὸν διδάσκοντα,[4]
ἐμὲ δὲ τὸν διασυρόμενον, ἀλλ' οὖν τῶν καιρῶν
ἡ καταστροφὴ ἐπαίδευσεν ἡμᾶς πρὸς μηδὲν
δυσκολαίνειν. πάλαι γὰρ τὰ τούτων ἀτιμότερα
συνήθη ἡμῖν γέγονε διὰ τὰς ἁμαρτίας ἡμῶν.
ἐγὼ τοίνυν, εἰ μὲν οὐδέπω τοῖς αὐτοῦ ἀδελφοῖς
δέδωκα πεῖραν τῆς ἐμαυτοῦ περὶ τὸν Θεὸν
αἱρέσεως,[5] οὐδὲ νῦν ἔχω τι ἀποκρίνασθαι· οὓς
γὰρ οὐκ ἔπεισεν ὁ μακρὸς χρόνος, πῶς συμπείσει
ἐπιστολὴ βραχεῖα ; εἰ δὲ ἐκεῖνα αὐτάρκη, λῆροι
νομιζέσθωσαν τὰ παρὰ τῶν διαβαλλόντων. πλήν
γε ὅτι, ἐὰν ἐπιτρέψωμεν στόμασιν ἀχαλινώτοις
καὶ καρδίαις ἀπαιδεύτοις λαλεῖν περὶ ὧν ἂν

---

[1] ἡμῶν add. Harl.   [2] οὕτω om. E.   [3] γάρ E.
[4] τοιούτους δὲ τοὺς ἀνεχομένους add. editi antiqi.
[5] προαιρέσεως Harl., Vat., et Clarom.

---

[1] Basil avoids mentioning the slanderer by name.

God that for the days or hours that are left to us
we may be preserved in the same disposition toward
you as in the past, during which we have been
conscious of having fallen short in nothing, be it
small or great.

But if the person we have in mind,[1] aspiring to
peer into the life of the Christians,[2] and also thinking
that his being associated with us may bring him a
certain degree of prestige, has recently proceeded
to trump up things which he has not heard and to
relate things of which he has gained no knowledge,
there is nothing surprising in that. But the surprising and indeed incredible thing is this—that he
finds as hearers of these slanders the truest to me of
the brethren among you, and not merely as hearers,
but even, it seems, as disciples. Even though, on
general grounds, it was incredible that such a man
as he should be the teacher and I the object of his
disparagement, yet the topsy-turvy condition of the
times has taught us to be vexed at nothing. For
charges more ignominious than these have for a
long time become familiar to us in punishment for
our sins. As for me, therefore, if I have never yet
given this fellow's brethren a proof of my opinions
regarding God, I certainly have no answer to give
now; for how will a brief letter persuade those
whom a long life has not convinced? But if that
life is in itself sufficient, let that which emanates
from the slanderers be considered mere nonsense.
Yet we must remember that if we suffer unbridled
mouths and uneducated minds to prattle about

[2] The intimation is that he cannot really enter into the
brotherhood of Christians, much as he would like to do so,
but can only peer at it.

ἐθέλωσιν,[1] καὶ ἕτοιμα ἔχωμεν πρὸς ὑποδοχὴν
τὰ ὦτα, οὐ μόνον ἡμεῖς τὰ τῶν ἄλλων παρα-
δεξόμεθα, ἀλλὰ καὶ ἕτεροι τὰ ἡμέτερα.

Τούτων δὲ αἴτιον ἐκεῖνο, ὃ πάλαι μὲν παρεκά-
λουν μὴ γίνεσθαι, νῦν δὲ ἀπαγορεύσας σιωπῶ,
τὸ μὴ συντυγχάνειν ἡμᾶς ἀλλήλοις. εἰ γὰρ κατὰ
τὰς ἀρχαίας συνθήκας, καὶ κατὰ τὴν ὀφειλομέ-
νην νῦν ταῖς ἐκκλησίαις παρ' ἡμῶν ἐπιμέλειαν,
τὰ πολλὰ τοῦ ἐνιαυτοῦ μετ' ἀλλήλων διή-
γομεν, οὐκ ἂν ἐδώκαμεν πάροδον τοῖς διαβάλ-
λουσι. σὺ[2] δέ, εἰ δοκεῖ, τούτους μὲν ἔα χαίρειν,
αὐτὸς δὲ παρακλήθητι συγκάμνειν ἡμῖν εἰς τὸν
προκείμενον ἀγῶνα καὶ συντυχεῖν μεθ' ἡμῶν τῷ
καθ' ἡμῶν στρατευομένῳ. εἰ γὰρ ὀφθῆς μόνον,
ἐφέξεις[3] αὐτοῦ τὴν ὁρμὴν καὶ τοὺς συγκροτου-
μένους ἐπὶ τῷ καταστρέψασθαι τὰ τῆς πατρίδος
πράγματα διαλύσεις, γνώριμον αὐτοῖς κατα-
στήσας, ὅτι αὐτὸς τῇ τοῦ Θεοῦ χάριτι τοῦ καθ'
ἡμᾶς συλλόγου κατάρχεις,[4] καὶ φράξεις πᾶν
ἄδικον στόμα τῶν λαλούντων κατὰ τοῦ Θεοῦ
ἀνομίαν. ἂν ταῦτα γένηται, αὐτὰ τὰ πράγματα
δείξει, τίς μὲν ὁ κατακολουθῶν σοι ἐπὶ τὰ καλά,
τίς δὲ ὁ μετοκλάζων καὶ προδιδοὺς δειλίᾳ τὸν
λόγον τῆς ἀληθείας. ἐὰν δὲ τὰ τῆς ἐκκλησίας
προδιδόμενα ᾖ, ὀλίγος[5] μοι λόγος διὰ ῥημάτων
πείθειν τοὺς τοσούτου με[6] τιθεμένους ἄξιον, ὅσον[7]
ἂν τιμήσωνται ἄνθρωποι οὔπω ἑαυτοὺς[8] μετρεῖν
δεδιδαγμένοι. μετ' οὐ πολὺ γάρ, τῇ τοῦ Θεοῦ

[1] θέλωσι E.
[3] ὑφέξεις E.
[5] οἱ δεῖς E.
[2] σοι E, editi antiqi.
[4] κατάρξεις editi antiqi.
[6] σε editi antiqi.

whatever they please, and if we hold our ears ready to receive, not only shall we receive a false idea of the affairs of the others, but they will do the same as to ours.

Now the cause of the present state of affairs is one which I have long urged you not to permit to arise, but which I now through very weariness of repetition pass over in silence—the fact that we do not meet one another. For if we, living up to our old agreements and to the responsibility which we now owe to the churches, were in the habit of spending the greater part of the year together, we should not have given access to these calumniators. But do you, if you approve, disregard these men, and of your own accord be pleased to co-operate with us in the struggle now at hand and to meet, in company with us, the enemy who is arrayed against us. For if you are merely seen, you will stop his attack and will utterly disperse those who are organizing themselves to overthrow their country, by making it known to them that you yourself by the grace of God are the leader of our forces, and that you will close every wicked mouth of such as utter lawlessness against God. If this is done, the facts themselves will show who it is that follows you to the goal of honour, and who it is that shifts hither and thither and in his cowardice betrays the word of truth. But if the interests of the Church are once betrayed, little need be said by me with the idea of persuading by words those who estimate my worth at what men may estimate it who have not yet learned to measure their own selves. For in no

---

[7] ὅσου E. [8] ἑαυτοῖς E.

χάριτι, ἡ διὰ τῶν ἔργων ἀπόδειξις τὰς συκοφαντίας ἐλέγξει, διοτι [1] προσδοκῶμεν ὑπὲρ τοῦ λόγου
τῆς ἀληθείας τάχα μέν τι καὶ μεῖζον πείσεσθαι·
εἰ δὲ μή, πάντως γε τῶν ἐκκλησιῶν καὶ τῶν
πατρίδων ἀπελαθήσεσθαι. ἐὰν δὲ καὶ μηδὲν τῶν
ἐλπιζομένων γένηται, οὐ μακράν ἐστι τὸ τοῦ
Χριστοῦ δικαστήριον. ὥστε, εἰ μὲν τὴν συντυχίαν, διὰ τὰς ἐκκλησίας ἐπιζητεῖς ἕτοιμος συνδραμεῖν ὅπουπερ ἂν προκαλῇ.[2] εἰ δέ, ἵνα τὰς
συκοφαντίας διαλύσω, οὐ σχολή μοι νῦν ἀποκρίνασθαι περὶ τούτων.

LXXII

Ἡσυχίῳ

Οἶδά σου καὶ τὴν πρὸς [3] ἡμᾶς ἀγάπην, καὶ
τὴν περὶ τὰ καλὰ σπουδήν. διόπερ χρήζων
δυσωπῆσαι τὸν ποθεινότατον υἱὸν Καλλισθένην,
ἡγησάμην, εἰ κοινωνόν σε λάβοιμι τῆς φροντίδος,
ῥᾷον κατορθώσειν τὸ σπουδαζόμενον. λελύπηται
ὁ ἀνὴρ κατὰ τοῦ λογιωτάτου Εὐστοχίου, καὶ
λελύπηται δικαίαν λύπην. ἐγκαλεῖ αὐτοῦ τοῖς
οἰκέταις θράσος κατ' αὐτοῦ καὶ ἀπόνοιαν. τοῦ-

---

[1] ὅτι E. [2] προσκαλῇ editi antiqi. [3] περί editi antiqi.

---

[1] Perhaps Basil is referring to martyrdom.
[2] Basil probably refers here both to Caesarea, the place of
his birth, and the Pontus, the region of his bringing-up.
Cf. Vol. I, p. 48, note 1.
[3] Written at about the same time as the preceding. On
Hesychius, cf. Letter XLIV.

great while, by the grace of God, the evidence of
our deeds will refute their slanders, because we
expect to suffer very soon some even greater misfortune [1] for the sake of the doctrine of truth; or,
if not that, then at least certainly to be banished
from the churches and from our countries. [2] But even
if none of these things to which we confidently look
forward comes to pass, the judgment of Christ is not
far off. Therefore, if you ask for the conference it
is for the churches' sake that I am ready to meet
with you wherever you summon me; but if it is in
order that I may refute these calumnies, then at
present I have no leisure to make any reply about
them.

LETTER LXXII

To Hesychius [3]

I am fully conscious both of your love for us and
of your zeal for what is honourable. Therefore, since
I am anxious that our most beloved son Callisthenes [4]
be placated, I have thought that, if I were to take
you as an associate in my design, I should more
easily bring to pass what I so strongly desire. He
has conceived a grievance against the most eloquent
Eustochius, and he has just grounds for his grievance. He accuses the servants of Eustochius of
insolence toward him, aye, and of madness. We
think it proper that he should be exhorted, being

---

[4] Callisthenes and Eustochius, mentioned below, were
both laymen of Cappadocia. Nothing is known about them
except such information as may be obtained from the present
and the following letters.

τὸν ἀξιοῦμεν παρακληθῆναι, ἀρκεσθέντα [1] τῷ
φόβῳ, ὃν ἐφόβησεν αὐτούς τε [2] τοὺς θρασυνο-
μένους καὶ τοὺς τούτων δεσπότας, καταλῦσαι
τὴν φιλονεικίαν, δόντα τὴν χάριν. οὕτω γὰρ
ἀμφότερα ὑπάρξει· [3] καὶ τὸ παρὰ ἀνθρώποις
σεμνόν, καὶ τὸ παρὰ Θεῷ εὐδόκιμον, ἐὰν τῷ φόβῳ
θελήσῃ τὸ μακρόθυμον ἀναμῖξαι. αὐτός τε οὖν,
εἴ τις σοι [4] προϋπάρχει φιλία πρὸς τὸν ἄνδρα
καὶ συνήθεια, αἴτησον παρ' αὐτοῦ τὴν χάριν
ταύτην· καὶ οὓς ἐὰν γνῷς ἐν τῇ πόλει δυναμένους
αὐτὸν δυσωπῆσαι, κοινωνοὺς λάβε τῆς φροντίδος,
εἰπὼν αὐτοῖς, ὅτι τὸ γινόμενον ἐμοὶ μάλιστα
κεχαρισμένον ἔσται.

Καὶ ἀπόπεμψαι τὸν συνδιάκονον πράξαντα [5]
ὧν ἕνεκεν ἀπεστάλη. αἰσχύνομαι γάρ, κατα-
φυγόντων πρός με τῶν ἀνθρώπων, μὴ δυνηθῆναι
αὐτοῖς γενέσθαι τι χρήσιμον.

LXXIII

Καλλισθένει

Ηὐχαρίστησα τῷ Θεῷ [6] τοῖς γράμμασιν ἐντυχὼν τῆς εὐγενείας σου· πρῶτον μέν, ὅτι ἀνδρὸς
τιμᾶν ἡμᾶς προαιρουμένου ἀφίκετό μοι προση-
γορία· καὶ γὰρ πολλοῦ μὲν [7] ἀξίαν τιθέμεθα
τῶν ἀρίστων ἀνδρῶν τὴν συντυχίαν· δεύτερον
δὲ εἰς εὐφροσύνην, τὸ μνήμης ἀγαθῆς τυγχάνειν.
σύμβολον δὲ μνήμης γράμματα, ἅπερ ἐπειδὴ

---

[1] ἀρκεσθῆναι παρακληθέντα E, Med.   [2] τε om. E.
[3] ὑπάρχει Harl.   [4] σοι om. E.
[5] τι add. E, editi antiqi.   [6] τῷ ἁγίῳ add. editi antiqi.

content with the fear which he has instilled into
the insolent servants themselves and into their
masters, to grant them forgiveness and put an end
to the quarrel. For in this way he will obtain two
things—the respect of men and the approval of
God—if he will consent to mingle forbearance with
the fear which he inspires. Do you, then, if you
have any well-established friendship or intimacy
with the man, ask this favour of him; and if you
happen to know those persons in the city who are
able to appease his anger, receive them as associates
in this design, telling them that the doing of this
thing will give me the greatest pleasure.

Send back our deacon, also, but only after he has
accomplished the purpose for which he was sent.
For I am ashamed, when the men in question have
taken refuge with me, that the rendering of some
service to them should prove beyond my powers.

LETTER LXXIII

To Callisthenes [1]

When I had read the letter of your Nobility, I
gave thanks to God: first, because greetings came
to me from a man who desired to honour us (for we
value highly association with the best men), and
secondly, because of the pleasure I received from
such kind remembrance. A letter, indeed, is a
token of remembrance, and when I received yours

---

[1] Of the same date as the preceding and on the same
subject. On Callisthenes, cf. the previous letter, note 2.

---

[7] μέν om. E.

ἐδεξάμην καὶ κατέμαθον τὸν ἐν αὐτοῖς νοῦν,
ἐθαύμασα ὅπως τῷ ὄντι κατὰ τὴν πάντων ὑπόληψιν πατρικὴν[1] ἀπένειμε[2] τὴν αἰδῶ. τὸ γὰρ
φλεγμαίνοντα καὶ ὠργισμένον καὶ ὁρμήσαντα
πρὸς τὴν τῶν λελυπηκότων ἄμυναν, παραλῦσαι
μὲν τὸ πολὺ τῆς σφοδρότητος, ἡμᾶς δὲ τοῦ
πράγματος κυρίους ποιήσασθαι, ἔδωκεν ἡμῖν
εὐφρανθῆναι ὡς[3] ἐπὶ τέκνῳ πνευματικῷ. ἀντὶ
οὖν τούτων τί ἄλλο λειπόμενόν ἐστιν ἢ εὔχεσθαί
σοι τὰ ἀγαθά; φίλοις μέν σε ἥδιστον εἶναι,
ἐχθροῖς δὲ φοβερόν, πᾶσι δὲ ὁμοίως αἰδέσιμον,
ἵνα καὶ οἱ τῶν προσηκόντων τι ἐλλελοιπότες,
αἴσθησιν λαβόντες τῆς ἐν σοὶ πραότητος, ἑαυτῶν
καθάψωνται, ὅτι εἰς τοιοῦτόν[4] σε ὄντα ἐξή-
μαρτον.

Ἐπειδὴ οὖν[5] προσέταξας τοὺς οἰκέτας ἐπὶ τὸν
τόπον ἐν ᾧ τὴν ἀταξίαν ἐπεδείξαντο διαχθῆναι,[6]
ἀξιῶ τὸν σκοπὸν μαθεῖν, καθ' ὃν ἐπιζητεῖ τοῦτο
ἡ χρηστότης σου. εἰ μὲν γὰρ αὐτὸς παρέσῃ καὶ
αὐτὸς εἰσπράξῃ[7] τῶν τετολμημένων τὴν δίκην,
παρέσονται μὲν οἱ παῖδες. τί γὰρ ἄλλο δεῖ
γενέσθαι, εἰ τοῦτό σοι κέκριται; πλὴν ἀλλ'
ἡμεῖς οὐκ οἴδαμεν ποίαν ἔτι χάριν εἰληφότες
ἐσόμεθα, ἐάν περ μὴ ἐξαρκέσωμεν[8] ἐξελέσθαι
τοὺς παῖδας τῆς τιμωρίας. εἰ δὲ αὐτόν σε ἡ
ἐπὶ τῆς λεωφόρου ἀσχολία καθέξει, τίς ὁ ὑποδεχόμενος ἐκεῖ τοὺς ἀνθρώπους; τίς δὲ ὁ μέλλων
αὐτοὺς ἀντὶ σοῦ ἀμύνεσθαι; ἀλλ' εἰ δοκεῖ σοι

---

[1] ἡμῖν add. E, editi antiqi. [2] ἀπένειμες editi antiqi.
[3] ὡς om. E. [4] τοσοῦτόν editi antiqi.
[5] δέ editi antiqi. [6] διαδεχθῆναι E.
[7] εἰσπράξεις editi antiqi. [8] ἐξαρκέσομεν editi antiqi.

and learned its purport, I marvelled that the respect
you accorded to me was in very truth, according to
the conception which all men have, that of a son to
a father. For the fact that a man who is blazing
with indignation and eager to take vengeance on
those who have injured him, should abandon for the
most part the vehemence of his emotions, and give
us full authority in the matter, afforded us such cause
for rejoicing as though it were in a spiritual son. In
return for this, therefore, what else is left than to
invoke blessings upon you—that you may be most
pleasing to your friends, formidable to your enemies,
and respected by all alike—in order that those who
have at all failed in their duties towards you, per-
ceiving the forbearance of your character, may blame
themselves for having wronged so admirable a man
as yourself ?

Since, therefore, you have given orders that the
slaves be taken to the place in which they exhibited
their rebellious attitude, I feel that I must learn
the object for which your Excellency demands this.
For if you are to be there in person and in person
to exact the penalty for their audacious deeds, the
slaves will indeed be there (for what other course is
possible, if this is your decision ?), yet as for ourselves,
on the other hand, we do not perceive what extra
favour we shall have received if our influence does
not suffice to secure for the slaves a remission of their
punishment. But if you yourself shall be detained
by the demands upon your time during the journey,
who is to receive the men at the designated place,
and who is to punish them in your stead ? But
if it is your wish that they be brought into your
presence and this is your absolute decision, then give

63

ἐλθεῖν αὐτοὺς εἰς ὄψιν καὶ τοῦτο πάντως κέκριται,
μέχρι Σασίμων κέλευσον γενέσθαι αὐτῶν τὴν
παράστασιν, καὶ αὐτοῦ δεῖξον σεαυτοῦ τὸ πρᾶον
τοῦ ἤθους καὶ μεγαλόθυμον. λαβὼν γὰρ ὑπο-
χειρίους τοὺς παροξύναντας, καὶ ἐν τούτῳ τὸ
εὐκαταφρόνητον [1] τῆς σεαυτοῦ [2] ἀξίας ἐπιδειξάμενος, ἄφες αὐτοὺς ἀβλαβεῖς, ὡς ἐν τοῖς προτέροις
γράμμασι παρεκαλέσαμεν, ἡμῖν μὲν διδοὺς τὴν
χάριν, παρὰ δὲ Θεοῦ τὴν ἐφ᾿ οἷς ποιεῖς ἀντίδοσιν
ἐκδεχόμενος.

Καὶ ταῦτα λέγω, οὐχ ὡς οὕτως ὀφείλοντος
τελεσθῆναι τοῦ πράγματος, ἀλλὰ συνενδιδοὺς τῇ
ὁρμῇ σου, καὶ φοβούμενος μή τι ὑπολείπηται [3]
ἄπεπτον τοῦ θυμοῦ, καὶ ὥσπερ ἐπὶ τῶν φλεγμαι-
νόντων ὀφθαλμῶν καὶ τὰ ἁπαλώτατα τῶν βοη-
θημάτων ὀδυνηρὰ φαίνεται, οὕτω καὶ νῦν ὁ
ἡμέτερος λόγος ἐξαγριάνῃ σε μᾶλλον ἢ κατα-
στείλῃ. ἐπεὶ τὸ εὐπρεπέστατον ἦν, καὶ σοὶ
μέγιστον κόσμον ἐνεγκεῖν δυνάμενον καὶ ἐμοὶ
ἀρκοῦν πρὸς τοὺς ἐμαυτοῦ φίλους καὶ ἡλικιώτας
εἰς σεμνολόγημα, τὸ ἡμῖν ἐπιτραπῆναι τὴν
ἐκδίκησιν. πάντως δὲ εἰ καὶ ὀμώμοσται σοὶ
δοῦναι αὐτοὺς [4] εἰς [5] τιμωρίαν κατὰ τοὺς νόμους,
οὔτε ἡ παρ᾿ ἡμῶν ἐπιτίμησις ἐλάττων ἐστὶν εἰς
ἐκδίκησιν, οὔτε ὁ θεῖος νόμος ἀτιμότερος τῶν
ἐμπολιτευομένων τῷ βίῳ νομίμων.

Ἀλλ᾿ ἦν δυνατὸν αὐτούς, ἐνταῦθα ἐπιστρα-
φέντας τοῖς ἡμετέροις νομίμοις, ἐν οἷς καὶ αὐτὸς
τὴν ἐλπίδα ἔχεις τῆς σωτηρίας, καὶ σὲ τῆς ἐπὶ
τῷ ὅρκῳ ἀνάγκης ἐλευθερῶσαι, καὶ αὐτοὺς

---

[1] ἀκαταφρόνητον E. [2] σῆς editi antiqi.
[3] ὑπολίπηται E. [4] αὐτεῖς E. [5] εἰς om. E.

orders that their appearance take place no farther away than Sasima, and there show the gentleness and magnanimity of your character. For having once taken into your power those who have angered you, and having by that act clearly indicated that your dignity is not to be made the object of contempt, send them away unharmed, as we besought you in our previous letter, to us granting that favour, but at God's hands awaiting the recompense for your deeds.

I say these things, moreover, not because I think the incident ought to be closed in this way, but by way of conceding something to your impetuous spirit, and because I am afraid that some part of your anger may remain undigested, and that just as, in the case of inflammation of the eyes, even the mildest remedies seem painful, so now our words may arouse your fury instead of calming it. For the fact is that the most befitting solution—the one which is capable of bringing you the greatest credit and is sufficient to enhance the dignity of my standing with my friends and contemporaries—would have been to entrust the punishment into our hands. And certainly, even if you have bound yourself by oath to give them over to the vengeance of the laws, a stern reprimand by us is no less effective in vindicating justice, nor is God's law held in slighter honour than the civil usages which play a part in the lives of men.

Nay, it would have been possible for them to be converted here in this place through the usages of our Church, in which you yourself have your hope of salvation, and thus to set you free from the obligation of your oath, and at the same time

65

σύμμετρον τοῖς ἡμαρτημένοις ἐκπληρῶσαι τὴν
δίκην.

Ἀλλὰ πάλιν μακρὰν ποιῶ τὴν ἐπιστολήν.
ὑπὸ γὰρ τοῦ σφόδρα σπουδάζειν πιθανός σοι
γενέσθαι, οὐδὲν τῶν εἰς διάνοιαν ἐρχομένων
ἀποσιωπῆσαι ἀνέχομαι, φοβούμενος μὴ παρὰ
τοῦτο ἄπρακτός μοι ἡ αἴτησις γένηται, ἐλλιπῶς
μου τὴν διδασκαλίαν ποιησαμένου. ἀλλ᾽, ὦ
τιμιώτατον καὶ γνήσιον θρέμμα τῆς Ἐκκλησίας,
βεβαίωσον καὶ ἐμοὶ τὰς ἐλπίδας, ἃς ἔχω νῦν
ἐπὶ σοὶ καὶ τὰς πάντων συμφώνως περὶ τῆς
σῆς ἐμμελείας καὶ πραότητος μαρτυρίας, καὶ
ἐπίστειλον τῷ στρατιώτῃ ἀπαλλαγῆναι ἡμῶν ἐν
τάχει, ὃς νῦν γε οὐδὲν ἐπαχθείας οὐδὲ ὕβρεως
ἐλλέλοιπε, μᾶλλον αἱρούμενός σε μὴ λυπῆσαι ἢ
πάντας ἡμᾶς οἰκείους ἔχειν καὶ φίλους.

LXXIV

Μαρτινιανῷ

Ἐμὲ τί οἴει πόσου ποτ᾽ ἂν τιμήσασθαι τὸ
εἰς ταὐτὸν ποθ᾽ ἡμᾶς ἀλλήλοις ἐλθεῖν καὶ ἐπὶ

---

[1] Of the year 371, and addressed to Martinianus, a personal
friend of Basil but otherwise unknown. There seems no
good reason for calling Martinianus an official of Cappadocia,
as Mr. B. Jackson does. On the other hand, the profusion of
literary allusions in the letter, and the compliments to the
knowledge of history and of mankind that Martinianus
possessed, suggest that he was a philosopher or man of letters.
Cf. W. M. Ramsay, Basil of Caesareia, *Expositor*, 5 Series,
Vol. III (1896), 54.

The policy of the Byzantine government had been uniformly
directed to subdividing the great provinces with a view to
diminishing the power of the provincial governors. Cappadocia was to be thus divided in 371 by the Emperor Valens,
resolved on this step probably by his enmity towards the
"orthodox" bishop. In any case, this subdivision would
naturally have been made sooner or later by an "orthodox"

themselves to pay the penalty commensurate with their crimes.

But again I am making my letter long. For since I am exceedingly anxious to convince you, I cannot allow myself to pass over in silence any of the ideas that come into my mind, fearing lest otherwise my request may prove unsuccessful,—if I fail to furnish an adequate presentation of the case. But, most honoured and true son of the Church, confirm both the hopes which I now have in you and the unanimous testimony of all to your moderation and gentleness, and command to depart from us at once the soldier, who up to now has omitted nothing in the way of annoyance and insolence, since he chooses rather to avoid offending you than to have us all as his devoted friends.

LETTER LXXIV

To Martinianus [1]

How highly, think you, would I for my part prize the privilege of our some day meeting one

bishop, solely as a political policy ; and as a matter of fact Cappadocia was later divided into three parts by Justinian. Valens' hatred for Basil, however, was exhibited by his leaving the smaller part of Cappadocia to the metropolis, Caesarea, and making the new province of Second Cappadocia decidedly larger. Caesarea was seriously affected by this change, and shrank to less than half its former size. Basil exerted himself to the utmost in its behalf, but the three letters (the present and two following) which he wrote entreating the intercession of certain influential persons with Valens in favour of Caesarea, are among the poorest in the collection. They are inflated and exaggerated in their description of the loss that would result to Caesarea, and show no appreciation of the causes that recommend the subdivision. The true greatness of Basil, however, appeared immediately afterwards, when Valens came to Caesarea.

67

πλεῖον σοὶ συγγενέσθαι, ὥστε πάντων ἀπολαῦσαι
τῶν ἐν σοὶ καλῶν; καὶ γὰρ εἰ μέγα πρὸς μαρτυρίαν παιδεύσεως τὸ πολλῶν ἀνθρώπων ἰδεῖν
ἄστεα, καὶ νόον γνῶναι, τοῦτο οἶμαι δι᾽ ὀλίγου
χαρίζεσθαι τὴν σὴν ὁμιλίαν. τί γὰρ διαφέρει
πολλοὺς ἰδεῖν κατὰ μέρος, ἢ ἕνα τὸν[1] πάντων
ὁμοῦ τὴν πεῖραν ἀναδεξάμενον; μᾶλλον δὲ ἐγὼ
καὶ πλεῖστον ἂν ἔχειν εἴποιμι τὸ διάφορον, ὅσα
ἀταλαίπωρον τὴν γνῶσιν τῶν καλῶν προξενεῖ,
καὶ καθαρὰν τῆς πρὸς τὸ χεῖρον ἐπιμιξίας συνά-
γει τὴν ἱστορίαν τῆς ἀρετῆς. εἴτε γὰρ πρᾶξις
ἀρίστη, εἴτε λόγος μνήμης ἄξιος, εἴτε πολιτεῖαι[2]
ἀνδρῶν ὑπερπεφυκότων τοὺς ἄλλους, πάντα τῷ
σῷ ταμιείῳ τῆς ψυχῆς ἐναπόκειται. ὥστε οὐκ
εἰς ἐνιαυτὸν μόνον, ὡς ὁ Ἀλκίνοος[3] τοῦ Ὀδυσσέως, ἀλλ᾽ εἰς πάντα μου τὸν βίον εὐξαίμην ἂν
σου ἀκούειν, καὶ μακρὸν ἄν μοι γενέσθαι τούτου
γε ἕνεκα τούτου, καὶ ταῦτα δυσκόλως πρὸς αὐτὸν
διακείμενος. τί δήποτ᾽ οὖν ἐπιστέλλω νῦν,
παρεῖναι δέον; ὅτι με[4] κάμνουσα ἡ πατρὶς
ἐπείγει πρὸς ἑαυτήν. οἷα γὰρ πέπονθεν, οὐκ
ἀγνοεῖς, ὦ ἄριστε· ὅτι Πενθέως τρόπον Μαινάδες
ὄντως τινές, δαίμονες,[5] αὐτὴν διεσπάσαντο.
διαιροῦσι γὰρ αὐτὴν καὶ ἐπιδιαιροῦσιν· ὥσπερ

---

[1] τῶν editi antiqi. [2] πολιτεῖα E.
[3] Ἀλκίνους E, editi antiqi. [4] κἀμέ E, MSS. Med.
[5] Perhaps a marginal gloss.

---

[1] Cf. *Odyssey*, I. 3 ff.: πολλῶν δ᾽ ἀνθρώπων ἴδεν ἄστεα καὶ νόον
ἔγνω, | πολλὰ δ᾽ ὅ γ᾽ ἐν πόντῳ πάθεν ἄλγεα ὃν κατὰ θυμόν, etc.
"Many were the men whose cities he saw and whose mind
he learned, aye, and many the woes he suffered in his heart
upon the sea, seeking to win his own life and the return of

another and of having for myself a longer association
with you, so as to enjoy all the noble qualities that
are yours? For if it is important as a proof of
education " to have seen the cities of many men
and to have learned their minds," [1] this boon is, I
think, conferred in a short time by converse with
you. For what superiority is there in seeing many
men one by one over seeing one single person who
has taken to himself the experience of all mankind?
Nay, rather should I say that there is the greatest
superiority in whatever provides without hardship
an acquaintance with what is noble, and brings
together, unsullied by any admixture of evil, the
entire record of virtue. For whether it be a noble
deed, or a saying worthy of remembrance, or the
polities of men who have surpassed all their fellows
in natural endowments, all these things are stored
away in the treasure-house of your soul. Therefore
not merely for a year, like Alcinous listening to
Odysseus,[2] but for my whole life I should pray that
I might listen to you, and that my life might be
prolonged on that account at least, even though
I am discontented with it. Why in the world, for
instance, am I now writing, when I ought to be
with you? It is because my afflicted country urges
me to hurry to succour her. For you are not unaware,
my good friend, of what she has suffered—that like
Pentheus she has been torn asunder by veritable
Maenads, demons in fact. They are dividing her,
and again dividing her, just as incompetent physicians

---

his comrades." Cf. also the imitation of Horace in *De
Arte Poetica*, 142 : Qui mores hominum multorum vidit et
urbes.

[2] Cf. *Odyssey*, Bks. 7, 8, 9.

οἱ κακοὶ τῶν ἰατρῶν, χαλεπώτερα τὰ ἕλκη
ποιοῦντες τῇ παρ' ἑαυτῶν ἀπειρίᾳ. ἐπεὶ οὖν
κέκμηκε κατατεμνομένη, λείπεται αὐτὴν θερα-
πεύειν, ὡς ἀρρωστοῦσαν. ἐπέστειλαν οὖν [1]
ἐπείγοντες ἡμᾶς οἱ πολῖται· καὶ ἀνάγκη ἀπαντᾶν,
οὐχ ὥς τι ὄφελος ἐσομένους τοῖς πράγμασιν,
ἀλλὰ τὴν ἐκ τῆς ἀπολείψεως μέμψιν ἐκκλίνοντας.
οἶσθα γάρ, ὡς εὔκολοι μὲν ἐλπίσαι οἱ ἀμηχα-
νοῦντες, εὔκολοι δέ που καὶ καταμέμψασθαι,
ἐπὶ τὸ παρεθὲν ἀεὶ τρέποντες τὰς αἰτίας.

Καίτοι ἔγωγε καὶ αὐτοῦ τούτου ἕνεκεν ἐδεόμην
σοι συνελθεῖν καὶ δοῦναι γνώμην· μᾶλλον δὲ παρακαλέσαι ἐνθυμηθῆναί τι νεανικὸν καὶ πρέπον τῷ
σεαυτοῦ φρονήματι, καὶ εἰς γόνυ κλιθεῖσαν τὴν
πατρίδα ἡμῶν μὴ περιιδεῖν, ἀλλὰ καταλαβόντα
τὸ στρατόπεδον εἰπεῖν μετὰ παρρησίας τῆς σῆς
μήτοι νομίζειν αὐτοὺς δύο κεκτῆσθαι ἀντὶ μιᾶς
ἐπαρχίας. οὐ γὰρ ἐξ ἄλλης τινὸς οἰκουμένης
ἐπεισήγαγον τὴν ἑτέραν,[2] ἀλλὰ παραπλήσιόν τι
πεποιήκασιν, ὥσπερ ἂν εἴ τις ἵππον ἢ βοῦν
κεκτημένος, εἶτα διχῇ διελὼν δύο νομίζοι ἔχειν
ἑνὸς ἄντι·[3] οὔτε γὰρ δύο ἐποίησε, καὶ τὸν ἕνα
διέφθειρεν· εἰπεῖν δὲ καὶ τοῖς παραδυναστεύουσι,
μὴ τοῦτον αὔξειν τὸν τρόπον τὴν βασιλείαν, οὐ
γὰρ ἐν ἀριθμῷ εἶναι τὴν δύναμιν, ἀλλ' ἐν τοῖς
πράγμασιν· ἐπεὶ νῦν γε ἡγούμεθα τοὺς μὲν ἀγνοίᾳ
τῆς ἀληθείας ἴσως, τοὺς δὲ τῷ μὴ βούλεσθαι

----

[1] γ' οὖν E.   [2] ἡμέραν E.   [3] ἀντὶ ἑνός E.

who make wounds worse because of their own in-
experience. Therefore, since she has become ill
under such dissection, the task remains to heal her
as a patient weakened by sickness. Accordingly
our fellow-citizens have written urging us to hasten
to them, and we must answer the summons, not
with the thought that we shall be of any help to
them in their difficulties, but in order to avoid the
censure that would be occasioned by our failing them.
For you know how prone to hope are those who are in
distress, but prone, methinks, also to find fault, ever
directing their charges against what has been left
undone.

And yet for this very reason I wanted to meet
you and express my mind to you ; or rather to beg
you to devise some vigorous measure, worthy of
your wisdom, and not to ignore our country when
she has fallen to her knees, but going to the court
to bid them with your characteristic frankness to
give up the notion that they possess two provinces
instead of one. For not from some other portion of
the earth have they brought in the second province,
but what they have done is about the same as if a
man, possessing a horse or an ox, should divide it into
two parts, and then consider that he had two animals
instead of one he had. For he has not created two
and he has destroyed the one. I wanted to urge you
also to tell those in authority not to try to increase
their kingdom in this fashion, for power consists,
not in numbers, but in actual things. And they
should be told, since we are of the opinion that they
now—some perhaps through ignorance of the truth,
others through their unwillingness to give offence
by their words, and others still through their un-

λυπεῖν τοῖς ῥήμασι, τοὺς [1] δὲ καὶ οὐ μέλον αὐτοῖς, περιορᾶν τὰ γινόμενα. εἰ μὲν οὖν ἦν [2] δυνατὸν αὐτὸν ἐλθεῖν πρὸς βασιλέα, τοῦτο κράτιστον μὲν τοῖς πράγμασι, πρέπον δέ σου τῇ καλῇ [3] τοῦ βίου προαιρέσει. εἰ δὲ βαρὺ ἄλλως καὶ διὰ τὴν ὥραν τοῦ ἔτους καὶ διὰ τὴν ἡλικίαν, ὡς αὐτὸς ἔφης, σύντροφον ἔχουσαν ἐν ἑαυτῇ τὸν ὄκνον, ἀλλὰ τό γε [4] ἐπιστεῖλαι πόνος οὐδείς. ὥστε, τὴν ἀπὸ τῶν γραμμάτων βοήθειαν χαριζόμενος [5] τῇ πατρίδι, πρῶτον μὲν σαυτῷ συνειδήσεις μηδὲν τῶν εἰς δύναμιν ἡκόντων ἐλλελοιπότι, ἔπειτα μέντοι καὶ τοῖς κάμνουσιν, αὐτῷ τῷ φαίνεσθαι συναλγῶν, ἀρκοῦσαν δώσεις παραμυθίαν. ἀλλ' εἴθε γὰρ ἦν [6] οἷόν τε, αὐτὸν ἐπιστάντα τοῖς πράγμασιν, ὄψει λαβεῖν αὐτὰ τὰ σκυθρωπά. οὕτω γὰρ ἂν ἴσως, ἀπ' αὐτῆς τῆς ἐναργείας [7] τῶν ὁρωμένων συγκινηθείς, ἀφῆκάς τινα φωνὴν πρέπουσαν καὶ τῇ σῇ μεγαλονοίᾳ καὶ τῇ κατηφείᾳ τῆς πόλεως. σὺ δὲ ἀλλ' ἡμῖν διηγουμένοις μὴ ἀπιστήσῃς. ἢ ὅτι Σιμωνίδου ὄντως ἤ τινος τοιούτου μελοποιοῦ ἐδεόμεθα, ἐναργῶς εἰδότος ἐπιστενάζειν τοῖς πάθεσι ; καίτοι τί λέγω Σιμωνίδην ; δέον Αἰσχύλον εἰπεῖν, ἢ εἰ δή τις ἕτερος, παραπλησίως ἐκείνῳ συμφορᾶς μέγεθος ἐναργῶς διαθέμενος, μεγαλοφώνως ὠδύρατο.

---

[1] τοῖς E.   [2] ἦν om. E.   [3] ὅλη editi antiqi.
[4] τό γε] τότε editi antiqi.   [5] χαρισάμενος editi antiqi.
[6] ἦν om. E.   [7] ἐνεργείας E.

concern for such matters—are permitting these things to happen. Now if it were possible for you to go to the Emperor himself, this would be the best thing in the circumstances, and would be in keeping with your noble course of life. But if it is difficult on general grounds and because of the season of the year and your age, which, as you yourself have said, is subject to an indwelling slothfulness, still there is no labour in writing a letter at least. Accordingly, if you do your country the service of helping her by letter, you will, in the first place, have the consciousness of not having failed her in anything within your power, and, in the second place, you will be giving, by the very fact that you show sympathy, sufficient consolation to those who are afflicted. But would that it had been possible for you to be present on the scene in person, and to see with your own eyes the melancholy sight as it is. For thus, perhaps, stirred by the very vividness of what you had seen, you would have sent forth a cry of protest befitting both your magnanimity and the sorrow of the city. Nevertheless, when we tell you the facts, do not refuse to believe us. Or is it that we had need of a Simonides [1] in very truth, or a poet of his powers, with skill to bewail in impressive language great disasters? Yet why do I say Simonides? I should have said Aeschylus,[2] or someone else who, setting forth impressively as he did a mighty disaster, with mighty voice made lamentation.

[1] Basil is probably thinking of Simonides' lament on those who died at Thermopylae.

[2] Basil probably has in mind Aeschylus' "Seven Against Thebes" and the Orestean trilogy.

Σύλλογοι μὲν γὰρ ἐκεῖνοι, καὶ λόγοι, αἱ[1] κατ' ἀγορὰν συντυχίαι τῶν ἐλλογίμων ἀνδρῶν, καὶ ὅσα πρότερον ἐποίει τὴν ἡμετέραν ὀνομαστὴν πόλιν[2] ἡμᾶς ἐπιλελοίπασιν· ὥστε τῶν περὶ παιδείαν καὶ λόγους ἧττον ἂν φανείη νῦν τις ἐμβαλὼν τῇ ἀγορᾷ ἢ Ἀθήνησι πρότερον οἱ ἀτιμίαν κατεγνωσμένοι, ἢ[3] τὰς χεῖρας ὄντες μὴ[4] καθαροί. ἀντεισῆκται δὲ τούτοις Σκυθῶν τινῶν ἢ Μασσαγετῶν ἀμουσία· μία δὲ φωνὴ ἀπαιτούντων καὶ ἀπαιτουμένων καὶ ξαινομένων ταῖς μάστιξι. στοαὶ δ' ἑκατέρωθεν σκυθρωπὸν ἐπηχοῦσαι[5] οἷον οἰκείαν δοκοῦσιν ἀφιέναι φωνὴν τοῖς γινομένοις ἐπιστενάζουσαι. γυμνάσια δὲ κεκλεισμένα καὶ νύκτας[6] ἀλαμπεῖς οὐκ ἐᾷ ἡμᾶς οὐδὲν λογίζεσθαι ἡ περὶ τοῦ[7] ζῆν ἀγωνία. κίνδυνος γὰρ οὐχ ὁ τυχών, τῶν κρατούντων ὑφαιρεθέντων, ὥσπερ ἐρείσμασι[8] πεσοῦσι συγκατενεχθῆναι τὰ πάντα. καὶ τίς ἂν λόγος τῶν κακῶν τῶν ἡμετέρων ἐφίκοιτο; οἱ μὲν οἴχονται φεύγοντες, μέρος τῆς βουλῆς ἡμῶν, οὐ τὸ φαυλότατον, τὴν ἀειφυγίαν Ποδανδοῦ[9] προτιμήσαντες. ὅταν δὲ Ποδανδὸν εἴπω, τὸν Κεάδαν με οἴου λέγειν τὸν Λακωνικόν, ἢ εἴ που[10] τῆς οἰκουμένης εἶδες βάραθρον αὐτοφυές, ἃ δὴ καὶ Χαρώνειά τισι προσαγορεύειν αὐτομάτως ἐπῆλθεν, ἀέρα νοσοποιὸν[11] ἀναπνέοντα. τοιούτῳ τινὶ ἐοικὸς

[1] τε add. E. [2] πάλαι E, editi antiqi.
[3] ἢ] οἱ (καί ante οἱ in marg. m. recen.) E. [4] οὐ E.
[5] ἀπηχοῦσαι Med. [6] νύκτες editi antiqi.
[7] τό editi antiqi. [8] ἐρείσματι E. [9] Προδανδοῦ E.
[10] εἴ που] ὅπου E. [11] φθοροποιόν editi antiqi.

---

[1] Modern Podando, in southern Cappadocia. Established by Valens as the capital of the new division of the province.

For the gatherings of old, the orations, the conversations of learned men in the market-place, and all that formerly made our city famous, have left us; in consequence there is now less likelihood of a learned or eloquent man's entering our Forum than that in former days at Athens men would appear in public who had been convicted of dishonour or were impure of hand. Instead of such men the unrefinement of Scythians or Massagete tribes has come in; we hear but one sound—the voices of men dunning and being dunned, of men lacerated with whips. The porticoes resounding on either side with melancholy echoes seem, as it were, to give forth a voice of their own as they lament over what is being done. As for our closed gymnasia and lampless nights, we cannot take thought of them at all because of our struggle to keep alive. For the danger is not slight that, since those in authority have been removed, the whole edifice will collapse, as it were, together with the falling of its props. What words, indeed, could match our misfortunes? Some have gone into exile, a part of our Council, and that not the most ignoble, preferring exile for life to Podandus.[1] But when I say Podandus, imagine that I say Laconian Ceades,[2] or any other pit made by nature which you may have seen anywhere in the world, such places as men have been led to designate instinctively as Charonian, since they exhale a deadly vapour. Like some such place as these I would have you consider this accursed

[2] The name given by the Spartans to the pit into which condemned criminals were thrown; cf. Pausanias, 4, 18, 4; Thucydides, 1, 134; Strabo, 8, 367.

νόμισον καὶ τὸ Ποδανδοῦ κακόν· τριῶν τοίνυν μοι-
ρῶν, οἱ μὲν φεύγουσιν αὐταῖς γυναιξὶ καὶ ἑστίαις
ἀπαναστάντες· οἱ δὲ ἀπάγονται ὥσπερ αἰχμάλω-
τοι, οἱ πλεῖστοι τῶν ἐν τῇ πόλει ἄριστοι, ἐλεεινὸν
φίλοις θέαμα, ἐχθροῖς δὲ εὐχὴν ἐκπληροῦντες, εἰ
δή τις γέγονεν ὅλως τοσοῦτον ἡμῖν ἐπαρασάμενος.
τριτάτη δέ που μοῖρα λέλειπται· οὗτοι δέ, τήν τε
ἀπόλειψιν τῶν συνήθων [1] οὐ φέροντες, καὶ ἅμα
τῆς χρείας ἀτονώτεροι [2] ἀπελεγχόμενοι, πρὸς
αὐτὸ τὸ ζῆν ἀπειρήκασι.

Ταῦτά σε φανερὰ ποιῆσαι πᾶσι παρακαλοῦμεν
τῇ σεαυτοῦ φωνῇ καὶ τῇ σεαυτοῦ παρρησίᾳ τῇ
δικαίᾳ, ἣν ἔχεις ἀπὸ τοῦ βίου, ἐκεῖνο σαφῶς
προειπόντα, ὅτι, ἐὰν μὴ ταχὺ μεταβουλεύσωνται,
οὐδ' ἕξουσιν εἰς οὓς τὴν φιλανθρωπίαν ἐνδείξονται.[3]
ἢ γὰρ γενήσῃ τι ὄφελος τοῖς κοινοῖς, ἢ τό γε τοῦ
Σόλωνος πεποιηκὼς ἔσῃ, ὃς τοῖς ἀπολειφθεῖσι τῶν
πολιτῶν ἀμύνειν [4] οὐκ ἔχων, τῆς ἀκροπόλεως ἤδη
κατεχομένης, τὰ ὅπλα ἐνδὺς πρὸ τῶν θυρῶν [5]
ἐκαθέζετο, εὔδηλος ὢν τῷ σχήματι τοῖς γινομένοις
οὐ συντιθέμενος. ἐκεῖνο δ' ἀκριβῶς οἶδα, ὅτι, καὶ
εἴ τίς σου νῦν τὴν γνώμην μὴ ἀποδέχοιτο, μικρὸν
ὕστερόν σοι [6] εὐνοίας τε ὁμοῦ καὶ συνέσεως τὴν
μεγίστην [7] δόξαν προσθήσει ὅταν ἴδῃ τὰ πράγματα κατὰ τὴν πρόρρησιν ἀπαντήσαντα.

---

[1] συνοίκων Med. Harl. [2] ἀπονώτερον E.
[3] ἐνδείξωνται editi antiqi.
[4] τῆς ἐλευθερίας add. editi antiqi.
[5] πυλῶν E. [6] σοι om. E, editi antiqi.
[7] μεγάλην E.

Podandus. Well then, of the three sections of our
city, some are going into exile, departing with their
wives and hearths; some are being led away as
captives, the majority of the best citizens of the
state, a miserable spectacle to their friends, but thus
fulfilling their enemies' prayers, if indeed any enemy
that ever lived has called down so terrible a curse
upon us. About a third part of the citizens is still
left here ; and these, because they cannot endure
the separation from their old acquaintances, and
being at the same time too weak to cope with the
necessities of their situation, despair of life itself.

We exhort you to make these circumstances known
to all with that voice of yours and with that righteous
boldness of speech which your condition of life con-
fers upon you, proclaiming this fact clearly—that
unless they quickly change their policies, they will
not have any to whom they may show their
benevolence. For you will either be of some assistance to the commonweal, or you will do as
Solon [1] did, who, being unable, when the Acropolis
already had been captured, to protect his fellow-
citizens who were left behind, put on his armour
and sat before the gates, making it clear by his
attitude that he was not a party to the things being
done. Moreover, I am absolutely certain of this,
that, even though there may be one who will not
now accept your decision in the matter, yet in a
short time he will assign to you the greatest renown
for both benevolence and wisdom, when he sees
events turning out in accordance with your pre-
dictions.

[1] This story is related in Plutarch, *Solon*, 30, and Diogenes
Laertius, 1, 49.

LXXV

Ἀβουργίῳ[1]

Πολλῶν ὄντων ἃ τὸ σὸν ἦθος ὑπὲρ τοὺς ἄλλους
εἶναι πεποίηκεν, οὐδὲν οὕτως ἴδιόν ἐστι σὸν ὡς ἡ
περὶ τὴν πατρίδα σπουδή, δικαίας αὐτῇ ἀποδι-
δόντος σου τὰς ἀμοιβάς, ἐξ ἧς ὁρμηθεὶς τοσοῦτος
ἐγένου, ὥστε διὰ πάσης τῆς οἰκουμένης γνώριμον
εἶναί σου τὴν περιφάνειαν. αὕτη τοίνυν ἡ πατρίς,
ἡ σὲ ἐνεγκοῦσα καὶ θρεψαμένη, εἰς τὴν τῶν
παλαιῶν διηγημάτων ἀπιστίαν περιελήλυθε·[2]
καὶ οὐκ ἄν τις ἐπιστὰς ἡμῶν τῇ πόλει, οὐδὲ τῶν
πάνυ συνήθων, αὐτὴν[3] γνωρίσειεν· οὕτως εἰς
πᾶσαν ἐρημίαν ἀθρόως μετεσκεύασται, πολλῶν
μὲν καὶ πρότερον αὐτῆς[4] ἀφαιρεθέντων τῶν[5]
πολιτευομένων, νῦν δὲ σχεδὸν ἁπάντων εἰς τὴν
Ποδανδὸν μετοικισθέντων. ὧν ἀκρωτηριασθέντες
οἱ λειπόμενοι καὶ αὐτοὶ εἰς πᾶσαν ἀπόγνωσιν
μεταπεπτώκασι,[6] καὶ πᾶσι τοσοῦτον ἐνεποίησαν[7]
τῆς ἀθυμίας τὸν ὄγκον, ὥστε σπανίζειν λοιπὸν
καὶ τῶν οἰκητόρων τὴν πόλιν, καὶ γεγενῆσθαι[8]
τὰ τῇδε ἐρημίαν δεινήν, ἐλεεινὸν μὲν φίλοις θέαμα,
πολλὴν δὲ χαρὰν καὶ εὐθυμίαν φέρον τοῖς πάλαι
ἐφεδρεύουσιν ἡμῶν τῷ πτώματι. τίνος οὖν ἐστι
χεῖρα ἡμῖν ὀρέξαι; ἢ τίνος συμπαθὲς[9] ἐφ᾽ ἡμῖν
ἀφεῖναι δάκρυον, ἀλλ᾽ οὐχὶ τῆς σῆς ἡμερότητος,

---

[1] Ἀβουργίῳ editi antiqi.   [2] ἐλήλυθε tres MSS.
[3] αὐτῇ E, Med.   [4] αὐτῆς om. E.   [5] τῶν om. E.
[6] καταπεπτώκασι editi antiqi.   [7] ἐνεποίησε E.
[8] γενέσθαι E.   [9] συμπαθεῖς E, editi antiqi.

---

[1] Written at about the same time as the preceding letter ;

LETTER LXXV

To Aburgius[1]

WHILE there are many qualities which have made your character superior to that of others, yet there is no trait so peculiarly your own as your zeal for your homeland, seeing that you render a just recompense to her from whom you were sprung and have reached so high an estate that your fame is known throughout the whole world. But now this very homeland herself, which bore and reared you, has reverted to the incredible condition of early legend; and no one of us, on revisiting the city, even one who had known her well, would recognize her, so completely has she been suddenly transformed into an utter solitude, since many of her citizens were even before this taken from her, and now almost all of them have emigrated to Podandus.[2] Mutilated by the loss of these, the remnants have themselves fallen into utter despair, and have produced in all the rest such an extreme measure of despondency, that the city now suffers a shortage even of inhabitants, and this district has become a terrible solitude, a spectacle inspiring pity in our friends, but affording great joy and satisfaction to those who have long waited for our fall. Whose privilege, therefore, is it to reach out a hand to us, whose is it to shed a tear of sympathy over us, if not your Clemency's, since you

---

another appeal to save Cappadocia from being divided into two provinces. Cf. Letter LXXIV, note 1. Letters XXXIII, CXLVII, CLXXVIII, CXCVI, and CCCIV are also addressed to Aburgius, an important layman, friend and compatriot of Basil.

[2] See previous letter, note 3.

COLLECTED LETTERS OF SAINT BASIL

ὃς καὶ ἀλλοτρίᾳ συμπαθοῖς πόλει τοιαῦτα καμ-
νούσῃ, μὴ ὅτι γε τῇ σε παραγαγούσῃ εἰς τὸν βίον ;
εἴ τις οὖν δύναμις, ταύτην νῦν ἐπὶ τῆς παρούσης
χρείας ἡμῖν ἐπίδειξαι.[1] πάντως δὲ μεγάλην ἔχεις
τὴν παρὰ τοῦ Θεοῦ ῥοπήν, ὃς ἐπ' οὐδενὸς καιροῦ
καταλέλοιπέ σε, καὶ πολλὰς ἔδωκέ σοι τῆς παρ'
ἑαυτοῦ[2] εὐμενείας τὰς ἀποδείξεις· μόνον ἐὰν
θελήσῃς ὅλως διαναστῆναι πρὸς τὴν ἐπιμέλειαν
ἡμῶν, καὶ τῇ προσούσῃ σοι δυνάμει χρήσασθαι
εἰς τὴν ὑπὲρ τῶν πολιτῶν βοήθειαν.

LXXVI

Σωφρονίῳ μαγίστρῳ

Τὸ μὲν μέγεθος τῶν καταλαβουσῶν συμφορῶν
τὴν πατρίδα ἡμῶν αὐτὸν ἐμὲ ἠνάγκαζε,[3] καταλαβόντα τὸ στρατόπεδον, τῇ τε σῇ μεγαλοφυΐᾳ
διηγήσασθαι τὴν κατέχουσαν ἡμῶν τὴν πόλιν
κατήφειαν, καὶ τοῖς λοιποῖς ὅσοι ἐπὶ μεγίστης
ἐστὲ δυνάμεως τῶν πραγμάτων. ἐπειδὴ δὲ ἥ τε
τοῦ σώματος ἀρρωστία καὶ ἡ τῶν ἐκκλησιῶν
ἐπιμέλεια κατέχει με, τέως διὰ γράμματος ἀποδύρασθαι πρὸς τὴν σὴν μεγαλόνοιαν ἐπείχθην,
γνωρίζων, ὅτι οὔτε σκάφος ἐν πελάγει πνεύμασι
βιαίοις καταβαπτισθὲν οὕτως ἀθρόως ἠφανίσθη
ποτέ, οὐ σεισμοῖς ἐκτριβεῖσα πόλις, οὐχ ὕδασιν
ἐπικλυσθεῖσα, εἰς ἀθρόον[4] ἀφανισμὸν ἐχώρησεν
οὕτως, ὡς ἡ ἡμετέρα τῇ καινῇ ταύτῃ τῶν πραγ-

---

[1] ἐπίδειξε E.   [2] αὐτοῦ editi antiqi.
[3] ἂν add. editi antiqi.
[4] εἰς ἀθρόον . . . παντελῇ] εἰς ἀπώλειαν ἐχώρησε παντελῶς
οὕτως ὡς ἡ ἡμετέρα . . . εἰς ἀθρόον ἦλθεν ἀφανισμόν editi antiqi.

would sympathize even with a foreign city labouring
under such misfortune, to say nothing of the city
that brought you into life? If, therefore, you have
any power to act, show it to us now in our present
need. But assuredly you do possess great strength
from God, who in no time of need has abandoned
you, and who has given you many proofs of His
goodwill—but only if you consent whole-heartedly
to rise up and take us under your care, and to
exercise the power which has come to you for the
assistance of your fellow-citizens.

LETTER LXXVI

To Sophronius, the Master [1]

The magnitude of the misfortunes which have
fallen upon our country was constraining me to go to
court and in person to describe the miseries which
now afflict our city, not only to your noble self, but
likewise to all others who, like you, are in positions
of greatest influence in the state. But since both
bodily ill-health and my solicitude for the churches
detains me, I have been compelled meanwhile to
pour out to your Magnanimity by letter my bitter
lamentations, making known to you that no
boat submerged on the high seas by violent winds
has ever disappeared so quickly, no city destroyed
by earthquakes or buried by floods of water has met
with such sudden effacement from the earth, as our
own, swallowed up by this new administration of our

---

[1] Of about the same date as the preceding, and on the
same general topic. For Sophronius, *magister officiorum*, cf.
Letter XXXII, note 1. Cf. also Letters XLVI, CLXXVII,
CLXXX, CXCIII, CCLXXII.

81

μάτων οἰκονομία καταποθεῖσα εἰς ἀπώλειαν
ἐχώρησε παντελῆ. καὶ μῦθος γέγονε τὰ ἡμέτερα.
οἴχεται μὲν γὰρ τὸ πολίτευμα· πᾶν δὲ τὸ
πολιτικὸν [1] σύνταγμα, τῇ περὶ τοὺς κρατοῦντας
ἀθυμίᾳ καταλιπὸν [2] τὴν ἐν τῇ πόλει οἴκησιν, διὰ
τῆς ἀγροικίας πλανᾶται. ἐπιλέλοιπε δὲ λοιπὸν
καὶ ἡ τῶν ἀναγκαίων διάθεσις, καὶ ὅλως ἀωρότα-
τον θέαμα γεγένηται ἡ πρότερον ἀνδράσι τε
λογίοις ἐπαγαλλομένη καὶ τοῖς λοιποῖς, οἷς
εὐθηνοῦνται πόλεις ἀνευδεῶς διάγουσαι.

Μίαν δὲ ἐνομίσαμεν ὡς ἐν δεινοῖς παραμυθίαν
εἶναι, τὸ ἐπιστενάξαι τοῖς πάθεσιν ἡμῶν πρὸς τὴν
σὴν ἡμερότητα, καὶ παρακαλέσαι, εἴ τις δύναμις,
χεῖρα ὀρέξαι τῇ πόλει ἡμῶν εἰς γόνυ κλιθείσῃ.
τὸν δὲ τρόπον δι᾽ οὗ ἂν γένοιο ἐν καιρῷ [3] τοῖς
πράγμασιν, αὐτὸς μὲν εἰσηγεῖσθαι οὐκ ἔχω, σοὶ
δὲ πάντως καὶ εὑρεῖν διὰ τὴν σύνεσιν ῥᾴδιον, καὶ
χρήσασθαι [4] τοῖς εὑρεθεῖσι, διὰ τὴν παρὰ Θεοῦ
σοι δεδομένην δύναμιν, οὐ χαλεπόν.

LXXVII

Ἀνεπίγραφος περὶ Θηρασίου

Ἓν καὶ τοῦτο τῆς ἀγαθῆς ἀρχῆς τοῦ μεγάλου
ἀπηλαύσαμεν Θηρασίου, τῆς σῆς λογιότητος τὴν

---

[1] πολιτῶν Vat.
[2] καταλιπόντες E, Harl., Reg. secundus, Clarom.
[3] σωτήρ add. editi antiqi.   [4] χρῆσθαι editi antiqi.

---

[1] Written at about the same time as the preceding, perhaps to the Elpidius mentioned in the following letter. The

affairs, has gone to utter destruction. And all that
was ours has become no more than a legend. For
gone is our government; and the whole body politic,
having abandoned its domicile in the city through despondency over the fate of its magistrates, is wandering aimlessly through the countryside. Aye, even
the marketing of the necessities of life has now
ceased, and the city, which formerly was wont to
glory both in its men of learning and in all else in
which cities abound which enjoy freedom from fear,
has become altogether a most unlovely spectacle.

Our sole consolation, considering the terrible
plight we are in, has seemed to be to bewail our
sufferings to your Clemency, and to urge you, if you
have influence, to stretch a hand to our city now
fallen to her knees. As to the means by which you
may opportunely intervene in the situation, I cannot
myself suggest them to you, but you by means of your
sagacity can assuredly discover them readily and,
once discovered, employ them without difficulty,
through the influence which God has given you.

LETTER LXXVII

Without Address, about Therasius [1]

This one advantage we enjoyed from the good
administration of the great Therasius—the visits

Therasius mentioned here appears to have been a governor of
Cappadocia, who was removed from his office after a brief
tenure of it, as the result of calumnious charges brought
against him by certain corrupt persons to whom his excellent
administration had caused annoyance. Therasius may be the
governor in whose behalf Basil wrote to Sophronius, the
prefect of Constantinople, in 372. Cf. Letter XCVI.

ἐπιδημίαν συνεχῶς ἡμῖν γινομένην. τὸ αὐτὸ δὲ
τοῦτο ἐζημιώθημεν στερηθέντες τοῦ ἄρχοντος.
ἀλλ᾽ ἐπειδὴ τὰ ἅπαξ ἡμῖν παρὰ τοῦ Θεοῦ
χαρισθέντα μένει βέβαια καὶ ταῖς ψυχαῖς
ἀλλήλων ἐνοικούμενα διὰ τῆς μνήμης, εἰ καὶ τοῖς
σώμασι διωρίσμεθα, γράφωμεν γοῦν συνεχῶς καὶ
φθεγγώμεθα[1] πρὸς ἀλλήλους τὰ ἀναγκαῖα, καὶ
μάλιστα νῦν, ὅτε ὁ χειμὼν τὴν ὀλιγοχρόνιον
ταύτην ἐκεχειρίαν ἐσπείσατο.

Ἐλπίζομεν δὲ μὴ ἀπολείψεσθαί σε τοῦ θαυμασιωτάτου ἀνδρὸς Θηρασίου, πρέπον εἶναι
κρίναντα κοινωνεῖν τῷ ἀνδρὶ τοιούτων φροντίδων,
ἤ γ᾽ οὐ μὲν οὖν[2] καὶ μάτην πρόφασιν ἀσμενίζοντα
παρέχουσάν σοι[3] ἰδεῖν τε τοὺς φίλους, καὶ παρ᾽
αὐτῶν θεαθῆναι. πολλὰ δὲ ἔχων εἰπεῖν καὶ περὶ
πολλῶν, εἰς τὴν συντυχίαν ὑπερεθέμην, οὐκ
ἀσφαλὲς εἶναι ἡγούμενος ἐπιστολαῖς τὰ τοιαῦτα
καταπιστεύειν.

LXXVIII

Ἀνεπίγραφος ὑπὲρ Ἐλπιδίου

Οὐκ ἔλαθεν ἡμᾶς ἡ ἀγαθή σου σπουδὴ περὶ τὸν
αἰδεσιμώτατον ἑταῖρον ἡμῶν Ἐλπίδιον, ὅπως τῇ
συνήθει σεαυτοῦ συνέσει ἔδωκας καιρὸν φιλανθρωπίας τῷ ἄρχοντι. ταύτην οὖν τὴν χάριν νῦν σε
τελειῶσαι παρακαλοῦμεν[4] διὰ τοῦ γράμματος,

---

[1] φθεγγόμεθα E.
[2] ἤ γ᾽ οὐ μὲν οὖν Capps, οὐ μὲν οὖν ed. Ben., ἡγούμενον
omnes MSS. et editi.
[3] σε E, Reg. secundus, Clarom.
[4] παρακαλῶ μέν editi antiqi.

LETTER LXXVIII

which your Excellence used continually to make to
us. But we have been robbed of even this, now that
we have been deprived of our governor. However,
since favours we have once received from God abide
steadfast and dwell through memory in the souls of
both of us, even though we have been separated in
body, let us at least write frequently and tell each
other of our necessities, and particularly at this
time when the storm has consented to this very
brief period of truce.

We hope, however, that you will not forsake that
most admirable man, Therasius, deeming it proper
to share with him matters of such concern, or
rather not without purpose availing yourself of an
excuse which provides you an opportunity to see
your friends and to be seen by them. However,
though I have much to say on various topics, I have
put them off until our meeting, not judging it safe
to entrust such matters to letters.

LETTER LXXVIII

WITHOUT ADDRESS, IN BEHALF OF ELPIDIUS[1]

WE have not failed to notice your kind interest in
our most venerable friend Elpidius, how in accordance with your usual sagacity you have given the
prefect an occasion for exercising his benevolence.
Therefore, we now urge you by this letter to complete
this favour and to remind the Prefect to place over

[1] Of the same date as the preceding. It is difficult to
identify this Elpidius. The cause of Basil's uneasiness seems
to be the general situation spoken of in the several letters
above.

καὶ ὑπομνῆσαι τὸν ἄρχοντα οἰκείῳ προστάγματι
ἐπὶ τῆς πατρίδος ἡμῶν καταστῆναι τὸν ἄνδρα
πᾶσαν σχεδὸν τὴν φροντίδα τῶν δημοσίων
ἐξηρτημένον. ὥστε πολλὰς ἕξεις καὶ εὐπροσώ-
πους ὑποβάλλειν προφάσεις τῷ ἄρχοντι, ἐξ ὧν
ἀναγκαίως ἐπιμένειν αὐτὸν τῇ πατρίδι ἡμῶν
προστάξει. οἷα δὲ τὰ ἐνταῦθα, καὶ ὅσου ἄξιος
τοῖς πράγμασιν ὁ ἀνήρ, πάντως οὐδὲν δεήσῃ παρ'
ἡμῶν διδαχθῆναι, αὐτὸς τῇ ἑαυτοῦ συνέσει
ἀκριβῶς ἐπιστάμενος.

LXXIX

Εὐσταθίῳ,[1] ἐπισκόπῳ Σεβαστείας

Καὶ πρὸ τοῦ δέχεσθαι τὰ γράμματα, ᾔδειν τὸν
πόνον ὃν ἔχεις ὑπὲρ πάσης ψυχῆς, ἐξαιρέτως δὲ
ὑπὲρ τῆς ἡμετέρας ταπεινώσεως, διὰ τὸ προβε-
βλῆσθαι ἐν τῷ ἀγῶνι τούτῳ· καὶ δεξάμενος[2]
παρὰ τοῦ αἰδεσιμωτάτου Ἐλευσινίου τὰ γράμ-

---

[1] Εὐσταθίῳ tantum habent E et Harl.
[2] δέ add. E, editi antiqi.

---

[1] Written in the year 371. Eustathius was bishop of
Sebaste or Sebasteia (modern Sivas), a town of the Pontus on
the northern bank of the Halys and capital of Armenia Minor
(c. A.D. 357–380). By his frequent changes of opinion,
Eustathius naturally lost the confidence of the rival schools
of theology, and was regarded with suspicion by all. However, he secured and for many years retained the affection
and respect of St. Basil.

On Basil's elevation to the episcopate in A.D. 370,
Eustathius showed the greatest joy, and expressed an
earnest desire to aid his friend in his new and responsible
office. The present letter exhibits the same kindly feeling
between the two bishops. On the plea that Basil would have

our country by an appropriate order the man who has dependent upon him nearly the whole care of its public affairs. Consequently you will be able to submit many fair-seeming reasons to the Prefect, which will of necessity induce him to order this man to remain in charge of our country. But what the situation is there, and how valuable the man is in the circumstances, you will certainly not need to be informed by us, since of your own sagacity you have accurate knowledge thereof.

LETTER LXXIX

To Eustathius, Bishop of Sebaste [1]

Even before receiving your letter, I was fully aware of the toil which you undergo for every soul, and especially for our own Humility,[2] because you must bear the brunt in this conflict; and when I received the letter from the most reverend Eleusinius,[3] and saw his very presence before me, I

need of fellow-helpers and counsellors, Eustathius recommended certain persons to his notice, who, as Basil later bitterly complained (Letter CCIII, 3), turned out to be spies of his actions and watchers of his words, interpreting all in a malevolent sense, and reporting his supposed heretical leanings to their chief. From the moment that Basil made this discovery until his death a bitter struggle was waged between the two. Basil was harassed continually until he died in A.D. 379, Eustathius himself dying soon after. Strangely enough, Peter, St. Basil's brother, succeeded Eustathius on the episcopal throne of Sebaste.

[2] A common title in Byzantine times.

[3] Known only from this letter. He was sent with the present letter, apparently to warn Basil of the approach of the Emperor Valens, and to express the apprehension he felt for the safety of Catholics, and especially for Basil himself.

ματα, καὶ αὐτὴν αὐτοῦ τὴν παρουσίαν θεασάμενος,
ἐδόξασα τὸ θεῖον[1] τὸ τοιοῦτο παραστάτην καὶ
συνασπιστὴν διὰ τῆς πνευματικῆς βοηθείας ἐν
τοῖς ὑπὲρ εὐσεβείας ἀγῶσι χαρισάμενον ἡμῖν.
γινωσκέτω δὲ ἡ ἀνυπέρβλητός σου θεοσέβεια
μέχρι νῦν προσβολὰς μέν τινας παρὰ τῶν
μεγάλων ἀρχόντων ἡμῖν γεγενῆσθαι, καὶ ταύτας
σφοδράς, τοῦ τε ἐπάρχου καὶ τοῦ περὶ τὸν κοιτῶνα
διαλεχθέντων ἰδιοπαθῶς[2] ὑπὲρ τῶν ἐναντίων·
τέως δὲ ἀτρέπτως ἡμᾶς πᾶσαν προσβολὴν ὑπο-
μεῖναι τῷ ἐλέει τοῦ Θεοῦ, τῷ χαριζομένῳ[3] ἡμῖν
τὴν συνεργίαν τοῦ Πνεύματος καὶ ἐνδυναμώσαντι[4]
ἡμῶν δι᾿ αὐτοῦ τὴν ἀσθένειαν.

LXXX

Ἀθανασίῳ, ἐπισκόπῳ Ἀλεξανδρείας

῾Όσον τῶν ἐκκλησιῶν τὰ ἀρρωστήματα ἐπὶ
τὸ μεῖζον πρόεισι, τοσοῦτον πάντες ἐπὶ τὴν σὴν
ἐπιστρεφόμεθα τελειότητα, μίαν ἑαυτοῖς ὑπολεί-
πεσθαι τῶν δεινῶν παραμυθίαν τὴν σὴν προστασίαν πεπιστευκότες· ὃς[5] καὶ τῇ δυνάμει τῶν
προσευχῶν καὶ τῷ[6] εἰδέναι τὰ βέλτιστα[7] τοῖς
πράγμασιν ὑποτίθεσθαι, διασώσασθαι ἡμᾶς ἐκ

---

[1] τὸ θεῖον Capps (on account of the following τό), τὸν Θεόν
MSS. et editi.
[2] καί add. E.
[3] τοῦ χαριζομένου Coisl. secundus, Reg. secundus.
[4] ἐνδυναμώσαντος Coisl. secundus, Reg. secundus.
[5] ὡς E, Med.   [6] τῷ] τό E.   [7] καὶ τό add. E.

---

[1] A title commonly applied to bishops in Byzantine
times.

glorified God, who, through His spiritual help, has
blessed us with such an assistant and comrade-in-
arms in our battles for the Faith. Let your unsurpassed Godliness[1] rest assured that up to the
present time some attacks, and these violent ones,
have been made upon us by high dignitaries, since
both the Prefect[2] and the High Chamberlain[3] have
spoken from peculiarly personal motives in favour of
our enemies; but so far we have fearlessly sustained
every attack through God's mercy, which is blessing
us with the assistance of the Spirit, and through
Him has strengthened our weakness.

LETTER LXXX

To Athanasius, Bishop of Alexandria[4]

THE more serious the maladies of the churches
become, the more we all turn to your Perfection,
firmly convinced that the sole consolation left to us
in our misfortunes is your patronage; for you,
through the efficacy of your prayers and through
your knowing how to offer the best suggestions in
difficulties, are believed by all alike, who are even

[2] The *Praefectus Praetorio*. During the later Empire, *i.e.*
after Diocletian, the *praefecti praetorio* lost their military
power with the suppression of the Praetorian Guards by Con-
stantine. Four prefects continued to be created, who
governed the same provinces as before. Their sphere was
essentially civil at this time, *i.e.* supreme administration of
justice and the finances.

[3] In the charge of the private apartments of the Imperial
palace was placed a favourite eunuch, who was styled *praepositus*, or *praepositus sacri cubiculi*, Prefect of the Sacred
Bed-chamber.

[4] Written in 371. Cf. Letter LXI, note 1.

τοῦ φοβεροῦ τούτου χειμῶνος παρὰ πάντων
ὁμοίως τῶν καὶ κατὰ μικρὸν ἢ ἀκοῇ ἢ πείρᾳ
γνωριζόντων τὴν τελειότητα σου πιστεύῃ.[1] διὸ
μὴ ἀνῇς καὶ προσευχόμενος ὑπὲρ τῶν ψυχῶν
ἡμῶν καὶ διεγείρων ἡμᾶς τοῖς γράμμασιν· ὧν εἰ
ᾔδεις ὁπόσον ἐστὶ τὸ ὠφέλιμον, οὐκ ἄν ποτε
παραπεσοῦσάν σοι γραμμάτων ἀφορμὴν πρὸς
ἡμᾶς ὑπερέβης. εἰ δὲ καταξιωθείημεν τῇ συνεργίᾳ
τῶν προσευχῶν τοῦ ἰδεῖν σε καὶ ἀπολαῦσαι τῶν
ἐν σοὶ ἀγαθῶν, καὶ προσθεῖναι τῇ ἱστορίᾳ τοῦ
ἡμετέρου βίου τὴν συντυχίαν τῆς μεγάλης σου
ὄντως καὶ ἀποστολικῆς ψυχῆς, πάντως ἂν ἑαυτοῖς[2]
ἐλογισάμεθα, ὧν ἐθλίβημεν[3] ἐν πάσῃ τῇ ζωῇ
ἡμῶν, ἀντίρροπον παρὰ τῆς τοῦ Θεοῦ φιλανθρωπίας ἐσχηκέναι παραμυθίαν.

LXXXI

Ἰννοκεντίῳ ἐπισκόπῳ[4]

Ὅσον εὐθύμησα δεξάμενος γράμματα τῆς ἀγάπης σου, τοσοῦτον ἐλυπήθην, ὅτι βάρος ἐπέθηκας
ἡμῖν φροντίδος τῆς ὑπερβαινούσης ἡμᾶς. πῶς γὰρ
δυνηθῶμεν ἀπὸ τοσούτου διαστήματος τοσαύτης
ἡμεῖς οἰκονομίας περιγενέσθαι; ἕως μὲν γὰρ
ὑμᾶς ἔχει ἡ Ἐκκλησία, ὡς ἰδίοις στηρίγμασιν
ἐπαναπαύεται, ἐὰν δέ τι περὶ τῆς ὑμετέρας ζωῆς
ὁ Κύριος οἰκονομήσῃ, τίνας δύναμαι[5] ὁμοτίμους

---

[1] πιστεύειν E.   [2] αὐτοῖς editi antiqi.
[3] ἐθλίβομαι editi antiqi.   [4] Ῥώμης add. absurde Clarom.
[5] δύναται E.

---

[1] Of the year 372. According to the supposition of

slightly acquainted with your Perfection either by
hearsay or by personal experience, to have saved us
from the present fearful tempest. Therefore do
not cease praying for our souls and arousing us by
your letters; for if you had known how helpful
these latter were, you would never have let pass any
opportunity that was offered to you of writing to
us. And if, through the co-operation of your
prayers, we should be accounted worthy of seeing
you, of enjoying the noble qualities that exist in you,
and of adding to the experiences of our life a
meeting with your truly great and apostolic soul, we
should assuredly consider that we had received from
the benevolence of God a consolation counter-
balancing the afflictions which we have endured
during our whole lifetime.

LETTER LXXXI

To Bishop Innocent [1]

Much as I rejoiced on receiving a letter from your
Affection,[2] even so I was troubled, because you have
put upon us a burden of care which surpasses our
strength. For how shall we be able, at so great a
distance, to prove equal to so important an administration? For although, so long as the Church has
you, it rests, as it were, upon its own foundations,
yet if the Lord make some dispensation regarding

Wittig, this letter belongs to St. John Chrysostom and is
addressed to Pope Innocent I. Cf. his "Studien zur Geschi-
chte des Papstes Innocenz I," in *Theologische Quartalschrift*,
84, 1902.

[2] "Your Affection" (ἀγάπη) was frequently used as a title
at this time.

COLLECTED LETTERS OF SAINT BASIL

ἐντεῦθεν ὑμῖν εἰς τὴν ἐπιμέλειαν τῶν ἀδελφῶν
ἐκπέμπειν; ὅπερ σὺ ἐπεζήτησας διὰ τῶν γραμμάτων, καλῶς ποιῶν καὶ ἐμφρόνως, βουλόμενος ζῶν
ἰδεῖν τὸν μετὰ σὲ μέλλοντα κυβερνᾶν τὸ ἐκλεκτὸν
ποίμνιον τοῦ Κυρίου· ὃ καὶ ὁ μακάριος Μωϋσῆς
καὶ ἐπεθύμησε καὶ εἶδεν· ἐπεὶ οὖν καὶ ὁ τόπος
μέγας καὶ περιβόητος, καὶ τὸ σὸν ἔργον παρὰ
πολλοῖς ὀνομαστόν, καὶ οἱ καιροὶ χαλεποί, μεγάλου
χρείαν ἔχοντες κυβερνήτου διὰ τὰς συνεχεῖς ζάλας
καὶ τοὺς ἐπανισταμένους κλύδωνας τῇ Ἐκκλησίᾳ,
οὐκ ἐνόμισα ἀσφαλὲς εἶναι τῇ ἐμῇ ψυχῇ ἀφωσιω-
μένως τῷ πράγματι χρήσασθαι, μάλιστα μεμνημένος ὧν ἔγραψας, ὅτι μέλλεις ἐπὶ τοῦ Κυρίου
ἀντικαθίστασθαί μοι, δικαζόμενος πρός με ὑπὲρ
τῆς ἀμελείας τῶν ἐκκλησιῶν.

Ἵνα οὖν μὴ εἰσέλθω εἰς κρίσιν μετὰ σοῦ, ἀλλὰ
μᾶλλον κοινωνόν σε εὕρω[1] τῆς ἀπολογίας μου
τῆς ἐπὶ τοῦ Χριστοῦ, περιβλεψάμενος ἐν τῷ
συνεδρίῳ τοῦ πρεσβυτερίου τοῦ κατὰ τὴν πόλιν,
ἐξελεξάμην τὸ τιμιώτατον[2] σκεῦος, τὸν ἔκγονον
τοῦ μακαρίου Ἑρμογένους, τοῦ τὴν μεγάλην καὶ
ἄρρηκτον[3] πίστιν γράψαντος ἐν τῇ μεγάλῃ
συνόδῳ· πρεσβύτερον τῆς ἐκκλησίας ἐκ πολλῶν
ἤδη ἐτῶν, εὐσταθῆ τὸν τρόπον, ἔμπειρον κανόνων,
ἀκριβῆ τὴν πίστιν, ἐν ἐγκρατείᾳ καὶ ἀσκήσει
μέχρι νῦν διάγοντα· εἰ καὶ ὅτι τὸ εὔτονον αὐτοῦ

[1] ἔξω editi antiqi. [2] τίμιον Harl., Med., et Clarom.
[3] ἄρρητον E, Harl., Clarom.

---

[1] He was the spiritual offspring of Hermogenes, having
been ordained by him. Hermogenes was bishop of Caesarea

your life, whom of like worth with yourself can I
send hence to care for our brethren? As to what
you have requested by your letter, acting rightly and
wisely in your desire, while still living, to behold
the one destined after you to guide the chosen flock
of the Lord—even as the blessed Moses both desired
and saw—since, now, your place is important and
famous, and your achievements renowned among
many, and the times are difficult, having need of a
great helmsman because of the continual storms and
the floods which rise against the Church, I have not
thought it safe for my soul to treat the matter per-
functorily, especially when I remember what you
have written, that you intend to oppose me before
the Lord, and charge me with neglect of the
churches.

In order, therefore, that I may not come into
litigation with you, but rather may find in you an
associate in my defence before Christ, having looked
about in the assembly of the presbyters belonging to
this city, I have chosen that most worthy vessel, the
offspring [1] of the blessed Hermogenes—who, in the
great Synod,[2] wrote the great and invincible creed.
The man of whom I speak has been a presbyter of
the Church already for many years, is firm of
character, well learned in the canons, strict in the
faith, and till now passing his life in continence
and asceticism—though in truth the rigour of his

in Cappadocia and predecessor of Dianius. Cf. Letters
CCXLIV, CCLXIII.
  [2] *i.e.*, at Nicaea. Basil seems to forget that it was
Leontius who was present at Nicaea as bishop of Caesarea,
although Hermogenes may have been present in lower orders,
and may have written the creed.

COLLECTED LETTERS OF SAINT BASIL

τῆς σκληραγωγίας λοιπὸν κατεδαπάνησε[1] τὴν
σάρκα· πτωχὸν καὶ μηδένα πορισμὸν[2] ἔχοντα
ἐν τῷ κόσμῳ τούτῳ, ὡς μηδὲ ἄρτου αὐτὸν εὐπορεῖν,
ἀλλὰ διὰ τῶν χειρῶν ἐκπλέκειν τὸν βίον μετὰ τῶν
ἀδελφῶν τῶν συνόντων αὐτῷ. τοῦτον ἐμοὶ βου-
λητόν ἐστιν ἀποστεῖλαι.

Εἰ οὖν καὶ αὐτὸς τοιούτου χρῄζεις ἀνδρός,
ἀλλὰ μὴ αὐτὸ τοῦτο νεωτέρου[3] τινὸς ἐπιτηδείου
μόνον πρὸς τὸ πέμπεσθαι καὶ τὰς βιωτικὰς
ἐξανύειν χρείας, ταχύ μοι διὰ πρώτης ἀφορμῆς
ἐπιστεῖλαι καταξίωσον, ἵνα πέμψω σοι τοῦτον
τὸν ἄνδρα, ἐκλεκτὸν ὄντα τοῦ[4] Θεοῦ, καὶ τῷ
πράγματι[5] ἐπιτήδειον, αἰδέσιμον τοῖς ἐντυγχά-
νουσι, καὶ ἐν πραότητι παιδεύοντα τοὺς ἀντι-
διατιθεμένους. ὃν ἠδυνάμην καὶ εὐθὺς ἐκπέμψαι·
ἀλλ' ἐπειδὴ αὐτὸς προλαβὼν ἐπεζήτησας ἄνθρωπον, τὰ μὲν ἄλλα καλὸν καὶ ἀγαπητὸν ἡμῖν, τοῦ
δὲ προειρημένου ἀνδρὸς παραπολὺ ἀποδέοντα,
ἠβουλήθην σοι φανερὰν γενέσθαι[6] τὴν ἐμαυτοῦ
γνώμην ἵν', εἰ χρῄζεις ἀνδρὸς τοιούτου,[7] ἢ
ἐκπέμψῃς τινὰ τῶν ἀδελφῶν τὸν συμπαραληψό-
μενον αὐτὸν περὶ τὰς νηστείας, ἢ ἐπιστείλῃς ἡμῖν,
ἐὰν μηδένα[8] ἔχῃς τὸν δυνάμενον τῆς μέχρις ἡμῶν
ὁδοιπορίας τὸν κάματον ὑποστῆναι.

---

[1] κατεδάμασε E, Harl., Clarom.
[2] παρισπασμόν Harl., Med., Clarom.
[3] τοῦτο νεωτέρου] αὐτονεωτέρου E.   [4] τοῦ om. E.

austere living has by now consumed his flesh—a
mendicant and possessed of no means in this world,
so that he cannot even provide himself with bread,
but through the labour of his hands ekes out his
existence in company with the brethren who are
with him. This is the man I propose to send you.

If, then, you yourself feel the need of such a man,
and not, in very truth, of some younger person, fit
only for messenger service and to perform the
common duties of life, be kind enough to write to
me at the very earliest opportunity, that I may
send you this man, who is the elect of God and
fitted for this duty, inspiring the respect of those
who meet him and schooling in gentleness his
opponents. I might have sent him to you at once,
but since you yourself anticipated me by asking for
a certain person, a man who, though in general
virtuous and beloved by us, yet falls far short of the
one whom I have just mentioned, I wished to make
my purpose clear to you, in order that, if you need a
person of this character, you may either send one of
the brethren at the time of the fast to escort him
hence, or write to us, if you have no one able to
undergo the labour of the journey all the way to
us.

---

⁵ γράμματι E.
⁶ καταστῆσαι editi antiqi.
⁷ τηλικούτου E.
⁸ ἐὰν μηδένα] ἐάν τινα E.

COLLECTED LETTERS OF SAINT BASIL

LXXXII

Ἀθανασίῳ, ἐπισκόπῳ Ἀλεξανδρείας

Ὅταν μὲν πρὸς τὰ πράγματα ἀποβλέψωμεν
καὶ τὰς δυσκολίας κατίδωμεν, ὑφ᾽ ὧν πᾶσα ἀγαθὴ
ἐνέργεια οἷον ὑπό τινος δεσμοῦ ἐμποδιζομένη κατέ-
χεται, εἰς ἀπόγνωσιν ἑαυτῶν ἐρχόμεθα παντελῆ·
ὅταν δὲ πάλιν πρὸς τὴν σὴν ἀπίδωμεν σεμνοπρέπειαν, καὶ λογισώμεθα, ὅτι σὲ ἰατρὸν τῶν ἐν ταῖς
ἐκκλησίαις ἀρρωστημάτων ὁ Κύριος ἡμῶν ἐτα-
μιεύσατο, ἀναλαμβάνομεν ἑαυτῶν τοὺς λογισμούς,
καὶ ἐκ τοῦ κατὰ τὴν ἀπόγνωσιν πτώματος πρὸς
τὴν ἐλπίδα¹ τῶν χρηστοτέρων διανιστάμεθα.
λέλυται πᾶσα Ἐκκλησία, ὡς οὐδὲ ἡ σὴ φρόνησις
ἀγνοεῖ. καὶ ὁρᾷς πάντως τὰ ἑκασταχοῦ, οἷον
ἀφ᾽ ὑψηλῆς τινος σκοπιᾶς τῆς τοῦ νοῦ θεωρίας·
ὅπως, καθάπερ ἐν πελάγει, πολλῶν ὁμοῦ συμ-
πλεόντων, ὑπὸ τῆς βίας τοῦ κλύδωνος πάντες ὁμοῦ
ἀλλήλοις προσρήγνυνται· καὶ γίνεται τὸ ναυάγιον,
πῆ μὲν ἐκ τῆς ἔξωθεν αἰτίας βιαίως κινούσης τὴν
θάλατταν, πῆ δὲ ἐκ τῆς τῶν ἐμπλεόντων² ταραχῆς
ἀντιβαινόντων ἀλλήλοις καὶ διωθουμένων. ἀρκεῖ

¹ πρὸς τὴν ἐλπίδα] τῇ ἐλπίδι Vat., Reg. uterque, Coisl.
secundus.
² πλεόντων E, Harl.

¹ Written late in the year 371. Cf. Loofs. According to
Tillemont (Note LX), the bishops referred to here by Basil,
as not in communion with him, are in all probability the
Macedonians.
² σεμνοπρέπεια, as frequently in Basil, is used here as a
title.

LETTER LXXXII

To Athanasius, Bishop of Alexandria [1]

WHENEVER we regard our affairs and perceive the difficulties by which every virtuous activity is held in check, hindered as it were by fetters, we arrive at absolute despair of ourselves; but when, on the other hand, we look at your Holiness [2] and consider that our Lord has appointed you the physician to heal the maladies of the churches, we resume our reflections and from the depths of our despair we rise to the hope of better things. The whole Church has been disrupted, as your Wisdom [3] is also not unaware. Furthermore, you assuredly can see, from the lofty watch-tower, [4] so to speak, of your mental vision, what is happening on every hand—how, as on the deep when many ships are sailing together, all are dashed together the one against the other by the violence of the waves, and the shipwreck occurs, partly, it is true, by reason of the external cause which violently agitates the sea, but partly from the confusion that reigns among the sailors, who jostle against and oppose one another. It is enough to

[3] φρόνησις, also a title, found in both Athanasius and Basil.

[4] Note the fitness of this figure as applied to the Bishop of Alexandria, who could still see the marble lighthouse erected at the eastern extremity of the island of Pharos by Ptolemy II. Note also the sophistic manner in which Basil develops this figure. In general we may say that sophistic influence is seen more in the development of the metaphor by Basil than in his frequent use of it. Cf. Campbell, 108 ff. For a similar use of this nautical metaphor, cf. De Spiritu Sancto, 30.

ἐπὶ τῆς εἰκόνος ἐᾶσαι τὸν λόγον, οὔτε τῆς σῆς
σοφίας ἐπιτρεπούσης τι πλέον, οὔτε τῆς καταστάσεως ἐπιτρεπούσης ἡμῖν τὴν παρρησίαν. καὶ
πρὸς ταῦτα[1] τίς ἱκανὸς κυβερνήτης; τίς ἀξιό-
πιστος διαναστῆσαι τὸν Κύριον ἐπιτιμῆσαι τῷ
ἀνέμῳ καὶ τῇ θαλάσσῃ; τίς ἕτερος ἢ ὁ ἐκ παιδὸς
τοῖς ὑπὲρ τῆς εὐσεβείας ἐναθλήσας ἀγῶσιν;

Ἐπεὶ οὖν ὥρμηται νῦν γνησίως πᾶν τὸ περὶ
ἡμᾶς ὑγιαῖνον κατὰ τὴν πίστιν εἰς τὴν πρὸς
τοὺς ὁμοδόξους κοινωνίαν καὶ ἕνωσιν, θαρροῦντος[2]
ἤλθομεν εἰς τὴν παράκλησίν σου τῆς ἀνεξικακίας,
ἐπιστεῖλαι πᾶσιν ἡμῖν ἐπιστολὴν μίαν, παραίνεσιν ἔχουσαν τῶν πρακτέων. οὕτω γὰρ βού-
λονται παρὰ σοῦ τὴν ἀρχὴν ὑπάρξαι αὐτοῖς τῶν
κοινωνικῶν διαλέξεων. ἐπειδὴ δὲ ἴσως ὕποπτοι
καταφαίνονταί[3] σοι τῇ μνήμῃ τῶν παρελθόντων,
ἐκεῖνο ποίησον, θεοφιλέστατε πάτερ· ἐμοὶ τὰς
πρὸς τοὺς ἐπισκόπους ἐπιστολὰς διάπεμψαι ἢ
διά τινος τῶν αὐτόθεν[4] πιστῶν, ἢ καὶ διὰ τοῦ
ἀδελφοῦ Δωροθέου τοῦ συνδιακόνου ἡμῶν, ἃς
ὑποδεξάμενος οὐ ρότερον δώσω, μὴ[5] λαβὼν τὰς
παρ' αὐτῶν ἀποκρίσεις· ἐὰν δὲ μή, Ἡμαρτηκὼς
ἔσομαι εἰς σὲ πάσας τὰς ἡμέρας τῆς ζωῆς μου.
πάντως δὲ οὐ[6] πλείονος ἄξιον φόβου τοῦτο τῷ

---

[1] ταύτας E.
[2] θαρροῦντες editi antiqi, sed ed. Haganoenis θαρροῦντας.
[3] καταφανήσονται E, editi antiqi.   [4] αὐτόθι E.
[5] ἤ editi antiqi.   [6] οὐδέ editi antiqi.

---

[1] Cf. Luke 8. 24: ὁ δὲ ἐγερθεὶς ἐπετίμησε τῷ ἀνέμῳ καὶ τῷ
κλύδωνι τοῦ ὕδατος. "But he arising rebuked the wind and
the rage of the water."
[2] The story of St. Athanasius, as a "boy bishop," is
related by Socrates, *Ecc. Hist.* 1, 15, and Rufinus, *Ecc. Hist.*

dismiss the topic with this simile, since your wisdom permits nothing more and the situation permits us no freedom of speech. But who is the helmsman capable of meeting these dangers? Who can be trusted to arouse the Lord that He may rebuke the wind and the sea?[1] Who other than he who from childhood[2] has struggled in the contests in defence of the faith?

Since, therefore, all about us that is sound as regards the faith is already nobly moving toward communion and unity with those of like belief, with confidence have we resorted to this appeal to urge your Patience[3] to write to us all one general letter, containing advice on the course of action we should adopt. For in this manner they wish the initiative in their discussions regarding their communion to be provided by you. But since perhaps they seem to you suspicious because of your recollection of the past, most God-beloved father, act as follows: Send to me the letters intended for the bishops, either by one of your own faithful there, or even by our brother, the deacon Dorotheus,[4] and when I have received them I shall not give them out until I am in possession of the bishops' answers; for, otherwise, " I will be guilty of sin against thee all the days of my life." [5] Assuredly these words could not have

---

1, 14. While playing a game of baptism with his companions, Athanasius was noticed by Alexander, who thereupon had him educated at the episcopal palace.

[3] ἀνεξικακία, used as a title here; Patience or Forbearance.

[4] The deacon used so frequently by Basil in the service of a messenger.

[5] Cf. Gen. 43. 9: ἡμαρτηκὼς ἔσομαι πρὸς σὲ πάσας τὰς ἡμέρας. "I will be guilty of sin against thee for ever." Judah is speaking to his father Jacob. Basil adds τῆς ζωῆς μου.

ἐξ ἀρχῆς εἰπόντι πρὸς τὸν πατέρα ἢ ἐμοὶ νῦν
πρὸς σὲ τὸν πνευματικὸν πατέρα λέγοντι. εἰ δὲ
τοῦτο παντὶ τρόπῳ ἀπηγόρευται παρὰ σοί, ἀλλ᾽
ἡμᾶς γε τῆς ἐπὶ τῇ διακονίᾳ αἰτίας ἄφες, ἀδόλως
καὶ ἀκατασκεύως, ἐπιθυμίᾳ τῆς εἰρήνης καὶ τῆς
πρὸς ἀλλήλους ἡμῶν συναφείας τῶν ὁμονοούντων
εἰς τὰ πρὸς τὸν¹ Κύριον, ἐπὶ τὴν πρεσβείαν ταύτην
καὶ μεσιτείαν² ἀφικομένους.

LXXXIII

Κηνσίτορι

᾽Εμοὶ πρὸς τὴν σὴν εὐγένειαν συνήθεια μὲν καὶ
ἡ κατ᾽ ὀφθαλμοὺς συντυχία πάνυ βραχεῖα γέγονε,
γνῶσις δὲ ἡ ἐξ ἀκοῆς, δι᾽ ἧς πολλοῖς συναπτόμεθα
τῶν ἐπιφανῶν, οὐκ ὀλίγη τε οὐδὲ εὐκαταφρόνητος.
εἰ δὲ καὶ σοί τις ἐκ τῆς φήμης περὶ ἡμῶν ὑπάρχει
λόγος, αὐτὸς ἂν εἰδείης ἄμεινον. τὸ δ᾽ οὖν σὸν
παρ᾽ ἡμῖν τοιοῦτόν ἐστιν οἷον εἴπομεν.³ ἐπειδὴ
δὲ⁴ ἐκάλεσέ σε ὁ Θεὸς εἰς πρᾶγμα φιλανθρωπίας
ἐπίδειξιν ἔχον, δι᾽ οὗ δυνατόν ἐστι διορθωθῆναι
ἡμῶν τὴν πατρίδα παντελῶς ἐδαφισθεῖσαν, ἡγοῦμαι πρέπειν μοι ὑπομνῆσαί σου τὴν χρηστότητα,
ἵνα ἐπ᾽ ἐλπίδι τῆς παρὰ Θεοῦ ἀνταποδόσεως
τοιοῦτον σεαυτὸν καταξιώσῃς παρασχέσθαι, ὥστε

---

¹ τόν om. E. ² καὶ μεσιτείαν om. E.
³ εἴποιμεν E, editi antiqi. ⁴ δέ om. E.

---

¹ Written in 372. The valuation of property and levying of
taxes were based on the census books (*libri censuales*) prepared

LETTER LXXXIII

inspired greater fear in the one who first addressed
them to his father than they inspire now in me as I
address them to my spiritual father. But if this idea
of communion has been entirely rejected by you, still
absolve us at least from all blame for our efforts,
since honestly and frankly, through a desire for peace
and mutual union among those who hold the same
beliefs about the Lord, have we entered upon this
embassy and mediation.

LETTER LXXXIII

To a Censitor [1]

My acquaintance and personal association with
your Nobility [2] has been very brief, but my knowledge of you by report, through which we are
brought in contact with many illustrious men, is
neither slight nor inconsiderable. But whether we
too have any reputation by report with you, you
yourself would be the better judge. However, your
reputation with us is what we have said. But since
God has called you to an office which affords opportunities of displaying kindness, one through which it
is possible to set upright again our country now
completely levelled with the earth, I think it proper
for me to bring a matter to your Excellency's [3] consideration, that in the hope of reward from God you
may deign so to conduct yourself as to be held

under the supervision of the *censitores*. The latter were
appointed by the Emperor, one for each province or smaller
unit of territory. The method of procedure was that followed
by the censor at Rome.

[2] A Byzantine title.

[3] Or "Goodness," also a Byzantine title.

COLLECTED LETTERS OF SAINT BASIL

ἀθανάτου μὲν τῆς μνήμης ἀξιοῦσθαι, γενέσθαι δὲ
αἰωνίων ἀναπαύσεων κληρονόμον, ἐκ τοῦ ἐλαφρο-
τέρας ποιῆσαι τοῖς καταπονουμένοις τὰς θλίψεις.

Ἐπειδὴ δὲ κἀμοί τίς ἐστι κτῆσις περὶ Χαμα-
νηνήν,[1] ἀξιῶ σε[2] προστῆναι αὐτῆς ὡς οἰκείας.
μὴ θαυμάζῃς[3] δέ, εἰ ἐμαυτοῦ λέγω τὰ τῶν φίλων,
μετὰ τῆς ἄλλης ἀρετῆς καὶ φιλίαν πεπαιδευμένος,
καὶ μεμνημένος τοῦ σοφῶς εἰπόντος, ἄλλον[4]
ἑαυτὸν εἶναι τὸν φίλον. τὴν τοίνυν κτῆσιν τὴν
διαφέρουσαν τῷδε, ταύτην ὡς ἐμαυτοῦ παρατί-
θεμαι τῇ τιμιότητί σου· καὶ παρακαλῶ, ἐπισκεψά-
μενον τὰ τῆς οἰκίας δυσχερῆ, δοῦναι αὐτοῖς καὶ
τῶν παρελθόντων χρόνων παραμυθίαν, καὶ πρὸς
τὸ μέλλον αἱρετὴν αὐτοῖς κατασκευάσαι τὴν
οἴκησιν, τὴν φευκτὴν καὶ ἀπηγορευμένην διὰ τὸ
πλῆθος τῆς ἐπικειμένης αὐτῇ συντελείας. σπου-
δάσω δὲ καὶ αὐτὸς περιτυχών σου τῇ κοσμιότητι
ἐντελέστερον περὶ ἑκάστου διαλεχθῆναι.

LXXXIV

Ἡγεμόνι

Σχεδὸν μὲν ἄπιστόν ἐστιν ὃ μέλλω γράφειν,
γεγράψεται δὲ τῆς ἀληθείας ἕνεκεν. ὅτι, πᾶσαν

[1] μηχανήν Med.   [2] ἀξιῶ σε] ἀξιῶσαι E.
[3] θαυμάσῃς E.   [4] ἄλλων E.

[1] Pythagoras is supposed to have been the first to utter
these words. They occur also in Aristotle, *Magna Moralia*,
II. 15 (ἕτερος ἐγώ), and in Cicero, *Laelius*, 21, 80 (*alter
idem*).

worthy of undying remembrance, and as to become an heir to eternal peace, for having lightened the burdens of such as are afflicted.

Since I too have a certain property in the vicinity of Chamanene, I request you to take care of it as you would of your own. But do not think it strange, if I call the property of my friends my own, since along with other virtues I have learned friendship, and have been mindful of the wise saying that a friend is another self.[1] This property, therefore, which belongs to him, I entrust to your Honour's[2] care just as if it were my own; and I urge you, after examining into the misfortunes of this household, to offer them both consolation for the past, and for the future to render desirable for them the residence which now is being shunned and abandoned on account of the multitude of taxes imposed upon it. I myself, moreover, shall be eager to meet your Decorum[3] and talk at greater length about each particular.

LETTER LXXXIV

To a Governor [4]

What I am about to write is almost incredible, but it shall be written for the sake of truth. It

---

[2] A Byzantine title.

[3] Also a Byzantine title.

[4] Written in 372. The person addressed is probably Elias, governor of Cappadocia. Basil here writes in behalf of an old man, whose four-year-old grandson has been placed on the senatorial roll, thus compelling his grandfather to serve again. Cf. also Letters XCIV and XCVI.

ἔχων ἐπιθυμίαν ὡς οἷόν τε ἦν πυκνότατα διαλέ-
γεσθαί σου τῇ καλοκἀγαθίᾳ, ἐπειδὴ εὖρον ταύτην [1]
γραμμάτων τὴν [2] ἀφορμήν, οὐκ ἐπέδραμον τῷ
ἑρμαίῳ, ἀλλ' ἀπώκνησα καὶ ἀνεδύην. τὸ οὖν
παράδοξον ἐν τούτῳ, ὅτι ἅπερ ηὐχόμην ὑπάρξαι, [3]
ταῦτα γενόμενα οὐκ ἐδεχόμην. αἴτιον δέ, ὅτι
αἰσχύνομαι δοκεῖν, μὴ φιλίας γε ἕνεκεν καθαρῶς,
ἀλλὰ χρείαν τινὰ θεραπεύων ἑκάστοτε, γράφειν.
ἀλλά με ἐκεῖνο εἰσῆλθεν (ὃ καὶ σὲ βούλομαι
διανοηθέντα, μήτοι νομίζειν ἡμᾶς ἐμπορικῶς μᾶλλον ἢ φιλικῶς ποιεῖσθαι τὰς διαλέξεις), ὅτι χρή
τι διάφορον ἔχειν τὰς τῶν ἀρχόντων προσρήσεις
παρὰ τοὺς ἰδιώτας. οὐ γὰρ ὁμοίως ἐντευκτέον
ἡμῖν ἰατρῷ τε ἀνδρὶ καὶ τῷ τυχόντι, οὔτε ἄρχοντι
δηλονότι καὶ ἰδιώτῃ· ἀλλὰ πειρατέον τοῦ μὲν ἐκ
τῆς τέχνης, τοῦ δὲ ἀπὸ τῆς ἐξουσίας ἀπολαύειν
εἰς τὰ ἡμέτερα. ὥσπερ οὖν τοῖς ἐν ἡλίῳ βαδί-
ζουσιν ἕπεται πάντως ἡ σκιά, κἂν αὐτοὶ μὴ
προέλωνται, οὕτω καὶ ταῖς πρὸς τοὺς ἄρχοντας
ὁμιλίαις ἀκολουθεῖ τι καὶ παρεμπόρευμα, ἡ τῶν
καμνόντων βοήθεια.

Τὴν μὲν οὖν πρώτην αἰτίαν τῆς ἐπιστολῆς
πληρούτω αὐτὸ τὸ προσειπεῖν σου τὴν μεγαλόνοιαν. ὅ, κἂν μηδεμία πρόφασις τῷ [4] γράφειν
προσῇ, ἀγαθὸν κεφάλαιον αὐτὸ χρὴ νομίζεσθαι.
προσείρησο [5] τοίνυν ἡμῖν, ὦ ἄριστε, καὶ φυλάττοιο

---

[1] τήν add. E. [2] τήν om. E. [3] ὑπάρξειν E, Med.
[4] τοῦ Harl., Med. [5] προσείποιο editi antiqi.

---

[1] A Byzantine title, as also " your Magnanimity " below.

is this,—that although I had every desire to converse with your Nobility [1] as often as possible, when I found this present occasion for writing, I did not rush at my good fortune, but hesitated and drew back. Now the strange part of all this is that, when that very opportunity came for which I prayed, I was not inclined to take it. And the reason is that I am ashamed to seem to write, not disinterestedly out of friendship, but serving some advantage on every occasion. However, the thought occurred to me (I want you as well to reflect on this point, and thus refrain from considering that we carry on our discussions with you after the manner of merchants rather than of friends), that some distinction should be made between words addressed to officials and those addressed to private persons. For we ought not to converse in the same manner with a physician as with any ordinary person, nor, obviously, with a magistrate in the same way as with a person in private station, but from the skill of the one and from the authority of the other we should try to derive some benefit for ourselves. Therefore, just as a shadow always pursues those who walk in the sun, even though they themselves do not so wish, so too in intercourse with magistrates there is an attendant incident of trafficking—assistance for the afflicted.

Accordingly, let our very salutation of your Magnanimity fulfil the primary cause of our letter; this, even if no other pretext for writing were at hand, should be considered a good subject in itself. Receive, then, our salutation, most excellent Sir, and may you be protected in every act of your life, as you pass from office to office and as you confer

τῷ βίῳ παντί, ἀρχὰς ἐξ ἀρχῶν ἀμείβων καὶ
ἄλλοτε ἄλλους ταῖς ἐπιστασίαις εὐεργετῶν. τοῦτο
γὰρ ἐμοί τε ποιεῖν σύνηθες, καὶ σοὶ ὀφειλόμενον
παρὰ τῶν καὶ κατὰ μικρὸν πεπειραμένων τῆς
περὶ τὸ ἄρχειν σου ἀρετῆς.

Μετὰ δὲ τὴν εὐχήν, δέξαι καὶ τὴν ὑπὲρ τοῦ
ἀθλίου γέροντος ἱκεσίαν, ὃν ἀφῆκε μὲν τῶν δημοσίων γράμμα βασιλικόν· μᾶλλον δὲ καὶ πρὸ τοῦ
βασιλέως αὐτὸ τὸ γῆρας ἔδωκεν αὐτῷ τὴν ἀναγκαίαν ἀτέλειαν. ἐβεβαίωσας δὲ καὶ αὐτὸς τὴν
ἄνωθεν χάριν αἰδοῖ τῆς φύσεως, καὶ προμηθείᾳ
τῶν δημοσίων, ἐμοὶ δοκεῖν, ὡς ἂν μὴ ἀνθρώπῳ
παρανοοῦντι [1] διὰ τὸν χρόνον κινδυνεύοι [2] τι τῶν
κοινῶν.

Δι' ἑτέρας δὲ ὁδοῦ πάλιν πῶς αὐτὸν ἔλαθες, ὦ
θαυμάσιε, παραγαγὼν εἰς τὸ μέσον; τὸν γὰρ
υἱϊδοῦν [3] αὐτοῦ, οὔπω τέταρτον ἔτος ἀπὸ γενέσεως
ἄγοντα, κελεύσας τοῦ βουλευτηρίου μετέχειν, τί
ἄλλο καὶ οὐχὶ τὸν πρεσβύτην διὰ τοῦ ἐκγόνου
πάλιν ἐξ ἀρχῆς παράγεις εἰς τὰ δημόσια ; ἀλλὰ
νῦν ἱκετεύομεν ἀμφοτέρων σε λαβεῖν τῶν ἡλικιῶν
οἶκτον, καὶ ἀμφοτέρους ἀνεῖναι διὰ τὰ προσόντα
ἑκατέρῳ ἐλεεινά. ὁ μὲν γὰρ οὐκ εἶδε [4] γονέας,
οὐδ' ἐγνώρισε, ἀλλὰ δι' ἀλλοτρίων χειρῶν εἰς τὸν
βίον τοῦτον εἰσῆλθεν, εὐθὺς [5] ἐκ σπαργάνων [6]
ἀμφοτέρων ὀρφανισθείς· ὁ δὲ τοσοῦτον ἐταμιεύθη
τῷ βίῳ, ὡς μηδὲν αὐτὸν εἶδος συμφορᾶς παρελ-
θεῖν· ἐπεῖδε μὲν γὰρ υἱοῦ τελευτὴν ἄωρον· εἶδε δὲ
οἶκον ἔρημον διαδόχων· ὄψεται δὲ νῦν, ἐὰν μή τι

[1] παρανομοῦντι editi antiqi.   [2] κινδυνεύῃ editi antiqi.
[3] υἱὸν γοῦν editi antiqi.   [4] οἶδε editi antiqi.

benefits now on some and now on others by your
government. For it is my custom to speak
thus, and it is due to you from those who have
experienced, even in small measure, the excellence
of your administration.

After my prayer, receive also my petition in behalf
of an unfortunate old man, whom an Imperial decree
has exempted from public burdens; nay, rather, old
age itself, even before the Emperor, had granted
him the inevitable exemption. You yourself, also,
have confirmed the Imperial favour by your respect
for Nature, and by your prudent care of the public
interests, as it seems to me, lest any public interest
should be endangered by a man whose mind is
becoming deranged through age.

But how, respected Sir, did you inadvertently
drag him again into the midst of public affairs by
another way? For when you commanded his grandson, not yet in his fourth year, to take his place in
the municipal senate, what else are you doing than
to drag the old man into public affairs afresh in the
person of his grandchild? But now we beseech you
to take pity upon the ages of both, and to exempt
both on account of what is worthy of pity in each.
For the one has not seen his parents, nor has he
known them, but he entered this life through alien
hands, having been bereft of both parents from his very
swaddling clothes; and the other has been granted
so long a period of life that he has escaped no form
of calamity. For he saw a son's untimely death;
he saw a house made destitute of its succession;
and he will now see (unless you yourself hit upon

---

⁵ εὐθύς om. E.　　　　　⁶ ἐπ᾽ add. E.

αὐτὸς ἄξιον τῆς σεαυτοῦ φιλανθρωπίας διανοηθῇς,
τὴν παραμυθίαν τῆς ἀπαιδίας, ταύτην ἀφορμὴν
αὐτῷ μυρίων γενησομένην κακῶν. οὐ γὰρ δήπου
τὸ παιδίον εἰς βουλευτὰς συντελέσει, ἢ ἐκλέξει
τὰς εἰσφοράς, ἢ στρατιώταις χορηγήσει τὸ σιτη-
ρέσιον, ἀλλ' ἀνάγκη πάλιν τοῦ ἀθλίου γέροντος
τὴν πολιὰν καταισχύνεσθαι. δὸς οὖν χάριν καὶ
τοῖς νόμοις ἀκόλουθον καὶ τῇ φύσει συμβαί-
νουσαν, τῷ μὲν προστάξας μέχρι τῆς τῶν ἀνδρῶν
ἡλικίας συγχωρηθῆναι, τὸν δὲ ἐπὶ τῆς κλίνης
ἀναμένειν τὸν θάνατον. πραγμάτων δὲ συνέχειαν
καὶ τὸ τῆς ἀνάγκης ἀπαραίτητον ἄλλοι προβαλ-
λέσθωσαν. οὐ γὰρ δὴ τοῦ σοῦ τρόπου ἢ κακῶς
πράττοντας περιιδεῖν, ἢ νόμων ὀλιγωρῆσαι, ἢ
φίλοις μὴ εἶξαι καθικετεύουσι, κἂν τὰ ἐξ ἀνθρώπων σε περιεστήκει[1] πράγματα.

LXXXV

Περὶ τοῦ μὴ δεῖν ὀρκοῦν[2]

Οὐ παυόμεθα κατὰ πᾶσαν σύνοδον διαμαρτυ-
ρόμενοι καὶ ἰδίᾳ ἐν ταῖς συντυχίαις περὶ τῶν
αὐτῶν διαλεγόμενοι, ὥστε τοὺς ὅρκους ἐπὶ τοῖς
δημοσίοις τελέσμασι μὴ ἐπάγεσθαι παρὰ τῶν
ἀπαιτητῶν τοῖς ἀγροίκοις. λειπόμενον ἦν[3] καὶ

[1] περιέστηκε editi antiqi.
[2] ὥστε παύσασθαι τοὺς τῶν δημοσίων πράκτορας τοὺς ὅρκους
τοῖς ὑποτελέσιν ἐπάγοντας Harl., Reg. secundus, Coisl.
secundus.
[3] οὖν add. Reg. secundus.

some remedy worthy of your kindness) that this consolation of his childlessness is destined to become the cause of countless troubles. For of course the child will not be counted among the senators, or collect taxes, or furnish provision-money for soldiers, but it will be necessary for the white locks of the wretched old man again to be put to shame. Grant, therefore, a favour both consistent with the laws and in agreement with Nature, ordering that exemption be granted to the one until he reach man's estate, and that the other be allowed to await his death in his bed. Let others offer the excuse of pressing business and inexorable necessity! For indeed it is not in keeping with *your* character either to allow men to suffer hardships, or to belittle the laws, or to refuse to yield to the petitions of your friends, even if the personal affairs of your subjects crowd upon your attention.

LETTER LXXXV

About there Being No Necessity of Taking the Oath [1]

We do not cease protesting solemnly at every synod and arguing on the same matter in our private conversations, namely, that in regard to the public taxes oaths should not be required of the farmers by the collectors. It was left to us, also by letter on

---

[1] Written in the year 372. For the distress of the Cappadocians under the heavy burden of taxation, cf. Letter LXXIV and note 1. A very disagreeable feature of the system of taxation was the practice of putting the people of the country under oath as to their inability to pay. The Church condemned the taking of oaths.

διὰ τοῦ γράμματος περὶ τῶν αὐτῶν ἐνώπιον Θεοῦ
καὶ ἀνθρώπων διαμαρτύρασθαι, ὅτι προσήκει
παύσασθαι ὑμᾶς[1] τὸν θάνατον ταῖς ψυχαῖς τῶν
ἀνθρώπων ἐπάγοντας, καὶ ἄλλους ἐπινοῆσαί τινας
τρόπους τῶν ἀπαιτήσεων, τὰς δὲ ψυχὰς συγχω-
ρῆσαι τοῖς ἀνθρώποις ἀτρώτους ἔχειν. ταῦτα
πρὸς σὲ γράφομεν, οὐχ ὡς σοῦ δεομένου τῆς ἐκ
τῶν λόγων παρακλήσεως (οἴκοθεν γὰρ ἔχεις τὰς
περὶ τὸ φοβεῖσθαι τὸν Κύριον[2] ἀφορμάς), ἀλλ'
ἵνα διὰ σοῦ πάντες οἱ ἀνεχόμενοί σου διδαχθῶσι
μὴ παροργίζειν τὸν ἅγιον, μηδὲ ἀπηγορευμένον
πρᾶγμα τῇ πονηρᾷ συνηθείᾳ εἰς ἀδιαφορίαν
κατάγειν. καὶ γὰρ οὔτε ὄφελός τι αὐτοῖς πρὸς
τὰς ἀπαιτήσεις ἐκ τῶν ὅρκων ἐστί, καὶ ὁμολο-
γούμενον κακὸν τῇ ψυχῇ προσλαμβάνουσιν.
ἐπειδὰν γὰρ καταμελετήσωσι[3] τὰς[4] ἐπιορκίας οἱ
ἄνθρωποι, οὐκέτι ἑαυτοὺς[5] ἐπείγουσι πρὸς τὴν
ἔκτισιν, ἀλλὰ ἀπάτης ὅπλον καὶ ἀναβολῆς
ἀφορμὴν ἐξευρῆσθαι αὐτοῖς τὸν ὅρκον οἴονται.

Εἴτε οὖν ὀξεῖαν ἐπάγει τὴν ἀνταπόδοσιν τοῖς
ἐπιωρκηκόσιν ὁ Κύριος, οὐχ ἕξουσι τοὺς ὑπα-
κούοντας, τῶν ὑπευθύνων ὑπὸ τῆς τιμωρίας
ἀναλωθέντων· εἴτε διὰ μακροθυμίας ἀνέχεται ὁ
Δεσπότης (ὃ προλαβὼν εἶπον, ὅτι οἱ πεπειραμένοι τῆς ἀνοχῆς τοῦ Κυρίου καταφρονοῦσιν
αὐτοῦ τῆς χρηστότητος), μὴ ἀνομείτωσαν διακενῆς, μηδὲ παροξυνέτωσαν ἐφ' ἑαυτοὺς τὸν Θεόν.
Εἴρηται ἡμῖν τὰ ἡμῖν ἐπιβάλλοντα· ὄψονται
οἱ ἀπειθοῦντες.

---

[1] ἡμᾶς E.   [2] τὸν Θεόν editi antiqi.
[3] καταμελήσωσι E, editi antiqi.

this same subject, to protest before God and men, that you should cease bringing death upon men's souls, but should think out some other methods of tax-exaction, and permit men to keep their souls uninjured. These things we are writing to you, not with the thought that you are in need of our written exhortation (for you have reasons at home for fearing the Lord), but in order that through you all who are subject to you may be taught not to rouse the Holy One to anger, and not to render a forbidden act a matter of indifference through evil habit. For the people derive no help from the oaths in combating the demand for taxes, but they do receive into their soul an acknowledged evil. For whenever men become fully practised in perjury, they no longer exert themselves to make payment, but think that the oath has been devised for them as an instrument of deception and a pretext for delay.

Now if the Lord brings swift retribution upon the perjured, the collectors will have none to answer their summons, for those will have been destroyed by God's punishment who have committed the perjury; and if the Master endures with patience (and as I have said before, those who have experienced the Lord's forbearance scorn His goodness), let them not transgress the law for no benefit,[1] nor yet provoke God against themselves.

We have spoken what is in keeping with our duty; those who do not obey will see to it.

---

[1] *i.e.* they will not escape their taxes even if they swear to their inability to pay them.

---

⁴ τὰς] τῆς E.   ⁵ αὐτούς E.

COLLECTED LETTERS OF SAINT BASIL

LXXXVI

Τῷ ἡγεμόνι

Οἶδα μεγίστην καὶ πρώτην σπουδὴν οὖσαν τῇ τιμιότητί σου πάντα[1] τρόπον χαρίζεσθαι τῷ δικαίῳ, δευτέραν δὲ τὸ καὶ τοὺς[2] φίλους εὖ ποιεῖν καὶ τῶν προσφευγόντων τῇ προστασίᾳ τῆς σῆς μεγαλονοίας ἀντιποιεῖσθαι. πάντα τοίνυν εἰς ταὐτὸν συνέδραμεν ἐπὶ τῆς παρούσης ὑποθέσεως. καὶ γὰρ δίκαιόν ἐστι τὸ πρᾶγμα, ὑπὲρ οὗ τὴν πρεσβείαν ποιούμεθα, καὶ ἡμῖν κεχαρισμένον, οὓς ἐν τοῖς φίλοις ἀριθμεῖν τοῖς σεαυτοῦ[3] κατηξίωσας, καὶ ὀφειλόμενον τοῖς τὴν στερρότητά σου εἰς τὴν ὑπὲρ ὧν πεπόνθασι βοήθειαν ἐπικαλουμένοις.

Σῖτον γάρ, ὃν μόνον εἶχε πρὸς[4] τὴν ἀναγκαίαν τοῦ βίου διαγωγὴν ὁ ποθεινότατος ἀδελφὸς Δωρόθεος, διήρπασάν τινες ἐν Βηρίσοις[5] τῶν τὰ δημόσια διοικεῖν πεπιστευμένων, εἴτε ἀφ' ἑαυτῶν ἐλθόντες ἐπὶ τὴν βίαν, εἴτε καὶ ἑτέρων αὐτοῖς ὑποθεμένων. πλὴν οὐδαμόθεν αὐτοῖς τὸ πρᾶγμα ἀνέγκλητον, τί γὰρ ἧττον ἀδικεῖ ὁ οἴκοθεν πονηρὸς ἢ ὁ ἑτέρων κακίᾳ ὑπηρετούμενος; καὶ τοῖς πεπονθόσιν ἡ ζημία ὁμοία. τοῦτον ἀξιοῦμεν, δι' ὧν ἀφηρέθη μὲν[6] ἀπολαβεῖν, καὶ μὴ ἐξεῖναι αὐτοῖς ἐπὶ ἑτέροις[7] τὴν αἰτίαν τῶν τετολμημένων ἀναφέρειν·[8] ὅσον δὲ[9] ἄξιον τὸ τὴν ἐκ τῆς σιτοδείας

---

[1] κατά E.   [2] τούς om. E.   [3] ἑαυτοῦ E, Med.
[4] πρὸς] εἰς E.   [5] Βηρίσσοις E.
[6] ἐξ αὐτῶν τὸ ἀφαιρεθέν add. editi Paris.
[7] ἑτέρους E.   [8] φέρειν E.
[9] ὅσου . . . τοσούτου] ὅσον . . . τοσοῦτον editi antiqi.

LETTER LXXXVI

To the Governor [1]

I know that the first and greatest object of your
Honour's zeal is to favour the cause of justice in
every way, and the second, to benefit your friends
and to take action in the interests of those who flee
to the protection of your Magnanimity. Hence we
are completely in accord in the present case. For
the thing for which we plead is just, and a favour to
us, whom you have deigned to number among your
friends, and an obligation due to those who implore
your Constancy for assistance in alleviating their
sufferings.

For the grain, which alone our very dear brother
Dorotheus possessed for meeting the necessities of
life, has been stolen by certain persons at Brisi of
those who are entrusted with the administration
of public affairs, whether they resorted to this act
of violence of their own accord, or were instigated
thereto by others. From no point of view, however,
is their action blameless. For in what respect does
he who is evil in himself commit less wrong than
he who serves the wickedness of others? To the
victims, moreover, the injury inflicted is the same.
We ask that Dorotheus shall get back the grain
from those by whom it was taken from him, and
that they should not be allowed to put the blame
for their audacity upon others. And as much as it

---

[1] Of the same year as the preceding. Some MSS. (Reg.
secundus and Bigot.) add to the present title: παραθετικὴ
ὑπὲρ πρεσβυτέρων περὶ καθαρπαγῆς σίτου, "of recommendation
in behalf of presbyters on the stealing of grain."

113

διαφυγεῖν ἀνάγκην, τοσούτου τὴν χάριν τιμη-
σόμεθα τὴν παρὰ τῆς σῆς μεγαλοφυΐας, ἐὰν ἄρα
δοῦναι καταξιώσῃς.

LXXXVII

Ἀνεπίγραφος ὑπὲρ τῶν αὐτῶν[1]

Ἐθαύμασα πῶς, σοῦ μεσιτεύοντος, τοσοῦτον
ἐτολμήθη κακὸν κατὰ τοῦ συμπρεσβυτέρου[2] ὥστε
ἣν μόνην εἶχεν ἀφορμὴν τοῦ βίου, ταύτην διαρπασ-
θῆναι, καὶ τὸ δεινότατον, ὅτι οἱ τοῦτο τετολμη-
κότες ἐπὶ σὲ[3] τὴν αἰτίαν ὧν πεποιήκασιν ἀνα-
φέρουσιν·[4] ὃν οὐχ ὅπως ἐπιτρέπειν τὰ τοιαῦτα
γίνεσθαι, ἀλλὰ καὶ παντὶ σθένει διακωλύειν
ἀκόλουθον ἦν, μάλιστα μὲν κατὰ πάντων, εἰ δ᾽
ἄρα, κατὰ γοῦν τῶν πρεσβυτέρων, καὶ τούτων
ὅσοι ἡμῖν ὁμόψυχοι, καὶ τὴν αὐτὴν τῆς εὐσεβείας
ὁδὸν πορευόμενοι. εἴ τι οὖν φροντίζεις τοῦ
ἀναπαῦσαι ἡμᾶς, ταχέως διορθωθῆναι τὰ γενόμενα
ποίησον. δύνασαι γὰρ σὺν Θεῷ καὶ ταῦτα καὶ
ἔτι μείζω τούτων κατορθοῦν, οἷς ἂν ἐθέλῃς.
ἐπέστειλα δὲ καὶ τῷ ἄρχοντι τῆς πατρίδος, ἵνα,
ἐὰν ἀφ᾽[5] ἑαυτῶν μὴ θελήσωσι ποιῆσαι τὰ δίκαια,
ἐκ[6] τῆς κινήσεως τῶν δικαστηρίων ἀναγκασθῶσι
ποιῆσαι.

---

[1] ἐπὶ κήσει E ; ἐπὶ ἐκδικήσει alii MSS. ; ἐπὶ οἰκήσει editi
antiqi.
[2] πρεσβυτέρου E, Med.   [3] ἐπὶ σέ om. E.
[4] εἰς add. E, editi antiqi.
[5] ἐφ᾽ editi antiqi.   [6] διά E

is worth to escape the privations of a famine, at so much shall we value the favour bestowed by your Magnanimity, if you deign to grant it.

LETTER LXXXVII

Without Address, on the Same Subject [1]

I am surprised that, with you acting as mediator, so great an outrage has been perpetrated against our presbyter [2]—that he has been plundered of the sole support of life which he possessed, and, worst of all, that the perpetrators of this deed lay the blame for the act which they have committed on you; for it was incumbent on you, not only not to allow such things to be done, but also, with all your power, to prevent their being done, if possible against any man, but if such things must be, against any presbyter at least, or, of presbyters, against such as are of like mind with us and are journeying along the same road of piety. If, therefore, you are at all concerned to put us at ease, see to it that what has been done be quickly rectified. For with God's help you can succeed in these and in still greater things for whomsoever you will. I have written also to the governor of my native land [3] in order that, if they do not wish to do what is right of themselves, they may be forced to do so under pressure of the courts.

---

[1] Of the same date and on the same subject as the preceding.

[2] *i.e.* Dorotheus. Cf. preceding letter.

[3] Cf. Letter VIII, Vol. I, p. 48, note 1.

COLLECTED LETTERS OF SAINT BASIL

LXXXVIII

Ἀνεπίγραφος, ἐπὶ ἀπαιτητῇ χρημάτων

Τὴν δυσκολίαν τῆς συγκομιδῆς τοῦ πραγ-
ματευτικοῦ χρυσίου πάντων μάλιστα ἡ σὴ
τιμιότης κατέμαθε· καὶ τῆς πενίας ἡμῶν οὐδένα
μάρτυρα τοιοῦτον ἔχομεν, οἷον σέ, ὃς ἐκ τῆς
μεγάλης φιλανθρωπίας καὶ συνέπαθες ἡμῖν καὶ
συμπεριηνέχθης μέχρι τοῦ παρόντος τὰ δυνατά,
οὐδαμοῦ τὸ πρᾷον τῆς ἑαυτοῦ τῶν τρόπων καταστάσεως ἐκ τῆς τῶν ἄνωθεν ἐπικειμένων ταραχῆς
παρακινήσας. ἐπεὶ οὖν ὑπολείπεται ἡμῖν ἐκ τοῦ
παντὸς σταθμοῦ ὀλίγον ἔτι χρυσίον, καὶ τοῦτο
ἀνάγκη ἐκ τοῦ ἐράνου, εἰς ὃν προετρεψάμεθα
πᾶσαν τὴν πόλιν, συγκομισθῆναι, παρακαλοῦμέν
σου τὴν ἡμερότητα μικρόν τι ἐκτεῖναι ἡμῖν τὴν
προθεσμίαν, πρὸς τὸ καὶ τοὺς ἔξω τῆς πόλεως
ὑπομνησθῆναι. ἐν ἀγροῖς γάρ ἐστι τὸ πολὺ τῶν
ἐν τέλει, ὡς οὐδὲ αὐτὸς ἀγνοεῖς. ἐὰν μὲν οὖν ᾖ
δυνατὸν παρὰ τοσάσδε λίτρας ἐκπεμφθῆναι,
τοσοῦτον γὰρ ἡμῖν ὑπολέλειπται, τοῦτο γενέσθαι
παρακαλοῦμέν σε· κἀκεῖνο ἐπαποσταλήσεται
ὕστερον· ἐὰν δὲ πᾶσα ᾖ ἀνάγκη ἀθρόον αὐτὸ
παραπεμφθῆναι τοῖς θησαυροῖς, ὅπερ ἐξ ἀρχῆς
ἠξιώσαμεν, πλατυτέραν ἡμῖν γενέσθαι τὴν προθεσμίαν.

---

[1] Of the same year as the preceding.

[2] The Benedictine editors remark on χρυσίον πραγμα-
τευτικόν (*aurum comparatitium*), that it was so called because
it was collected for the purpose of providing troops with
equipment, according to Gothofredus on *Cod. Theod.*, 7, 6, 3.
The provinces of the East, with the exception of Osroene
and Isauria, contributed gold instead of actual equipment.

LETTER LXXXVIII

LETTER LXXXVIII

WITHOUT ADDRESS, FOR A TAX-COLLECTOR [1]

THE difficulty of collecting gold furnished by
contribution [2] your Honour has learned better than
anyone else; moreover, we have no witness of
our poverty better qualified than yourself, who out
of your great kindness have both sympathized with
us and, up to the present, have shown us indulgence
as far as possible, never allowing the mildness of
your disposition to be altered by the distraction
occasioned by those in high authority who beset you. Since, therefore, a small amount of the
whole sum we owe is still lacking, and this must
be got together from the general contribution
which we have urged the city as a whole to make,
we beseech your Clemency to favour us by extending the period of grace a little in order that those
who are absent from the city may be notified. For
most of the magistrates are in the country, as you
yourself are not unaware. Now, if it is possible that
the money, less this particular number of pounds (for
this is the sum we still lack), be sent, we ask you
that this be done; and the above-named shortage
will be dispatched later; but if it is absolutely
necessary that the stated sum be forwarded to the
treasury all at once, then grant us what we asked in
the first place, namely, that the period of grace be
extended for us.

A law by Valens on this subject and dated 368 reads: Omnem
canonem vestium ex Kal. Sept. ad Kal. Aprilis largitionibus
trade, proposita Rectori provinciae vel eius officio condem-
nationis poena; that is, the gold must be paid between Sept.
1 and April 1. Since Basil is here pleading for an extension
of time, if not exemption, this letter may be dated shortly
before April 1.

COLLECTED LETTERS OF SAINT BASIL

LXXXIX

Μελετίῳ, ἐπισκόπῳ Ἀντιοχείας

Ὁ ἀγαθὸς Θεός, παρασχόμενος ἡμῖν προφάσεις προσηγοριῶν πρὸς τὴν σὴν τιμιότητα, τὸ
σφοδρὸν τοῦ πόθου παραμυθεῖται. μάρτυς γὰρ
αὐτὸς τῆς ἐπιθυμίας ἡμῶν ἣν ἔχομεν εἰς τὸ
θεάσασθαί σου τὸ¹ πρόσωπον, καὶ ἀπολαῦσαι
τῆς ἀγαθῆς σου καὶ ψυχωφελοῦς διδασκαλίας.
καὶ νῦν δὲ διὰ τοῦ εὐλαβεστάτου καὶ σπουδαιο-
τάτου ἀδελφοῦ Δωροθέου τοῦ συνδιακόνου ἐρχο-
μένου παρακαλοῦμέν σε προηγουμένως προσεύχεσθαι ὑπὲρ ἡμῶν, ἵνα μὴ πρόσκομμα ὦμεν
τῷ λαῷ, μηδὲ ἐμπόδιον ταῖς ὑμετέραις εὐχαῖς
πρὸς τὸ δυσωπῆσαι τὸν Κύριον. ἔπειτα καὶ
ὑπομιμνήσκομεν καταξιῶσαί σε πάντα τυπῶσαι
διὰ τοῦ προειρημένου ἀδελφοῦ, καὶ εἴ τι δεῖ
ἐπισταλῆναι τοῖς κατὰ τὴν δύσιν, διὰ τὸ ὀφείλειν
ἀναγκαίως καὶ δι' ἡμετέρου αὐτοῖς ἀπενεχθῆναι
γράμματα, αὐτὸν ὑπαγορεῦσαι τὰς ἐπιστολάς.
ἡμεῖς γὰρ ἐπιτυχόντες Σαβίνου, τοῦ παρ' αὐτῶν
ἀποσταλέντος διακόνου, ἐπεστείλαμεν² πρός τε
τοὺς Ἰλλυριοὺς καὶ πρὸς τοὺς κατὰ τὴν Ἰταλίαν

¹ σου τὸ] τοῦτο editi antiqi.
² ἀπεστείλαμεν E, editi antiqi.

---

¹ Written before Easter 372. On Meletius, bishop of
Antioch, cf. Letters LVII and LXVIII.
² A deacon of the church of Antioch, and attached to the
communion of Meletius. The year before (371) he had been
the bearer of two letters from Basil to Athanasius, entreating
him to use his influence with the Western Church to inter-

LETTER LXXXIX

To Meletius, Bishop of Antioch [1]

The good God, by affording us opportunities of addressing your Honour, assuages the intensity of our longing. For He Himself is a witness of the desire which we have to behold your countenance and to enjoy your good and soul-profiting instruction. And now through our most pious and zealous brother, the deacon Dorotheus,[2] who is setting out, we beseech you, primarily, to pray for us that we may not be a stumbling-block to the people, nor a hindrance to your own prayers for the placation of the Lord. And, secondly, we suggest that you deign to arrange all things through the brother just mentioned, and if there is any need of writing to those in the West, it being an urgent obligation that letters be sent to them from our side also, that you yourself dictate the letters. For we, on meeting the deacon Sabinus, who had been sent by them, have written to the Illyrians and to the

pose and heal the schism of the Church of Antioch, by inducing all the orthodox to join with Meletius and his party. Cf. Letters XLVIII, L, and LII. At the close of 371 Basil again sent Dorotheus to Athanasius, with letters to Pope Damasus and the Western bishops, asking for assistance in his efforts to unite the East. Cf. Letter LII. Dorotheus spent the winter in Italy negotiating to no purpose, and returned in 372 to Athanasius and Basil, bringing letters from Damasus which bore witness to the community of their faith, but offered no real assistance. Cf. Letters LXI, LXII, and CCLXXIII. Basil is now sending Dorotheus to Meletius requesting him to draw up more urgent letters to the bishops of the West. These letters, however, are to be sent to Rome, not by Dorotheus, but by the deacon Sabinus.

καὶ Γαλλίαν [1] ἐπισκόπους, καί τινας τῶν ἰδίως πρὸς ἡμᾶς ἐπιστειλάντων. εὔλογον δὲ ὡς ἀπὸ κοινοῦ [2] τῆς συνόδου ἀποσταλῆναί τινα τὸν κομίζοντα δεύτερα γράμματα, ἅπερ αὐτὸς κέλευσον τυπωθῆναι.

Καὶ περὶ τοῦ αἰδεσιμωτάτου ἐπισκόπου Ἀθανασίου ἀκριβῶς γινώσκουσαν τὴν τελείαν σου φρόνησιν ὑπομιμνήσκομεν, ὅτι ἀμήχανον τοῖς παρ' ἐμοῦ γράμμασιν ἐπιδοῦναι ἢ [3] ποιῆσαί τι τῶν ὀφειλομένων, ἐὰν μὴ καὶ παρ' ὑμῶν, τῶν τότε τὴν κοινωνίαν αὐτοῦ ἀναβαλλομένων, δέξηταί τινα τρόπον. αὐτὸς γὰρ λέγεται πάνυ ὡρμῆσθαι πρὸς τὸ συναφθῆναι ἡμῖν, καὶ τὰ κατὰ δύναμιν συμβαλέσθαι, λυπεῖσθαι δέ, ὅτι καὶ τότε παρεπέμφθη ἀκοινώνητος, καὶ ἔτι νῦν [4] ἀτελεῖς μένουσιν αἱ ὑποσχέσεις.

Τὰ δὲ κατὰ τὴν ἀνατολὴν ὅπως διάκειται οὐκ ἔλαθε πάντως τὰς ἀκοὰς τῆς θεοσεβείας σου, καὶ δι' ἑαυτοῦ δὲ ἀκριβέστερον πάντα ὁ προειρημένος ἀδελφὸς διηγήσεται. ὃν καταξίωσον εὐθὺς ἐκπέμψαι μετὰ τὸ Πάσχα, διὰ τὸ ἀναμένειν τὰς ἀπὸ Σαμοσάτων ἀποκρίσεις· οὗ καὶ τὴν προθυμίαν ἀπόδεξαι, καὶ εὐχαῖς αὐτὸν ἐνισχύσας, πρόπεμψον εἰς τὰ προκείμενα.

---

[1] καὶ Γαλλίαν om. Vat., Reg. secundus.
[2] κοινῆς editi antiqi.   [3] καί editi antiqi.   [4] νῦν om. E.

---

[1] Tillemont holds that this cannot apply to Athanasius the Great, because it is unlikely that Meletius would refuse him communion. Maran (*Vita Basilii*, xxii), however,

bishops in Italy and Gaul, and to certain ones who had sent letters to us privately. It would be prudent that a messenger be sent carrying a second letter from the common synod, and do you yourself command this letter to be written.

Now regarding the most reverend bishop Athanasius, we must remind your perfect wisdom, which knows all accurately, that it is impossible to promote or accomplish any of those things which are necessary by means of letters from me, unless he receives his communion in some way from you also, who once deferred giving it. For he himself is said to have made every effort to unite with us, and, on his part, to have done all in his power; but he is now grieving, they say, because on the occasion in question he was sent away without communion, and because the promises which were made to him remain even yet unfulfilled.[1]

How conditions are in the East has assuredly not escaped the ears of your Holiness, and the brother whom we have mentioned above will in person relate everything more accurately. Be kind enough to send him away immediately after Easter, since he is awaiting the replies of the Samositans; approve his zeal, and having fortified him with your prayers send him forth upon his present business.

shows not only that the circumstances fit in, but that the statement of Meletius' refusal is borne out by Letter CCLVIII, 3. It seems that Athanasius himself was so far committed to the other side in the Antiochene dispute that he could not recognize Meletius.

XC

Τοῖς ἁγιωτάτοις ἀδελφοῖς καὶ ἐπισκόποις τοῖς ἐν
τῇ δύσει [1]

Ὁ ἀγαθὸς Θεός, ὁ ἀεὶ ταῖς θλίψεσι τὰς παρακλήσεις παραζευγνύς, ἔδωκεν ἡμῖν καὶ νῦν ἐπὶ [2]
τῷ πλήθει τῶν ὀδυνῶν εὑρέσθαι τινὰ μετρίαν
παράκλησιν ἐκ [3] τῶν γραμμάτων, ἃ παρὰ τῆς
ὑμετέρας ὀρθότητος ὁ τιμιώτατος πατὴρ ἡμῶν
Ἀθανάσιος [4] ὁ ἐπίσκοπος δεξάμενος διεπέμψατο
ἡμῖν, ὑγιοῦς πίστεως μαρτυρίαν, καὶ τῆς ἀνε-
πηρεάστου ὑμῶν ὁμονοίας καὶ συμπνοίας ἀπόδειξιν ἔχοντα, ὥστε καὶ ποιμένας ἀναδεικνύναι [5]
τοῖς ἴχνεσι τῶν πατέρων ἀκολουθοῦντας καὶ τὸν
λαὸν τοῦ Κυρίου μετ᾽ ἐπιστήμης ποιμαίνοντας.
ταῦτα πάντα ηὔφρανεν [6] ἡμᾶς τοσοῦτον, ὥστε
λῦσαι ἡμῶν τὴν κατήφειαν, καὶ μειδίαμά τι βραχὺ
ταῖς ψυχαῖς ἡμῶν ἐμποιῆσαι ἀπὸ τῆς σκυθρωπῆς
ταύτης τῶν πραγμάτων καταστάσεως,[7] ἐν ᾗ νῦν
καθεστήκαμεν.

Ἐπέτεινε δὲ ἡμῖν τὴν παράκλησιν ὁ Κύριος
διὰ τοῦ υἱοῦ ἡμῶν τοῦ εὐλαβεστάτου συνδιακόνου
Σαβίνου, ὃς καὶ τὰ παρ᾽ ὑμῖν καλὰ διηγησάμενος
ἀκριβῶς ἔθρεψεν ἡμῶν τὰς ψυχάς· καὶ τὰ ἡμέτερα δέ,[8] τῇ πείρᾳ μαθών, ἐναργῶς ὑμῖν ἀναγγελεῖ, ἵνα προηγουμένως μὲν διὰ τῆς ἐκτενοῦς καὶ
φιλοπόνου δεήσεως τῆς πρὸς τὸν Κύριον συνα-

---

[1] ἐπισκόποις δυτικοῖς συνοδική, " A synodical letter to the
bishops of the West," E.

[2] ἐν E.   [3] τε add. E.   [4] Ἀθανάσιος om. Regii duo.

[5] ἀποδειχθῆναι Reg. secundus, Coisl. secundus. τούς add. E,
editi antiqi.

LETTER XC

To the Most Holy Brethren and Bishops of the West [1]

THE good God, who always yokes consolations with afflictions, has granted us even now amid the present multitude of woes that we should find a certain measure of consolation in the letters which our most honoured father, Bishop Athanasius, received from your orthodox selves and forwarded to us, being as they are a testimony to your sound faith, giving proof of your unalterable unanimity and concord, so that they show clearly that the shepherds are following the footsteps of the fathers and with knowledge are feeding the people of the Lord. All this has delighted us to such a degree as to dissolve our dejection and to engender in our souls a faint smile, as it were, after the gloom of the state of affairs in which we at present find ourselves.

And the Lord has increased our consolation through our son, the most reverend deacon Sabinus, who by his accurate account of the goodly situation among you has nourished our souls; and our condition in turn he will report to you plainly when he becomes familiar with it through experience, in order that, in the first place, you may unite with us in our struggle by your earnest and untiring prayer to the

---

[1] Written before Easter of 372. Newman takes this letter and also Letter XCII in close connexion with Letter LXX, which appears to be addressed to Pope Damasus.

---

⁶ εὔφρανεν E. ⁷ κινήσεως quattuor MSS. ⁸ δέ om. E.

γωνίζησθε ἡμῖν, ἔπειτα δὲ καὶ τὴν ἐνδεχομένην
ὑμῖν[1] παραμυθίαν ταῖς καταπονουμέναις ἐκκλησίαις εἰσενέγκασθαι μὴ παραιτήσησθε. κέκμηκε
γὰρ τὰ ἐνταῦθα, ἀδελφοὶ τιμιώτατοι, καὶ ἀπείρη-
κε πρὸς τὰς συνεχεῖς προσβολὰς τῶν ἐναντίων
ἡ Ἐκκλησία, ὥσπερ τι πλοῖον ἐν πελάγει μέσῳ
ταῖς ἐπαλλήλοις πληγαῖς τῶν κυμάτων βασα-
νιζόμενον, εἰ μή τις γένοιτο ταχεῖα ἐπισκοπὴ
τῆς ἀγαθότητος τοῦ Κυρίου. ὥσπερ οὖν ἡμεῖς
ἴδιον ἑαυτῶν ἀγαθὸν ποιούμεθα τὴν ὑμετέραν[2]
πρὸς ἀλλήλους σύμπνοιάν τε καὶ ἑνότητα, οὕτω
καὶ ὑμᾶς παρακαλοῦμεν συμπαθῆσαι ἡμῶν ταῖς
διαιρέσεσι, καὶ μή, ὅτι τῇ θέσει τῶν τόπων
διεστήκαμεν, χωρίζειν ἡμᾶς ἀφ' ἑαυτῶν, ἀλλ' ὅτι
ἑνούμεθα τῇ κατὰ τὸ Πνεῦμα κοινωνίᾳ, εἰς τὴν
ἑνὸς σώματος ἡμᾶς συμφωνίαν ἀναλαμβάνειν.

Γνώριμα δὲ τὰ θλίβοντα ἡμᾶς, κἂν ἡμεῖς μὴ
λέγωμεν· εἰς πᾶσαν γὰρ τὴν οἰκουμένην λοιπὸν
ἐξήχηται. καταπεφρόνηται τὰ τῶν πατέρων
δόγματα· ἀποστολικαὶ παραδόσεις ἐξουδένωνται·
νεωτεροποιῶν[3] ἀνθρώπων ἐφευρέματα ταῖς ἐκκλησίαις ἐμπολιτεύεται· τεχνολογοῦσι λοιπόν,
οὐ[4] θεολογοῦσιν, οἱ ἄνθρωποι· ἡ τοῦ κόσμου
σοφία τὰ πρωτεῖα φέρεται, παρωσαμένη τὸ
καύχημα τοῦ σταυροῦ. ποιμένες ἀπελαύνονται,
ἀντεισάγονται δὲ λύκοι βαρεῖς, διασπῶντες τὸ
ποίμνιον τοῦ Χριστοῦ. οἶκοι εὐκτήριοι ἔρημοι
τῶν ἐκκλησιαζόντων· αἱ ἐρημίαι πλήρεις τῶν
ὀδυρομένων. οἱ πρεσβύτεροι ὀδύρονται, τὰ παλαιὰ

---

[1] ἡμῖν E.   [2] ἡμετέραν E.
[3] ἐξουδένωνται· νεωτεροποιῶν] ἐξουθένηνται, νεωτέρων tres
Regii, Coisl. secundus.
124

Lord, and secondly, that you may not refuse to
bring all the consolation in your power to our suffering churches. For here all things are sick, most
reverend brethren, and in the face of the continuous
attacks of her enemies the church has given up the
struggle—like a ship in mid-sea when it is buffeted
by the successive blows of the waves—unless it
receive some speedy visitation of the goodness of
the Lord. Therefore, just as we consider your
agreement and unity with one another as a special
blessing for us, so too we beg you to sympathize
with our dissensions and not, because we are
separated by our respective geographical positions,
to sever us from yourselves, but, inasmuch as we are
united in the communion of the Spirit, to take us
into the harmony of one single body.

The evils which afflict us are well known, even
if we do not now mention them, for long since have
they been re-echoed through the whole world. The
teachings of the Fathers are scorned; the apostolic
traditions are set at naught; the fabrications of
innovators are in force in the churches; these men,
moreover, train themselves in rhetorical quibbling
and not in theology; the wisdom of the world
takes first place to itself, having thrust aside the
glory of the Cross. The shepherds are driven away,
and in their places are introduced troublesome
wolves who tear asunder the flock of Christ. The
houses of prayer are bereft of those wont to assemble
therein; the solitudes are filled with those who
weep. The elders weep, comparing the past with

---

⁴ οὐ] καὶ οὐχί E.

συγκρίνοντες τοῖς παροῦσιν· οἱ νέοι ἐλεεινότεροι,
μὴ εἰδότες οἵων ἐστέρηνται.

Ταῦτα ἱκανὰ μὲν κινῆσαι πρὸς[1] συμπάθειαν
τοὺς τὴν Χριστοῦ ἀγάπην πεπαιδευμένους·
συγκρινόμενος δὲ τῇ ἀληθείᾳ τῶν πραγμάτων
ὁ λόγος παρὰ πολὺ τῆς ἀξίας αὐτῶν ἀπολείπεται.
εἴ τι οὖν παραμύθιον ἀγάπης, εἴ τις κοινωνία
Πνεύματος, εἴ τινα[2] σπλάγχνα οἰκτιρμῶν,[3]
κινήθητε πρὸς τὴν ἀντίληψιν ἡμῶν. λάβετε
ζῆλον εὐσεβείας, ἐξέλεσθε ἡμᾶς τοῦ χειμῶνος
τούτου. λαλείσθω καὶ παρ᾽ ἡμῖν μετὰ παρρησίας
τὸ ἀγαθὸν ἐκεῖνο κήρυγμα τῶν πατέρων, τὸ
καταστρέφον μὲν τὴν δυσώνυμον αἵρεσιν τὴν[4]
Ἀρείου, οἰκοδομοῦν[5] δὲ τὰς ἐκκλησίας ἐν τῇ
ὑγιαινούσῃ διδασκαλίᾳ ἐν ᾗ ὁ Υἱὸς ὁμοούσιος
ὁμολογεῖται τῷ Πατρί, καὶ τὸ Πνεῦμα τὸ ἅγιον
ὁμοτίμως συναριθμεῖταί τε καὶ συλλατρεύεται·
ἵνα ἣν ὑμῖν[6] ἔδωκεν ὁ Κύριος ὑπὲρ τῆς ἀληθείας
παρρησίαν, καὶ τὸ ἐπὶ τῇ ὁμολογίᾳ τῆς θείας[7]
καὶ σωτηρίου Τριάδος καύχημα, τοῦτο καὶ ἡμῖν
διὰ τῶν ὑμετέρων εὐχῶν καὶ τῆς συνεργίας ὑμῶν
χαρίσηται. τὸ δὲ καθέκαστον αὐτὸς ὁ προειρημένος συνδιάκονος ἀναγγελεῖ ὑμῶν τῇ ἀγάπῃ.
καὶ πᾶσι δὲ τοῖς γενομένοις κανονικῶς παρὰ τῆς
ὑμετέρας τιμιότητος συνεθέμεθα, τὸν ἀποστολικὸν
ὑμῶν ζῆλον ὑπὲρ τῆς ὀρθοδοξίας ἀποδεξάμενοι.

---

[1] εἰς editi antiqi.   [2] τινα] τι E.
[3] καὶ οἰκτιρμοί E.   [4] τοῦ E.
[5] στερεοῦν editi antiqi, οἰκονομοῦν Harl., Regius.

the present; the young are more to be pitied, since they know not of what they have been deprived.

These facts are sufficient to move to sympathy those who have been taught the love of Christ; yet my speech in comparison with the true state of things falls far short of a worthy presentation of them. If, then, there is any consolation of love, if there is any communion of the Spirit, if there are any bowels of mercy, be moved to our assistance. Take up the zeal of piety, and rescue us from this storm. And let us also pronounce with boldness that good dogma [1] of the Fathers, which overwhelms the accursed heresy of Arius, and builds the churches on the sound doctrine, wherein the Son is confessed to be consubstantial with the Father, and the Holy Spirit is numbered with them in like honour and so adored; in order that the Lord through your prayers and your co-operation may also bestow upon us that fearlessness in the cause of truth, and that glory in the confession of the divine and saving Trinity, which He has given to you. The deacon whom we have mentioned will himself announce everything in detail to your Affection. Moreover, with all that has been done canonically by your Honours we are in agreement, having welcomed your apostolic zeal for orthodoxy.

---

[1] Basil in general seems to use δόγματα in the sense of doctrines and practices privately and tacitly sanctioned in the Church, and he reserves κηρύγματα for what is now usually understood as δόγματα.

---

[6] ἡμῖν E.   [7] ἀληθείας editi antiqi.

XCI

Οὐαλεριανῷ, ἐπισκόπῳ Ἰλλυριῶν[1]

Χάρις τῷ Κυρίῳ,[2] τῷ δόντι ἡμῖν ἀρχαίας
ἀγάπης καρπὸν ἰδεῖν ἐν τῇ σῇ καθαρότητι, ὅς
γε τοσοῦτον διεστὼς τῷ σώματι, συνῆψας ἡμῖν
σεαυτὸν[3] διὰ γράμματος, καὶ τῷ πνευματικῷ
σου καὶ ἁγίῳ πόθῳ περιπτυξάμενος ἡμᾶς, ἀμύθητόν τι[4] φίλτρον ταῖς ψυχαῖς ἡμῶν ἐνεποίησας.
ἔργῳ γὰρ ἐμάθομεν τῆς παροιμίας τὴν δύναμιν,
ὅτι "Ὥσπερ ψυχῇ διψώσῃ ψυχρὸν ὕδωρ, οὕτως
ἀγγελία ἀγαθὴ ἐκ γῆς[5] μακρόθεν.

Δεινὸς γάρ ἐστι παρ' ἡμῖν λιμὸς ἀγάπης,
ἀδελφὲ τιμιώτατε. καὶ ἡ αἰτία πρόδηλος, ὅτι
διὰ τὸ πληθυνθῆναι τὴν ἀνομίαν ἐψύγη[6] τῶν
πολλῶν ἡ ἀγάπη. διὰ τοῦτο καὶ πολλοῦ ἄξιον
ἡμῖν ἐφάνη τὸ γράμμα, καὶ ἀμειβόμεθά σε διὰ
τοῦ αὐτοῦ ἀνδρὸς τοῦ εὐλαβεστάτου συνδιακόνου
ἡμῶν καὶ ἀδελφοῦ Σαβίνου· δι' οὗ καὶ γνωρί-
ζομέν σοι ἑαυτούς καὶ παρακαλοῦμέν σε ἐπα-

---

[1] Ἰλλυρικοῦ Harl., Reg. secundus, Coisl. secundus.
[2] Θεῷ nonnulli MSS.   [3] ἑαυτόν E.   [4] τό E, Med.
[5] γῆς] sic E, Med., Harl. τῆς alii MSS. et editi.
[6] ψυγήσεται E.

---

[1] Before Easter of 372. St. Valerianus, bishop of Aquileia,
is first mentioned as being present at the council of Rome
in 371. Cf. Theodoret, *H.E.* 2, 17. He presided at the
council held in 381 at Aquileia against the Arian bishops
Palladius and Secundinus, although he took small part in
the discussion, St. Ambrose being the leader of the Catholics.
He was also at the council at Rome in 382. Cf. Theodoret,

LETTER XCI

LETTER XCI

To Valerian, Bishop of the Illyrians[1]

Thanks be unto the Lord, who has permitted us to see in your Purity the fruit of pristine love;[2] for you, though so far separated in body, have united yourself to us by letter, and embracing us with your spiritual and holy yearning you have engendered in our souls an ineffable affection. For by experience we have learned the force of the proverb that: "As cold water to a thirsty soul, so is good tidings from a far country."[3]

For terrible among us is the famine of love, most honoured brother. And the cause is manifest: "because iniquity has abounded, the charity of many has grown cold."[4] For this reason, indeed, your letter has seemed of great worth to us, and we are answering you through the same person, our most reverend deacon and brother, Sabinus; and through him, moreover, we both make our own con-

---

H.E. 5, 9. The date of his death is uncertain. He is commemorated on Nov. 27. Under his rule there grew up at Aquileia that group of people of whom Jerome was the most famous, and which he calls in his chronicle (A.D. 378) "a company of the blessed." Dorotheus or Sabinus had brought letters from Athanasius, and Sabinus one from Valerianus, and Basil is here taking the opportunity to reply.

[2] *i.e.* an exemplification of Christian love as taught in the early Church.

[3] Cf. Prov. 25. 25: ὥσπερ ὕδωρ ψυχρὸν ψυχῇ διψώσῃ προσηνές, οὕτως ἀγγελία ἀγαθὴ ἐκ γῆς μακρόθεν.

[4] Cf. Matt. 24. 12: καὶ διὰ τὸ πληθυνθῆναι τὴν ἀνομίαν, ψυγήσεται ἡ ἀγάπη τῶν πολλῶν.

"And because iniquity hath abounded, the charity of many shall grow cold."

γρυπνεῖν ταῖς ὑπὲρ ἡμῶν προσευχαῖς, ἵνα δῷ
ποτὲ ὁ ἅγιος Θεὸς καὶ τοῖς ἐνταῦθα πράγμασι
γαλήνην καὶ ἡσυχίαν, καὶ ἐπιτιμήσῃ τῷ ἀνέμῳ
τούτῳ καὶ τῇ θαλάσσῃ, ὥστε παύσασθαι ἡμᾶς
τοῦ σάλου καὶ τῆς ἀνατροπῆς, ἐν ᾗ νῦν καθεστήκαμεν, ἀεὶ καταποντισθήσεσθαι[1] παντελῶς
ἀναμένοντες.

Ἀλλὰ τοῦτο μεγάλως[2] ἐν τοῖς παροῦσιν ὁ
Κύριος ἡμῖν ἐχαρίσατο, τὸ ὑμᾶς ἀκούειν ἐν
ἀκριβεῖ συμφωνίᾳ καὶ ἑνότητι εἶναι πρὸς ἀλλήλους, καὶ ἀκωλύτως παρ' ὑμῖν τὸ κήρυγμα τῆς
εὐσεβείας περιαγγέλλεσθαι. ὁτεδήποτε γὰρ
(εἴπερ μὴ συγκέκλεισται λοιπὸν ὁ χρόνος τοῦ
κόσμου τούτου, ἀλλ' ἔτι ἡμέραι τῆς ἀνθρωπίνης
ζωῆς ὑπολείπονται) ἀνάγκη παρ' ὑμῶν ἀνανεω-
θῆναι τὴν πίστιν τῇ ἀνατολῇ, καὶ ὧν ἐλάβετε
παρ' αὐτῆς ἀγαθῶν, τούτων ἐν καιρῷ παρασχέσθαι αὐτῇ τὴν ἀντίδοσιν. τὸ γὰρ ὑγιαῖνον
ἐνταῦθα μέρος καὶ τὴν τῶν πατέρων εὐσέβειαν
ἐκδικοῦν ἱκανῶς κέκμηκε, πολλαῖς καὶ ποικίλαις
μηχανημάτων προσβολαῖς ἐν τῇ ἑαυτοῦ μεθοδείᾳ
τοῦ διαβόλου αὐτὸ κατασείσαντος. ἀλλ' εὐχαῖς
ὑμετέραις τῶν ἀγαπώντων τὸν Κύριον σβεσθείη
μὲν ἡ πονηρὰ καὶ λαοπλάνος αἵρεσις τῆς Ἀρείου
κακοδοξίας· ἀναλάμψειε δὲ ἡ ἀγαθὴ τῶν πατέρων
ἡμῶν διδασκαλία τῶν συνελθόντων κατὰ τὴν
Νίκαιαν, ὥστε σύμφωνον τῷ σωτηρίῳ βαπτίσματι τὴν δοξολογίαν ἀποπληροῦσθαι[3] τῇ μακαρίᾳ
Τριάδι.

dition known to you and beseech you to be vigilant in your prayers for us, in order that the holy God may some day grant calm and repose to our concerns here, and may rebuke this wind and sea, so that we can find rest from the tempest-tossing and confusion in which we now find ourselves, ever waiting to be plunged utterly into the deep.

But this great blessing the Lord has bestowed upon us in our present situation—that we hear that you are in strict harmony and unity with one another, and that without hindrance the proclamation of the true faith is being made among you. For at some time (unless the period of this world is now closed, but if days of human existence alone still remain) there must come from you a renewal of the faith for the East, and in due time you must render her a recompense for the blessings which you have received from her. For that portion of us here that is sound and that guards the true doctrine of our fathers has become quite weary, since the devil in his craftiness has struck it down by the many and cunning assaults of his machinations. But by the prayers of you who love the Lord may that wicked and deceiving heresy, the false doctrine of Arius, be extinguished ; may the good teaching of our fathers who met at Nicaea shine forth again, so that the doxology in harmony with saving baptism may be duly rendered to the Blessed Trinity.

---

[1] καταποντίζεσθαι editi antiqi.   [2] μέγας editi antiqi.
[3] ἀναπληροῦσθαι E.

XCII

Πρὸς Ἰταλοὺς καὶ Γάλλους

Τοῖς θεοφιλεστάτοις καὶ ὁσιωτάτοις ἀδελφοῖς[1] συλλειτουργοῖς[2] κατὰ τὴν Ἰταλίαν καὶ Γαλλίαν ὁμοψύχοις ἐπισκόποις Μελέτιος, Εὐσέβειος, Βασίλειος, Βάσσος, Γρηγόριος, Πελάγιος, Παῦλος, Ἄνθιμος, Θεόδοτος, Βῖθος, Ἀβραάμιος, Ἰοβῖνος,[3] Ζήνων, Θεοδώρητος, Μαρκιανός, Βάραχος, Ἀβραάμιος, Λιβάνιος, Θαλάσσιος, Ἰωσήφ, Βοηθός, Ἰάτριος,[4] Θεόδοτος, Εὐστάθιος, Βαρσούμας, Ἰωάννης, Χοσρόης,[5] Ἰωσάκης,[6] Νάρσης, Μάρις, Γρηγόριος, Δαφνός,[7] ἐν Κυρίῳ χαίρειν.

Φέρει μέν τινα παραμυθίαν ταῖς ὀδυνωμέναις ψυχαῖς καὶ στεναγμὸς πολλάκις ἐκ βάθους τῆς καρδίας ἀναπεμπόμενος, καί που καὶ δάκρυον ἀποστάξαν τὸ πολὺ τῆς θλίψεως διεφόρησεν. ἡμῖν δὲ οὐχ, ὅσον[8] στεναγμὸς καὶ δάκρυον, παραμυθίαν ἔχει τὸ ἐξειπεῖν ἡμῶν τὰ πάθη πρὸς τὴν ἀγάπην ὑμῶν· ἀλλά τις ἡμᾶς καὶ ἐλπὶς χρηστοτέρα θάλπει, ὡς τάχα ἄν, εἰ ἐξαγγείλαιμεν ὑμῖν τὰ λυποῦντα ἡμᾶς, διαναστήσαιμεν[9] ὑμᾶς πρὸς

---

[1] ἀδελφοῖς om. E.   [2] τοῖς add. E.

[3] Ἰοβῖνος Vat. ; Σαβῖνος editi antiqi.

[4] Ἀτρεῖος Vat., Coisl. secundus, Reg. secundus.

[5] Χρυσορόης Coisl. secundus, Reg. secundus.

[6] Ἰσάκης Reg. secundus ; Ἰσάκις Coisl. secundus ; Ἰώσακις Harl.

[7] καὶ οἱ λοιποί add. ed. antiqi ; καὶ οἱ σὺν αὐτοῖς ἀδελφοί add. Med.

[8] ὅσην Regii duo, Coisl. secundus.

[9] διαναστήσωμεν duo MSS. ; διαναστήσαντες Harl. ; διαναστήσομεν editi antiqi.

LETTER XCII

To the Italians and Gauls[1]

To our most God-beloved and holy brethren, co-workers in Italy and Gaul, bishops of like mind with us, we, Meletius,[2] Eusebius,[3] Basil,[4] Bassus,[5] Gregory,[6] Pelagius,[7] Paul, Anthimus,[8] Theodotus,[9] Vitus,[10] Abraham,[11] Jobinus,[12] Zeno,[13] Theodoretus, Marcianus, Barachus, Abraham,[14] Libanius, Thalassius, Joseph, Boethus, Iatrius,[15] Theodotus, Eustathius,[16] Barsumas, John, Chosroes, Iosaces,[17] Narses, Maris, Gregory,[18] Daphnus, send you greetings in the Lord.

Even a groan repeatedly uttered from the depths of the heart brings some degree of consolation to souls in affliction, and doubtless, too, a falling tear has swept away the greater portion of our anguish. But the telling of our woes to your Charity means for us, not consolation such as groans and tears may bring; nay, there is also hope for better things that warms us, a hope that perhaps, if we should announce to you the causes of our affliction, we might rouse you to take those measures for our

---

[1] Written in 372. [2] Of Antioch.
[3] Of Samosata. [4] Of Caesarea.
[5] Tillemont (*Basil*, Note LII) suggests Barses of Edessa.
[6] The elder, of Nazianzus. [7] Of Laodicea.
[8] Of Tyana. [9] Of Nicopolis. [10] Of Carrhae.
[11] Of Batnae. [12] Of Perrha. [13] Of Tyre.
[14] Of Urimi in Syria.
[15] Maran would read Otreius of Melitine for Iatrius.
[16] Of Sebasteia.
[17] Maran would read Isaaces, identifying him with the Isacoces of Armenia Major.
[18] Probably Gregory of Nyssa, lately consecrated.

τὴν ἀντίληψιν ἡμῶν, ἣν πάλαι μὲν[1] προσεδοκήσαμεν παρ' ὑμῶν ταῖς κατὰ τὴν ἀνατολὴν
ἐκκλησίαις γενήσεσθαι, οὐδέπω[2] δὲ τετυχήκαμεν,
πάντως τοῦ[3] ἐν σοφίᾳ τὰ ἡμέτερα διοικοῦντος
Θεοῦ, κατὰ τὰ ἀθεώρητα αὐτοῦ τῆς δικαιοσύνης
κρίματα, πλείονι χρόνῳ παραταθῆναι ἡμᾶς[4] ἐν
τοῖς πειρασμοῖς τούτοις οἰκονομήσαντος. οὐ γὰρ
δήπου ἠγνοήσατε τὰ καθ' ἡμᾶς, ἀδελφοὶ τιμιώτατοι, ὧν ἡ ἀκοὴ καὶ ἐπὶ[5] τὰ ἔσχατα τῆς οἰκουμένης ἐξέδραμεν·[6] οὐδὲ ἀσυμπαθεῖς που ὑμεῖς
πρὸς τοὺς ὁμοψύχους τῶν ἀδελφῶν, μαθηταὶ
ὑπάρχοντες τοῦ Ἀποστόλου, τοῦ πλήρωμα εἶναι
τοῦ νόμου τὴν πρὸς τὸν πλησίον ἀγάπην διδά-
σκοντος. ἀλλ' ὅπερ εἴπαμεν, ἐπέσχεν ὑμῶν τὴν
ὁρμὴν ἡ δικαία τοῦ Θεοῦ κρίσις, ἐκπληρωθῆναι
ἡμῖν τὴν διατεταγμένην ἐπὶ ταῖς ἁμαρτίαις ἡμῶν
θλίψιν ἐπιμετροῦσα.[7] ἀλλὰ νῦν γοῦν, καὶ πρὸς
τὸν ὑπὲρ τῆς ἀληθείας ζῆλον καὶ τὴν ἡμετέραν
συμπάθειαν, διαναστῆναι ὑμᾶς παρακαλοῦμεν,
πάντα μαθόντας, καὶ ὅσα πρὸ τούτου τὰς ἀκοὰς
ὑμῶν διέφυγε, παρὰ τοῦ εὐλαβεστάτου ἀδελφοῦ
ἡμῶν τοῦ συνδιακόνου Σαβίνου, ὃς δυνήσεται
ὑμῖν καὶ ὅσα τὴν ἐπιστολὴν διαφεύγει παρ'
ἑαυτοῦ διηγήσασθαι· δι' οὗ παρακαλοῦμεν ὑμᾶς
ἐνδύσασθαι σπλάγχνα οἰκτιρμοῦ, καὶ ἀποθέσθαι
μὲν πάντα ὄκνον, ἀναλαβεῖν δὲ τὸν κόπον τῆς
ἀγάπης· καὶ μήτε ὁδοῦ μῆκος, μήτε τὰς κατ'
οἶκον ἀσχολίας, μήτ' ἄλλο τι τῶν ἀνθρωπίνων
ὑπολογίσασθαι.

---

[1] μέν om. E.   [2] οὐδέποτε editi antiqi.
[3] τὰ πάντα add. E, editi antiqi.   [4] ὑμᾶς E.
[5] εἰς editi antiqi.   [6] διέδραμεν editi antiqi.

relief which we have long been expecting would
come from you to the churches in the East, but
which we have not yet received—surely for the
reason that God, who in His wisdom disposes our
affairs, has ordained according to the inscrutable
judgments of His justice that we should be racked
in these trials for a still longer period. For you
surely have not remained ignorant how affairs are
amongst us, most honoured brethren, whereof the
rumour has gone forth to the uttermost parts of the
world; nor are you, methinks, without sympathy
for brethren of like mind with yourselves, being
disciples of the Apostle,[1] who teaches that the love
of neighbour is the fulfilling of the law. But, as
we have said, it is the righteous judgment of God,
meting out to us for fulfilment the suffering appointed for our offences, that has restrained your
interest in our behalf. But now at least, by your
zeal for the truth and by the sympathy you have for
us, we implore you to rouse yourselves, when you
have learned the whole story, even what has hitherto
escaped your ears, from our most revered brother,
the deacon Sabinus, who will be able to relate to you
by word of mouth whatever is not contained in our
letter. Through him we beseech you to put on the
bowels of mercy, to cast aside all hesitation, and to
take up the labour of love; and to take into consideration neither length of journey, nor the business you
may have at home, nor any other concern of man.

[1] Cf. Rom. 13, 10: ἡ ἀγάπη τῷ πλησίον κακὸν οὐκ ἐργάζεται·
πλήρωμα οὖν νόμου ἡ ἀγάπη.
"The love of our neighbour worketh no evil. Love
therefore is the fulfilling of the law."

---

[7] ἐπιμετρήσασα editi antiqi.

Οὐ γὰρ περὶ μιᾶς ἐκκλησίας ὁ κίνδυνος, οὐδὲ δύο ἢ τρεῖς αἱ τῷ χαλεπῷ τούτῳ χειμῶνι παραπεσοῦσαι.[1] σχεδὸν γὰρ ἀπὸ τῶν ὅρων τοῦ Ἰλλυρικοῦ μέχρι Θηβαΐδος τὸ τῆς αἱρέσεως κακὸν ἐπινέμεται. ἧς τὰ πονηρὰ σπέρματα πρότερον μὲν ὁ δυσώνυμος Ἄρειος κατεβάλετο, ῥιζωθέντα δὲ διὰ βάθους ὑπὸ πολλῶν τῶν ἐν μέσῳ φιλοπόνως τὴν ἀσέβειαν γεωργησάντων, νῦν τοὺς φθοροποιοὺς καρποὺς ἐξεβλάστησεν.[2] ἀνατέτραπται μὲν γὰρ τὰ τῆς εὐσεβείας δόγματα, συγκέχυνται δὲ ἐκκλησίας θεσμοί. φιλαρχίαι δὲ τῶν μὴ φοβουμένων τὸν Κύριον ταῖς προστασίαις ἐπιπηδῶσι· καὶ ἐκ τοῦ προφανοῦς λοιπὸν ἆθλον δυσσεβείας ἡ προεδρία πρόκειται· ὥστε ὁ τὰ χαλεπώτερα βλασφημήσας εἰς ἐπισκοπὴν [3] λαοῦ προτιμότερος. οἴχεται σεμνότης ἱερατική· ἐπιλελοίπασιν οἱ ποιμαίνοντες μετ᾽ ἐπιστήμης [4] ποίμνιον τοῦ Κυρίου, οἰκονομίας πτωχῶν εἰς ἰδίας ἀπολαύσεις καὶ δώρων διανομὰς παραναλισκόντων ἀεὶ [5] τῶν φιλαρχούντων. ἠμαύρωται κανόνων ἀκρίβεια. ἐξουσία τοῦ ἁμαρτάνειν πολλή· οἱ γὰρ διὰ σπουδῆς ἀνθρωπίνης [6] παρελθόντες ἐπὶ τὸ ἄρχειν ἐν αὐτῷ τούτῳ τῆς σπουδῆς τὴν χάριν ἀνταναπληροῦσι, τῷ πάντα πρὸς ἡδονὴν ἐνδιδόναι [7] τοῖς ἁμαρτάνουσιν. ἀπόλωλε κρίμα δίκαιον· πᾶς τις τῷ θελήματι τῆς καρδίας αὐτοῦ πορεύεται. ἡ πονηρία ἄμετρος, οἱ λαοὶ

---

[1] περιπεσοῦσαι editi antiqi.
[2] ἐξεβλάστησαν E, editi antiqi.
[3] ἐπίσκοπον alii MSS.   [4] τό add. E.
[5] ἀεὶ] πάντα Med., Harl.
[6] διὰ σπουδῆς ἀνθρωπίνης] σπουδαῖς ἀνθρωπίναις editi antiqi.

For the danger is not confined to a single church,
nor are there two or three only which have been
overthrown by this fierce tempest. For we can
almost say that the curse of this heresy is spreading
out from the borders of Illyricum to the Thebaid;
its baneful seeds were formerly scattered by the
infamous Arius, and, taking deep root through the
efforts of many who have cultivated them assiduously
in the meantime, they have now produced their
death-dealing fruits. For the teachings of the true
faith have been overthrown and the ordinances of
the Church have been set at naught. The lust for
office on the part of men who do not fear the Lord
leaps upon the positions of high authority, and quite
openly now the foremost place is offered as a prize
for impiety; and consequently that man who has
uttered the more horrible blasphemies is accounted
the more worthy of the episcopal direction of the
people. Gone is the dignity of the priesthood.
None are left to tend the flock of the Lord with
knowledge, while ambitious men ever squander the
sums collected for the poor on their own pleasures
and for the distribution of gifts. The strict
observance of the canons has been weakened.
Licence to commit sin has become widespread; for
those who have come into office through the favour
of men take this very means of returning thanks
for the favour—conceding to sinners whatever will
conduce to their pleasure. Just judgment is dead;
each and every one proceeds according to the whim
of his own heart. Wickedness goes beyond all

COLLECTED LETTERS OF SAINT BASIL

ἀνουθέτητοι, οἱ προεστῶτες ἀπαρρησίαστοι·
δοῦλοι γὰρ τῶν δεδωκότων τὴν χάριν, οἱ δι'
ἀνθρώπων ἑαυτοῖς τὴν δυναστείαν κατακτη-
σάμενοι. ἤδη δὲ καὶ ὅπλον τισὶ τοῦ πρὸς ἀλλήλους πολέμου ἡ ἐκδίκησις δῆθεν τῆς ὀρθοδοξίας
ἐπινενόηται, καὶ τὰς ἰδίας ἔχθρας ἐπικρυψάμενοι·
ὑπὲρ τῆς εὐσεβείας ἐχθραίνειν κατασχηματί-
ζονται. ἄλλοι δέ, τὸν ἐπὶ τοῖς αἰσχίστοις ἐκ-
κλίνοντες ἔλεγχον, τοὺς λαοὺς εἰς τὴν κατ'
ἀλλήλων φιλονεικίαν ἐκμαίνουσιν, ἵνα τοῖς κοινοῖς
κακοῖς τὸ καθ' ἑαυτοὺς συσκιάσωσι.

Διὸ καὶ ἄσπονδός ἐστιν ὁ πόλεμος οὗτος, τῶν
τὰ πονηρὰ εἰργασμένων τὴν κοινὴν εἰρήνην, ὡς
ἀποκαλύπτουσαν αὐτῶν τὰ κρυπτὰ τῆς αἰσχύνης,
ὑφορωμένων. ἐπὶ τούτοις γελῶσιν οἱ ἄπιστοι,
σαλεύονται οἱ ὀλιγόπιστοι· ἀμφίβολος ἡ πίστις,
ἄγνοια κατακέχυται τῶν ψυχῶν, διὰ τὸ μιμεῖσθαι[1]
τὴν ἀλήθειαν τοὺς δολοῦντας τὸν λόγον ἐν κα-
κουργίᾳ. σιγᾷ μὲν γὰρ τὰ τῶν εὐσεβούντων
στόματα, ἀνεῖται δὲ πᾶσα βλάσφημος γλῶσσα.
ἐβεβηλώθη τὰ ἅγια, φεύγουσι τοὺς εὐκτηρίους
οἴκους οἱ ὑγιαίνοντες τῶν λαῶν ὡς ἀσεβείας
διδασκαλεῖα, κατὰ δὲ τὰς ἐρημίας πρὸς τὸν ἐν
οὐρανοῖς Δεσπότην μετὰ στεναγμῶν καὶ δακρύων
τὰς χεῖρας αἴρουσιν. ἔφθασε γὰρ[2] πάντως καὶ
μέχρις ὑμῶν τὰ γινόμενα[3] ἐν ταῖς πλείσταις τῶν
πόλεων, ὅτι οἱ λαοὶ σὺν γυναιξὶ καὶ παιδίοις[4]
καὶ αὐτοῖς τοῖς πρεσβύταις,[5] πρὸ τῶν τειχῶν
ἐκχυθέντες, ἐν τῷ ὑπαίθρῳ τελοῦσι τὰς προσευχάς, φέροντες πάσας τὰς ἐκ τοῦ ἀέρος κακο-

---

[1] μισεῖσθαι Med.   [2] δέ editi antiqi.

138

bounds, the laity are deaf to admonition, their
leaders are without freedom of speech ; for those
who have obtained power for themselves through
the favour of men are the slaves of those who have
conferred the favour. And already, to serve them
as a weapon in their warfare with one another,
"the vindication of orthodoxy," forsooth, has been
devised by some, and they, concealing their private
enmities, pretend that they hate one another for
religion's sake ! Still others, to avoid exposure for
their shameful deeds, inflame the laity to mutual
strife in order that they may use the public ills to
screen their own conduct.

Hence this is a truceless war, for the perpetrators
of these evil deeds dread a general peace on the
ground that it will lay bare their hidden acts of
shame. At this state of affairs unbelievers laugh,
those of little faith waver ; the true faith is am-
biguous ; ignorance is poured down upon souls by
reason of the fact that those who maliciously falsify
doctrine imitate the truth. For the lips of the
pious are silent, yet every blasphemous tongue is let
loose. Holy things have been profaned, those of
the laity who are sound in faith flee the houses of
prayer as schools of impiety, and in the solitudes
they raise their hands with groans and tears to the
Master in heaven. For surely what is happening in
most of our cities has already reached even you—
that the laity with their wives, their children, and
even their aged, having poured forth in front of
the walls, offer up their prayers under the open
sky, enduring all the discomforts of the weather

---

[3] γενόμενα editi antiqi.   [4] παισί editi antiqi.
[5] πρεσβυτέροις E.

παθείας σὺν πολλῇ τῇ μακροθυμίᾳ, τὴν παρὰ
τοῦ Κυρίου ἀντίληψιν ἀναμένοντες.

Τίς θρῆνος τῶν συμφορῶν τούτων ἄξιος ; ποῖαι
πηγαὶ δακρύων κακοῖς τοσούτοις ἀρκέσουσιν ;[1]
ἕως οὖν ἔτι δοκοῦσιν ἑστάναι τινές, ἕως ἔτι ἴχνος
τῆς παλαιᾶς καταστάσεως διασώζεται,[2] πρὶν
τέλεον ταῖς ἐκκλησίαις ἐπέλθῃ[3] τὸ ναυάγιον,
ἐπείχθητε πρὸς ἡμᾶς, ἐπείχθητε ἤδη, ναὶ δεόμεθα,
ἀδελφοὶ γνησιώτατοι· δότε χεῖρα τοῖς εἰς γόνυ
κλιθεῖσι. συγκινηθήτω ἐφ' ἡμῖν τὰ ἀδελφικὰ
ὑμῶν σπλάγχνα, προχυθήτω δάκρυα συμπαθείας.
μὴ περιίδητε τὸ ἥμισυ τῆς οἰκουμένης ὑπὸ τῆς
πλάνης καταποθέν· μὴ ἀνάσχησθε ἀποσβεσθῆναι
τὴν πίστιν, παρ' οἷς πρῶτον ἐξέλαμψε.

Τί οὖν ποιήσαντες ἀντιλήψεσθε τῶν πραγμάτων, καὶ πῶς τὸ πρὸς τοὺς θλιβομένους συμπαθὲς
ἐπιδείξεσθε,[4] οὐ παρ' ἡμῶν πάντως δεήσει μαθεῖν[5]
ὑμᾶς, ἀλλ' αὐτὸ τὸ Πνεῦμα τὸ ἅγιον ὑμῖν ὑπο-
θήσεται. πλήν γε ὅτι τάχους χρεία πρὸς τὸ
περισώσασθαι τοὺς περιλειφθέντας, καὶ παρουσίας ἀδελφῶν πλειόνων, ὥστε πλήρωμα εἶναι
συνόδου τοὺς ἐπιδημοῦντας, ἵνα μὴ μόνον ἐκ τῆς
τῶν ἀποστειλάντων σεμνότητος, ἀλλὰ καὶ ἐκ τοῦ
οἰκείου ἀριθμοῦ τὸ ἀξιόπιστον εἰς διόρθωσιν ᾖ,[6]
καὶ τὴν ἐν Νικαίᾳ γραφεῖσαν παρὰ τῶν πατέρων
ἡμῶν πίστιν ἀνανεώσωνται,[7] καὶ τὴν αἵρεσιν ἐκ-
κηρύξωσι,[8] καὶ ταῖς ἐκκλησίαις τὰ εἰρηνικὰ
διαλέξονται, τοὺς τὰ αὐτὰ φρονοῦντας συνά-
γοντες[9] εἰς ὁμόνοιαν. τοῦτο γὰρ δήπου τὸ

---

[1] ἐπαρκέσουσι editi antiqi. [2] διασώζηται E.
[3] ἐπελθεῖν Reg. duo. [4] ἐπιδείξησθε E, Harl.
[5] μανθάνειν editi antiqi. [6] ᾖ Capps, οἱ MSS. et editi.
[7] ἀνανεώσωνται Capps : ἀνανεώσονται MSS. et editi.

with great patience, while they await assistance from the Lord.

What song of lamentation can do justice to such calamities as these? What fountains of tears will be adequate for such misfortunes? Therefore, while some still seem to keep their feet, while a trace of the old order of things is still preserved, before complete shipwreck comes upon our churches, hasten to us, yes, hasten to us at once, we implore you, most true and dear brethren; stretch forth your hands to us who have fallen to our knees. Let your fraternal hearts be moved in our behalf, let your tears of sympathy be poured forth. Do not suffer half the world to be swallowed up by error; do not allow the faith to be extinguished in those lands where it first flashed forth.

What action you must take, then, to assist us, and how you are to show sympathy to those in affliction, surely you will not need to learn from us, but the Holy Spirit himself will direct you. But remember that there is need of haste, if those who are still left are to be saved, and of the presence of several brethren, that they in visiting us may complete the number of the synod, so that by reason not only of the high standing of those who have sent them, but also of the number of the delegates they themselves constitute, they may have the prestige to effect a reform; and may restore the creed which was written by our fathers at Nicaea, may banish the heresy, and may speak to the churches a message of peace by bringing those of like convictions into unity. For this, clearly, is the most pitiful

---

8 ἐκκηρύξουσι tres MSS. ; ἐκριζώσουσι editi antiqi.
9 συναγαγόντες E, Harl.

πάντων ἐλεεινότατον ὅτι καὶ τὸ δοκοῦν ὑγιαίνειν
ἐφ᾿ ἑαυτὸ ἐμερίσθη· καὶ περιέστηκεν ἡμᾶς, ὡς
ἔοικε, παραπλήσια πάθη τοῖς ποτὲ κατὰ τὴν
Οὐεσπασιανοῦ πολιορκίαν τὰ Ἱεροσόλυμα περι-
σχοῦσιν. ἐκεῖνοί τε γὰρ ὁμοῦ μὲν τῷ¹ ἔξωθεν
συνείχοντο πολέμῳ, ὁμοῦ δὲ καὶ τῇ ἔνδοθεν
στάσει τῶν ὁμοφύλων καταναλίσκοντο. ἡμῖν δὲ
πρὸς τῷ φανερῷ πολέμῳ τῶν αἱρετικῶν ἔτι καὶ
ὁ² παρὰ τῶν δοκούντων ὀρθοδοξεῖν³ ἐπαναστὰς
πρὸς ἔσχατον ἀσθενείας τὰς⁴ ἐκκλησίας κατή-
γαγεν. ἐφ᾿ ἅπερ καὶ μάλιστα τῆς παρ᾿ ὑμῶν
χρῄζομεν βοηθείας, ὥστε τοὺς τὴν ἀποστολικὴν
ὁμολογοῦντας πίστιν, ἃ παρεπενόησαν⁵ σχίσματα
διαλύσαντας, ὑποταγῆναι τοῦ λοιποῦ τῇ αὐθεντίᾳ
τῆς Ἐκκλησίας, ἵνα ἄρτιον γένηται τὸ σῶμα τοῦ
Χριστοῦ, πᾶσι τοῖς μέλεσιν εἰς ὁλοκληρίαν
ἐπανελθόν, καὶ μὴ μόνον τὰ παρ᾿ ἑτέροις μακαρί-
ζωμεν ἀγαθά, ὅπερ νῦν ποιοῦμεν, ἀλλὰ καὶ τὰς
ἡμετέρας αὐτῶν ἐπίδωμεν ἐκκλησίας τὸ ἀρχαῖον
καύχημα τῆς ὀρθοδοξίας ἀπολαβούσας. τῷ ὄντι
γὰρ τοῦ ἀνωτάτου μακαρισμοῦ ἄξιον τὸ τῇ
ὑμετέρᾳ θεοσεβείᾳ χαρισθὲν παρὰ τοῦ Κυρίου τὸ
μὲν κίβδηλον ἀπὸ τοῦ δοκίμου καὶ καθαροῦ δια-
κρίνειν, τὴν δὲ τῶν πατέρων πίστιν ἄνευ τινὸς
ὑποστολῆς κηρύσσειν· ἣν καὶ ἡμεῖς ἐδεξάμεθα,
καὶ ἐπέγνωμεν ἐκ τῶν ἀποστολικῶν χαρακτήρων
μεμορφωμένην, συνθέμενοι καὶ αὐτῇ καὶ πᾶσι
142

condition of all—that even that group of us which
is apparently sound has become divided against
itself; and we are encircled, as it seems, by like
calamities to those which once fell on Jerusalem
during the siege of Vespasian. For the inhabitants
of that city were at one and the same time being
hemmed in by the war waged from outside and
wasted by the dissension of their own people inside.
And so it is with us : in addition to the open war
waged by heretics, the other war that has come
upon us from those who are supposed to be orthodox
has reduced the churches to the last degree of
weakness. It is against this that we are especially
in need of your assistance, that those who confess
the apostolic faith, having put an end to the schisms
of their own devising, may henceforth become subject
to the authority of the Church, that the body of
Christ, having returned to unity in all its parts, may
be made perfect, and that we may not only felicitate
the good fortunes of others, as we now do, but
may also see our own churches recover their ancient
glory of orthodoxy. For truly it is a thing that calls
for the highest felicitation, that it has been granted
by the Lord to your piety to distinguish the spurious
from the approved and the pure, and to proclaim
the faith of the fathers without any evasion. This
faith we too have received, and we recognized it
from the apostolic traits with which it was characterized, having submitted ourselves both to it and

---

1 τά E.   2 δ] ἡ E.
3 ὁμοδοξεῖν Harl., Vat., Reg. primus.
4 τῆς E.
5 ἃ παρεπενόησαν] ἅπερ ἐπενόησαν editi antiqi.

τοῖς ἐν τῷ συνοδικῷ γράμματι κανονικῶς καὶ
ἐνθέσμως δεδογματισμένοις.

XCIII

Πρὸς Καισαρίαν¹ πατρικίαν, περὶ κοινωνίας

Καὶ τὸ κοινωνεῖν δὲ καθ' ἑκάστην ἡμέραν, καὶ
μεταλαμβάνειν τοῦ ἁγίου σώματος καὶ αἵματος
τοῦ Χριστοῦ, καλὸν καὶ ἐπωφελές, αὐτοῦ σαφῶς
λέγοντος· ὁ τρώγων μου τὴν σάρκα, καὶ πίνων
μου τὸ αἷμα, ἔχει ζωὴν αἰώνιον. τίς γὰρ ἀμφι-
βάλλει, ὅτι τὸ μετέχειν συνεχῶς τῆς ζωῆς οὐδὲν
ἄλλο² ἐστὶν ἢ ζῆν πολλαχῶς; ἡμεῖς μέντοιγε
τέταρτον καθ' ἑκάστην ἑβδομάδα κοινωνοῦμεν, ἐν
τῇ Κυριακῇ, ἐν τῇ τετράδι, καὶ ἐν τῇ παρασκευῇ,
καὶ τῷ Σαββάτῳ, καὶ ἐν ταῖς ἄλλαις ἡμέραις ἐὰν
ᾖ μνήμη ἁγίου³ τινός.

Τὸ δὲ ἐν τοῖς τοῦ διωγμοῦ καιροῖς ἀναγκάζεσθαι

¹ πρὸς Καισάριον πατρίκιον περὶ κοινωνίας Colbertinus MS. ;
in quodam codice Regio occurrit fragmentum huius epistolae
sic inscriptum : ἐκ τῆς πρὸς Καισάριον ἐπιστολῆς.
² τι add. quidam MSS.   ³ μάρτυρος editi antiqi.

---

¹ For this synodical letter, cf. Theodoret 1, 8 and Socrates
1, 9.   The Benedictine editors are surprised that Basil shows
agreement with this synodical letter, since it defines the Son
as τῆς αὐτῆς ὑποστάσεως καὶ οὐσίας (of the same essence and
substance).   It is, however, not in the synodical letter, but
in the anathemas originally appended to the creed, that it is
denied that He is of a different substance or essence.   Even
here it is not said positively that He is of the same substance
or essence.   For a discussion of these theological terms, cf.
Letters VIII and XXXVIII with notes.

to all the doctrines which have been canonically and legally promulgated in the synodical letter.[1]

LETTER XCIII

To The Patrician, Caesaria,[2] on Communion

And also to take communion every day, that is to say, to partake of the holy body and blood of Christ, is good and beneficial, since He himself clearly says: "He that eateth My flesh, and drinketh My blood, hath everlasting life."[3] For who can doubt that sharing continually in the life is nothing else than living in many ways? We for our part, however, take communion four times each week—on Sunday, on Wednesday, on Friday, and on Saturday[4]—and on the other days only when there is a com-memoration of a saint.[5]

On the question of a person being compelled, in

[2] Written in 372. Note that some MSS. read Caesarius. Tillemont (*Basil*, Note XXXIV) says that Arnaud does not consider this letter as Basil's, but that he gives no reason for denying its authenticity. Tillemont himself thinks that it is a fragment of a letter, and indeed the first words appear to be a continuation. Although it is lacking in many manuscripts, there appears no worthy reason for doubting its authorship.

[3] John 6. 54.

[4] The Greek meanings are literally: Lord's Day, the Fourth, Preparation, and Sabbath.

[5] Note the variant reading μάρτυρος, "of a martyr." Basil in a letter to Saint Ambrose (CXCVII) says the same honour was accorded to Saint Dionysius of Milan at his place of burial as to a martyr. Gregory Thaumaturgus at Neocaesarea, Athanasius, and Basil, all received like honour soon after death.

τινα, μὴ παρόντος ἱερέως ἢ λειτουργοῦ, τὴν κοινωνίαν λαμβάνειν τῇ ἰδίᾳ χειρί, μηδαμῶς εἶναι βαρὺ
περιττόν ἐστιν ἀποδεικνύναι, διὰ τὸ καὶ[1] τὴν
μακρὰν συνήθειαν τοῦτο δι᾽ αὐτῶν τῶν πραγμάτων
πιστώσασθαι. πάντες γὰρ οἱ κατὰ τὰς ἐρήμους[2]
μονάζοντες, ἔνθα μὴ ἔστιν ἱερεύς, κοινωνίαν οἴκοι
κατέχοντες ἀφ᾽ ἑαυτῶν μεταλαμβάνουσιν. ἐν
Ἀλεξανδρείᾳ δὲ καὶ ἐν Αἰγύπτῳ ἕκαστος καὶ
τῶν ἐν λαῷ τελούντων ὡς ἐπὶ τὸ πλεῖστον ἔχει
κοινωνίαν ἐν τῷ οἴκῳ αὐτοῦ, καὶ ὅτε βούλεται[3]
μεταλαμβάνει δι᾽ ἑαυτοῦ. ἅπαξ γὰρ τὴν θυσίαν
τοῦ ἱερέως τελειώσαντος καὶ δεδωκότος, ὁ λαβὼν
αὐτὴν ὡς ὅλην ὁμοῦ, καθ᾽ ἑκάστην μεταλαμβάνων,
παρὰ τοῦ δεδωκότος εἰκότως μεταλαμβάνειν[4] καὶ
ὑποδέχεσθαι πιστεύειν ὀφείλει. καὶ γὰρ καὶ ἐν
τῇ ἐκκλησίᾳ ὁ ἱερεὺς ἐπιδίδωσι τὴν μερίδα καὶ
κατέχει αὐτὴν ὁ ὑποδεχόμενος μετ᾽ ἐξουσίας
ἁπάσης, καὶ οὕτω προσάγει τῷ στόματι τῇ ἰδίᾳ
χειρί. ταὐτὸν τοίνυν ἐστὶ τῇ δυνάμει, εἴτε μίαν
μερίδα δέξεταί τις παρὰ τοῦ ἱερέως, εἴτε πολλὰς
μερίδας ὁμοῦ.

[1] καί om. E.   [2] ἐρημίας multi MSS.
[3] καὶ ὅτε . . . ἑαυτοῦ om. E, editi antiqi.
[4] μεταλαμβάνει E, alii MSS.

---

[1] Cf. Catholic Encyclopaedia, under "Eucharist." In
general it is by Divine and ecclesiastical right that the laity
should as a rule receive communion only from the consecrated
hand of the priest. Cf. *Trent Sess.* XIII, cap. VIII. The

times of persecution when no priest or ministrant
is present, to take communion with his own hand, it
is superfluous to point out that this is in no wise sinful, since long custom has sanctioned this practice
from the very force of circumstances. For all who
live the monastic life in the solitudes, where there is
no priest, keep the communion at home and partake
of it from their own hands. At Alexandria also and
in Egypt, each person, even those belonging to the
laity, as a rule keeps the communion in his own
home, and partakes of it with his own hands when
he so wishes. For when the priest has once consummated the offering and has given it, he who has
received it ought confidently to believe that he is
partaking of it, even as he has received it, all at
once, even when he partakes of it daily. So it is
when the rite is performed in the church also—the
priest hands over the portion, and the recipient in
receiving it has complete right of possession, and by
such right raises it to his mouth with his own hand.
It is, therefore, in respect of authority, one and the
same thing, whether a communicant receives a single
portion from the priest or many portions at once.[1]

practice of the laity giving themselves Holy Communion was
formerly, and is to-day, allowed only in case of necessity. In
early Christian times it was customary for the faithful to
take the Blessed Sacrament to their homes and communicate
privately, a custom to which Basil refers above. Cf. also
Justin Martyr, *Apol.* I, 85 ; Tertullian, *De Orat.* XIX, and
Ad Uxor. II, 5 ; Cyprian, *De Lapis*, CXXXII ; and Jerome,
Letter CXXV. Up to the ninth century it was usual for the
priest to place the Sacred Host in the right hand of the
recipient, who kissed it and then placed it in his own mouth.
Women, from the fourth, to the ninth centuries, were
required to have a cloth wrapped about their right hand in
this ceremony.

XCIV

Ἠλίᾳ ἄρχοντι τῆς ἐπαρχίας[1]

Ὥρμησα μὲν καὶ αὐτὸς καταλαβεῖν σου τὴν
τιμιότητα, ὡς ἂν μὴ τῇ ἀπολείψει ἔλαττόν τι
ἔχοιμι τῶν διαβαλλόντων· ἀλλ' ἐπειδὴ ἡ ἀρρωστία
τοῦ σώματος διεκώλυσε, σφοδρότερον πολλῷ τῆς
συνηθείας ἐπιθεμένη, ἀναγκαίως ἦλθον ἐπὶ τὸ
γράμμα. ἐγὼ τοίνυν, ὦ θαυμάσιε, συντυχὼν
πρώην τῇ τιμιότητί σου, ὥρμησα μὲν καὶ περὶ
πάντων τῶν κατὰ τὸν βίον μου πραγμάτων
ἀνακοινώσασθαί σου τῇ φρονήσει,[2] ὥρμησα δὲ
καὶ τῶν ἐκκλησιῶν ἕνεκα[3] ποιήσασθαί τινα λόγον,
ὡς ἂν μὴ ταῖς μετὰ ταῦτα διαβολαῖς χώρα τις
ὑπολείποιτο.[4] ἀλλ' ἐπέσχον ἐμαυτόν, λογιζόμενος
περίεργον εἶναι παντελῶς, καὶ πέρα τοῦ μέτρου
φιλότιμον, ἀνδρὶ τοσοῦτον[5] πλῆθος πραγμάτων
ἐξηρτημένῳ ἔτι καὶ τὰς ἔξω τῶν ἀναγκαίων
ἐπιβάλλειν φροντίδας. ὁμοῦ τε,[6] εἰρήσεται γὰρ
τἀληθές, καὶ ἄλλως ὤκνησα μήποτε εἰς ἀνάγκην
ἔλθωμεν ταῖς κατ' ἀλλήλων ἀντιλογίαις τρῶσαι
τὴν ψυχήν σου, ὀφείλουσαν ἐν τῇ καθαρᾷ περὶ
τὸν Θεὸν εὐλαβείᾳ τέλειον τὸν μισθὸν τῆς θεοσεβείας[7] καρποῦσθαι. τῷ ὄντι γάρ, ἐάν σε πρὸς
ἑαυτοὺς ἐπιστρέψωμεν[8] ἡμεῖς, ὀλίγην σοι σχολὴν
πρὸς τὰ δημόσια καταλείψομεν, καὶ παραπλήσιον
ποιήσομεν, ὥσπερ ἂν εἴ τις κυβερνήτην, νεοπαγῆ

---

[1] τῷ ἄρχοντι τῆς ἐπαρχίας E, Med.   [2] φροντίσει E.
[3] τοῦ add. editi antiqi.   .   [4] ὑπολίποιτο E.
[5] τοσούτῳ E.   [6] τε] δέ E.
[7] θεότητος E.   [8] ἐπιστρέψωμεν editi antiqi.

148

LETTER XCIV

To Elias, Governor of the Province [1]

I MYSELF have been eager to visit your Honour, lest through failure to do so I should fare worse than my calumniators; but since the ill-health of my body has prevented it, besetting me much more violently than usual, of necessity I have had recourse to writing. When, therefore, respected Sir, I recently met your Honour, I strongly desired to communicate with your wisdom concerning all my temporal affairs, and I desired, too, to hold converse with you in behalf of the churches, so that no room should be left for slanders hereafter. But I checked myself, deeming it altogether officious and unduly zealous to load additional and unnecessary cares on a man already weighed down with such a multitude of duties. At the same time—for the truth must be told—I hesitated especially through fear of being forced, by any controversy we might have with one another, to wound your soul, which in its pure piety toward God is entitled to reap the perfect reward of religion. For truly, if we turn your attention to ourselves, we shall leave you scant leisure for your public duties, and we shall be acting like a man who would burden with an additional cargo a pilot who guides a newly-built ship in the midst of a great

[1] Written in 372, at the departure of Valens. On Elias, governor of Cappadocia, cf. also Letters LXXXIV, XCVI. In the present letter, Basil defends himself from the calumnies brought against him by his enemies regarding the church and the hospital he had recently established in the suburbs of Caesarea. Cf. Greg. Naz., *Oratio* XX; Theodoret, *Ecc. Hist.* IV, 19; and Sozomen, VI, 34.

ναῦν ἐν μεγάλῳ κλύδωνι διευθύνοντα, τῇ προσ-
θήκῃ τοῦ φόρτου καταβαρύνοι, δέον ἀφαιρεῖν τι
τῶν ἀγωγίμων καὶ συνεπικουφίζειν ὡς δυνατόν.
ὅθεν μοι δοκεῖ καὶ βασιλεὺς ὁ μέγας, τὴν πολυ-
πραγμοσύνην ἡμῶν ταύτην καταμαθών, ἐᾶσαι
ἡμᾶς ἐφ᾽ ἑαυτῶν τὰς ἐκκλησίας οἰκονομεῖν.

Τοὺς μέντοι ταῖς ἀδόλοις ἀκοαῖς σου παρε-
νοχλοῦντας ἐρωτηθῆναι βούλομαι, τί χεῖρον ἔχει
τὰ δημόσια παρ᾽ ἡμᾶς; ἢ τί μικρὸν ἢ μεῖζον τῶν
κοινῶν ἐκ τῆς ἡμετέρας περὶ τὰς ἐκκλησίας
οἰκονομίας ἠλάττωται; πλὴν εἰ μή τις λέγοι
βλάβην τοῖς πράγμασι φέρειν, οἶκον εὐκτήριον
μεγαλοπρεπῶς[1] κατεσκευασμένον[2] ἀναστῆσαι τῷ
Θεῷ ἡμῶν, καὶ περὶ αὐτὸν οἴκησιν, τὴν μὲν ἐλευ-
θέριον ἐξῃρημένην[3] τῷ κορυφαίῳ, τὰς δὲ ὑποβε-
βηκυίας τοῖς θεραπευταῖς τοῦ θείου διανενεμη-
μένας ἐν τάξει,[4] ὧν ἡ χρῆσις κοινὴ πρός τε ὑμᾶς
τοὺς ἄρχοντας καὶ τοὺς παρεπομένους ὑμῖν. τίνα
δὲ ἀδικοῦμεν, καταγώγια τοῖς ξένοις οἰκοδομοῦντες,
τοῖς τε[5] κατὰ πάροδον ἐπιφοιτῶσι καὶ τοῖς θεραπείας τινὸς διὰ τὴν ἀσθένειαν δεομένοις, καὶ τὴν
ἀναγκαίαν τούτοις παραμυθίαν ἐγκαθιστῶντες,
τοὺς νοσοκομοῦντας, τοὺς ἰατρεύοντας, τὰ νωτο-
φόρα, τοὺς παραπέμποντας; τούτοις ἀνάγκη καὶ
τέχνας ἕπεσθαι, τάς τε πρὸς τὸ ζῆν ἀναγκαίας, καὶ
ὅσαι πρὸς εὐσχήμονα βίου διαγωγὴν ἐφευρέθησαν·
οἴκους πάλιν ἑτέρους ταῖς ἐργασίαις ἐπιτηδείους,
ἅπερ πάντα τῷ μὲν τόπῳ κόσμος, τῷ δὲ ἄρχοντι
ἡμῶν σεμνολόγημα, ἐπ᾽ αὐτὸν τῆς εὐφημίας ἐπα-

---

[1] μεγαλοπρεπές editi antiqi.   [2] κατεσκευασμένον E.
[3] ἐξηρτημένην alii MSS.   [4] ἐν τάξει] ἐντάξαι editi antiqi.
[5] τε om. E.

storm, when he ought rather to relieve him of a portion of his freight and lighten the vessel as far as possible. It is for this reason, it seems to me, that the great Emperor, on his part, having learned about this officious tendency of ours, has allowed us to govern the churches ourselves.

I wish, however, that those who keep annoying your honest ears be asked what harm the state receives at our hands; or what, either small or great, of the public interests has suffered injury through our government of the churches; unless, indeed, someone may say that it inflicts injury upon the state to raise in honour of our God a house of prayer built in magnificent fashion, and, grouped about it, a residence, one portion being a generous home reserved for the bishop, and the rest subordinate quarters for the servants of God's worship arranged in order—access to all of which is alike free to you magistrates yourselves and to your retinue. And whom do we wrong when we build hospices for strangers, for those who visit us while on a journey, for those who require some care because of sickness, and when we extend to the latter the necessary comforts, such as nurses, physicians, beasts for travelling and attendants?[1] There must also be occupations to go with these men, both those that are necessary for gaining a livelihood, and also such as have been discovered for a decorous manner of living. And, again, they need still other buildings equipped for their pursuits, all of which are an ornament to the locality, and a source of pride to our governor, since their fame redounds to your

[1] One of the duties of the clergy at this time was to act as guides and escort. Cf. Letters XCVIII and CCXLIII.

νιούσης. ὅς γε οὐδὲ τούτου ἕνεκεν πρὸς τὴν
ἐπιστασίαν ἡμῶν ἐξεβιάσθης, ὡς μόνος ἐξαρκῶν
τῷ μεγέθει τῆς γνώμης τά τε κατερρυηκότα τῶν
ἔργων[1] ἀναλαβεῖν, καὶ οἰκίσαι τὰς ἀοικήτους,
καὶ ὅλως εἰς πόλεις τὰς ἐρημίας μετασκευάσαι.
τὸν οὖν εἰς ταῦτα συνεργοῦντα ἐλαύνειν καὶ
ὑβρίζειν, ἢ τιμᾶν καὶ περιέπειν, ἀκολουθότερον
ἦν; καὶ μὴ οἰηθῇς, ὦ ἄριστε, λόγον μόνον εἶναι
τὰ παρ' ἡμῶν· ἤδη γάρ ἐσμεν ἐν τῷ ἔργῳ, τὰς
ὕλας τέως συμποριζόμενοι.

Τὰ μὲν οὖν πρὸς τὴν τοῦ ἄρχοντος ἀπολογίαν
τοιαῦτα. ἃ δὲ δεῖ πρὸς τὰς τῶν φιλαιτίων μέμψεις,
ὡς Χριστιανῷ καὶ φίλῳ πεφροντικότι ἡμῶν τῆς
ὑπολήψεως ἀποκρίνασθαι, ἀναγκαῖον νῦν ἀποσιωπῆσαι, ὡς καὶ μακρότερα τοῦ μέτρου τῆς ἐπιστολῆς, καὶ ἄλλως οὐκ ἀσφαλῆ[2] γράμμασιν
ἀψύχοις καταπιστεύεσθαι. ἵνα δὲ μὴ τὸν πρὸ
τῆς συντυχίας χρόνον ταῖς διαβολαῖς τινων ὑπαχ-
θείς, ὑφεῖναί τι τῆς περὶ ἡμᾶς εὐνοίας ἀναγκασθῇς,
τὸ τοῦ Ἀλεξάνδρου ποίησον. καὶ γὰρ ἐκεῖνόν
φασι, διαβαλλομένου τινὸς τῶν συνήθων, τὴν
μὲν ἑτέραν τῶν ἀκοῶν ἀνεῖναι τῷ διαβάλλοντι,
τὴν δὲ ἑτέραν ἐπιμελῶς ἐπιφράξασθαι τῇ χειρί,
ἐνδεικνύμενον ὅτι δέοι τὸν ὀρθῶς κρίνειν μέλλοντα
μὴ ὅλον εὐθὺς τοῖς προλαβοῦσιν ἀπάγεσθαι, ἀλλὰ
τὸ ἥμισυ τῆς ἀκροάσεως ἀκέραιον διασώζειν πρὸς
ἀπολογίαν τῷ μὴ παρόντι.

[1] τῶν ἔργων] τῷ χρόνῳ sex alii MSS.; τῷ χρόνῳ add. editi
antiqi.
[2] ἀσφαλές E.

---

[1] Of this story about Alexander cf. Letter XXIV.

credit. Nor was it, indeed, on this account that you have been forced to give attention to our affairs —that, namely, you, by reason of the magnitude of your wisdom, are competent single-handed to restore the works which have fallen into ruin, to people the uninhabited areas, and in general to transform the solitudes into cities! Was it, therefore, the more consistent course to harass and insult the man who co-operates with you in these works, or rather to honour him and show him every consideration? And do not think, most excellent Sir, that our protest consists of words alone; for we are already in action, being engaged meanwhile in getting our materials together.

So much, then, for our defence to you as the governor. But as to the answer which we ought to make to you as a Christian and as a friend solicitous of our reputation, in reply to the criticisms of the censorious, this we must pass over in silence at this time as being not only too long for the compass of this letter, but also unsafe to be trusted to soulless written characters. But in order that during the time before our meeting you may not, being gradually influenced by the slanders of certain persons, be forced to relinquish to some extent your goodwill toward us, do what Alexander did. For they say that when a friend of his was being slandered he gave the slanderer free access to one ear, but carefully obstructed the other with his hand, showing that he who intends to judge justly ought not to be at once wholly carried away by those who get at him first, but should keep half his hearing uncontaminated for the plea of the absent party.[1]

XCV

Εὐσεβίῳ, ἐπισκόπῳ Σαμοσατωι

Πάλαι ἐπιστείλας τῇ θεοσεβείᾳ σου ἄλλων τέ
τινων ἕνεκεν καὶ τοῦ συντυχεῖν ἡμᾶς ἀλλήλοις,
διήμαρτον τῆς ἐλπίδος, οὐκ ἀφικομένων τῶν γραμμάτων εἰς τὰς χεῖρας τῆς σῆς τιμιότητος, τοῦ
μακαρίου διακόνου Θεοφράστου δεξαμένου μὲν τὰ
γράμματα ἡμῶν ἐπί τινα περιοδείαν ἀναγκαίως
ἀποδημούντων,[1] μὴ διαπεμψαμένου δὲ τῇ θεοσεβείᾳ σου, τῷ προκαταληφθῆναι τῇ ἀρρωστίᾳ ὑφ'
ἧς ἐτελεύτησεν. ὅθεν τοσοῦτον ὕστερος ἦλθον
τοῦ καιροῦ πρὸς τὸ γράφειν, ὥστε μηδὲ ὄφελός
τι ἐλπίζειν ἐκ τῆς ἐπιστολῆς ἔσεσθαι ταύτης, εἰς
στενὸν παντελῶς κατακλεισθέντος τοῦ χρόνου.
ὁ γάρ τοι θεοφιλέστατος ἐπίσκοπος Μελέτιος καὶ
Θεόδοτος ἐπέταξαν ἡμῖν πρὸς αὐτοὺς διαβῆναι,
ἀγάπης τε ἐπίδειγμα τὴν[2] συντυχίαν ποιούμενοι,
καί τινα καὶ διόρθωσιν γενέσθαι τῶν νῦν παρα-
λυπούντων βουλόμενοι. ἀπέδειξάν τε ἡμῖν χρόνον
μὲν τῆς συντυχίας τὰ μέσα τοῦ προσιόντος μηνὸς
Ἰουνίου, τόπον δὲ Φαργαμοῦν[3] τὸ χωρίον, ἐπίση-
μον μαρτύρων περιφανείᾳ[4] καὶ πολυανθρωπίᾳ
συνόδου τῆς κατὰ ἔτος ἕκαστον παρ' αὐτοῖς τελου-

---

[1] ἀποδημοῦντος editi antiqi.   [2] σήν add. E.
[3] Φαρμαγοῦν E.   [4] ἐπιφανείᾳ E.

---

[1] Placed by Loofs in May of 372.   For Eusebius cf. earlier
letters.
[2] Probably the bearer of a letter from Basil to Meletius in

LETTER XCV

To Eusebius, Bishop of Samosata [1]

ALTHOUGH I long ago wrote to your Piety in regard both to other matters and especially our meeting each other, I was disappointed in my hope, since my letters did not reach the hands of your Honour; for the blessed deacon Theophrastus [2] received the letters from us as we were setting out upon an unavoidable journey abroad, [3] but did not deliver them to your Piety on account of his being seized beforehand by the illness whereof he died. For this reason I have set about writing to you so tardily in comparison with the proper moment that I do not even hope that any benefit will come from this letter, since the time has been reduced to absolutely the scantiest margin. For the most God-beloved bishops, Meletius and Theodotus, [4] bade us go over to them, making such a visit a proof of my love, and also desiring that some amendment might be formed of the things which now trouble them. Moreover, they set as the time of our meeting the middle of the approaching month of June, and as the place, Phargamos, made illustrious by the glory of martyrs and by the largely attended synod held

371. Cf. Letter LVII. μακάριος, "blessed," as usual in Christian Greek, here means "deceased."

[3] περιοδεία may here mean the regular tour of a bishop to the parishes of his diocese.

[4] Theodotus of Nicopolis was disturbed about Basil's being in communion with Eustathius. On Meletius, bishop of Antioch, cf. Letters LVII, LXVIII, LXXXIX, CXX, CXXIX, CCXVI and notes.

μένης. ἐπεὶ δὲ ἔδει με, μετὰ τὴν ἐπάνοδον μαθόντα
τὴν κοίμησιν τοῦ μακαρίου διακόνου, καὶ τὰς
ἐπιστολὰς ἀργὰς παρ' ἡμῖν κειμένας, μὴ ἡσυ-
χάσαι, διὰ τὸ ἔτι ἡμέρας ἡμῖν τριάκοντα καὶ τρεῖς
ἐπὶ τὴν προθεσμίαν ὑπολελεῖφθαι, ἀπέστειλα κατὰ
σπουδὴν τῷ αἰδεσιμωτάτῳ ἀδελφῷ Εὐσταθίῳ τῷ
συλλειτουργῷ ἡμῶν τὰ γράμματα ταῦτα, ὥστε δι'
αὐτοῦ παραπεμφθῆναί σου τῇ σεμνότητι,[1] καὶ
πάλιν ἐν τάχει ἀνακομισθῆναι ἡμῖν τὰς ἀποκρίσεις. εἰ μὲν γὰρ δυνατὸν ἢ ἄλλως ἄρεσκον
σοι παραγενέσθαι, καὶ αὐτοὶ παρεσόμεθα· εἰ δὲ
μή, αὐτοὶ μέν, ἂν ὁ Θεὸς θέλῃ, τὸ περυσινὸν
ἀποτίσομεν χρέος τῆς συντυχίας, ἐὰν μή τι πάλιν
ἐπιγένηται ἡμῖν ἐξ ἁμαρτιῶν κώλυμα· τὴν δὲ τῶν
ἐπισκόπων ἔντευξιν εἰς ἕτερον χρόνον ὑπερθησόμεθα.

XCVI

Σωφρονίῳ μαγίστρῳ

Καὶ τίς οὕτω φιλόπολις, ὃς τὴν ἐνεγκοῦσαν καὶ
θρεψαμένην πατρίδα ἴσα γονεῦσι τιμῶν, ὡς αὐτὸς
σύ, κοινῇ τε πάσῃ τῇ πόλει καὶ ἰδίᾳ ἑκάστῳ τὰ
ἀγαθὰ συνευχόμενος, καὶ οὐκ εὐχόμενος μόνον,
ἀλλὰ καὶ βεβαιῶν τὰς εὐχὰς διὰ σαυτοῦ;[2]
δύνασαι γάρ που σὺν Θεῷ τὰ τοιαῦτα, καὶ δύναιό
γε ἐπὶ μήκιστον, οὕτω χρηστὸς ὤν.

Ἀλλ' ὅμως ἐπὶ σοῦ ὄναρ ἐπλούτησεν ἡ πατρὶς

---

[1] τιμιότητι editi antiqi.   [2] διὰ σαυτοῦ] δι' ἑαυτοῦ E.

Written in 372, on the removal of Elias as governor of

there every year. And since it was imperative for
me, after learning on my return home that the now
blessed deacon had fallen asleep, and that the letters
were still lying here untouched, not to be idle,
seeing that only thirty-three days are still left before
the appointed time, I have sent this letter in all haste
to our most reverend brother and fellow-worker,
Eustathius, that through him it may be forwarded
to your Majesty and that your reply may be
speedily returned to us. For if it is possible or,
in general, pleasing to you to come, we ourselves
also shall be there ; but if not we shall, God willing,
ourselves discharge last year's debt and meet you,
unless some obstacle again arise, on account of our
sins, to prevent it ; and we shall defer the meeting
of the bishops to another time.

LETTER XCVI

To Sophronius, Master[1]

What man is so patriotic, honouring equally with
his parents the fatherland which gave him birth
and reared him, as are you yourself, who invoke
blessings for the whole city in common and for each
individual citizen, and not praying only, but also
confirming your prayers by your personal efforts ?
For it is doubtless by God's aid that you are able to
do such things, and may you for the longest time
continue to be able, excellent man that you are.

But nevertheless it was under you that our city

Cappadocia. Cf. Letters LXXXIV and XCIV, which Basil
addresses to Elias.

ἡμῶν, ἄνδρα μὲν ἔχουσα τὸν τὴν ἐπιμέλειαν
αὐτῆς ἐπιτραπέντα, οἷον οὔ φασιν ἄλλον οἱ τὰ
παλαιότατα τῶν παρ᾽ ἡμῖν ἐπιστάμενοι ἐπὶ τῶν
ἀρχικῶν [1] θρόνων πρότερον ἀναβῆναι, ἐπηρείᾳ δέ
τινων ἀφαιρεθεῖσα ταχέως, οἳ τὸ ἐλεύθερον τοῦ
ἀνδρὸς καὶ ἀθώπευτον τοῦ πρὸς αὐτὸν πολέμου
ἀφορμὴν ἐποιήσαντο, καὶ διαβολὰς αὐτῷ κατε-
σκεύασαν, λαθόντες τὰς ἀκοὰς τῆς σῆς τελειότητος. διὸ πανδημεὶ πάντες σκυθρωπάζομεν,
ζημιωθέντες ἄρχοντα μόνον δυνάμενον εἰς γόνυ
κλιθεῖσαν ἤδη τὴν πόλιν ἡμῶν ἀνορθῶσαι, ἀληθῆ [2]
φύλακα τοῦ δικαίου, εὐπρόσιτον τοῖς ἀδικουμένοις,
φοβερὸν τοῖς παρανομοῦσιν, ἴσον καὶ πένησι καὶ
πλουσίοις, καὶ τὸ μέγιστον, τὰ τῶν Χριστιανῶν
πράγματα πρὸς τὴν ἀρχαίαν ἐπανάγοντα τιμήν.
τὸ γάρ, ὅτι ἀδωρότατος ὢν ἴσμεν ἀνθρώπων, καὶ
οὐδενὶ [3] παρὰ τὸ δίκαιον χαριζόμενος, ὡς μικρότερα
τῆς λοιπῆς ἀρετῆς τοῦ ἀνδρὸς παρελίπομεν.

Ταῦτα ὀψὲ μὲν [4] τοῦ καιροῦ μαρτυροῦμεν,
ὥσπερ οἱ μονῳδοῦντες ἑαυτοὺς [5] παραμυθούμενοι,
οὐχὶ τοῖς πράγμασί τι ποιοῦντες χρήσιμον.
πλὴν οὐδὲ τοῦτο ἄχρηστον, ἐν τῇ μεγάλῃ σου
ψυχῇ τὴν μνήμην τοῦ ἀνδρὸς ἀποκεῖσθαι, [6] χάριν
τε εἰδέναι ὡς εὐεργέτῃ [7] τῆς ἐνεγκούσης, καὶ εἴ τις
ἐπιφύοιτο αὐτῷ τῶν διὰ τὸ μὴ προτιμηθῆναι τοῦ
δικαίου χαλεπαινόντων, ὑπερμαχεῖν καὶ προΐ-
στασθαι, πᾶσι ποιήσαντα φανερόν, ὅτι οἰκεῖον
σεαυτῷ τὸν ἄνδρα τίθεσαι, ἀρκοῦσαν ἀφορμὴν εἰς

[1] τῶν ἀρχικῶν θρόνων] τὸν ἀρχικὸν θρόνον editi antiqi.
[2] ἀκριβῆ editi antiqi. [3] οὐδέν multi MSS.
[4] μέν om. E. [5] ἑαυτοῖς E, editi antiqi.
[6] καί add. E.

became rich as in a dream, because it had in charge of its administration a man whose like never before ascended the governor's seat, as those declare who are familiar with our ancient history, and then, through the malicious spite of a certain man, was speedily deprived of him—men who made the generosity of the man and his immunity from flattery an excuse for their war upon him, and trumped up against him calumnies, deceiving the ears of your Perfection. Therefore we are one and all, the entire people, dejected at having been deprived of a governor who alone is able to raise again our city, which had already been brought to its knees, who is a true guardian of justice, easy of access for the victims of injustice, terrible to law-breakers, fair to both poor and rich, and, greatest of all, who was restoring Christianity to its ancient honour. For the fact that he was the most incorruptible man we know, and that he never granted a favour in violation of justice, we have passed over as of less significance than the man's other virtues.

But to these things we are bearing witness too late, when the proper season is past, just like those who console themselves by singing dirges but do nothing useful to better their condition. Yet this is not useless—that the recollection of the man should be stored up in your great soul, and that you should feel grateful to him as the benefactor of the land that bore you; and, if any of those who are angry at not having been preferred to this just man should attack him, that you should fight for him and defend him, making it clear to all that you hold this man as one closely bound to you, considering

---

οἰκειότητα τὴν ἀγαθὴν περὶ αὐτοῦ μαρτυρίαν
τιθέμενος καὶ τὴν τῶν πραγμάτων πεῖραν, οὐ
κατὰ τὴν τῶν χρόνων ἀναλογίαν ὑπάρχουσαν.
ἃ γὰρ οὐδ' ἂν ἐν πολλοῖς ἔτεσι παρ' ἄλλου
γένοιτο, ταῦτα ἐν ὀλίγῳ παρ' αὐτοῦ κατώρθωται.
ἀρκοῦσα δ' ἡμῖν [1] χάρις καὶ τῶν συμβάντων παραμυθία, ἐὰν καὶ βασιλεῖ συστήσῃς αὐτόν, καὶ τὰς
ἐπενεχθείσας αὐτῷ διαβολὰς ἀποσκευάσῃ. ταῦτά
σοι πᾶσαν [2] οἴου τὴν πατρίδα διὰ μιᾶς τῆς ἡμετέρας [3] φωνῆς διαλέγεσθαι, καὶ κοινὴν εἶναι πάντων εὐχήν, γενέσθαι τι τῷ ἀνδρὶ διὰ τῆς σῆς
τελειότητος δεξιόν.

XCVII

Τῇ βουλῇ Τυάνων

Ὁ ἀνακαλύπτων βαθέα καὶ φανερῶν βουλὰς
καρδιῶν Κύριος ἔδωκε καὶ τοῖς ταπεινοῖς σύνεσιν
τῶν δυσθεωρήτων, ὥς τινες οἴονται, τεχνασμάτων.
οὐδὲν οὖν ἡμᾶς ἔλαθεν, οὔτε τῶν πεπραγμένων τι
κεκρυμμένον. ἀλλ' ὅμως ἡμεῖς οὔτε ὁρῶμεν οὔτε
ἀκούομεν ἄλλο τι ἢ τὴν εἰρήνην τοῦ Θεοῦ καὶ ὅσα [4]
πρὸς αὐτὴν φέρει. εἰ γὰρ καὶ ἕτεροι δυνατοί, καὶ
μεγάλοι, καὶ ἑαυτοῖς πεποιθότες, ἀλλ' ἡμεῖς οἱ μη-

---

[1] ἡ add. E. [2] πᾶσαν om. E.
[3] ἡμέρας E. [4] τοιαῦτα E, editio Paris.

---

[1] Written in 372. Valens was ever hostile to Cappadocia.
Partly to vent his wrath upon it, and partly to obtain a
greater amount of revenue, he had in 370 determined to
divide it into two provinces. Podandus, an insignificant

as sufficient grounds for the attachment the excellent testimony you receive concerning him and also your experience of his deeds—an experience which is not in accordance with the example of the times. For that which could not have been brought about by another in many years has been accomplished in a short time by him. It will be a sufficient favour to us, and a consolation for our afflictions, if you will recommend him to the Emperor, and will do away with the slanders that have been brought against him. Consider that your whole country is addressing these words to you through our single voice, and that it is the common prayer of all that something favourable may come to the man through your Perfection.

LETTER XCVII

To the Senate of Tyana [1]

He who reveals hidden things and makes manifest the counsels of the heart, even the Lord, has bestowed upon the lowly a knowledge of artifices which some think are difficult to understand. Therefore nothing has escaped our notice, nor has anything that has been done remained concealed from us. Yet we ourselves, nevertheless, neither see nor hear anything but the peace of God and whatsoever leads to it. For even if others are powerful, and great, and confident in themselves, we, on the

town at the foot of Mt. Taurus, was to be the chief seat of the new province, and half of the executive was transferred there. The resulting dismay and dejection of Caesarea are depicted vividly by Basil in Letters LXXIV, LXXV, and LXXVI.

δέν, καὶ τοῦ μηδενὸς ἄξιοι· ὥστε οὐκ ἄν ποτε¹ τοσοῦτον ἑαυτοῖς λάβοιμεν, ὡς ἐν τῇ μονώσει
δύνασθαι νομίσαι περιέσεσθαι τῶν πραγμάτων,
ἀκριβῶς εἰδότες, ὅτι πλέον ἡμεῖς τῆς ἑνὸς ἑκάστου
τῶν ἀδελφῶν ἐπικουρίας δεόμεθα ἢ ὅσον ἡ ἑτέρα
τῶν χειρῶν τῆς ἑτέρας. ἐπεὶ καὶ ἐξ αὐτῆς τῆς
τοῦ σώματος ἡμῶν κατασκευῆς τὸ ἀναγκαῖον τῆς
κοινωνίας ὁ Κύριος ἡμᾶς ἐδίδαξεν. ὅταν γὰρ
πρὸς αὐτὰ ταῦτα ἀπίδω² τὰ μέλη ἡμῶν, ὅτι ἓν
οὐδὲν ἑαυτῷ πρὸς ἐνέργειαν αὔταρκες, πῶς ἐμαυτὸν
λογίσομαι ἐξαρκεῖν ἑαυτῷ πρὸς τὰ τοῦ βίου
πράγματα; οὔτε γὰρ ἂν ποὺς ἀσφαλῶς βαδίσειε,
μὴ συνυποστηρίζοντος τοῦ ἑτέρου, οὔτε ὀφθαλμὸς
ὑγιῶς ἴδοι, μὴ κοινωνὸν ἔχων τὸν ἕτερον καὶ μετ'
αὐτοῦ συμφώνως προσβάλλων τοῖς ὁρατοῖς. ἡ
ἀκοὴ ἀκριβεστέρα ἡ δι' ἀμφοῖν τοῖν πόροιν τὴν
φωνὴν δεχομένη, καὶ ἀντίληψις κραταιοτέρα τῇ
κοινωνίᾳ τῶν δακτύλων. καὶ ἁπαξαπλῶς οὐδὲν
οὔτε τῶν ἐκ φύσεως οὔτε τῶν ἐκ προαιρέσεως
κατορθουμένων ὁρῶ ἄνευ τῆς τῶν ὁμοφύλων
συμπνοίας ἐπιτελούμενον· ὅπου γε καὶ αὐτὴ ἡ
προσευχὴ μὴ ἔχουσα τοὺς συμφωνοῦντας ἀδρανεσ-
τέρα ἐστὶ πολλῷ ἑαυτῆς, καὶ ὁ Κύριος ἐπηγγείλατο μέσος γενήσεσθαι μεταξὺ δύο ἢ τριῶν
ἐπικαλουμένων αὐτὸν ἐν ὁμονοίᾳ. καὶ αὐτὴν δὲ
τὴν οἰκονομίαν ὁ Κύριος κατεδέξατο, ἵνα εἰρηνο-

¹ ὥστε οὐκ ἄν . . . ὡς] μηδενὸς οὐκ ἄν ποτε τοσοῦτον ἑαυτοὺς
ὑπολάβοιμεν, ὥστε editi antiqi.

contrary, are nothing, and worth nothing; consequently we would never attribute so much to ourselves as to consider that single-handed we could surmount our difficulties, for we know very clearly that we need the help of each and every brother more than one hand needs the other. Indeed, from the very constitution of our bodies the Lord has taught us the necessity of the community. For whenever I look upon these very limbs of ours, and see that no one of them is sufficient in itself to produce action, how can I reason that I of myself suffice to cope with the difficulties of life? For one foot could not make a stride safely unless the other supported it, nor could the eye see accurately unless it had the other as its partner and, working in harmony with it, cast its glance upon the objects of sight. The hearing is more exact when it receives sound through both its channels; and the grasp of the hand is stronger through the combined efforts of the fingers. And to sum up, I see that none of those things which are accomplished either by nature or by deliberate choice is completed without the union of the related forces; since, in truth, even prayer itself, if it be not voiced by many together, is much less efficacious than it might be, and the Lord has promised that He would be in the midst of two or three who should invoke Him together.[1] And indeed the reason why the Lord took up his very stewardship was that He might

---

[1] Cf. Matt. 18, 20 : οὗ γάρ εἰσι δύο ἢ τρεῖς συνηγμένοι εἰς τὸ ἐμὸν ὄνομα, ἐκεῖ εἰμὶ ἐν μέσῳ αὐτῶν. "For where there are two or three gathered together in My name, there am I in the midst of them."

---

[2] ἀπίδωμεν editi antiqi.

ποιήσῃ διὰ τοῦ αἵματος τοῦ σταυροῦ αὐτοῦ εἴτε
τὰ ἐπὶ τῆς γῆς εἴτε τὰ ἐν τοῖς οὐρανοῖς.

Ὥστε, διὰ ταῦτα πάντα, ἐν εἰρήνῃ μένειν τὰς
λειπομένας ἡμῶν ἡμέρας εὐχόμεθα, ἐν εἰρήνῃ δὲ
γενέσθαι τὴν κοίμησιν ἡμῶν αἰτοῦμεν. ὑπὲρ
ταύτης οὐδὲ πόνον ἐλλείπειν[1] ὅντινα οὖν ἔγνωκα,
οὐ ταπεινόν τι φθέγξασθαι ἢ ποιῆσαι, οὐχ ὁδοιπορίας μῆκος ὑπολογίσασθαι, οὐκ ἄλλο τι τῶν
ὀχληρῶν[2] ὑποστείλασθαι, ὥστε τῶν μισθῶν τῆς
εἰρηνοποιίας ἐπιτυχεῖν. κἂν μὲν ἔπηταί[3] τις
ταῦτα καθηγουμένοις ἡμῖν, τοῦτο ἄριστον, καὶ
εὐχὴ[4] τυγχάνει πέρας· ἐὰν δὲ πρὸς τὴν ἐναντίαν
ἀφέλκῃ,[5] ἐγὼ μὲν οὐδὲ οὕτω τῆς ἐμαυτοῦ κρίσεως
ἀποστήσομαι. αὐτὸς δὲ ἕκαστος τῆς οἰκείας
ἐργασίας ἐν ἡμέρᾳ τῆς ἀνταποδόσεως τοὺς καρποὺς ἐπιγνώσεται.

XCVIII

Εὐσεβίῳ, ἐπισκόπῳ Σαμοσάτων

Πάνυ ὡρμημένος καταλαβεῖν τὴν Νικόπολιν,
μετὰ τὸ δέξασθαι τὰ παρὰ τῆς ὁσιότητός[6] σου
γράμματα ἄρνησιν ἔχοντα τῆς ἀφίξεως, παρείθην
ἀπὸ[7] τῆς ἐπιθυμίας[8] καὶ πάσης ὁμοῦ τῆς ἀσθενείας ἀνεμνήσθην. ἦλθε δέ μοι εἰς ἔννοιαν καὶ ἡ
τῶν κεκληκότων ἀφοσίωσις, ὅτι, παροδικὴν πρὸς

---

[1] λείπειν E. [2] μοχθηρῶν E, Harl., Vat.
[3] ἔποιτο editi antiqi.
[4] εὐχή Capps ; εὐχῆς MSS. et editi.
[5] ἐφέλκοι τῆς αὐτῆς editi antiqi.
[6] κοσμιότητος vulgata. [7] ὑπό E, editi antiqi.

through the blood of His cross establish peace both on earth and in heaven.[1]

Therefore, on account of all this, we pray that we may abide in peace for the rest of our days, and in peace we ask that our last sleep may come upon us. For the sake of this peace, therefore, I have determined to neglect no effort whatever, not to omit anything as too humble to say or do, not to take into account the length of any journey, and not to shrink before any irksome thing, if so I may obtain the rewards of peace-making. And if anyone follows us who are leading the way in this matter, that is excellent, and my prayer is fulfilled ; but if anyone pulls in an opposite direction, I will not be moved thereby to renounce my decision. But each one himself on the day of retribution will acknowledge the fruits of his own works.

LETTER XCVIII

To Eusebius, Bishop of Samosata [2]

Although I had been exceedingly eager to visit Nicopolis, yet, after receiving the letter of your Holiness containing the statement that you were not going there, I relinquished my desire, and at the same time remembered all my infirmities of health. Moreover, the perfunctory manner of those who had invited me came to my mind—that after extending

---

[1] *i.e.*, by His Incarnation, the community of Man and God.
[2] According to Loofs (p. 25), this letter was written at Sebaste in the middle of June 372.

---

[3] ἀθυμίας E, Harl., editi antiqi.

ἡμᾶς ποιησάμενοι τὴν κλῆσιν διὰ τοῦ αἰδεσιμωτάτου ἀδελφοῦ Ἑλληνίου τοῦ ἐξισοῦντος Να-
ζιανζόν, δεύτερον περὶ τῶν αὐτῶν ὑπομιμνήσκοντα [1]
ἢ ὁδηγοῦντα ἡμᾶς οὐ κατηξίωσαν [2] ἀποστεῖλαι.
ἐπεὶ οὖν ὕποπτοι αὐτοῖς ἐσμὲν διὰ τὰς [3] ἁμαρτίας
ἡμῶν, ἐφοβήθημεν μή που τὸ φαιδρὸν αὐτοῖς τῆς
πανηγύρεως τῇ παρουσίᾳ ἡμῶν ἐπιθολώσωμεν.
μετὰ μὲν γὰρ τῆς σῆς μεγαλοφυΐας καὶ πρὸς τοὺς
μεγάλους ἀποδύσασθαι πειρασμοὺς οὐκ ὀκνοῦμεν,
ἄνευ δὲ σοῦ οὐδὲ ταῖς τυχούσαις θλίψεσιν
ἀντιβλέψαι αὐτάρκως ἔχομεν. ἐπεὶ οὖν ἐκκλησιαστικῶν ἔνεκεν γίνεσθαι ἡμῶν ἡ πρὸς αὐτοὺς
ἔντευξις ἔμελλε, τὸν μὲν τῆς πανηγύρεως καιρὸν
παρελίπομεν, εἰς ἡσυχίαν δὲ καὶ ἀτάραχον διαγωγὴν τὴν συντυχίαν ὑπερεθέμεθα, καὶ προῃρή-
μεθα καταλαβόντες τὴν Νικόπολιν διαλεχθῆναι
περὶ τῶν ταῖς ἐκκλησίαις ἀναγκαίων τῷ θεοφιλεστάτῳ ἐπισκόπῳ Μελετίῳ, εἰ μέλλοι παραι-
τεῖσθαι τὴν ἐπὶ Σαμόσατα [4] ὁδόν· εἰ δὲ μή, αὐτῷ [5]
συνδραμούμεθα, ἐὰν παρ' ἀμφοτέρων τοῦτο ἡμῖν
κατάδηλον γένηται, παρά τε αὐτοῦ ἐκείνου
ἀντιγράψαντος ἡμῖν περὶ τούτων (ἐπεστείλαμεν
γάρ), καὶ παρὰ τῆς σῆς θεοσεβείας.

Ἐπισκόποις δὲ τοῖς ἐκ τῆς δευτέρας Καππα-
δοκίας συντυγχάνειν ἐμέλλομεν· οἵ, ἐπειδὴ ἑτέρας

---

[1] ὑπομνήσκοντα Harl.   [2] οὐ κατηξίωσαν] οὐκ ἠξίωσαν E.
[3] τὰς] τῆς E.   [4] Σαμοσάτων Harl.
[5] αὐτοῦ E, editi antiqi.

---

[1] A surveyor of Customs at Nazianzus, and confidential
friend of both Basil and Gregory Nazianzene. He was an
Armenian by race, was married, and the father of a family.

to us a passing invitation through our most reverend
brother, Hellenius,[1] regulator of taxes at Nazianzus,
they did not think it worth while to send a messenger
to remind us of this same matter again or to act as
our escort.   Since, then, because of our sins we are
suspected by them, we feared lest perchance by our
presence we might disturb their joy of the festival.
For in company with your Magnanimity we do not
shrink from stripping ourselves for even great trials,
but without you we are not self-reliant enough to
face even ordinary afflictions.   Hence, inasmuch as
our meeting with them was to be concerned with
ecclesiastical matters, we have let pass the occasion
of the festival, we have postponed our meeting to a
period of peace and tranquillity, and we have determined to visit Nicopolis and to take up the question
of the needs of the churches with the most God-
beloved bishop Meletius,[2] in case he should decline
to make the journey to Samosata.   But if he should
not   decline,   we   shall   travel   thither   with   him,
provided this be made clear to us by you both—by
him through a letter written to me in reply regarding this matter (for we have written to him), and by
your Piety.

It was also our intention to meet the bishops of
Cappadocia Secunda ; but they, when they had been

He had a brother who, like himself, had acquired reputation
by his eloquence.   Both were employed in the administration
of justice.   In 371 Hellenius conveyed a letter from Gregory
to Basil ; cf. Basil, Letter LXXI.   Hellenius' official title was
ἐξισωτής (peraequator), whose chief duty was to conduct extraordinary local revisions of taxes.   Such officials were directly
responsible to the praetorian prefects.

    [2] For this Meletius, cf. Letters LVII, LXVIII, LXXXIX,
CXX, CXXIX, and CCXVI.

ὠνομάσθησαν ἐπαρχίας, ἐνόμισαν ἀθρόως καὶ
ἀλλοεθνεῖς καὶ ἀλλόφυλοι πρὸς ἡμᾶς γεγενῆσθαι
οἳ τοσοῦτον ἡμᾶς ἠγνόησαν, ὅσον οἱ μηδὲ τὴν
ἀρχὴν πεπειραμένοι,[1] μηδὲ εἰς λόγους ποτὲ
ἀφικόμενοι.[2] προσεδοκᾶτο δὲ καὶ ἑτέρα συντυχία
τοῦ αἰδεσιμωτάτου ἐπισκόπου Εὐσταθίου, ἡ καὶ
γενομένη ἡμῖν. διὰ γὰρ τὸ παρὰ πολλῶν κατα-
βοᾶσθαι αὐτὸν ὡς περὶ τὴν πίστιν παραχα-
ράσσοντά τι, ἀφικόμεθα αὐτῷ εἰς λόγους, καὶ
εὕρομεν σὺν Θεῷ πρὸς πᾶσαν ὀρθότητα εὐγνωμόνως
ἀκολουθοῦντα. τὰ δὲ τῶν ἐπισκόπων γράμματα
παρὰ τὴν αἰτίαν αὐτῶν ἐκείνων οὐκ ἐκομίσθη τῇ
τιμιότητί σου, οὓς ἐχρῆν τὰ παρ' ἡμῶν δια-
πέμψασθαι· ἀλλὰ καὶ ἐμὲ παρῆλθε, τῇ συνεχείᾳ
τῶν φροντίδων ἐκκρουσθέντα τῆς μνήμης.

Τὸν δ' ἀδελφὸν[3] Γρηγόριον κἀγὼ ἠβουλόμην[4]
οἰκονομεῖν ἐκκλησίαν τῇ αὐτοῦ φύσει σύμμετρον.
αὕτη δὲ ἦν πᾶσα εἰς ἓν συναχθεῖσα ἡ ὑφ' ἡλίῳ.[5]
ἐπειδὴ[6] δὲ τοῦτο ἀδύνατον, ἔστω ἐπίσκοπος, μὴ
ἐκ τοῦ τόπου σεμνυνόμενος, ἀλλὰ τὸν τόπον
σεμνύνων ἀφ' ἑαυτοῦ. ὄντως γὰρ μεγάλου ἐστὶν
οὐ τοῖς μεγάλοις μόνον ἀρκεῖν, ἀλλὰ καὶ τὰ μικρὰ
μεγάλα ποιεῖν τῇ ἑαυτοῦ δυνάμει.

---

[1] πεπειρασμένοι editi antiqi.   [2] ἀφικνούμενοι editi antiqi.
[3] ἐμόν, τόν, add. editi antiqi.   [4] ἐβουλόμην E.
[5] ὑφ' ἡλίῳ] ὑφήλιος Med. ; ὑφ' ἥλιον Bigot., Reg. secundus,
Coisl. secundus.
[6] ἐπεί editi antiqi.

---

[1] Cf. previous letter and note.
[2] According to Tillemont, this reference is to Basil's own
brother, Gregory of Nyssa. Maran, however (*Vita Basilii*,
xxiv), thinks this false, due partly to the introduction into
the text of the word ἐμόν, which he eliminates. He points

named as of another province,[1] immediately thought
that they had become of a different race and stock
from us, and they ignored us as thoroughly as would
those who have never had acquaintance with us at
all and have never come into converse with us.
Another meeting, too, with the most reverend bishop
Eustathius was expected by us, and this actually
took place. For since he was being denounced by
many on the ground that he was falsifying the faith
in some way, we entered into conference with him,
and we found him, by God's grace, candidly in
harmony with all orthodoxy. The letter of the
bishop was not delivered to your Honour through
the fault of those same persons who should have
forwarded the letter from us; but the matter
escaped my attention, having been driven from my
memory by continual cares.

I also had wished that my brother Gregory[2] were
governing a church commensurate with his talents.
But such a church would be the whole church under
the sun merged into one! But since this is impossible,
let him be a bishop, not receiving dignity from his
see, but himself conferring dignity upon the see.
For it is the part of a truly great man not merely to
be equal to great things, but also to make little
things great by his own power.

out also that Gregory of Nyssa, although unwilling to accept
consecration, never objected after it took place, and was
even sent to Nazianzus to console the younger Gregory, who
was in distress under like circumstances. Furthermore,
Gregory of Nyssa was consecrated in the regular manner, on
the demand of the people and clergy with the assent of the
bishops of the province. Cf. Letter CCXXV. On the other
hand, Gregory the younger was consecrated to Sasima without
these formalities. Hence it is probably the latter who is
here referred to.

Τί δὲ δεῖ [1] ποιῆσαι τῷ Παλματίῳ, μετὰ
τοσαύτας παρακλήσεις τῶν ἀδελφῶν ἔτι ὑπηρε-
τοῦντι τῷ Μαξίμῳ πρὸς τοὺς διωγμούς; ἀλλ'
ὅμως οὐδὲ νῦν ὀκνοῦσιν ἐπιστεῖλαι· παραγενέσθαι
γὰρ καὶ ὑπὸ ἀσθενείας [2] σώματος καὶ ὑπὸ ἀσχολιῶν οἰκειακῶν οὐκ ἐπιτρέπονται.

Γίνωσκε μέντοι, θεοφιλέστατε πάτερ, ὅτι πάνυ [3]
χρῄζει τῆς παρουσίας σου τὰ ἡμέτερα, καὶ
ἀνάγκη σε τὸ τίμιον γῆρας ἔτι ἅπαξ κινῆσαι,
ὑπὲρ τοῦ στῆσαι περιφερομένην λοιπὸν καὶ ἐγγὺς
πτώματος οὖσαν τὴν Καππαδοκίαν.

XCIX

Τερεντίῳ Κόμητι

Πάνυ πολλὴν σπουδὴν ἐνστησάμενος πειθαρ-
χῆσαι μερικῶς γοῦν καὶ τῷ βασιλικῷ προστάγματι

---

[1] ποιῆσαι Med.   [2] τοῦ add. E.
[3] πᾶν editi antiqi.

---

[1] Otherwise unknown.
[2] Governor of Cappadocia, successor of Elias, and himsel
succeeded by Antipater. Cf. Tillemont, note 58. Although,
as here indicated, he persecuted the orthodox, in the next
year, when he was removed from office and accused of
embezzlement of public funds, he had no warmer advocate
than Basil. There are three letters of Basil in his behalf to
influential laymen, begging them to befriend him in his
extremity; to Aburgius (Letter CXLVII); to Trajan (Letter
CXLVIII), and another inscribed, probably falsely, to Trajan
(Letter CXLIX). The persecutions here mentioned may
not be persecutions in the ecclesiastical sense, but severe
exactions of tribute.

LETTER XCIX

But what is to be done in the case of Palmatius,[1] who after so many admonitions from his brethren still supports Maximus[2] in his persecutions? Yet even now they do not hesitate to write to him; for they are not permitted to visit him on account of bodily ill-health[3] and their pressing duties at home.

Now be assured, most God-beloved father, that our situation needs your presence exceedingly, and you must bestir your venerable age once again, that you may give support to Cappadocia, which is even now tottering and near its fall.

LETTER XCIX

To Count Terentius[4]

ALTHOUGH at the outset I felt very great eagerness to obey, in part at least, both the Imperial

---

[3] Probably of Palmatius himself.

[4] Written from Satala in July or August 372. Cf. Loofs, 27. Terentius was general and count under Valens, and, though orthodox, held the Arian emperor's favour. Ammianus Marcellinus (27, 12; and 30, 1) belittles him because of his Christianity. Basil addresses the present letter to Terentius, who is in Iberia, in command of twelve legions, and details the difficulties, caused chiefly by Theodotus, in the way of carrying out the Emperor's order to supply Armenia with bishops. The Emperor's order had been enforced by a private letter from Terentius himself.

A still longer letter from Basil to Terentius, written during the Antiochene schism, A.D. 375, seeking to divert him from the side of Paulinus to that of Meletius, is Letter CCXIV.

Another letter of Basil's (CV) is addressed to the daughters of Terentius, who were deaconesses at Samosata.

καὶ τῷ φιλικῷ τῆς σῆς τιμιότητος γράμματι, οὗ
ἐγὼ πάντα λόγον καὶ πᾶσαν γνώμην γέμειν ὀρθῆς
προαιρέσεως καὶ ἀγαθῆς διανοίας πεπίστευκα, εἰς
ἔργον ἀγαγεῖν τὴν προθυμίαν οὐκ ἐπετράπην.[1]
αἴτιον δὲ τὸ μὲν πρῶτον καὶ ἀληθέστατον αἱ ἐμαὶ
ἁμαρτίαι, πανταχοῦ μοι προαπαντῶσαι καὶ
ὑποσκελίζουσαί μου τὰ διαβήματα· ἔπειτα καὶ ἡ
τοῦ δοθέντος ἡμῖν εἰς συνεργίαν ἐπισκόπου πρὸς
ἡμᾶς ἀλλοτρίωσις. οὐκ οἶδα γὰρ ὅ τι παθὼν ὁ
αἰδεσιμώτατος ἀδελφὸς ἡμῶν Θεόδοτος, ὁ ἐπαγ-
γειλάμενος ἡμῖν ἐξ ἀρχῆς πάντα συμπράξειν, καὶ
προθύμως ἡμᾶς ἀπὸ Γητασῶν ἐπὶ Νικόπολιν
καταγαγών,[2] ἐπειδὴ εἶδεν ἡμᾶς ἐπὶ τῆς πόλεως,
οὕτως ἡμᾶς ἐβδελύξατο, καὶ οὕτως ἐφοβήθη τὰς
ἁμαρτίας ἡμῶν, ὡς μήτε εἰς ἑωθινὴν εὐχὴν μήτε
εἰς ἑσπερινὴν ἀνασχέσθαι ἡμᾶς παραλαβεῖν·
δίκαια μὲν ποιῶν, ὡς πρὸς ἡμᾶς, καὶ πρέποντα
τῷ ἐμῷ βίῳ, οὐ λυσιτελοῦντα δὲ τῇ κοινῇ καταστάσει τῶν ἐκκλησιῶν βουλευόμενος. τὴν δὲ
αἰτίαν τούτων προέφερεν ἡμῖν, ὅτι ἠνεσχόμεθα εἰς
κοινωνίαν τὸν αἰδεσιμώτατον ἐπίσκοπον Εὐστάθιον
παραδέξασθαι. τὸ μέντοι γενόμενον παρ' ἡμῶν
τοιοῦτόν ἐστιν.

Ἡμεῖς, κληθέντες εἰς σύνοδον παρὰ τοῦ
ἀδελφοῦ Θεοδότου τελουμένην[3] καὶ ὁρμήσαντες
δι' ἀγάπην ὑπακοῦσαι τῇ κλήσει, ἵνα μὴ δόξωμεν
ἄπρακτον καὶ ἀργὴν ποιεῖσθαι τὴν συντυχίαν,

---

[1] ἐτράπην editi antiqi.   [2] καταγαγεῖν editi antiqi.
[3] τελειουμένην editi antiqi.

---

[1] Bishop of Nicopolis in Lesser Armenia, an aged prelate
of high character and unquestioned orthodoxy. Theodotus
was greatly respected by St. Basil, but he was extremely

ordinance and the friendly letter of your Honour,
whose every word and every thought I am convinced
is filled with right purpose and good intentions,
I was not permitted to turn my desire into action.
And the reason, the primary and the truest one, is
my sins, which come forth to meet me on every
side and trip my steps; and, secondly, our alienation
from the bishop assigned to co-operate with us.
For I do not know what has happened to our most
reverend brother Theodotus,[1] that after promising
us in the beginning to help in every way, and
eagerly bringing us down from Getasa to Nicopolis,
yet when he saw us in the city he so loathed us,
and so feared our sins, that he could not bring
himself to take us with him to either morning or
evening prayers; what he did was just, so far as we
are concerned, and befitting my life, but was not
working for the best interests of the common
organization of the churches. But he alleged to us
as the cause of this treatment the fact that we had
received the most reverend bishop Eustathius into
communion. What we have done, however, is this :

When we were summoned to a synod which was
being held by our brother Theodotus, and for
charity's sake were eager to obey the summons, in
order that we should not seem to render the meeting
futile and of no effect, we made a special effort to

annoyed at Basil's reluctance to sever connexions with
Eustathius of Sebaste. On this very account he refused to
co-operate with Basil in giving bishops to Lesser Armenia,
and he virtually excommunicated Basil on the latter's arrival,
by invitation, at Nicopolis. Brotherly relations between the
two, however, were later re-established. Two of Basil's
extant letters are addressed to Theodotus : Letters CXXI
and CXXX.

ἐσπουδάσαμεν εἰς λόγους ἐλθεῖν τῷ προειρημένῳ
ἀδελφῷ Εὐσταθίῳ. καὶ προετείναμεν αὐτῷ τὰ
περὶ τῆς πίστεως ἐγκλήματα, ὅσα προφέρουσιν
αὐτῷ οἱ περὶ τὸν ἀδελφὸν Θεόδοτον, καὶ ἠξιώσαμεν, εἰ μὲν ἕπεται τῇ ὀρθῇ πίστει, φανερὸν ἡμῖν
καταστῆσαι, ὥστε ἡμᾶς εἶναι κοινωνικούς· εἰ δὲ
ἀλλοτρίως ἔχει, ἀκριβῶς εἰδέναι, ὅτι καὶ ἡμεῖς
ἕξομεν πρὸς αὐτὸν ἀλλοτρίως. πολλῶν τοίνυν
γενομένων λόγων πρὸς ἀλλήλους, καὶ πάσης
ἐκείνης τῆς ἡμέρας ἐν τῇ περὶ τούτων σκέψει
δαπανηθείσης, καταλαβούσης λοιπὸν τῆς ἑσπέ-
ρας, διεκρίθημεν ἀπ᾽ ἀλλήλων, εἰς οὐδὲν ὁμο-
λογούμενον πέρας τὸν λόγον[1] προαγαγόντες. τῇ
δὲ ἑξῆς πάλιν, ἔωθεν συγκαθεσθέντες, περὶ τῶν
αὐτῶν διελεγόμεθα, ἐπελθόντος ἤδη καὶ τοῦ
ἀδελφοῦ Ποιμενίου, τοῦ πρεσβυτέρου τῆς Σεβαστείας, καὶ σφοδρῶς ἡμῖν τὸν ἐναντίον γυμνάζοντος
λόγον. κατὰ μικρὸν οὖν ἡμεῖς τε, ὑπὲρ ὧν ἔδοξεν
ἡμῖν ἐγκαλεῖν, ἀπελυόμεθα, κἀκείνους εἰς τὴν[2]
τῶν ἐπιζητουμένων ὑφ᾽ ἡμῶν συγκατάθεσιν
προηγάγομεν,[3] ὥστε χάριτι τοῦ Κυρίου εὑρεθῆναι
ἡμᾶς μηδὲ εἰς τὸ σμικρότατον πρὸς ἀλλήλους
διαφερομένους. οὕτω τοίνυν περὶ ἐννάτην που
ὥραν ἀνέστημεν ἐπὶ τὰς προσευχάς, εὐχαριστή-
σαντες τῷ Κυρίῳ τῷ δόντι ἡμῖν τὸ αὐτὸ φρονεῖν
καὶ τὸ αὐτὸ λέγειν. ἐπὶ τούτοις ἔδει με καὶ
ἔγραφόν τινα παρὰ τοῦ ἀνδρὸς ὁμολογίαν λαβεῖν,
ὥστε καὶ τοῖς ἐναντιουμένοις αὐτῷ φανερὰν

---

[1] τῶν λόγων E, τὸν λόγον in marg. manu recente.
[2] ὑπέρ add. E.   [3] προσηγάγομεν editi antiqi.

---

[1] Otherwise unknown.

enter into conference with our brother Eustathius just mentioned. And we presented to him the charges regarding his faith, such as our brother Theodotus and his followers bring against him, and we asked him, in case he followed the orthodox Faith, to make this fact manifest to us so that we might be in communion with him; but if he was otherwise disposed, we asked him to know clearly that we too should be otherwise disposed toward him. Thereupon, after we had conversed much with each other, and after the whole of that day had been consumed in the examination of these matters, evening having now fallen, we parted from each other without having brought our discussion to any conclusion to which we could both agree. But after we had again assembled on the morning of the following day, we were entering upon a discussion of the same subject, when our brother, Poimenius,[1] presbyter of Sebasteia, entered our conference also, and began vigorously to press the opposing doctrine against us.[2] Little by little we for our part, accordingly, kept clearing away the charges upon the strength of which they seemed to accuse us, and we brought them to such an assent regarding the subjects of our investigation that by the grace of the Lord we found ourselves to be differing from one another not even in the smallest point. Thus, therefore, somewhere about the ninth hour we arose for prayer, thanking the Lord who had given us to think and speak the same things. In confirmation of this I ought to have obtained also a written confession from the man, so that his assent might

[2] "Us" and "we" here mean the writer, St. Basil, and not Basil and Eustathius.

γενέσθαι τὴν συγκατάθεσιν, καὶ τοῖς λοιποῖς
ἱκανὴν εἶναι τοῦ ἀνδρὸς τῆς προαιρέσεως τὴν
ἀπόδειξιν. ἀλλ' ἐβουλήθην αὐτὸς ὑπὲρ[1] πολλῆς
ἀκριβείας, τοῖς ἀδελφοῖς συντυχὼν τοῖς περὶ
Θεόδοτον, παρ' αὐτῶν λαβεῖν γραμματεῖον
πίστεως, καὶ αὐτὸ[2] προτεῖναι τῷ προειρημένῳ·
ἵνα ἀμφότερα γένηται, ἥ τε ὀρθὴ πίστις παρ'
αὐτοῦ ὁμολογηθῇ,[3] καὶ αὐτοὶ πληροφορηθῶσι,
μηδεμίαν ἔχοντες ἀντιλογίας ὑπόθεσιν ἐκ τοῦ τὰς
παρ' αὐτῶν προτάσεις παραδεχθῆναι. ἀλλὰ
πρὶν μαθεῖν τίνος ἔνεκεν συνετύχομεν, καὶ τί
ἡμῖν ἐκ τῆς ὁμιλίας κατώρθωται, οἱ περὶ τὸν
ἐπίσκοπον Θεόδοτον οὐκέτι ἡμᾶς εἰς τὴν σύνοδον
προτρέψασθαι κατηξίωσαν. ἀλλ' ἀπὸ μέσης
ἀνεζεύξαμεν[4] τῆς ὁδοῦ, ἀθυμήσαντες, ὅτι ἀτελεῖς
ἡμῖν ποιοῦσι τοὺς ὑπὲρ τῆς εἰρήνης τῶν ἐκκλησιῶν
καμάτους.

Μετὰ ταῦτα τοίνυν, ἐπειδὴ κατέλαβεν ἡμᾶς ἡ
ἀνάγκη τῆς ἐπὶ τὴν Ἀρμενίαν ὁδοῦ, εἰδὼς τοῦ
ἀνδρὸς τὸ ἰδιότροπον καὶ βουλόμενος ὑπὸ[5] μάρτυρι ἀξιοπίστῳ αὐτός τε ὑπὲρ τῶν πεπραγμένων
ἀπολογήσασθαι κἀκεῖνον πληροφορῆσαι, ἦλθον
ἐπὶ τὰ Γήτασα τὸν ἀγρὸν τοῦ θεοφιλεστάτου
ἐπισκόπου Μελετίου, συμπαρόντος μοι[6] καὶ
αὐτοῦ τοῦ προειρημένου Θεοδότου· καὶ οὕτως
ἐκεῖ, ἐπειδὴ ἐνεκλήθημεν παρ' αὐτοῦ ἐπὶ τῇ[7]
πρὸς Εὐστάθιον συναφείᾳ, εἶπον τὸ[8] ἐκ τῆς συν-

---

[1] ὑπέρ R.J.D., ὑπό MSS. et editi. [2] οὗτοι E.
[3] ὁμολογῆται tres MSS. recen. [4] ἀνέζευξαν editi antiqi.
[5] ἐπί nonnulli MSS. [6] μου E.
[7] ἐπὶ τῇ . . . συναφείᾳ] περὶ τῆς . . . συναφείας nonnulli
MSS.

be made clear also to those who oppose him and might be for the rest a sufficient demonstration of the man's convictions. But I desired on my own account, for the sake of complete accuracy, to meet our brothers, the followers of Theodotus, receive from them a written testimonial of faith, and present this to the afore-mentioned Theodotus ; my purpose was that two things might be accomplished, namely, that the orthodox Faith should be confessed by him, and that his followers should themselves be fully informed, they having thus no ground for controversy by reason of the fact that the propositions had been accepted by themselves. But before learning for what reason Eustathius and I had met, and what success had been achieved by us as a result of our conference, the followers of the bishop Theodotus no longer deemed it proper to invite us to the synod. But in the middle of our journey we turned back, disheartened that they were rendering of no avail our labours in behalf of the peace of the churches.

After this, therefore, when the necessity of a journey to Armenia fell upon us, being well acquainted with the peculiar character of the man and desirous of having the support of a most trustworthy witness in defending myself for my actions and of giving him full information, I came to Getasa, the field of the most God-beloved bishop Meletius, the afore-mentioned Theodotus being also present at the time ; and thus in that place, when we were accused by him on the ground of our connexion with Eustathius, I told him of the happy outcome of our

---

[8] τὸ . . . κατόρθωμα] τὰ . . . κατορθώματα E.

COLLECTED LETTERS OF SAINT BASIL

τυχίας κατόρθωμα, ὅτι ἔλαβον αὐτὸν εἰς πάντα
ἡμῖν ὁμοδοξοῦντα. ὡς δὲ διεβεβαιοῦτο ἔξαρνον
γεγενῆσθαι μετὰ τὴν ἀφ' ἡμῶν ἀναχώρησιν, καὶ
διαβεβαιοῦσθαι αὐτὸν τοῖς ἰδίοις αὐτοῦ[1] μαθηταῖς, ᾗ μὲν εἰς μηδὲν ἡμῖν περὶ τῆς πίστεως
συντεθεῖσθαι, ἀπήντων ἐγὼ πρὸς ταῦτα (καὶ
σκόπει, θαυμασιώτατε, εἰ μὴ δικαιοτάτας[2] καὶ
ἀναντιρρήτους ἐποιούμην πρὸς τοῦτο τὰς ἀποκρίσεις), ὅτι ἐγὼ μὲν πέπεισμαι, εἰκάζων ἐκ τῆς
λοιπῆς εὐσταθείας τοῦ ἀνδρός, μὴ οὕτως αὐτὸν
κούφως περιτρέπεσθαι πρὸς τὰ ἐναντία, μηδὲ νῦν
μὲν ὁμολογεῖν νῦν δὲ ὑπὲρ ὧν εἶπεν ἀρνεῖσθαι,
ἄνδρα καὶ τὸ ὑπὲρ τῶν τυχόντων ψεῦδος ὡς
φοβερὸν ἀποφεύγοντα, μὴ ὅτι γε περὶ τῶν
τηλικούτων πραγμάτων καὶ οὕτω παρὰ πᾶσι
βεβοημένων,[3] ἑλέσθαι ἄν ποτε ἐναντιωθῆναι τῇ
ἀληθείᾳ. εἰ δὲ ἄρα καὶ ἀληθῆ εἶναι συμβῇ τὰ
θρυλλούμενα παρ' ὑμῶν, προτεῖναι αὐτῷ γραμματεῖον πᾶσαν ἔχον τῆς ὀρθῆς πίστεως τὴν ἀπόδειξιν χρή. ἐὰν μὲν οὖν εὕρω αὐτὸν συντιθέμενον
ἐγγράφως, ἐπιμενῶ τῇ κοινωνίᾳ· ἐὰν δὲ λάβω
ἀναδυόμενον, ἀποστήσομαι αὐτοῦ τῆς συναφείας.
ἀποδεξαμένου τὸν λόγον τοῦ ἐπισκόπου Μελετίου
καὶ τοῦ ἀδελφοῦ Διοδώρου τοῦ συμπρεσβυτέρου
(παρῆν γὰρ τοῖς γινομένοις), συνθέμενος ὁ αἰδεσιμώτατος ἀδελφὸς Θεόδοτος ἐκεῖ, καὶ παρακα-
λέσας ἡμᾶς κατελθεῖν ἐπὶ Νικόπολιν, ἵνα καὶ
τὴν ἐκκλησίαν αὐτοῦ ἐπισκεψώμεθα, καὶ αὐτὸν
λάβωμεν τῆς μέχρι Σατάλων ὁδοιπορίας συνέμπορον, καταλιπὼν[4] ἡμᾶς ἐν Γητάσοις, ἐπειδὴ

[1] ἑαυτοῦ E.
[2] δικαιοτάτως καὶ ἀναντιρρήτως Reg. primus et Bigot.

178

meeting, that I found him agreeing with us in
every belief. But as he kept maintaining that
Eustathius had denied all this after taking his departure from us, and had personally declared to his
own disciples that in truth he had not come into
any agreement whatever on the question of faith,
I met these charges (and observe, most respected
Sir, whether I did not make the most just and
irrefutable replies thereto) by saying that I was
convinced, basing my judgment on the general
stability of the man's character, that he would not
be so lightly turned to opposite views, that he would
not now agree and now deny what he had just
said, and that a man who shuns falsehood even in
trivial affairs as a fearful thing, to say nothing of
matters of such importance and so talked of by all,
would never choose to gainsay the truth. But if he
did do this, and if what is common talk among you
should turn out to be true, we ought to propose
to him a written statement containing a complete
proof of his orthodox faith. If, then, I find that
he affirms his agreement in writing, I shall remain
in communion with him; but if I catch him drawing
back, I shall sever all connexions with him. Although the bishop Meletius and our brother Diodorus,
the presbyter (for he was present while all this was
going on), accepted this decision, and although our
most reverend brother Theodotus agreed on that
occasion, and urged us to go down to Nicopolis in
order that we should not only visit his church but
also take him as a fellow-traveller on our journey
as far as Satala, yet he left us at Getasa, and when

---

[3] βεβοημένον E ; διαβεβοημένων editi antiqi.

[4] συνέμπορον, καταλιπών] συνέκπορον καταλιπόντα editi antiqi.

κατελάβομεν τὴν Νικόπολιν, ἐπιλαθόμενος ὧν
τε παρ' ἐμοῦ[1] ἤκουσεν.[2] ὧν τε συνέθετο ἡμῖν,
ἐκείναις ταῖς ὕβρεσι καὶ ταῖς ἀτιμίαις, ἃς
μικρῷ πρόσθεν διηγησάμην, καταισχύνας ἡμᾶς
ἀπέπεμψε.

Πῶς οὖν ἦν δυνατόν μοι, τιμιωτάτη κεφαλή,[3]
ποιῆσαί τι τῶν προστεταγμένων, καὶ δοῦναι
ἐπισκόπους τῇ Ἀρμενίᾳ, οὕτω πρός με τοῦ
κοινωνοῦ τῆς φροντίδος διατεθέντος, παρ' οὗ ἐγὼ
προσεδόκων τοὺς ἐπιτηδείους ἄνδρας εὑρήσειν;
διὰ τὸ εἶναι ἐν τῇ παροικίᾳ αὐτοῦ καὶ εὐλαβεῖς
καὶ συνετοὺς καὶ τῆς γλώττης ἐμπείρους καὶ τὰ
λοιπὰ ἰδιώματα τοῦ ἔθνους ἐπισταμένους· ὧν
εἰδὼς τὰ ὀνόματα, ἑκὼν[4] σιωπήσομαι, ἵνα μή
τι ἐμπόδιον γένηται πρὸς τὸ ἐν ἑτέρῳ γοῦν χρόνῳ
χρησιμευθῆναι τὴν Ἀρμενίαν.

Καὶ νῦν γενόμενος μέχρι Σατάλων ἐν τοιούτῳ
σώματι, τὰ μὲν λοιπὰ ἔδοξα τῇ τοῦ Θεοῦ χάριτι
καθιστᾶν, εἰρηνεύσας τοὺς τῆς Ἀρμενίας ἐπισκόπους, καὶ διαλεχθεὶς αὐτοῖς τὰ πρέποντα, ὥστε
ἀποθέσθαι τὴν συνήθη ἀδιαφορίαν[5] καὶ ἀναλαβεῖν τὴν γνησίαν τοῦ Κυρίου ὑπὲρ τῶν ἐκκλησιῶν σπουδήν, δοὺς αὐτοῖς καὶ τύπους περὶ τῶν
ἀδιαφόρως κατὰ τὴν Ἀρμενίαν παρανομουμένων,
ὅπως αὐτοῖς προσῆκεν ἐπιμελεῖσθαι. ἐδεξάμην
δὲ καὶ ψηφίσματα παρὰ τῆς ἐκκλησίας Σατάλων,
παράκλησιν ἔχοντα δοθῆναι αὐτοῖς παρ' ἡμῶν
ἐπίσκοπον. ἐπιμελὲς δέ μοι τοῦτο ἐγένετο, καὶ
τὴν περιχυθεῖσαν βλασφημίαν τῷ ἀδελφῷ ἡμῶν

---

[1] τε παρ' ἐμοῦ] παρ' ἡμῶν E.   [2] ἤκουσαν editi antiqi.
[3] κεφαλῇ E.   [4] ἑκουσίως editi antiqi.

we arrived at Nicopolis, forgetful alike of what he
had heard from me and what he had agreed to with
us, he put us to shame with those acts of insolence
and indignity which I mentioned a little while ago,
and sent us away.

How then was it possible for me, most honoured
Sir, to perform any of the commands laid upon me,
and to furnish bishops to Armenia, when my associate
in the business was thus disposed towards me, the
man through whom I expected to discover the
suitable men? The reason is that in his parish
there are pious and sagacious persons, who are
skilled in the language and are well versed in the
other peculiarities of that nation. Although I know
their names, I shall willingly remain silent, lest
anything should arise to prevent their being of
service to Armenia at another time.

And now having come to Satala in such a state of
body, I seem, by the grace of God, to have settled
all other questions; for I have established peace
among the bishops of Armenia, and have argued
with them in befitting terms to put aside their
customary indifference, and to take up again the
true zeal of the Lord in behalf of the churches;
I have also given them rules regarding those acts,
due to indifference, which are committed throughout
Armenia in violation of the law, to show them how
it is fitting that they should take heed of those
things. I have received, too, a voted decision from
the church of Satala, with the request that a bishop
be given them by us. This matter has concerned
me, and also to investigate the slander which has

---

[5] διαφοράν Bigot., Reg. secundus, Coisl. secundus.

COLLECTED LETTERS OF SAINT BASIL

Κυρίλλῳ τῷ ἐπισκόπῳ Ἀρμενίας ἀνερευνῆσαι·
καὶ διὰ τῆς χάριτος τοῦ Θεοῦ εὕρομεν αὐτὴν
ψευδῶς κινηθεῖσαν ἐκ διαβολῆς τῶν μισούντων
αὐτόν· ἣν καὶ φανερῶς ὡμολόγησαν ἐφ᾽ ἡμῶν.
καὶ ἐδόξαμεν μετρίως ἡμεροῦν πρὸς αὐτὸν τὸν ἐν
Σατάλοις λαόν, ὥστε μηκέτι αὐτοῦ τὴν κοινωνίαν
φεύγειν. εἰ δὲ μικρὰ ταῦτα καὶ οὐδενὸς ἄξια,
ἀλλὰ παρ᾽ ἡμῶν οὐδὲν ἦν πλέον δυνατὸν γενέσθαι,
διὰ τὴν ἐκ τῆς τοῦ διαβόλου περιεργίας ἡμῶν
αὐτῶν πρὸς ἀλλήλους ἀσυμφωνίαν. ταῦτά με
ἔδει[1] σιωπᾶν, ἵνα μὴ δόξω δημοσιεύειν ἐμαυτοῦ
τὰ ὀνείδη· ἀλλ᾽ ἐπειδὴ οὐκ ἦν ἄλλως ἀπολογή-
σασθαί σου τῇ μεγαλοφυΐᾳ, εἰς ἀνάγκην ἦλθον
πᾶσαν τῶν γεγονότων τὴν ἀλήθειαν διηγήσασθαι.

C

Εὐσεβίῳ, ἐπισκόπῳ Σαμοσάτων

Οὕτως εἶδον τὰ γράμματα τῆς ἀγάπης σου ἐν
τῇ γείτονι χώρᾳ τῆς Ἀρμενίας,[2] ὡς ἂν ἴδοιεν οἱ
θαλαττεύοντες πυρσὸν ἐν πελάγει πόρρωθεν
φρυκτωρούμενον, ἄλλως τε κἂν ἀγριαίνουσά πως
τύχοι[3] ἡ θάλασσα ὑπ᾽ ἀνέμων. καὶ γὰρ φύσει
μὲν ἡδὺ καὶ παρηγορίαν ἔχον πολλὴν τὸ τῆς σῆς
σεμνότητος γράμμα, τότε δὲ μάλιστα τὴν ἀπ᾽
αὐτοῦ[4] χάριν ὁ καιρὸς συνηύξησεν,[5] ὃν ὁποῖος

---

[1] ταῦτά με ἔδει] ταῦτα ἔδει μέν editi antiqi.
[2] τῶν Ἀρμενίων editi antiqi.   [3] τύχῃ editi antiqi.
[4] ἀπ᾽ αὐτοῦ] ἐπ᾽ αὐτῷ E, Harl.
[5] προσηύξησεν editi antiqi.

182

been heaped upon our brother, Cyril, the bishop of
Armenia; and through the grace of God we have
found that it was falsely fomented by the calumny
of his enemies, and this the latter have openly
confessed before us. And it seems that in a measure
we have reconciled the laity in Satala to him, so that
they no longer avoid his communion. Now if these
things are trivial and of no importance, on the other
hand there was nothing further which we could do,
owing to our discord between one and another,
caused by the busy activity of the devil. I ought
to have kept silent on these matters, that I may
not appear to be spreading abroad the reproaches
against myself; but since I could make my defence
to your Magnanimity in no other way, I have found
it necessary to relate the whole truth of what has
taken place.

LETTER C

To Eusebius, Bishop of Samosata [1]

I BEHELD the letter of your Charity in this neighbouring country of Armenia, with the same feelings
with which men at sea would behold a beacon fire
shining from afar upon the deep, especially if the sea
should chance to be in an angry state by reason of
the winds. For the letter of your August Reverence,
though naturally possessing sweetness and great
consolation, then especially had its charm enhanced
by the occasion of its arrival. What the occasion

---

[1] According to Loofs (30), written from Armenia in July
or August 372. Previous letters addressed by Basil to
Eusebius of Samosata are XXVII, XXX, XXXI, XXXIV,
XLVII, XLVIII, XCV, XCVIII.

ἦν, καὶ ὅπως ἡμᾶς λυπήσας, ἐγὼ μὲν οὐκ ἂν
εἴποιμι, κρίνας ἅπαξ ἐπιλαθέσθαι [1] τῶν λυπηρῶν·
ὁ μέντοι συνδιάκονος ἡμῶν διηγήσεταί σου τῇ
θεοσεβείᾳ.

Ἐμὲ δὲ ἐπέλιπε παντελῶς τὸ σῶμα, ὥστε μηδὲ
τὰς σμικροτάτας κινήσεις δύνασθαι ἀλύπως
φέρειν. πλὴν ἀλλ' εὔχομαι δυνηθῆναί μοι τὴν
παλαιὰν ἐπιθυμίαν νῦν γοῦν διὰ τῆς βοηθείας
τῶν σῶν προσευχῶν ἐκπληρωθῆναι· εἰ καὶ ὅτι
πολλήν μοι πεποίηκε τὴν δυσκολίαν ἡ ἀποδημία
αὕτη, τοσούτῳ χρόνῳ ἀμεληθέντων τῶν κατὰ τὴν
ἡμετέραν ἐκκλησίαν πραγμάτων. ἐὰν δὲ ὁ Θεός,
ἕως ἐσμὲν ὑπὲρ γῆς, καταξιώσῃ ἡμᾶς ἰδεῖν ἐπὶ
τῆς ἐκκλησίας ἡμῶν τὴν σὴν θεοσέβειαν, ὄντως
ἀγαθὰς ἐλπίδας καὶ ἐπὶ τοῖς μέλλουσιν ἕξομεν,
ὡς οὐ πάντῃ ἐσμὲν [2] ἀπόβλητοι τῶν δωρεῶν τοῦ
Θεοῦ. τοῦτο γοῦν, ἐὰν ᾖ δυνατόν, παρακαλοῦμεν
ἐπὶ τῆς συνόδου γενέσθαι, ἣν δι' ἔτους ἄγομεν ἐπὶ
τῇ μνήμῃ τοῦ μακαρίου [3] μάρτυρος Εὐψυχίου
προσεγγιζούσῃ λοιπὸν κατὰ τὴν ἑβδόμην ἡμέραν
τοῦ Σεπτεμβρίου μηνός. καὶ γὰρ καὶ φροντίδος
ἄξια ἡμῖν περίκειται [4] πράγματα τῆς παρὰ σοῦ
δεόμενα συνεργίας, εἴς τε κατάστασιν ἐπισκόπων
καὶ εἰς βουλὴν καὶ σκέψιν τῶν μελετωμένων καθ'
ἡμῶν παρὰ τῆς χρηστότητος Γρηγορίου τοῦ

---

[1] ἐκλαθέσθαι E.
[2] γενησόμεθα editi antiqi.
[3] μακαριωτάτου editi antiqi.
[4] πρόκειται E.

was, and how it pained us, I should not myself speak, having determined once and for all to forget my grievances. Our deacon, however, will relate everything to your Piety.

My body has failed me so completely that I am unable to make even the slightest movement without pain. However, I pray that now, at any rate, my old desire can be fulfilled through the assistance of your prayers; although it is true that this absence abroad has caused me great difficulties, since the affairs of our own church have been neglected for so long a time. Yet if God, while we are still on earth, will deem us worthy to see your Piety in our church, we shall have truly bright hopes for the future also, that we shall not be wholly excluded from the gifts of God. This, then, if it be possible, we beg you to have take place at the synod which we convene every year on the seventh of September in memory of the blessed Eupsychius,[1] an event which is now approaching. Moreover, we are encompassed by matters worthy of serious attention which stand in need of your assistance, namely, the question of establishing bishops, and the matter of investigating and deliberating about the actions meditated against us by Gregory of Nyssa in his

[1] Eupsychius appears in the Roman calendar, and his martyrdom is celebrated on April 9 (*Boll. Acta. SS.* April 9). He suffered in the reign of Julian for the part he took in the demolition of a temple to Fortune. Cf. Sozomen, *Ecc. Hist.* V, 11. Julian gave orders that the temple should be rebuilt. This order was never fulfilled, but a church was erected on the spot, dedicated to the memory of Eupsychius. Basil here entreats Eusebius of Samosata to be present at the festival of Eupsychius, and in Letter CCLII he summons the bishops of Pontus to the festival of the dedication of this church.

Νυσσαέως ὃς συνόδους συγκροτεῖ κατὰ τὴν
Ἄγκυραν καὶ οὐδένα τρόπον ἐπιβουλεύων ἡμῖν
ἀφίησιν.

CI

Παραμυθητική[1]

Εὐχῆς ἄξιον ἦν, πρώτην διαπεμπομένους
ἐπιστολήν, εὐθυμοτέραν ἔχειν[2] τὴν τῶν γραμμάτων ὑπόθεσιν. οὕτω γὰρ ἂν ἡμῖν τὰ κατὰ
γνώμην ὑπῆρξε, διότι πᾶσι βουλόμεθα τοῖς ἐν
εὐσεβείᾳ ζῆν προαιρουμένοις πάντα τὸν βίον εἰς
ἀγαθὸν εὐοδοῦσθαι. ἀλλ᾽ ἐπειδὴ ὁ διοικῶν τὴν
ζωὴν ἡμῶν Κύριος, κατὰ τὴν ἄρρητον αὐτοῦ
σοφίαν πάντως πρὸς τὸ σύμφερον τῶν ψυχῶν
τῶν ἡμετέρων ταῦτα ᾠκονόμησε γενέσθαι, δι᾽ ὧν
σοι μὲν ὀδυνηρὰν κατέστησε τὴν ζωήν, ἡμᾶς δέ,
τοὺς τῇ κατὰ Θεὸν ἀγάπῃ συνημμένους, εἰς
συμπάθειαν ἤγαγε, μαθόντας παρὰ τῶν ἀδελφῶν
ἡμῶν ἐν οἷς γέγονας, ἀναγκαῖον ἡμῖν ἐφάνη τὴν
ἐνδεχομένην παράκλησιν προσαγαγεῖν σοι. εἰ
μὲν οὖν ἦν δυνατὸν καὶ διαβῆναι μέχρι τοῦ τόπου
ἐν ᾧ συμβαίνει διάγειν σου τὴν εὐγένειαν, περὶ
παντὸς ἂν τοῦτο ἐποιησάμην. ἐπεὶ δὲ καὶ ἡ τοῦ
σώματος ἀρρωστία καὶ τῶν συνεχόντων ἡμᾶς
πραγμάτων τὸ πλῆθος καὶ αὐτὴν ταύτην ἣν
ὑπέστημεν ὁδὸν ἐπὶ πολλῇ τῶν καθ᾽ ἡμᾶς
ἐκκλησιῶν ζημίᾳ παρεσκεύασε, διὰ γραμμάτων

---

[1] τῇ ὁμοζύγῳ Ἀρινθαίου add. editi antiqi ; πρός τινα θλίψεσιν
ἀδικήτοις περιπεσόντα Regius secundus ; τινὶ θλίψεσιν ἀδικήτοις
περιπεσόντι Bigot.
[2] σχεῖν E.

simplicity,[1] who convenes synods at Ancyra, and in no way ceases to plot against us.

LETTER CI

Consolatory [2]

It were worthy of prayer that in sending our first letter to you we might have had a more cheerful subject about which to write. If that had been so, everything would have been as we wished, for we desire that the whole life of all who choose to live in true religion should prosper well. But since the Lord who dispenses our lives has surely arranged these things according to His ineffable wisdom for the good of our souls, and so has made your life a life of sorrow, and has brought us, who are joined to you by the love of God, to feel sympathy for your plight, on hearing from our brothers in what troubles you were, it seemed that we must send you all possible consolation. Now if it had been possible to cross over to where your Nobility happens to live, I should have considered it of the greatest importance to do so. But since our bodily weakness and the manifold duties which occupy us caused even this journey which we had in mind to involve great harm to the churches under our care, we were eager to

---

[1] As the Benedictine edition points out, this opposition was due not to want of affection but to want of tact. For a similar display of lack of tact on the part of Gregory of Nyssa, cf. Letter LVIII.

[2] Written in 372. Editions anterior to the Benedictine add to the title τῇ ὁμοζύγῳ ᾽Αρινθαίου, "to the wife of Arinthaeus," but no manuscript known to us contains it.

ἐπισκέψασθαί σου τὴν σεμνότητα προεθυμήθημεν,
ὑπομιμνήσκοντες, ὅτι αἱ θλίψεις αὗται οὐκ ἀργῶς
τοῖς δούλοις τοῦ Θεοῦ παρὰ τοῦ ἐπισκοποῦντος
ἡμᾶς Κυρίου γίνονται, ἀλλὰ ἐπὶ δοκιμασίᾳ τῆς
ἀληθινῆς πρὸς τὸν κτίσαντα ἡμᾶς Θεὸν ἀγάπης.
ὡς γὰρ τοὺς ἀθλητὰς οἱ τῶν ἀγώνων κάματοι τοῖς
στεφάνοις προσάγουσιν, οὕτω καὶ τοὺς Χριστια-
νοὺς ἡ ἐν τοῖς[1] πειρασμοῖς δοκιμασία πρὸς τὴν
τελείωσιν ἄγει, ἐὰν μετὰ τῆς πρεπούσης ὑπομονῆς
ἐν εὐχαριστίᾳ πάσῃ τὰ οἰκονομούμενα παρὰ τοῦ
Κυρίου καταδεξώμεθα.

Ἀγαθότητι Δεσπότου διοικεῖται τὰ πάντα.
οὐδὲν τῶν συμβαινόντων ἡμῖν ὡς λυπηρὸν ὑποδέχεσθαι χρή, κἂν πρὸς τὸ παρὸν ἅπτηται τῆς
ἀσθενείας ἡμῶν. εἰ γὰρ καὶ τοὺς λόγους ἀγνοοῦ-
μεν, καθ᾿ οὓς ἕκαστον τῶν γινομένων[2] ὡς καλὸν
παρὰ τοῦ Δεσπότου ἡμῖν ἐπάγεται, ἀλλ᾿ ἐκεῖνο
πεπεῖσθαι ὀφείλομεν, ὅτι πάντως συμφέρει τὸ
γινόμενον ἢ ἡμῖν διὰ τὸν τῆς ὑπομονῆς μισθὸν ἢ
τῇ παραληφθείσῃ ψυχῇ, ἵνα μή, ἐπὶ πλέον τῇ
ζωῇ ταύτῃ ἐπιβραδύνασα τῆς ἐμπολιτευομένης
τῷ βίῳ κακία ἀναπλησθῇ. εἰ μὲν γὰρ ἐν τῇ
ζωῇ ταύτῃ ἡ τῶν Χριστιανῶν ἐλπὶς περιώριστο,
εἰκότως χαλεπὸν ἂν ἐνομίσθη τὸ θᾶττον δια-
ζευχθῆναι τοῦ σώματος· εἰ δὲ ἀρχὴ τοῦ ἀληθινοῦ
βίου τοῖς κατὰ Θεὸν ζῶσίν ἐστι τὸ τῶν δεσμῶν
τούτων τῶν σωματικῶν τὴν ψυχὴν ἐκλυθῆναι, τί
λυπούμεθα, ὡς καὶ[3] οἱ μὴ ἔχοντες ἐλπίδα; παρακλήθητι οὖν μὴ ὑποπεσεῖν τοῖς πάθεσιν, ἀλλὰ
δεῖξαι ὅτι ὑπέρκεισαι καὶ ὑπερῆρας.

---

[1] αὐτοῖς add. editi antiqi.   [2] γιγνομένων E.
[3] καί om. E.

visit your August Reverence by letter, and to remind you that these afflictions do not come in vain to God's servants from the Lord who watches over us, but as a test of their genuine love for the God who created us. For as the toils of their contests bring athletes their crowns, so the test which comes to Christians through their tribulations leads them on to perfection, if with fitting patience in all thanksgiving we accept the Lord's dispensations.

By the goodness of God are all things disposed. Nothing that happens to us should be accepted as grievous, even if for the present it touches our weakness. For even if we are ignorant of the words according to which everything that happens is brought to us as a blessing from God, yet we should at least be convinced of this—that assuredly whatever happens is good, either for us through the reward won by our patience or for the soul which we have received, lest by tarrying longer in this world the soul be contaminated by the wickedness which inheres in human life. For if the hope of Christians were limited to this life, the early separation from the body would reasonably be thought hard; but if for those who live according to God the beginning of the true life is the release of the soul from these bodily bonds, why then are we sorrowful even as those who have no hope?[1] Therefore, I beg of you, do not succumb to your woes, but show that you stand above them and have transcended them.

---

[1] Cf. 1 Thess. 4, 12: οὐ θέλω δὲ ὑμᾶς ἀγνοεῖν, ἀδελφοί, περὶ τῶν κεκοιμημένων, ἵνα μὴ λυπῆσθε, καθὼς καὶ οἱ λοιποὶ οἱ μὴ ἔχοντες ἐλπίδα. "And we will not have you ignorant, brethren, concerning them that are asleep, that you be not sorrowful, even as others who have no hope."

CII

Σαταλεῦσι πολίταις

Ἐγὼ τάς τε ἰδίας ὑμῶν παρακλήσεις καὶ τὰς
τοῦ λαοῦ παντὸς δυσωπηθείς, καὶ ἐδεξάμην[1] τὴν
φροντίδα τῆς καθ᾽ ὑμᾶς ἐκκλησίας, καὶ ὑπε-
σχόμην ὑμῖν ἐνώπιον Κυρίου μηδὲν ἐλλείψειν τῶν
εἰς δύναμιν ἐμὴν ἡκόντων. διὸ ἠναγκάσθην, κατὰ
τὸ γεγραμμένον,[2] οἷον τῆς κόρης τοῦ ἐμοῦ ὀφθαλμοῦ ἄψασθαι. οὕτως τὸ ὑπέρβαλλον τῆς καθ᾽
ὑμᾶς τιμῆς οὐδενός μοι συνεχώρησεν εἰς μνήμην
ἐλθεῖν, οὐ συγγενείας, οὐ τῆς ἐκ παιδὸς συνηθείας
τῆς ὑπαρχούσης μοι πρὸς τὸν ἄνδρα, πρὸ τῶν
παρ᾽ ὑμῶν αἰτηθέντων· ἀλλὰ πάντων μὲν τῶν
ἰδίᾳ μοι ὑπαρχόντων πρὸς αὐτὸν εἰς οἰκειότητος
λόγον ἐπιλαθόμενος, μὴ ὑπολογισάμενος δὲ μηδὲ
τοῦ στεναγμοῦ τὸ πλῆθος, ὃ καταστενάξει μου
ὁ λαὸς ὁ τὴν προστασίαν αὐτοῦ ζημιωθείς, μὴ
πάσης αὐτοῦ τῆς συγγενείας τὸ δάκρυον, μὴ
μητρὸς αὐτοῦ γηραιᾶς καὶ ἐπὶ μόνῃ τῇ παρ᾽ αὐτοῦ
θεραπείᾳ σαλευούσης τὴν θλῖψιν εἰς καρδίαν
λαβών· πάντων ὁμοῦ τοιούτων ὄντων[3] καὶ τοσού-
των ἀλογήσας, ἑνὸς ἐγενόμην, τοῦ τὴν ὑμετέραν
ἐκκλησίαν κατακοσμῆσαι μὲν τῇ τοῦ τηλικούτου
ἀνδρὸς προστασίᾳ, βοηθῆσαι δὲ αὐτῇ ἐκ τῆς
χρονίας ἀπροστασίας εἰς γόνυ λοιπὸν κλιθείσῃ,

---

[1] κατεδεξάμην Harl.   [2] εἰρημένον Harl., Med.
[3] ἀλγεινῶν Med.

---

[1] Placed by the Benedictine edition in 372, but by Loofs
(20 f.) in 373. This letter concerns the appointment of a

LETTER CII

To the Citizens of Satala[1]

STIRRED to shame by your own pleadings as well as by those of all the laity, I have taken over the care of your church, and have promised you before the Lord to leave nothing undone which is within my power. Therefore, as it is written, I was forced to touch, as it were, the apple of my eye.[2] Thus my overwhelming respect for you has not permitted me to call to mind either ties of relationship or my intimacy with the man which dates from childhood, before what has been requested by you; but, forgetting all that passed privately between him and me in the nature of friendship, paying no heed to the multitude of lamentations which the people uttered against me when deprived of his rule, or to the tears of all his relatives, not taking to heart the affliction of his aged mother whose only anchor is his care of her; disregarding one and all the many and serious considerations of this sort, I became engrossed with but one concern—to adorn your church with the leadership of such a man, and to succour it, bowed to its knees as it was from the long lack of leadership, and standing in need

bishop for the see of Satala in the north-east of Armenia Minor.

[2] Cf. Zech. 2, 8: διότι τάδε λέγει Κύριος Παντοκράτωρ Ὀπίσω δόξης ἀπέσταλκέν με ἐπὶ τὰ ἔθνη τὰ σκυλεύσαντα ὑμᾶς, διότι ὁ ἁπτόμενος ὑμῶν ὡς ἁπτόμενος τῆς κόρης τοῦ ὀφθαλμοῦ αὐτοῦ. "For thus saith the Lord of hosts: After the glory he hath sent me to the nations that have robbed you: for he that toucheth you, toucheth the apple of my eye."

καὶ πολλῆς καὶ δυνατῆς χειραγωγίας εἰς τὸ
διαναστῆναι δεομένῃ.[1]

Τὰ μὲν οὖν ἡμέτερα τοιαῦτα. τὰ δὲ παρ' ὑμῶς
ἀπαιτοῦμεν λοιπὸν μὴ ἐλάττονα φανῆναι τὴν
ἡμετέρας ἐλπίδος καὶ τῶν ὑποσχέσεων ἃς πε-
ποιήμεθα τῷ ἀνδρί, ὅτι πρὸς οἰκείους καὶ φίλους
αὐτὸν ἐξεπέμψαμεν, ἑκάστου ὑμῶν ὑπερβαλέσθαι
τὸν ἕτερον ἐν τῇ περὶ τὸν ἄνδρα σπουδῇ καὶ
ἀγάπῃ προθυμουμένου. ὅπως οὖν ἐπιδείξησθε[2]
τὴν καλὴν ταύτην φιλοτιμίαν, καὶ τῷ ὑπερβάλ-
λοντι τῆς θεραπείας παρακαλέσητε αὐτοῦ τὴν
καρδίαν, ὥστε λήθην μὲν αὐτῷ ἐγγενέσθαι πατρίδος, λήθην δὲ συγγενῶν,[3] λήθην δὲ λαοῦ
τοσοῦτον ἐξηρτημένου τῆς προστασίας αὐτοῦ
ὅσον παιδίον νεαρὸν τῆς μητρῴας θηλῆς.

Προαπεστείλαμεν δὲ Νικίαν, ὥστε τὰ γενόμενα
φανερὰ καταστῆσαι τῇ τιμιότητι ὑμῶν, καὶ
προλαβόντας ὑμᾶς ἑορτάζειν καὶ εὐχαριστεῖν τῷ
Κυρίῳ τῷ δι' ἡμῶν[4] καταξιώσαντι τὴν εὐχὴν
ὑμῶν ἐκπληρωθῆναι.

CIII

Σαταλεῦσιν[5]

Ἤγαγεν εἰς ἔργον ὁ Κύριος τοῦ λαοῦ αὐτοῦ[6]
τὰ αἰτήματα, καὶ ἔδωκεν αὐτῷ διὰ τῆς ἡμετέρας
ταπεινώσεως ποιμένα ἄξιον μὲν τοῦ ὀνόματος,
καὶ οὐ κατὰ τοὺς πολλοὺς καπηλεύοντα τὸν

---

[1] δεομένης editi antiqi.   [2] ἐπιδείξεσθε editi antiqi.
[3] συγγενείας editi antiqi.   [4] ἡμᾶς editi antiqi.
[5] ἀνεπίγραφος ἐπὶ ἐκκλησίᾳ E.   [6] αὐτοῦ om. E.

of some great and powerful guidance to enable it to rise again.[1]

So much regarding ourselves. And now we beg you, on your part, not to fall short of our hopes, or of the assurances which we made the man, that you to whom we sent him are devoted friends, each one of you being eager to surpass the other in zeal for him and in love. Therefore see that you display that noble rivalry, and cheer his heart by the overwhelming force of your solicitude, that he may come to forget his fatherland, his relatives, and his people, who have been as dependent on his protection as is a young child on its mother's breast.

We have sent Nicias[2] on ahead to tell your honourable selves what has happened, and that you on receiving the news may hold festival and give thanks to the Lord who has seen fit through us to fulfil your prayer.

LETTER CIII

To the People of Satala[3]

The Lord has brought the prayers of His people to a fulfilment, and through our humble instrumentality has given them a shepherd worthy of the name, one who does not, like most men,

[1] The person Basil has in mind is Poemenius. Cf. Letter CXXII.
[2] Otherwise unknown.
[3] Of the same date as the preceding, and on the same general topic.

λόγον, δυνάμενον δὲ καὶ ὑμῖν[1] τοῖς τὴν ὀρθότητα
τοῦ κηρύγματος ἀγαπῶσι καὶ τὴν κατ᾽ ἐντολὰς[2]
τοῦ Κυρίου ζωὴν καταδεξαμένοις ἀρέσκειν καθ᾽
ὑπερβολὴν ἐν τῷ ὀνόματι[3] τοῦ Κυρίου τοῦ
πληρώσαντος αὐτὸν τῶν πνευματικῶν αὐτοῦ
χαρισμάτων.

CIV

Μοδέστῳ ὑπάρχῳ

Αὐτὸ τὸ γράφειν πρὸς ἄνδρα τοσοῦτον, κἂν
μηδεμία πρόφασις ἑτέρα προσῇ, μέγιστόν ἐστι
τῶν εἰς τιμὴν φερόντων τοῖς αἰσθανομένοις· διότι
αἱ πρὸς τοὺς παμπληθὲς[4] τῶν λοιπῶν ὑπερέ-
χοντας ὁμιλίαι μεγίστην τοῖς ἀξιουμένοις[5] περιφάνειαν προξενοῦσιν. ἐμοὶ δ᾽ ὑπὲρ πατρίδος
πάσης ἀγωνιῶντι ἀναγκαία πρὸς τὴν σὴν μεγαλόνοιαν ἡ ἔντευξις, ἧς ἱκετεύω πράως καὶ κατὰ τὸν
σεαυτοῦ τρόπον ἀνασχέσθαι, καὶ χεῖρα ὀρέξαι
τῇ πατρίδι ἡμῶν εἰς γόνυ ἤδη[6] κλιθείσῃ.[7] ἔστι
δὲ ὑπὲρ οὗ ἱκετεύομέν[8] σε τὸ πρᾶγμα τοιοῦτον.
Τοὺς τῷ Θεῷ ἡμῶν ἱερωμένους, πρεσβυτέρους

---

[1] ἡμῖν editi antiqi.   [2] ἐντολήν E.
[3] ῥήματι editi antiqi.   [4] παμπληθεῖς editi antiqi.
[5] τήν add. E.   [6] ἤδη om. E.
[7] ἐλθούσῃ editi antiqi.   [8] ἱκετεύωμεν E.

---

[1] Written in 372; on the taxation of the clergy. Modestus
was Prefect of the Praetorium, and a persecutor of Catholics
under Valens. At the command of Valens, he offered Basil
the choice between deposition and communion with the
Arians. Shortly after this, Modestus fell seriously ill, which

make traffic of the title, but who is capable in the extreme of satisfying you who love the orthodox doctrine and have accepted the life that is in accordance with the Lord's commands, in the name of the Lord who has filled him with His spiritual blessings.

LETTER CIV

To the Prefect Modestus[1]

The very act of writing to so great a man, even if there be no other excuse, is most conducive to honour in the eyes of the discerning; for intercourse with men who are overwhelmingly superior to the rest of mankind affords the greatest distinction to such as are deemed worthy of it. As for me, as I strive earnestly for my country as a whole, I must needs address to your Magnanimity this petition (which I entreat you to suffer calmly even according to your character), that you stretch forth a helping hand to our fatherland now bowed to its knees. And the matter regarding which we seek your help is this.

Those who are consecrated to our God, that is

he regarded as divine judgment for his insolence towards Basil. Modestus at once summoned the holy man to his sick bed, and, humbly begging pardon for his behaviour, commended himself to his prayers. Modestus soon recovered, which he attributed to Basil's intercessions, and he accordingly regarded him with the greatest reverence. Henceforth Basil's influence with Modestus was so great that he was constantly importuned for letters of favour to the Prefect. Six of these letters of St. Basil are extant: the present one, CX, CXI, CCLXXIX, CCLXXX, and CCLXXXI.

καὶ διακόνους, ὁ παλαιὸς κῆνσος ἀτελεῖς ἀφῆκεν.[1]
οἱ δὲ νῦν ἀπογραψάμενοι, ὡς οὐ λαβόντες παρὰ
τῆς ὑπερφυοῦς σου ἐξουσίας πρόσταγμα,[2] ἀπε-
γράψαντο, πλὴν εἰ μὴ πού τινες ἄλλως εἶχον
ὑπὸ τῆς ἡλικίας τὴν ἄφεσιν. δεόμεθα οὖν
μνημόσυνον τῆς σῆς εὐεργεσίας τοῦτο ἡμῖν ἀφεθῆναι,[3] παντὶ τῷ ἐπιόντι χρόνῳ ἀγαθὴν περὶ
σοῦ μνήμην διαφύλαττον, καὶ συγχωρηθῆναι κατὰ
τὸν παλαιὸν νόμον τῆς συντελείας τοὺς ἱερα-
τεύοντας·[4] καὶ μὴ εἰς πρόσωπον τῶν νῦν κατα-
λαμβανομένων γενέσθαι τὴν ἄφεσιν (οὕτω γὰρ
εἰς τοὺς διαδόχους ἡ χάρις μεταβήσεται, οὓς οὐ
πάντως συμβαίνει τοῦ ἱερατεύειν ἀξίους εἶναι),
ἀλλὰ κατὰ τὸν ἐν τῇ ἐλευθέρᾳ ἀπογραφῇ τύπον
κοινήν τινα συγχώρησιν κληρικῶν γενέσθαι, ὥστε
ὑπὸ τῶν οἰκονομούντων τὰς ἐκκλησίας τοῖς ἑκάστοτε λειτουργοῦσι τὴν ἀτέλειαν δίδοσθαι.

Ταῦτα καὶ τῇ σῇ μεγαλοφυΐα ἀθάνατον τὴν
ἐπὶ τοῖς ἀγαθοῖς δόξαν διαφυλάξει, καὶ τῷ
βασιλικῷ οἴκῳ πολλοὺς τοὺς ὑπερευχομένους
παρασκευάσει, καὶ αὐτοῖς τοῖς δημοσίοις μέγα
παρέξει ὄφελος, ἡμῶν οὐ πάντως τοῖς κληρικοῖς,
ἀλλὰ τοῖς ἀεὶ καταπονουμένοις τὴν ἀπὸ τῆς ἀτε-
λείας παραμυθίαν παρεχομένων· ὅπερ[5] οὖν καὶ
ἐπὶ τῆς ἐλευθερίας[6] ποιοῦμεν, ὡς ἔξεστι γνῶναι
τῷ βουλομένῳ.

---

[1] ἀφῆκαν editi antiqi.   [2] προστάματα E, Harl.
[3] ἐναφεθῆναι editi antiqi.
[4] τῆς . . . ἱερατεύοντας] τὴν συντελείαν τοῖς ἱερατεύουσι E.
[5] ὥσπερ editi antiqi.   [6] ἐλευθέρας E.

---

[1] The Benedictine edition notes that the words "presbyters
and deacons" are probably a marginal gloss, which crept

presbyters and deacons,[1] the earlier census left immune from taxation. But the present registrars, alleging that they had received no authorization from your high Lordship, have enrolled them, with the exception perhaps of some who are otherwise exempt because of old age. Therefore we ask that this exemption be granted us as a memorial of your beneficence, which will protect your good name for all future time, and that according to the old law those who act as priests be exempt from contribution, and that the exemption be not granted to the persons of those who now receive it (for in that case the favour would pass to their heirs, who might not be at all worthy of priestly duties), but that a general concession be granted the clergy according to the draft of the open register,[2] so that exemption may be given by those who regulate the affairs of the churches to such as on each occasion are in the service.

This will not only keep the glory of the good deeds of your great Lordship immortal, but it will also increase the number of those who pray for the Imperial house, and will confer a great benefit even upon the public revenues, since we give the relief which is derived from our immunity from taxation, not altogether to the clergy, but to those who are at any time in distress; indeed, this is just what we do when we are free to do so, as anyone who wishes may find out.

into the text early in the MSS. tradition, since all the MSS. seem to have it. Moreover, by ἱερωμένους and all cognate words Basil always means the whole clergy. Cf. Letter IV and note.

[2] Probably the public census list.

CV

Διακόνοις θυγατράσι Τερεντίου Κόμητος [1]

Ἐγὼ καὶ Σαμοσάτοις ἐπιστὰς προσεδόκησα
συντεύξασθαι τῇ κοσμιότητι ὑμῶν· καὶ ἐπειδὴ
διήμαρτον τῆς συντυχίας, οὐ μετρίως ἤνεγκα τὴν
ζημίαν, λογιζόμενος πότε εἴη ἢ ἐμοὶ δυνατὸν πάλιν
πλησιάσαι τοῖς καθ' ὑμᾶς χωρίοις ἢ [2] ὑμῖν [3]
αἱρετὸν τὴν ἡμετέραν καταλαβεῖν. ἀλλ' ἐκεῖνα
μὲν κείσθω ἐν τῷ θελήματι τοῦ Κυρίου.

Τὸ δὲ νῦν ἔχον, ἐπειδὴ εὗρον τὸν υἱὸν Σωφρόνιον
πρὸς ὑμᾶς ἐξορμῶντα, ἡδέως αὐτῷ τὴν ἐπιστολὴν
ἐπέθηκα [4] ταύτην, προσηγορίαν ὑμῖν κωμίζουσαν
καὶ τὴν ἡμετέραν γνώμην δηλοῦσαν, ὅτι οὐ
διαλιμπάνομεν τῇ τοῦ Θεοῦ χάριτι μεμνημένοι
ὑμῶν, καὶ εὐχαριστοῦντες ὑπὲρ ὑμῶν τῷ Κυρίῳ
ὅτι ἀγαθῆς ῥίζης ἀγαθὰ βλαστήματά ἐστε,
ἔγκαρπα τοῖς ἀγαθοῖς ἔργοις, καὶ τῷ ὄντι ὡς
κρίνα ἐν μέσῳ ἀκανθῶν. τὸ γὰρ ὑπὸ τοσαύτης
διαστροφῆς τῶν παραφθειρόντων τὸν λόγον τῆς
ἀληθείας περικυκλουμένας μὴ ἐνδοῦναι πρὸς τὰς
ἀπάτας, μηδὲ τὸ ἀποστολικὸν τῆς πίστεως
κήρυγμα καταλιπούσας πρὸς τὴν νῦν ἐπιπολά-
ζουσαν καινοτομίαν [5] μετατεθῆναι, πῶς οὐχὶ
μεγάλης μὲν πρὸς τὸν Θεὸν εὐχαριστίας ἄξιον,
μεγάλους δὲ ὑμῖν ἐπαίνους δικαιότατα προξενεῖ;

---

[1] Φερεντίου κόμητος editi antiqi.   περὶ πίστεως add. quidam
MSS.
[2] εἰ add. E.
[3] ἢ ὑμῖν] ἢ εἰ ὑμῖν editi antiqi.
[4] ἐπέδωκα editi antiqi.
[5] κενοφωνίαν E.

LETTER CV

To the Deaconesses, Daughters of Count Terentius [1]

When I visited Samosata I expected to meet your Modesties; and when I missed this meeting, I did not bear the disappointment lightly, wondering when it might either be possible for me to visit your country again or convenient for you to visit ours. However, let all this rest with the will of the Lord.

As to the present, when I found that my son Sophronius [2] was setting out in your direction, I gladly entrusted him with this letter, which conveys to you our greetings, and makes known our mind—that by God's grace we never cease to be mindful of you, and to thank the Lord for you that you are goodly scions of a goodly stock, fruitful in good works, and in very truth like lilies among thorns. [3] For that you have not given way to deceptions, surrounded as you are by the gross perversity of men who destroy the word of truth, and that you have not abandoned the apostolic proclamation of faith and gone over to the popular novelty of the day—does this not call for great thanksgiving to God, and does it not most justly bring you great commendation? You have

---

[1] Written in the autumn of 372. Cf. Loofs 33. For Count Terentius, cf. Letter XCIX and note.

[2] Perhaps the disciple of Eustathius, noted in Letter CXIX.

[3] Cf. Cant. 2, 2 : Ὡς κρίνον ἐν μέσῳ ἀκανθῶν, οὕτως ἡ πλησίον μοῦ ἀνὰ μέσον τῶν θυγατέρων. " As the lily among thorns, so is my love among the daughters."

εἰς Πατέρα καὶ Υἱὸν καὶ ἅγιον Πνεῦμα πεπιστεύ-
κατε· μὴ προδῶτε ταύτην τὴν παρακαταθήκην·
πατέρα τὴν πάντων ἀρχήν· Υἱὸν μονογενῆ, ἐξ
αὐτοῦ γεννηθέντα, ἀληθινὸν Θεόν, τέλειον ἐκ τε-
λείου, εἰκόνα ζῶσαν, ὅλον δεικνύντα ἐν ἑαυτῷ τὸν
Πατέρα· Πνεῦμα ἅγιον, ἐκ Θεοῦ τὴν ὕπαρξιν ἔχον,[1]
τὴν πηγὴν τῆς ἁγιότητος, δύναμιν ζωῆς παρεκτι-
κήν, χάριν τελειοποιόν, δι' οὗ υἱοθετεῖται ἄνθρωπος,
καὶ ἀπαθανατίζεται[2] τὸ θνητόν, συνημμένον Πατρὶ
καὶ Υἱῷ κατὰ πάντα ἐν δόξῃ καὶ[3] ἀϊδιότητι, ἐν
δυνάμει καὶ βασιλείᾳ, ἐν δεσποτείᾳ καὶ θεότητι,
ὡς καὶ ἡ τοῦ σωτηρίου βαπτίσματος παράδοσις
μαρτυρεῖ.

Οἱ δὲ κτίσμα λέγοντες ἢ τὸν Υἱὸν ἢ τὸ Πνεῦμα,
ἢ ὅλως αὐτὸ[4] εἰς τὴν λειτουργικὴν καὶ δουλικὴν
κατάγοντες τάξιν, μακράν εἰσι τῆς ἀληθείας, ὧν
φεύγειν προσήκει τὰς κοινωνίας καὶ ἐκτρέπεσθαι
τοὺς λόγους ὡς δηλητήρια ὄντα[5] ψυχῶν· ἐὰν δέ
ποτε δῷ[6] ἡμῖν ὁ Κύριος γενέσθαι κατὰ ταὐτόν,
πλατύτερον ὑμῖν τοὺς περὶ τῆς πίστεως ἐκθησό-
μεθα λόγους, ὥστε μετ' ἀποδείξεων γραφικῶν καὶ
τὸ τῆς ἀληθείας ἰσχυρὸν καὶ τὸ σαθρὸν τῆς
αἱρέσεως ὑμᾶς ἐπιγνῶναι.

CVI

Στρατιώτῃ

Ὑπὲρ πολλῶν ἔχοντες εὐχαριστεῖν τῷ Κυρίῳ,
ὧν καὶ ἠξιώθημεν παρ' αὐτοῦ ἐπὶ τῆς ἐπιδημίας

---

[1] ὕπαρξιν ἔχον] ὕπαρχον quidam MSS.
[2] ἐπαθανατίζεται editi antiqi.   [3] ἐν add. E.

believed in Father, Son, and Holy Ghost; do not prove false to this sacred trust: Father, the beginning of all things; only begotten Son, born from Him, true God, Perfect from Perfect, living image, displaying the Father entirely in Himself; Holy Spirit, with His subsistence from God, fount of Holiness, power that gives life, grace that gives perfection, whereby man is adopted, and the mortal made immortal, joined to the Father and the Son in every phase of glory and eternity, of power and royalty, of sovereignty and divinity, as even the tradition of the baptism of salvation doth testify.

Those who speak of the Son or the Spirit as a creature, or who in general place the Spirit in the category of servile and slavish things, are far from the truth, and we should avoid communion with these and turn away their words as being snares for the soul. But if ever the Lord grants that we be together again, we shall so set forth to you at greater length the doctrine of the Faith, that by proofs taken from Scripture you may recognize the strength of the truth and the rottenness of the heresy.

LETTER CVI

To a Soldier[1]

ALTHOUGH we can thank the Lord for many things of which in our travels we have been considered

[1] Written in 372.

ἡμῶν,[1] μέγιστον ἀγαθὸν ἐκρίναμεν τὴν γνῶσιν
τῆς σῆς τιμιότητος, τὴν παρὰ τοῦ ἀγαθοῦ Δεσπότου παρασχεθεῖσαν ἡμῖν. ἔγνωμεν γὰρ ἄνδρα
δεικνύντα, ὅτι καὶ ἐν τῷ στρατιωτικῷ βίῳ δυνατὸν
τῆς πρὸς Θεὸν ἀγάπης τὸ τέλειον διασῶσαι, καὶ
ὅτι οὐκ ἐν τῇ περιβολῇ τῆς ἐσθῆτος, ἀλλ᾽ ἐν τῇ
διαθέσει τῆς ψυχῆς ὁ Χριστιανὸς ὀφείλει χαρακ-
τηρίζεσθαι.

Καὶ τότε οὖν μετὰ πάσης ἐπιθυμίας συνετύγ-
χομέν σοι, καὶ νῦν, ὁσάκις ἂν εἰς μνήμην ἔλθωμεν,
μεγίστης ἀπολαύομεν εὐφροσύνης. ἀνδρίζου
τοίνυν, καὶ ἴσχυε, καὶ τὴν πρὸς Θεὸν ἀγάπην
τρέφειν καὶ πολυπλασιάζειν ἀεὶ σπούδαζε, ἵνα
σοι καὶ ἡ τῶν ἀγαθῶν παρ᾽ αὐτοῦ χορηγία ἐπὶ
μεῖζον προΐῃ. ὅτι δὲ καὶ ἡμῶν μέμνησαι, οὐδεμιᾶς ἑτέρας ἀποδείξεως προσδεόμεθα, τὴν ἐκ τῶν
πραγμάτων ἔχοντες μαρτυρίαν.

CVII

Ἰουλίττῃ ἐλευθέρᾳ

Πάνυ ἠθύμησα τοῖς γράμμασιν ἐντυχὼν τῆς
εὐγενείας σου, ὅτι σε πάλιν αἱ αὐταὶ περιέχουσιν
ἀνάγκαι. καὶ τί δεῖ ποιεῖν πρὸς ἀνθρώπους οὕτω
παλίμβολον[2] ἐπιδεικνυμένους τὸ ἦθος, καὶ ἄλλοτε
ἄλλα λέγοντας, καὶ ταῖς ἰδίαις ὁμολογίαις μὴ
ἐμμένοντας; εἰ γὰρ μετὰ τὰς ἐπ᾽[3] ἐμοῦ καὶ τοῦ

---

[1] ὑμῶν E.   [2] παλίμβουλον E.
[3] ἀπ᾽ editi antiqi.

---

[1] Written in 372. Julitta, a widow lady of Cappadocia, is
being harassed by the guardian of her heirs. Basil writes

worthy by Him, yet we have counted as the greatest blessing that acquaintance with your Honour which was granted us by the good Master. For we have come to know a man who proves that even in military life one may preserve the perfection of love for God, and that a Christian should be marked, not by the fashion of his clothing, but by the disposition of his soul.

Now at the time we were quite eager to meet you, and now, as often as we call you to memory, we experience the greatest pleasure. Therefore play the man, and be strong, and always strive to foster and increase your love of God, that the supply of the blessings He bestows upon you may grow greater and greater. Moreover, that you on your part are mindful of us we need no further proof, for we have the witness of your deeds.

LETTER CVII

To the Widow Julitta [1]

I was very angry when I read in the letter of your Nobility that the same difficulties again beset you. And how should we deal with men who display such perverse natures, and say one thing on one occasion and another on another, and never abide by their agreements? For if, after making such promises in the presence of myself and the ex-

this and the next two letters in an effort to relieve her of these troubles. Tillemont, though on insufficient grounds, is inclined to identify her with other widows (ἐλευθέραι), to whom Basil addressed letters.

ἀπὸ ὑπάρχων ὑποσχέσεις, νῦν, ὡς μηδενὸς εἰρη-
μένου, οὕτω στενοχωρεῖ τὴν προθεσμίαν, ἔοικε
παντελῶς ἀπηρυθριακέναι πρὸς ἡμᾶς ὁ ἀνήρ.

Πλὴν ἀλλ' ἐπέστειλα αὐτῷ, ἐντρέπων αὐτὸν
καὶ ὑπομιμνήσκων τῶν αὐτοῦ ὑποσχέσεων. ἐπέστειλα δὲ καὶ Ἑλλαδίῳ, τῷ οἰκείῳ τοῦ ὑπάρχου,
ἵνα δι' αὐτοῦ διδαχθῇ τὰ κατὰ σὲ ὁ ὕπαρχος.[1]
αὐτὸς γὰρ μέχρι τοσούτου θαρρῆσαι δικαστῇ
τοσούτῳ οὐκ ἐνόμισα ἐπίβαλλον[2] εἶναί μοι, διὰ
τὸ μηδέ πω περὶ ἰδιωτικοῦ πράγματος αὐτῷ
ἐπεσταλκέναι, καὶ ὑφορᾶσθαι κατάγνωσίν τινα,
ὡς οἶδας, εὐκόλως τῶν μεγάλων ἀνδρῶν ἀγριαι-
νόντων πρὸς τὰ τοιαῦτα· εἰ μέντοι τι ἔσται
ὄφελος, ἔσται τοῦτο διὰ Ἑλλαδίου, ἀνθρώπου
καὶ χρηστοῦ καὶ περὶ ἡμᾶς διακειμένου, καὶ Θεὸν
φοβουμένου, καὶ παρρησίαν ἀμύθητον ἔχοντος
πρὸς τὸν ἄρχοντα. δυνατὸς δὲ ὁ ἅγιος διαγαγεῖν[3]
σε πάσης θλίψεως, μόνον ἐὰν ἀληθινῇ καὶ γνησίᾳ
καρδίᾳ ἐπελπίσωμεν ἐπ' αὐτόν.

CVIII

Τῷ κηδεμόνι τῶν κληρονόμων Ἰουλίττης

Ἐθαύμασα ἀκούσας ὅτι, τῶν χρηστῶν ἐκείνων
καὶ πρεπόντων τῇ σῇ ἐλευθερίᾳ ὑποσχέσεων ἐπιλαθόμενος, νῦν σφοδροτάτην καὶ ἀπαραίτητον
ἐπάγεις τὴν ἀπαίτησιν τῇ ἀδελφῇ τῇδε· καὶ τί
εἰκάσω ἐκ τῶν λεγομένων οὐκ ἔχω. σοί τε γὰρ

---

[1] ἔπαρχος E.   [2] ἐπιβάλλειν E.
[3] διάγειν editio Paris.

prefects, the man now, as if nothing had been said, shortens the time of grace as you report, he seems to have utterly lost all sense of shame before us.

However, I did write to him, rebuking him and reminding him of his promises. And I wrote also to Helladius,[1] one of the Prefect's household, that the Prefect might be informed of your affairs through him. For I did not think that it was incumbent upon me to make bold to such an extent myself with so important an officer, because I had never written to him about a matter of private business, and I feared some censure—for, as you know, men of high station are easily incensed over such matters. If, however, there is to be any assistance forthcoming, it will be through Helladius, a good man, well disposed towards us, God-fearing, and enjoying untold freedom of speech with the Prefect. But the Holy One can guide you through every affliction, if only with a true and sincere heart we place our hopes in Him.

LETTER CVIII

To the Guardian of the Heirs of Julitta[2]

I have been surprised to hear that you, forgetting those excellent promises which were so becoming to your generosity, now place a very harsh and rigorous demand on this sister of ours; and I do not know what to think of these reports. For I am not only

---

[1] This Helladius, except for the present letter and Letter CIX, is unknown.

[2] Of the same date as the preceding and on the same general topic.

COLLECTED LETTERS OF SAINT BASIL

πολλὴν παρὰ τῶν πεπειραμένων σου μαρτυρου-
μένην ἐλευθερίαν σύνοιδα, καὶ τῶν ὑποσχέσεών
σου μέμνημαι ὧν ἐποίησας ἐπ’ ἐμοῦ καὶ τοῦδε,[1]
λέγων ἐλάττονα μὲν γράφειν χρόνον, πλείονα δὲ
συγχωρήσειν διὰ τὸ[2] βούλεσθαι συμπεριφέρεσθαι
τῇ ἀνάγκῃ τοῦ πράγματος, καὶ συγγνώμην παρέχειν τῇ ἐλευθέρᾳ ἀναγκαζομένῃ τοσοῦτον ἀθρόως
ἐκ τῆς οἰκίας προΐεσθαι χρῆμα.

Τίς οὖν ἡ αἰτία δι’ ἣν ἡ τοσαύτη μεταβολὴ
γέγονεν ἐγὼ νοεῖν οὐκ ἔχω. πλὴν ὅπερ ἂν ᾖ,
παρακαλῶ σε, μεμνημένον τῆς σεαυτοῦ ἐλευ-
θεριότητος καὶ πρὸς τὸν Κύριον ἀπιδόντα τὸν
ἀμειβόμενον τὰς χρηστὰς προαιρέσεις, δοῦναι τὸν
καιρὸν ὃν ἐξ ἀρχῆς ὑπέσχου τῆς ἀνέσεως, ἵνα
δυνηθῶσι συμπωλήσαντες τὰ ἑαυτῶν διαλῦσαι
τὸ χρέος. δῆλον δὲ ὅτι κἀκείνων μέμνημαι, ὅτι
ὑπέσχου, εἰ λάβοις τὸ ὁμολογηθὲν χρυσίον, πάντα
τὰ ὁμολογηθέντα χαρτία, καὶ τὰ ἐπὶ τῶν ἀρχόντων πραχθέντα καὶ τὰ ἰδιωτικῶς γενόμενα,[3] παρα-
δώσειν τῇ προειρημένῃ.

Παρακαλῶ οὖν, καὶ ἡμᾶς τίμησον καὶ κτῆσαι
παρὰ τῷ Κυρίῳ μεγάλην ἑαυτῷ εὐλογίαν, ἀνα-
μνησθεὶς τῶν σεαυτοῦ ὑποσχέσεων, γινώσκων ὅτι
ἄνθρωπος εἶ καὶ αὐτὸς[4] ἀναμένειν ὀφείλεις τοὺς
καιροὺς ἐν οἷς δεηθήσῃ τῆς παρὰ τοῦ Θεοῦ ἀντι-
λήψεως· ἣν μὴ ἀποκλείσῃς σεαυτῷ διὰ τῆς
παρούσης σκληρότητος, ἀλλ’ εὐτρέπισον τοὺς
οἰκτιρμοὺς τοῦ Θεοῦ ἐπὶ σαυτόν, πᾶσαν χρηστότητα
καὶ ἐπιείκειαν τοῖς καταπονουμένοις ἐπιδειξάμενος.

[1] καὶ τοῦδε] τοῦ δὲ λόγου conj. Combefisius.
[2] διὰ τὸ] δεῖ τῷ E, editi antiqi.
[3] γινόμενα editi antiqi.   [4] καί add. E.

acquainted with your great liberality, to which those who have experienced it bear witness, but I also remember the promises made by you in the presence of myself and this man;[1] for you said that, though you were naming a shorter time in writing, you would grant a longer term because you wished to meet the necessities of the case, and that you were showing indulgence to the widow in view of her being under the necessity of paying out so great a sum of money from her substance all at once.

Now what the cause is of this great change that has taken place in you I cannot understand. But whatever it is, I beg you, remembering your own generosity, and gazing upon the Lord who requites good resolutions, to grant the term of grace which you promised in the beginning, that they may be able to sell their property and discharge the debt. And it is evident that I remember this also very well—that you promised, if you should receive the sum agreed upon, to give back to the aforesaid widow all the stipulated documents, both those that were done in the presence of the magistrates and those that were executed privately.

Do you, accordingly, I pray, both honour us and obtain great praise for yourself with the Lord by being mindful of your promises, realizing that you are a man and must expect occasions when you will yourself need help from God; and do not exclude yourself from this help by persisting in your present severity, but make ready God's mercies for yourself by showing every kindness and clemency to those who are in distress.

[1] *i.e.* the ex-prefect.

CIX

Ἑλλαδίῳ Κόμητι

Πάνυ παραιτούμενος δι᾽ ὄχλου εἶναι τῇ χρηστό-
τητί σου διὰ τὸ μέγεθος τῆς περὶ ὑμᾶς ἀρχῆς, ἵνα
μὴ δόξω ἀμέτρως ἐμφορεῖσθαι τῆς φιλίας ὑμῶν,
ὅμως ὑπὸ τῶν ἀναγκῶν ἡσυχάζειν οὐκ ἐπιτρέ-
πομαι. τὴν γοῦν ἀδελφὴν τήνδε, καὶ πρὸς γένος
ἡμῖν οὖσαν καὶ διὰ χηρείαν καταπονουμένην καὶ
παιδὸς ὀρφανοῦ πράγματος[1] φροντίζουσαν, ἐπεὶ
εἶδον λοιπὸν ὑπὲρ δύναμιν ἀφορήτοις ἀνάγκαις
συνεχομένην, κατελεήσας καὶ παθὼν τὴν ψυχὴν
ἔσπευσα παρακαλέσαι σε, ἵνα, εἴ τις δύναμις, τῷ
ἀποσταλέντι παρ᾽ αὐτῆς ἀνθρώπῳ καταξιώσῃς
συμπρᾶξαι, πρὸς τὸ ὅπερ αὐτὴ παριοῦσα[2] ὑπέσχετο ὑφ᾽ ἡμῶν, ἤδη τοῦτο αὐτὴν ἀποδοῦσαν τῆς
εἰς τὸ πλέον ἐπηρείας ἀπαλλαγῆναι. ὑπέσχετο
γὰρ τὸ κεφάλαιον δοῦσα συγχωρεῖσθαι τοὺς
τόκους.

Νῦν τοίνυν οἱ φροντίζοντες αὐτῆς τῶν κληρο-
νόμων μετὰ τὸ κεφάλαιον καὶ τὴν τῶν τόκων
εἴσπραξιν ἐπιχειροῦσι ποιήσασθαι. ὡς οὖν εἰδὼς
ὅτι Κύριός ἐστιν ὁ τὰ τῶν χηρῶν καὶ ὀρφανῶν
ἰδιοποιούμενος, οὕτω σπούδασον χρήσασθαι ἑαυτὸν τῇ σπουδῇ τῇ ὑπὲρ τοῦ πράγματος ἐπ᾽ ἐλπίδι
τῆς παρ᾽ αὐτοῦ τοῦ Θεοῦ ἡμῶν μισθαποδοσίας.
οἶμαι γὰρ καὶ τὴν ἡμερότητα τοῦ θαυμασιωτάτου
ἐπάρχου[3] μαθοῦσαν ὅτι τὸ κεφάλαιον ἐκτέτισται,

---

[1] πραγμάτων E.
[2] παριοῦσα Bigot. alter secunda manu, περιοῦσα alii MSS. et
editi.   [3] ὑπάρχου conj. ed. Ben.

LETTER CIX

To Count Helladius [1]

ALTHOUGH I must earnestly beg pardon for troubling your Excellency in view of the magnitude of the office you hold, lest I shall seem to be making an immoderate use of your friendship, yet I am not permitted by my necessities to hold my peace. At any rate, when I beheld this sister (a relative of ours, suffering the affliction of widowhood, and anxious about the substance of her fatherless son)—when, I say, I beheld her beset beyond her strength with intolerable hardships, being filled with pity for her and sick at heart, I have hastened to urge you, if it is in any way possible, to deign to co-operate to this end with the messenger whom she has sent, that, namely, since this woman has already paid the amount she promised in person and in our presence, she may be freed from all further spiteful annoyance. For she promised to pay the principal on condition of being relieved of the interest.

Now, then, those who act as guardians of her heirs, the principal having been paid, are trying to exact payment of the interest also. Therefore, do you, as one who knows that the Lord makes the affairs of widows and orphans His own, yourself strive to employ all your zeal in this matter in the hope of the reward which our God Himself will give. For I think that our kind and most admirable Prefect, on learning that the principal has been paid, will

---

[1] On the same subject as the two preceding letters, and of the same time. Except for the present letter and Letter CVII, this Helladius is unknown.

209

συμπαθήσειν τῷ ἐλεεινῷ λοιπὸν καὶ ἀθλίῳ οἴκῳ
εἰς γόνυ κλιθέντι καὶ οὐκέτι ἀρκοῦντι ταῖς ἔξωθεν
αὐτῷ ἐπαγομέναις ἐπηρείαις. παρακαλῶ οὖν, καὶ
τῇ ἀνάγκῃ σύγγνωθι δι᾽ ἣν ὤχλησά[1] σοι, καὶ τῷ
πράγματι σύμπραξον κατὰ τὴν δύναμιν, ἣν ἔδωκέ
σοι ὁ Χριστὸς χρηστῷ καὶ ἀγαθῷ τὸν τρόπον
ὄντι, καὶ εἰς ἀγαθὸν οἷς ἔλαβες κεχρημένῳ.

CX

Μοδέστῳ ὑπάρχῳ

Ὅσης ἡμῖν τιμῆς καὶ παρρησίας μεταδίδως, τῇ
ἡμερότητι τοῦ τρόπου καταβαίνειν πρὸς ἡμᾶς ἀνε-
χόμενος, τοσαύτην σοι καὶ ἔτι πλείω ἐν παντὶ
τῷ βίῳ παρὰ τοῦ ἀγαθοῦ ἡμῶν Δεσπότου τὴν
αὔξησιν γενέσθαι[2] τῆς περιφανείας εὐχόμεθα.
ἐμὲ δὲ καὶ πάλαι ἐπιθυμοῦντα γράφειν καὶ ἀπολαύειν τῆς παρὰ σοῦ τιμῆς, κατεῖχεν ἡ πρὸς τὸ
ὑπερέχον αἰδώς, εὐλαβούμενον μήποτε νομισθῶ
ἀμέτρως ἐμφορεῖσθαι τῆς παρρησίας.

Νῦν δὲ ὁμοῦ μὲν καὶ τὸ λαβεῖν τὴν ἐξουσίαν[3]
τοῦ ἐπιστέλλειν παρὰ τῆς ἀπαραβλήτου σου
μεγαλοφυΐας, ὁμοῦ δὲ καὶ χρεία τῶν καταπονουμένων ἐξεβιάσατό με πρὸς τὸ θαρσεῖν. εἴ τις οὖν
καὶ παρὰ τῶν μικρῶν ἐπὶ τοῖς μεγίστοις[4] ἱκετηρίας
ἰσχύς, παρακλήθητι, θαυμασιώτατε, φιλανθρώπῳ
νεύματι ἐλεεινῇ ἀγροικίᾳ τὴν σωτηρίαν χαρίσας-

---

[1] ἠνόχλησα conj. ed. Ben.   [2] γεγενέσθαι E.
[3] Νῦν . . . ἐξουσίαν om. E.   [4] μεγάλοις E.

sympathize with this pitiful and wretched household,
which is now bowed to its knee and is no longer able
to cope with the spitefulness which is visited upon
it from the outside. Therefore, I entreat you (and
pardon the necessity which forces me to trouble you),
lend your assistance to this matter also according to
the power which Christ has given to you, who are
noble and of good character and have always
employed for a good end what you have received.

LETTER CX

To the Prefect Modestus [1]

What measure of honour and of frankness in
speech you bestow upon us, when in the kindness
of your heart you consent to condescend to us, may
that same measure and still more of enhancement of
your fame be given to you throughout your life by
our good Master, we pray. Although I have long
wished to write and to take advantage of the honour
you show me, yet respect for your higher station
restrained me, careful as I was lest I be thought to
avail myself unduly of the freedom you accord me.

But now two things—my having received permission from your incomparable Magnanimity to
write, and likewise the need of those who are in
distress—have constrained me to be bold. So if the
prayers of the small are of any avail with the great,
be pleased, most admirable Sir, by your benign assent
to bestow salvation upon a pitiful rustic people, and
give orders that the tax on iron be made tolerable

[1] Written in 372, on the tribute of iron paid at Mount
Taurus. On Modestus, cf. Letter CIV and note.

θαι, καὶ τοῖς τὸν Ταῦρον οἰκοῦσι τὸν σιδηροφόρον
φορητὴν προστάξαι γενέσθαι τὴν τοῦ σιδήρου
συντέλειαν, ὡς μὴ εἰς ἅπαξ αὐτοὺς ἐκτριβῆναι,
ἀλλὰ διαρκῆ αὐτῶν εἶναι τὴν ὑπηρεσίαν τοῖς
δημοσίοις· οὗ μάλιστα πάντων μέλειν τῇ ἀξια-
γάστῳ σου φιλανθρωπίᾳ πεπείσμεθα.

CXI

Μοδέστῳ ὑπάρχῳ

Ἄλλως μὲν οὐκ ἂν ἐθάρρησα δι᾽ ὄχλου γενέσθαι
τῇ μεγαλοφυΐᾳ σου, εἰδὼς καὶ ἐμαυτὸν μετρεῖν
καὶ τὰς ἐξουσίας γνωρίζειν. ἐπειδὴ δὲ εἶδον
ἄνδρα φίλον ἐναγωνίως διακείμενον ἐπὶ τῷ μετα-
κληθῆναι, ἀπετόλμησα αὐτῷ δοῦναι τὴν ἐπιστολὴν
ταύτην, ἵνα ἀνθ᾽ ἱκετηρίας[1] αὐτὴν προβαλλόμενος
τύχῃ τινὸς φιλανθρωπίας. πάντως δέ, εἰ καὶ
ἡμεῖς οὐδενὸς λόγου ἄξιοι, ἀλλ᾽ αὐτὸ τὸ μέτριον[2]
ἱκανὸν δυσωπῆσαι τὸν φιλανθρωπότατον τῶν
ὑπάρχων[3] καὶ ἡμῖν δοῦναι συγγνώμην, ἵνα, εἰ
μὲν μηδὲν πεπλημμέληται τῷ ἀνδρί, σωθῆναι
αὐτὸν δι᾽ αὐτὴν τὴν ἀλήθειαν, εἰ δὲ καὶ ἥμαρτεν,
ἀφεθῆναι αὐτῷ δι᾽ ἡμᾶς τοὺς ἱκετεύσαντας.

Οἷα δὲ τὰ ἐνταῦθα τῶν πραγμάτων ἐστί, τίς
μᾶλλον ἐπίσταται σοῦ, τοῦ καὶ ἐπιβλέποντος τὰ
παρ᾽ ἑκάστῳ[4] σαθρὰ καὶ τῇ θαυμασίᾳ προμηθείᾳ
τὰ πάντα διακρατοῦντος;

---

[1] ἱκεσίας Reg. uterque, Coisl. secundus.
[2] μέτρον editi antiqi.
[3] ἐπάρχων E, Med.
[4] ἑκάστου editi antiqi.

for the inhabitants of the iron-bearing Taurus, so that they may not be ruined once for all, but that their service to the treasury of the state may continue to be rendered—an object in which beyond all others we are convinced that your admirable Benevolence is concerned.

LETTER CXI

To the Prefect Modestus [1]

In other circumstances I should not have made bold to trouble your Excellency, knowing both how to measure my own importance and how to estimate the powers of others. But when I saw a friend in great distress of mind by reason of a summons, I ventured to give him this letter, that by casting it before you in lieu of the suppliant's token [2] he might obtain a measure of kindness. But in any case, even if we are of no account, yet our very restraint will suffice to placate the most kind-hearted of prefects and to secure us forgiveness, to the end that, if the man has done no wrong, he may be saved through the influence of the truth itself, but if he has indeed sinned, that his sin may be forgiven him through us who make supplication.

But as to our own situation here, who is better informed than you, who both observe what is corrupt in every man and by your wonderful forethought keep all things under your control?

[1] Of the same date as the preceding. For Modestus, cf. Letter CIV and note.
[2] An olive-branch held in the hands of a suppliant, as a symbol of his condition and claim.

CXII

Ἀνδρονίκῳ ἡγεμόνι [1]

Εἰ μὲν οὕτως εἶχον σώματος, ὥστε ῥαδίως ὑπομένειν ὁδοιπορίας δύνασθαι καὶ τὰ τοῦ χειμῶνος
δυσχερῆ φέρειν, οὐκ ἂν ἐπέστελλον, ἀλλ' αὐτὸς
παρὰ [2] τὴν σὴν μεγαλοψυχίαν ἐβάδιζον δυοῖν [3]
ἕνεκεν· τοῦ τε παλαιὸν [4] ὑποσχέσεως ἐκτῖσαι
χρέος (οἶδα γὰρ ὁμολογήσας παρέσεσθαι τῇ
Σεβαστείᾳ καὶ ἀπολαῦσαί [5] σου τῆς τελειότητος·
ὅπερ ἐποίησα μέν, διήμαρτον δὲ τῆς συντυχίας,
μικρὸν κατόπιν τῆς σῆς καλοκἀγαθίας παραγενό-
μενος), ἑτέρου δέ, τοῦ τὴν πρεσβείαν δι' ἐμαυτοῦ
πληρῶσαι, ἣν ἀποστεῖλαι [6] τέως ἀπώκνουν, μικρότερον ἐμαυτὸν κρίνων ἢ ὥστε τοιαύτης τυγχάνειν
χάριτος, καὶ ἅμα λογιζόμενος, ὅτι οὔτε ἄρχοντα [7]
οὔτε ἰδιώτην ὑπὲρ οὐδενὸς ἄν τις λέγων διὰ γραμμάτων πείσειεν οὕτως, ὡς αὐτὸς παρών, καὶ τὰ
μὲν ἀπολυόμενος [8] τῶν ἐγκλημάτων, τὰ δὲ ἱκε-
τεύων, τοῖς δὲ συγγνώμην παραιτούμενος ἔχειν·
ὧν οὐδὲν ἂν [9] ῥαδίως δι' ἐπιστολῆς γένοιτο. πᾶσιν
οὖν τούτοις ἐν ἀντιθείς, σὲ τὴν θείαν κεφαλήν,
καὶ ὅτι ἐξαρκέσει τὴν γνώμην ἐνδείξασθαί σοι,
ἣν περὶ τοῦ πράγματος ἔχομεν, τὰ δὲ λοιπὰ
προσθήσεις παρὰ σεαυτοῦ, [10] πρὸς τὴν ἐγχείρησιν
οὐκ ἀπώκνησα.

---

[1] ὑπὲρ τοῦ πρεσβυτέρου add. E.   πρὸ πρεσβυτέρου add. Vat.,
Med.
[2] πρός editi antiqi.   [3] δυαῖν E.   [4] παλαιᾶς E.
[5] ἀπολαύσειν editi antiqi.   [6] ὑποστῆναι E, editi antiqi.
[7] ἄρχονται E.   [8] ἀποδυόμενος E.   [9] ἄν om. E.

LETTER CXII

To Andronicus, General [1]

If I were strong enough in body to be able easily to endure travelling and to bear the hardships of winter, I should not now be writing to you, but should be proceeding to your Magnanimity in person with two purposes in view—to discharge the long-standing debt of a promise (for I know that I agreed to visit Sebasteia and enjoy the company of your Perfection; and I did go there, but missed meeting you, since I arrived a little too late for your noble self), and, secondly, to perform in person the mission which I have thus far hesitated to fulfil by a communication, since I judged myself too insignificant a person to obtain such a favour, and at the same time considered that no one in pleading another's cause could win over an official or a private citizen so well by stating his case in writing as by being present in person, orally disposing of some of his client's charges, pleading excuse for others, and asking pardon for the rest—none of which things could easily be done by letter. So, weighing against these disadvantages one single advantage—yourself, a god-like man—and considering that it will suffice to indicate to you the judgment we have concerning the affair, to which you will add out of your own knowledge what is lacking, I have not shrunk from making this attempt.

[1] Written in 372. Andronicus, to whom this letter is addressed, and Domitian, an offender, in whose behalf the letter is written, are otherwise unknown.

---

¹⁰ παρὰ σεαυτοῦ] παρ' ἑαυτοῦ E.

Ἀλλ' ὁρᾷς ὅπως κύκλῳ περίειμι ὀκνῶν καὶ
ἀναδυόμενος τὴν αἰτίαν ἐκφαίνειν ὑπὲρ ὧν ποιοῦμαι
τοὺς λόγους. Δομετιανὸς οὗτος ἐπιτήδειος ἡμῖν
ἐστὶν[1] ἐκ τῶν γονέων ἄνωθεν, ὥστε ἀδελφοῦ μηδ'
ὁτιοῦν διαφέρειν. τί γὰρ ἄν τις μὴ τἀληθῆ λέγοι ;
εἶτα τὴν αἰτίαν μαθόντες ἀφ' ἧς ταῦτα πέπονθεν,
ἄξιον εἶναι τοῦ παθεῖν οὕτως ἔφαμεν. μηδὲ[2] γὰρ
ἔστω μηδείς, ὃς μικρὸν ἢ μεῖζον εἰς τὴν σὴν
ἀρετὴν ἀμελήσας[3] τὴν τιμωρίαν ἐκφύγοι. ἀλλ'
ὁρῶντες τοῦτον περιδεῶς καὶ ἀδόξως ζῶντα, καὶ
ἐπὶ τῇ σῇ ψήφῳ κειμένην αὐτοῦ τὴν σωτηρίαν,
ἀρκοῦσαν αὐτὸν ἔχειν τὴν δίκην ἐκρίναμεν.
μεγαλόψυχόν τε ὁμοῦ καὶ φιλάνθρωπον διανοη-
θῆναί σε περὶ αὐτοῦ ἱκετεύομεν. τὸ μὲν γὰρ τοὺς
ἀντιτείνοντας ὑπὸ χεῖρα λαμβάνειν ἀνδρείου τε
καὶ ἄρχοντος ὡς ἀληθῶς, τὸ δὲ τοῖς ὑποπεπτωκόσι
χρηστὸν εἶναι καὶ πρᾶον μεγαλοφροσύνῃ πάντων
καὶ ἡμερότητι διαφέροντος. ὥστε ὑπάρξει σοι
βουληθέντι ἐν τῷ αὐτῷ τήν τε πρὸς τὸ ἀμύνασθαι
καὶ τὴν εἰς τὸ σώζειν, ὡς ἂν ἐθέλοις,[4] ἐπιδείξασθαι
μεγαλοψυχίαν. τοῦτο μέτρον ἀρκοῦν Δομετιανῷ
τῆς κολάσεως, τῶν προσδοκωμένων ὁ φόβος καὶ
ὧν ἄξιον οἶδεν ἑαυτὸν παθεῖν ὄντα. τούτοις
μηδὲν εἰς τιμωρίαν προσθεῖναι αὐτῷ ἱκετεύομεν.
καὶ γὰρ ἐκεῖνο σκόπει, ὅτι κύριοι μὲν τῶν ἠδικη-
κότων πολλοὶ τῶν πρότερον[5] ἤδη γεγόνασιν, ὧν
οὐδεὶς πρὸς τοὺς ὕστερον διεπέμφθη λόγος·
ἀφῆκαν δὲ τὴν ὀργὴν οἱ φιλοσοφίᾳ τοὺς πολλοὺς
ὑπεράραντες, ὧν ἀθάνατος ἡ μνήμη τῷ χρόνῳ[6]

[1] ἐστίν om. E. [2] μή E.
[3] ἁμαρτήσας editi antiqi. [4] ἐθέλῃς editi antiqi.
[5] προτέρων E.

216

But you see how I go about in a circle, hesitating and shrinking from making known the reason why I am writing this letter. This man Domitian is a friend of ours, as our parents were friends long before, so that he differs not at all from a brother. For why should one not tell the truth? Then on learning the reason why he is in his present plight, we declared that he deserved to suffer so. For let there be no man who, after slighting your Virtuous Self in any matter small or great, shall escape the penalty. But when we saw that this man lived in fear and ignominy, and that his salvation rested with your decision, we judged that he had received sufficient punishment; and we now beg you to consider his case with both magnanimity and kindness. For to keep the rebellious under one's hand is truly the part of a strong man and a ruler, but to be kind and gentle to the fallen is the mark of one who surpasses all men in magnanimity and kindness. And thus it will be within your power, if you so wish, to exhibit with the same person magnanimity both in exacting punishment and, as you would prefer, in granting succour. This is a sufficient measure of chastisement for Domitian—his fear of what lies in store for him, and of the punishment which he well knows he deserves to suffer. To all this we beg you to add nothing by way of vengeance. And consider this also, that there have been many among those who have gone before us who have exercised power over wrong-doers, of these no record has been passed on to posterity; but of those who, transcending the many through philosophy, have abated their wrath, an immortal remembrance has been handed down to

---

⁶ βίῳ Vat., Reg. secundus, Coisl. secundus.

παντὶ παραδέδοται. προσκείσθω δὲ καὶ τοῦτο
τοῖς περὶ σοῦ διηγήμασι. δὸς ἡμῖν, τοῖς ὑμνεῖν
προαιρουμένοις τὰ σά, τὰς[1] ἐν τοῖς ἄνω χρόνοις
ᾀδομένας[2] φιλανθρωπίας ὑπερβαλέσθαι. οὕτω
καὶ Κροῖσος τῷ παιδοφόνῳ τὴν ὀργὴν ἀφεῖναι
λέγεται, ἑαυτὸν παραδόντι εἰς τιμωρίαν· καὶ
Κῦρος ὁ μέγας αὐτῷ τούτῳ τῷ Κροίσῳ φίλος
γενέσθαι μετὰ τὴν νίκην. τούτοις σε συναριθ-
μήσομεν, καὶ, ὅση δύναμις ἡμετέρα, ταῦτα
ἀναγορεύσομεν, εἴπερ μὴ μικροί τινες εἶναι
παντάπασιν ἀνδρὸς τοσούτου κήρυκες νομισ-
θείημεν.

Ἐκεῖνο δὲ ἐπὶ πᾶσιν εἰπεῖν ἀναγκαῖον, ὅτι τοὺς
ὁτιοῦν ἀδικοῦντας οὐχ ὑπὲρ τῶν ἤδη γεγενημένων
κολάζομεν (τίς[3] γὰρ ἂν γένοιτο μηχανὴ μὴ γεγενῆσθαι τὰ πεπραγμένα ;), ἀλλ’ ὅπως ἂν ἢ αὐτοὶ
πρὸς τὸ λοιπὸν ἀμείνους γένοιντο, ἢ ἑτέροις
ὑπάρξειαν τοῦ σωφρονεῖν παράδειγμα.[4] τούτων
τοίνυν οὐθέτερον ἐνδεῖν[5] ἄν τις ἐν τῷ παρόντι
φήσειεν· αὐτός τε γὰρ καὶ μετὰ τὸν θάνατον
τούτων μεμνήσεται, τούς τε λοιποὺς τεθνάναι τῷ
δέει πρὸς τοῦτον ἀφορῶντας οἴομαι. ὥσθ’ ὅπερ
ἂν προσθῶμεν τῇ τιμωρίᾳ, τὴν ὀργὴν ἡμῶν αὐτῶν
ἀποπιμπλάναι δόξομεν· ὃ πολλοῦ δεῖν ἐπὶ σοῦ
ἀληθὲς εἶναι φαίην ἂν ἔγωγε, καὶ οὐδὲν ἂν τούτων
τῶν λόγων προήχθην εἰπεῖν, εἰ μὴ μείζονα τῷ
διδόντι τὴν χάριν ἐνεώρων ἢ τοῖς λαμβάνουσιν.
οὐδὲ γὰρ ὀλίγοις ἔσται καταφανὴς ἡ μεγαλοψυχία
τοῦ τρόπου. Καππαδόκαι γὰρ ἅπαντες ἀποσκο-
ποῦσι τὸ μέλλον, οἷς εὐξαίμην ἂν μετὰ τῶν

---

[1] τά E.   [2] ᾀδόμενα E.   [3] τί E.
[4] παραδείγματα Reg. uterque et Coisl. secundus.

all time. And let this also be added to the reports
about you.   Grant to us, who would fain hymn your
praises, to surpass the songs of good deeds sung in
previous ages.   Thus even Croesus[1] is said to have
abated his wrath against the slayer of his son who
had given himself up for punishment; and Cyrus
the Great is said to have become friendly to this
very Croesus[2] after his victory over him. With
these shall we number you, and with all our power
shall we proclaim these deeds, unless we be considered as an altogether too insignificant herald of
so great a man.

And this plea we must always utter on every
occasion, that we punish those who do any wrong,
not for what has already taken place (for what means
can there be of undoing what has been done?), but
that they may either become better themselves in
future, or may be an example to teach wisdom to
others.   So one might say that neither of these
conditions is lacking in the present case ; for Domitian
himself will remember these things even after his
death, and I imagine that his fellows are frightened
to death through looking at him. Thus if we add
anything to his punishment, we shall seem to be
glutting our own anger, which I would say is far
from being the truth in your case, and I could not
have induced myself to say any of these things, did
I not see that the reward is greater for him who
gives than for those who receive. For not to a
mere few will the magnanimity of your character
be known. For all the Cappadocians are regarding
the future, and it would be my prayer that they

---

[1] Cf. Herodotus 1, 45.   [2] Cf. Herodotus 1, 88.

COLLECTED LETTERS OF SAINT BASIL

λοιπῶν ἀγαθῶν τῶν προσόντων σοι καὶ ταύτην[1]
ἀπαριθμήσασθαι.

Ὀκνῶ δὲ τοῦ γράφειν παύσασθαι, ἡγούμενός
μοι ζημίαν οἴσειν τὸ παρεθέν. τοσοῦτόν γε μὴν
προσθήσω, ὅτι πολλῶν ἐπιστολὰς[2] ἔχων ἐξαιτου-
μένων αὐτὸν πασῶν ἡγήσατο προτιμοτέραν εἶναι
τὴν παρ' ἡμῶν, οὐκ οἶδά που[3] μαθὼν εἶναί τινα
ἡμῶν λόγον παρὰ τῇ σῇ τελειότητι. ὅπως οὖν
μήτε αὐτὸς ψευσθῇ τῶν ἐλπίδων, ἃς ἐφ' ἡμῖν
ἔσχε, καὶ ἡμῖν ὑπάρξῃ πρὸς τοὺς ἐνταῦθα σεμνο-
λογεῖσθαι, παρακέκλησο, δέσποτα ἀνυπέρβλητε,
ἐπινεῦσαι πρὸς τὴν αἴτησιν. πάντως δὲ οὐδενὸς
χεῖρον τῶν πώποτε φιλοσοφησάντων ἐπέσκεψαι
τὰ ἀνθρώπινα, καὶ οἶδας ὡς καλὸς θησαυρὸς πᾶσι
τοῖς δεομένοις ὑπουργεῖν προαποκείμενος.[4]

CXIII

Τοῖς ἐν Ταρσῷ πρεσβυτέροις

Συντυχὼν τῷδε, πολλὴν ἔσχον τῷ ἁγίῳ Θεῷ
τὴν χάριν, ὅτι με καὶ διὰ τῆς αὐτοῦ παρουσίας
ἀπὸ πολλῶν θλίψεων παρεμυθήσατο, καὶ τὴν
ὑμετέραν ἀγάπην ἐναργῶς ἔδειξε δι' αὐτοῦ.
σχεδὸν γὰρ τὸν πάντων ὑμῶν περὶ τὴν ἀλήθειαν
ζῆλον ἐν τῇ τοῦ ἑνὸς ἀνδρὸς προαιρέσει κατέμαθον.
ἃ μὲν οὖν τῇ ἰδίᾳ διελέχθημεν πρὸς ἀλλήλους αὐτὸς
ὑμῖν ἀπαγγελεῖ·[5] ἃ δὲ παρ' ἐμοῦ γνωρισθῆναι
ὑμῶν προσῆκε τῇ ἀγάπῃ, ταῦτά ἐστιν.

[1] τοῦτο editi antiqi.　　[2] ἐπιστολῶν E.
[3] οἶδά που] οἶδ' ὅπως editi antiqi.
[4] προαποκείμενός ἐστι editi antiqi.

might number this also with the rest of the virtues which you possess.

Yet I hesitate to cease writing, thinking that what has been omitted will cause me harm. So much at any rate I shall add, that although he had letters from many who were interceding for him, he considered the one from us to be more valuable than them all, having learned, I know not where, that a word from us was of weight with your Perfection. Therefore that he on his part may not be deceived in the hopes which he has placed in us, and that there may be for us some occasion for glorification before our people, be pleased, most illustrious master, to assent to our request. And assuredly you, no less than any of the philosophers of the past, have studied human life, and you know how goodly a treasure is laid up for all who help the needy.

LETTER CXIII

To the Presbyters at Tarsus [1]

ON meeting this man, I was very grateful to the Holy God, because by sending him to me after many afflictions He comforted me, and through him gave clear proof of your love. For I can almost say that in the purpose of this one man I learned the zeal for the truth which all of you possess. Now, what we discussed privately with one another he himself will report to you; but what your charity may fittingly learn from me is the following.

[1] Written in 372, and maintaining that the Nicene Creed alone should be required of the brethren.

---

[5] ἐπαγγελεῖ editi antiqi.

Ὁ καιρὸς πολλὴν ἔχει ῥοπὴν πρὸς καταστροφὴν
τῶν ἐκκλησιῶν, καὶ τοῦτο πολὺν ἔχομεν ἤδη
χρόνον ἐξ οὗ καταμανθάνομεν. οἰκοδομὴ δὲ Ἐκκλησίας, καὶ σφαλμάτων διόρθωσις, καὶ συμ-
πάθεια μὲν πρὸς τοὺς ἀσθενοῦντας ὑπερασπισμὸς
δὲ πρὸς τοὺς ὑγιαίνοντας τῶν ἀδελφῶν οὐδὲ εἷς.
ἀλλ' οὔτε βοήθημα ἢ θεραπευτικὸν [1] τῆς προ-
κατασχούσης νόσου, ἢ προφυλακτικὸν τῆς προσδοκωμένης οὐδέν. καὶ ὅλως ἔοικε λοιπὸν ἡ τῆς
Ἐκκλησίας κατάστασις (ἵνα ἐναργεῖ χρήσωμαι
τῷ ὑποδείγματι, κἂν εὐτελέστερον εἶναι δοκῇ)
ἱματίῳ παλαιῷ, ὑπὸ τῆς τυχούσης προφάσεως
ῥᾳδίως καταρρηγνυμένῳ, ὃ πρὸς τὴν ἐξ ἀρχῆς
ἰσχὺν ἐπανελθεῖν πάλιν ἀδυνατεῖ. ὡς οὖν ἐν
καιρῷ τοιούτῳ, μεγάλης χρεία τῆς σπουδῆς καὶ
πολλῆς τῆς ἐπιμελείας εὐεργετηθῆναί τι τὰς ἐκκλησίας. εὐεργεσία δέ ἐστιν ἑνωθῆναι τὰ τέως
διεσπασμένα.[2] ἕνωσις δ' ἂν γένοιτο, εἰ βουλη-
θείημεν, ἐν οἷς μηδὲν βλάπτομεν τὰς ψυχάς,
συμπεριενεχθῆναι τοῖς ἀσθενεστέροις.

Ἐπεὶ οὖν πολλὰ στόματα ἤνοικται κατὰ τοῦ
Πνεύματος τοῦ ἁγίου καὶ πολλαὶ γλῶσσαι
ἠκόνηνται εἰς τὴν κατ' αὐτοῦ βλασφημίαν,
ἀξιοῦμεν ὑμᾶς, ὅσον ἐστὶν ἐφ' ὑμῖν,[3] εἰς ὀλίγον
ἀριθμὸν περιστῆσαι τοὺς βλασφημοῦντας· καὶ
τοὺς μὴ λέγοντας κτίσμα τὸ Πνεῦμα τὸ ἅγιον
δέχεσθαι εἰς κοινωνίαν, ἵνα μόνοι καταλειφθῶσιν
οἱ βλάσφημοι, καὶ ἢ καταισχυνθέντες ἐπανέλθωσι
πρὸς τὴν ἀλήθειαν, ἢ ἐπιμένοντες τῇ ἁμαρτίᾳ
ἀναξιόπιστοι ὦσι διὰ τὴν ὀλιγότητα. μηδὲν

---

[1] προθεραπευτικόν Med.   [2] διεσπαρμένα duo MSS.

The spirit of the times is much inclined to the destruction of the churches, and it is now a long time since we have learned this. As for the establishment of the Church, the correction of errors, sympathy for the brethren who are weak and protection of those who are sound—of these things not one! Nay, there is neither remedy nor cure for the disease which is already upon us, nor means of precaution against that which we await. And, in short, the condition of the Church now (to use a vivid example, even if it seems to be rather mean) is like that of an old cloak, which, being easily torn by an ordinary strain, cannot be again restored to its original strength. In such times, therefore, as these there is need of great diligence and much care that the churches may be in some way benefited. And a benefit it is that the parts which have hitherto been broken apart be united again. And a union might be effected if we should be willing to show indulgence to the weaker, whenever we can do so without causing harm to souls.

Since, therefore, the mouths of many have been opened against the Spirit, and many tongues have been whetted to utter blasphemy against Him, we believe that you ought, in so far as it is in your power, to reduce the number of blasphemers to a small number; those who do not call the Holy Spirit a creature should be received in communion with you, that the blasphemers may be left alone, and either, being put to shame, may return to the truth, or, abiding in their error, may be considered unworthy of belief by reason of the smallness of their

---

[3] ἡμῖν editi antiqi.

τοίνυν πλέον ἐπιζητῶμεν, ἀλλὰ προτεινώμεθα
τοῖς βουλομένοις ἡμῖν συνάπτεσθαι ἀδελφοῖς
τὴν ἐν Νικαίᾳ πίστιν· κἂν ἐκείνῃ συνθῶνται,
ἐπερωτῶμεν καὶ τὸ μὴ δεῖν λέγεσθαι κτίσμα τὸ
Πνεῦμα τὸ ἅγιον, μηδὲ κοινωνικοὺς αὐτῶν εἶναι
τοὺς λέγοντας. πέρα δὲ τούτων [1] ἀξιῶ μηδὲν
ἐπιζητεῖσθαι παρ' ἡμῶν. πέπεισμαι γάρ, ὅτι τῇ
χρονιωτέρᾳ συνδιαγωγῇ καὶ τῇ ἀφιλονείκῳ συγ-
γυμνασίᾳ, καὶ εἴ τι δέοι πλέον προστεθῆναι εἰς
τράνωσιν, δώσει ὁ Κύριος ὁ πάντα συνεργῶν εἰς
ἀγαθὸν τοῖς ἀγαπῶσιν αὐτόν.

CXIV

Τοῖς ἐν Ταρσῷ περὶ Κυριακόν [2]

῞Οσον ἐστὶ τὸ τῆς εἰρήνης ἀγαθόν, τί χρὴ
λέγειν πρὸς ἄνδρας υἱοὺς τῆς εἰρήνης; ἐπεὶ οὖν
τὸ μέγα τοῦτο καὶ θαυμαστὸν καὶ πᾶσι περι-
σπούδαστον τοῖς ἀγαπῶσι τὸν Κύριον κινδυνεύει
λοιπὸν εἰς ὄνομα ψιλὸν περιστῆναι διὰ τὸ
πληθυνθῆναι τὴν ἀνομίαν, ψυγείσης λοιπὸν ἐν
τοῖς πολλοῖς τῆς ἀγάπης, οἶμαι προσήκειν μίαν
ταύτην εἶναι σπουδὴν τοῖς γνησίως καὶ ἀληθινῶς
δουλεύουσι τῷ Κυρίῳ, τὸ ἐπαναγαγεῖν πρὸς
ἕνωσιν τὰς ἐκκλησίας τὰς πολυμερῶς καὶ πολυ-

---

[1] πέρα δὲ τούτων . . . παρ' ἡμῶν] παρὰ δὲ τούτων . . . παρ'
ὑμῶν editi antiqi.
[2] τοῖς αὐτοῖς περὶ Κυριακὸν παραπλήσια editi antiqi.

---

[1] Cf. Rom. 8. 28: οἴδαμεν δὲ ὅτι τοῖς ἀγαπῶσι τὸν θεὸν πάντα
συνεργεῖ εἰς ἀγαθὸν τοῖς κατὰ πρόθεσιν κλητοῖς οὖσιν. "And
we know that to them that love God, all things work

number. Let us then seek nothing more, but merely propose the Creed of Nicaea to the brethren who wish to join us; and if they agree to this, let us demand also that the Holy Spirit shall not be called a creature, and that those who do so call Him shall not be communicants with them. But beyond these things I think nothing should be insisted upon by us. For I am convinced that by longer association together and by mutual experience without strife, even if there should be need of some addition being made for clarification, the Lord who worketh all things together unto good to such as love Him [1] will concede this.

LETTER CXIV

To Cyriacus and his Followers at Tarsus [2]

Why need I tell men who are the sons of peace how great is the blessing of peace? So, since this boon, great and wonderful and eagerly sought by all who love the Lord, is now in danger of being reduced to a mere name, "because iniquity hath abounded, the charity in many having now grown cold," [3] I think that those who really and truly labour for the Lord should have this one aim—to bring back into union the churches that have been severed from one another "at sundry times and in

together unto good, to such as, according to His purpose, are called to be saints."

[2] Written in 372, and, like the preceding letter, on the sufficiency of the Nicene Creed. The Cyriacus to whom this letter is addressed has not been identified.

[3] Cf. Matt. 24, 12: καὶ διὰ τὸ πληθυνθῆναι τὴν ἀνομίαν, ψυγήσεται ἡ ἀγάπη τῶν πολλῶν. "And because iniquity hath abounded, the charity of many shall grow cold."

τρόπως ἀπ᾽ ἀλλήλων διατμηθείσας. ὁ δὴ καὶ
αὐτὸς ἐπιχειρῶν ποιεῖν οὐκ ἂν δικαίως πολυ-
πράγμονος αἰτίαν λάβοιμι. οὐδὲν γὰρ οὕτως
ἴδιόν ἐστι Χριστιανοῦ ὡς τὸ εἰρηνοποιεῖν· διὸ καὶ
τὸν ἐπ᾽ αὐτῷ μισθὸν μέγιστον ἡμῖν ὁ Κύριος
ἐπηγγείλατο. συντυχὼν τοίνυν τοῖς ἀδελφοῖς
καὶ θεασάμενος αὐτῶν πολὺ μὲν τὸ φιλάδελφον
καὶ τὸ περὶ ὑμᾶς ἀγαπητικόν, πολλῷ δὲ ἔτι πλέον
τὸ φιλόχριστον[1] καὶ τὸ περὶ τὴν πίστιν ἀκριβές
τε καὶ εὔτονον, καὶ ὅτι πολλὴν ἀμφοτέρων ποιοῦν-
ται σπουδήν, τῆς τε ὑμετέρας ἀγάπης μὴ χω-
ρίζεσθαι καὶ τὴν ὑγιαίνουσαν πίστιν μὴ κατα-
προδοῦναι, ἀποδεξάμενος αὐτῶν τὴν ἀγαθὴν
προαίρεσιν ἐπιστέλλω τῇ σεμνότητι ὑμῶν, παρακαλῶν πάσῃ ἀγάπῃ ἔχειν αὐτοὺς ἡνωμένους
γνησίως καὶ πάσης ἐκκλησιαστικῆς φροντίδος
κοινωνούς· ἐγγυησάμενος καὶ αὐτοῖς τὴν ὑμετέραν
ὀρθότητα, ὅτι καὶ αὐτοὶ τῇ τοῦ Θεοῦ χάριτι τῷ
ὑπὲρ τῆς ἀληθείας ζήλῳ πρὸς πάντα ἐστὲ παρα-
τεταγμένοι, ὅσαπερ ἂν δέῃ[2] παθεῖν ὑπὲρ τοῦ
λόγου τῆς ἀληθείας.

Ἔστι δέ, ὡς ἐμαυτὸν πείθω, τὰ οὔτε ὑμῖν
ὑπεναντία, καὶ τοῖς προειρημένοις τῶν ἀδελφῶν
αὐτάρκη πρὸς πληροφορίαν, ταῦτα, ὁμολογεῖν
ὑμᾶς τὴν ὑπὸ τῶν πατέρων ἡμῶν ἐκτεθεῖσαν
πίστιν τῶν ἐν Νικαίᾳ ποτὲ συνελθόντων, καὶ
μηδεμίαν τῶν ἐκεῖ λέξεων ἀθετεῖν, ἀλλ᾽ εἰδέναι
ὅτι τριακόσιοι δέκα καὶ ὀκτώ, ἀφιλονείκως συνιόν-
τες, οὐκ ἄνευ τῆς τοῦ ἁγίου Πνεύματος ἐνεργείας

[1] φιλόχρηστον Ε. [2] δέοι editi antiqi.

[1] Cf. Heb. 1, 1: πολυμερῶς καὶ πολυτρόπως πάλαι ὁ Θεὸς

divers manners." [1] When I myself also attempt to
accomplish this result I could not justly be accused
of officiousness. For no activity is so peculiarly
Christian as making peace; wherefore the reward
for this which the Lord has promised us is the
highest. So, after meeting the brethren, and
observing how great is their brotherly love,[2] and their
affection towards you, and how much greater still is
their love for Christ and their strictness and vigour
in the faith, and seeing that they were very zealous
for two things—not to be separated from your
charity and not to betray the sound faith—
accepting their good purpose I am writing to your
August Reverence, urging with all charity that you
hold them truly united and sharing in all the
solicitude of the Church ; I have vouched to them
also for your orthodoxy, saying that you likewise, by
the grace of God, have in your zeal for the truth
made yourselves ready to suffer whatever may be
needful in behalf of the doctrine of truth.

The following conditions, I am convinced, are not
contrary to your own feelings, and are satisfactory
to the above-mentioned brothers by way of information—that you profess the faith as set forth by the
Fathers who once assembled at Nicaea, and deny no
one of the statements made there, but realize that
three hundred and eighteen, coming together without
strife, spoke not without the agency of the Holy

λαλήσας τοῖς πατράσιν ἐν τοῖς προφήταις. "God, who at
sundry times and in divers manners spoke in times past to
the fathers by the prophets."

[2] Cf. Matt. 5, 9 : μακάριοι οἱ εἰρηνοποιοὶ ὅτι αὐτοὶ υἱοὶ Θεοῦ
κληθήσονται. "Blessed are the peace-makers : for they shall
be called the children of God."

ἐφθέγξαντο· προσθεῖναι δὲ τῇ πίστει ἐκείνῃ καὶ
τὸ μὴ χρῆναι λέγειν κτίσμα τὸ Πνεῦμα τὸ ἅγιον,
μὴ μέντοι μηδὲ τοῖς λέγουσι κοινωνεῖν, ἵνα καθαρὰ
ᾖ τοῦ Θεοῦ ἡ Ἐκκλησία, μηδὲν ζιζάνιον ἑαυτῇ
παραμεμιγμένον ἔχουσα. ταύτης αὐτοῖς τῆς
πληροφορίας παρὰ τῆς εὐσπλαγχνίας ὑμῶν
προτεθείσης, καὶ αὐτοὶ πρέπουσαν ὑμῖν ὑποταγὴν
ἕτοιμοί εἰσι παρασχέσθαι. αὐτὸς γὰρ ἐγγυῶμαι
τὸ μέρος τῶν ἀδελφῶν, ὡς εἰς οὐδὲν ἀντεροῦσιν,
ἀλλὰ πᾶσαν ὑμῖν ἐπιδείξονται εὐταξίας ὑπερ-
βολήν, ἑνὸς τούτου αὐτοῖς τοῦ ἐπιζητουμένου παρ'
αὐτῶν ὑπὸ τῆς ὑμετέρας τελειότητος ἑτοίμως
παρασχεθέντος.

CXV

Σιμπλικίᾳ αἱρετικῇ [1]

Ἀβούλως οἱ ἄνθρωποι καὶ μισοῦσι τοὺς κρείτ-
τονας καὶ φιλοῦσι τοὺς χείρονας. διὸ δὴ καὶ

---

[1] Βασίλειος add. E.

---

[1] Written in 372 or 373. The tone of this letter is wholly
unworthy of St. Basil, and not at all like that of the other
letters. There is, however, no other reason for doubting its
authenticity. The circumstances which led to the writing of
this letter may be learned from Gregory Nazianzenus, Letter
XXXVIII. It seems that a certain church in Cappadocia,
long without a bishop, had elected a slave of a certain
Simplicia, a wealthy and generous lady but of suspected
orthodoxy. Basil and Gregory unwisely ordained the man
without the consent of her owner, who threatened Basil
with the vengeance of her slaves and eunuchs. In the
present letter, Basil replies to her threats. After Basil died,
she harassed Gregory in an effort to get the ordination annulled.
Cf. Maran, *Vita Basilii*, XXV. The Migne edition states
that the codex Caesareus LXVII contains the following
prefatory note for this letter:

Spirit; and that you add to the aforesaid Creed that one must not speak of the Holy Spirit as a creature, nor have communion with those who so speak of Him, in order that the Church of God may be pure, having no darnel mixed with it. When this assurance has been given them from the goodness of your heart, they in turn are ready to offer you fitting obedience. For I myself vouch to you in behalf of the brethren that they will offer no opposition, but will show you a full abundance of good discipline, provided that this one thing which is demanded by them be readily granted by your Perfection.

LETTER CXV

To the Heretic Simplicia [1]

Foolish it is for men both to hate their superiors and to love their inferiors. Wherefore I myself now

τοῦ αὐτοῦ ἐπιστολὴ πρὸς Σιμπλικίαν περὶ εὐνούχων αὐτῆς. αἱρετικὴ ἦν αὕτη. ἀρρωστήσαντος δὲ τοῦ μακαρίου Βασιλείου, καὶ εἰσιόντος ἔν τινι λουτρῷ λούσασθαι, ἡ αὐτὴ Σιμπλικία προστάττει εὐνούχοις καὶ κορασίοις ῥιφῆναι τὰ σάβανα αὐτοῦ ἔξω· καὶ παρευθὺς ἡ δικαία κρίσις τοῦ θεοῦ ἀνεῖλέ τινας ἐξ αὐτῶν· καὶ ἡ αὐτὴ Σιμπλικία ἔπεμψε χρήματα τῷ αὐτῷ μακαρίῳ Βασιλείῳ ἐξιλεουμένη τὸ πταῖσμα· ὁ δέ, μὴ δεξάμενος, ἔγραψεν αὐτῇ ταῦτα.

"Letter of the same to Simplicia, about her eunuchs. She was a heretic. Now when Basil was ill, and was entering a bath to wash, the same Simplicia ordered her eunuchs and maids to throw his towels outside; and straightway the just judgment of God destroyed some of them; and the same Simplicia sent money to the same blessed Basil to make amends for her insult; but he would not receive them and wrote this to her." The writer of this comment was evidently unacquainted with the letter of Gregory of Nazianzus quoted above.

229

COLLECTED LETTERS OF SAINT BASIL

αὐτὸς κατέχω τὴν γλῶτταν, σιωπῇ τῶν ἐμῶν
ὕβρεων πνίγων τὸν ὄνειδον. ἐγὼ δὲ μενῶ τὸν
ἄνωθεν δικαστήν, ὃς οἶδε πᾶσαν κακίαν ἐν τέλει
ἀμύνεσθαι. κἂν γὰρ ὑπὲρ ψάμμον ἐκχέῃ[1] τις
χρήματα, βλάπτει ψυχήν, πατήσας τὸ δίκαιον.
ἀεὶ γὰρ θυσίαν Θεός, οὐχ ὡς χρῄζων, οἶμαι, ζητεῖ,
ἀλλὰ θυσίαν πολυτελῆ τὴν εὐσεβῆ καὶ δικαίαν
γνώμην δεχόμενος. ὅταν δέ τις ἑαυτὸν παρα-
βαίνων πατῇ, κοινὰς λογίζεται τὰς εὐχάς.

Σαυτὴν οὖν τῆς ἐσχάτης ἡμέρας ὑπόμνησον,
καὶ ἡμᾶς, εἰ βούλει, μὴ δίδασκε. ἴσμεν σου
πλείονα, καὶ[2] ταῖς ἔνδοθεν ἀκάνθαις οὐ τοσοῦτον
συμπνιγόμεθα· οὔτε ἐν ὀλίγοις καλοῖς δεκα-
πλασίονα κακίαν ἐπιμίγνυμεν. ἐπήγειρας ἡμῖν
σαύρας τε καὶ φρύνους, ἐαρινὰ δῆθεν θηρία, πλὴν
ὅμως ἀκάθαρτα. ἀλλ' ἥξει πτερὸν[3] ἄνωθεν τὸ
ταῦτα νεμόμενον. ἐμοὶ γὰρ λόγος, οὐχ ὡς σὺ
νομίζεις, ἀλλ' ὡς οἶδε κρίνειν Θεός. εἰ δὲ καὶ
μαρτύρων χρεία, οὐ δοῦλοι στήσονται, οὐδὲ
εὐνούχων γένος ἄτιμον καὶ πανώλεθρον· τοῦτο δὴ
τοῦτο, ἄθηλυ, ἄνανδρον, γυναικομανές, ἐπίζηλον,
κακόμισθον, ὀξύθυμον, θηλυδριῶδες,[4] γαστρίδου-
λον, χρυσομανές, ἀπηνές, κλαυσίδειπνον, εὐμετά-
βλητον, ἀμετάδοτον, πάνδοχον, ἀπροσκορές, μανι-
κὸν καὶ ζηλότυπον· καὶ τί γὰρ ἔτι εἰπεῖν ; σὺν
αὐτῇ τῇ γενέσει σιδηροκατάδικον. πῶς οὖν
τούτων[5] γνώμη ὀρθή, ὧν καὶ οἱ πόδες στρεβλοί ;
οὗτοι σωφρονοῦσι μὲν ἄμισθα διὰ σιδήρου·
μαίνονται δὲ ἄκαρπα δι' οἰκείαν αἰσχρότητα.
οὐχ οὗτοι στήσονται τῆς κρίσεως μάρτυρες, ἀλλ'

---

[1] ἐκχέει editi antiqi. [2] ἐν add. E.
[3] πτηνόν Regius secundus et Coisl. secundus.
[4] θηλυδρῶδες E. [5] τούτῳ E.

230

check my tongue, by silence smothering the indignity of the insults offered me. But I shall await
the Judge above, who knows how in the end to
avenge all evil. For even if anyone pour out money
like sand, he but harms his soul, having trampled on
justice. For God always demands a sacrifice, not, I
think, because He needs it, but because He accepts
the pious and just mind as a costly sacrifice. But
when anyone by transgression tramples upon himself,
He considers his prayers profane.

Therefore be mindful of the last day, and, if you
please, do not try to teach us. We know more than
you, and are not so choked up within by thorns, nor
do we mingle a tenfold evil with a few virtues. You
have roused against us lizards and toads,[1] beasts of
spring forsooth, but nevertheless unclean. But there
will come a bird from above to feed on these. For
it matters to me, not how you think, but how God
knows how to judge. And if there be need also of
witnesses, slaves will not stand forth, nor any disreputable and utterly accursed race of eunuchs,—
yes, I mean just that—a race, neither feminine nor
masculine, woman-mad, envious, of evil wage, quick
to anger, effeminate, slaves to the belly, money-mad,
coarse, grumbling about their dinner, fickle, stingy,
ready to accept anything, disgusting, crazed, jealous
—and yet why say more?—at their very birth
doomed to the knife! How then can these possess
true judgment, whose very feet are twisted? They
are chaste without reward—thanks to the knife;
and they rave with passion without fruition—thanks
to their own lewdness. These will not stand as
witnesses at the judgment, but the eyes of just

---

[1] Apparently the slaves and eunuchs.

ὀφθαλμοὶ δικαίων, καὶ ὄψεις ἀνδρῶν τελείων· ὅσοι
τότε ὁρῶσι, πρὸς ἃ βλέποντες νῦν εἰσὶ συνέσει.

CXVI

Φιρμίνῳ

Καὶ σπάνιά σου τὰ γράμματα, καὶ μικρὰ
ταῦτα, ἢ ὄκνῳ τοῦ γράφειν, ἢ ἄλλως, τὸν ἐκ
τοῦ πλήθους κόρον διαφεύγειν οἰκονομοῦντος,
ἤπου καὶ πρὸς βραχυλογίαν ἑαυτὸν συνεθίζοντος.
ἡμῖν μέντοι οὐδὲν ἐξαρκεῖ, ἀλλὰ κἂν ὑπερβάλλῃ
τῷ πλήθει, τῆς ἐπιθυμίας ἐστὶν ἐλάττω διὰ τὸ
βούλεσθαι [1] ἕκαστα περὶ σοῦ μανθάνειν, πῶς μέν
σοι τὸ σῶμα ἔχει, ὅπως δέ σοι τὰ τῆς ἀσκήσεως,
καὶ πότερον ἐπιμένεις τοῖς ἐξ ἀρχῆς ἐγνωσμένοις
ἤ τι καὶ μετεβουλεύσω, πρὸς τὰ συμπίπτοντα
τὴν γνώμην μετατιθέμενος.[2]

Εἰ μὲν οὖν ὁ αὐτὸς διέμεινας [3] σεαυτῷ, οὐκ ἂν
πλῆθος γραμμάτων ἐπεζητοῦμεν, ἀλλ᾽ ἐξήρκει
ἡμῖν τοσοῦτον· ὁ δεῖνα τῷ δεῖνι· ὑγιαίνειν ἡμᾶς
ἴσθι, καὶ ἔρρωσο. ἐπεὶ δὲ ἀκούομεν ἃ [4] καὶ
λέγειν αἰσχυνόμεθα, καταλιπόντα σε τὴν τῶν
μακαρίων προγόνων τάξιν, ἐπὶ τὸν πρὸς πατρὸς
πάππον αὐτομολεῖν καὶ Βρεττάνιον σπουδάζειν
γενέσθαι ἀντὶ Φιρμίνου, ἐπιζητοῦμεν αὐτὰ ταῦτα

---

[1] πάνθ᾽ add. editi antiqi.   [2] μεταθέμενος editi antiqi.
[3] διέμενες Med.   [4] ἀκούομεν ἃ] τὰ ἀκουόμενα E.

---

[1] Written about 372. Firminus, his father of like name,
and his grandfather, Bretannius, are known only from this
letter. It seems that Firminus had at one time resolved to

men and the countenances of whole men—all who then see with their eyes that which they now gaze upon with their understanding.

LETTER CXVI

To Firminus [1]

YOUR letters are rare, and these brief, either through reluctance to write, or for some other reason—because you plan to avoid the satiety that comes from numbers, or perhaps are even accustoming yourself to brevity of speech. We, however, are not at all satisfied, but even if there is an exceedingly great number, it falls short of our desire because we wish to know everything about you—how your health is, how it is with your practice of asceticism, and whether you abide by your original determination, or have made some change, altering your purpose to suit the circumstances.

Now if you had remained consistent with yourself, we should not be asking for a great number of letters, but so much would be enough for us: "So-and-so to So-and-so; rest assured that we are well, and good health to you." But since we hear what we are ashamed even to mention,—that you, forsaking the ranks of your blessed forefathers, have deserted to your paternal grandfather and are ambitious to become a Bretannius rather than a Firminus, these

become an ascetic. Later, however, he abandoned asceticism and joined the army, intent upon a military career. Basil, on hearing this, wrote the present letter. He exhorts him to abandon army life and imitate his father, who distinguished himself in civic duties, rather than his grandfather, Bretannius, who won military fame.

ἀκοῦσαι,[1] καὶ τοὺς λογισμοὺς μαθεῖν καθ᾽ οὓς
ἐπὶ ταύτην ἐλθεῖν τοῦ βίου τὴν ὁδὸν ὑπήχθης.
ἀλλ᾽ ἐπειδὴ αὐτὸς ἀπεσιώπησας αἰδοῖ τοῦ βου-
λεύματος, ἡμεῖς σε παρακαλοῦμεν μήτε[2] βου-
λεύεσθαι αἰσχύνης ἄξια, καὶ εἴ τι[3] ὑπέδραμέ
σου τὸν νοῦν, ἀπελάσαντα τοῦτο τῆς διανοίας
σεαυτοῦ γενέσθαι πάλιν, καὶ μακρὰ χαίρειν
εἰπόντα στρατείᾳ καὶ ὅπλοις καὶ ταῖς ἐπὶ[4] στρατοπέδου ταλαιπωρίαις, καταλαβεῖν τὴν πατρίδα, ἀρκοῦν πρὸς ἀσφάλειαν βίου καὶ πρὸς
πᾶσαν περιφάνειαν τὸ ἐξίσου τοῖς προγόνοις
κρατῆσαι τῆς πόλεως ἡγησάμενον· ὅπερ ἀπόνως
σοι παραγενήσεσθαι πεπιστεύκαμεν, πρός τε τὴν
ἐκ φύσεως ἐπιτηδειότητα ἀφορῶντες καὶ πρὸς τὴν
ἐρημίαν τῶν ἐνισταμένων. εἴτε οὖν μὴ γέγονεν
ἐξ ἀρχῆς ἡ γνώμη, εἴτε γενομένη πάλιν ἐκβέ-
βληται, γνώρισον[5] ἡμῖν ἐν τάχει· εἰ δέ, ὃ μὴ
γένοιτο, τὰ αὐτὰ μένει βουλεύματα, αὐτάγγελτος
ἡμῖν ἡκέτω ἡ συμφορά· γραμμάτων δὲ οὐ
δεόμεθα.

CXVII

Ἀνεπίγραφος, ἐπὶ ἀσκήσει

Ἐγὼ καὶ ἄλλως ὀφείλεσθαι τῇ ὑμετέρᾳ τιμιότητι ἐμαυτὸν νομίζω, καὶ τὸ νῦν δὲ τοῦτο φρόν-

---

[1] παρὰ σοῦ add. editio Paris.   [2] μήποτε E.
[3] καί add. E.   [4] τοῦ add. E.
[5] δήλωσον editi antiqi.

---

[1] Written about 372. This is clearly the answer of

very things we want to hear from you, and to learn
the considerations that have influenced you to enter
upon this manner of life. But because you yourself
have been silent through shame of your plan, we
exhort you never to plan things which call for shame,
and if any such thing has entered your mind, to
expel it from your thoughts and regain the mastery
over yourself, and, bidding a long farewell to military
life and to arms and to the toils of the camp, to
return to your native country, since as regards
security of life and all glory it is enough to be the
ruler, like your forefathers, of your own city through
your leadership; and in this we are confident that
you can succeed without difficulty, as we observe,
not only the fitness for rule which nature has given
you but also the absence of opponents. Whether,
therefore, this has not been your intention from the
beginning, or, having once been in your mind, has
been rejected again, inform us at once; but if, on
the other hand (and may it not come to pass), your
plans remain the same, let the misfortune come to
us self-announced, and we need no letters.

LETTER CXVII

WITHOUT INSCRIPTION, ON ASCETICISM [1]

FOR other reasons I consider myself indebted to
your Honour, and now the present anxiety in which

Firminus to the preceding letter, and there appears no
reason for doubting its authenticity. This and all the other
unaddressed letters do not appear in MSS. of the Aa family,
but this is probably due to their having been unknown. Cf.
Bessières 156, 159, 160.

τισμα, ἐν ᾧ ἐσμέν, ἀναγκαίως ἡμᾶς ὑπευθύνους
ταῖς τῶν τοιούτων πραγμάτων ὑπηρεσίαις καθί-
στησι, κἂν οἱ τυχόντες ὦσιν[1] οἱ ἐπιτάττοντες,
μὴ ὅτι ὑμεῖς οἱ πολλοῖς δικαίοις καὶ ἄλλοις πρὸς
ἡμᾶς συναπτόμενοι. τὰ μὲν οὖν παρελθόντα εἰς
ἐξέτασιν ἀγαγεῖν οὐκ ἀναγκαῖον· ἐπεὶ ἐνῆν εἰπεῖν,
ὅτι ἡμεῖς ἐγενόμεθα ἑαυτοῖς τῶν[2] ταράχων αἴτιοι,
τῆς ἀγαθῆς ἐκείνης ἀσκήσεως καὶ μόνης ἀγούσης
πρὸς σωτηρίαν φιλονεικήσαντες ἀποστῆναι· διὸ
τάχα καὶ τῷ ταράχῳ τούτῳ εἰς πειρασμὸν
παρεδόθημεν.

Ἀλλ’ ἐκεῖνα μὲν γέγονε καὶ ὑπομνήσεως ἠξιώθη,
ὥστε μὴ δεύτερον ἡμᾶς τοῖς ὁμοίοις περιπεσεῖν.
τὰ δὲ ἐφεξῆς, πάνυ βούλομαι πληροφορεῖσθαί
σου τὴν εὐλάβειαν, ὅτι τοῦ Θεοῦ συγχωροῦντος
ῥᾶστα ἡμῖν προσχωρήσει, τοῦ πράγματος καὶ
ἐννόμου ὄντος καὶ οὐδὲν ἔχοντος βαρύ, καὶ τῶν
φίλων ἡμῶν πολλῶν[3] ἑτοίμως χαριζομένων, ὄντων
ἐν τῷ στρατοπέδῳ. τυπωθήσεται οὖν παρ’ ἡμῶν
δέησις, κατὰ τὴν ὁμοιότητα τοῦ προσδοθέντος
λιβέλλου τῷ βικαρίῳ, ἐν ᾗ ἐὰν μή τις γένηται
παρολκή, εὐθέως ἀποπεμψόμεθα τὴν ἐκ τοῦ
γράμματος[4] ἄδειαν παρεχόμενοι. πέπεισμαι δὲ

---

[1] εἰσίν E, editi antiqi. [2] τῶν om. E.
[3] πολλῶν om. Vat., Med. [4] πράγματος E.

---

[1] The civil government of the Empire was distributed into
thirteen dioceses. The first of these was subject to the
jurisdiction of the *court* of the East. The place of the
Augustal praefect of Egypt was no longer filled by a Roman

we find ourselves also of necessity places us under obligation for services in troubles of this kind, even if those who lay their commands upon us are ordinary persons and not, like yourself, men who are joined to us by many other just claims. Now it is not necessary to bring the past into review; for I might say that we were the cause of our own disturbances, since we strove to abandon that goodly practice of asceticism which alone leads to salvation; and so perhaps we were given over to this disturbance also by way of temptation.

But those matters are past, and have been considered worthy of mention only that we may not a second time fall into the same difficulties. As to the next step, however, I am quite anxious that your Reverence be informed that, God granting, it will easily turn out as we wish, the matter being lawful and involving no difficulty, and our friends at court, who are many, are glad to do us a favour. So a petition will be drawn up by us, modelled on the document that has been handed to the Vicar,[1] according to which, if there is no delay, we shall be quickly sent home by merely producing the permit based upon the writ.[2] And I am convinced that in

knight; but the name was retained. The eleven remaining dioceses—Asiana, Pontica, Thrace, Macedonia, Dacia, Pannonia or Western Illyricum, Italy, Africa, Gaul, Spain, and Britain—were governed by twelve *vicars* or *vice-prefects*.

[2] That a written discharge was necessary is plainly seen from Letter CXXIII of Gregory Nazianzenus, who thus addressed a certain Ellelichus: "Mamanta, the slave Reader, whose father was a soldier, was consecrated to God on account of his noble character. Give him to God and to us, but do not let him be numbered among vagabond soldiers. Give him his freedom in writing, so that he may not be threatened by others." Cf. Migne, Vol. 32, 534, note 99.

ἐν τοιούτοις μεῖζον τῶν βασιλικῶν προσταγμά-
των τὴν προαίρεσιν ἡμῶν ἰσχύειν, ἣν ἐὰν ἄτρεπτον
καὶ ἀκλινῆ ἐκ τοῦ κατὰ τὴν ἀκμὴν βίου ἐπιδει-
ξώμεθα, ἀνεπιχείρητος ἡμῖν καὶ ἄσυλος διὰ τῆς
τοῦ Θεοῦ βοηθείας τῆς παρθενίας ἡ φυλακὴ εἴη.

Τὸν δὲ ἐγχειρισθέντα ἡμῖν παρὰ σοῦ ἀδελφὸν
καὶ ἐθεασάμεθα ἡδέως, καὶ ἔχομεν ἐν τοῖς γνω-
ρίμοις, εὐχόμενοι ἄξιον εἶναι τοῦ Θεοῦ καὶ τῆς
σῆς μαρτυρίας.

CXVIII

Ἰοβίνῳ, ἐπισκόπῳ Πέρρης

Ἔχω σε χρεώστην ὀφλήματος ἀγαθοῦ. ἐδά-
νεισα γάρ σοι χρέος ἀγάπης, ὃ χρή με ἀπολαβεῖν
σὺν τόκῳ, ἐπειδὴ καὶ ὁ Κύριος ἡμῶν τὸ τοιοῦτον
εἶδος τῶν τόκων οὐ παραιτεῖται. ἀπόδος τοίνυν,
ὦ φίλη κεφαλή, ἐπιστὰς ἡμῶν τῇ πατρίδι. τοῦτο
μὲν οὖν ἐστιν αὐτὸ τὸ κεφάλαιον. τίς δὲ ἡ
προσθήκη; τὸ σὲ εἶναι τὸν παραγινόμενον, ἄνδρα
τοσοῦτον ἡμῶν διαφέροντα ὅσῳ[1] πατέρες εἰσὶ
βελτίους παίδων.

[1] ὅσον E.

such matters our principles are more powerful than
the royal mandates, and that if we show them to be
unswerving and without deviation from the very
highest life, with the help of God the keeping of our
celibacy would be unassailable and inviolate.

We were not only glad to see the brother whom
you entrusted to us, but we also count him among
our friends, praying that he may be worthy of God
and of your testimony.

LETTER CXVIII

To Jovinus, Bishop of Perrha [1]

I consider you a debtor for a goodly debt. For I
made you a loan, an obligation of love, which I ought
to get back with interest, since even our Lord does
not deprecate usury of this kind. Therefore, pay it
back, my dear friend, by a visit to our land. That
would be, to be sure, only the principal itself. But
what would be the increase? The fact that it is
you who pay the visit, a man so far superior to us
as parents are better than their children.

[1] Written at the end of 372, or at the beginning of 373.
This letter is an excellent example of the spirit of the Second
Sophistic period of Greek rhetoric. The entire letter is
a rather far-fetched metaphor. Basil has already visited
Jovinus, and his visit is compared to a loan out at interest.
That Jovinus repaid the visit we learn from Letter CXXVII.

The MSS. vary between Jovinus and Jobinus. Further-
more, all do not agree in qualifying Jovinus as Bishop of
Perrha. Some MSS. read Κέρρης, and others Πέργης. Tille-
mont and Maran, however, prefer the reading Πέρρης of six
MSS. (4 Vat. Reg., 2nd Coisl., and Paris). Perrha was in
Syria and not far from the seat of Eusebius of Samosata.

CXIX

Εὐσταθίῳ, ἐπισκόπῳ Σεβαστείας

Καὶ διὰ τοῦ αἰδεσιμωτάτου καὶ εὐλαβεστάτου
ἀδελφοῦ μου [1] Πέτρου προσφθέγγομαί σου τὴν
ἀγάπην,[2] παρακαλῶν σε ὡς διὰ πάσης προφάσεως
καὶ νῦν προσεύχεσθαι ὑπὲρ ἐμοῦ, ἵνα, μεταβαλ-
λόμενος [3] ἀπὸ τοῦ φευκτοῦ [4] τούτου καὶ βλαβεροῦ
τρόπου, γένωμαί ποτε ἄξιος τοῦ ὀνόματος τοῦ
Χριστοῦ. πάντως δέ, κἂν ἐγὼ μὴ λέγω, διαλεχ-
θήσεσθε πρὸς ἀλλήλους περὶ τῶν καθ᾽ ἡμᾶς, καὶ
γνωρίσει σοι τὴν ἀκρίβειαν τῶν πεπραγμένων,
ὥστε μὴ παραδεχθῆναι ἀβασανίστως τὰς πονηρὰς
καθ᾽ ἡμῶν ὑπονοίας, ἃς εἰκὸς κατασκευάζειν τοὺς
καὶ παρὰ τὸν τοῦ Θεοῦ φόβον καὶ παρὰ τὴν τῶν
ἀνθρώπων ὑπόληψιν εἰς ἡμᾶς ἐξυβρίσαντας. οἷα
γὰρ ἡμῖν ἐνεδείξατο ὁ γενναῖος Βασίλειος, ὃν
ἀντὶ φυλακτηρίου τῆς ἐμῆς ζωῆς παρὰ τῆς σῆς
εὐλαβείας ὑπεδεξάμην, ἐγὼ μὲν καὶ εἰπεῖν αἰσ-
χύνομαι· εἴσῃ δὲ τὰ καθ᾽ ἕκαστον παρὰ τοῦ
ἀδελφοῦ ἡμῶν διδαχθείς. καὶ τοῦτο λέγω οὐκ
ἐκεῖνον ἀμυνόμενος (εὔχομαι γὰρ αὐτῷ μὴ λογισ-

---

[1] μου om. E. [2] καί editi antiqi.
[3] μεταβαλόμενος E, Reg. secundus, Bigot. alter.
[4] ἀπευκτοῦ editi antiqi.

---

[1] Written at the end of 372 or beginning of 373. It deals
with the untrustworthiness of a certain Basil and Sophronius,
two henchmen of Eustathius, by whom they had been recommended to Basil. Eustathius was ruined by his love of
power and self-aggrandizement, which was probably the
source of his hypocrisy. Basil was loath to break with
Eustathius because of their mutual interest in asceticism,

LETTER CXIX

To Eustathius, Bishop of Sebaste [1]

I ADDRESS you, my dear friend, through my most
reverend and pious brother Peter,[2] urging you on
every occasion and especially now to pray for me,
that, being transformed from this present abhorrent
and harmful nature, I may one day become worthy
of the name of Christ. But assuredly, even if I do
not speak, you and he will converse with one another
about our affairs, and he will make known to you
every detail of what has happened, so that you may
not admit without investigation the base suspicions
against us, which these men are likely to trump up,
who, regardless of the fear of God or of our reputation among men, have heaped insults upon us.
For what sort of charges the noble [3] Basil has
brought against us, the man whom I received from
your Reverence as a guard of my life, I am indeed
ashamed to say; but you will know every detail on
being informed by our brother. And this I say, not
to avenge myself upon this Basil (for I pray that it

and for a long time was blind to Eustathius' duplicity and
Arian proclivities. As subsequent letters show, the present
letter records the first of a series of events that eventually
brought about a break between the two. Cf. Letter LXXXIX
(and note), which is also addressed to Eustathius. For
Eustathius' persistent heresy, cf. Letters CXXX, CCXXIII
and CCXLIV.

[2] The present letter and Letter CCIII, written to the
bishops of the Pontus, were carried by one named Peter,
whom St. Basil designates as brother. It is uncertain
whether this Peter is Basil's own brother or a spiritual
brother.

[3] Ironical. For this Basil, cf. note 1.

241

θῆναι παρὰ τοῦ Κυρίου), ἀλλὰ βεβαίαν μοι τὴν
παρὰ σοῦ ἀγάπην μεῖναι ἡμῖν διοικούμενος, ἣν
φοβοῦμαι μὴ διασαλεύσωσι ταῖς ὑπερβολαῖς τῶν
διαβολῶν, ἃς εἰκὸς αὐτοὺς κατασκευάσαι εἰς
ἀπολογίαν τοῦ πταίσματος. ὅπερ[1] δ' ἂν κατη-
γορήσωσιν ἡμῶν, ἐκεῖνο παρὰ τῆς σῆς ἀγχινοίας
ἐξεταζέσθωσαν, εἰ ἐνεκάλεσαν ἡμῖν, εἰ τὴν[2] διόρθωσιν τοῦ ἁμαρτήματος οὗ νῦν ἡμῖν ἐπάγουσιν
ἐπεζήτησαν, εἰ ὅλως φανερὰν ἑαυτῶν τὴν πρὸς
ἡμᾶς λύπην κατέστησαν. νῦν δέ, ἐν φαιδρῷ τῷ
προσώπῳ καὶ πεπλασμένοις[3] ἀγάπης ῥήμασιν
ἀμύθητόν τινα δόλου καὶ πικρίας βυθὸν τῇ ψυχῇ
συγκαλύπτοντες, διὰ τῆς ἀνελευθέρου φυγῆς[4]
ἐφανέρωσαν. ἐφ' ᾧ ὅσον μὲν ἡμῖν[5] ἐποιήσαντο
πένθος, ὅσον δὲ τὸν γέλωτα τοῖς ἀεὶ τὸν εὐλαβῆ
βίον ἐν τῇ ἀθλίᾳ ταύτῃ πόλει βδελυσσομένοις καὶ
τέχνην πρὸς τὸ πιστευθῆναι καὶ σχηματισμὸν
εἰς ἀπάτην τὸ πλάσμα τῆς σωφροσύνης[6] διαβε-
βαιουμένοις ἐπιτηδεύεσθαι, πάντως, κἂν ἡμεῖς
μὴ διηγησώμεθα, γνώριμον τῇ συνέσει σου. ὡς
μηδὲν ἐπιτήδευμα οὕτως ὕποπτον εἶναι πρὸς
κακίαν λοιπὸν τοῖς ἐνταῦθα, ὡς τὸ ἐπάγγελμα
τοῦ ἀσκητικοῦ βίου.

Ἃ πῶς χρὴ[7] θεραπευθῆναι, τῆς σῆς ἂν εἴη
συνέσεως φροντίσαι.[8] τὰ γὰρ παρὰ Σωφρονίου
συρραπτόμενα[9] ἐγκλήματα ἡμῖν οὐκ ἀγαθῶν
ἐστι προοίμια, ἀλλ' ἀρχὴ διαιρέσεως καὶ χωρισ-

---

[1] οὗπερ Medicaeus, Regius primus, Bigot. alter.
[2] εἰ τὴν . . . εἰ ὅλως] τὴν . . . ἢ ὅλως editi antiqi.
[3] τετιμημένοις tres MSS.   [4] σιωπῆς E, editi antiqi.
[5] ἡμῖν . . . δέ] προξενοῦμεν E.
[6] ταπεινοφροσύνης E, Harl., Reg. secundus.
[7] ἃ πῶς] ὅπως οὖν E, editi antiqi.

may not be laid to his account by our Lord), but to
make sure that your love for me shall abide steadfast, since I fear that these men may shake it by the
exaggerated slanders which they have probably
trumped up in defence of their error. But whatever
accusation these persons may bring against us, let
them be examined by you with all your acumen as to
this--first, whether they have brought a formal complaint against us, secondly, whether they have sought
the rectification of the error for which they now attack
us, and, finally, whether they have made their grievance against us entirely clear. But as the case now
stands, though they conceal within their souls, under
their beaming countenances and their counterfeit
expressions of affection, a depth of treachery and
bitterness that defies description, yet through their
ignoble flight they have made their grievance manifest. How much sorrow they have brought upon us
in this matter, and how much occasion for ridicule
they have furnished to those in this unhappy city
who constantly express their contempt for the pious
life and assert that our pretended practice of
chastity is but a trick to get ourselves trusted and
a pose intended to deceive, assuredly all this, even if
we refrain from stating it, is well known to your
sagacity; and the result is that no mode of life is so
suspected as vicious by the people here as is the profession of asceticism.

How these things should be remedied would be
the proper concern of your sagacity to devise. For
the charges concocted against us by Sophronius are
not a prelude of good things, but a beginning of

---

8 φροντίς Vat.; καὶ φροντίδος tres alii MSS.
9 συνερραμμένα editi antiqi.

μοῦ καὶ σπουδῇ τοῦ καὶ τὴν ἐν ἡμῖν ἀγάπην
ἀποψυγῆναι. ὃν ὑπὸ τῆς σῆς εὐσπλαγχνίας
παρακαλοῦμεν κατασχεθῆναι ἀπὸ τῆς βλαβερᾶς
ταύτης ὁρμῆς, καὶ πειραθῆναι τῇ παρ' ἑαυτοῦ
ἀγάπῃ κατασφίγγειν μᾶλλον τὰ διστάμενα καὶ
μὴ[1] τοῖς πρὸς διάστασιν[2] ὡρμημένοις συνεπι-
τείνειν τὸν χωρισμόν.

CXX

Μελετίῳ, ἐπισκόπῳ Ἀντιοχείας

Γράμματα ἐδεξάμην παρὰ τοῦ θεοφιλεστάτου
ἐπισκόπου Εὐσεβίου, προστάσσοντα πάλιν γρα-
φῆναι τοῖς δυτικοῖς περί τινων ἐκκλησιαστικῶν.
καὶ ἐβουλήθη παρ' ἡμῶν τυπωθῆναι τὴν ἐπιστολὴν ὑπογραφῆναι δὲ παρὰ πάντων τῶν[3]
κοινωνικῶν. ἐπεὶ οὖν οὐχ εὗρον ὅπως ἐπιστείλω
περὶ ὧν ἐπέταξε, παρέπεμψα τὸ ὑπομνηστικὸν
τῇ θεοσεβείᾳ σου, ἵνα καὶ αὐτῷ ἐντυχὼν καὶ
τοῖς ἀναφερομένοις παρὰ τοῦ ποθεινοτάτου ἀδελ-

---

[1] καὶ μὴ] ἤ E.   [2] τὸ διαστασιάζειν editi antiqi.
[3] τῶν om. E.

---

[1] Probably written in A.D. 372. Letters CXX, CXXI,
CXXII, CXXIX, and CXXX are all related in the matter
of chronology. Tillemont and the Benedictine editors agree
in the actual dating, although they differ in the identity of
certain persons. Loofs (p. 29), in treating of these letters,

division and separation and an incentive to the cooling even of the charity within us. We urge that this man be restrained by your kindness of heart from this hurtful impulse of his, and that your affection rather strive to tighten that which is falling apart and not to increase the tendency to schism in those who are eager for disagreement.

LETTER CXX

To Meletius, Bishop of Antioch [1]

I HAVE received a letter from the most God-beloved bishop Eusebius, enjoining that we write again to the Westerners concerning certain ecclesiastical affairs. He wished, furthermore, that the letter be drawn up by us but signed by all those in communion. Since, therefore, I have not discovered how to write about those things which he has enjoined, I am sending his memorandum to your Godliness in order that when you have read it and given heed to the matters reported by our most

raises questions which he does not himself answer satisfactorily. Indeed in several places his arrangement seems to be contradicted by certain facts contained in the letters themselves. I have retained the chronology of Tillemont and the Benedictines.

For the identity of Meletius, cf. Letter LXVI, note 4. Previous letters addressed to Meletius are LVII, LXVIII, and LXXXIX. In this letter Basil continues his support of the claims of Meletius, now exiled in Armenia, as the regular Catholic bishop of Antioch, and he complains of the irregular ordination of Faustus as bishop of an Armenian see by Anthimus of Tyana, one of his opponents.

φοῦ Σαγκτισσίμου τοῦ συμπρεσβυτέρου προσέ-
χων,[1] αὐτὸς καταξιώσῃς ὡς παρίσταταί σοι[2]
περὶ τούτων τυπῶσαι, ἡμῶν ἑτοίμως ἐχόντων
καὶ[3] αὐτῷ συνθέσθαι καὶ ταχέως ποιῆσαι περι-
κομισθῆναι[4] τοῖς κοινωνικοῖς, ὥστε τὰς πάντων
ὑπογραφὰς ἔχοντα ἀπελθεῖν τὸν μέλλοντα ὁρμᾶν
πρὸς τοὺς κατὰ τὴν δύσιν ἐπισκόπους. ταχέως[5]
ἡμῖν τὸ παριστάμενον τῇ ὁσιότητί σου γνωρισθῆναι κέλευσον, ἵνα μὴ ἀγνοῶμεν τὰ δόξαντά
σοι.

Περὶ δὲ τῶν τυρευομένων[6] ἢ καὶ ἤδη ἐσκευωρη-
μένων καθ᾽ ἡμῶν ἐν τῇ Ἀντιοχείᾳ ἀνοίσει[7] ὁ
αὐτὸς ἀδελφὸς τῇ τιμιότητί σου, ἐάν περ μὴ
προλαβοῦσα ἡ φήμη τῶν γενομένων φανερὰ
ποιήσῃ τὰ πεπραγμένα. καὶ γὰρ ἐγγύς ἐστιν
ἡ ἐλπὶς τῆς ἐκβάσεως τῶν ἀπειλουμένων.
γινώσκειν δὲ βούλομαι τὴν εὐλάβειάν σου, ὅτι
ὁ ἀδελφὸς Ἄνθιμος Φαῦστον, τὸν συνόντα τῷ

---

[1] προσχών E.
[2] παρίσταταί σοι] καταξιώσαις editi antiqi.
[3] σοι add. editi antiqi.   [4] παρακομισθῆναι E.
[5] οὖν add. editi antiqi.   [6] πορευομένων alii editi.
[7] ἀνύσει E, Med., Reg. secundus.

---

[1] Tillemont argues that Sanctissimus because of his Latin
name was a priest from the West. The Benedictine editor,
however, prefers to consider him a presbyter of Antioch,
since Roman names were at this time quite commonly given

beloved brother Sanctissimus,[1] our presbyter, you
may yourself deign to write as seems best to you
about these affairs; for we are ready both to agree to
this and to cause it to be sent quickly around to
those in communion with us, so that the messenger
who is about to set out to visit the bishops of the
West may have the signatures of all when he departs.
Order whatever seems best to your Holiness to be
quickly made known to me, in order that we may not
be ignorant of your decisions.

And as regards what is being devised or even
what has already been fabricated against us at
Antioch, the same brother will inform your Honour,
unless previously the report of what has happened
shall have made clear what has been done. For in
truth hope is at hand that these threats will pass
away. But I wish your Reverence to know that our
brother Anthimus [2] has ordained and made a bishop

to Greeks. The latter seems correct, because Sanctissimus
displays unusual interest in Eastern affairs, and Basil calls
him his " most beloved," and " fellow-presbyter," and sends
him on several important missions. The following is a
chronology of his known journeys :

374. The Easterners send Sanctissimus and Dorotheus to
the West in the early spring.

375. Sanctissimus and Dorotheus return to the East through
Thrace. They probably visit Eusebius of Samosata, who was
exiled to Thrace in 374.

376. Sanctissimus makes an extensive tour of the East.

377. The Easterners communicate with the Westerners
through Sanctissimus to procure the condemnation of
Apollinarius and Eustathius.

[2] In 371 Anthimus, a contentious and ambitious prelate,
claimed to be metropolitan of Cappadocia Secunda with his
diocese Tyana as a metropolitan see. He was joined by
those prelates who opposed Basil's election to the see of
Caesarea.

πάπα,¹ ἐπίσκοπον ἐχειροτόνησε, μηδὲ ψήφους
δεξάμενος, καὶ τῷ τόπῳ χειροτονήσας ² τοῦ αἰδεσιμωτάτου ἀδελφοῦ Κυρίλλου· ὥστε στάσεων
ἐμπλῆσαι τὴν Ἀρμενίαν. ἵνα ³ τοίνυν μὴ κατα-
ψεύσωνται ἡμῶν,⁴ μηδὲ αὐτοὶ τὴν αἰτίαν σχῶμεν
τῆς ἀταξίας τῶν γενομένων, ἐγνώρισα ταῦτα τῇ
σεμνότητί σου. δῆλον δέ, ὡς καὶ αὐτὸς καταξιώσεις γνώριμα ποιῆσαι τοῖς λοιποῖς. ἡγοῦμαι
γὰρ πολλοὺς λυπήσειν τὴν ἀταξίαν ταύτην.

CXXI

Θεοδότῳ, ἐπισκόπῳ Νικοπόλεως ⁵

Πολὺς ὁ χειμὼν καὶ ἐπὶ τὸ μακρότατον παρα-
ταθείς, ὡς μηδὲ τὰς διὰ γραμμάτων παραμυθίας
ῥᾳδίως ἡμῖν ὑπάρχειν. ὅθεν ὀλιγάκις οἶδα καὶ
ἐπιστείλας τῇ εὐλαβείᾳ σου καὶ δεξάμενος γράμματα. ἀλλ᾽ ἐπειδὴ ὁ ποθεινότατος ἀδελφὸς ἡμῶν

¹ πάππῳ Coisl. secundus, Reg. secundus.
² τῷ τόπῳ χειροτονήσας . . . ἐμπλῆσαι] καταχειροτονήσας
. . . ἐμπληρῶσαι editi antiqi.
³ ὅρα editi antiqi. ⁴ ὑμῶν E.
⁵ Ἀρμενίας add. Harl. Ἀρμενίας μικρᾶς add. editi antiqi,
nonnulli MSS.

---

[1] All information about Faustus is procured from Letters
CXX, CXXI, and CXXII of St. Basil. Smith and Wace
infer that he was Bishop of Satala, but Tillemont and the
Benedictine editors prove this to be untenable.

[2] The title pope (papa) was originally employed with great
latitude. In the East it has always been used to designate
simple priests. In the West, however, it seems from the
beginning to have been restricted to bishops. It was probably
in the fourth century that it became a distinctive title of the

LETTER CXXI

of Faustus,[1] him who associates with the pope,[2] without having received votes, and having appointed him in the place of our most reverend brother Cyril; and in consequence Armenia has become filled with schisms. Therefore, that they may not lie against us, and that we ourselves may not be held responsible for the confusion produced by what has happened, I have made these things known to your August Reverence. And obviously you yourself will deign to make this known to the rest. For I think that the present confusion will distress many.

LETTER CXXI

To Theodotus, Bishop of Nicopolis[3]

The winter is severe and very long drawn out, so that it is not easily within our power to have the consolation of even a letter. It is for this reason, I realize, that I have seldom either written to your Reverence or received a letter from you. But since

Roman Pontiff. Gregory VII finally prescribed that it be confined to the successors of Peter. To whom Basil here refers is an enigma.

[3] On the same subject, and of the same date as the preceding; one of the two (cf. CXXX) extant letters of St. Basil to Theodotus. Theodotus, Bishop of Nicopolis and Metropolitan of Lesser Armenia, was an aged prelate of noble character and unquestioned soundness of faith, and was highly esteemed by Basil. Theodotus, however, suspected Eustathius of Sebaste of unsound doctrine, and when Basil, who at first felt a warm friendship for Eustathius, was reluctant to give credence to these suspicions and even endeavoured to clear them away, he turned his suspicions upon Basil himself. Theodotus then became openly cold and discourteous, and refused to co-operate with Basil in the appointing of bishops to Lesser Armenia.

Σαγκτίσσιμος[1] ὁ συμπρεσβύτερος τὴν μέχρις
ὑμῶν ὁδοιπορίαν ὑπέστη, δι᾽ αὐτοῦ καὶ προσφθέγγομαί[2] σου τὴν κοσμιότητα,[3] καὶ παρακαλῶ
προσεύχεσθαι ὑπὲρ ἐμοῦ καὶ χρῆσαι τὴν ἀκοὴν
τῷ προειρημένῳ,[4] ὥστε παρ᾽ αὐτοῦ διδαχθῆναι
τὰ τῶν ἐκκλησιῶν ἐν οἵοις[5] ἐστὶ καὶ τὴν δυνατὴν
σπουδὴν εἰσενέγκασθαι εἰς τὰ προκείμενα.

Γίνωσκε δὲ ὅτι Φαῦστος γράμματα ἔχων ἧκε
πρὸς ἡμᾶς παρὰ[6] πάπα, ἀξιοῦντα αὐτὸν γενέσθαι
ἐπίσκοπον. ἐπειδὴ δὲ ᾐτήσαμεν ἡμεῖς,[7] μαρτυρίαν τῆς σῆς εὐλαβείας καὶ τῶν λοιπῶν ἐπισκόπων, καταφρονήσας ἡμῶν πρὸς Ἄνθιμον ᾤχετο,
καὶ παρ᾽ αὐτοῦ λαβὼν τὴν χειροτονίαν χωρὶς
ἡμετέρας ὑπομνήσεως ἐπανῆκε.

CXXII

Ποιμενίῳ, ἐπισκόπῳ Σατάλων

Πάντως ἐπεζήτησας[8] γράμματα παρὰ τῶν
Ἀρμενίων, ὅτε ἐπανῆκαν διὰ σοῦ, καὶ τὴν αἰτίαν
ἔμαθες, δι᾽ ἣν οὐκ ἔδωκα αὐτοῖς τὴν ἐπιστολήν.
εἰ μὲν οὖν εἶπον φιλαλήθως, ἔδωκας ἡμῖν αὐτόθεν

---

[1] Σαγκτήσιμος E, editi antiqi.
[2] προσφθεγγόμεθα E, Med.
[3] τιμιότητα E.   [4] εἰρημένῳ E.   [5] οἷς E.
[6] τοῦ add. E.   [7] ᾐτησάμην ἡμεῖς om. E, Med.
[8] ἐπιζητήσας editi antiqi.

---

[1] Cf. note 1, p. 246.
[2] Cf. note 1, p. 248.
[3] Cf. note 2, p. 248.
[4] Cf. note 2, p. 247.

our most beloved brother Sanctissimus,[1] the presbyter, has undertaken the journey to you, through
him I salute your Decorum, and beseech you to pray
for me and to lend audience to the aforesaid, that
you may be informed by him in what condition the
affairs of the churches are and bring all possible zeal
to bear upon the matters aforementioned.

But be informed that Faustus [2] came to us with a
letter from a pope,[3] asking that he be made bishop.
But when we asked for a testimonial from your
Reverence and from the rest of the bishops, showing
contempt for us, he went to Anthimus,[4] and after
receiving the election from him without any mention
being made of us, he returned.

LETTER CXXII

To Poemenius, Bishop of Satala [5]

You must certainly have asked the Armenians for
a letter as they returned through your country, and
must have learned the reason why I had not given
them the letter. Now if they spoke with regard for
the truth, you granted us forgiveness on the spot;

[5] Written at the end of 372 or beginning of 373. Poemenius,
Bishop of Satala in Armenia, was a near relation of Basil, and
had been brought up with him in close intimacy. In 372
Valens commissioned Basil to appoint bishops to the vacant
sees in Armenia, among which was Satala. In compliance
with Imperial orders and the earnest petitions of both
magistrates and people, St. Basil appointed Poemenius to
the see in Satala. Cf. Letter CII, where Basil earnestly
commends his friend to the good offices of his new flock. In
the present letter reference is also made to the uncanonical
appointment of Faustus by Anthimus, on which cf. the
letters immediately preceding.

τὴν συγγνώμην· εἰ δὲ ἀπεκρύψαντο ἐκεῖνοι, ὅπερ
οὐκ¹ εἰκάζω—ἀλλὰ παρ' ἡμῶν ἄκουε.

Ὁ τὰ πάντα γενναῖος Ἄνθιμος, ὁ διὰ μακροῦ
χρόνου τὴν πρὸς ἡμᾶς εἰρήνην σπεισάμενος,
ἐπειδὴ εὗρε καιρὸν ἑαυτοῦ τε² κενοδοξίαν ἐκπληρῶσαι καὶ ἡμῖν λύπην τινὰ προξενῆσαι,
ἐχειροτόνησε τὸν Φαῦστον ἰδίᾳ αὐθεντίᾳ καὶ
ἰδίᾳ χειρί, οὐδενὸς ὑμῶν ἀναμείνας ψῆφον καὶ
ἡμῶν καταγελάσας ἀκριβολογουμένων περὶ τὰ
τοιαῦτα. ἐπεὶ οὖν συνέχεε μὲν παλαιὰν εὐταξίαν, κατεφρόνησε δὲ καὶ ὑμῶν, παρ' ὧν ἀνέμενον
ἐγὼ τὴν μαρτυρίαν δέξασθαι, ἐποίησε δὲ πρᾶγμα
οὐκ οἶδα εἰ εὐάρεστον τῷ Θεῷ, τούτου ἕνεκεν³
λυπηθεὶς πρὸς αὐτούς, οὐδεμίαν ἔδωκα ἐπιστολὴν
πρὸς οὐδένα τῶν Ἀρμενίων, οὐδὲ πρὸς τὴν σὴν
εὐλάβειαν. ἀλλ' οὐδὲ εἰς κοινωνίαν ἐδεξάμην
τὸν Φαῦστον, φανερῶς διαμαρτυρόμενος, ὅτι εἰ
μὴ ὑμέτερά μοι κομίσειε γράμματα, πάντα τὸν
χρόνον ἔσομαι καὶ αὐτὸς ἠλλοτριωμένος καὶ τοὺς
ὁμοψύχους μοι⁴ οὕτω διαθήσω πρὸς αὐτὸν
ἔχειν.

Εἰ μὲν οὖν ἰάσιμα τὰ γενόμενα, σπούδασον
αὐτός τε ἐπιστεῖλαι μαρτυρῶν αὐτῷ, εἰ ὁρᾷς
ἀγαθὴν τοῦ ἀνδρὸς τὴν ζωήν, καὶ τοὺς ἄλλους
προτρέψασθαι· εἰ δὲ ἀνίατα, καὶ τοῦτό μοι
φανερὸν ποίησον, ὥστε μηκέτι με αὐτοῖς καθόλου
προσέχειν, εἰ καὶ ὅτι, ὡς ἔδειξαν, ὥρμηνται
λοιπὸν πρὸς τὸν Ἄνθιμον ἑαυτῶν⁵ μεταθεῖναι
τὴν κοινωνίαν, ἡμῶν καὶ τῆς ἐκκλησίας ταύτης,
ὡς ἑώλων εἰς φιλίαν, καταφρονήσαντες.

¹ οὖν E.   ² τήν add. E.   ³ ἕνεκα E.

252

but if they concealed the facts, which I do not suppose—well, hear our story:

The in all respects noble Anthimus, he who long ago made his peace with us, when he found an opportunity of satisfying his own conceit and of causing some vexation to us, consecrated Faustus by his own authority and with his own hand, waiting for the vote of no one of you and ridiculing us for being scrupulous about such matters. Since, then, he was violating an ancient orderly practice and had showed contempt even for you, from whom I was waiting to receive the testimonial, and had committed an act which I am inclined to consider displeasing to God, I, feeling aggrieved at the Armenians on this account, gave them no letter to anyone in Armenia, not even to your Reverence. Moreover, I did not even receive Faustus into communion, plainly giving witness that unless he should bring me a letter from you, I myself would be permanently estranged and would dispose those of like mind with me also to be so disposed toward him.

Now, if what has happened admits of a remedy, do you yourself hasten to write, bearing witness for him, if you see that the life of the man is good, and to urge the rest to do likewise. But if the situation is incurable, make this also clear to me, that I may no longer pay any attention to them at all—even if you must say that they have undertaken, as they have indicated, to transfer their communion to Anthimus, in contempt of us and this church, having grown stale as regards friendship.

CXXIII

Οὐρβικίῳ μονάζοντι

Ἔμελλες ἡμῖν παρέσεσθαι (καὶ τὸ ἀγαθὸν ἐγγὺς) ἄκρῳ γοῦν δακτύλῳ καταψύξαι[1] ἡμᾶς ἐν τοῖς πειρασμοῖς φλεγομένους. εἶτα τί; αἱ ἁμαρτίαι ἡμῶν ἀντέβησαν καὶ διεκώλυσαν τὴν ὁρμήν, ἵν' ἀθεράπευτα κάμνωμεν. ὥσπερ γὰρ ἐν τοῖς κύμασι τὸ μὲν λήγει, τὸ δὲ ἀνίσταται, τὸ δὲ ἤδη φρίκῃ μελαίνεται, οὕτω καὶ τῶν ἡμετέρων κακῶν τὰ μὲν πέπαυται, τὰ δὲ πάρεστι, τὰ δὲ προσδοκᾶται· καὶ μία τῶν κακῶν ἡμῖν, ὡς ἐπὶ τὸ πλεῖστον, ἀπαλλαγή, εἶξαι τῷ καιρῷ καὶ ὑπεξελθεῖν τοῖς διώκουσιν.

Ἀλλὰ καὶ πάρεσο ἡμῖν,[2] ἢ παραμυθούμενος, ἢ καὶ γνώμην δώσων, ἢ καὶ προπέμψων,[3] πάντως δὲ αὐτῷ τῷ ὀφθῆναι ῥάους ποιήσων. καὶ τὸ μέγιστον, εὔχου, καὶ ὑπερεύχου, μὴ καὶ τοὺς λογισμοὺς ἡμῶν βαπτισθῆναι ὑπὸ τοῦ κακοῦ καὶ τοῦ[4] κλύδωνος, ἀλλ' ἐν πᾶσι διαφυλάσσειν τῷ Θεῷ τὸ εὐχάριστον, ἵνα μὴ ἐν τοῖς κακοῖς δούλοις ἀριθμηθῶμεν, ἀγαθύνοντι μὲν ἐξομολογούμενοι, παιδεύοντι δὲ διὰ τῶν ἐναντίων μὴ

---

[1] καταψύξων editi antiqi.
[2] πάρεσο ἡμῖν] ἡμῖν ἧκε μόλις editi antiqi.
[3] προσπέμψων editi antiqi.
[4] καὶ τοῦ om. quinque MSS.

---

[1] Written in 373, to Urbicius, a monk, about whom nothing is known, except for the present letter and Letter CCLXII. Basil here writes for consolation and advice. The period 372–374 was one of intense personal suffering for

LETTER CXXIII

To Urbicius, a Monk [1]

You were on the point of visiting us (and the blessing was near), to cool us with but the tip of your finger as we burned in the midst of temptations. Then what? Our sins stood in the way and prevented your setting out, that in our sickness we might find no healing. For just as among the waves one sinks, another rises, and a third is already turning black with rippling, so too with our troubles— some have ceased, others are at hand, and others are being awaited; and the one relief from our evils is, for the most part, to yield to the occasion and to withdraw from before our pursuers.

But pray do visit us, either to console us, or to give advice, or to send us on our way, but in any case by the very sight of you to make us easier at heart. And—most important of all—pray, and pray again, that our reason be not submerged by the flood of evil, but that in all things we may keep ourselves pleasing to God, in order that we may not be numbered among the wicked servants who thank Him when He grants blessings, but when He chastises through the opposite means do

St. Basil. He and his lifelong friend Gregory of Nazianzus had become estranged; Theodotus, Bishop of Nicopolis, for whom Basil had great esteem, had suspected him of heresy, and refused to co-operate with him in appointing bishops in Lesser Armenia; he had at last been forced to see the treachery and ingratitude of his former friend, Eustathius of Sebaste; and, finally, Eusebius of Samosata, his intimate and confidential counsellor, had been exiled to Thrace by the Emperor Valens.

προστιθέμενοι· ἀλλὰ καὶ δι' αὐτῶν τῶν δυσχερῶν
ὠφελώμεθα, μᾶλλον αὐτῷ πιστεύοντες, ὅτε καὶ
μᾶλλον χρῄζομεν.

CXXIV

Θεοδώρῳ [1]

Λέγουσί τινες τοὺς ἑαλωκότας τῷ πάθει τοῦ
ἔρωτος, ὅταν κατά τινα βιαιοτέραν ἀνάγκην τῶν
ποθουμένων ἀπάγωνται, εἰ πρὸς τὴν εἰκόνα τῆς
ἀγαπηθείσης μορφῆς ἀποβλέψειαν, τὸ σφοδρὸν
ἀναπαύειν τοῦ πάθους διὰ τῆς ἐν ὀφθαλμοῖς
ἀπολαύσεως. εἰ μὲν οὖν ἀληθῆ ταῦτα ἢ [2] μὴ
λέγειν οὐκ ἔχω· ὃ δέ μοι πρὸς τὴν σὴν συμβέ-
βηκεν ἀγαθότητα οὐ πόρρω τῶν εἰρημένων ἐστίν.
ἐπειδὴ γὰρ γέγονέ τις διάθεσις ἐμοὶ πρὸς τὴν
ἱερὰν καὶ ἄδολόν σου ψυχήν, ἵν' οὕτως εἴπω,
ἐρωτική, τὸ δὲ ἀπολαύειν τῶν ποθουμένων, ὡς
οὐδὲ ἄλλο τι τῶν ἀγαθῶν, οὐκ ἐν εὐκολίᾳ ἡμῖν
ἐστι διὰ τὴν ἐκ τῶν ἁμαρτιῶν ἐναντίωσιν, ἐνόμισα
εἰκόνα τῆς ἀγαθότητός σου ἐναργεστάτην ἐν τῇ
τῶν εὐλαβεστάτων ἡμῶν ἀδελφῶν παρουσίᾳ
ἑωρακέναι. καὶ εἰ δίχα τούτων συνέβη τῇ σῇ
με περιτυχεῖν γνησιότητι, ἐλογισάμην ἂν ἐν σοὶ
κἀκείνους ἑωρακέναι· διότι τῆς ἀγάπης, λέγω,
τοσοῦτον ἐν ἑκάστῳ ὑμῶν τὸ μέτρον ἐστίν, ὡς
ἐπίσης τὴν περὶ τοῦ πλείονος ἑκάστῳ φιλονεικίαν
ἐμφαίνεσθαι. ἐπὶ τούτοις ηὐχαρίστησα τῷ ἁγίῳ
Θεῷ, καὶ εὔχομαι, εἴπερ ἔτι ὑπολείπεταί τις

---

[1] ἀσπαστική add. Reg. secundus, Coisl. secundus, editi
antiqi.

not submit. Nay, let us derive benefit even from
our very difficulties, trusting in Him the more when
we stand the more in need.

LETTER CXXIV

To Theodorus[1]

SOME say that those who are seized with the
passion of love, whenever through some unusually
urgent necessity they are parted from the object of
their desire, if they can look upon the semblance of
the beloved form in a picture, can check the violence
of their passion through the pleasure they derive
from the sight. Now whether this is true or not
I cannot say; but that which has happened to me
regarding your Goodness is not far from what I
have described. For since I had conceived with
respect to your holy and guileless soul what I may
call an amatory disposition, but the enjoyment of
the object of our desire, like all other blessings, is
made difficult for us by the opposition of our sins, I
thought that I saw a very distinct image of your
Goodness in the presence of our very reverend
brothers. And if, in their absence, I had fallen
in with your Nobility, I should have considered that
in you I had seen them also; for the measure of my
love, I mean, is so great in the case of each of you
that there appears in me an eager desire for the
advantage of each in equal degree. For this I have
thanked the holy God, and I pray, if any period of

[1] Written in A.D. 373. The identity of this Theodorus is
quite unknown.

[2] ᾗ editi antiqi.

χρόνος ζωῆς, γενέσθαι μοι διὰ σοῦ τὴν ζωὴν
ἡδεῖαν, ὡς τό γε νῦν ἄθλιον πρᾶγμα τὸ ζῆν καὶ
φευκτὸν εἶναι ἡγοῦμαι, τῆς τῶν φιλτάτων συν-
ουσίας κεχωρισμένον.[1] οὐ γάρ ἐστι, κατὰ τὴν
ἐμὴν κρίσιν, ἐφ' ᾧ τις ἂν εὐθυμήσειε, τῶν ἀληθῶς
ἀγαπώντων διεζευγμένος.

CXXV

Ἀντίγραφον Πίστεως ὑπαγορευθείσης παρὰ τοῦ
ἁγιωτάτου[2] Βασιλείου, ᾗ ὑπέγραψεν Εὐστάθιος ὁ Σεβαστείας ἐπίσκοπος.

Τοὺς προληφθέντας ἑτέρᾳ πίστεως ὁμολογίᾳ
καὶ μετατίθεσθαι πρὸς τὴν τῶν ὀρθῶν συνάφειαν

---

[1] κεχωρισμένος editio secunda Paris.
[2] μεγάλου editi antiqi.

---

[1] Written in 373. This letter represents but one step in
Basil's gradual disillusionment as to the character of
Eustathius of Sebaste. On Eustathius, cf. Letters LXXIX,
and CXIX with notes. The series of incidents leading up
to Basil's break with Eustathius may be described briefly as
follows :

Theodotus, bishop of Nicopolis, had invited St. Basil to
attend a Synodical meeting at Nicopolis. Basil, on his way
there, interviewed Eustathius, which at once barred him
from attending the synod. Grieved and humiliated at this
treatment from Theodotus, Basil returned home and sought
counsel from Eusebius of Samosata. This occurred in May
of 372. In the following June or July he again returned to
Armenia, not only to confer with Meletius but also to comply
with an order from the Emperor to place bishops in the
vacant sees of that province. On account of the coolness
between himself and Theodotus, Basil went first to Getasa,
the home of Meletius, and there, in the presence of reliable

life be yet left to me, that my life be made sweet
through you, since for the present, at least, I consider life a wretched thing and to be avoided,
separated as it is from association with those most
dear. For, in my opinion, there is nothing for
which a man may be joyful if he be separated from
those who truly love him.

LETTER CXXV

A Transcript of Faith Dictated by the most
    Holy Basil, to Which Eustathius, the Bishop
    of Sebaste, Subscribed [1]

Those who have formerly been committed to an
unorthodox confession of Faith and wish to pass

witnesses, he justified his conduct with Eustathius and
refuted the accusations of Theodotus. The latter, who was
present, maintained that Eustathius had denied any agreement with Basil's propositions. Accordingly, to satisfy
Theodotus, Basil offered to make Eustathius sign a profession of faith containing all the articles of the Nicene
Creed. Theodotus accepted the plan, and promised to assist
Basil in appointing bishops in Armenia. However, upon his
arrival in Nicopolis, Theodotus forgot all that had passed
and virtually excommunicated Basil. Under these circumstances, Basil was prevented from making the appointments.
Fatigued, disappointed, and grieved over the turn of affairs,
he returned home only to find sadly neglected conditions in
his own diocese.

St. Basil made a third visit to Armenia in the year 373,
probably on account of the ordination of Faustus. It was
on this trip that the people of Armenia demanded an assurance of the orthodoxy of Eustathius. St. Basil willingly
offered to go in person to Eustathius and have him sign
a profession of faith. The present letter was accordingly
drafted. Some think it is written by St. Basil together
with Theodotus, while others believe that it has the tone of a

COLLECTED LETTERS OF SAINT BASIL

βουλομένους, ἢ καὶ νῦν πρῶτον ἐν τῇ κατηχήσει
τοῦ λόγου τῆς ἀληθείας ἐπιθυμοῦντας γενέσθαι,
χρὴ τὴν ὑπὸ τῶν μακαρίων πατέρων ἐν τῇ κατὰ
Νίκαιάν ποτε συγκροτηθείσῃ συνόδῳ γραφεῖσαν
πίστιν. τὸ δὲ αὐτὸ τοῦτο χρήσιμον ἂν εἴη καὶ
πρὸς τοὺς ὑπονοουμένους ἐναντίως ἔχειν τῇ
ὑγιαινούσῃ διδασκαλίᾳ καὶ συσκιάζοντας ἑαυτῶν
ἀποφυγαῖς εὐπροσώποις τὸ τῆς κακοδοξίας
φρόνημα. καὶ γὰρ καὶ τούτοις αὐτάρκης ἡ
ἐγκειμένη πίστις. ἢ γὰρ διορθώσαιντο ἑαυτῶν
τὴν ἐν τῷ κρυπτῷ νόσον, ἢ συγκαλύπτοντες
αὐτὴν¹ ἐν τῷ βάθει, αὐτοὶ μὲν τὸ κρίμα τῆς
ἀπάτης βαστάσουσιν, ἡμῖν δὲ τὴν ἀπολογίαν
κούφην ἐν τῇ ἡμέρᾳ τῆς κρίσεως παρασκευά-
σουσιν, ὅτε ἀποκαλύψει ὁ Κύριος τὰ κρυπτὰ
τοῦ σκότους, καὶ φανερώσει τὰς βουλὰς τῶν
καρδιῶν. λαμβάνειν τοίνυν αὐτοὺς ὁμολογοῦντας
προσήκει, ὅτι πιστεύουσι κατὰ τὰ ῥήματα τὰ
ὑπὸ τῶν Πατέρων ἡμῶν ἐκτεθέντα ἐν τῇ Νικαίᾳ
καὶ κατὰ τὴν ὑγιῶς ὑπὸ τῶν ῥημάτων τούτων
ἐμφαινομένην διάνοιαν.

Εἰσὶ γάρ τινες οἱ καὶ ἐν ταύτῃ τῇ πίστει

---

¹ ἑαυτήν E.

---

synodical decree.   At any rate, a meeting was arranged and
the transcript signed in the presence of witnesses. For Basil's
own account of the signing, cf. Letter CCXLIV, sec. 2. But
Basil's suspicions, once aroused, were not easily allayed. He
accordingly proposed another meeting so that the prelates of
Caesarea and Sebaste might be united with one another and
their communion for the future be sincere. Both the place
and the date were decided upon, but Eustathius and his
colleagues failed to keep the appointment.

In spite of all efforts on the part of Eusebius of Samosata
to effect a reconciliation and finally to win Eustathius to the

over into unity with the orthodox, or those who now for the first time wish to be instructed in the doctrine of truth, must be taught in the articles of Faith as drawn up by the blessed Fathers in the synod once convened at Nicaea. And this same thing would also be useful for those who are suspected of being opposed to the sound doctrine and who seek to cloak with specious subterfuges their unorthodox views. For even for these the creed embodied therein suffices. For either they may correct their hidden malady, or, if they still conceal it in the depth of their hearts, they will themselves bear the responsibility for their deception, but for us they will make easy our defence on the Day of Judgment, when the Lord "will reveal the hidden things of darkness and will make manifest the counsels of the heart." [1] It is therefore fitting to receive them when they confess that they believe according to the words set forth by our Fathers at Nicaea and according to the meaning disclosed by those words when soundly interpreted.

For there are some who even in this creed pervert

Nicene faith, Eustathius, shortly after signing the present letter, renounced communion with Basil and openly attacked him on the ground of Apollinarism. Although pained at the duplicity of his former friend, and distressed over his false charges, Basil for about three years maintained a discreet silence. He then for the first time openly defended himself against the slanders of Eustathius. Cf. Letter CCXXIII.

[1] 1 Cor. 4, 5: ὥστε μὴ πρὸ καιροῦ τι κρίνετε, ἕως ἂν ἔλθῃ ὁ Κύριος, ὃς καὶ φωτίσει τὰ κρυπτὰ τοῦ σκότους, καὶ φανερώσει τὰς βουλὰς τῶν καρδιῶν· καὶ τότε ὁ ἔπαινος γενήσεται ἑκάστῳ ἀπὸ τοῦ Θεοῦ. "Therefore judge not before the time ; until the Lord come, who both will bring to light the hidden things of darkness, and will make manifest the counsels of the heart ; and then shall every man have praise from God."

COLLECTED LETTERS OF SAINT BASIL

δολοῦντες τὸν λόγον τῆς ἀληθείας καὶ πρὸς τὸ
ἑαυτῶν βούλημα τὸν νοῦν τῶν ἐν αὐτῇ ῥημάτων
ἕλκοντες. ὅπου γε καὶ Μάρκελλος ἐτόλμησεν, ἀσε-
βῶν εἰς τὴν ὑπόστασιν τοῦ Κυρίου ἡμῶν Ἰησοῦ
Χριστοῦ καὶ ψιλὸν αὐτὸν ἐξηγούμενος λόγον,
ἐκεῖθεν προφασίσασθαι[1] τὰς ἀρχὰς εἰληφέναι,
τοῦ ὁμοουσίου τὴν διάνοιαν κακῶς ἐξηγούμενος.[2]
καί τινες τῶν ἀπὸ τῆς δυσσεβείας τοῦ Λίβυος
Σαβελλίου, ὑπόστασιν καὶ οὐσίαν ταὐτὸν εἶναι
ὑπολαμβάνοντες, ἐκεῖθεν ἕλκουσι τὰς ἀφορμὰς
πρὸς τὴν κατασκευὴν τῆς ἑαυτῶν βλασφημίας, ἐκ
τοῦ ἐγγεγράφθαι τῇ πίστει, ὅτι Ἐὰν δέ τις λέγῃ[3]
ἐξ ἑτέρας οὐσίας ἢ ὑποστάσεως τὸν Υἱόν, ἀναθεματίζει ἡ καθολικὴ καὶ ἀποστολικὴ ἐκκλησία.
οὐ γὰρ ταὐτὸν εἶπον ἐκεῖ[4] οὐσίαν καὶ ὑπόστασιν.
εἰ γὰρ μίαν καὶ τὴν αὐτὴν ἐδήλουν ἔννοιαν αἱ
φωναί, τίς χρεία ἦν ἑκατέρων; ἀλλὰ δῆλον ὅτι,
ὡς τῶν μὲν ἀρνουμένων τὸ ἐκ τῆς οὐσίας εἶναι
τοῦ Πατρός, τῶν δὲ λεγόντων οὔτε ἐκ τῆς οὐσίας
ἀλλ' ἐξ ἄλλης τινὸς ὑποστάσεως, οὕτως ἀμφότερα,
ὡς ἀλλότρια τοῦ ἐκκλησιαστικοῦ φρονήματος,
ἀπηγόρευσαν. ἐπεὶ ὅπου γε τὸ ἑαυτῶν ἐδήλουν

---

[1] προφασίζεσθαι Coisl. secundus, Reg. secundus.
[2] ἐξηγούμενος om. E.
[3] λέγει Harl.; λέξῃ editi antiqi.
[4] ἐκεῖνοι editi antiqi.

---

[1] Marcellus of Ancyra was one of the bishops present at
the Councils of Ancyra and Nicaea. He was a strong
opponent of Arianism, but in his zeal to combat Arius
adopted the opposite extreme of modified Sabellianism. He
was several times condemned, dying deprived of his see in
374. Marcellus confused the Personality of God, declaring
that God was originally only one Personality, but at the

the doctrine of truth and stretch the sense of the
words in it to suit their own purpose. For instance,
even Marcellus,[1] acting impiously toward the person [2]
of our Lord Jesus Christ and explaining Him as
mere "Word," had the effrontery to profess that he
had taken his principles from that creed, perversely
explaining the meaning of "consubstantial." And
some of those from the impious sect of the Libyan
Sabellius,[3] understanding person and substance to
be the same, draw from that creed the beginnings
they use for the establishment of their own blasphemy,
from the fact of its having been written in the creed
that "if anyone says the Son is of a different substance or person, the Catholic and Apostolic Church
anathematizes him." For it is not said therein that
the substance and the person are the same. For if
the words revealed one and the same meaning, what
was the need of each separately? But it is evident
that, since some denied that the Son is of the
substance of the Father, and others said that He
was not of the substance but of some other person,
thus they condemned both positions as foreign to
the opinion of the Church. For, when they came

creation of the universe the Word or Logos went out from
the Father and was God's activity in the world. This Logos
became incarnate in Christ and was thus constituted Son of
God. The Holy Ghost likewise went forth as the third
Divine Personality from the Father and from Christ accord-
ing to St. John 20, 22. At the consummation of all things,
however, Christ and the Holy Ghost will return to the
Father, and the Godhead will be again an absolute Unity.
Cf. Cath. Encycl. under Marcellus of Ancyra. Cf. also
Jerome, *De Vir. Ill.* 86.

[2] For a definition of the theological terms used in this
letter, cf. Letter VIII and note.

[3] For Sabellius, cf. Introduction, Vol. I.

φρόνημα, εἶπον ἐκ τῆς οὐσίας τοῦ Πατρὸς τὸν
Υἱόν, οὐκέτι προσθέντες καὶ τὸ ἐκ τῆς ὑποστάσεως. ὥστε ἐκεῖνο μὲν ἐπ' ἀθετήσει κεῖται τοῦ
πονηροῦ φρονήματος, τοῦτο δὲ φανέρωσιν ἔχει τοῦ
σωτηρίου δόγματος. δεῖ τοίνυν ὁμολογεῖν ὁμοούσιον
τὸν Υἱὸν τῷ Πατρί, καθὼς γέγραπται, ὁμολογεῖν
δὲ ἐν ἰδίᾳ μὲν ὑποστάσει τὸν Πατέρα, ἐν ἰδίᾳ δὲ
τὸν Υἱόν, καὶ ἐν ἰδίᾳ τὸ Πνεῦμα τὸ ἅγιον, καθὰ
καὶ αὐτοὶ σαφῶς[1] ἐκδεδώκασιν. αὐτάρκως γὰρ
καὶ σαφῶς[2] ἐνεδείξαντο εἰπόντες, φῶς ἐκ φωτός,
ὅτι ἕτερον μὲν τὸ γεννῆσαν φῶς, ἕτερον δὲ τὸ
γεννηθέν, φῶς μέντοι καὶ φῶς· ὥστε ἕνα καὶ
τὸν αὐτὸν εἶναι τὸν τῆς οὐσίας λόγον. ἐγκείσθω
δὴ ἡμῖν καὶ αὐτὴ ἡ πίστις ἡ κατὰ Νίκαιαν
συγγραφεῖσα.

Πιστεύομεν εἰς ἕνα Θεὸν Πατέρα[3] παντοκράτορα, πάντων ὁρατῶν τε καὶ ἀοράτων ποιητήν.
καὶ εἰς ἕνα Κύριον[4] Ἰησοῦν Χριστὸν τὸν Υἱὸν
τοῦ[5] Θεοῦ, γεννηθέντα ἐκ τοῦ Πατρὸς Μονογενῆ,
τουτέστιν, ἐκ τῆς οὐσίας τοῦ Πατρός· Θεὸν ἐκ
Θεοῦ, φῶς ἐκ φωτός, Θεὸν ἀληθινὸν ἐκ Θεοῦ
ἀληθινοῦ· γεννηθέντα, οὐ ποιηθέντα· ὁμοούσιον
τῷ Πατρί, δι' οὗ τὰ πάντα ἐγένετο, τά τε ἐν τῷ
οὐρανῷ καὶ τὰ[6] ἐν τῇ γῇ· τὸν δι' ἡμᾶς τοὺς ἀνθρώπους καὶ διὰ τὴν ἡμετέραν σωτηρίαν κατελθόντα,[7]
καὶ σαρκωθέντα, ἐνανθρωπήσαντα, παθόντα, καὶ
ἀναστάντα τῇ τρίτῃ ἡμέρᾳ, ἀνελθόντα εἰς τοὺς[8]
οὐρανούς, ἐρχόμενον κρῖναι ζῶντας καὶ νεκρούς.
καὶ εἰς τὸ ἅγιον Πνεῦμα. τοὺς δὲ λέγοντας· Ἦν

---

[1] εὐσεβῶς Harl., Regius.
[2] σοφῶς Harl. secunda manu, editi antiqi.
[3] Πατέρα om. E.   [4] ἡμῶν add. editi antiqi.

to revealing their opinion, they said that the Son
was of the substance of the Father, not going on
to add "of the person." Thus the former statement
is laid down as a rejection of faulty opinion, while
the latter contains the declaration of the doctrine
of salvation. It is necessary, therefore, to confess
the Son as of the same substance as the Father, as it
is written, and to confess the Father in His own
proper person, and the Son in His own, and the
Holy Ghost in His own, according as the Fathers
themselves have clearly set forth. For sufficiently
and clearly have they shown this when they said,
"Light of Light, the One which begot Light and
the Other which was begotten, and yet Light and
Light," so that the definition of the substance is
one and the same. Now let the creed itself, composed at Nicaea, be added by us.

We believe in one God the Father Almighty,
maker of all things, visible and invisible, and in
one Lord Jesus Christ, the Son of God, born of the
Father, the only Begotten, that is, of the substance
of the Father; God of God, Light of Light, true God
of true God; begotten not made; consubstantial
with the Father, by whom all things were made,
both in heaven and on earth; who for us men and
for our salvation came down and was incarnate, and
was made Man. He suffered and arose on the third
day, and He ascended into heaven and shall come
to judge the living and the dead. And in the Holy
Ghost. And as for such who say "There was a time

---

5 τοῦ om. E.   6 καὶ τὰ] τά τε E.
7 ἐκ τῶν οὐρανῶν add. editiones Paris. et secunda Basil.
8 τούς om. E.

ποτέ, ὅτε οὐκ ἦν, καὶ πρὶν γεννηθῆναι οὐκ ἦν,
καὶ ὅτι ἐξ οὐκ ὄντων ἐγένετο, ἢ ἐξ ἑτέρας
ὑποστάσεως ἢ οὐσίας φάσκοντας εἶναι ἢ τρεπτὸν
ἢ ἀλλοιωτὸν τὸν Υἱὸν τοῦ Θεοῦ, τοὺς τοιούτους
ἀναθεματίζει ἡ καθολικὴ καὶ ἀποστολικὴ Ἐκκλησία.

Ἐπεὶ οὖν ἐνταῦθα τὰ μὲν ἄλλα ἀρκούντως
καὶ ἀκριβῶς διώρισται, τὰ μὲν ἐπὶ διορθώσει
τῶν βλαβέντων, τὰ δὲ εἰς προφυλακὴν τῶν
προσδοκωμένων ὑποφυήσεσθαι· ὁ δὲ περὶ τοῦ
Πνεύματος λόγος ἐν παραδρομῇ κεῖται οὐδεμιᾶς
ἐξεργασίας ἀξιωθεὶς διὰ τὸ μηδέπω τότε τοῦτο
κεκινῆσθαι τὸ ζήτημα, ἀλλ' ἀνεπιβούλευτον
ἐνυπάρχειν[1] ταῖς τῶν πιστευόντων ψυχαῖς τὴν
περὶ αὐτοῦ διάνοιαν· κατὰ μικρὸν δὲ προϊόντα
τὰ πονηρὰ τῆς ἀσεβείας σπέρματα, ἃ πρότερον
μὲν ὑπὸ Ἀρείου τοῦ προστάτου τῆς αἱρέσεως
κατεβλήθη, ὕστερον δὲ ὑπὸ τῶν τὰ ἐκείνου κακῶς
διαδεξαμένων, ἐπὶ λύμῃ τῶν ἐκκλησιῶν ἐξετράφη,
καὶ ἡ ἀκολουθία τῆς ἀσεβείας εἰς τὴν κατὰ τοῦ
Πνεύματος βλασφημίαν ἀπέσκηψεν·[2] ἀναγκαῖον
πρὸς τοὺς μὴ φειδομένους ἑαυτῶν, μηδὲ προορω-
μένους τὴν ἄφυκτον ἀπειλήν, ἣν τοῖς βλασφη-
μοῦσιν εἰς τὸ Πνεῦμα τὸ ἅγιον ὁ Κύριος ἡμῶν
ἐπανετείνατο,[3] ἐκεῖνο προτείνειν, ὅτι χρὴ αὐτοὺς
ἀναθεματίζειν τοὺς λέγοντας κτίσμα τὸ Πνεῦμα
τὸ ἅγιον, καὶ τοὺς νοοῦντας οὕτω, καὶ τοὺς μὴ
ὁμολογοῦντας αὐτὸ φύσει ἅγιον εἶναι, ὡς ἔστι
φύσει ἅγιος ὁ Πατήρ, καὶ φύσει ἅγιος ὁ Υἱός,
ἀλλ' ἀποξενοῦντας[4] αὐτὸ τῆς θείας καὶ μακαρίας
φύσεως. ἀπόδειξις δὲ τοῦ ὀρθοῦ φρονήματος τὸ

[1] ὑπάρχειν E. [2] ἐπέσκηψεν E, Regius.

266

when He was not," and "Before He was begotten He was not," or that "He came into existence from what was not," or who profess that the Son of God is of a different person or substance, or that He changeth, or is variable, such as these the Catholic and Apostolic Church anathematizes.

Since, therefore, all points with but one exception have been sufficiently and accurately defined herein, some as an emendation for what had been perverted, and others as a precaution against what was expected to arise—for the doctrine of the Holy Ghost was laid down cursorily, not being considered as necessary of elaboration, because at that time this question had not yet been agitated, but the sense of it was unassailably inherent in the souls of the faithful—but since, coming forth little by little, the baneful seeds of impiety, which had been sown before by Arius, the author of the heresy, and later by those who wickedly succeeded to his opinions, have been nurtured to the harm of the churches, and the succession of impiety has broken forth into blasphemy against the Spirit, in view of these things it is necessary to hold before those who have no pity for themselves nor foresee the inevitable threat which our Lord held over those who blaspheme the Holy Ghost, this conclusion—that we must anathematize those who call the Holy Spirit a creature, both those who think so, and those who will not confess that He is holy by nature, even as the Father is holy by nature, and as the Son is holy by nature, but deprive Him of His divine and blessed nature. And the proof of orthodox opinion

---

³ ἐπανετείνετο E.   ⁴ ξενοῦντας E.

μὴ χωρίζειν αὐτὸ Πατρὸς καὶ Υἱοῦ (δεῖ γὰρ
ἡμᾶς βαπτίζεσθαι μέν, ὡς παρελάβομεν· πιστεύειν δέ, ὡς βαπτιζόμεθα· δοξάζειν δέ, ὡς
πεπιστεύκαμεν, Πατέρα καὶ Υἱὸν καὶ ἅγιον
Πνεῦμα), ἀφίστασθαι δὲ τῆς κοινωνίας τῶν
κτίσμα λεγόντων, ὡς φανερῶς βλασφημούντων·
ἐκείνου διωμολογημένου (ἀναγκαία γὰρ ἡ ἐπιση-
μείωσις διὰ τοὺς συκοφάντας), ὅτι οὔτε ἀγέννητον
λέγομεν τὸ Πνεῦμα τὸ ἅγιον· ἕνα γὰρ οἴδαμεν
ἀγέννητον καὶ μίαν τῶν ὄντων ἀρχήν, τὸν
Πατέρα τοῦ Κυρίου ἡμῶν Ἰησοῦ Χριστοῦ· οὔτε
γεννητόν· ἕνα γὰρ μονογενῆ ἐν τῇ παραδόσει τῆς
πίστεως δεδιδάγμεθα· τὸ δὲ Πνεῦμα τῆς ἀληθείας
ἐκ τοῦ Πατρὸς ἐκπορεύεσθαι διδαχθέντες, ἐκ τοῦ
Θεοῦ εἶναι ὁμολογοῦμεν ἀκτίστως. ἀναθεματίζειν δὲ καὶ τοὺς λειτουργικὸν λέγοντας τὸ
Πνεῦμα τὸ ἅγιον, ὡς διὰ τῆς φωνῆς ταύτης εἰς
τὴν τοῦ κτίσματος κατάγοντας τάξιν. τὰ γὰρ
λειτουργικὰ πνεύματα κτίσματα ἡμῖν ἡ Γραφὴ
παρέδωκεν, εἰποῦσα, ὅτι Πάντες εἰσὶ λειτουργικὰ
πνεύματα εἰς διακονίαν ἀποστελλόμενα. διὰ δὲ
τοὺς πάντα φύροντας καὶ μὴ φυλάσσοντας τὴν ἐν
τοῖς εὐαγγελίοις διδασκαλίαν, ἀναγκαῖόν ἐστι καὶ
τοῦτο προσδιαστείλασθαι [1] ὅτι φεύγειν δεῖ καὶ
τοὺς τὴν ἀκολουθίαν ἣν παρέδωκεν ἡμῖν ὁ Κύριος
ἐναμείβοντας, ὡς φανερῶς μαχομένους τῇ εὐσεβείᾳ,[2] καὶ Υἱὸν μὲν προτάσσοντας [3] τοῦ Πατρός,
Υἱοῦ δὲ τὸ Πνεῦμα τὸ ἅγιον προτιθέντας.
ἀκίνητον γὰρ καὶ ἀπαρεγχείρητον φυλάσσειν

---

[1] προδιαστείλασθαι E.   [2] ἀληθείᾳ editi antiqi.
[3] προστάσσοντας E.

is not to separate Him from the Father and the Son (for we must be baptized as we have received the words of baptism, and we must believe as we are baptized, and we must give glory as we have believed, to the Father, the Son, and the Holy Ghost), but to abstain from communion with those, as open blasphemers, who call Him a creature; since this point is agreed upon (for comment is necessary because of the slanders), that we neither speak of the Holy Spirit as unbegotten—for we recognize One unbegotten and One Beginning of all existing things, the Father of our Lord Jesus Christ—nor speak of Him as begotten—for we have been taught One only begotten in the tradition of our Faith; and having been taught that the Spirit of Truth proceeds from the Father, we confess it to be from God without any act of creation. And we must anathematize also those who speak of the Holy Ghost as ministering, on the ground that by this expression they lower Him to the order of creatures. For Scripture has handed down to us the ministering spirits as creatures, saying, "All are ministering spirits sent to minister." [1] And on account of those who confuse everything and do not preserve the teaching of the Gospel, it is necessary to lay down this principle also—that we must avoid those who change the order which our Lord had left us, as being clearly enemies of religion, and place the Son before the Father and put the Holy Spirit before the Son. For it is meet that we keep unaltered

---

[1] Cf. Heb. 1, 14: οὐχὶ πάντες εἰσὶ λειτουργικὰ πνεύματα, εἰς διακονίαν ἀποστελλόμενα διὰ τοὺς μέλλοντας κληρονομεῖν σωτηρίαν; "Are they not all ministering spirits, sent to minister for them who shall receive the inheritance of salvation?"

προσήκει τὴν ἀκολουθίαν, ἣν ἐξ αὐτῆς τοῦ Κυρίου
τῆς φωνῆς παρελάβομεν, εἰπόντος· Πορευθέντες,
μαθητεύσατε πάντα τὰ ἔθνη, βαπτίζοντες αὐτοὺς
εἰς τὸ ὄνομα τοῦ Πατρὸς καὶ τοῦ Υἱοῦ καὶ τοῦ
ἁγίου Πνεύματος.

Ὑπογραφὴ Εὐσταθίου ἐπισκόπου.[1]

Εὐστάθιος ἐπίσκοπος σοὶ Βασιλείῳ ἀναγνοὺς
ἐγνώρισα, καὶ συνήνεσα τοῖς προγεγραμμένοις.
ὑπέγραψα δὲ συμπαρόντων μοι τῶν ἀδελφῶν, τοῦ
ἡμετέρου Φρόντωνος, καὶ τοῦ χωρεπισκόπου
Σεβήρου, καὶ ἄλλων τινῶν κληρικῶν.

CXXVI

Ἀταρβίῳ[2]

Παραγενόμενοι μέχρι τῆς Νικοπόλεως ἐπ'
ἐλπίδι τοῦ καὶ τὰς κινηθείσας ταραχὰς ἐπανορ-
θώσασθαι καὶ τὴν ἐνδεχομένην ἐπαγαγεῖν παραμυθίαν τοῖς ἀτάκτως καὶ παρὰ τὸν ἐκκλησια-
στικὸν θεσμὸν γενομένοις,[3] σφόδρα ἠθυμήσαμεν
μὴ καταλαβόντες σου τὴν χρηστότητα, ἀλλὰ
μαθόντες ἐξεληλακέναι σε πρὸς πᾶσαν ἔπειξιν,[4]
καὶ ταῦτα μεσούσης σχεδὸν τῆς συνόδου τῆς παρ'
ὑμῶν τελουμένης. διὸ ἀναγκαίως ἐπὶ τὸ γράμμα
ἤλθομεν, δι' οὗ ὑπομιμνήσκομεν ἀπαντῆσαι πρὸς

---

[1] Ὑπογραφὴ Εὐσταθίου ἐπισκόπου] καὶ ὑπέγραψεν Εὐστάθιος ὁ
Σεβαστείας ἐπίσκοπος Harl., Regius.
[2] Νικοπόλεως add. Clar. Νεοκαισαρείας add. E, Med.
[3] γεγενημένοις E, Med. [4] ἐπίδειξιν E.

---

[1] Matt. 28, 19.
[2] Fronto was a priest under the jurisdiction of Theodotus,
Bishop of Nicopolis, to whose see he was elevated after the

and untampered with that order which we received from the very words of Our Lord, when He said, " Going teach ye all nations, baptizing them in the name of the Father, and of the Son, and of the Holy Ghost." [1]

Signature of Eustathius, Bishop.

I, Eustathius, bishop, after reading to you, Basil, have understood, and have approved what has been written above. And I have signed in the presence of my brothers, our Fronto,[2] the suffragan-bishop Severus,[3] and certain other members of the clergy.

LETTER CXXVI

To Atarbius [4]

Arriving at Nicopolis in the hope of setting right the troubles which had been stirred up and of providing all possible relief for what had happened irregularly and contrary to ecclesiastical law, we were greatly disappointed when we did not meet your Goodness, but learned that you had departed in all haste and indeed almost in the middle of the synod which was being held by you. Therefore we must have recourse to writing, through which we bid you

latter's death. However, he did not possess Theodotus' firmness of character, for he fell into heresy.

[3] Known only from this passage.

[4] Of the year 373. For Atarbius, Bishop of Neocaesarea, cf. Letter LXV. He was a relative of Basil, and the leader of the Neocaesareans in their revolt against Basil. Cf. Letter CCVII. The present letter is an excellent example of the firm and tactful way in which Basil dealt with such as wandered from the orthodox faith and as even had wronged himself.

ἡμᾶς, ἵνα αὐτὸς διὰ σαυτοῦ παραμυθήσῃ ἡμῶν
τὴν λύπην, ἣν μέχρι θανάτου λελυπήμεθα,
ἀκούσαντες ἐπὶ μέσης τῆς ἐκκλησίας τετολμῆσθαι
πράγματα οὔπω μέχρι τῆς ἡμέρας ταύτης εἰς
ἀκοὴν ἡμετέραν ἐλθόντα. καὶ ταῦτα μὲν εἰ καὶ
λυπηρὰ καὶ βαρέα, ἀλλ' ἔτι φορητά, διὰ τὸ εἰς
ἄνθρωπον γεγενῆσθαι, ὃς τὴν ὑπὲρ ὧν πέπονθεν
ἐκδίκησιν τῷ Θεῷ ἐπιτρέψας, ὅλος ἐστὶ τῆς
εἰρήνης καὶ τοῦ μηδὲν παρὰ τὴν αὐτοῦ[1] αἰτίαν
βλαβερὸν γίνεσθαι[2] τῷ λαῷ τοῦ Θεοῦ.

Ἐπειδὴ δέ τινες τῶν τιμίων καὶ πάσης πίστεως
ἀξίων ἀδελφῶν ἀπήγγειλαν ἡμῖν, ὡς περὶ τὴν
πίστιν καινοτομουμένων τινῶν καὶ λαλουμένων
παρὰ σοῦ ὑπεναντίως τῇ ὑγιαινούσῃ διδασκαλίᾳ,
ἐπὶ τούτοις[3] πλέον συγκινηθέντες, καὶ πολὺν
ἀγῶνα ἀγωνιάσαντες τοῦ[4] μὴ πού τι[5] πρὸς τοῖς
μυρίοις τραύμασιν, οἷς πέπονθεν ἡ Ἐκκλησία
παρὰ τῶν εἰς τὴν ἀλήθειαν τοῦ Εὐαγγελίου
ἐξαμαρτόντων,[6] ἔτι καὶ ἄλλο ἀναφυῆ κακόν, ἀνα-
νεωθείσης τῆς παλαιᾶς τοῦ ἐχθροῦ τῆς Ἐκκλησίας Σαβελλίου αἱρέσεως (τούτοις γὰρ οἱ ἀδελφοὶ
ἀπήγγειλαν[7] ἡμῖν συγγενῆ εἶναι τὰ εἰρημένα),
τούτου ἕνεκεν ἐπεστείλαμεν, ἵνα μὴ ὀκνήσῃς
μικρὸν διάστημα κινηθεὶς καταλαβεῖν[8] ἡμᾶς, καὶ
τὴν ἐπὶ τούτοις πληροφορίαν παρασχόμενος, ἡμῶν
τε τὴν ὀδύνην καταπραῦναι, καὶ τὰς[9] τοῦ Θεοῦ
ἐκκλησίας παραμυθήσασθαι, τὰς νῦν ἀφορήτως
καὶ βαρέως ἐπί τε τοῖς πεπραγμένοις καὶ ἐπὶ τοῖς
θρυλλουμένοις εἰρῆσθαι παρὰ σοῦ λυπουμένας.

¹ ἑαυτοῦ Ε.   ² γενέσθαι Ε, editi antiqi.
³ τούτῳ Ε.   ⁴ τοῦ om. Ε.
⁵ τε editi antiqi.   ⁶ ἐξαμαρτανόντων Med. et Bigot.

to meet us, that you yourself in person may console
our grief, which has distressed us unto death, for
we heard that in the midst of the Church you dared
a thing which has never before this day come to our
hearing. But even these things, even if they are
painful and severe, are yet endurable, because they
have happened to a man who has entrusted to God
the requital of his sufferings and is wholly desirous
of peace and of having nothing harmful happen,
through any fault of his, to the people of God.

But since some of our honoured brothers who are
worthy of every trust have announced to us that
certain innovations in regard to the faith are being
made by you, and that things are being said by you
contrary to sound teaching, being aroused the more
on this account, and being in great distress lest perchance, in addition to the countless wounds which the
Church has suffered at the hands of those who have
erred against the truth of the Gospel, still another
evil may spring up, if there be a renewal of the
ancient heresy of Sabellius,[1] the enemy of the
Church (for our brothers announced that the words
spoken by you were akin to his), on this account we
have written, that you may not hesitate to rouse
yourself and undertake a short journey to us, and,
by furnishing us full information on these points, to
assuage our grief and to solace the churches of God,
which are now unbearably and seriously grieved at
what has been done and at what is generally
reported to have been said by you.

[1] Vol. I, Introduction.

---

[7] ἀπήγγελον editi antiqi.   [8] παραλαβεῖν E.
      [9] τοῦ add. E.

CXXVII

Εὐσεβίῳ, ἐπισκόπῳ Σαμοσάτων

Ὁ φιλάνθρωπος Θεὸς ὁ συμμέτρους ταῖς θλίψεσι τὰς παρακλήσεις συνάπτων καὶ παρακαλῶν τοὺς ταπεινούς, ἵνα μὴ λάθωσιν ὑπὸ τῆς περισσοτέρας λύπης καταποθέντες, ἴσην ταῖς ἐπιγενομέναις ἡμῖν κατὰ τὴν Νικόπολιν ταραχαῖς τὴν παραμυθίαν ἐπήγαγε, τὸν θεοφιλέστατον ἐπίσκοπον Ἰοβῖνον ἐν καιρῷ ἐπιστήσας· ὃς ὅπως εὐκαίρως ἡμῖν ἐπεφάνη, αὐτὸς διηγησάσθω. ἡμεῖς γὰρ φειδόμενοι τοῦ μήκους τῆς ἐπιστολῆς σιωπήσομεν, καὶ ἵνα μὴ δόξωμεν τοὺς ἐκ μεταβολῆς ἀγαπητοὺς ἡμῖν γενομένους[1] οἱονεὶ τῇ ὑπομνήσει τοῦ σφάλματος στηλιτεύειν.

Ἀλλὰ παράσχοι ὁ ἅγιος Θεὸς ἐπιστῆναί σε τοῖς ἡμετέροις τόποις, ὥστε περιπτύξασθαι μὲν τὴν σὴν σεμνοπρέπειαν, διηγήσασθαι δὲ τὰ καθ' ἕκαστον. πέφυκε γάρ πως τὰ κατὰ τὴν πεῖραν λυπήσαντα ψυχαγωγίαν τινὰ[2] ἔχειν ἐν διηγήμασι.[3] πλὴν ἀλλ' ὑπὲρ ὧν τελείως μὲν ὡς πρὸς τὴν εἰς ἡμᾶς ἀγάπην, προηγουμένως δὲ καὶ

---

[1] γινομένους E, Med.   [2] τινά om. E.
[3] πολλήν add. editi antiqi.

---

[1] Written about June 373. All that is definitely known of Eusebius of Samosata is learned from the letters of St. Basil the Great and St. Gregory of Nazianzus. He was instrumental in the consecration of Meletius as Bishop of Antioch, and was his staunch supporter during the long

LETTER CXXVII

To Eusebius, Bishop of Samosata [1]

Our merciful God, who applies consolations commensurate with our afflictions and consoles the downhearted, lest unaware they be overwhelmed by excessive grief, has brought to us a solace equal to the troubles that befell us at Nicopolis, having caused the most God-beloved bishop, Jovinus, to come opportunely; and how very opportunely he appeared to us, let him himself tell. For we, to spare a long letter, shall say nothing ourselves, and also that we may not seem to denounce as it were publicly by the mention of their error those who by a change of heart have become dear to us.

But may the holy God grant that you may come to our region, so that I may embrace your August Reverence, and recount to you every particular. For it is natural somehow that matters which have grieved us when we experienced them can afford a certain gratification when we recount them. However, as regards those matters in which our most God-beloved bishop has been active—with complete

years of schism and exile. It was likewise through his efforts that Basil was elevated to the see of Caesarea. This was the beginning of a mutual and unbroken friendship. After Easter in 374, Eusebius was exiled to Thrace. He was recalled in 378, and on his return to Samosata was martyred. Previous letters addressed to him are XXVII, XXX, XXXI, XXXIV, XLVII, XLVIII, XCV, XCVIII, and C.

Shortly after Basil's return from Nicopolis, whither he had gone to investigate the trouble caused by the uncanonical consecration of Faustus, Jovinus paid him a visit and rallied to his support. Jovinus himself is apparently the bearer of this letter, telling the good news to Eusebius.

στιβαρῶς ὡς πρὸς τὴν τῶν κανόνων ἀκρίβειαν ὁ
θεοφιλέστατος ἐπίσκοπος ἐκινήθη, ἐπαίνεσον
αὐτόν, καὶ εὐχαρίστησον τῷ Κυρίῳ, ὅτι τὰ σὰ
θρέμματα πανταχοῦ τὸν χαρακτῆρα τῆς σῆς
σεμνότητος δείκνυσιν.

CXXVIII

Εὐσεβίῳ, ἐπισκόπῳ Σαμοσάτων

Ἐγὼ τὴν περὶ τὸ εἰρηνεύεσθαι τὰς ἐκκλησίας
τοῦ Κυρίου [1] σπουδὴν ἔργῳ μὲν ἐνδείξασθαι ἀξίως
οὔπω δεδύνημαι, ἐν δὲ τῇ καρδίᾳ μου τοσαύτην
ἔχειν ἐπιθυμίαν φημί, ὥστε ἡδέως ἂν καὶ τὴν
ζωὴν τὴν ἐμαυτοῦ προέσθαι ὑπὲρ τοῦ τὴν ὑπὸ
τοῦ πονηροῦ ἐξαφθεῖσαν φλόγα τοῦ μίσους κατα-
σβεσθῆναι. καὶ εἰ μὴ τῆς ἐπιθυμίας ἕνεκεν τῆς
κατὰ τὴν εἰρήνην ἠνεσχόμην ἐγγίσαι τοῖς κατὰ
Κολώνειαν τόποις, μὴ εἰρηνευθείη μοι [2] ἡ ζωή.
εἰρήνην μέντοι τὴν ἀληθινὴν τὴν ὑπ' αὐτοῦ τοῦ
Κυρίου καταλειφθεῖσαν ἡμῖν ἐπιζητῶ· καὶ ὃ
παρεκάλεσά [3] μοι εἰς πληροφορίαν ὑπάρξαι, οὐκ
ἄλλο τι ἐπιθυμοῦντός ἐστιν ἢ τῆς ἀληθινῆς
εἰρήνης, κἂν ἄλλως τινὲς διαστρέφοντες τὴν
ἀλήθειαν ἐξηγῶνται. ἐκεῖνοι μὲν οὖν κεχρήσθω-

---

[1] Θεοῦ quattuor MSS.   [2] μου E.
[3] ὃ παρεκάλεσα] ὅπερ ἐκάλεσα editi antiqi.

---

[1] Written in 373. For Eusebius, see preceding letters.
This letter is Basil's reply to a letter from Eusebius, in
which Eusebius attempted to effect a reconciliation between
Basil and Eustathius of Sebaste. On Eustathius of Sebaste,
see preceding letters.

success as far as his love towards us is concerned, and especially and with great vigour so far as the exact observance of the canons is concerned—give him praise, and thank the Lord, that your disciples everywhere display the character of your Holiness.

LETTER CXXVIII

To Eusebius, Bishop of Samosata [1]

I have not yet been able in a worthy manner to give practical proof of my zeal for establishing peace among the churches of the Lord, but in my heart I cherish, I affirm, so great a desire that I would gladly even lay down my life to extinguish this flame of hatred that has been stirred up by the evil one. And if it was not on account of this desire of peace that I consented to visit the region of Colonia,[2] may my life enjoy no peace. But it is the true peace left us by the Lord Himself that I am seeking; and what I demanded should be put into my hands as a guarantee,[3] is the act of one who desires nothing other than the true peace, even though certain persons [4] distort the truth and

[2] Letters CCXXVII and CCXXVIII are addressed to the clergy and magistrates of Colonia in Armenia. This was probably the place at which, in the presence of Basil and others, Eustathius was to subscribe to the Creed as defined in Letter CXXV.

[3] *i.e.* of the orthodoxy of Eustathius of Sebaste.

[4] Probably the two monks, Basil and Euphronius, who had been recommended to St. Basil's service by Eustathius, and who had busied themselves spreading calumnies about St. Basil. Cf. Letter CXIX.

σαν ταῖς γλώσσαις αὐτῶν ἐφ᾽ ἃ βούλονται·
πάντως γὰρ αὐτοῖς ποτὲ τῶν ῥημάτων τούτων
μεταμελήσει.

Τὴν δὲ σὴν ὁσιότητα παρακαλῶ μεμνῆσθαι τῶν
ἐξ ἀρχῆς προτάσεων, καὶ μὴ παράγεσθαι ἄλλας
ἀποκρίσεις ἀντ᾽ ἄλλων ἐρωτημάτων δεχόμενον,[1]
μηδὲ ποιεῖν ἐνεργὰ τὰ σοφίσματα τῶν ἄνευ τῆς
περὶ τὸ λέγειν δυνάμεως ἀπ᾽ αὐτῆς μόνης τῆς
γνώμης δεινότατα πάντων τὴν ἀλήθειαν κακουρ-
γούντων. προέτεινα γὰρ ἁπλᾶ καὶ σαφῆ καὶ
εὐμνημόνευτα ῥήματα· εἰ τοὺς μὴ δεχομένους τὴν
ἐν Νικαίᾳ πίστιν παραιτούμεθα εἰς κοινωνίαν,
καὶ εἰ μετὰ τῶν κτίσμα λέγειν τὸ Πνεῦμα τὸ
ἅγιον ἀποτολμώντων τὸ μέρος ἔχειν οὐκ ἀνεχόμεθα. ὁ δέ,[2] ἀντὶ τοῦ πρὸς ἔπος ταῖς ἐρωτήσε-
σιν ἀποκρίνασθαι, ἐκεῖνα ἡμῖν ἐρραψῴδησεν
ἅπερ ἀπέστειλας· καὶ τοῦτο οὐκ ἀφελείᾳ[3] γνώμης,
ὡς ἄν τῳ δόξαι,[4] οὐδὲ τῷ μὴ δύνασθαι συνορᾶν τὸ
ἀκόλουθον. ἀλλ᾽ ἐκεῖνο λογίζεται, ὅτι ἀρνούμενος
μὲν ἡμῶν τὴν πρότασιν, τοῖς λαοῖς ἑαυτὸν κατάδηλον ποιήσει, συντιθέμενος δὲ ἡμῖν, τῆς μεσότητος
ἀποστήσεται, ἧς οὐδὲν αὐτῷ μέχρι τοῦ νῦν γέγονε
προτιμότερον. μὴ τοίνυν ἡμᾶς κατασοφιζέσθω,
μηδὲ μετὰ τῶν ἄλλων καὶ τὴν σὴν παρακρουέσθω
φρόνησιν· ἀλλὰ σύντομον ἡμῖν λόγον ἀποστει-
λάτω πρὸς τὸ ἐρώτημα, ἢ ὁμολογῶν τὴν κοινωνίαν
πρὸς τοὺς ἐχθροὺς τῆς πίστεως, ἢ ἀρνούμενος.
ἐὰν ταῦτα συμπείσῃς αὐτὸν καὶ πέμψῃς μοι
ὀρθὰς καὶ οἵας εὔχομαι τὰς ἀποκρίσεις, ἐγώ εἰμι

[1] δεχομένην editi antiqi.　　[2] ὁ δέ] οὐδέ E.
[3] ἀφελείᾳ E.
[4] ἄν τῳ δόξαι] αὐτῷ δόξαι E, editi antiqi.

interpret it otherwise. So let them employ their
tongues as they will, for assuredly they will some
day regret such words.

But I urge your Holiness[1] to be mindful of the
primary propositions, and not to be led astray by
accepting answers which do not correspond to the
questions, and not to render effective the quibbles
of men who, lacking all ability to speak on the
strength of their mere opinions, corrupt the truth
most dreadfully of all men. For I set forth propositions in terms which were simple, clear, and
easily remembered :—whether we shall forbid the
admission to our communion of those who do not
accept the Nicaean Creed, and whether we shall
refuse to have any participation with those who
dare to call the Holy Spirit a creature. But he,
instead of answering my questions word for word,
recited the very same statements that you have
written us ; and this he did with no simplicity of
mind, as one might think, nor through any inability to realize the outcome. On the contrary,
he has this in mind,—that if he denies our proposition, he will make his true self clear to the people,
but that if he agrees with us, he will be withdrawing
from the middle course, which has thus far been decidedly preferable to him. So do not let him outwit
us, and do not let him deceive your wisdom as he has
done with the rest; but let him send us a succinct
answer to the question, either confessing communion
with the enemies of the faith or denying it. If you
win him over to this and the answers you send me
are direct and such as I pray for, I am the one who

---

[1] A title given in Byzantine times to bishops and monks,
and sometimes to emperors.

ὁ τὰ κατόπιν πάντα ἡμαρτηκώς· ἐγὼ δέχομαι
πᾶσαν τὴν αἰτίαν ἐκείνην ἐπ' ἐμαυτόν· τότε με
ἀπαίτει ταπεινοφροσύνης ἐπίδειξιν. ἕως δ' ἂν
μηδὲν γένηται τούτων, σύγγνωθι, θεοφιλέστατε
πάτερ, μὴ δυναμένῳ μετὰ ὑποκρίσεως θυσια-
στηρίῳ Θεοῦ παρεστάναι.[1] εἰ γὰρ μὴ τοῦτο
ἐφοβούμην, τίνος ἕνεκεν ἐμαυτὸν ἐχώριζον Εὐΐππίου, τοιούτου μὲν τὰ περὶ λόγους, τοσοῦτον δὲ
χρόνῳ[2] προήκοντος, τοσαῦτα δὲ τῆς πρὸς ἡμᾶς
φιλίας δίκαια κεκτημένου ; εἰ δὲ ἐκεῖνα καλῶς καὶ
προσηκόντως ὑπὲρ τῆς ἀληθείας ἐπράξαμεν, γελοῖον δή που τοῖς τὰ αὐτὰ ἐκείνῳ λέγουσι διὰ
τῆς τῶν εὐφυῶν τούτων καὶ χαριέντων μεσότητος
συναπτόμενον φαίνεσθαι.

Οὐ μὴν οὐδὲ παντελῶς μοι δοκεῖ τῶν μὴ δεχο-
μένων τὴν πίστιν ἀλλοτριοῦν ἑαυτούς, ἀλλὰ
ποιήσασθαί τινα τῶν ἀνδρῶν ἐπιμέλειαν κατὰ
τοὺς παλαιοὺς θεσμοὺς τῆς ἀγάπης, καὶ ἐπιστεῖλαι αὐτοῖς ἀπὸ μιᾶς γνώμης, πᾶσαν παράκλησιν μετ' εὐσπλαγχνίας προσάγοντας, καὶ τὴν
τῶν πατέρων πίστιν προτεινομένους προκαλεῖσθαι
αὐτοὺς εἰς συνάφειαν· κἂν μὲν πείσωμεν, κοινῶς
αὐτοῖς ἑνωθῆναι· ἐὰν δὲ ἀποτύχωμεν, ἀρκεῖσθαι
ἡμᾶς ἀλλήλοις, τὸν δὲ ἐπαμφοτερισμὸν τοῦτον
ἐξορίσαι τοῦ ἤθους, ἀναλαβόντας τὴν εὐαγγε-
λικὴν καὶ ἄδολον πολιτείαν, ᾗ συνέζων οἱ ἐξ

---

[1] παριστάναι editi antiqi.　　　　[2] χρόνον editi antiqi.

---

[1] The superlative form of this adjective was used in
Christian times as a title applied to bishops, monks,
deacons, and emperors.

have been utterly at fault in the past; I take all
the blame upon myself; then you may demand of
me a proof of humility. But as long as none of
these things comes to pass, forgive me, most god-
beloved [1] father, if I cannot as a hypocrite stand at
God's altar. For if it were not for my fear of
hypocrisy, why did I separate myself from Euippius,[2]
so eminent in letters, so advanced in years, possessing so many claims to friendship with us? And if
on that occasion we acted nobly and properly in
support of the truth, surely it would be ridiculous
for me to appear to be united with those who,
through the mediation of these clever and charming
persons, make the same assertions as he made.

And yet it does not seem best to me to estrange
ourselves entirely from those who do not accept the
faith, but we should show some concern for these
men according to the old laws of charity and should
with one accord write letters to them, offering every
exhortation with kindliness, and proffering to them
the faith of the Fathers we should invite them to
join us; and if we convince them, we should be
united with them in communion; but if we fail, we
should ourselves be content with one another, and
should remove this present uncertainty from our
way of life, taking up again that evangelical and
guileless polity in which they lived who from the

---

[2] Euippius: a bishop of Arianizing doctrines, from whom
Basil felt it necessary for the cause of truth to separate
altogether. Cf. Letter LVI. Eustathius of Sebaste, in
A.D. 360, violently declaimed against Euippius as not deserving the name of bishop, but in A.D. 376, Eustathius
united with him and recognized the bishops and presbyters
he had ordained. Cf. Letters CCXXVI, CCXXXIX,
CCXLIV, CCLI.

COLLECTED LETTERS OF SAINT BASIL

ἀρχῆς προσελθόντες τῷ λόγῳ. ἦν γάρ, φησί,
τῶν πιστευσάντων καρδία καὶ ψυχὴ μία. ἐὰν
μὲν οὖν πεισθῶσί σοι, ταῦτα ἄριστα. εἰ δὲ μή,
γνωρίσατε τοὺς πολεμοποιούς, καὶ παύσασθε
ἡμῖν τοῦ λοιποῦ περὶ διαλλαγῶν ἐπιστέλλοντες.

CXXIX

Μελετίῳ, ἐπισκόπῳ Ἀντιοχείας

Ἤιδειν ὅτι ξενίσει τὴν ἀκοὴν τῆς τελειότητός
σου τὸ νῦν ἐπιφυὲν ἔγκλημα τῷ πάντα εἰπεῖν
εὐκόλῳ Ἀπολιναρίῳ. καὶ γὰρ οὐδὲ αὐτὸς τὸν
πρὸ τούτου χρόνον ἤμην ἐπιστάμενος ἔχειν·
ἀλλὰ νῦν οἱ Σεβαστηνοὶ διερευνησάμενοί ποθεν
αὐτὰ εἰς τὸ μέσον ἤνεγκαν, καὶ περιφέρουσι
σύνταγμα, ἐξ οὗ μάλιστα καὶ ἡμᾶς καταδικά-
ζουσιν, ὡς τὰ αὐτὰ φρονοῦντας, ἔχον ῥήσεις

---

[1] Cf. Acts, 4, 32: τοῦ δὲ πλήθους τῶν πιστευσάντων ἦν ἡ
καρδία καὶ ἡ ψυχὴ μία. "And the multitude of believers had
but one heart and one soul."

[2] The Benedictine edition has assigned the composition of
this letter to A.D. 373. Loofs presents rather unconvincing
arguments for both this letter and the following (CXXX) being
written in the summer of 375.
The addressee of this letter, St. Meletius, Bishop of
Antioch, was born in Melitene, Lesser Armenia, and died at
Antioch in 381. He apparently believed that truth lay in
delicate distinctions, but his formula was so indefinite that it
is difficult even to-day to grasp it clearly. He was neither a
thorough Nicene nor a decided Arian, and he passed alter-
nately as an Anomean, a Homoiousian, a Homoian, or a
Neo-Nicene, seeking always to remain outside any inflexible
classification. After his death his name long remained for the

beginning adhered to the Word.[1] "For," he says, "the believers had but one heart and one soul." If, then, they obey you, that will be best. But if not, recognize the instigators of the trouble, and henceforth cease writing to me about a recon ciliation.

LETTER CXXIX

To Meletius, Bishop of Antioch [2]

I knew that the charge which has now sprung up against Apollinaris,[3] that man who is so ready to say anything, would surprise the ears of your Perfection.[4] For in fact not even I myself was aware until the present time that the situation was as it is ; but now the Sebastenes, having sought out these matters from some source, have brought them before the public, and they are circulating a document from which they bring accusations chiefly against us as well, on the ground that we hold the same views as those expressed in the document. It contains such

Eastern faithful a rallying sign and a synonym of orthodoxy.

Basil here writes to refute the charges made against him of teaching heresy, and he names Apollinaris as the real author of the heretical document used as evidence. He considers other matters also, including the action taken upon his case at the court.

[3] Apollinaris (Ἀπολινάριος) the Younger, Bishop of Laodicea, flourished during the first half of the fourth century. He was highly esteemed by Basil, it seems, until the year 376. He taught that Christ had a human body and a human sensitive soul, but no rational mind, the Divine Logos taking the place of this last.

[4] Byzantine title.

τοιαύτας· ὥστε πανταχῆ συνεζευγμένως, μᾶλλον
δὲ ἡνωμένως τῇ ἑτερότητι νοεῖν ἀναγκαῖον τὴν
πρώτην ταυτότητα, καὶ δευτέραν καὶ τρίτην
λέγοντας τὴν αὐτήν. ὅπερ γάρ ἐστι πρώτως ὁ
Πατήρ, τοῦτό ἐστι δευτέρως ὁ Υἱός, καὶ τρίτως
τὸ Πνεῦμα. αὖθις δὲ ὅπερ ἐστὶ πρώτως τὸ
Πνεῦμα τοῦτο δευτέρως τὸν Υἱόν, καθὸ δὴ καὶ ὁ
Κύριός ἐστι τὸ Πνεῦμα· καὶ τρίτως τὸν Πατέρα
καθὸ δὴ Πνεῦμα ὁ Θεός. καὶ ὡς βιαιότερον
σημᾶναι[1] τὸ ἄρρητον, τὸν Πατέρα πατρικῶς Υἱὸν
εἶναι, τὸν δὲ Υἱὸν υἱικῶς Πατέρα. καὶ ὡσαύτως
ἐπὶ τοῦ Πνεύματος, καθὸ δὴ εἷς Θεὸς ἡ Τριάς.

Ταῦτά ἐστι τὰ θρυλλούμενα, ἃ οὐδέποτε
δύναμαι πιστεῦσαι πλάσματα εἶναι τῶν περι-
φερόντων,[2] εἰ καὶ ὅτι ἐκ τῆς καθ᾿ ἡμῶν[3] συκοφαντίας οὐδὲν λογίζομαι αὐτοῖς ἀτόλμητον εἶναι.
γράφοντες γάρ τισι τῶν καθ᾿ ἑαυτούς, καὶ προσθέντες[4] τὴν καθ᾿ ἡμῶν διαβολήν, ἐπήγαγον
ταῦτα, ῥήματα μὲν αἱρετικῶν ὀνομάσαντες,[5] τὸν
δὲ πατέρα τῆς συγγραφῆς ἀποκρυψάμενοι, ἵνα
τοῖς πολλοῖς ἡμεῖς νομισθῶμεν εἶναι οἱ λογο-
γράφοι.[6] πλὴν ἀλλ᾿ οὐκ ἂν μέχρι τοῦ καὶ[7]
ῥήματα συνθεῖναι προῆλθεν αὐτῶν ἡ ἐπίνοια, ὥς
γε ἐμαυτὸν πείθω. ὅθεν, ὑπὲρ τοῦ καὶ τὴν καθ᾿
ἡμῶν κρατοῦσαν βλασφημίαν ἀπώσασθαι, καὶ
δεῖξαι πᾶσιν, ὡς οὐδὲν ἡμῖν ἐστι[8] κοινὸν πρὸς
τοὺς ἐκεῖνο λέγοντας, ἠναγκάσθημεν μνησθῆναι

---

[1] σημαίνει E.
[2] προφερόντων editi antiqi.
[3] ἡμᾶς E, Regius primus.
[4] προθέντες Coisl. secundus, Reg. secundus.
[5] ὀνομάζοντες editi antiqi.

statements as these : " Consequently it is necessary to conceive of the first identity in every case conjointly, or rather unitedly with the dissimilarity, saying that the second and the third are the same. For what the Father is first, the Son is secondly, and the Spirit thirdly. And again, what is first the Spirit, this is secondly the Son—inasmuch as the Lord is the Spirit—and thirdly the Father—inasmuch as the Spirit is God." And in order to express this unspeakable thought more forcefully : " That the Father is paternally the Son, and the Son is filially the Father. And in like manner with the Holy Ghost, inasmuch as the Trinity is one God."

These are the things that are being noised about, but I can never believe that these are fabrications of those who are spreading them abroad, although, on account of their slanderous charges against us, I consider that nothing is beyond the limits of their effrontery. For when writing to some of their own adherents, and after making this false accusation against us, they added the words mentioned above, calling them the expressions of heretics, but concealing the name of the father of the document, in order that to people at large we might be considered the author. However, their intelligence could not have carried them to the point of actually composing these statements, as I am convinced. Hence, for the sake of repudiating the charge of blasphemy that is prevalent against us, and of showing to all that we have nothing in common with those who say such things, we have been forced to mention this

---

[6] ὀλιγογράφοι E.   [7] μέχρι τοῦ καί] τοῦ μέχρι E.
[8] ἐστί om. E.

τοῦ ἀνδρός, ὡς προσεγγίζοντος τῇ ἀσεβείᾳ τοῦ
Σαβελλίου. καὶ ταῦτα μὲν εἰς τοσοῦτον.

Ἀπὸ δὲ τοῦ στρατοπέδου ἧκέ τις ἀγγέλλων,
ἐπὶ τῇ πρώτῃ κινήσει τοῦ κρατοῦντος, ἣν ἐκίνη-
σαν αὐτὸν οἱ τὰς διαβολὰς ἡμῶν[1] καταχέοντες,
γεγενῆσθαί τινα καὶ δευτέραν γνώμην, ὥστε μὴ
δοθῆναι ἡμᾶς ἐκδότους τοῖς κατηγόροις, μήτε
παραδοθῆναι ἡμᾶς τῷ ἐκείνων θελήματι, ὅπερ ἦν
ἐξ ἀρχῆς ὁρισθέν· ἀλλά τινα γενέσθαι τέως
ἀναβολήν. ἐὰν οὖν ἢ ταῦτα μένῃ, ἢ τούτων
τι δόξῃ φιλανθρωπότερον, σημανοῦμέν σου τῇ
θεοσεβείᾳ. ἐὰν δὲ κρατῇ τὰ πρότερα, οὐδὲ τοῦτό
σε λήσεται.

Ὁ μέντοι ἀδελφὸς Σαγκτίσσιμος πάντως ἐστὶ
παρ' ὑμῖν πάλαι, καὶ ἃ ἐπιζητεῖ δῆλα γέγονε τῇ
τελειότητί σου. εἰ οὖν φαίνεται ἀναγκαῖόν τι
ἔχειν ἡ πρὸς τοὺς δυτικοὺς ἐπιστολή, καταξίωσον
τυπώσας αὐτὴν διαπέμψασθαι[2] ἡμῖν, ὥστε
ποιῆσαι ὑπογραφῆναι παρὰ τῶν ὁμοψύχων καὶ
ἑτοίμην ἔχειν τὴν ὑπογραφήν, ἐν χάρτῃ κεχωρισ-
μένῳ ἐντετυπωμένην,[3] ὃν δυνάμεθα συνάψαι τῷ
παρὰ τοῦ ἀδελφοῦ ἡμῶν τοῦ συμπρεσβυτέρου

---

[1] ἡμῖν editi antiqi.
[2] καταξίωσον . . . διαπέμψασθαι] καταξίαν . . . διαπέμψαι
editi antiqi.
[3] ἐντετυπωμένην om. E.

---

[1] i.e. Apollinaris.
[2] Sabellius affirmed that there exists in God only a single
person, and that this unity or monad (μονάς) constitutes the
absolute being of God. When the divine essence departed
from its quiet and inactivity, manifesting itself and acting,

man's name [1] as one who is approaching the impiety of Sabellius.[2] But let so much suffice on this matter.

But a messenger has come from the court, saying that after the first excitement of the Emperor, to which he was impelled by those who were pouring out their slanders against us, a second resolution was determined upon—that we should not be surrendered to our accusers, nor should we be placed at the mercy of their will, as was decreed in the first place ; but that up to the present there has been delay. Therefore, if these matters remain as they are, or if some more kindly action is decided on, we shall inform your Godliness.[3] And if the former course prevail, this also will not be concealed from you.

But our brother Sanctissimus, at all events, has been with you for a long time, and your Perfection has become fully aware of what he has in mind. So, if the letter to the people of the West appears to contain anything that is important for us, be pleased to draft it and send it to us, in order that we may get it subscribed to by those of the same mind as ourselves, and that we may have the subscription ready, written upon a separate sheet of paper, which we can fasten to the sheet which is being carried around to us by our brother the pres-

---

it was called the Word (λόγος). It is the Word which created the world ; and again it is the Word which undertook the salvation of humanity. For this work it took three successive modes of existence : three aspects (πρόσωπα), three denominations (ὀνόματα), corresponding to the three economies which succeed each other in the order of salvation : Father, Son, and Holy Ghost. But these three modes of existence are transitory and accidental. Each of them is to cease at the same time as the object which necessitates each.

[3] A title usually given to the bishops in Byzantine times.

περικομιζομένῳ.[1] ἐγὼ μὲν γὰρ οὐδὲν εὑρὼν[2]
συνεκτικὸν ἐν τῷ ὑπομνηστικῷ, οὐκ ἔσχον ὑπὲρ
οὗ ἐπιστείλω τοῖς ἐν τῇ δύσει. τὰ μὲν γὰρ ἀναγκαῖα προείληπται· τὰ δὲ περιττὰ γράφειν παντελῶς μάταιον. περὶ δὲ τῶν αὐτῶν ἐνοχλεῖν μὴ
καὶ γελοῖον εἴη;

Ἐκείνη δέ μοι ἔδοξεν ὥσπερ ἀγύμναστος εἶναι
ἡ ὑπόθεσις καὶ χώραν παρέχειν γράμμασι,[3] τὸ
παρακαλέσαι αὐτοὺς μὴ ἀκρίτως δέχεσθαι τὰς
κοινωνίας τῶν ἐκ τῆς ἀνατολῆς ἀφικνουμένων,
ἀλλ' ἅπαξ μίαν μερίδα ἐκλεξαμένους, τοὺς λοιποὺς
ἐκ τῆς μαρτυρίας τῶν κοινωνικῶν προσλαμ-
βάνεσθαι· καὶ μὴ παντὶ τῷ πίστιν γράφοντι ἐπὶ
προφάσει δὴ τῆς ὀρθοδοξίας προστίθεσθαι. οὕτω
γὰρ εὑρεθήσονται τοῖς μαχομένοις κοινωνοῦντες,
οἱ τὰ μὲν ῥήματα πολλάκις τὰ αὐτὰ προβάλλον-
ται, μάχονται δὲ ἀλλήλοις ὅσον οἱ πλεῖστον
διεστηκότες. ἵν' οὖν μὴ ἐπὶ πλεῖον ἡ αἵρεσις
ἐξάπτηται[4] τῶν πρὸς ἀλλήλους διαστασιαζόντων
ἀντιπροβαλλομένων τὰ παρ' αὐτῶν γράμματα,
παρακληθῆναι αὐτοὺς ἔδει κεκριμένας ποιεῖσθαι
καὶ τὰς τῶν ἐντυγχανόντων αὐτοῖς κοινωνίας καὶ
τὰς ἐγγράφως γινομένας κατὰ τὸν τύπον τῆς
Ἐκκλησίας.

---

[1] κομιζομένου E.
[2] οὐδὲν εὑρὼν] οὐδὲν εὗρον Harl. ; οὐχ εὑρών editi antiqi.
[3] γράμματι editi antiqi.

byter. For since I found in the memorandum
nothing especially important, I had no grounds for
writing to those in the West. For those things
which were necessary have been anticipated ; and to
write what is superfluous is wholly vain. And
would it not even be ridiculous to trouble them
about the same matters ?

But the following subject seemed to me to be as
it were undeveloped and to offer grounds for writing
—the matter of urging them not to receive indis-
criminately the communion of those coming from the
East, but after once choosing a single portion of
them, to accept the rest on the testimony of these
already in communion ; and of urging them not to take
into communion everyone who writes down the
Creed as a supposed proof of orthodoxy. For thus
they will find themselves to be in communion with
men prone to fight, who often put forward statements of doctrine which are identical, but then
proceed to fight with one another as violently as
the men who are of diametrically opposite opinions.
In order, then, that heresy may not flame out still
more on the part of those who in their conflict with
one another bring forward their opposing formulae,
the people of the West ought to be urged to
exercise discrimination as regards both communion
with those who come to them by chance and
communion based upon a written document according to the law of the Church.[1]

[1] From this passage and from Letter CCXXIV the Benedictine editors perceive two kinds of communion : (1) personal,
in the Eucharist and prayer, and (2) by letter.

---

[4] ἐξαπατῆται editi antiqi.

CXXX

Θεοδότῳ, ἐπισκόπῳ Νικοπόλεως

Καλῶς καὶ προσηκόντως ἡμῶν καθήψω, τιμιώτατε ὡς ἀληθῶς καὶ ποθεινότατε ἀδελφέ, ὅτι ἐξ
οὗ ἀνεχωρήσαμεν τότε τῆς σῆς εὐλαβείας τὰς
περὶ τῆς πίστεως ἐκείνας προτάσεις τῷ Εὐσταθίῳ
φέροντες, οὐδέν σοι οὔτε μικρὸν οὔτε μεῖζον τῶν
κατ’ αὐτὸν ἐδηλώσαμεν. ἐγὼ δὲ οὐχ ὡς εὐκατα-
φρονήτων [1] τῶν παρ’ αὐτοῦ γενομένων εἰς ἡμᾶς
ὑπερεῖδον, ἀλλ’ ὡς εἰς πάντας λοιπὸν τοὺς ἀνθρώπους διαβοηθείσης τῆς φήμης, καὶ οὐδενὸς τῆς
παρ’ ἡμῶν διδασκαλίας εἰς τὸ τὴν προαίρεσιν τοῦ
ἀνδρὸς διδαχθῆναι προσδεομένου. τοῦτο γὰρ καὶ
αὐτὸς ἐπενόησεν, ὥσπερ φοβούμενος μὴ ὀλίγους
σχῇ τῆς ἑαυτοῦ γνώμης μάρτυρας, εἰς πᾶσαν
ἐσχατιὰν τὰς ἐπιστολὰς ἃς καθ’ ἡμῶν συνέγραψε
διαπεμψάμενος. τῆς μὲν οὖν κοινωνίας ἡμῶν
αὐτὸς ἀπέρρηξεν ἑαυτόν, μήτε κατὰ τὸν ὡρισ-
μένον τόπον συνδραμεῖν ἡμῖν ἀνασχόμενος, μήτε
τοὺς μαθητὰς ἑαυτοῦ παραγαγών, ὅπερ ὑπέσχετο·
ἀλλὰ καὶ ἡμᾶς στηλιτεύων ἐν πανδήμοις συνό-

---

[1] καταφρονήτων editi antiqi.

---

[1] For the date of this letter, see note 1 of the preceding
letter. Theodotus, Bishop of Nicopolis, a staunch friend of
Basil, died in A.D. 375. He is mentioned in Letters XCII,
XCV, XCIX, CXXI, CCXXIX, and CCXXXVII.

LETTER CXXX

To Theodotus, Bishop of Nicopolis [1]

NOBLY and fittingly have you upbraided us, most honoured in very truth and beloved brother, because, since the time when we departed from your Reverence, bringing those propositions concerning the Faith to Eustathius,[2] we have informed you of nothing either small or great in regard to his affairs. But as for me, it was not because I regarded as contemptible the charges which have been instigated by him against us that I have overlooked the matter, but because the report has now been noised abroad to the whole world, and because nobody needs any instruction from us as regards the purposes of this man. For he contrived this result himself—as if he were afraid that he would have but a few witnesses of his opinion—by sending to most distant parts the letters which he wrote against us. He of his own accord has thus severed himself from communion with us, for he did not fulfil his intention of meeting us at the appointed place, nor did he bring his disciples as he had promised; but he denounced us in the general synods,

---

[2] Eustathius of Sebaste, 300–377. He was bishop of Sebaste in 356, and was one of the founders of monasticism. He had studied under Arius, and wavered between semi-Arianism throughout his life. He was a close friend of Basil until the latter recognized his true character in 372 or 373. He had once signed the Nicene Creed, for he together with Theophilus and Silvanus went on a mission to Rome in 365-6, and acknowledged their adherence to the Nicene Creed before Pope Liberius. Cf. Letter CCXLV. He seems to have been a vacillating character, and it is said that he signed practically all the creeds of his age.

COLLECTED LETTERS OF SAINT BASIL

δοις, μετὰ τοῦ Κίλικος Θεοφίλου, γυμνῇ καὶ
ἀπαρακαλύπτῳ τῇ βλασφημίᾳ ὡς ἀλλότρια τῆς
ἑαυτοῦ¹ διδασκαλίας ταῖς ψυχαῖς τοῦ λαοῦ
ἐνσπείραντας δόγματα. ἱκανὰ μὲν οὖν ἦν καὶ
ταῦτα πᾶσαν ἡμῶν τὴν πρὸς αὐτὸν συνάφειαν
διαλῦσαι. ἐπειδὴ δὲ καὶ εἰς Κιλικίαν ἐλθών, καὶ
συντυχὼν Γελασίῳ τινί, πίστιν αὐτῷ ἐξέθετο, ἣν
μόνον² ἦν Ἀρείου συγγράψαι καὶ εἴ τις αὐτοῦ
γνήσιος μαθητής, τότε δὴ καὶ πλέον πρὸς τὸν
χωρισμὸν ἐβεβαιώθημεν, λογισάμενοι, ὅτι οὔτε
Αἰθίοψ ἀλλάξει ποτὲ τὸ δέρμα αὐτοῦ, οὔτε
πάρδαλις τὰ ποικίλματα αὐτῆς, οὔτε ὁ ἐν διαστρό-
φοις δόγμασι συντραφεὶς ἀποτρίψασθαι δύναται
τὸ κακὸν τῆς αἱρέσεως.

Ἐπενεανιεύσατο δὲ τούτοις καὶ γράψας καθ᾽
ἡμῶν, μᾶλλον δὲ συγγράψας λόγους μακροὺς
πάσης λοιδορίας καὶ συκοφαντίας γέμοντας· ὑπὲρ
ὧν οὐδὲν ἀπεκρινάμεθα τέως, διὰ τὸ διδαχθῆναι
παρὰ τοῦ ἀποστόλου, μὴ ἑαυτοὺς ἐκδικεῖν, ἀλλὰ
διδόναι τόπον τῇ ὀργῇ· καὶ ἅμα ἐννοήσαντες τὸ
βάθος τῆς ὑποκρίσεως, μεθ᾽ ἧς πάντα τὸν χρόνον
ἡμῖν προσηνέχθη, ἀφασίᾳ τινὶ ὑπ᾽ ἐκπλήξεως
κατεσχέθημεν.

Εἰ δὲ καὶ μηδὲν ἦν ἐκείνων, τὸ ὑπόγυον τοῦτο,
τὸ τολμηθὲν αὐτῷ, τίνι οὐκ ἂν φρίκην καὶ

¹ αὐτοῦ editi antiqi.   ² μόνον editi antiqi.

---

[1] Theophilus was bishop of Castabala (also called Hiero-
polis) on the river Pyramis in Cilicia, whither he was trans-
lated from Eleutheropolis. Cf. Letters CCXLIV. and
CCXLV. He was on friendly terms with St. Basil at one
time, and was sent to Rome on an embassy. See note
above.

he along with the Cilician Theophilus,[1] saying
with bare and undisguised slander that we were
sowing a different doctrine from his in the souls
of the people. Accordingly, these circumstances
sufficed for our severing all connexions with him.
And when, having come into Cilicia and having met
there a certain Gelasius,[2] he set forth his creed to
him, a creed to which only an Arius could subscribe
or a real disciple of Arius, then in truth were we
more strongly confirmed in our separation from him,
considering that neither will an Ethiopian ever
change his skin, nor a leopard her spots,[3] nor is a
man who has been nourished on perverted doctrines
able to rid himself of the evil of heresy.

He has added to these acts of effrontery by
writing against us, or rather by composing long
tracts filled with every abuse and calumny ; regarding which we have hitherto made no reply, because
we have been taught by the apostle not to avenge
ourselves, but to give place unto wrath ;[4] and,
moreover, having considered the depth of the
hypocrisy which has characterized his dealings with
us at all times, we have been seized with a sort of
speechlessness through astonishment.

But even if none of these things had been, in whom
would not this last piece of audacity on his part

[2] This Gelasius is otherwise unknown.
[3] Cf. Jer. 13, 23 : εἰ ἀλλάξεται Αἰθίοψ τὸ δέρμα αὐτοῦ καὶ
πάρδαλις τὰ ποικίλματα αὐτῆς ; καὶ ὑμεῖς δυνήσεσθε εὖ ποιῆσαι
μεμαθηκότες τὰ κακά. " If the Ethiopian can change his skin,
or the leopard his spots : you also may do well, when you
have learned evil."
[4] Cf. Rom. 12, 19 : μὴ ἑαυτοὺς ἐκδικοῦντες, ἀγαπητοί, ἀλλὰ
δότε τόπον τῇ ὀργῇ. " Revenge not yourselves, my dearly
beloved ; but give place unto wrath."

ἀποστροφὴν παντελῆ τοῦ ἀνδρὸς ἐνεποίησεν;
ὅς γε, ὡς ἀκούω (εἴ γε ἀληθὴς ὁ λόγος καὶ μὴ
πλάσμα ἐστὶν ἐπὶ διαβολῇ συντεθέν), ὅτι καὶ
ἀναχειροτονῆσαί τινας ἐτόλμησεν, ὃ μέχρι σήμερον
οὐδεὶς τῶν αἱρετικῶν ποιήσας φαίνεται. πῶς
οὖν δυνατὸν πράως φέρειν ἡμᾶς τὰ τοιαῦτα καὶ
ἰάσιμα εἶναι νομίζειν τοῦ ἀνδρὸς τὰ ἁμαρτήματα;
μὴ τοίνυν ψευδέσι λόγοις παράγεσθε, μηδὲ
ὑπονοίαις ἀνδρῶν πάντα εὐκόλως πρὸς τὸ κακὸν
ἐκλαμβανόντων πείθεσθε, ὡς ἄρα ἡμεῖς ἀδιά-
φορα¹ τιθέμεθα τὰ τοιαῦτα. γίνωσκε γάρ,
ποθεινότατε ἡμῖν καὶ τιμιώτατε, ὅτι οὔπω οἶδα
τοσοῦτον πένθος ἄλλοτε τῇ ψυχῇ μου παραδεξά-
μενος, ὅσον νῦν, ὅτε ἤκουσα τῶν ἐκκλησιαστικῶν
θεσμῶν τὴν σύγχυσιν. ἀλλὰ μόνον εὔχου, ἵνα
δῴη ἡμῖν ὁ Κύριος μηδὲν κατὰ θυμὸν ἐνεργεῖν,
ἀλλ' ἔχειν τὴν ἀγάπην, ἥτις οὐκ ἀσχημονεῖ, οὐ
φυσιοῦται. ὅρα γὰρ ὅπως² οἱ μὴ ἔχοντες ταύτην ἐπήρθησαν μὲν ὑπὲρ τὰ μέτρα τὰ ἀνθρώπινα, ἐνασχημονοῦσι δὲ τῷ βίῳ, κατατολμῶντες
πράξεων, ὧν ὁ παρελθὼν χρόνος οὐκ ἔχει τὰ
ὑποδείγματα.

---

¹ ἀδιάφορα Coisl. secundus, Reg. secundus.
² πῶς editi antiqi.

---

¹ Cf. 1 Cor. 13, 4 and 5: ἡ ἀγάπη μακροθυμεῖ, χρηστεύεται·
οὐ φυσιοῦται, οὐκ ἀσχημονεῖ, οὐ ζητεῖ τὰ ἑαυτῆς. ἡ ἀγάπη οὐ

have produced a chill of horror and a complete
aversion for the man? For he, as I hear (if the
report be true and not a figment made up for the
purpose of calumny), has presumed also to re-ordain
certain men, a thing which up to the present no one
of the heretics appears to have done. How, then, is
it possible for us to endure such things mildly and to
consider that the errors of the man are curable?
Therefore, do not be led astray by his false words;
nor give credence to the suspicions of men who are
easily inclined to understand everything in a bad
sense, who assume, for instance, that we regard such
matters as of indifferent importance. For we wish
you to know, most beloved and honoured friend,
that I do not recall having ever received such deep
grief in my soul as at this moment, when I have
heard of the confusion in the ecclesiastical laws. But
only pray that the Lord may grant us to do nothing
in anger, but to have charity, which does not act
unseemly, and is not puffed up.[1] For, behold how
those who do not have this charity have been raised
above the bounds proper to men, and are now living
a most unseemly life, daring to commit deeds of
which the past possesses no examples.[2]

ζηλοῖ· ἡ ἀγάπη οὐ περπερεύεται, οὐ παροξύνεται, οὐ λογίζεται
τὸ κακόν. "Charity is patient, is kind: charity envieth not,
dealeth not perversely; is not puffed up; is not ambitious,
seeketh not her own, is not provoked to anger, thinketh no
evil."

[2] The Benedictine editors remark that Basil is not correct
in maintaining that there was no heretical precedent for such
actions. The Arians are charged with it in the Book of the
Prayers of Faustus and Marcellinus, *Bib. Patr.* V, 655. Cf.
also Constantius' letter to the Ethiopians against Fru-
mentius; Athan., *Apol. ad Const.* 31.

CXXXI

Ὀλυμπίῳ

Ὄντως ἡ τῶν ἀπροσδοκήτων ἀκοὴ ἱκανή ἐστι
ποιῆσαι ἀνθρώπου[1] ἠχῆσαι ἀμφότερα τὰ ὦτα.
ὃ καὶ ἐμοὶ νῦν συνέβη. εἰ γὰρ[2] καὶ τὰ μάλιστα
γεγυμνασμέναις μου λοιπὸν ταῖς ἀκοαῖς προ-
σέπεσε[3] τὰ περιφερόμενα καθ' ἡμῶν ταῦτα
συντάγματα, διὰ τὸ καὶ πρότερον αὐτὸν ἐμὲ
δεδέχθαι τὴν ἐπιστολήν, πρέπουσαν μὲν ταῖς
ἐμαῖς ἁμαρτίαις, οὐ μὴν προσδοκηθεῖσάν ποτε
γραφήσεσθαι παρὰ τῶν ἐπιστειλάντων· ἀλλ'
ὅμως τὰ δεύτερα τοσαύτην ὑπερβολὴν ἐφάνη
ἡμῖν ἔχειν ἐν ἑαυτοῖς τῆς πικρίας, ὥστε ἐπι-
σκοτῆσαι τοῖς προλαβοῦσι. πῶς γὰρ οὐ μικροῦ
τῶν φρενῶν ἔξω ἐγενόμην τῶν ἐμαυτοῦ, ἐντυχὼν
τῇ πρὸς τὸν εὐλαβέστατον ἀδελφὸν Δαζίναν[4]
ἐπιστολῇ, μυρίων μὲν ὕβρεων καὶ κατηγοριῶν
ἀφορήτων γεμούσῃ καθ' ἡμῶν καὶ ἐπαναστάσεων,
ὡς ἐν τοῖς χαλεπωτάτοις ἡμῶν κατὰ τῆς Ἐκκλησίας βουλεύμασιν εὑρεθέντων; εὐθὺς δὲ καὶ
ἀποδείξεις τοῦ ἀληθεῖς εἶναι τὰς καθ' ἡμῶν
βλασφημίας ἐπήχθησαν ἀπὸ συγγράμματος οὐκ
οἶδα ὑπὸ τίνος γραφέντος. μέρη μὲν γὰρ ἐπέγνων,
ὁμολογῶ, παρὰ[5] τοῦ Λαοδικέως Ἀπολιναρίου

---

[1] ἄνθρωπον Reg. secundus, Bigot., Coisl. secundus.
[2] γάρ om. E.   [3] προσέπεσον editi antiqi.
[4] Δεζίναν Med., Clarom.   [5] περί editi antiqi.

---

[1] Written in about 373, to Olympius, a wealthy layman of
Neocaesarea and intimate friend of Basil. The subject of
the letter is the same as that of the several preceding.

LETTER CXXXI

To Olympius [1]

Truly the hearing of unexpected news is enough to make both ears of a man ring. This has now happened to me also. For although the reports of those writings which are being circulated against us have reached my ears, already exceedingly well practised in such matters (for even before that I myself had received the letter, which indeed befitted my sins, but which I never thought would be written by those who sent it), nevertheless the later reports have proven to have in them so great an excess of bitterness as to obscure all that has gone before. For how could I help becoming almost out of my senses when I read the letter addressed to our very reverend brother Dazinas,[2] a letter teeming with countless insults, with intolerable accusations against us and assaults, as though I had been detected in the most shameful plans against the Church? For example, proofs of the truth of the slanders against me were drawn from a work written by someone, I know not whom. For I did indeed recognize, I confess, that parts had been written by Apollinarius [3]

Other letters addressed to this Olympius are IV, XII, XIII, and CCXI.

[2] In this letter Eustathius accused Basil of bad faith and of Apollinarian errors.

[3] Apollinarius the Younger flourished in the latter half of the fourth century, and was at first highly esteemed by Athanasius and Basil, for his classical culture, piety, and steadfastness to the Nicene Creed during the Arian controversy. Later he became the author of the Christological heresy which bears his name.

COLLECTED LETTERS OF SAINT BASIL

γεγράφθαι, καὶ αὐτὰ οὐδὲ ἀναγνοὺς ἐξ ἔργου
ποτέ, ἀλλ᾽ ἀκούσας ἑτέρων ἀπαγγειλάντων· ἄλλα
δέ τινα εὗρον ἐγγεγραμμένα,[1] ἃ μήτε ἀνέγνων
ποτέ, μήτε [2] ἑτέρου λέγοντος ἤκουσα· καὶ τούτων
ὁ μάρτυς ἐν οὐρανῷ πιστός. πῶς οὖν οἱ τὸ
ψεῦδος ἀποστρεφόμενοι, οἱ τὴν ἀγάπην πλήρωμα
εἶναι τοῦ νόμου δεδιδαγμένοι, οἱ τὰ ἀσθενήματα
τῶν ἀδυνάτων βαστάζειν ἐπαγγελλόμενοι, ταύτας
ἡμῖν κατεδέξαντο τὰς συκοφαντίας ἐπενεγκεῖν
καὶ ἀπ᾽ [3] ἀλλοτρίων συγγραμμάτων ἡμᾶς κατα-
κρῖναι,[4] πολλὰ λογισάμενος κατ᾽ ἐμαυτόν, ἐπινοεῖν
τὴν αἰτίαν οὐκ ἔχω, εἰ μή, ὅπερ ἐξ ἀρχῆς εἶπον,
μέρος ἔκρινα εἶναι τῶν ὀφειλομένων μοι διὰ τὰς
ἁμαρτίας κολάσεων καὶ τὴν ἐπὶ τούτοις λύπην.

Πρῶτον μὲν γὰρ κατεπένθησα τῇ ψυχῇ, ὅτι
ὠλιγώθησαν αἱ ἀλήθειαι ἀπὸ τῶν υἱῶν τῶν
ἀνθρώπων· ἔπειτα δὲ καὶ ἐφοβήθην αὐτὸς περὶ
ἐμαυτοῦ, μή ποτε πρὸς ταῖς ἄλλαις ἁμαρτίαις
καὶ τὴν μισανθρωπίαν πάθω, οὐδὲν πιστὸν ἐν
οὐδενὶ λογιζόμενος εἶναι, εἴπερ οἱ εἰς τὰ μέγιστα
παρ᾽ ἐμοῦ πιστευθέντες τοιοῦτοι μὲν περὶ ἐμέ,
τοιοῦτοι δὲ περὶ αὐτὴν ἐφάνησαν τὴν ἀλήθειαν.
γίνωσκε τοίνυν, ἀδελφέ, καὶ πᾶς ὅστις τῆς
ἀληθείας φίλος, μήτε ἐμὰ εἶναι τὰ συντάγματα,
οὔτε ἀρέσκεσθαι [5] αὐτοῖς, ἐπεὶ μὴ τῇ ἐμῇ γνώμῃ
συγγεγράφθαι. εἰ δὲ ἐπέστειλά ποτε πρὸ
πολλῶν ἐνιαυτῶν [6] Ἀπολιναρίῳ ἢ ἄλλῳ τινί,
ἐγκαλεῖσθαι οὐκ ὀφείλω, οὔτε γὰρ αὐτὸς [7] ἐγκαλῶ,
εἴ τις ἐκ τῆς ἑταιρίας τινὸς εἰς αἵρεσιν ἀπεσχίσθη

---

[1] γεγραμμένα E.   [2] ἤ E.   [3] ἐπ᾽ E.
[4] κατακρίνειν E., Harl., Reg. primus, Clarom.

of Laodicea, although I had never read them in his book but had merely heard others relate them; but I found certain other things written therein which I have never read nor heard anybody else state, and of these the faithful Witness is in heaven. How, therefore, those who scorn falsehood, who have been taught that charity is the fulfilment of the law, who profess to bear the infirmities of the weak, could have brought themselves to assail us with these calumnies and to condemn us from the writings of other men, this is a thing for which, though I have pondered deeply, I cannot discover the reason, unless, as I said in the beginning, I must conclude that the sorrow caused me by these things is a part of the punishments due me on account of my sins.

For, in the first place, I grieved in my soul, that truths had been made of little account by the sons of men; and, in the second place, I was also afraid for myself, lest some time, in addition to my other sins, I should also experience a hatred of mankind, reflecting that no trust is to be placed in any man, inasmuch as those who were most freely trusted by me have shown themselves so false to me and so false to truth itself. Know then, brother, and everyone who is a lover of truth, that these writings are not mine, nor are they pleasing to me, for they have not been composed according to my convictions. And if I ever wrote, many years ago, to Apollinarius or to any other person, I ought not to be blamed. For I, on my part, do not find fault, if any member of anybody's group has detached himself to go into heresy

---

⁵ ἀρκεῖσθαι editi antiqi.   ⁶ ἐτῶν editi antiqi
      ⁷ ἐγώ add. editi antiqi.

(οἴδατε δὲ πάντως τοὺς ἄνδρας, κἂν ὀνομαστὶ μὴ
λέγω), διότι ἕκαστος τῇ ἰδίᾳ ἁμαρτίᾳ ἀποθανεῖται.
Ταῦτα νῦν μὲν ἀπεκρινάμην πρὸς τὸν ἀπο-
σταλέντα τόμον,[1] ἵνα αὐτός τε εἰδείης τὴν ἀλήθειαν
καὶ τοῖς βουλομένοις μὴ κατέχειν ὡς ἐν ἀδικίᾳ
τὴν ἀλήθειαν φανερὰν καταστήσῃς. ἐὰν δὲ δέῃ
καὶ πλατύτερον ὑπὲρ ἑκάστου τῶν ἐπενεχθέντων
ἡμῖν ἀπολογήσασθαι, καὶ τοῦτο ποιήσομεν, τοῦ
Θεοῦ συνεργοῦντος. ἡμεῖς, ἀδελφὲ Ὀλύμπιε,
οὔτε τρεῖς θεοὺς λέγομεν, οὔτε Ἀπολιναρίῳ
κοινωνοῦμεν.

CXXXII

Ἀβραμίῳ, ἐπισκόπῳ Βατνῶν

Πάντα τὸν ἀπὸ τοῦ μετοπώρου χρόνον ἠγνόησα
περὶ τῆς εὐλαβείας σου, ὅπου [2] διάγεις. καὶ γὰρ
πεπλανημένας τὰς φήμας εὕρισκον, τῶν μὲν
ἀπαγγελλόντων ἐν Σαμοσάτοις διατρίβειν σου
τὴν εὐλάβειαν, τῶν δὲ ἐν τῇ χώρᾳ, ἄλλων δὲ περὶ
τὰς βάτνας αὐτὰς διαβεβαιουμένων ἑωρακέναι·
διὸ οὐδὲ συνεχῶς ἐπέστειλα. νῦν δὲ μαθὼν ἐν
Ἀντιοχείᾳ διάγειν, ἐν τῇ οἰκίᾳ τοῦ αἰδεσιμωτάτου
Σατορνίνου τοῦ κόμητος, ἔδωκα τὴν ἐπιστολὴν
προθύμως τῷ ποθεινοτάτῳ καὶ εὐλαβεστάτῳ

---

[1] ἀλλά add. editi antiqi.   [2] ὅπως E.

---

[1] Cf. Letter CXXV ; also Greg. Naz. *Orat.* I and XXIX.
[2] Placed by the Benedictines in 373. Loofs prefers the
spring of 375 as the date of composition ; cf. pp. 28 ff. and
46 ff. Abramius or Abraham was bishop of Batnae in

(and you certainly know the men, even if I do not call them by name), for each one will perish by his own sin.

These answers I have made at the present time regarding the book that was sent, in order that you yourself may know the truth and may make it clear to such as do not wish to restrain the truth as guilty of an injustice. But if it is necessary to defend myself even more extensively regarding each of the charges brought against us, this also shall we do, God being our helper. As for us, Brother Olympius, we neither say that there are three Gods, nor do we keep communion with Apollinarius.[1]

LETTER CXXXII

To Abramius, Bishop of Batnae[2]

During the whole time since late autumn I have been ignorant of the whereabouts of your Reverence. For I kept receiving misleading rumours, some saying that your Reverence was sojourning in Samosata, others that you were in the country, while others maintained that they had seen you near Batnae itself. On this account I did not write regularly. But having just learned that you are staying in Antioch at the house of the most venerable Count Saturninus,[3] I have eagerly entrusted this letter to our most beloved and revered brother,

Osrhoene near the Euphrates. His name appears with those of Meletius, Eusebius, Basil, and others in the letter written by the bishops of the East to those of Italy and Gaul. Cf. Letter XCII. He also was present at the Council of Constantinople in 381.

[3] This Saturninus is not otherwise known.

ἀδελφῷ Σαγκτισσίμῳ τῷ συμπρεσβυτέρῳ,[1] δι᾽ οὗ
προσφθέγγομαί σου τὴν ἀγάπην, παρακαλῶν
ὅπουπερ ἂν ᾖς μεμνῆσθαι μάλιστα μὲν τοῦ Θεοῦ,
εἶτα καὶ ἡμῶν, οὓς ἀγαπᾶν ἐξ ἀρχῆς προείλου, καὶ
ἔχειν ἐν τοῖς οἰκειοτάτοις ἀριθμουμένους.

CXXXIII

Πέτρῳ, ἐπισκόπῳ Ἀλεξανδρείας

Τῆς μὲν σωματικῆς φιλίας ὀφθαλμοὶ πρόξενοι
γίνονται, καὶ ἡ διὰ μακροῦ χρόνου ἐγγινομένη
συνήθεια βεβαιοῖ· τὴν δὲ ἀληθινὴν ἀγάπην ἡ τοῦ
Πνεύματος δωρεὰ συνίστησι, συνάπτουσα μὲν τὰ
μακρῷ διεστῶτα τόπῳ, γνωρίζουσα δὲ ἀλλήλοις
τοὺς ἀγαπητούς, οὐ διὰ σωματικῶν χαρακτήρων,
ἀλλὰ διὰ τῶν τῆς ψυχῆς [2] ἰδιωμάτων. ὃ δὴ καὶ
ἐφ᾽ ἡμῶν ἡ τοῦ Κυρίου χάρις ἐποίησε, παρασχο-
μένη ἡμᾶς ἰδεῖν σε τοῖς τῆς ψυχῆς ὀφθαλμοῖς,
καὶ περιπτύξασθαί σε τῇ ἀγάπῃ τῇ ἀληθινῇ, καὶ
οἰονεὶ συμφυῆναί σοι καὶ πρὸς μίαν ἐλθεῖν ἕνωσιν
ἐκ τῆς κατὰ τὴν πίστιν κοινωνίας. πεπείσμεθα
γάρ σε ἀνδρὸς τοσούτου θρέμμα ὑπάρχοντα, καὶ
τὴν ἐκ παλαιοῦ διατριβὴν μετ᾽ αὐτοῦ λαχόντα,
τῷ αὐτῷ πορεύεσθαι πνεύματι, καὶ τοῖς αὐτοῖς
στοιχεῖν τῆς εὐσεβείας δόγμασι.

Διὸ καὶ προσφθεγγόμεθά σου τὴν τιμιότητα,
καὶ παρακαλοῦμεν μετὰ τῶν ἄλλων καὶ τὴν περὶ

---

[1] ἡμῶν add. editi antiqi.　　　[2] ἀρετῆς editi antiqi.

---

[1] Cf. Letters CXX and CXXI.

Sanctissimus,[1] our presbyter, through whom I salute your Charity, begging that wherever you are you will be mindful especially of God, then also of us, whom from the beginning you chose to cherish and to number among your most intimate friends.

LETTER CXXXIII

To Peter, Bishop of Alexandria [2]

Eyes are promoters of bodily friendship, and the intimacy engendered through long association strengthens such friendship. But true love is formed by the gift of the Spirit, which brings together objects separated by a wide space, and causes loved ones to know each other, not through the features of the body, but through the peculiarities of the soul. This indeed the favour of the Lord has wrought in our case also, making it possible for us to see you with the eyes of the soul, to embrace you with the true love, and to grow one with you, as it were, and to enter into a single union with you through communion according to faith. For we are convinced that you, having been the spiritual nursling of so great a man, and having been favoured with long association with him, walk in the same spirit as he and are guided by the same dictates of piety.

Therefore we salute your Honour, and entreat you to take over from him, among other things, the

[2] Written in 373, to Peter, Bishop of Alexandria. This Peter had succeeded Athanasius in May 373, by the latter's request, who died on May 2 of that year. Basil begs him to follow in the footsteps of Athanasius: in love for God, for the brotherhood, and for Basil himself.

ἡμᾶς διάθεσιν τοῦ μεγάλου ἀνδρὸς διαδέξασθαι·
ἐπιστέλλειν τε ἡμῖν συνήθως τὰ κατὰ σαυτόν,
καὶ ἐπιμελεῖσθαι τῆς πανταχοῦ ἀδελφότητος τοῖς
αὐτοῖς σπλάγχνοις καὶ τῇ αὐτῇ προθυμίᾳ, ᾗ καὶ
ὁ μακαριώτατος[1] ἐκεῖνος περὶ πάντας ἐχρῆτο
τοὺς ἀγαπῶντας τὸν Θεὸν ἐν ἀληθείᾳ.

CXXXIV

Παιονίῳ πρεσβυτέρῳ

"Οσον ηὔφρανας ἡμᾶς τοῖς γράμμασιν εἰκάζεις
που πάντως αὐτοῖς οἷς ἐπέστειλας· οὕτω τὸ καθα-
ρὸν τῆς καρδίας, ἀφ' ἧς προῆλθεν ἐκεῖνα τὰ
ῥήματα, ἀκριβῶς ἐκ τῶν γραμμάτων κατεμηνύετο.
καὶ γὰρ[2] ὁλκὸς μὲν ὕδατος δείκνυσι τὴν οἰκείαν
πηγήν, λόγου δὲ φύσις τὴν προενεγκοῦσαν αὐτὸν
καρδίαν χαρακτηρίζει. ὥστε ἄτοπόν τε καὶ πολὺ
τοῦ εἰκότος παρηλλαγμένον πεπονθέναι ὁμολογῶ.
σπουδάζων γὰρ ἀεὶ γράμμασιν ἐντυγχάνειν τῆς
τελειότητός σου, ἐπειδὴ ἔλαβον εἰς χεῖρας τὴν
ἐπιστολὴν καὶ ἀνέγνων αὐτήν, οὐχ ἥσθην μᾶλλον
τοῖς ἐπεσταλμένοις, ἢ ἠνιάθην τὴν ζημίαν, ὁπόση
γέγονεν ἡμῖν κατὰ τὸν τῆς σιωπῆς χρόνον,
διαλογιζόμενος.

'Αλλ' ἐπειδὴ ἤρξω γράφειν, μὴ διαλίπῃς[3]

---

[1] μακάριος E.   [2] καί add. editi antiqi.
[3] διαλίποις multi MSS. non vetustissimi.

---

[1] Written in 373. Paeonius is otherwise unknown.
Letters CXXXIV, CXXXV, CCXXIII, CCCXXXIII and
CCCXXXIV have been quoted in certain studies of the
history of stenography. A. Schramm (*Korrespondenzblatt,*

great man's disposition toward us, to send me word
of your affairs regularly, and to take care of the
brotherhood everywhere with the same kindliness
and the same zeal which that most blessed one
employed toward all those who in truth love God.

LETTER CXXXIV

To the Presbyter Paeonius [1]

How much pleasure you gave us by your letter you
no doubt fully surmise from the very tones you used
in writing it; so accurately was the purity of heart
whence those words proceeded revealed by what you
wrote. For as a rill of water reveals its own true
source, so the nature of one's speech shows the
character of the heart that brought it forth. So I
confess that I have experienced a strange and very
unusual thing. For though always eager to read a
letter from your Perfection,[2] when I had taken the
letter in my hands and read it, I was not so much
delighted by the message you had sent as I was
vexed at the thought of how great a loss I had
sustained during your period of silence.

But since you have begun to write, do not cease

Amtliche Zeitschr. des k. Stenographischen Instituts zu
Dresden, 1903 (XLVIII), 221 and 241 ff.) would conclude
from the present letter that Basil himself was a master of
tachygraphy, and did not scorn to give instruction in it. F.
Maier (*idem*, 1904 (XLIX) 42 ff.) rightly objects to this conclusion. In any case Basil employed tachygraphy, and had
his difficulties with it. Cf. the present letter, and Letter
CXXX.

[2] A Byzantine title, used usually of priests.

τοῦτο ποιῶν. εὐφρανεῖς γὰρ πλέον ἢ οἱ τὰ
πολλὰ χρήματα τοῖς φιλοπλούτοις διαπεμπό-
μενοι· τῶν δὲ γραφέων οὐδείς μοι παρῆν, οὔτε
τῶν καλλιγραφούντων οὔτε τῶν ταχυγράφων.
οὓς γὰρ[1] ἔτυχον ἐξασκήσας, οἱ μὲν ἀνέδραμον
ἐπὶ τὴν πρώτην τοῦ βίου συνήθειαν, οἱ δὲ ἀπειρήκασι πρὸς τοὺς πόνους, χρονίαις ἀρρωστίαις
κεκακωμένοι.

CXXXV

Διοδώρῳ,[2] πρεσβυτέρῳ Ἀντιοχείας

Ἐνέτυχον τοῖς ἀποσταλεῖσι βιβλίοις παρὰ τῆς
τιμιότητός σου. καὶ τῷ μὲν δευτέρῳ ὑπερήσθην,
οὐ διὰ τὴν βραχύτητα μόνον, ὡς εἰκὸς ἦν τὸν
ἀργῶς πρὸς πάντα καὶ ἀσθενῶς λοιπὸν διακείμενον, ἀλλ᾽ ὅτι πυκνόν τε ἅμα ἐστὶ ταῖς ἐννοίαις,
καὶ εὐκρινῶς ἐν αὐτῷ ἔχουσιν αἵ τε ἀντιθέσεις
τῶν ὑπεναντίων καὶ αἱ πρὸς αὐτὰς ἀπαντήσεις·
καὶ τὸ τῆς λέξεως ἁπλοῦν τε καὶ ἀκατάσκευον
πρέπον ἔδοξέ μοι εἶναι προθέσει Χριστιανοῦ, οὐ
πρὸς ἐπίδειξιν μᾶλλον ἢ κοινὴν ὠφέλειαν συγ-
γράφοντος.[3] τὸ δὲ πρότερον, τὴν μὲν δύναμιν
ἔχον τὴν αὐτὴν ἐν τοῖς πράγμασι, λέξει δὲ πολυ-

---

[1] καί add. E. [2] Θεοδώρῳ E, Med.
[3] γράφοντος editi antiqi.

---

[1] Written in 373. Cf. previous letter and note. This is
an exceedingly interesting letter, especially for the student
of the history of literary criticism. It contains Basil's ideas
on the rhetoric of his day, which were exactly such as a
person of good taste would hold to-day, although in all
probability a unique position in Basil's time. And we must

doing so. For you give more pleasure than do those
who distribute large sums of money to the avari-
cious. But no one of my scribes has been at hand,
either caligraphist or shorthand writer. For of
those whom I have trained, some have gone back to
their former manner of life, and the others have
abandoned their labours, having been afflicted with
chronic maladies.

LETTER CXXXV

To Diodorus, Presbyter of Antioch [1]

I HAVE read the books sent me by your Honour.
And with the second I was exceedingly pleased, not
only because of its brevity, which was likely to
please a man who is inactive in all matters and in
poor health besides, but because it is at once close-
packed with ideas, and both the objections of our
opponents and our answers to them are set forth in
the work with the utmost clarity; and its simple
and unlaboured style seemed to me to befit the
purpose of a Christian, who writes not so much for
display as for general edification. But the former
work, which is of the same importance as to subject-
matter, but is adorned with richer diction, with

say that St. Basil in his own works was consistent with this
theory. He also characterizes at some length Plato's style
and that of Aristotle and Theophrastus.
This Diodorus was a pupil of Silvanus, bishop of Tarsus.
Cf. Theodoret, *Hist. Eccl.* 4, 24. In Letter XVI Theodoret
speaks of his obligations to him as a teacher. In 378,
Diodorus became bishop of Tarsus. Only a few fragments of
his works are extant, for the major portion, it is said, was
destroyed by the Arians. Cf. also Basil's Letter CLX.

τελεστέρᾳ καὶ σχήμασι ποικίλοις καὶ διαλογικαῖς
χάρισι κεκομψευμένον, πολλοῦ μοι ἐφάνη καὶ
χρόνου πρὸς τὸ ἐπελθεῖν[1] καὶ πόνου διανοίας
πρὸς τὸ καὶ συλλέξαι τὰς ἐννοίας καὶ παρα-
κατασχεῖν αὐτὰς τῇ μνήμῃ δεόμενον. αἱ γὰρ
ἐν τῷ μεταξὺ παρεμβαλλόμεναι διαβολαὶ τῶν
ὑπεναντίων καὶ συστάσεις τῶν ἡμετέρων, εἰ
καὶ γλυκύτητάς τινας ἐπεισάγειν δοκοῦσι διαλεκ-
τικὰς[2] τῷ συγγράμματι, ἀλλ᾽ οὖν τῷ[3] σχολὴν
καὶ διατριβὴν ἐμποιεῖν διασπῶσι μὲν τὸ συνεχὲς
τῆς ἐννοίας καὶ τοῦ ἐναγωνίου λόγου τὸν τόνον
ὑποχαυνοῦσιν.

Ἐκεῖνο γὰρ πάντως συνεῖδέ[4] σου ἡ ἀγχίνοια,
ὅτι καὶ τῶν ἔξωθεν φιλοσόφων οἱ τοὺς διαλόγους
συγγράψαντες, Ἀριστοτέλης μὲν καὶ Θεόφραστος,
εὐθὺς αὐτῶν ἥψαντο τῶν πραγμάτων, διὰ τὸ
συνειδέναι ἑαυτοῖς τῶν Πλατωνικῶν χαρίτων τὴν
ἔνδειαν. Πλάτων δὲ τῇ ἐξουσίᾳ τοῦ λόγου ὁμοῦ
μὲν τοῖς δόγμασι μάχεται, ὁμοῦ δὲ καὶ παρα-
κωμῳδεῖ τὰ πρόσωπα, Θρασυμάχου μὲν τὸ θρασὺ
καὶ ἰταμὸν διαβάλλων, Ἱππίου δὲ τὸ κοῦφον
τῆς διανοίας καὶ χαῦνον, καὶ[5] Πρωταγόρου τὸ
ἀλαζονικὸν καὶ ὑπέρογκον. ὅπου δὲ ἀόριστα
πρόσωπα ἐπεισάγει τοῖς διαλόγοις, τῆς μὲν
εὐκρινείας ἕνεκεν τῶν πραγμάτων κέχρηται τοῖς
προσδιαλεγομένοις,[6] οὐδὲν δὲ ἕτερον ἐκ τῶν
προσώπων ἐπεισκυκλεῖ ταῖς ὑποθέσεσιν· ὅπερ
ἐποίησεν ἐν τοῖς Νόμοις.

Δεῖ οὖν καὶ ἡμᾶς τοὺς οὐ κατὰ φιλοτιμίαν

---

[1] ἐξελθεῖν editi antiqi.
[2] γλυκύτητας . . . διαλεκτικάς] γλυκυτάτας . . . διαλέξεις
Med., Harl.

figures of divers kinds, and with charms peculiar to
the dialogue, seemed to me to require a great deal
of time to peruse and much mental labour to grasp
its ideas and to retain them in the memory. For
the accusations of our opponents and the arguments
in defence of our own side which have been worked
into the context, even though they do seem to add
some dialectic attractions to the work, yet by causing
delay and waste of time disrupt the continuity of the
thought and loosen the tension of the argumentative
attack.

For assuredly your quick wit realizes this—that
those philosophers outside the faith who wrote
dialogues, Aristotle and Theophrastus for instance,
at once grappled with the facts themselves, because
they realized their own lack of the literary graces of
Plato. But Plato with the power of his eloquence at
one and the same time both attacks opinions and
ridicules the persons who represent them, attacking
the rashness and recklessness of Thrasymachus, the
levity and conceit of Hippias, and the boastfulness
and pompousness of Protagoras.[1] But whenever he
introduces indefinite characters into his dialogues, he
uses his interlocutors merely for the sake of giving
clarity to his subject matter, and brings nothing else
from the characters into the arguments; just as he
did in the *Laws*.

So it is necessary also for us, who do not set out

---

[1] *i.e.*, in the *Republic*, the *Hippias*, and the *Protagoras*
respectively.

---

[3] τό E.   [4] συνοῖδε Harl., secunda manu.
[5] καὶ] τοῦ δέ E.   [6] προδιαλεγομένοις tres MSS.

ἐρχομένους ἐπὶ τὸ γράφειν, ἀλλ' ὑποθήκας καταλιμπάνειν ὠφελίμων λόγων τῇ ἀδελφότητι προε-
λομένους, ἐὰν μέν τι πᾶσι προκεκηρυγμένον ἐπὶ
αὐθαδείᾳ τρόπου πρόσωπον ὑποβαλλώμεθα,[1]
τινὰ καὶ ἀπὸ[2] προσώπου ποιότητος παραπλέκειν
τῷ λόγῳ, εἴπερ ὅλως ἐπιβάλλει ἡμῖν διαβάλλειν
ἀνθρώπους, τῶν πραγμάτων ἀφεμένους.[3] ἐὰν δὲ
ἀόριστον ᾖ τὸ διαλεγόμενον, αἱ πρὸς τὰ πρόσωπα
διαστάσεις[4] τὴν μὲν συνάφειαν διακόπτουσι,
πρὸς οὐδὲν δὲ πέρας χρήσιμον ἀπαντῶσι.[5]

Ταῦτα εἶπον ἵνα δειχθῇ, ὅτι οὐκ εἰς κόλακος
χεῖρας ἀπέστειλάς σου τοὺς πόνους, ἀλλὰ ἀδελφῷ
τῷ γνησιωτάτῳ ἐκοινώνησας τῶν καμάτων.
εἶπον δὲ οὐ πρὸς ἐπανόρθωσιν τῶν γεγραμμένων,
ἀλλὰ πρὸς φυλακὴν τῶν μελλόντων. πάντως
γὰρ ὁ τοσαύτῃ περὶ τὸ γράφειν ἕξει καὶ σπουδῇ
κεχρημένος οὐκ ἀποκνήσει γράφων· ἐπειδὴ οὐδὲ
οἱ τὰς ὑποθέσεις παρέχοντες ἀπολήγουσιν. ἡμῖν
δὲ ἀρκέσει μὲν ἀναγινώσκειν τὰ ὑμέτερα· τοῦ δὲ
δύνασθαι γράφειν τι τοσοῦτον ἀποδέομεν, ὅσον
μικροῦ δέω λέγειν, καὶ τοῦ ὑγιαίνειν, ἢ καὶ τοῦ
μετρίαν σχολὴν ἄγειν ἀπὸ τῶν πραγμάτων.

Ἀπέστειλα δὲ νῦν διὰ τοῦ ἀναγνώστου τὸ
μεῖζον καὶ πρότερον, ἐπελθὼν αὐτὸ ὡς ἐμοὶ
δυνατόν. τὸ δὲ δεύτερον[6] παρακατέσχον, βουλόμενος αὐτὸ μεταγράψαι, καὶ μὴ εὐπορῶν τέως[7]
τινὸς τῶν εἰς τάχος γραφόντων. μέχρι γὰρ
τοσαύτης ἦλθε πενίας τὰ ἐπίφθονα Καππαδοκῶν.

---

[1] χρή add. E.   [2] τῆς τοῦ add. E.
[3] ἀφεμένοις editi antiqi.   [4] διατάσεις editi antiqi.
[5] τοῦ λόγου add. editi antiqi.

to write for worldly honour, but propose to bequeath
to the brethren admonitions on edifying subjects, if
we introduce a character already well known to the
world for rashness of conduct, to weave something
derived from the quality of the character into the
treatise, if it is at all incumbent upon us to
censure men who neglect their duties. But if the
material brought into the dialogue be indefinite,
digressions against persons break its unity and tend
to no useful end.

All this I have said that it might be shown that
you have not sent your work into the hands of a
flatterer, but that you have given to a most sincere
brother a share in your toils. And I have spoken,
not to correct what has been written, but as a
warning for future writings. For assuredly a man
who has employed such aptitude and enthusiasm for
writing will not refrain from writing; since there
is no shortage of persons to supply you with subjects.
For us it will suffice to read what you write; but we
fall as far short of being able to write anything ourselves, as, I may almost say, of enjoying good health,
or of having even a modicum of leisure from active
affairs.

I have now sent back to you through the lector the
first and larger of your works, after reading it to the
best of my ability. The second, however, I have
kept, wishing to copy it, although as yet I am not
provided with any fast copyist. For to such a state
of poverty has the once envied condition of the
Cappadocians come !

---

⁶ καὶ μικρότερον add. editi Paris.   ⁷ τέος E.

CXXXVI

Εὐσεβίῳ, ἐπισκόπῳ Σαμοσάτων

Ἐν οἷοις ἡμᾶς ὄντας κατέλαβεν ὁ χρηστὸς
Ἰσαάκης[1] αὐτός σοι ἄμεινον διηγήσεται, εἰ καὶ
μὴ ἀρκοῦσαν ἔχει τὴν γλῶσσαν, ὥστε τραγικῶς
ἐξαγγεῖλαι τὸ ὑπεραῖρον τῶν παθῶν, τοσοῦτον
ἦν τῆς ἀρρωστίας τὸ μέγεθος. καὶ τὸ εἰκὸς δὲ
παντὶ γνώριμον τῷ ἐμὲ καὶ κατὰ βραχὺ ἐπιστα-
μένῳ. εἰ γὰρ ἐν τῇ δοκούσῃ εὐεξίᾳ τῶν ἀπε-
γνωσμένων πρὸς τὸ ζῆν ἀσθενέστερον διεκείμην,
γινώσκειν ἔξεστι τίς ἂν ἤμην ἐπὶ τῆς ἀρρωστίας.
καίτοιγε ἐχρῆν (δὸς γὰρ τῷ πυρετῷ συγγνώμην
ἐρεσχελοῦντι), ἐπειδή μοι κατὰ φύσιν ἦν τὸ
νοσεῖν, ἐν τῇ μεταβολῇ ταύτῃ[2] τῆς ἕξεως ὑγείας[3]
μοι νῦν τὸ κράτιστον περιεῖναι. ἀλλ' ἐπειδὴ
μάστιξ τοῦ Κυρίου ἐστὶ προσθήκαις ταῖς κατὰ
τὴν ἡμετέραν ἀξίαν τὸ ἀλγεινὸν ἐπιτείνουσα,
ἀσθένειαν ἐπὶ τῇ ἀσθενείᾳ προσεκτησάμην, ὥστε
τὸ ἀπὸ τούτου καὶ παιδὶ φανερὸν εἶναι, ὅτι πᾶσα
ἀνάγκη οἰχήσεσθαι[4] ἡμῖν τὸ ἔλυτρον τοῦτο,[5]
πλὴν εἰ μή που ἄρα ἡ τοῦ Θεοῦ φιλανθρωπία
ἡμῖν ἐν τῇ μακροθυμίᾳ αὐτοῦ[6] χρόνους εἰς μετά-
νοιαν χαριζομένῃ,[7] ποιήσειε καὶ νῦν, ὡς καὶ
πολλάκις πρότερον, λύσιν τινὰ καὶ πόρον[8] ἐκ
τῶν ἀμηχάνων δεινῶν.[9] ταῦτα μὲν οὖν ἕξει ὡς
αὐτῷ φίλον καὶ ἡμῖν συμφέρον.

---

[1] Ἰσαάκιος editi antiqi.   [2] ταύτης quattuor MSS.
[3] ὑγιείας E.   [4] οἰχήσεται E, Harl., Med.
[5] τούτου editi antiqi.   [6] καί add. E.
[7] χαριζομένου E.   [8] καί add. E.   [9] κακῶν E.

LETTER CXXXVI

To Eusebius, Bishop of Samosata [1]

In what condition the excellent Isaac [2] has found us he himself will relate to you better, even though his tongue is inadequate to proclaim in tragic fashion the transcendence of my sufferings, such was the seriousness of my illness. But probably this was known to everyone who was never so slightly acquainted with me. For if when in apparent good health I was really weaker than those of whose lives we despair, one may understand what I must have been during that illness. And yet I really ought (for you must grant indulgence to the fever that harasses me), since sickness used to be my natural state, in my present change of condition to be enjoying the best of health. But since it is the scourge of the Lord that goes on extending our bad health by new additions according to our deserts, I have acquired one infirmity after another, so that the result is plain to a child—that this shell of ours must quite certainly depart, unless perchance the mercy of God, in His magnanimity granting us the grace of a period of time for repentance, should now also, as on so many former occasions, bring about some release and some means of escape from our desperate straits. These things, however, shall be according to His pleasure and our own profit.

[1] Written in 373. This Eusebius was Bishop of Samosata on the Euphrates from 360 to 373. He was orthodox of faith, and a friend of Basil, Gregory Nazianzene, and Meletius, Bishop of Antioch. Cf. Letters XXVII, XXX, XXXI, XXXIV, etc.

[2] Otherwise unknown.

Τὰ δὲ τῶν ἐκκλησιῶν ὅπως οἴχεται καὶ προπέ-
ποται, ἡμῶν τῆς οἰκείας ἀσφαλείας ἕνεκεν τὰ τῶν
πλησίον περιορώντων καὶ οὐδὲ τοῦτο συνορᾶν
δυναμένων, ὅτι τῇ τοῦ κοινοῦ κακοπραγίᾳ[1] καὶ
τὸ καθ᾽ ἕκαστον συναπόλλυται, τί χρὴ καὶ
λέγειν; ἄλλως τε καὶ πρὸς ἄνδρα, ὃς πόρρωθεν
ἕκαστα προειδώς, καὶ προδιεμαρτύρω καὶ προε-
κήρυξας, καὶ αὐτός τε προεξανέστης, καὶ τοὺς
λοιποὺς συνεπήγειρας, ἐπιστέλλων, αὐτὸς παρα-
γινόμενος, τί οὐ ποιῶν, τίνα φωνὴν οὐκ ἀφιείς!
ὧν μεμνήμεθα μὲν[2] ἐφ᾽ ἑκάστῳ τῶν ἐκβαινόν-
των, ὠφελούμεθα δὲ ἀπ᾽ αὐτῶν οὐκέτι. καὶ νῦν
εἰ μὴ αἱ ἁμαρτίαι ἀντέστησάν μοι, καὶ τὸ μὲν
πρῶτον ὁ εὐλαβέστατος καὶ ἀγαπητὸς ἀδελφὸς
ἡμῶν Εὐστάθιος ὁ συνδιάκονος, εἰς νόσον χαλεπὴν
καταπεσών, εἰς ὅλους με δύο παρέτεινε μῆνας,
ἡμέραν ἐξ ἡμέρας τὴν σωτηρίαν αὐτοῦ περι-
μένοντα· ἔπειτα δὲ οἱ σὺν ἐμοὶ πάντες ἠσθένησαν,
ὧν τὰ μὲν καταλείμματα[3] ἐξαριθμήσεται[4] ὁ
ἀδελφὸς Ἰσαάκης· τὸ δὲ τελευταῖον αὐτὸς ἐγὼ
τῇ νόσῳ κατεσχέθην ταύτῃ· ἐπεὶ πάλαι ἂν ἤμην
παρὰ[5] τὴν σὴν τιμιότητα, οὐκ ὄφελός τι τοῖς
κοινοῖς παρεχόμενος, ἀλλ᾽ ἐμαυτῷ μέγα κέρδος
ἐκ τῆς συντυχίας σου[6] κτώμενος. καὶ γὰρ
ἐγνώκειν ἔξω τῶν ἐκκλησιαστικῶν γενέσθαι
βελῶν διὰ τὸ ἀφύλακτον ἡμῶν πρὸς τὰ σκευω-
ρούμενα[7] παρὰ τῶν ἐναντίων. σώζοι σε τῷ βίῳ

---

[1] δυσπραγίᾳ Reg. secundus, Coisl. secundus.
[2] μέν om. E.   [3] ἐγκαταλείμματα E.
[4] ἐξαριθμηθήσεται E.   [5] πρός E.
[6] σου om. E.   [7] σκαιωρούμενα Harl., Paris., Clarom.

---

[1] Cf. Dem. *Olynth.* 3, 22, 34 : προπέτοται τῆς αὐτίκα χάριτος

As for the interests of the churches—how they
have gone to ruin and have been lightly sacrificed,[1]
while we, consulting our own personal safety, neglect
the good of our neighbours and are unable to see
even this, that the ruin of each of us is involved in
the common disaster—why need I say a word?
And especially so to a man like you who, foreseeing
everything long in advance, made protest and issued
proclamation beforehand, and not only was the first
to rise up yourself, but also helped to rouse the rest,
writing them letters, visiting them in person,
omitting what act, leaving what word unspoken!
These things we do indeed remember after each event
happens, but we no longer derive profit from them.
And now if my sins had not stood in my way,—that
is, first of all, our most reverend and beloved brother
and deacon, Eustathius,[2] falling grievously ill, caused
me no great anxiety for two whole months as I
waited day after day for his return to health; and
next, all my associates fell ill (of which things our
brother Isaac will enumerate all that I omit); and,
last of all, I myself was seized by this present
illness—but for these things I should long ago have
been by the side of your Honour, not lending you
any aid in the common cause, but deriving great
gain for myself from your company. For I had
decided to get out of the way of the missiles of the
ecclesiastics because I had no means of protecting
myself against the contrivances of my adversaries.
May the mighty hand of God preserve you unto

τὰ τῆς πόλεως πράγματα. "The interests of the state have
been lightly sacrificed for mere present pleasure."

[2] This deacon enjoyed Basil's confidence, and once conveyed another letter for him to Eusebius of Samosata. Cf.
Letter XLVII.

παντὶ ἡ μεγάλη τοῦ Θεοῦ χείρ, τὸν γενναῖον
φύλακα τῆς πίστεως καὶ νήφοντα τῶν ἐκκλησιῶν
προστάτην· καὶ καταξιώσειεν ἡμᾶς πρὸ τῆς
ἐξόδου τῆς συντυχίας σου ἐπ᾽ ὠφελείᾳ τῶν
ψυχῶν ἡμῶν.

CXXXVII

Ἀντιπάτρῳ

Νῦν μοι δοκῶ μάλιστα ἐπαισθάνεσθαι τῆς
ζημίας, ἢν ὑπομένω διὰ τὸ ἀρρωστεῖν, ὁπότε,
ἀνδρὸς τοιούτου τὴν πατρίδα ἡμῶν ἐφέποντος,
αὐτὸς ἀπεῖναι διὰ τὴν ἐπιμέλειαν τοῦ σώματος
ἀναγκάζομαι. μῆνα γὰρ ὅλον ἤδη προσκαθέζομαι [1] τῇ ἐκ τῶν αὐτοφυῶς θερμῶν [2] ὑδάτων θεραπείᾳ ὡς δή τι ὄφελος ἐντεῦθεν ἕξων. ἔοικα δὲ
διακενῆς πονεῖν ἐπὶ τῆς ἐρημίας, ἢ καὶ γέλωτος
τοῖς πολλοῖς ἄξιος εἶναι φαίνεσθαι, μηδὲ τῆς
παροιμίας ἀκούων τῆς οὐδὲν ἀπὸ θερμῶν ὄφελος
εἶναι τοῖς τεθνηκόσι λεγούσης.

Διόπερ καὶ οὕτως ἔχων βούλομαι πάντα παρεὶς
καταλαβεῖν σου τὴν σεμνοπρέπειαν, ὥστε τῶν ἐν
σοὶ καλῶν ἀπολαύειν καὶ τὰ κατὰ τὸν οἶκον τὸν
ἐμαυτοῦ πράγματα διὰ τῆς σῆς ὀρθότητος εὐπρε-
πῶς διαθέσθαι. ἐμὸς γάρ ἐστιν ἴδιος ὁ τῆς σεμνοτάτης μητρὸς ἡμῶν Παλλαδίας οἶκος, ἢν οὐ μόνον ἡ
τοῦ γένους οἰκειότης ἡμῖν συνάπτει, ἀλλὰ καὶ τὸ τοῦ

---

[1] μῆνα . . . προσκαθέζομαι om. E; ἤδη om. Harl., Med.,
editi antiqi. προσκαθέσομαι editi antiqi.

[2] αὐτοφυῶς θερμῶν om. E.

---

[1] Written in 373. Antipater, governor of Cappadocia,

all mankind, you who are the noble guardian of the faith and the vigilant champion of the churches; and before our departure from this life may He deem us worthy of an interview with you for the good of our soul.

LETTER CXXXVII

To Antipater [1]

At this time I seem to be most sensible of the loss which I suffer in being sick, when, on the occasion of a man like you succeeding to the governorship of our country, I am myself compelled to be absent because of the care I must take of my body. For during a whole month already have I been assiduously undergoing the treatment of the naturally hot waters, expecting to receive some benefit therefrom. But it seems that I toil quite uselessly in this solitary place, or that I even show myself deserving of ridicule in the eyes of the many for not heeding the proverb which says, "Warm baths are of no use to the dead."

Wherefore, in spite of my present condition, I desire, putting aside everything else, to go to your gracious self, that I may have the benefit of your excellent qualities and through your uprightness may fittingly arrange the affairs of my own house. For my very own is the house of our most revered mother Palladia, whom not only the kinship of family binds to us, but also the goodness of her

to whom Basil recommends the protection of Palladia, his old friend and relative. Cf. Letters CLXXXVI and CLXXXVII. Palladia is otherwise unknown.

τρόπου δεξιὸν ἀντὶ μητρὸς ἡμῖν εἶναι πεποίηκεν.
ἐπεὶ οὖν κεκίνηταί τις ταραχὴ περὶ τὸν οἶκον αὐτῆς,
ἀξιοῦμέν σου τὴν μεγαλόνοιαν μικρὸν ὑπερθέσθαι
τὴν ἐξέτασιν καὶ ἀναμεῖναι ἡμῶν τὴν παρουσίαν,
οὐχ ὥστε διαφθαρῆναι τὸ δίκαιον (μυριάκις γὰρ
ἂν ἀποθανεῖν ἑλοίμην ἢ τοιαύτην αἰτῆσαι χάριν
παρὰ δικαστοῦ φίλου τοῖς νόμοις καὶ τῷ δικαίῳ),
ἀλλ᾿ ὥστε ἃ οὐκ εὐπρεπὲς ἐμοὶ γράφειν, ταῦτα
ἀπὸ στόματος ἀπαγγέλλοντός μου μαθεῖν. οὕτω
γὰρ οὔτε αὐτὸς τῆς ἀληθείας διαμαρτήσῃ, οὔτε
ἡμεῖς πεισόμεθά τι τῶν ἀβουλήτων. δέομαι οὖν,
τοῦ προσώπου ἐν ἀσφαλείᾳ ὄντος καὶ κατεχο-
μένου παρὰ τῆς τάξεως, ἀνεπαχθῆ ταύτην χάριν
καὶ ἀνεπίφθονον ἡμῖν καταθέσθαι.

CXXXVIII

Εὐσεβίῳ, ἐπισκόπῳ Σαμοσάτων

Τίνα με οἴει ψυχὴν ἐσχηκέναι, ὅτε τὴν ἐπιστολὴν ἐδεξάμην τῆς θεοσεβείας σου; εἰ μὲν γὰρ
πρὸς τὴν ἐν τῷ γράμματι ἀπεῖδον διάθεσιν, εὐθὺς
ὥρμων πέτεσθαι τὴν εὐθὺς [1] Σύρων, εἰ δὲ πρὸς τὴν
ἀρρωστίαν τοῦ σώματος, ὑφ᾿ ἧς πεπεδημένος
ἐκείμην, ᾐσθανόμην οὐχὶ τοῦ πέτεσθαι μόνον
ἀλλὰ καὶ τοῦ ἐπὶ τῆς κλίνης στρέφεσθαι
ἐνδεῶς ἔχων. πεντηκοστὴν γὰρ ταύτην ἡμέραν
ἦγον ἐν τῇ ἀρρωστίᾳ, καθ᾿ ἣν ἐπέστη ἡμῖν
ὁ ἀγαπητὸς καὶ σπουδαιότατος ἀδελφὸς ἡμῶν
συνδιάκονος Ἐλπίδιος· πολλὰ μὲν τῷ πυρετῷ

[1] εὐθύ E.

character has caused to be a second mother to us.
So, since some trouble has been stirred up concerning
her house, we ask your Magnanimity to postpone
your inquiry a little while, and to await our presence,
not that justice may be foiled (for I should prefer
to die ten thousand times than to ask such a favour
of a judge who is a lover of the laws and of justice),
but that you may learn from me by word of mouth
those things which it does not become me to write.
For thus you yourself will neither fail of the truth
nor shall we suffer anything we would fain avoid. I
therefore ask you, since the person in question is
in safe custody and is held by the soldiers, to grant
us this favour as one that can give no offence or
cause any odium.

LETTER CXXXVIII

To Eusebius, Bishop of Samosata [1]

Into what state of mind, think you, did I come
when I received the letter of your Holiness? [2] For
if I looked at the spirit of your letter, I was straightway eager to fly straight to Syria, but if at the
weakness of my body, because of which I lay
fettered, I realized that I was incapable not only
of flying but even of turning over on my bed. For
that day on which Elpidius,[3] our beloved and most
excellent brother and deacon, arrived was the fiftieth

---

[1] Written in 373. On Eusebius, Bishop of Samosata, cf.
Letters XXVII, XXX, XXXI, XXXIV, XLVII, etc.

[2] Byzantine title, commonly given to bishops.

[3] Elpidius, a deacon at whose hands Basil received the
present letter from Eusebius of Samosata, and by whom
Basil sent a letter of consolation to the Egyptian bishops in
exile for the faith in Palestine (Letter CCLXV).

δαπανηθείς, ὃς ἀπορίᾳ τῆς τρεφούσης αὐτὸν
ὕλης, τῇ ξηρᾷ ταύτῃ σαρκὶ οἷον θρυαλλίδι
κεκαυμένῃ περιειλούμενος, μαρασμὸν [1] καὶ χρονίαν
ἐπήγαγεν ἀρρωστίαν· τὰ δὲ ἐφεξῆς, ἡ ἀρχαία
πληγή μου, τὸ ἧπαρ τοῦτο διαδεξάμενον, ἀπέ-
κλεισε μέν με [2] τῶν σιτίων, ἀπεδίωξε δὲ τῶν
ὀμμάτων τὸν ὕπνον, ἐν μεθορίοις δὲ κατέσχε
ζωῆς καὶ θανάτου, τοσοῦτον ζῆν ἐπίτρεπον,[3]
ὅσον τῶν ἀπ' αὐτοῦ δυσχερῶν ἐπαισθάνεσθαι.
ὥστε καὶ ὕδασιν ἐχρησάμην αὐτοφυῶς θερμοῖς
καί τινας παρ' ἰατρῶν ἐπιμελείας κατεδεξάμην.
ἅπαντα δὲ ἤλεγξε τὸ νεανικὸν τοῦτο κακόν· ὅ, τοῦ
μὲν ἔθους παρόντος, κἂν ἄλλος ἐνέγκοι, ἀμελε-
τήτως δὲ προσπεσόντος οὐδεὶς οὕτως ἀδαμάντινος
ὥστε ἀντισχεῖν.

Ὑφ' οὗ πολὺν ὀχληθεὶς χρόνον, οὐδέποτε οὕτως
ἠνιάθην ὅσον νῦν, ἐμποδισθεὶς παρ' αὐτοῦ πρὸς
τὴν συντυχίαν τῆς ἀληθινῆς ἀγάπης σου. οἵας
γὰρ ἀπεστερήθημεν [4] θυμηδίας οἶδα καὶ αὐτός, εἰ
καὶ ἄκρῳ δακτύλῳ τοῦ γλυκυτάτου μέλιτος τῆς
παρ' ὑμῖν ἐκκλησίας ἀπεγευσάμην πέρυσιν.

Ἐγὼ δὲ καὶ ἄλλων ἀναγκαίων ἕνεκεν πραγμάτων ἐδεόμην εἰς ταὐτὸν [5] γενέσθαι τῇ θεοσεβείᾳ σου
καὶ περὶ πολλῶν μὲν ἀνακοινώσασθαι, πολλὰ δὲ
μαθεῖν. καὶ γὰρ οὐδέ ἐστιν ἐνταῦθα οὐδὲ ἀγάπης
ἀληθινῆς ἐπιτυχεῖν. ὅταν δὲ καὶ πάνυ τις ἀγα-
πῶντα εὕροι,[6] οὐκ ἔστιν ὁ δυνάμενος παραπλησίως
τῇ τελείᾳ σου φρονήσει καὶ τῇ ἐμπειρίᾳ, ἣν ἐκ

---

[1] μαρασμώδη E, Harl., Med., editi antiqi.
[2] με om. E.   [3] ἐπιτρέπων editi antiqi.
[4] ἀπεστερήθην editi antiqi.   [5] εἰς ταὐτό Harl.

I had spent in this illness; I was greatly wasted by
the fever which, through lack of fuel to nourish it,
enfolded this withered flesh of mine as though it
were a burnt wick and brought on languor and prolonged weakness; and then next this liver of mine
(my ancient scourge), following the fever, barred me
from foods, drove sleep from my eyes, and kept me
on the verge of life and death, allowing me only so
much of life as to keep me sensible of its discomforts. Therefore I resorted to the use of naturally
hot waters and received some attention from
physicians. But all these things were put to shame
by this lusty malady, which, if one were accustomed
to it, anybody might endure, but when it attacks
without warning, no one is so hardy as to withstand.

Though I have been troubled by this disease for
a long time, never have I been so distressed as now,
since I have been prevented by it from meeting with
your true Charity.[1] Of what gladness of heart we
have been deprived I myself also know, even though
it was with but my finger-tip that I tasted last year
of the very sweet honey of your church.

Because of other pressing matters as well I wanted
to meet with your Holiness and both to consult with
you about many things and to learn many things
from you. For here it is not possible to meet with
even genuine charity. But though one may at times
find a person who shows even very great charity,
there exists no one who is able, in a manner comparable with your perfect wisdom and the experience

---

[1] Byzantine title.

---

[6] εὔρῃ editi antiqi.

COLLECTED LETTERS OF SAINT BASIL

πολλῶν τῶν περὶ τὰς ἐκκλησίας συνελέξω καμάτων, δοῦναι γνώμην ἡμῖν περὶ τῶν προκειμένων.
Τὰ μὲν οὖν ἄλλα οὐκ ἐνῆν γράφειν· ἃ δ' οὖν
καὶ ἐξενεγκεῖν ἀσφαλὲς ταῦτά ἐστιν. ὁ πρεσβύτερος Εὐάγριος, ὁ υἱὸς Πομπηϊανοῦ τοῦ Ἀντιο-
χέως, ὁ συναπάρας ποτὲ ἐπὶ τὴν δύσιν τῷ
μακαρίῳ Εὐσεβίῳ ἐπανῆκε νῦν ἐκ τῆς Ῥώμης,
ἀπαιτῶν ἡμᾶς ἐπιστολὴν αὐτὰ τὰ παρ' ἐκείνων
γεγραμμένα ἔχουσαν αὐτολεξεὶ (ἀνεκόμισε δὲ
ἡμῖν εἰς τοὐπίσω τὰ παρ' ἡμῶν, ὡς οὐκ ἀρέσαντα
τοῖς ἀκριβεστέροις τῶν ἐκεῖ), καὶ πρεσβείαν τινὰ
δι' ἀνδρῶν ἀξιολόγων ἤδη κατεπείγεσθαι, ὑπὲρ
τοῦ εὐπρόσωπον ἔχειν ἀφορμὴν τοὺς ἄνδρας τῆς
ἐπισκέψεως ἡμῶν.
Οἱ κατὰ Σεβάστειαν τὰ ἡμέτερα φρονοῦντες,
Εὐσταθίου τὸ ὕπουλον τῆς κακοδοξίας ἕλκος
ἀπογυμνώσαντες, ἀπαιτοῦσί τινα παρ' ἡμῶν ἐκκλησιαστικὴν[1] ἐπιμέλειαν.

[1] αὐτῶν add. E.

---

[1] Evagrius, known as of Antioch, the dates of whose birth and death are uncertain. He was consecrated bishop over one of the parties at Antioch in 388–389. He went to Italy with Eusebius, Bishop of Vercelli, and at the death of that prelate returned to Antioch in company with St. Jerome. He was probably the ascetic who trained St. John Chrysostom in monastic discipline. He belonged to the Eustathian division of the orthodox church at Antioch. He also aided Pope Damasus in getting the better of his rival Ursinus. After nine or ten years he returned to the East, stopping *en route* at Caesarea to visit Basil (373). Later, from Antioch, Evagrius wrote Basil a harsh letter, accusing him of love of strife and controversy. Basil's reply is a model of courteous sarcasm. Later Evagrius became the instrument for prolonging the schism. Cf. Theodoret, *Ecc. Hist.* 5, 23 ; and St. Basil, Letter CLVI.

which you have gathered from your many labours
for the churches, to offer advice on the matters
which lie before us.

Now there are some things which I cannot put in
writing; the things which I can set forth with safety
are these: The presbyter Evagrius,[1] son of Pompeianus[2] of Antioch, who formerly went to the
West in company with Eusebius[3] of blessed memory,
has now returned from Rome, demanding from us
a letter containing the very things written by them
word for word (and our own letter he has brought
back to us again on the ground that it was not
pleasing to the more strict of the people there),
and he also asks that a sort of embassy of influential
men be sent in haste, that the men may have a
reasonable occasion for visiting us.

Those at Sebaste who feel as we do, having laid
bare the festering ulcer of Eustathius'[4] evil doctrine,
demand from us some ecclesiastical attention.

[2] Pompeianus of Antioch, the father of Evagrius, was,
according to St. Jerome, a descendant of the officer of that
name who accompanied Aurelian against Zenobia of Palmyra
(273).

[3] St. Eusebius, Bishop of Vercelli, 283–371. According
to St. Ambrose, he was the first bishop of the West to
unite the monastic with the clerical life; cf. Ambrose,
Letter LXIII, *Ad Vercellenses*. Entirely orthodox, at the
synod of Milan (355), he refused to sign the document
condemning St. Athanasius. In 363, on his return to
Vercelli from exile, he became one of the chief opponents
of the Arian bishop Amentius of Milan. The Church
honours him as a martyr on December 16.

[4] Eustathius of Sebaste (*circ.* 300–377), one of the chief
founders of monasticism in Asia Minor and for a time the
intimate friend of St. Basil. He hesitated all his life
between the various forms of Arianism, and finally became
the leader of the Pneumatomachians condemned by the
First Council of Constantinople.

'Ικόνιον πόλις ἐστὶ τῆς Πισιδίας, τὸ μὲν παλαιὸν
μετὰ τὴν μεγίστην ἡ πρώτη, νῦν δὲ καὶ αὐτὴ
προκάθηται[1] μέρους, ὅ, ἐκ διαφόρων τμημάτων
συναχθέν, ἐπαρχίας ἰδίας οἰκονομίαν ἐδέξατο.
αὕτη καλεῖ[2] καὶ ἡμᾶς εἰς ἐπίσκεψιν,[3] ὥστε αὐτῇ
δοῦναι ἐπίσκοπον. τετελευτήκει γὰρ ὁ Φαυστῖνος.

Εἰ οὖν δεῖ μὴ κατοκνεῖν τὰς ὑπερορίους χειροτο-
νίας, καὶ ποίαν τινὰ χρὴ δοῦναι τοῖς Σεβαστηνοῖς
ἀπόκρισιν, καὶ πῶς πρὸς τὰς τοῦ Εὐαγρίου διατε-
θῆναι γνώμας, ἐδεόμην διδαχθῆναι αὐτὸς δι᾽ ἐμαυτοῦ συντυχὼν τῇ τιμιότητί σου, ὧν[4] πάντων ἀπεστερήθην διὰ τὴν παροῦσαν ἀσθένειαν. ἐὰν μὲν
οὖν ᾖ τινος ἐπιτυχεῖν ταχέως πρὸς ἡμᾶς ἀφικνου-
μένου, καταξίωσον περὶ πάντων ἀποστεῖλαί μοι
τὰς ἀποκρίσεις· εἰ δὲ μή, εὖξαι ἐλθεῖν ἐπὶ νοῦν
μοι, ὅπερ εὐάρεστον ᾖ τῷ Κυρίῳ. ἐν δὲ τῇ
συνόδῳ μνήμην ἡμῶν κέλευσον γενέσθαι, καὶ
αὐτὸς δὲ πρόσευξαι ὑπὲρ ἡμῶν, καὶ τὸν λαὸν
συμπαράλαβε, ἵνα τὰς λειπομένας ἡμέρας ἢ ὥρας
τῆς παροικίας ἡμῶν καταξιωθῶμεν δουλεῦσαι, ὡς
ἔστιν εὐάρεστον τῷ Κυρίῳ.

CXXXIX

Τοῖς Ἀλεξανδρεῦσιν

Ἡμᾶς μὲν ἡ ἀκοὴ τῶν γεγενημένων κατά τε τὴν
Ἀλεξάνδρειαν καὶ τὴν λοιπὴν Αἴγυπτον διωγμῶν

---

[1] προκάθηται] πρώτη κάθηται tres MSS.   [2] καλεῖ om. E.
[3] κεκλήκει add. E.   [4] ὡς Harl., Med.

---

[1] i.e. Antioch.
[2] For Faustinus cf. Letter CLXI. He was succeeded by
John I, who in turn was succeeded by Amphilochius.

LETTER CXXXIX

Iconium is a city of Pisidia, in olden times the first after the greatest,[1] and now also it is the capital of that territory which, made up of different sections, has received the management of its own government. This city urges me to make it a visit, that we may give it a bishop. For Faustinus[2] has died.

Whether, therefore, I should not decline these ordinations beyond our borders, and what sort of an answer I should give to the Sebastines, and how I should be disposed toward the propositions of Evagrius, on all these matters I need to be instructed by a personal meeting with your Honour, but I have been deprived of all this by my present ill-health. If, then, it is possible to find anyone who is coming to us soon, deign to send me your answers on all these questions; but if not, pray that there may come to my mind that thing which is most pleasing to the Lord. And order that remembrance of us be made in the synod, and do you yourself pray for us, and join the people with you in prayer, that we may be thought worthy to serve during the remaining days or hours of our sojourn as is acceptable to the Lord.

LETTER CXXXIX

To the Alexandrians [3]

Long since has the rumour reached us of the persecutions that have taken place throughout Alexandria and the rest of Egypt, and it has rent

[3] Written in 373 to the Alexandrians to console them and to encourage them to great constancy, harassed as they were by a terrible persecution. The persecution referred to is the one caused by Valens, who tortured the Eastern Catholics from 369 to the end of his reign.

COLLECTED LETTERS OF SAINT BASIL

πάλαι κατέλαβε, καὶ διέθηκε τὰς ψυχάς, ὡς εἰκὸς
ἦν. ἐλογισάμεθα γὰρ τὸ ἔντεχνον τοῦ διαβολικοῦ
πολέμου· ὃς [1] ἐπειδὴ εἶδεν ἐν τοῖς παρὰ τῶν
ἐχθρῶν διωγμοῖς πληθυνομένην τὴν Ἐκκλησίαν
καὶ μᾶλλον θάλλουσαν, μετέστρεψεν ἑαυτοῦ
τὴν βουλήν,[2] καὶ οὐκέτι ἐκ τοῦ προφανοῦς πολεμεῖ,
ἀλλὰ κεκρυμμένα ἡμῖν τὰ ἔνεδρα [3] τίθησι, καλύπ-
των αὐτοῦ τὴν ἐπιβουλὴν διὰ τοῦ ὀνόματος ὃ
περιφέρουσιν, ἵνα καὶ πάθωμεν τὰ αὐτὰ τοῖς
πατράσιν ἡμῶν, καὶ μὴ δόξωμεν πάσχειν ὑπὲρ
Χριστοῦ, διὰ τὸ Χριστιανῶν ὄνομα ἔχειν καὶ τοὺς
διώκοντας. ταῦτα λογιζόμενοι πολὺν χρόνον
ἐκαθέσθημεν ἐπὶ τῇ ἀγγελίᾳ τῶν γεγενημένων [4]
ἐκπεπληγμένοι. καὶ γὰρ τῷ ὄντι ἤχησαν [5] ἡμῶν
ἀμφότερα τὰ ὦτα μαθόντα τὴν ἀναιδῆ καὶ μισάν-
θρωπον αἵρεσιν τῶν διωξάντων ὑμᾶς, ὅτι οὐχ
ἡλικίαν ᾐδέσθησαν, οὐ τοὺς ἐν τῇ πολιτείᾳ [6]
καμάτους, οὐ λαῶν ἀγάπην· ἀλλὰ καὶ ᾐκίσαντο
τὰ σώματα, καὶ ἠτίμωσαν, καὶ ἐξορίαις παρέδωκαν,
καὶ διήρπασαν τὰς ὑπάρξεις ὧν εὑρεῖν ἠδυνήθη-
σαν, οὔτε τὴν παρὰ ἀνθρώπων κατάγνωσιν [7]
ἐντρεπόμενοι, οὔτε τὴν φοβερὰν τοῦ δικαίου κριτοῦ
ἀνταπόδοσιν προορώμενοι. ταῦτα ἡμᾶς ἐξέπληξε
καὶ μικροῦ ἔξω ἐποίησε τῶν λογισμῶν. συνεισῆλθε
δὲ τούτοις τοῖς διαλογισμοῖς κἀκείνη ἡ ἔννοια·
ἆρα μὴ ἐγκατέλιπεν ἑαυτοῦ τὰς ἐκκλησίας παντελῶς ὁ Κύριος ; ἆρα μὴ ἐσχάτη ὥρα ἐστί, καὶ ἡ
ἀποστασία διὰ τούτων λαμβάνει τὴν εἴσοδον, ἵνα
λοιπὸν ἀποκαλυφθῇ ὁ ἄνομος, ὁ υἱὸς τῆς ἀπωλείας,
326

our hearts, as was natural. For we took thought of
the ingenuity of the devil's warfare,—how the devil,
when he saw the Church multiplying and flourishing
still more amid the persecutions of its enemies,
changed his plan, and no longer fights openly, but
places hidden snares for us, concealing his plot by
means of the name which his followers bear, that we
may suffer as our fathers did and yet not seem to
suffer for Christ, because of the fact that our persecutors also bear the name of Christians. Considering these things we sat for a long time amazed at the
report of what had happened. For in truth both
our ears rang on learning of the shameless and cruel
heresy of your persecutors, in that they showed no
respect for age, nor for the labours of a life well
spent, nor for charity toward the people ; nay, they
even tortured their bodies, and dishonoured them,
and gave them over to exile, and plundered the
property of whomsoever they could find, neither
giving heed to the condemnation of men nor looking
forward to the fearful requital of the just Judge.
These things have stricken us and have almost put
us out of our senses. And along with these reflections there comes into our mind this thought also :
Has not the Lord abandoned His churches utterly ?
Is not this the last hour, when apostasy uses these
means to gain entrance, " so that at length the man
of sin may be revealed, the son of perdition, who

---

¹ πῶς editi antiqi.
² ἑαυτοῦ τὴν βουλὴν] αὐτοῦ τὴν ἐπιβουλήν editi antiqi.
³ κεκρυμμένα ἡμῖν τὰ ἔνεδρα] κεκρυμμένας ἡμῖν τὰς ἔνεδρας E.
⁴ γενομένων Coisl. secundus, tres Regii.
⁵ ἤχησεν E   ⁶ πολιᾷ editi antiqi.
⁷ κατάκρισιν E, Med.

ὁ ἀντικείμενος, καὶ ὑπεραιρόμενος ἐπὶ πάντα λεγόμενον Θεὸν ἢ σέβασμα ;

Πλὴν εἴτε πρόσκαιρός ἐστιν ὁ πειρασμός, βαστάσατε αὐτόν, οἱ καλοὶ τοῦ Χριστοῦ ἀγωνισταί· εἴτε καὶ τῇ παντελεῖ φθορᾷ τὰ πράγματα παραδίδοται,[1] μὴ ἀκηδιάσωμεν πρὸς τὰ παρόντα, ἀλλ' ἀναμείνωμεν τὴν ἐξ οὐρανῶν ἀποκάλυψιν καὶ ἐπιφάνειαν τοῦ μεγάλου Θεοῦ καὶ Σωτῆρος ἡμῶν Ἰησοῦ Χριστοῦ. εἰ γὰρ πᾶσα ἡ κτίσις λυθήσεται καὶ μεταποιηθήσεται τὸ σχῆμα τοῦ κόσμου τούτου, τί θαυμαστὸν καὶ ἡμᾶς, μέρος ὄντας τῆς κτίσεως, παθεῖν τὰ κοινὰ πάθη καὶ παραδοθῆναι θλίψεσιν, ἃς κατὰ τὸ μέτρον τῆς δυνάμεως ἡμῶν ἐπάγει ἡμῖν ὁ δίκαιος κριτής, οὐκ ἐῶν ἡμᾶς πειρασθῆναι ὑπὲρ ὃ δυνάμεθα, ἀλλὰ διδοὺς σὺν τῷ πειρασμῷ καὶ τὴν ἔκβασιν, τοῦ δυνηθῆναι[2] ὑπενεγκεῖν ;

Ἀναμένουσιν ὑμᾶς, ἀδελφοί, οἱ τῶν μαρτύρων στέφανοι· ἕτοιμοί εἰσιν οἱ χοροὶ τῶν ὁμολογητῶν προτεῖναι ὑμῖν τὰς χεῖρας καὶ ὑποδέξασθαι ὑμᾶς εἰς τὸν ἴδιον ἀριθμόν. μνήσθητε τῶν πάλαι ἁγίων, ὅτι οὐδεὶς τρυφῶν οὐδὲ[3] κολακευόμενος τῶν στεφάνων τῆς ὑπομονῆς ἠξιώθη, ἀλλὰ πάντες, διὰ μεγάλων θλίψεων πυρωθέντες, τὸ δοκίμιον ἐπεδείξαντο.[4] οἱ μὲν γὰρ ἐμπαιγμῶν καὶ μαστίγων πεῖραν ἔλαβον, ἄλλοι δὲ ἐπρίσθησαν, οἱ

---

[1] παραδίδονται editi antiqi. [2] ἡμᾶς add. E.
[3] οὐ editi antiqi. [4] ὑπεδείξαντο E.

opposeth and is lifted up above all that is called
God or that is worshipped "? [1]

Yet if the trial be momentary, bear it, brave
champions of Christ; or even if all has been given
over to utter destruction, let us not grow listless in
the face of present circumstances, but let us await
the revelation from heaven and the epiphany of our
great God and Saviour, Jesus Christ. For if all
creation shall be dissolved and the scheme of this
world be transformed, what wonder is it that we also,
being a part of creation, should suffer the common
doom and be given over to afflictions, which the
just Judge brings upon us according to the measure
of our strength, "not permitting us to be tempted
above that which we are able, but granting also with
temptation issue, that we may be able to bear it"? [2]

There await you, brothers, the martyrs' crowns;
the choirs of the confessors are ready to extend to
you their hands and to receive you among their own
number. Remember the saints of old, that no one
of them who indulged himself or yielded to flattery
was thought worthy of the crown of patient endur-
ance, but that they all, having through great afflictions
been tried by fire, proved their metal. For some
"had trial of mockeries and stripes," while others
"were cut asunder," and still others "were put to

---

[1] 2 Thess. 2. 4.

[2] Cf. 1 Cor. 10. 13: πειρασμὸς ὑμᾶς οὐκ εἴληφεν εἰ μὴ ἀνθρώπινος·
πιστὸς δὲ ὁ Θεός, ὃς οὐκ ἐάσει ὑμᾶς πειρασθῆναι ὑπὲρ ὃ δύνασθε,
ἀλλὰ ποιήσει σὺν τῷ πειρασμῷ καὶ τὴν ἔκβασιν τοῦ δύνασθαι ὑμᾶς
ὑπενεγκεῖν. "Let no temptation take hold on you, but such
as is human. And God is faithful, who will not suffer you to
be tempted above that which you are able; but will make
also with temptation issue, that you may be able to bear
it."

δὲ[1] ἐν φόνῳ μαχαίρας ἀπέθανον. ταῦτά ἐστι
τὰ σεμνολογήματα τῶν ἁγίων. μακάριος ὁ
καταξιωθεὶς τῶν ὑπὲρ Χριστοῦ παθημάτων.
μακαριώτερος δὲ ὁ πλεονάσας ἐν τοῖς παθήμασι·
διότι οὐκ ἄξια τὰ παθήματα τοῦ νῦν καιροῦ πρὸς
τὴν μέλλουσαν δόξαν ἀποκαλυφθῆναι[2] εἰς
ἡμᾶς.

Εἰ μὲν οὖν ἦν δυνατὸν αὐτόν με παραγενέσθαι,
οὐδὲν ἂν προετίμησα τῆς συντυχίας ὑμῶν, ὥστε
καὶ ἰδεῖν τοὺς ἀθλητὰς τοῦ Χριστοῦ, καὶ περιπτύξασθαι, καὶ κοινωνῆσαι τῶν προσευχῶν καὶ
τῶν πνευματικῶν ἐν ὑμῖν χαρισμάτων. ἐπειδὴ δὲ
τὸ σῶμά μοι λοιπὸν ὑπὸ χρονίας νόσου κατανά-
λωται, ὡς μηδὲ ἀπὸ τῆς κλίνης δύνασθαί με
καταβαίνειν, καὶ οἱ ἐφεδρεύοντες ἡμῖν πολλοί, ὡς
λύκοι ἅρπαγες, ἐπιτηροῦντες καιρὸν πότε δυνηθῶσι διαρπάσαι τὰ πρόβατα τοῦ Χριστοῦ,
ἀναγκαίως ἐπὶ τὴν διὰ τοῦ γράμματος ἐπίσκεψιν
ἦλθον, παρακαλῶν προηγουμένως μὲν ἐκτενεῖς
τὰς ὑπὲρ ἐμοῦ ποιεῖσθαι ὑμᾶς δεήσεις, ἵνα
καταξιωθῶ τὰς γοῦν λειπομένας ἡμέρας ἢ ὥρας
δουλεῦσαι τῷ Κυρίῳ κατὰ τὸ εὐαγγέλιον τῆς
βασιλείας, ἔπειτα καὶ συγγνώμην ἔχειν μου τῇ
ἀπολείψει καὶ τῇ βραδυτῆτι ταύτῃ τῶν γραμμάτων. μόλις γὰρ ηὐπορήσαμεν ἀνθρώπου τοῦ
δυναμένου ἐξυπηρετήσασθαι ἡμῶν τῇ ἐπιθυμίᾳ·
λέγομεν δὲ τὸν υἱὸν ἡμῶν Εὐγένιον τὸν μονά-
ζοντα, δι' οὗ παρακαλῶ εὔξασθαι ὑπὲρ ἡμῶν καὶ
τῆς Ἐκκλησίας πάσης, καὶ ἀντιγράψαι ἡμῖν τὰ
περὶ ὑμῶν, ἵνα γνόντες εὐθυμότερον διατεθῶμεν.

[1] ἐπρίσθησαν, οἱ δὲ] ἐπειράσθησαν. ἐπρίσθησαν E.
[2] ἀποκαλύπτεσθαι E.

330

death by the sword." [1] These are the proud boasts
of the saints. Blessed is he who is deemed worthy
of suffering for Christ! And more blessed is he
who abounds in sufferings; for "the sufferings of
this time are not worthy to be compared with the
glory to come that shall be revealed in us." [2]

Now if it had been possible for me to be with you
in person, I should have preferred nothing to such
meeting with you, that I might see the athletes of
Christ, and embrace you, and to share in your prayers
and in your spiritual acts of grace. But since my
body has been wasted by a long sickness, so that I
am not even able to leave my bed, and since they are
many who lie in wait for us, like rapacious wolves,
watching for an opportunity when they may be able
to seize the sheep of Christ, of necessity have I been
reduced to visit you by letter, urging you above all
to make earnest supplications for me, that I may be
thought worthy to spend at least the remaining days
or hours in serving the Lord according to the Gospel
of His kingdom, and, in the second place, asking you
to grant me pardon for my absence and for the tardi-
ness of this letter. For with difficulty have we
found a man who is able to carry out our desire; we
mean our son Eugenius, the monk, through whom I
ask you to pray for us and for the entire Church, and
to write us in answer about your affairs, that on
being informed we may be of better cheer.

---

[1] Cf. Heb. 11. 36-37 : ἕτεροι δὲ ἐμπαιγμῶν καὶ μαστίγων
πεῖραν ἔλαβον ἔτι δὲ δεσμῶν καὶ φυλακῆς· ἐλιθάσθησαν, ἐπρίσθησαν,
ἐπειράσθησαν, ἐν φόνῳ μαχαίρας ἀπέθανον. " And others had
trial of mockeries and stripes, moreover also of bonds and
prisons. They were stoned, they were cut asunder, they
were tempted, they were put to death by the sword."
[2] Rom. 8. 18.

CXL

Τῇ Ἀντιοχέων Ἐκκλησίᾳ [1]

Τίς δώσει μοι πτέρυγας, ὡσεὶ περιστερᾶς; καὶ
πετασθήσομαι [2] πρὸς ὑμᾶς καὶ καταπαύσω τὸν
πόθον ὃν ἔχω ἐπὶ τῇ συντυχίᾳ τῆς ὑμετέρας ἀγάπης. νυνὶ δὲ οὐχὶ πτερύγων ἐνδεῶς ἔχω μόνον,
ἀλλὰ καὶ αὐτοῦ τοῦ σώματος, πάλαι μέν μοι ὑπὸ
μακρᾶς τῆς [3] ἀρρωστίας πεπονηκότος, νῦν δὲ ὑπὸ
τῶν συνεχῶν θλίψεων παντελῶς συντετριμμένου.
τίς γὰρ οὕτως ἀδαμάντινος τὴν ψυχήν, τίς οὕτω
παντελῶς ἀσυμπαθὴς καὶ ἀνήμερος, ὡς [4] ἀκούων
τοῦ πανταχόθεν ἡμᾶς [5] προσβάλλοντος στεναγμοῦ,
οἷον ἀπό τινος χοροῦ κατηφοῦς κοινόν τινα
θρῆνον καὶ σύμφωνον προσηχοῦντος, μὴ οὐχὶ
παθεῖν τὴν ψυχήν, καὶ κατακαμφθῆναι εἰς γῆν,
καὶ ταῖς ἀμηχάνοις ταύταις μερίμναις παντελῶς
ἐκτακῆναι; ἀλλὰ δυνατὸς ὁ ἅγιος Θεὸς δοῦναί
τινα λύσιν τῶν ἀμηχάνων καὶ χαρίσασθαι ἡμῖν
τινὰ τῶν μακρῶν πόνων ἀναπνοήν. ὥστε καὶ
ὑμᾶς τὴν αὐτὴν ἔχειν ἀξιῶ παράκλησιν καὶ τῇ
ἐλπίδι τῆς παρακλήσεως χαίροντας ὑμᾶς τὸ παρὸν
ἀλγεινὸν τῶν θλίψεων ὑπομένειν. εἴτε γὰρ
ἁμαρτημάτων ἀποτίννυμεν δίκας, ἱκαναὶ αἱ
μάστιγες πρὸς παραίτησιν [6] λοιπὸν τῆς ἐφ᾽ ἡμῖν
ὀργῆς τοῦ Θεοῦ· εἴτε εἰς τοὺς ὑπὲρ τῆς εὐσεβείας
ἀγῶνας διὰ τῶν πειρασμῶν τούτων κεκλήμεθα,[7]
δίκαιος ὁ ἀθλοθέτης μὴ ἐᾶσαι ἡμᾶς πειρασθῆναι

---

[1] τῇ ἐκκλησίᾳ Ἀντιοχείας παραμυθητική E.
[2] πετανθήσομαι Regius.   [3] τῆς om. E.   [4] ὅς E.
[5] ἡμῖν Reg. secundus, Coisl. secundus.

LETTER CXL

LETTER CXL

To the Church of Antioch [1]

" Who will give me wings like a dove, and I will fly " [2] to you and end the longing which I have for converse with your Charity? But as it is I lack, not only wings, but my very body also, for it has suffered for a long time from my chronic illness and is now quite crushed by its continuous afflictions. For who is so hard of heart, who so wholly without sympathy and kindness, that, when he hears the lamentations which assail us from all sides, issuing as it were from a doleful choir intoning in unison a kind of universal dirge, does not suffer at heart, and is not bowed down to earth, and is not utterly wasted away by their present desperate anxieties? But the holy God has power to grant relief from our desperate straits and to bless us with a respite from our prolonged labours. So I feel that you also may well possess the same consolation, and, rejoicing in the hope of that consolation, endure the present pain of your afflictions. For if we are paying a penalty for sins, our scourging will suffice to appease henceforth God's wrath towards us, or if through these trials we have been called into the contest on behalf of the true religion, the arbiter of the contest is just and

---

[1] Written in 373.

[2] Cf. Psal. 54. 7 : καὶ εἶπα Τίς δώσει μοι πτέρυγας ὡσεὶ περιστερᾶς, καὶ πετασθήσομαι καὶ καταπαύσω; "And I said : Who will give me wings like a dove, and I will fly and be at rest?"

---

[6] παρέκτισιν editi antiqi.   [7] βεβλιούμεθα editi antiqi.

333

COLLECTED LETTERS OF SAINT BASIL

ὑπὲρ ὃ δυνάμεθα ὑπενεγκεῖν, ἀλλ᾽ ἐπὶ τοῖς προ
πεπονημένοις ἀποδοῦναι ἡμῖν τὸν τῆς ὑπομονῆς
καὶ τῆς εἰς αὐτὸν ἐλπίδος στέφανον. μὴ οὖν
ἀποκάμωμεν ἐναθλοῦντες εἰς τοὺς ὑπὲρ τῆς εὐσε
βείας ἀγῶνας, μηδὲ δι᾽ ἀνελπιστίας τὰ πονηθέντα
ἡμῖν προώμεθα. οὐ γὰρ μία πρᾶξις ἀνδρείας οὐδὲ
βραχὺς πόνος τὸ τῆς ψυχῆς καρτερὸν διαδείκνυ
σιν, ἀλλ᾽ ὁ δοκιμάζων ἡμῶν τὰς καρδίας διὰ μακ
ρᾶς καὶ παρατεταμένης τῆς δοκιμασίας βούλεται
ἡμᾶς τῆς δικαιοσύνης στεφανίτας ἀποδειχ
θῆναι.[1]

Μόνον ἀνένδοτον φυλασσέσθω τὸ φρόνημα
ἡμῶν, ἄσειστον τὸ στερέωμα τῆς εἰς Χριστὸν
πίστεως διατηρείσθω, καὶ ἥξει ἐν τάχει ὁ ἀντι
ληψόμενος ἡμῶν· ἥξει καὶ οὐ χρονιεῖ. προσδέχου
γὰρ θλῖψιν ἐπὶ θλίψει, ἐλπίδα ἐπ᾽ ἐλπίδι, ἔτι
μικρόν, ἔτι μικρόν. οὕτως οἶδε ψυχαγωγεῖν τῇ
ἐπαγγελίᾳ τοῦ μέλλοντος τοὺς ἑαυτοῦ τροφίμους
τὸ Πνεῦμα τὸ ἅγιον. μετὰ γὰρ τὰς θλίψεις ἡ
ἐλπίς, ἐκ τοῦ σύνεγγυς δὲ πάρεστι τὰ ἐλπιζό
μενα. κἂν γὰρ ὅλον τις εἴποι τὸν ἀνθρώπινον
βίον, σμικρότατόν ἐστι διάστημα παντελῶς,
συγκρίσει ἐκείνου τοῦ ἀπεράντου αἰῶνος τοῦ ἐν
ταῖς ἐλπίσιν ἀποκειμένου.

Πίστιν δὲ ἡμεῖς οὔτε παρ᾽ ἄλλων γραφομένην
ἡμῖν νεωτέραν παραδεχόμεθα, οὔτε αὐτοὶ τὰ τῆς
ἡμετέρας διανοίας γεννήματα παραδιδόναι τολμῶ
μεν, ἵνα μὴ ἀνθρώπινα ποιήσωμεν[2] τὰ τῆς εὐσε
βείας ῥήματα· ἀλλ᾽ ἅπερ παρὰ τῶν ἁγίων πατέρων
δεδιδάγμεθα, ταῦτα τοῖς ἐρωτῶσιν ἡμᾶς διαγγέλλο
μεν. ἔστι τοίνυν ἐκ πατέρων ἐμπολιτευομένη τῇ

[1] ἀναδειχθῆναι editi antiqi.

334

will not permit us to be tried beyond what we can endure,[1] nay, for what we have already endured He will give us the crown of patience and of our hope in Him. So let us not weary of the contest in the struggle for the true religion, and let us not in despair give up the fruits of our labours. For it is not a single act of courage nor yet a labour for a brief space that proves the soul's strength, but He who makes trial of our hearts wishes by means of a long and protracted trial that we may be appointed winners of the crown of righteousness.

Only let our spirits be kept unyielding, the steadfastness of our faith in Christ maintained unshaken, and presently He will come who will take our part ; He will come and not delay. For you must look forward to affliction upon affliction, hope upon hope, for yet a little while, yet a little while. Thus does the Holy Spirit know how to beguile his nurslings by the promise of the future. For beyond the afflictions is hope, and near at hand are the objects of our hope. For even if one should speak of the whole of human life, it is indeed a very short span altogether as compared with that endless eternity which lies yonder in our hopes.

As to creed, we accept no newer creed written for us by others, nor do we ourselves make bold to give out the product of our own intelligence, lest we make the words of our religion the words of man; but rather that which we have been taught by the holy Fathers do we make known to those who question us. We have, then, enfranchised in our church

---

[1] Cf. 1 Cor. 10. 13. See previous letter, p. 329, note 2.

---

[2] λογίζωνται editi antiqi.

ἐκκλησίᾳ ἡμῶν ἡ γραφεῖσα παρὰ τῶν ἁγίων
πατέρων πίστις τῶν κατὰ τὴν Νίκαιαν συνελθόν-
των·[1] ἣν ἡγούμεθα μὲν διὰ στόματος εἶναι καὶ
παρ᾽ ὑμῖν, οὐ παραιτούμεθα δέ, ἵνα μὴ ὄκνου
ἔγκλημα ἀπενεγκώμεθα, καὶ αὐτὰ τὰ ῥήματα
ἐνσημᾶναι τῷ γράμματι. ἔστι δὲ ταῦτα. πιστεύομεν εἰς ἕνα Θεὸν Πατέρα παντοκράτορα,
ὁρατῶν τε πάντων καὶ ἀοράτων ποιητήν. καὶ εἰς
ἕνα Κύριον Ἰησοῦν Χριστὸν τὸν Υἱὸν τοῦ Θεοῦ,
γεννηθέντα ἐκ τοῦ Πατρὸς μονογενῆ· τουτέστιν,
ἐκ τῆς οὐσίας τοῦ Πατρός· φῶς ἐκ φωτός, Θεὸν
ἀληθινὸν ἐκ Θεοῦ ἀληθινοῦ· γεννηθέντα οὐ ποιη-
θέντα, ὁμοούσιον τῷ Πατρί, δι᾽ οὗ τὰ πάντα
ἐγένετο, τά τε ἐν τῷ οὐρανῷ καὶ τὰ ἐν τῇ γῇ. τὸν
δι᾽ ἡμᾶς τοὺς ἀνθρώπους καὶ διὰ τὴν ἡμετέραν
σωτηρίαν κατελθόντα·[2] σαρκωθέντα, ἐνανθρωπήσαντα, παθόντα, καὶ ἀναστάντα τῇ τρίτῃ ἡμέρᾳ·
ἀνελθόντα εἰς οὐρανούς, ἐρχόμενον κρῖναι ζῶντας
καὶ νεκρούς. καὶ εἰς τὸ ἅγιον Πνεῦμα. τοὺς δὲ
λέγοντας, ἦν ποτέ, ὅτε οὐκ ἦν· καί, πρὶν γεννηθῆναι οὐκ ἦν· καί, ὅτι ἐξ οὐκ ὄντων ἐγένετο· ἢ
ἐξ ἑτέρας ὑποστάσεως ἢ οὐσίας φάσκοντας εἶναι,
ἢ τρεπτόν, ἢ ἀλλοιωτὸν τὸν Υἱὸν τοῦ Θεοῦ, τούτους
ἀναθεματίζει ἡ καθολικὴ καὶ ἀποστολικὴ Ἐκκλησία.

Πιστεύομεν τούτοις. ἐπειδὴ δὲ ἀδιόριστός

----
[1] ἡμῖν add. E.

from the time of the Fathers the creed which
was written by the holy Fathers convened at
Nicaea; and this we believe is repeated among you
also, but, in order that we may not incur the
charge of reluctance, we do not refuse to put into
writing the very words themselves. They are as
follows: "We believe in one God, the Father
Almighty, Maker of all things visible and invisible.
And in one Lord, Jesus Christ, the Son of God, born
of the Father, the only begotten, that is, the substance
of the Father. Light of light, true God of true
God; begotten, not made, consubstantial with the
Father, by whom all things were made both in
heaven and on earth. Who for us men and for
our salvation came down; and was incarnate and
was made man; suffered and rose again on the third
day. He ascended into heaven, and shall come to
judge the living and the dead. And (we believe) in
the Holy Ghost. But as for those who say 'There
was when He was not,' and 'Before He was begotten
He was not,' or that 'He came into existence from
what was not,' or who profess that the Son of God is
of a different person or substance, or that the Son of
God is changeable or variable, these the Catholic and
Apostolic Church anathematizes." [1]

This do we believe. But since the doctrine of the

[1] The Benedictine editors point out that Saint Leontius
brought the Nicene Creed to Caesarea, and that Hermogenes,
the successor of Leontius, bravely defended it, according to
Letter LXXXI. Hermogenes' successor, Dianius, however,
signed several Arian formulae, but the Nicene Creed continued to be maintained. Furthermore, in Letter LI Dianius
is described as supporting it.

[2] ἐκ τῶν οὐρανῶν add. editi antiqi.

ἐστιν ὁ περὶ τοῦ ἁγίου Πνεύματος λόγος, οὔπω
τότε τῶν πνευματομάχων ἀναφανέντων, τὸ χρῆναι ἀναθεματίζεσθαι τοὺς λέγοντας τῆς κτιστῆς
εἶναι καὶ δουλικῆς φύσεως τὸ Πνεῦμα τὸ ἅγιον
ἐσίγησαν. οὐδὲν γὰρ ὅλως τῆς θείας καὶ μακαρίας
Τριάδος κτιστόν.

CXLI

Εὐσεβίῳ, ἐπισκόπῳ Σαμοσάτων

Ἐδεξάμην ἤδη δύο ἐπιστολὰς παρὰ τῆς ἐνθέου
καὶ τελειοτάτης φρονήσεώς σου, ὧν ἡ μὲν ὑπέγρα-
φεν ἡμῖν ἐναργῶς, ὅπως μὲν προσεδοκήθημεν ὑπὸ
τοῦ λαοῦ τοῦ ὑπὸ τὴν χεῖρα τῆς ὁσιότητός σου,
ὅσον δὲ ἐλυπήσαμεν ἀπολειφθέντες τῆς ἁγιωτάτης
συνόδου. ἡ δὲ ἑτέρα, ἡ παλαιοτέρα μέν, ὡς
εἰκάζω τῷ γράμματι, ὕστερον δὲ ἡμῖν ἀποδοθεῖσα,
διδασκαλίαν περιεῖχε πρέπουσάν σοι καὶ ἡμῖν
ἀναγκαίαν, μὴ καταρραθυμεῖν τῶν ἐκκλησιῶν τοῦ
Θεοῦ, μηδὲ κατὰ μικρὸν προΐεσθαι τοῖς ὑπεναν-
τίοις τὰ πράγματα, ἀφ' ὧν τὰ μὲν ἐκείνων αὐξήσει,

---

[1] They flourished in the countries adjacent to the Helles-
pont. They denied the divinity of the Holy Ghost, hence
the name Pneumatomachi or Combators against the Spirit.
Macedonius, their founder, was intruded into the see of
Constantinople by Arians (A.D. 342) and enthroned by
Constantius, who had for a second time expelled Paul, the
Catholic bishop. They are sometimes called Macedonians,
after the name of their founder.

[2] *i.e.* the Fathers of Nicaea.

[3] Written in 373. In this letter Basil answers two complaints of Eusebius: that Basil had not come to him, and
that Basil should take up more energetically the defence of
orthodoxy.

Holy Spirit had not yet been defined, for no Pneu-matomachi [1] had as yet arisen at that time, they [2] were silent about the need of anathematizing those who say that the Holy Spirit is of a created and servile nature. For nothing at all in the divine and blessed Trinity is created.

LETTER CXLI

To Eusebius, Bishop of Samosata [3]

I HAVE already received two letters from your divine and consummate Wisdom,[4] and one of these vividly described to us how we had been expected by the people under the episcopal sway of your Holiness, and how much disappointment we occa-sioned by being absent from the most holy synod. The other letter, of an earlier date, as I judge by the writing, but delivered to us after the first-mentioned, contained an admonition which does credit to your-self and is necessary for us—not to neglect the churches of God nor little by little to surrender the control of affairs to our adversaries, with the result that their interests will increase and ours will be

---

St. Eusebius, Bishop of Samosata (Commagene), died in 379. His feast is celebrated on June 22 by the Greeks and June 21 by the Latins. His life reflects more than any other the unrest and troubles of the Eastern Church between 361 and 379. Eusebius was a moderate partisan of the Creed of Nicaea. He was threatened by Constantius, and, under Valens, could only traverse his diocese in disguise in order to sustain the faith of his people. A decree of 373 banished him to Thrace. Finally, when after the death of Valens (376) he returned to Commagene, an Arian woman killed him by hitting him with a stone. Cf. Tillemont, note 64.

[4] A title in Byzantine times.

τὰ δὲ ἡμέτερα μειωθήσεται. καὶ οἶμαι πρὸς
ἑκατέραν ἀποκεκρίσθαι· πλὴν ἀλλὰ καὶ νῦν,
ἐπειδὴ ἄδηλον εἰ οἱ πιστευθέντες τὴν διακονίαν
διέσωσαν ἡμῶν τὰς ἀποκρίσεις, περὶ τῶν αὐτῶν
ἀπολογοῦμαι· πρὸς μὲν τὴν ἀπόλειψιν ἀληθεσ-
τάτην πρόφασιν γράφων, ἧς οἶμαι τὴν ἀκοὴν
καὶ μέχρι τῆς σῆς ὁσιότητος διαβεβηκέναι, ὅτι
ὑπὸ ἀρρωστίας κατεσχέθην τῆς μέχρις αὐτῶν με
τῶν πυλῶν τοῦ θανάτου καταγαγούσης. καὶ ἔτι
καὶ νῦν, ἡνίκα ἀπέστελλον περὶ τούτων, λείψανα
φέρων τῆς ἀρρωστίας ἔγραφον. ταῦτα δέ ἐστι
τοιαῦτα, ὥστε ἐξαρκεῖν ἑτέρῳ νοσήματα[1] εἶναι
δύσφορα.

Πρὸς δὲ τό, ὅτι οὐ ῥαθυμίᾳ ἡμετέρᾳ τὰ τῶν
ἐκκλησιῶν τοῖς ἐναντίοις προδέδοται, εἰδέναι
βούλομαι τὴν θεοσέβειάν σου, ὅτι οἱ κοινωνικοὶ
δῆθεν ἡμῖν τῶν ἐπισκόπων, ἢ ὄκνῳ, ἢ τῷ πρὸς
ἡμᾶς ὑπόπτως ἔχειν ἔτι καὶ μὴ καθαρῶς, ἢ τῇ
παρὰ τοῦ διαβόλου ἐγγινομένῃ πρὸς τὰς ἀγαθὰς
πράξεις ἐναντιώσει, συνάρασθαι[2] ἡμῖν οὐκ ἀνέχον-
ται. ἀλλὰ σχήματι μὲν δῆθεν οἱ πλείους ἐσμὲν
μετ' ἀλλήλων, προστεθέντος ἡμῖν καὶ τοῦ χρηστοῦ Βοσπορίου, ἀληθείᾳ δὲ πρὸς οὐδὲν ἡμῖν τῶν
ἀναγκαιοτάτων συναίρονται· ὥστε με καὶ ὑπὸ τῆς
ἀθυμίας ταύτης τὸ πλεῖστον μέρος πρὸς τὴν
ἀνάληψιν ἐμποδίζεσθαι, συνεχῶς μοι τῶν ἀρ-

---

[1] ἑτέρων νοσήματα E ; ἑτέρῳ νοσήματα Harl., Med. ; ἑτέρων
νοσήματι editi antiqi.

diminished. I think I have answered both letters; but since it is not clear whether those entrusted with the mission succeeded in delivering our replies, I shall now defend myself once more as regards these same matters. As regards my absence, I am writing a most truthful excuse, the report of which, I think, has travelled even to your Holiness —that I was detained by an illness which brought me down to the very gates of death. And again even now, as I tell you about these things, I am writing while still suffering the after-effects of my illness. And these are of such a character that for another man they would pass for maladies not easy to endure.

As to the other matter, to explain that it is through no negligence on our part that the interests of the churches have been surrendered to our adversaries, I wish your Reverence to know that the bishops who pretend to be in communion with us, either because of reluctance, or again on account of being suspicious of us and not frank and open towards us, or finally on account of the opposition to good works which is fomented by the devil, do not permit themselves to assist us. But while ostensibly the majority of us are united with one another, the excellent Bosporius [1] also having been added to our number, yet in reality they render us no assistance in the most urgent matters; consequently my recovery is being hindered for the most part by my discouragement, since all

---

[1] Bosporius, an intimate friend of Basil, was Bishop of Colonia in Cappadocia Secunda. Cf. Letter LI.

---

[2] συναίρεσθαι editi antiqi.

ρωστημάτων ἐκ τῆς σφοδρᾶς λύπης ἀποστρε-
φόντων.[1]

Τί δ' ἂν ποιήσαιμι μόνος, τῶν κανόνων, ὡς καὶ
αὐτὸς οἶδας, ἐνὶ τὰς τοιαύτας οἰκονομίας μὴ συγ-
χωρούντων ; καίτοι τίνα θεραπείαν οὐκ ἐθερά-
πευσα ; ποίου κρίματος αὐτοὺς οὐκ ἀνέμνησα τὰ
μὲν διὰ γραμμάτων, τὰ δὲ καὶ διὰ τῆς συντυχίας ; ἦλθον γὰρ καὶ μέχρι τῆς [2] πόλεως κατὰ
ἀκοὴν τοῦ ἐμοῦ θανάτου. ἐπεὶ δὲ ἔδοξε τῷ Θεῷ
ζῶντας ἡμᾶς παρ' αὐτῶν καταληφθῆναι, διελέχθημεν αὐτοῖς τὰ εἰκότα. καὶ παρόντα μὲν αἰδοῦνται,
καὶ ὑπισχνοῦνται τὰ εἰκότα πάντα, ἀπολειφθέντες
δὲ πάλιν πρὸς τὴν ἑαυτῶν ἀνατρέχουσι γνώμην.
ταῦτα καὶ ἡμεῖς τῆς κοινῆς καταστάσεως τῶν
πραγμάτων ἀπολαύομεν, προδήλως τοῦ Κυρίου
ἐγκαταλιπόντος ἡμᾶς, τοὺς διὰ τὸ πληθυνθῆναι
τὴν ἀνομίαν ψύξαντας τὴν ἀγάπην. ἀλλὰ
πρὸς πάντα ἡμῖν ἀρκεσάτω ἡ μεγάλη σου καὶ
δυνατωτάτη πρὸς Θεὸν ἱκεσία. τάχα γὰρ ἂν
ἢ γενοίμεθά τι τοῖς πράγμασι χρήσιμοι, ἢ
διαμαρτόντες [3] τῶν σπουδαζομένων, φύγοιμεν τὴν
κατάκρισιν.

---

[1] ὑποστρεφόντων E.
[2] τῆς om. E.

the symptoms of my disease continually recur as the result of my exceeding grief.

But what can I do single-handed, when the Canons,[1] as you yourself well know, do not grant to one man the appropriate administrative powers? And yet what remedy is there that I have not applied? What decision have I failed to bring to their attention, partly by letters, and partly by personal interviews? For they even came to the city at a report of my death. But since it was pleasing to God that they should find us still alive, we addressed them in language proper to such an occasion. They are reverent in my presence, and promise all that they should, but on leaving me they once more return to their own opinion. In all this we, as well as others, are but feeling the effect of the general condition of affairs, for the Lord has clearly abandoned us, seeing that we have grown cold in our love on account of the widespread increase of lawlessness. But to combat all this let your great and most powerful supplication to God assist us. For perhaps we may be of some use in the situation, or, if we fail in what we desire, may escape condemnation.

[1] These canons, which were falsely ascribed to the apostles, are sometimes cited by Basil among the canonical epistles. He seems here to refer to the 27th, where it is ordained that in each province the bishops should not initiate anything of an important character without the opinion or consent of him who is first in rank among them, and that each one should be content with those things which belong to his own district; but he should not do anything without the good-will of all. Basil was very scrupulous in observing this canon. Cf. the note of the Benedictine editors.

---

[3] διαμαρτάνοντες editi antiqi.

CXLII

Νουμεραρίῳ ἐπάρχων[1]

Συνήγαγον μὲν[2] πάντας ἐν τῇ συνόδῳ τοῦ μακαρίου μάρτυρος Εὐψυχίου τοὺς ἀδελφοὺς ἡμῶν τοὺς χωρεπισκόπους, ὥστε γνωρίμους ποιῆσαι τῇ τιμιότητί σου. ἐπεὶ δὲ ἀπελείφθης, διὰ γραμμάτων αὐτοὺς ἀναγκαῖόν ἐστι προσαχθῆναί σου τῇ τελειότητι. γνώριζε τοίνυν τὸν ἀδελφὸν τόνδε ἄξιον ὄντα τοῦ πιστεύεσθαι παρὰ τῆς σῆς φρονήσεως διὰ τὸν φόβον τοῦ Κυρίου. καὶ ἅπερ ἂν τῶν πτωχῶν ἕνεκεν ἀναφέρῃ σου τῇ ἀγαθῇ προαιρέσει, καταξίωσον ὡς ἀληθεύοντι πείθεσθαι καὶ τὴν δυνατὴν ἐπικουρίαν παρέχεσθαι τοῖς καταπονουμένοις. καταξιώσεις δὲ δηλονότι καὶ πτωχοτροφίαν τῆς συμμορίας τῆς ὑπ' αὐτὸν ἐπισκέψασθαι καὶ πάντῃ ἀνεῖναι τῆς συντελείας. τοῦτο γὰρ ἤδη καὶ τῷ ἑταίρῳ σου συνήρεσε τὴν μικρὰν κτῆσιν τῶν πενήτων ἀλειτούργητον καταστῆσαι.

---

[1] ἐπαρχιῶν Reg. secundus, Coisl. secundus.
[2] συνήγαγον μὲν] συνηγάγομεν E, Reg. secundus.

---

[1] Written in 373. Νουμεραρίῳ is merely the transcription of a Latin title. There were two Numerarii in every province. The Benedictine editors remark that Valens had decreed in 365 that the Numerarii of the Consulares and Praesides should henceforth be called *tabellarii*. But perhaps that law was little observed, or, as has happened in many other letters of Basil, the heading has been added since Basil's time by the scribes.

LETTER CXLII

To the Prefects' Accountant[1]

I CONVENED all our brethren, the Chorepiscopi,[2] at the synod of the blessed martyr Eupsychius,[3] in order to introduce them to your Honour. But since you were absent, it is now necessary that they be introduced to your Perfection by letter. Know, then, that this present brother is worthy of being trusted by your Wisdom through his fear of the Lord. Moreover, whatever matters he may refer to your goodwill as regards the welfare of the poor, deign to believe him as a man who speaks the truth and to offer to the afflicted the greatest assistance possible. In particular, you will have the kindness to inspect the home for the poor in the district under his care, and to exempt it entirely from taxation. For it has already pleased your colleague also to make the small property of the poor immune from assessment.

[2] Cf. Letter LIII and note.
[3] Eupsychius appears in the Roman calendar, and his martyrdom is celebrated on April 9. During the reign of Julian he assisted in the demolition of a temple of Fortune in the city of Caesarea in Cappadocia. All who took part in this affair were condemned either to death or banishment (cf. Sozomen, *H. E.* 5, 11). Eupsychius was beheaded, but the temple of Fortune was never rebuilt. In its place a church in memory of Eupsychius was erected. To the festival of the dedication of this church Basil summoned all the bishops of Pontus by a letter which is still extant (Letter CCLII). Furthermore, we find Basil eagerly entreating Eusebius of Samosata to be present at the festival of Eupsychius on Sept. 7, 372 (cf. Basil, Letter C ; also Greg. Naz., Letters XXVI and XXVII).

345

CXLIII

Ἑτέρῳ νουμεραρίῳ

Εἰ μὲν αὐτῷ μοι δυνατὸν ἦν συμπαρεῖναι τῇ τιμιότητί σου, δι᾽ ἐμαυτοῦ ἂν πάντως ἀνήνεγκα περὶ ὧν ἐβουλόμην καὶ προέστην τῶν καταπονουμένων. ἐπεὶ δέ με ἀρρωστία σώματος καὶ ἀσχολίαι πραγμάτων ἀφέλκουσιν,[1] ἀντ᾽ ἐμαυτοῦ σοι τὸν ἀδελφὸν τόνδε τὸν χωρεπίσκοπον συνίστημι, ὥστε σε αὐτῷ γνησίως προσχόντα χρήσασθαι συμβούλῳ, ὡς φιλαλήθως καὶ ἐμφρόνως δυναμένῳ συμβουλεῦσαι περὶ τῶν πραγμάτων. τὸ γὰρ πτωχοτροφεῖον τὸ παρ᾽ αὐτοῦ οἰκονομούμενον ἐπειδὰν καταξιώσῃς θεάσασθαι (ὄψει γάρ, εὖ οἶδα, καὶ οὐ παραδραμῇ, ἐπειδὴ οὐδὲ ἄπειρος[2] εἶ τοῦ ἔργου, ἀλλ᾽, ὡς ὁ δεῖνά μοι ἀνήνεγκεν, ἐν τῶν ἐν τῇ Ἀμασείᾳ ἐξ ὧν ἔδωκέ σοι ὁ Κύριος διατρέφεις), ἐπειδὰν οὖν ἴδῃς καὶ τοῦτο, πάντα αὐτῷ παρέξῃ[3] τὰ ἐπιζητούμενα. ἤδη γάρ μοι καὶ ὁ ἑταῖρός σου κατεπηγγείλατο φιλανθρωπίαν τινὰ περὶ τὰ πτωχοτροφεῖα. τοῦτο δὲ λέγω, οὐχ ἵνα ἄλλον αὐτὸς μιμήσῃ (σὲ γὰρ εἰκὸς ἑτέροις εἶναι

---

[1] ἀνθέλκουσιν editi antiqi.   [2] ἄπορος E, Reg. secundus.
[3] παρέξεις editi antiqi.

---

[1] Written in 373. Cf. previous letter, note 1.
[2] Cf. Letter LIII and note.
[3] A city in the Pontus, situated on the Iris.
[4] By the word "colleague" here is not meant the other accountant to whom the previous letter is addressed, because in that letter also Basil remarks that he has been promised

LETTER CXLIII

To the Other Accountant [1]

If it had been possible for me to call upon your Honour, I should certainly have brought to your attention in person the matters about which I wished to consult you, and I should have championed the cause of the afflicted. Since, however, illness of body and the pressure of affairs detain me, I am now recommending to you in my place this brother, the chorepiscopus,[2] that you, paying him sincere attention, may treat him as your counsellor, since he is able truthfully and prudently to advise you concerning our affairs. For instance, when you are kind enough to look at the home for the poor that is administered by him (for you will see it, I am sure, and will not pass it by, since you are not unfamiliar with the work, but, as a certain person has informed me, you are supporting one of the homes at Amasea [3] with the means which the Lord has bestowed upon you)—when, therefore, you see this home also, you will furnish him with whatever he requests. For already your colleague [4] has also promised me some beneficence for the homes for the poor. But I am saying this, not to induce you to imitate another (for there is every reason why

help for the poor by the addressee's colleague. Since there were but two accountants, this probably refers to another officer who had very similar duties. The Benedictine editors conjecture him to be the prefects' officer (τρακτευτὴς τῶν ἐπάρχων), to whom the next letter is addressed, and who is asked to fulfil certain promises he has made. However, it may be that Basil, to gain his end, is craftily telling each of the two what the other has promised.

347

τῶν καλῶν ἡγεμόνα), ἀλλ' ἵνα γνῷς ὅτι δὴ περὶ
αὐτῶν τούτων καὶ ἄλλοι ἡμᾶς ἐδυσωπήθησαν.[1]

CXLIV

Τρακτευτῇ τῶν ἐπάρχων

Γνωρίζεις πάντως τόνδε ἐκ τῆς κατὰ τὴν πόλιν
συντυχίας, ὅμως δέ σοι αὐτὸν καὶ διὰ τῆς ἐπιστολῆς προσάγομεν συνιστῶντες, ὅτι εἰς πολλά
σοι τῶν σπουδαζομένων χρήσιμος ἔσται, διὰ τὸ
καὶ συνετῶς καὶ εὐλαβῶς δύνασθαι ὑποτίθεσθαι
τὰ πρακτέα. ἃ δὲ ἐμοὶ εἰς τὸ οὖς διελέχθης,
ταῦτα νῦν ἐστὶ καιρὸς ἐπιδείξασθαι, ἐπειδάν σοι
ὁ προειρημένος ἀδελφὸς τὰ τῶν πτωχῶν ὑπο-
δείξῃ.

CXLV

Εὐσεβίῳ, ἐπισκόπῳ Σαμοσάτων

Οἶδα τοὺς μυρίους πόνους[2] σου, οὓς ἀνέτλης
ὑπὲρ τῶν ἐκκλησιῶν τοῦ Θεοῦ, καὶ τῶν ἀσχολιῶν
τὸ πλῆθος οὐκ ἀγνοῶ, ἃς ἔχεις, τὴν οἰκονομίαν οὐ
παρέργως ἀλλὰ κατὰ τὸ θέλημα τοῦ Κυρίου
διατιθέμενος. καὶ τὸν ἐκ γειτόνων ὑμῖν ἐπικα-
θήμενον ἐννοῶ,[3] ᾧ ἀνάγκη ὑμᾶς, ὥσπερ ὄρνιθας

---

[1] ἐδυσώπησαν E, editi antiqi.
[2] κόπους quattuor MSS.　　　[3] ἐννοῶ om. E.

---

[1] Written in 373 and on the same occasion.

you should be the leader of the rest in noble deeds), but in order that you may know that others also regarding these very matters have shown us a reverent respect.

LETTER CXLIV

To the Prefects' Officer [1]

You are surely acquainted with this man through your interview with him in the city, but nevertheless we are introducing and commending him to you also by letter, because he will be useful to you in many matters which now engage your attention, as he is a man capable of advising you intelligently and piously as to what must be done. And now you will have the opportunity of giving proof of the things you once whispered into my ear, when the brother whom we have mentioned shall have laid before you the condition of the poor.

LETTER CXLV

To Eusebius, Bishop of Samosata [2]

I know the innumerable tasks which you have taken upon yourself in defence of the churches of God, and I am not unaware of the multitude of activities which occupy you, since you conduct your administration in no cursory manner but in accordance with the will of the Lord. And I bear in mind him [3] who besieges you from close at hand, to avoid whom each one of you must, like birds cowering before

[2] Written in 373. For this Eusebius, cf. Letter CXLI, p. 339, note 3.
[3] *i.e.* Valens.

ἀετῷ ὑποπτήσσοντας, μὴ πόρρω τῆς σκέπης
ἕκαστον ἀποτρέχειν. τούτων με οὐδὲν λέληθεν.
ἀλλ᾽ ὁ πόθος πρᾶγμα βίαιον, καὶ ἐλπίσαι τὰ μὴ
ἐνδεχόμενα καὶ ἐγχειρῆσαι τοῖς ἀδυνάτοις·[1] μᾶλλον
δὲ ἡ ἐπὶ Κύριον ἐλπὶς ἰσχυρότατον πάντων. οὐ
γὰρ ἀλόγῳ ἐπιθυμίᾳ, ἀλλ᾽ ἰσχύϊ πίστεως προσδοκῶ καὶ πόρον ἐν ἀμηχάνοις φανήσεσθαι καὶ
πάντων ῥᾳδίως σε[2] τῶν κωλυμάτων περιγε-
νήσεσθαι, πρὸς τὸ ἰδεῖν σε τὴν φιλτάτην τῶν
ἐκκλησιῶν, καὶ μέντοι καὶ[3] ὀφθῆναι παρ᾽ αὐτῆς·
ὃ πάντων αὐτῇ τῶν ἀγαθῶν προτιμότατον, τῷ σῷ
προσβλέψαι προσώπῳ καὶ τῆς σῆς ἀκοῦσαι
φωνῆς. μὴ τοίνυν αὐτῇ τὰς ἐλπίδας ἀτελεῖς
καταστήσῃς. καὶ γὰρ πέρυσιν ἀπὸ τῆς Συρίας
ἐπανελθών, ἣν ἐδεξάμην ἐπαγγελίαν, ταύτην
διακομίσας, πῶς οἴει μετέωρον αὐτὴν κατέστησα
ταῖς ἐλπίσι ; μὴ οὖν εἰς ἄλλον καιρὸν ὑπέρθῃ τὴν
ἐπίσκεψιν αὐτῆς,[4] ὦ θαυμάσιε. καὶ γὰρ ἐὰν ᾖ
δυνατὸν ἰδεῖν αὐτήν ποτε, ἀλλ᾽ οὐχὶ καὶ μεθ᾽
ἡμῶν, οὓς ἐπείγει ἡ νόσος ἀπᾶραι λοιπὸν τοῦ
ὀδυνηροῦ τούτου βίου.

CXLVI

Ἀντιόχῳ [5]

Οὐκ ἔχω μέμψασθαί σοι[6] ἀργίαν οὐδὲ ῥᾳθυ-
μίαν, ὅτι καιροῦ παραπεσόντος[7] γραμμάτων ἀπε-

---

[1] ποιεῖ add. editi antiqi.
[2] ῥᾳδίως σε] περιγενέσθαι editi antiqi.
[3] καὶ] κἂν E.   [4] αὐτῶν Harl.
[5] τῷ αὐτῷ ἐπισκόπῳ E.   [6] σου E.
[7] παρεμπεσόντος editi antiqi.

an eagle, never stray far from your place of shelter.
None of these facts has escaped me. However,
desire is a powerful thing, forcing one both to hope
for that which is unattainable and to undertake that
which is impossible; nay, rather, our hope in the
Lord is the strongest of all.[1] For not by means
of unreasoning desire but through the strength of
faith I expect that a way will appear in desperate
straits and that you will easily surmount all obstacles,
so that you may see your most beloved church, and,
moreover, may also be seen by her; and this she
holds in esteem above all blessings—to gaze upon
your countenance, and to listen to your voice.
Therefore do not cause her hopes to be unfulfilled.
For when, returning from Syria last year, I brought
with me the promise which I had received, to what
pitch of hopeful expectation do you think I raised
her? Accordingly, do not defer to another occasion
your visit to her, admirable sir. For even if it is
possible to see her some day, it may not, however,
be possible to see her and also us, since our sickness
is urging us soon to depart from this painful life.

LETTER CXLVI

To Antiochus [2]

I CANNOT blame you for laziness or indifference,
because when an opportunity for writing was at

[1] Cf. St. Augustine *in Ps.* 3: "Vita vere mortalis spes
est vitae immortalis"; and St. Greg., *Moral.*: "Spes in
aeternitatem animum erigit, et idcirco nulla mala sentit."
Cf. also Ovid, *Pont.* 1, 7.

[2] Written in 373 to Antiochus, the nephew of Eusebius,
Bishop of Samosata. Letters CLVII, CLVIII, and CLXVIII
are also addressed to him.

σιώπησας. ἦν γὰρ διὰ τῆς τιμίας ἐμοὶ χειρὸς
διεπέμψω προσηγορίαν πολλῶν ἐπιστολῶν τιμιω-
τέραν ποιοῦμαι. ἀντὶ οὖν ταύτης προσαγορεύω
σε, καὶ παρακαλῶ σπουδαίως ἀντέχεσθαι τῆς
κατὰ ψυχὴν σωτηρίας, πάντα τὰ πάθη τῆς
σαρκὸς παιδαγωγοῦντα τῷ λόγῳ, καὶ διηνεκῶς
τὴν περὶ Θεοῦ ἔννοιαν, οἷον ἐν ναῷ τινι ἁγιωτάτῳ,
τῇ σαυτοῦ ψυχῇ ἐνιδρυμένην ἔχοντα· ἐπὶ πάσης
δὲ πράξεως καὶ παντὸς λόγου πρὸ ὀφθαλμῶν
λαμβάνειν τὸ τοῦ Χριστοῦ [1] δικαστήριον, ὥστε
σοι τὰς κατὰ μέρος ἐνεργείας συναχθείσας ἐπὶ
τῆς ἀκριβοῦς ἐκείνης καὶ φοβερᾶς ἐξετάσεως
δόξαν ἐν τῇ ἡμέρᾳ τῆς ἀνταποδόσεως ἐνεγκεῖν,
ἐπὶ πάσης τῆς κτίσεως τῶν ἐπαίνων ἀξιουμένῳ.
εἰ δὲ καταδέχοιτο τὴν μέχρις ἡμῶν ὁδὸν ὁ μέγας,
οὐ μικρὸν κέρδος ἰδεῖν σε μετ' αὐτοῦ ἐπὶ τῆς
ἡμετέρας.

CXLVII

Ἀβουργίῳ

Μῦθον ἐνόμιζον τέως τὰ τοῦ Ὁμήρου, ὅτε
ἐπῄειν αὐτοῦ τὸ ἕτερον μέρος τῆς ποιήσεως, ἐν ᾧ
τὰ τοῦ Ὀδυσσέως πάθη μεταδιδάσκει. ἀλλ'
ἐκεῖνα τὰ μυθικὰ τέως καὶ ἄπιστα πάνυ ἡμᾶς
πιθανὰ νομίζειν ἐδίδαξεν ἡ περὶ τὸν πάντα ἄριστον
Μάξιμον περιπέτεια. καὶ γὰρ καὶ [2] οὗτος ἄρχων

---

[1] Κυρίου editi antiqi. [2] καί om. E.

---

[1] *i.e.* Eusebius of Samosata.
[2] Written in 373. Basil asks his friend Aburgius to use
his influence in behalf of Maximus, former governor of
Cappadocia, who has been unjustly accused of embezzlement,

352

hand you kept your silence. For the greeting which you sent me in your honoured hand I hold in greater esteem than many letters. I therefore in turn send my greetings to you, and I exhort you to cleave zealously to the salvation of your soul, moderating all the affections of the flesh by reason, and constantly keeping the thought of God firmly established in your soul, as in a most holy temple ; and in every word and in every deed hold before your eyes the judgment of Christ, so that, when all your several activities have been brought before that strict and terrible scrutiny, they may bring you glory on the day of reward, when you are accounted worthy of praise in the presence of every creature. And if that great man [1] should take upon himself a journey to us, it would be no small gain to see you with him in our country.

LETTER CXLVII

To Aburgius [2]

I used to think the works of Homer fable, whenever I read the second part of his poem in which he gives his strange version of the sufferings of Odysseus. But what formerly seemed to me fabulous and incredible the calamity which has befallen our most excellent Maximus has taught me to consider as altogether probable. For Maximus was a ruler over

stripped of his office and property, and forced to flee to Caesarea. Aburgius was a wealthy layman, to whom Basil often appealed in behalf of his unfortunate acquaintances and friends. Other letters to Aburgius are XXXIII, LXXV, CXCVI, CLXXVIII, and CCCIV. On Maximus, cf. Letter XCVIII.

353

ἐγένετο ἔθνους οὐ φαυλοτάτου, ὥσπερ ἐκεῖνος ὁ
στρατηγὸς τῶν Κεφαλλήνων. καὶ πολλὰ χρήματα
ἄγων ἐκεῖνος γυμνὸς ἐπανῆλθε, καὶ τοῦτον οὕτως
ἡ συμφορὰ διέθηκεν, ὡς κινδυνεῦσαι ἐν ἀλλοτρίοις
ῥάκεσιν ὀφθῆναι τοῖς οἴκοι.[1] καὶ ταῦτα πέπονθε,
Λαιστρυγόνας τάχα που ἐφ᾽ ἑαυτὸν παροξύνας,
καὶ Σκύλλῃ περιπεσὼν ἐν γυναικείᾳ μορφῇ
κυνείαν ἐχούσῃ ἀπανθρωπίαν καὶ ἀγριότητα.
ἐπεὶ οὖν μόλις αὐτῷ ὑπῆρξε τὸν ἄφυκτον
τοῦτον διανήξασθαι κλύδωνα, σὲ δι᾽ ἡμῶν ἱκετεύει,
ἀξιῶν αἰδεσθῆναι τὴν κοινὴν φύσιν καὶ ἐπὶ ταῖς
παρ᾽ ἀξίαν αὐτοῦ συμφοραῖς ἀλγήσαντα, μὴ
σιωπῇ κρύψαι τὰ κατ᾽ αὐτόν, ἀλλὰ διαγγεῖλαι
τοῖς ἐν δυνάμει, ὥστε μάλιστα μὲν καὶ γενέσθαι
τινὰ αὐτῷ βοήθειαν πρὸς τὴν σκευωρηθεῖσαν [2]
ἐπήρειαν· εἰ δὲ μή, δημοσιευθῆναι γοῦν τὴν
προαίρεσιν τοῦ εἰς αὐτὸν ἐμπαροινήσαντος.
ἀρκοῦσα γὰρ τῷ ἠδικημένῳ παραμυθία ἡ τῶν
ἐπιβουλευσάντων αὐτῷ τῆς πονηρίας φανέρωσις.

CXLVIII

Τραϊανῷ

Πολλὴν φέρει τοῖς καταπονουμένοις παραμυθίαν καὶ τὸ ἔχειν ἀποδύρασθαι τὰς ἑαυτῶν
συμφοράς, καὶ μάλιστα ὅταν ἀνδρῶν ἐπιτύχωσι
δυναμένων ἐκ τῆς τοῦ τρόπου καλοκἀγαθίας

---

[1] οἰκείοις editi antiqi.   [2] σκαιωρηθεῖσαν Harl., Clarom.

[1] Written in 373.   Another appeal in behalf of Maximus ;
cf. preceding letter.   The Trajan addressed here may be the

no mean people, just as Odysseus was the war-chief
of the Cephallenians. Odysseus took with him
great riches, but on his return was empty-handed,
and Maximus has been reduced by his misfortune to
such a plight that he is very likely to appear to his
people at home in borrowed rags. And all this he
has suffered, perhaps because he has aroused some
Laestrygones against himself, or has fallen in with a
Scylla, woman in shape but dog in savagery and
fierceness. Since, then, he has barely been able to
swim out of this present engulfing sea of trouble, he
supplicates you through us, asking you to respect our
common kind and out of compassion for his unmerited
sufferings not to hide his affairs in silence, but bring
them to the notice of those in authority, in order, if
possible, that he may have some assistance to
combat the malice that has been worked up against
him, or, if this is not possible, that at least the
intention of the man who has dealt outrageously
with him may be made known to the public. For it
is satisfying comfort to a man who has suffered from
injustice to have the wickedness of his persecutors
brought to light.

LETTER CXLVIII

To Trajan [1]

It brings great comfort to men in trouble to be
able to lament their misfortunes, especially when
they meet with those who by reason of the nobility
of their character are able to sympathize with suffer-

commander-in-chief of the army under Valens ; but this is
by no means certain.

συμπαθῆσαι τοῖς ἀλγεινοῖς. ὅθεν καὶ ὁ αἰδεσιμώτατος ἀδελφὸς Μάξιμος, ὁ τῆς πατρίδος ἡμῶν
ἡγησάμενος, παθὼν οἷα οὐδέπω¹ τις ἀνθρώπων
ἕτερος, καὶ πάντων μὲν γυμνωθεὶς τῶν προσόντων,
ὅσα τε ἦν αὐτῷ πατρῷα καὶ ὅσα ἐκ προτέρων
πόνων ὑπῆρχε² συνειλεγμένα, κακοπαθήσας δὲ τῷ
σώματι μυρία ταῖς ἄνω καὶ κάτω πλάναις, καὶ
οὐδὲ αὐτὴν τὴν ἐπιτιμίαν ἀνεπηρέαστον διασώσας,
ἧς ἕνεκα πάντα πονεῖν τοῖς ἐλευθέροις σύνηθες,
πολλὰ μὲν πρὸς ἡμᾶς³ περὶ τῶν συμβάντων
αὐτῷ ἀπωλοφύρατο, ἠξίωσε δὲ δι' ἡμῶν ὡς ἐν
κεφαλαίῳ φανερὰν γενέσθαι σοι τὴν περιστᾶσαν
αὐτῷ τῶν κακῶν Ἰλιάδα. κἀγώ, ἐπειδὴ ἄλλως
οὐδὲν ἀφελεῖν αὐτοῦ τῶν δεινῶν ἠδυνήθην, ἑτοίμως
ταύτην ἔδωκα τὴν χάριν· τὸ ὀλίγα ἐκ πολλῶν ὧν
ἤκουσα παρ' αὐτοῦ διαγγεῖλαι τῇ κοσμιότητί σου,
ἐπειδὴ αὐτὸς ἐρυθριᾶν μοι ἐδόκει τὰς ἑαυτοῦ
συμφορὰς ἐναργῶς διηγήσασθαι.

Εἰ γὰρ καὶ οὐ⁴ πονηρὸν τὸν ἠδικηκότα συνίστησι τὰ γενόμενα,⁵ ἀλλ' οὖν γε τὸν πεπονθότα
τῆς ἐλεεινοτάτης ὄντα μερίδος δείκνυσιν, ἐπειδὴ
αὐτὸ τὸ περιπεσεῖν τοῖς θεηλάτοις κακοῖς ἀπόδει-
ξίν πως ἔχειν δοκεῖ τοῦ παραδεδόσθαι τοῖς πάθεσιν. ἀλλ' ἀρκεῖ αὐτῷ πρὸς παραμυθίαν τῶν
συμβάντων τὸ εὐμενεῖ αὐτὸν προσβλέψαι τῷ
ὄμματί σε καὶ τὴν πολυαρκῆ χάριν, ἧς πάντες
ἀπολαύοντες δαπανᾶν οὐ δύνανται, τὴν τῆς σῆς
ἡμερότητος λέγω, καὶ ἐπ' αὐτὸν ἀφεθῆναι. ὅτι
δὲ καὶ ἐν δικαστηρίοις μεγάλη αὐτῷ ἀφορμὴ
πρὸς τὴν νίκην ἡ παρὰ σοῦ ῥοπή, πάντες ἀκριβῶς

¹ οὔπω E, editi antiqi.   ² ὑπῆρχε om. E.
³ ὑμᾶς E.

356

ing. For this reason our most honourable brother
Maximus, the late governor of our country, after
experiencing such misfortunes as no other man ever
did, having been stripped of all his possessions, both
those which he had inherited and those that had
been amassed by his former labours, and having
endured a thousand bodily sufferings because of his
wanderings from place to place, and having been
unable to keep unassailed by malice even his civil
rights, in defence of which freemen are wont to endure everything—after all this he has bewailed to us
at length what has happened to him, and has asked
that through us there be made known to you in
summary the Iliad of woes which envelops him.
And as I was unable to relieve him of his distress in
any other way, I readily granted this favour—to
report to your Decorum an account of a few of the
many things I have heard from him, inasmuch as he
seemed to me to be too modest to give you a plain
account of his troubles himself.

For even if the facts of the case do not prove the
author of the injustice to be a wicked man, yet they
at least show the victim's lot to be the most pitiful
of all, since the very fact of his having fallen into
divinely inflicted distress seems somehow to be proof
of his having been delivered over to his sufferings. But
it suffices to console him for what has befallen if you
but look upon him with a kindly eye and extend to
him that abundant grace which all men draw upon but
cannot exhaust—I mean the grace of your leniency.
And that the weight of your influence in the
tribunal will be a great step towards victory we are

---

⁴ οὐ add. Capps.   ⁵ γεγονότα editi antiqi.

πεπείσμεθα. δικαιότατος δὲ πάντων καὶ αὐτὸς
οὗτος, ὁ τὴν ἐπιστολὴν ἡμῶν, ὥς τι ὄφελος αὐτῷ
ἐσομένην, ἐπιζητήσας· ὃν μετὰ τῶν ἄλλων
ἴδοιμεν τῇ κατὰ δύναμιν αὐτοῦ[1] φωνῇ τὴν σὴν
εὐφημοῦντα σεμνότητα.

CXLIX

Τραϊανῷ

Καὶ αὐτὸς ὑπέβαλες ὀφθαλμῷ τὴν κακοπάθειαν
τοῦ πρότερον μὲν εὐδοκίμου, νῦν δὲ ἐλεεινοτάτου
πάντων Μαξίμου, τοῦ ἄρξαντος τῆς πατρίδος
ἡμῶν, ὡς οὐκ ὤφελεν![2] οἶμαι γὰρ ἂν πολλοῖς
ἀπευκτὴν ἔσεσθαι τὴν τῶν ἐθνῶν ἀρχήν, εἰ πρὸς
τοιοῦτον[3] πέρας μέλλουσι καταστρέφειν αἱ προ-
στασίαι. ὥστε τί δεῖ ἡμᾶς τὰ καθ᾽ ἕκαστον
ἀπαγγέλλειν, ὧν τε εἴδομεν, ὧν τε ἠκούσαμεν,
ἀνδρὶ διὰ πολλὴν τῆς διανοίας ὀξύτητα ἱκανῷ ἐξ
ὀλίγων τῶν πραχθέντων στοχάσασθαι τὰ λειπόμενα; πλὴν ἐκεῖνό γε εἰπών, ἴσως οὐ περιττός
σοι φανήσομαι, ὅτι πολλῶν ὄντων καὶ δεινῶν τῶν
εἰς αὐτὸν τολμηθέντων πρὸ τῆς σῆς παρουσίας,
τοιαῦτα γέγονε τὰ μετὰ ταῦτα, ὡς φιλανθρωπίαν
ποιῆσαι νομισθῆναι τὰ φθάσαντα. τοσαύτην
εἶχεν ὑπερβολὴν ὕβρεως καὶ ζημίας καὶ τῆς
εἰς αὐτὸ τὸ σῶμα κακοπαθείας, τὰ δὴ ὕστερον
αὐτῷ παρὰ τοῦ κρατοῦντος ἐξευρεθέντα. καὶ νῦν

---

[1] αὐτοῦ om. E. [2] ὤφειλεν editi antiqi.
[3] τοιοῦτο E.

---

[1] Written in 373. Another appeal for Maximus. The

all convinced with certainty. And this man who has asked the present letter of us, in the hope that it would be of some help to him, is himself also the most upright of men; and may we see him among the rest voicing with all his might the praises of your August Reverence.

LETTER CXLIX

To Trajan[1]

You yourself have seen with your own eyes the distress of Maximus, once held in high repute, but now the most pitiful of all mortals, the late Prefect of our country—would that he had never been such! For I think that the governorship of peoples would be avoided by many if their high position were likely to come to such an end. So what need is there of our relating in detail what we have seen and heard to a man who by great keenness of mind is able to conjecture from a few events all that is left untold? But in saying the following perhaps I shall not seem to you to be going too far— that although many and terrible were the outrages perpetrated upon him before your arrival, those which followed were of such a character that the earlier must be reckoned as acts of kindness. Such was the excess of abuse and loss of property and even bodily injury in the measures lately devised against him by the ruler. And now he has come

MSS. give this letter as to the same Trajan; cf. previous letters. If this Trajan is the one suggested in note 1 of the previous letter, he could have had no personal knowledge of the troubles of Maximus. However, the identity of this Trajan is by no means certain.

ἔμφρουρος ἥκει τὰ λείψανα τῶν ὧδε κακῶν αὐτοῦ
ἀποπληρώσων, ἐὰν μὴ σὺ τὴν μεγάλην σαυτοῦ
χεῖρα ὑπερσχεῖν ἐθελήσῃς τῷ καταπονουμένῳ.
περιττὸν μὲν οὖν οἶδα ποιῶν, τὴν σὴν χρηστότητα
εἰς φιλανθρωπίαν παρακαλῶν. πλὴν ἀλλ᾽ ἐπειδὴ
βούλομαι γενέσθαι χρήσιμος τῷ ἀνδρί, ἱκετεύω
σου τὴν σεμνοπρέπειαν προσθεῖναί τι τῇ ἐκ
φύσεως περὶ τὸ καλὸν σπουδῇ δι᾽ ἡμᾶς, ὥστε
ἐναργὲς τῷ ἀνδρὶ γενέσθαι τῆς ὑπὲρ αὐτοῦ παρακλήσεως ἡμῶν τὸ ὄφελος.

CL

Ἀμφιλοχίῳ, ὡς παρὰ Ἡρακλείδου

Ἐγὼ καὶ τῶν ὁμιληθέντων ἡμῖν πρὸς ἀλλήλους
ποτὲ μέμνημαι, καὶ ὧν τε αὐτὸς εἶπον, ὧν τε
ἤκουσα παρὰ τῆς εὐγενείας σου, οὐκ ἐπιλέλησμαι.
καὶ νῦν βίος μέν με δημόσιος οὐ κατέχει. εἰ γὰρ
καὶ τῇ καρδίᾳ ὁ αὐτός εἰμι καὶ οὔπω τὸν παλαιὸν
ἀπεδυσάμην ἄνθρωπον, πλὴν τῷ γε σχήματι, καὶ
τῷ μακρὰν ἐμαυτὸν ποιῆσαι τῶν τοῦ βίου πραγμάτων, ἔδοξα λοιπὸν οἷον ἐπιβεβηκέναι τῆς ὁδοῦ
τῆς κατὰ Χριστὸν πολιτείας. καθέζομαι δὲ ἐπ᾽
ἐμαυτοῦ, ὥσπερ οἱ εἰς πέλαγος ἀφιέναι μέλλοντες
ἀποσκοπεύων[1] τὸ μέλλον. οἱ μὲν γὰρ πλέοντες

[1] σκοπεύων E.

[1] Written in 373. Amphilochius, later consecrated Bishop
of Iconium, had abandoned his practice of the law and was
living in retirement at Ozizala, not far from Nazianzus, the
see of his uncle Gregory. The following letters of St. Basil
addressed to Amphilochius have been preserved : CLXI,
CLXXVI, CXC, CXCI, CC, CCI, CCII, CCXVIII, CCXXXI,

under guard to finish off the remnants of the evils
suffered here, unless you are willing to stretch out
your mighty hand to protect the victim of misfortune.
I know that I am doing a superfluous thing when I
exhort your Excellency to do an act of kindness.
But as I desire to be of some service to the man, I
beg your Grace to add something to your natural
zeal for the good, and this on our account, that the
man may know clearly the benefit derived from our
intercession in his behalf

LETTER CL

To Amphilochius, as if from Heracleidas [1]

I remember the matter which we once discussed
together, and I have not forgotten both what I
myself said and what I heard from your Nobility.
And now public life does not hold me back.   For
although I am the same at heart and have not yet
put off the old man—except at least ostensibly, that
is, by having removed myself far from the affairs of
life—I seem to have entered, as it were, upon the
way that is in accordance with Christ's polity.   And
I sit by myself, scanning the future as do those who
are about to put out to sea.   For those who sail

CCXXXII, CCXXXIII, CCXXXIV, CCXXXV, CCXXXVI,
and CCXLVIII, besides those dealing with the canons.
    Heracleidas, a young friend of Amphilochius and also a
retired lawyer, was living at St. Basil's famous hospital at
the time this letter was written.   This letter was written to
Amphilochius in the name of Heracleidas to explain why
Heracleidas had not joined him in his retirement, to describe
what Heracleidas was doing at Caesarea, and to urge Amphilochius to get in touch with St. Basil, if possible, so that he
might learn from him many needed lessons.

ἀνέμων χρήζουσι πρὸς τὴν εὔπλοιαν, ἡμεῖς δὲ
τοῦ χειραγωγήσοντος ἡμᾶς καὶ ἀσφαλῶς διὰ τῶν
ἁλμυρῶν κυμάτων τοῦ βίου παραπέμψοντος.
χρήζειν γὰρ ἐμαυτὸν λογίζομαι πρῶτον μὲν
χαλινοῦ πρὸς τὴν νεότητα, ἔπειτα κέντρων πρὸς
τὸν δρόμον τῆς εὐσεβείας. τούτων δὲ πρόξενος
λόγος [1] δηλονότι, νῦν μὲν παιδαγωγῶν ἡμῶν τὸ
ἄτακτον, νῦν δὲ τὸ νωθρὸν τῆς ψυχῆς διεγείρων.
πάλιν μοι χρεία φαρμάκων ἑτέρων, ὥστε τὸν ἐκ
τῆς συνηθείας ἀποπλύνασθαι ῥύπον. οἶδας γὰρ
ὅτι ἡμεῖς, οἱ πολὺν χρόνον ἐνεθισθέντες τῇ ἀγορᾷ,
ἀφειδῶς μὲν ἔχομεν τῶν ῥημάτων, ἀφυλάκτως δὲ
πρὸς τὰς ἐν τῇ διανοίᾳ συνισταμένας ἐκ τοῦ
πονηροῦ [2] φαντασίας. ἡττήμεθα δὲ καὶ τιμῆς
καὶ τὸ ἐφ' ἑαυτοῖς τι φρονεῖν οὐ ῥᾳδίως ἀποτιθέ-
μεθα. πρὸς ταῦτα μεγάλου μοι δεῖν καὶ ἐμπείρου
λογίζομαι διδασκάλου. ἔπειτα μέντοι καὶ τὸν
ὀφθαλμὸν τῆς ψυχῆς ἀποκαθαρθῆναι, ὥστε πᾶσαν
τὴν ἀπὸ τῆς ἀγνοίας ἐπισκότησιν, οἱονεί τινα
λήμην, ἀφαιρεθέντα, δύνασθαι ἐνατενίζειν τῷ
κάλλει τῆς δόξης τοῦ Θεοῦ, οὐ μικροῦ ἔργου
κρίνω, οὐδ' ἐπ' ὀλίγον τὴν ὠφέλειαν φέρειν.

Ἃ καὶ τὴν σὴν λογιότητα συνορᾶν, καὶ ἐπιθυ-
μεῖν ὑπάρξαι τινὰ εἰς ταύτην τὴν βοήθειαν
ἀκριβῶς ἐπίσταμαι [3] καὶ ἐάν ποτε δῷ ὁ Θεὸς
εἰς ταὐτὸν ἀφικέσθαι τῇ κοσμιότητί σου, δηλονότι
πλείονα μαθήσομαι ὑπὲρ ὧν φροντίζειν με χρή.
νῦν γὰρ ὑπὸ πολλῆς ἀμαθίας οὐδὲ ὅσων [4] ἐνδεής
εἰμι γνωρίζειν δύναμαι· πλήν γε ὅτι οὐδὲν μετε-
μέλησέ μοι τῆς πρώτης ὁρμῆς, οὔτε ὀκλάζει μου

---

[1] τις add. E.
[2] τοῦ πονηροῦ] τῆς πονηρίας quinque MSS.

require winds for a fine voyage, while we require someone to lead us by the hand and escort us safely over the briny billows of life. For I consider that I myself require, first of all a bridle to restrain my youth, then spurs for the race of piety. And that which provides these two things is manifestly reason, at one time schooling our insubordination, at another rousing up the sluggishness of our souls. Again, I have need of other remedies to wash away the stains contracted from habit. For you know that we who have been for a long time accustomed to public life are unsparing of speech and are not on our guard against the images which are stirred up in our minds by the evil one. And we are easy victims to preferment and cannot easily lay aside some degree of pride in ourselves. In guard against these things I think that I have need also of a great and experienced teacher. Then, moreover, the task of cleansing the eye of the soul, so that, when once freed, as from a kind of rheum, from all the darkness of ignorance, it may be able to look steadily upon the beauty of the glory of God, calls, I judge, for no small labour and brings no small benefit.

I know full well that your Eloquence perceives all this, and that you desire that someone shall be at hand to render such aid; that if ever God grants that I have a meeting with your Decorum, I shall certainly learn more regarding those matters about which I must needs be concerned. For now, on account of my great ignorance, I cannot even know how many things I lack; and yet I by no means regret this first attempt, nor does my soul sink at the

---

³ πέπεισμαι E, Med.   ⁴ ὅσον E.

ἡ ψυχὴ πρὸς τὸν σκοπὸν τοῦ κατὰ Θεὸν βίου,
ὅπερ ἠγωνίασας ἐπ᾽ ἐμοί, καλῶς καὶ προσηκόντως
ἑαυτῷ ποιῶν, μήποτε στραφεὶς εἰς τὰ ὀπίσω
στήλη γένωμαι ἁλός, ὅπερ γυνή τις ἔπαθεν,
ὥσπερ [1] ἀκούω. ἀλλ᾽ ἔτι μέν με [2] καὶ αἱ ἔξωθεν
ἀρχαὶ συστέλλουσιν, ὥσπερ λειποτάκτην τινὰ
τῶν ἀρχόντων ἀναζητούντων.[3] ἐπέχει δέ με
μάλιστα ἡ ἐμοῦ αὐτοῦ καρδία, ἐκεῖνα μαρτυροῦσα
ἑαυτῇ ἅπερ εἴρηκα.

Ἐπειδὴ δὲ συνθηκῶν ἐμνήσθης, καὶ κατηγο-
ρεῖν ἐπηγγείλω, γελάσαι με ἐποίησας ἐν ταύτῃ
τῇ κατηφείᾳ μου, ὅτι ἔτι ῥήτωρ εἶ καὶ τῆς
δεινότητος οὐκ ἀφίστασαι. ἐγὼ γὰρ οὕτω [4]
νομίζω, εἰ μὴ πάντη ὡς ἀμαθὴς διαμαρτάνω τῆς
ἀληθείας, μίαν εἶναι ὁδὸν τὴν πρὸς Κύριον
ἄγουσαν, καὶ πάντας τοὺς πρὸς αὐτὸν πορευο-
μένους συνοδεύειν ἀλλήλοις καὶ κατὰ μίαν συνθή-
κην τοῦ βίου πορεύεσθαι. ὥστε ποῦ ἀπελθὼν
χωρισθῆναί σου δύναμαι καὶ μὴ μετὰ σοῦ ζῆν
καὶ μετὰ σοῦ δουλεύειν Θεῷ, ᾧ κοινῇ προσε-
φύγομεν; τὰ μὲν γὰρ σώματα ἡμῶν τόποις
διασταθήσεται, ὁ δὲ τοῦ Θεοῦ ὀφθαλμὸς κοινῇ
ἀμφοτέρους ἐφορᾷ [5] δηλονότι, εἴπερ οὖν ἄξιος
καὶ ὁ ἐμὸς βίος ὑπὸ τῶν ὀφθαλμῶν τοῦ Θεοῦ
ἐποπτεύεσθαι· ἀνέγνων γάρ που ἐν Ψαλμοῖς, ὅτι

---

[1] ὥς E.   [2] με om. E.
[3] ἀνεπιζητούντων editi antiqi.   [4] οὕτως E.
[5] ὁρᾷ E.

[1] Cf. Gen. 19. 26 : καὶ ἐπέβλεψεν ἡ γυνὴ αὐτοῦ εἰς τὰ ὀπίσω,
καὶ ἐγένετο στήλη ἁλός. "And his wife, looking behind her,
was turned into a statue of salt."

prospect of the life that is in accordance with God—
the matter which caused you, rightly and in a
manner befitting yourself, to be anxious about me,
lest turning back I might become a "statue of salt,"
as I hear happened to a certain woman.[1] And yet
it is true that powers from without still hamper me,
like officers who seek to bring back a deserter; but
most of all it is my own heart which restrains me,
bearing witness to itself to the very things that I
have mentioned.

But when you mentioned agreements, and
announced that you would be the accuser, you made
me laugh in spite of my present dejection, because
you still play the rôle of a public man and have not
given up cleverness.[2] As for me, this is my opinion
—that, unless in my ignorance I have altogether
missed the truth, there is only one way leading to
the Lord, and all who travel toward Him are
companions of one another and travel according to
one agreement as to life. Consequently, where can
I go and yet be separated from you, and not live
with you and with you serve God, to whom we have
both together fled? For though our bodies will be
separated in space, yet the eye of God is assuredly
gazing upon us both in common—if indeed my life is
worthy to be looked upon by the eyes of God; for I
have read somewhere in the Psalms that "the eyes of

[2] Apparently Amphilochius and Heracleidas had made an
agreement with each other to abstain from public life.
Heracleidas having broken this agreement, Amphilochius
threatened to bring action against him. The parallel in Attic
law is in cases of ἀτιμία (loss of civil rights), when a public
man is debarred from δημοσία (public service); and ἀγγέλλειν
is the technical term for the denunciation.

Ὀφθαλμοὶ Κυρίου ἐπὶ δικαίους. ἐγὼ μὲν γὰρ
εὔχομαι καὶ σοὶ καὶ παντὶ τῷ παραπλησίως [1]
σοι προαιρουμένῳ καὶ τῷ σώματι συνεῖναι, καὶ
πᾶσαν νύκτα καὶ ἡμέραν μετὰ σοῦ κλίνειν τὰ
γόνατα πρὸς τὸν Πατέρα ἡμῶν τὸν ἐν τοῖς
οὐρανοῖς, καὶ εἴ τις ἄλλος ἀξίως ἐπικαλούμενος
τὸν Θεόν. οἶδα γὰρ τὴν ἐν ταῖς προσευχαῖς
κοινωνίαν πολὺ τὸ κέρδος φέρουσαν.[2] ἐὰν δέ,
ὁσάκις ὑπάρξῃ μοι ἐν διαφόρῳ γωνιδίῳ [3] παρερ-
ριμμένῳ [4] στενάζειν, ἀκολουθήσει μοι πάντως τὸ
ψεύδεσθαι, μάχεσθαι μὲν [5] πρὸς τὸν λόγον οὐκ
ἔχω, ἤδη δὲ ὡς ψεύστου [6] ἐμαυτὸν κατακρίνω,
εἴ τι τοιοῦτον κατὰ τὴν παλαιὰν ἀδιαφορίαν
ἐφθεγξάμην, ὅ [7] με τῷ κρίματι τοῦ ψεύδους
ὑπόδικον καθιστᾷ.

Γενόμενος δὲ πλησίον Καισαρείας, ὥστε γνωρίσαι τὰ πράγματα, καὶ αὐτῇ παραβαλεῖν τῇ πόλει
μὴ ἀνασχόμενος, τῷ πλησίον προσέφυγον πτωχο-
τροφείῳ, ὥστε ἐκεῖ μαθεῖν περὶ ὧν ἐβουλόμην.
εἶτα κατὰ συνήθειαν ἐπιδημήσαντι τῷ θεοφιλεστάτῳ ἐπισκόπῳ ἀνήνεγκα περὶ ὧν ἐπέταξεν
ἡμῖν ἡ λογιότης σου. καὶ ἃ μὲν ἀπεκρίνατο,
οὔτε τῇ μνήμῃ φυλαχθῆναι παρ' ἡμῶν δυνατὸν
ἦν, καὶ ἐπιστολῆς ὑπερέβαινε μέτρον· ὡς ἐν
κεφαλαίῳ δὲ περὶ τῆς ἀκτημοσύνης ἐκεῖνο ἔφη
τὸ μέτρον εἶναι, ὥστε εἰς τὸν ἔσχατον χιτῶνα
ἕκαστον ἑαυτῷ περιιστάναι [8] τὴν κτῆσιν. καὶ
παρείχετο ἡμῖν ἐκ τοῦ Εὐαγγελίου τὰς ἀποδείξεις·
μίαν μέν, ὡς Ἰωάννου τοῦ βαπτιστοῦ εἰπόντος·

---

[1] παραπλήσιον editi antiqi.   [2] ἔχουσαν tres MSS. recent.
[3] γονιδίῳ editi antiqi.   [4] παρερριμένως E.
[5] μέν add. E, editi antiqi.   [6] ψεύστης E.

the Lord are upon the just." [1] For I do indeed pray
to be with you in the body also, as well as with everyone who makes a choice similar to yours, and every
night and day to bend my knees with you before
our Father who is in heaven, as well as with anyone
else who worthily calls upon God. For I know that
association in prayer brings great gain. But if,
whenever I happen to utter a complaint as I lie cast
aside in a corner different from yours, the charge of
falsehood is certain to follow me, I cannot fight
against the accusation, but forthwith condemn
myself as a liar, if I ever during my earlier period of
indifference said anything which makes me liable to
the charge of falsehood. [2]

But when I came near enough to Caesarea to
observe the situation, refraining, however, from visiting the city itself, I took refuge in the neighbouring
poor-house, that I might gain there the information I
wished. Then I laid before the most God-beloved
bishop, who had come to visit the place according to
custom, the matters as to which your Eloquence had
instructed us. And though it was impossible for us to
keep in memory what he said in reply, and it passed
beyond the limits of a letter, yet in general on the
subject of poverty he said that this was the measure,
—that each should limit his possession to the last
tunic. And he furnished us with proofs from the
Gospel—one from John the Baptist, who said : " He

---

[1] Cf. Psal. 33. 16 : ὅτι ὀφθαλμοὶ Κυρίου ἐπὶ δικαίους, καὶ ὦτα
αὐτοῦ εἰς δέησιν αὐτῶν. " The eyes of the Lord are upon the
just : and His ears unto their prayers."

[2] Amphilochius had apparently found fault with Heracleidas
in consequence of a complaint, and had accused him of
repenting having entered upon the ascetic life.

---

[7] ἅ E.   [8] παριστῆσαι E, Med.

COLLECTED LETTERS OF SAINT BASIL

Ὁ ἔχων δύο χιτῶνας μεταδότω τῷ μὴ ἔχοντι·
ἑτέραν δέ, ὡς τοῦ Κυρίου τοῖς μαθηταῖς ἀπαγο-
ρεύσαντος μὴ[1] ἔχειν δύο χιτῶνας. προσετίθει δὲ[2]
τούτοις καὶ[3] τό· Εἰ θέλεις τέλειος εἶναι, ὕπαγε,
πώλησόν σου τὰ ὑπάρχοντα, καὶ δὸς πτωχοῖς.
ἔλεγε δὲ καὶ τὴν τοῦ μαργαρίτου παραβολὴν
εἰς τοῦτο φέρειν· ὅτι ὁ ἔμπορος ὁ εὑρὼν τὸν
πολύτιμον μαργαρίτην ἀπελθὼν ἐπώλησεν ἑαυτοῦ
πάντα τὰ ὑπάρχοντα καὶ ἠγόρασεν ἐκεῖνον. προσετίθει δὲ τούτοις, ὅτι οὐδὲ ἑαυτῷ τινα ἐπιτρέπειν
χρὴ τὴν τῶν χρημάτων διανομήν, ἀλλὰ τῷ τὰ τῶν
πτωχῶν οἰκονομεῖν πεπιστευμένῳ.[4] καὶ τοῦτο
ἀπὸ τῶν Πράξεων ἐπιστοῦτο· ὅτι πωλοῦντες τὰ
προσόντα αὐτοῖς, φέροντες ἐτίθουν παρὰ τοὺς
πόδας τῶν ἀποστόλων, καὶ παρ᾽ ἐκείνων διεδίδοτο
ἑκάστῳ, καθότι ἄν τις χρείαν εἶχεν. ἔλεγε γὰρ
ἐμπειρίας χρῄζειν τὴν διάγνωσιν τοῦ ἀληθῶς δεομένου καὶ τοῦ κατὰ πλεονεξίαν αἰτοῦντος. καὶ ὁ
μὲν τῷ θλιβομένῳ διδοὺς τῷ Κυρίῳ ἔδωκε, καὶ
παρ᾽ αὐτοῦ λήψεται τὸν μισθόν· ὁ δὲ τῷ περιερ-
χομένῳ παρασχόμενος παντὶ προσέρριψε κυνί,
φορτικῷ μὲν διὰ τὴν ἀναίδειαν, οὐκ ἐλεεινῷ δὲ
διὰ τὴν ἔνδειαν.

Περὶ δὲ τοῦ πῶς χρὴ βιοῦν ἡμᾶς καθ᾽ ἡμέραν,

[1] μή om. E.   [2] καί add. E.
[3] καί om. E.   [4] ἐμπεπιστευμένῳ editi antiqi.

---

[1] Luke 3. 11.
[2] Cf. Matt. 10. 9 and 10: μὴ κτήσησθε χρυσόν, μηδὲ
ἄργυρον, μηδὲ χαλκὸν εἰς τὰς ζώνας ὑμῶν, μὴ πήραν εἰς ὁδόν, μηδὲ
δύο χιτῶνας, μηδὲ ὑποδήματα μηδὲ ῥάβδαν. "Do not possess
gold, nor silver, nor money in your purses·: nor scrip for
your journey, nor two coats, nor shoes, nor a staff."
[3] Matt. 19. 21.

that hath two coats, let him give to him that hath none " ; [1] and another from our Lord, who warns His disciples not to have two tunics.[2] He added to these this also : " If thou wilt be perfect, go sell what thou hast and give it to the poor." [3] And he said too that the parable of the pearl referred to this—that the merchant who found the precious pearl went away, sold all his possessions and bought it. And he added to these words that it was not necessary for anyone to take upon himself the distribution of his goods, but only to commit this task to him to whom the management of the alms of the poor had been entrusted. And he proved this from the Acts,[4] to wit : " Selling their goods they took and laid the price of the things before the feet of the Apostles, and distribution was made by them to everyone according as he had need." For he said that experience was necessary for distinguishing between the man who is truly in need and the man who begs through avarice. And while he who gives to the afflicted has given to the Lord, and will receive his reward from Him, yet he who gives to every wanderer casts it to a dog, that is troublesome on account of his shamelessness, but not pitiable because of his need.

And as to how we should live day by day, he had

---

[4] Cf. Acts 4. 34 and 35 : οὐδὲ γὰρ ἐνδεής τις ὑπῆρχεν ἐν αὐτοῖς· ὅσοι γὰρ κτήτορες χωρίων ἢ οἰκιῶν ὑπῆρχον, πωλοῦντες ἔφερον τὰς τιμὰς τῶν πιπρασκομένων, καὶ ἐτίθουν παρὰ τοὺς πόδας τῶν ἀποστόλων· διεδίδοτο δὲ ἑκάστῳ καθότι ἄν τις χρείαν εἶχεν. "For neither was there anyone needy among them. For as many as were owners of lands or houses, sold them, and brought the price of the things they sold, and laid it down before the feet of the apostles. And distribution was made to everyone, according as he had need." It is to be noted that Basil's "by them" does not appear in the Acts.

ὀλίγα μὲν ἔφθη εἰρηκὼς ὡς πρὸς τὸ τῆς ὑποθέσεως
μέγεθος· πλὴν ἀλλ' ἐβουλόμην παρ' αὐτοῦ ἐκείνου
σε μαθεῖν. ἐμὲ γὰρ ἀφανίζειν τὴν ἀκρίβειαν τῶν
διδαγμάτων οὐκ εὔλογον. ηὐχόμην δὲ μετὰ σοῦ
ποτὲ καταλαβεῖν αὐτόν, ἵνα καὶ τῇ μνήμῃ ἀκριβῶς
φυλάξας τὰ λεχθέντα, καὶ τῇ σεαυτοῦ συνέσει
προσεξεύρῃς τὰ λείποντα. ἐκεῖνο γὰρ μέμνημαι
ἐκ τῶν πολλῶν ὧν ἤκουσα, ὅτι ἡ περὶ τοῦ πῶς
χρὴ ζῆν τὸν Χριστιανὸν διδασκαλία οὐ τοσοῦτον
δεῖται λόγου ὅσον τοῦ καθημερινοῦ ὑποδείγματος.
καὶ οἶδα ὅτι, εἰ μή σε κατεῖχεν ὁ δεσμὸς τῆς
γηροκομίας τοῦ πατρός, οὐκ ἂν οὔτε αὐτὸς ἄλλο
τι προετίμησας τῆς συντυχίας τοῦ ἐπισκόπου, οὔτ'
ἂν ἐμοὶ συνεβούλευσας καταλιπόντι τοῦτον εἰς
ἐρημίας πλανᾶσθαι. τὰ μὲν γὰρ σπήλαια καὶ
αἱ πέτραι ἀναμένουσιν ἡμᾶς, αἱ δὲ παρὰ τῶν
ἀνδρῶν ὠφέλειαι οὐκ ἀεὶ ἡμῖν παραμένουσιν.
ὥστε, εἰ ἀνέχῃ μου συμβουλεύοντος, τυπώσεις
τὸν πατέρα μικρὸν ἐπιτρέπειν σοι ἀναχωρεῖν
αὐτοῦ καὶ περιτυγχάνειν[1] ἀνδρὶ πολλὰ καὶ ἐκ
τῆς ἑτέρων πείρας καὶ ἐκ τῆς οἰκείας συνέσεως
καὶ εἰδότι καὶ παρέχειν τοῖς προσιοῦσιν[2] αὐτῷ
δυναμένῳ.

CLI

Εὐσταθίῳ ἀρχιάτρῳ[3]

Εἴ τι ὄφελος ἡμετέρων[4] γραμμάτων, μηδένα
χρόνον διαλίπῃς ἐπιστέλλων ἡμῖν καὶ διεγείρων[5]
ἡμᾶς πρὸς τὸ γράφειν. αὐτοὶ μὲν γὰρ προδήλως

[1] συντυγχάνειν Med. [2] προσοῦσιν E.
[3] ἀρχιητρῷ Harl., E. [4] ὑμετέρων E, Vat. [5] ἐγείρων E.

time enough to say only a little considering the
importance of the subject; but I should prefer you
to have learnt about this from the man himself. For
it is not fitting that I should spoil the precision of
his instructions. But I prayed that I might some
time visit him in company with you, in order that
you, guarding his words carefully in your memory,
might by the application of your own intelligence
find out in addition whatever he left unsaid. For of
the many things that I heard, I remember this—
that teaching a Christian how he ought to live does
not call so much for words as for daily example.
And I know that, if you were not chained by the
obligation of caring for your aged father, you yourself would have preferred nothing to a talk with the
bishop, nor would you have counselled me to leave
this person and go wandering in the desert. For
while the caves and the rocks will wait for us, yet
the aid which true men can give will not always
abide with us. Wherefore, if you will permit me to
advise you, you will press upon your father to permit
you to leave him for a little while and to betake
yourself to a man who both knows much from the
experience of others, as well as from his own wisdom,
and can impart it to those who come to him.

LETTER CLI

To Eustathius, a Physician [1]

If there is any profit in our letters, at no time
cease writing to us and urging us to write. For we

[1] Written in 373. Cf. also Letter CLXXXIX, which is
addressed to the same Eustathius but may well belong to
Gregory of Nyssa.

ἡδίους γινόμεθα ἐντυγχάνοντες ἐπιστολαῖς συνε-
τῶν ἀνδρῶν ἀγαπώντων τὸν Κύριον· εἰ δὲ καὶ
αὐτοί τι ἄξιον σπουδῆς εὑρίσκετε[1] παρ᾽ ἡμῖν,
ὑμέτερον εἰδέναι τῶν ἐντυγχανόντων. εἰ μὲν οὖν
μὴ ὑπὸ τοῦ πλήθους τῶν ἀσχολιῶν ἀπηγόμεθα,
οὐκ ἂν τῆς ἐκ τοῦ γράφειν συνεχῶς εὐφροσύνης
ἀπειχόμεθα. ὑμεῖς δέ, οἷς ἐλάττους αἱ φροντίδες,
ὁσάκις ἂν οἷόν τε ᾖ κατακηλεῖτε ἡμᾶς τοῖς γράμμασι. καὶ γὰρ τὰ φρέατά φασιν ἀντλούμενα
βελτίω γίνεσθαι. ἐοίκασι δέ σου[2] αἱ ἐξ ἰατρικῆς
παραινέσεις εἰς πάρεργον χωρεῖν, οὐχ ἡμῶν ἐπα-
γόντων τὸν σίδηρον, ἀλλ᾽ ἑαυτοῖς ἐκπιπτόντων
τῶν ἀπαχρειουμένων.

Ὁ μὲν οὖν τοῦ Στωϊκοῦ λόγος· ἐπειδή, φησί,
μὴ γίνεται τὰ πράγματα ὡς βουλόμεθα, ὡς γίνεται
βουλόμεθα.[3] ἐγὼ δὲ τοῖς μὲν πράγμασι τὴν
γνώμην συγκατατίθεσθαι[4] οὐ καταδέχομαι, τὸ
δὲ ἀβουλήτως τινὰς ποιεῖν τι τῶν ἀναγκαίων οὐκ
ἀποδοκιμάζω. οὔτε γὰρ ὑμῖν τοῖς ἰατροῖς τὸ
καίειν τὸν ἄρρωστον ἢ ἄλλως ποιεῖν ἀλγεῖν
βουλητόν· ἀλλ᾽ οὖν καταδέχεσθε πολλάκις τῇ
δυσχερείᾳ τοῦ πάθους ἑπόμενοι· οὔτε[5] οἱ πλέοντες
ἑκουσίως ἐκβάλλουσι τὰ ἀγώγιμα, ἀλλ᾽ ὥστε
διαφυγεῖν τὰ ναυάγια ὑφίστανται τὴν ἐκβολήν,
τὸν ἐν πενίᾳ βίον τοῦ ἀποθανεῖν προτιμῶντες.
ὥστε καὶ ἡμᾶς οἵου ἀλγεινῶς μὲν καὶ μετὰ μυρίων
ὀδυρμῶν φέρειν τὸν χωρισμὸν τῶν ἀφισταμένων,
φέρειν δ᾽ οὖν ὅμως· ἐπειδὴ τοῦ Θεοῦ καὶ τῆς

---

[1] εὑρήσετε editi antiqi.   [2] σοι E.
[3] βουλώμεθα editi antiqi.
[4] συμμετατίθεσθαι Harl., Reg. primus, et Vat.
[5] οὔτε] οἵ τε E.

on our part are certainly made more happy by reading letters from wise men who love the Lord, and if you on your part find anything worth while in ours, it is for you who read them to know. If, then, we were not distracted by our manifold duties, we should not refrain from the pleasure of writing constantly; but do you, whose cares are less, console us as often as is possible by writing. For, as they say, "Wells become better for being used." And your advice drawn from the art of medicine seems to go for naught, since it is not we who are applying the knife, but those who resort to its use are being driven out by each other.[1]

Now a Stoic saying goes: "Since things do not happen as we wish, we wish them as they happen." But as for me, though I cannot accommodate my mind to things as they are, yet I do not object to men in certain situations doing unwillingly a thing that is inevitable. For neither is it the wish of you physicians to cauterize the sick or cause them pain in any other way (although you do often consent to it in recognition of the seriousness of the malady), nor do navigators willingly throw overboard their cargo,[2] but with a view to escaping shipwreck they submit to this throwing overboard, preferring life in poverty to death. So pray believe that we also, while enduring with sorrow and countless lamentations the separation from those who leave our ranks, yet endure it nevertheless; because to the lovers of

---

[1] Eustathius, the bishop, and his followers are using the knife upon each other.

[2] According to the Benedictine editors the cargo thrown overboard represents the loss of unity suffered by the Sebastenes when they left the communion of Eustathius. Cf. Letter CCXXXVII.

ἐπ᾽ αὐτὸν[1] ἐλπίδος οὐδὲν τοῖς τῆς ἀληθείας
ἐρασταῖς προτιμότερον.

CLII

Οὐΐκτορι στρατηλάτῃ

Ἄλλῳ μέν τινι μὴ ἐπιστέλλων, τάχα ἂν
δεξαίμην δικαίως ἔγκλημα ῥᾳθυμίας ἢ λήθης.
σοῦ δὲ πῶς ἔστιν ἐπιλαθέσθαι, οὗ παρὰ πᾶσιν
ἀνθρώποις λαλεῖται τὸ ὄνομα; πῶς δὲ καταρρα-
θυμῆσαι,[2] ὃς πάντων σχεδὸν τῶν κατὰ τὴν οἰκουμένην τῷ ὕψει τῶν ἀξιωμάτων ὑπερανέστηκας·
ἀλλὰ δήλη ἡμῶν ἡ αἰτία τῆς σιωπῆς· ὀκνοῦμεν
δι᾽ ὄχλου γίνεσθαι[3] ἀνδρὶ τοσούτῳ. εἰ δὲ πρὸς
τῇ λοιπῇ σου ἀρετῇ καὶ τοῦτο κατεδέξω, οὐ μόνον
πεμπόμενα παρ᾽ ἡμῶν δέχεσθαι γράμματα, ἀλλὰ
καὶ ἐλλειφθέντα ἐπιζητεῖν, ἰδοὺ καὶ γράφομεν
νῦν τεθαρρηκότως[4] καὶ γράψομέν γε εἰς[5] τὸ
ἐφεξῆς, εὐχόμενοι τῷ ἁγίῳ Θεῷ δοθῆναί σοι τὴν
ἀμοιβὴν τῆς περὶ ἡμᾶς τιμῆς. ὑπὲρ δὲ τῆς
Ἐκκλησίας προέλαβες ἡμῶν τὰς παρακλήσεις,
πάντα ποιήσας ὅσα ἂν ἡμεῖς ἐπεζητήσαμεν. ποιεῖς
δὲ οὐκ ἀνθρώποις χαριζόμενος, ἀλλὰ Θεῷ τῷ
τιμήσαντί σε, ὃς τὰ μὲν ἔδωκεν ἐν τῇ νῦν ζωῇ
ἀγαθά, τὰ δὲ δώσει ἐν τῷ μέλλοντι αἰῶνι, ἀνθ᾽
ὧν μετὰ ἀληθείας ἐπορεύθης τὴν ὁδὸν αὐτοῦ,
ἀκλινῆ τὴν καρδίαν ἐν τῇ ὀρθότητι τῆς πίστεως
ἀπ᾽ ἀρχῆς εἰς τέλος διασωσάμενος.

---

[1] ἐπ᾽ αὐτὸν] ἑαυτῶν E.
[2] οὗ παρὰ . . . καταρρᾳθυμῆσαι om. E.
[3] γενέσθαι multi MSS.
[4] τεθαρρηκότες editi antiqi.   [5] πρός editi antiqi.

truth "nothing is to be preferred to God and to our hope in Him."

LETTER CLII

To Victor, the General[1]

Were I to neglect writing to any other man, I should perhaps justly incur the charge of carelessness or forgetfulness. But in your case how is it possible to forget one whose name is on the lips of everyone, or to become careless about one who surpasses in the loftiness of his honours almost all who dwell on earth? But the reason for our silence is clear: we hesitate to disturb so great a man. But if in addition to your other virtues you possess this one also,—that you not only accept such letters as we do send but also miss those which we have failed to send, behold! we write now with confidence and in the future too shall write, praying to the holy God that recompense be given you for the honour you show us. Moreover, you have anticipated our appeals on behalf of the Church, having done all that we could have asked. And in what you do you seek to win favour, not with men, but with God who has honoured you, who has given you some blessings in this present life and will give you others in the world to come, in recompense for your travelling His way with truth, keeping your heart unswervingly in the orthodox faith from the beginning to the end.

[1] Written in 373. Victor was a distinguished general under Valens, a man of high character, consul in 369, and an orthodox Christian. Cf. Gregory Nazianzene, Letters CXXXIII and CXXXIV. In 378 he united with Trajanus, Arintheus, and other generals in remonstrating with Valens on his Arianism. Cf. Theod., *H. E.*, 4, 30; and Amm. Marc. 31, 7.

CLIII

Βίκτορι ἀπὸ ὑπάτων

Ὁσάκις ἂν ἡμῖν ὑπάρξῃ γράμμασιν ἐντυχεῖν
τῆς κοσμιότητός σου, τοσαυτάκις χάριν ὁμολογοῦμεν τῷ Θεῷ, ὅτι διαμένεις καὶ μεμνημένος ἡμῶν
καὶ ὑπ' οὐδεμιᾶς διαβολῆς τὴν ἀγάπην ἐλαττῶν,
ἣν ἅπαξ κρίσει τῇ ὀρθοτάτῃ ἢ συνηθείᾳ χρηστῇ
ἀναλαβεῖν κατεδέξω. εὐχόμεθα οὖν τῷ ἁγίῳ
Θεῷ καὶ σὲ διαμεῖναι ἐν τῇ ὁμοίᾳ πρὸς ἡμᾶς
διαθέσει, καὶ ἡμᾶς ἀξίους εἶναι τῆς παρὰ σοῦ
τιμῆς, ἣν τιμᾷς ἡμᾶς διὰ τοῦ γράμματος.

CLIV

Ἀσχολίῳ, ἐπισκόπῳ Θεσσαλονίκης [1]

Καλῶς ἐποίησας, καὶ κατὰ τὸν τῆς πνευματικῆς
ἀγάπης νόμον, κατάρξας τῶν πρὸς ἡμᾶς γραμμάτων καὶ τῷ ἀγαθῷ ὑποδείγματι πρὸς τὸν
ὅμοιον ζῆλον ἡμᾶς ἐκκαλεσάμενος. καὶ γὰρ ἡ μὲν
τοῦ κόσμου φιλία ὀφθαλμῶν δεῖται καὶ συντυχίας,
ὥστε ἐκεῖθεν ἀρχὴν τῆς συνηθείας γενέσθαι, οἱ δὲ
πνευματικῶς ἀγαπᾶν εἰδότες οὐ τῇ σαρκὶ προξένῳ
κέχρηνται τῆς φιλίας, ἀλλὰ τῇ τῆς πίστεως

---

[1] Ἀσχολίῳ μονάζοντι καὶ πρεσβυτέρῳ Coisl. secundus, Reg.
secundus, Vat. et Paris. Ἀσχολίῳ μονάζοντι Reg. primus,
Bigot.

---

[1] Written in 373, and in all probability to the same Victor
as is addressed in the previous letter.

LETTER CLIII

To Victor, the Ex-Consul [1]

As often as it falls to our lot to read a letter from
your Decorum, so often do we acknowledge our
thanks to God, that you both continue to be mindful
of us and that you maintain undiminished by any
slander the love which once for all through sound
judgment or through excellent habit you deigned
to assume for us. We therefore pray to the holy
God that you may persist in the same disposition
towards us, and that we on our part may be worthy
of the honour which you show us by writing to us.

LETTER CLIV

To Ascholius, Bishop of Thessalonica [2]

You have acted rightly, and according to the law
of spiritual charity, in writing to us first and in
challenging us by your good example to the like
zeal. For while worldly love needs the eyes and
personal contact that there may arise thence a beginning of intimacy, yet those who know how to
love in the spiritual way do not depend upon the
flesh to promote their love, but through the fellow-

---

[2] Written in 373. St. Ambrose (Letter XV, 12) says of
Ascholius : Ad summum sacerdotium a Macedonicis obsecratus
populis, electus a sacerdotibus. Letter XV of St. Ambrose
was written to the church at Thessalonica on the occasion of
Ascholius' death. Ascholius baptized Theodosius at Thessa-
lonica in 380, before his Gothic war, and was present at the
Council of Constantinople in 381. Cf. Letters CLXIV and
CLXV, also Socrates, *Ecc. Hist.* V, 6 and 8.

COLLECTED LETTERS OF SAINT BASIL

κοινωνίᾳ πρὸς τὴν πνευματικὴν συνάφειαν ἄγονται.
χάρις οὖν τῷ Κυρίῳ τῷ παρακαλέσαντι ἡμῶν
τὰς καρδίας ἐν τῷ δεῖξαι[1] ὅτι οὐκ ἐν πᾶσι κατέ-
ψυκται ἡ ἀγάπη, ἀλλ᾽ εἰσί που τῆς οἰκουμένης οἱ
τῆς Χριστοῦ μαθητείας τὸν χαρακτῆρα δεικνύντες.
καὶ τοίνυν ἔδοξέ μοι τὸ καθ᾽ ὑμᾶς ἐοικέναι πρᾶγμα
ἄστροις ἐν νυκτερινῇ συναφείᾳ·[2] ἄλλοις κατ᾽
ἄλλα μέρη τοῦ οὐρανοῦ διαλάμπουσιν, ὧν
χαρίεσσα μὲν ἡ λαμπρότης, χαριέστερον δὲ δήπου
τὸ ἀπροσδόκητον. τοιοῦτοι δὲ καὶ ὑμεῖς οἱ τῶν
ἐκκλησιῶν φωστῆρες, ὀλίγοι παντελῶς καὶ
εὐαρίθμητοι ἐν τῇ σκυθρωπῇ ταύτῃ καταστάσει,
οἷον ἐν σκοτομήνῃ διαφαινόμενοι, πρὸς τῷ ἐκ τῆς
ἀρετῆς χαρίεντι, ἔτι καὶ τῷ σπανίῳ τῆς εὑρέσεως
τὸ περιπόθητον ἔχοντες.

Ἐγνώρισε δέ σου τὴν διάθεσιν ἡμῖν τὸ γράμμα
αὐτάρκως. εἰ γὰρ καὶ μικρὸν ἦν τῷ πλήθει τῶν
συλλαβῶν, ἀλλὰ τῇ γε ὀρθότητι τῆς διανοίας
ἀρκοῦσαν ἡμῖν τῆς προαιρέσεως τὴν ἀπόδειξιν
ἔδωκε. τὸ γὰρ περὶ τὸν μακαριώτατον Ἀθανά-
σιον ἐσπουδακέναι δεῖγμα ἐναργέστατον τοῦ
ὑγιῶς[3] ἔχειν περὶ τὰ μέγιστα. ἀντὶ οὖν τῆς ἐπὶ
τοῖς γράμμασιν εὐφροσύνης πολλὴν οἴδαμεν
χάριν τῷ τιμιωτάτῳ υἱῷ ἡμῶν Εὐφημίῳ· ᾧ
καὶ αὐτὸς εὔχομαι πᾶσαν ὑπάρχειν βοήθειαν
ἐξ ἁγίου· καὶ σὲ συνεύχεσθαι ἡμῖν παρακαλῶ, ὅπως ἂν ἀπολάβοιμεν αὐτὸν ἐν τάχει
μετὰ τῆς κοσμιωτάτης ὁμόζυγος[4] αὐτοῦ, θυγα-
τρὸς δὲ ἡμῶν ἐν Κυρίῳ. παρακλήθητι δὲ
καὶ αὐτὸς μὴ ἐν προοιμίοις ἡμῖν στῆσαι τὴν

---

[1] ἐκ τοῦ δεῖξαι editi antiqi.   [2] συννεφείᾳ E.
[3] ἁγίως editi antiqi.

ship of the faith are brought to the union of the
spirit. So thanks be to the Lord who has consoled
our hearts by showing that charity has grown cold
in all men, but that there exist somewhere in the
world men who display the mark of Christ's teaching! And indeed your function has seemed to me
like that of the stars in nightly concurrence: they
illuminate one portion of the heavens after another,
and while their brightness is delightful, more delightful still, methinks, is the suddenness of their
coming. Such are you who are lights of the churches,
very few and easily numbered in this present gloomy
state of affairs, shining as in a moonless night, not
only giving delight through your virtue, but also
arousing, by the rarity with which you are found,
our deep affection.

Your letter made known sufficiently your disposition towards us. For even if it was brief in
the number of its syllables, yet in the integrity of
its sentiments it gave us an adequate proof of your
purpose. For the zeal you have shown for the most
blessed Athanasius gives the clearest possible evidence of your soundness in the matters of greatest
importance. In return, then, for the joy received
from your letter we express our great thanks to our
most honoured son Euphemius,[1] for whom I also pray
that all assistance may be at hand from the Holy
One. I urge you also to join us in our prayer, that
we may soon receive him back accompanied by his
most discreet wife, our daughter in the Lord. And
as for yourself, we beg you not to stop our happiness

---

[1] The bearer of the letter from Ascholius to Basil.

⁴ συζύγου editi antiqi.

COLLECTED LETTERS OF SAINT BASIL

εὐφροσύνην, ἀλλὰ διὰ τῆς ἀεὶ παραπιπτούσης προφάσεως ἐπιστέλλειν καὶ τὴν πρὸς ἡμᾶς διάθεσιν τῷ πυκνῷ τῆς ὁμιλίας αὔξειν, καὶ τὰ περὶ τῶν αὐτοῦ[1] ἐκκλησιῶν, ὅπως ἔχει κατὰ τὴν συμφωνίαν, σημαίνειν· περὶ δὲ[2] τῶν ἐνταῦθα προσεύχεσθαι, ὥστε γενέσθαι καὶ παρ' ἡμῖν γαλήνην μεγάλην, ἐπιτιμήσαντος τοῦ Κυρίου ἡμῶν τῷ ἀνέμῳ καὶ τῇ θαλάσσῃ.

CLV

Ἀνεπίγραφος ἐπὶ ἀλείπτῃ

Πρὸς πολλὰς τὰς διὰ τῆς ἐπιστολῆς ἣν πρώτην καὶ μόνην κατηξίωσεν ἡμῖν ἡ εὐγένειά σου διαπέμψασθαι ἐγγεγραμμένας κατηγορίας ἀπορῶ[3] ἀπολογήσασθαι, οὐ διὰ τὴν τοῦ δικαίου ἔνδειαν, ἀλλὰ διὰ τὸ ἐν πλήθει τῶν ἐπιφερομένων δύσκολον εἶναι τῶν καιριωτέρων τὴν προτίμησιν, καὶ ὅθεν δεῖ πρῶτον ἡμᾶς ἄρξασθαι τῆς θεραπείας. ἢ τάχα δεῖ αὐτῇ[4] τῇ τάξει τῶν γεγραμμένων χρησαμένους ὁδῷ πρὸς ἕκαστον ἀπαντᾶν.

Τοὺς ἐπὶ Σκυθίαν ἀπαίροντας ἐντεῦθεν μέχρι σήμερον οὐκ ἐγνωρίσαμεν· ἀλλ' οὐδὲ τῶν ἐκ τῆς οἰκίας[5] ὑπέμνησαν ἡμᾶς, ὥστε προσειπεῖν σε[6]

---

[1] σαυτοῦ editi antiqi.   [2] τε E.   [3] ἀπορῶν E.
[4] δεῖ αὐτῇ] δι' αὐτήν E.   [5] οἰκείας editi antiqi.
[6] σε om. E.

---

[1] Written in 373. According to the Benedictine edition the person addressed is Julius Soranus, a relative of Basil and a duke of Scythia. The sub-title may have been added by a copyist. It applies to Soranus, inasmuch as he was "a

380

at its beginning, but on every pretext that arises to write and thus enhance your disposition towards us by frequent communication, and to keep us informed about the condition of your churches as regards harmony ; and as for our own affairs, we beg you to pray that a great calm may come about among us also, after our Lord has rebuked the wind and the sea.

LETTER CLV

WITHOUT ADDRESS, ON THE CASE OF A TRAINER [1]

As regards the many accusations which are contained in the first and only letter which your Nobility has deigned to send us, I am at a loss how to defend myself, not through lack of a just cause, but through the fact that in the multitude of the charges brought it is difficult to make a choice of the more apposite and to know at what point we should first begin our healing treatment of the matter. Or perhaps we should employ the very order of the written items and methodically meet them one by one.

Until to-day we had no knowledge of those who are departing hence for Scythia ; in fact, no member even of your household suggested to us that we

---

trainer" (ἀλείπτης) and encourager of martyrs. In Letter CLXIV Basil calls Ascholius "trainer" of the martyr Sabas. On the present letter and Letters CLV, CLXIV, and CLXV, which have to do with transferring the remains of the Gothic martyr Sabas (died April 372) to Caesarea in Cappadocia, cf. G. Pfeilschefter, *Ein neues Werk des Wulfila, Veröffentlichungen aus dem Kirchenhistor*, Seminar, München, 1907, pp. 192-224. This letter is one of the earliest references to the preservation of the relics of martyrs.

δι' αὐτῶν, καίτοι πάνυ διὰ σπουδῆς τιθεμένους ἐπὶ
πάσης προφάσεως προσφθέγγεσθαί σου τὴν τιμιότητα. ἐπιλαθέσθαι δέ σου ἐν προσευχαῖς ἀδύνατον,
εἰ μὴ πρότερον τοῦ ἔργου ἡμῶν ἐπιλαθώμεθα, εἰς ὃ
ἔταξεν ἡμᾶς ὁ Κύριος. μέμνησαι γὰρ πάντως τῶν
κηρυγμάτων τῶν ἐκκλησιαστικῶν, πιστὸς ὢν τῇ
τοῦ Θεοῦ χάριτι, ὅτι καὶ ὑπὲρ τῶν ἐν ἀποδημίαις
ἀδελφῶν δεόμεθα, καὶ ὑπὲρ τῶν ἐν ταῖς[1] στρατείαις
ἐξεταζομένων, καὶ ὑπὲρ παρρησιαζομένων διὰ τὸ
ὄνομα Κυρίου, καὶ ὑπὲρ τῶν τοὺς πνευματικοὺς
καρποὺς ἐπιδεικνυμένων, ἐν τῇ ἁγίᾳ Ἐκκλησίᾳ
τὰς εὐχὰς ποιούμεθα· ὧν πάντως ἐν τοῖς πλείοσιν[2]
ἢ καὶ ἐν τοῖς πᾶσι νομίζομεν καὶ τὴν σὴν ἐμπερι-
λαμβάνεσθαι τιμιότητα. ἰδίᾳ δέ σου ἡμεῖς πῶς
ἂν ἐπιλαθώμεθα, τοσαῦτα ἔχοντες τὰ κινοῦντα
ἡμᾶς πρὸς μνήμην, ἀδελφὴν τοιαύτην, ἀδελφιδοὺς[3]
τοιούτους, συγγένειαν οὕτω χρηστήν, οὕτως
ἀγαπῶσαν ἡμᾶς, οἶκον, οἰκέτας, φίλους, ἐξ ὧν, κἂν
μὴ βουλώμεθα, ἀναγκαίως ὑπομιμνησκόμεθά σου
τῆς ἀγαθῆς προαιρέσεως ;

Περὶ δὲ τοῦδε ὁ ἀδελφὸς ὁ δεῖνα οὐδὲν ἡμῖν
ἤνεγκεν ἐπαχθές, οὐδὲ παρ' ἡμῶν βλάπτουσα
αὐτόν τις κρίσις ἐξενήνεκται οὐδεμία. τρέψον οὖν
τὴν λύπην ἐπὶ τοὺς τὰ ψευδῆ διηγησαμένους,
ἀπολύσας πάσης μέμψεως καὶ τὸν χωρεπίσκοπον
καὶ ἐμέ. εἰ δέ τινα δίκην γυμνάζει ὁ σχολαστικὸς
ὁ δεῖνα, ἔχει δικαστήρια δημόσια καὶ νόμους.
ἀξιῶ οὖν ὑμᾶς ἐπὶ τούτοις μηδεμίαν ἔχειν
μέμψιν.

---

[1] ταῖς om. E.   [2] χρόνοις E, editi antiqi.
[3] ἀδελφικήν E.

should salute you through them, although we are
eagerly disposed to salute your Honour on every
occasion. And we cannot forget you in our prayers,
unless we first forget the labours to which the Lord
has appointed us. For you surely remember, since
by the grace of God you are faithful, the invocations [1]
of the Church—that we both make supplication for
our brethren who are sojourning abroad, and offer
prayers in the Holy Church for those who are
enrolled in military service, and for those who speak
out boldly for the sake of the name of the Lord,
and for those who show the fruits of the Spirit; and
certainly in the greater number of these prayers, or
even in all of them, we consider that your Honour
also is included. And in private how can we forget
you when we have so many things to prompt us to
remember you—such a sister, such nephews, a kins-
folk so good, so affectionate towards us, house, household, and friends, on account of whom, even if we
do not wish it, we are constrained to remember
your goodwill?

But in regard to this present matter a certain
brother has brought us no unpleasant news, nor has
any decision whatever been given out by us which
might cause injury to him. Therefore turn your
indignation against those who have made the false
statements, absolving the chorepiscopus and myself
from all blame. And if this certain learned fellow is
making ready any legal action, he has public courts
and laws. Therefore I request you to put no blame
on us in these matters.

---

[1] κηρύγματα here seems to denote an appointed liturgy.
For a similar meaning of the word, cf. Cyprian, Letter
LXXV, from Firmilianus.

Αὐτὸς δὲ ὅσα ποιεῖς ἀγαθά, σεαυτῷ θησαυρίζεις·
καὶ ἢν παρέχῃ ἀνάπαυσιν τοῖς διὰ τὸ ὄνομα τοῦ
Κυρίου διωκομένοις, ταύτην σεαυτῷ ἐν ἡμέρᾳ τῆς
μισθαποδοσίας προετοιμάζεις. καλῶς δὲ ποιήσεις,
ἐὰν καὶ λείψανα μαρτύρων τῇ πατρίδι ἐκπέμψῃς,[1]
εἴπερ, ὡς ἐπέστειλας ἡμῖν, ὁ ἐκεῖ διωγμὸς ποιεῖ
καὶ νῦν μάρτυρας τῷ Κυρίῳ.

CLVI

Εὐαγρίῳ πρεσβυτέρῳ

Τοσοῦτον ἀπέσχον τοῦ δυσχερᾶναι πρὸς τὸ
μῆκος τῶν γραμμάτων, ὥστε καὶ μικρά μοι ἔδοξεν
εἶναι ἡ ἐπιστολὴ ὑπὸ τῆς κατὰ τὴν ἀνάγνωσιν
ἡδονῆς. τί γὰρ ἥδιον ἄκουσμα τοῦ τῆς εἰρήνης
ὀνόματος; ἢ[2] τί τοῦ ὑπὲρ τῶν τοιούτων βουλεύεσ-
θαι ἱεροπρεπέστερον καὶ μᾶλλον τῷ Κυρίῳ
κεχαρισμένον; σοὶ μὲν οὖν παράσχοι ὁ Κύριος
τὸν μισθὸν τῆς εἰρηνοποιίας, οὕτω καλῶς προαιρουμένῳ καὶ σπουδαίως ἐγκειμένῳ πράγματι
μακαριστῷ. ἡμᾶς δὲ νόμιζε, τιμία κεφαλή,
ἕνεκα[3] μὲν τοῦ προῃρῆσθαι καὶ εὔχεσθαι ἰδεῖν
ποτὲ τὴν ἡμέραν ἐν ᾗ πάντες τὸν αὐτὸν πληρώ-
σουσι σύλλογον, οἱ ταῖς διανοίαις ἀλλήλων μὴ
ἀπεσχισμένοι, μηδενὶ παραχωρεῖν τῶν εἰς τὴν
σπουδὴν τούτων πρωτείων. καὶ γὰρ ἂν εἴημεν

---

[1] ἐκπέμψῃ E.   [2] ἤ om. Harl., Med.
[3] ἕνεκεν E.

---

[1] Written in the late autumn of 373 ; cf. Loofs 31, note 3.
Evagrius, commonly known as of Antioch to distinguish him

As for yourself, whatever good deeds you perform, you are laying them up as a treasure for yourself; and whatever alleviation you render to those who are being persecuted for the sake of the name of the Lord, this you are preparing for yourself on the day of reward. And you will do well, if you send the relics of martyrs to your native land, since, as you have written us, the persecution which is taking place there is even now making martyrs to the Lord.

LETTER CLVI

To Evagrius, the Presbyter [1]

So far was I from being displeased at the length of your letter, that it seemed even short to me because of the pleasure I got from reading it. For what is sweeter to the ears than the name of peace? Or what is more befitting the sacred office and more pleasing to the Lord than to deliberate on matters such as these? Therefore may the Lord render to you the reward of peace-making, you who so nobly undertake and so zealously pursue a most blessed work. But know, honoured sir, that—on account of the choice we have made and the prayers we offer that we may yet see the day when all those who are not divided from one another in mind shall fill the same assembly—of those foremost in zeal for this end we yield to none. For we would truly be the

from others of the same name, especially Evagrius the historian. The dates of his birth and his death are uncertain, but he is known to have been consecrated by the dying Paulinus in 388 (an act which prolonged the Meletian schism at Antioch), and seems to have lived until at least 392 ; cf. Letter CXXXVIII.

COLLECTED LETTERS OF SAINT BASIL

ὡς ἀληθῶς πάντων ἀνθρώπων ἀτοπώτατοι, σχίσ-
μασι καὶ κατατομαῖς ἐκκλησιῶν ἐφηδόμενοι,[1]
καὶ μὴ τὴν συνάφειαν τῶν μελῶν τοῦ σώματος
τοῦ Χριστοῦ τὸ μέγιστον τῶν ἀγαθῶν τιθέμενοι.
ὅσον μέντοι τῆς ἐπιθυμίας ἡμῖν περίεστι, τοσοῦτον
γίνωσκε τῆς δυνάμεως ἐνδεῖν. οὐ γὰρ ἀγνοεῖ σου
ἡ τελεία φρόνησις, ὅτι τὰ χρόνῳ κρατυνθέντα
πάθη πρῶτον μὲν χρόνου δεῖται πρὸς τὴν διόρθωσιν, ἔπειτα ἰσχυρᾶς καὶ εὐτονωτέρας ἀγωγῆς,[2] εἰ
μέλλοι[3] τις τοῦ βάθους αὐτοῦ καθικνεῖσθαι, ὥστε
πρόρριζα ἐξελεῖν τῶν καμνόντων τὰ ἀρρωστήματα. οἶδας δὲ ὃ λέγω, καὶ εἰ δεῖ τρανότερον
εἰπεῖν, οὐδεὶς ὁ φόβος.

Τὴν φιλαυτίαν ἔθει μακρῷ ταῖς ψυχαῖς ἐρριζω-
θεῖσαν εἷς ἀνὴρ ἀνελεῖν οὐχ οἷός τε, οὐδ' ἐπιστολὴ
μία, οὐδὲ χρόνος βραχύς. τὰς γὰρ ὑπονοίας καὶ
τὰς ἐξ ἀντιλογιῶν παρατριβὰς παντελῶς ἀναιρεθῆ-
ναι, μὴ ἀξιοπίστου τινὸς μεσιτεύοντος τῇ εἰρήνῃ,
ἀμήχανον. καὶ εἰ μὲν ἐπέρρει ἡμῖν τὰ παρὰ τῆς
χάριτος καὶ ἦμεν δυνατοὶ λόγῳ καὶ ἔργῳ καὶ τοῖς
πνευματικοῖς χαρίσμασι δυσωπῆσαι τοὺς ἀντι-
διατιθεμένους, ἔδει κατατολμῆσαι τοῦ τοσούτου
πράγματος. τάχα δὲ οὐδ' ἂν τότε συνεβούλευσας
ἡμῖν μόνοις ἐλθεῖν ἐπὶ τὴν ἐπανόρθωσιν, ὄντος τοῦ
ἐπισκόπου τῇ τοῦ Θεοῦ χάριτι, ᾧ ἡ φροντὶς ἀνῆκε[4]
προηγουμένως τῆς ἐκκλησίας· ὃν οὔτε αὐτὸν ἐλθεῖν πρὸς ἡμᾶς οἷόν τε, καὶ ἡμῖν ἀποδημήσειν[5]
τέως ὑπὸ τοῦ χειμῶνος οὐ ῥᾴδιον, μᾶλλον δὲ
παντελῶς ἀδύνατον, οὐ μόνον καθότι τὸ σῶμά

[1] ἐνηδόμενοι Harl., Reg. secundus.
[2] διαγωγῆς editi antiqi.   [3] μέλοι E.
[4] ἀνήκει editi antiqi.   [5] ἀποδημεῖν editi antiqi.

most unnatural of all men, if we rejoiced in the
schisms and divisions of the churches, and did not
consider the union of the members of the body of
Christ to be the greatest of all blessings. However,
you should know that our power is as deficient as
our desire is abundant. For your perfect wisdom
is not unaware of the fact that evils which have
been strengthened by time need time first of all for
their correction, then a strong and vigorous method
of treatment, if one is to get at the very bottom
of them, so as to tear out by the roots the complaints of the ailing. But you know what I mean,
and if it is necessary to speak more clearly, there
is no cause for fear.

Self-love, when rooted in the mind by long habit,
no one man can eradicate, no one letter, no short
time. For the complete elimination of suspicions
and of the clashes arising from controversies is
impossible, unless there be some trustworthy man
to act as a mediator in the interest of peace. And
if all the strength of divine grace should flow upon
us, and if we were able by word and deed and the
gifts of the Spirit to move our opponents, then it
would be necessary for me to undertake so great
a task. Yet perhaps even in that case you would
not have advised us to set about the work of correction all alone, since he[1] who by the grace of
God is the bishop is the man upon whom the care
of his church falls chiefly ; and it is not possible for
him to come to us in person, and because of the
winter it is not easy for us in the meantime to go
abroad, or rather it is altogether impossible, not

---

[1] Meletius of Antioch.

μοι[1] ὑπὸ μακρᾶς ἀρρωστίας ἀπείρηκεν, ἀλλ᾽ ὅτι
καὶ αἱ τῶν Ἀρμενιακῶν ὁρῶν αἱ[2] ὑπερβάσεις
μικρὸν ὕστερον ἄβατοι[3] γίνονται καὶ τοῖς πάνυ
καθ᾽ ἡλικίαν σφριγῶσι. γράμματι δὲ αὐτῷ
σημᾶναι[4] ταῦτα οὐ παραιτήσομαι. οὐ μέντοι
προσδοκῶ τι ἐκ τῶν γραμμάτων ἀξιόλογον ἀπο-
βήσεσθαι, τῆς τε τοῦ ἀνδρὸς ἀκριβείας στοχαζό-
μενος καὶ αὐτῆς τῆς φύσεως τῶν γραμμάτων· ὅτι
οὐ πέφυκεν ἐναργῶς δύνασθαι δυσωπεῖν ὁ διαπεμ-
πόμενος λόγος. πολλὰ γὰρ δεῖ εἰπεῖν, πολλὰ καὶ
ἀντακοῦσαι, καὶ λῦσαι τὰ ὑποπίπτοντα, καὶ
ἀνθυπενεγκεῖν[5] τὰ ὑφορμοῦντα, ὧν οὐδὲν δύναται
ὁ ἐν τοῖς γράμμασι λόγος, ἀργὸς καὶ ἄψυχος ἐν
τῷ χάρτῃ διερριμμένος.

Πλὴν ἀλλ᾽, ὅπερ ἔφην, οὐκ[6] ἀποκνήσω γράψαι.
γίνωσκε μέντοι, ὡς ἀληθῶς εὐλαβέστατε καὶ
πολυπόθητε ἡμῖν[7] ἀδελφέ, ὅτι οὐδεμία μοι πρὸς
οὐδένα τῇ τοῦ Θεοῦ χάριτι ἰδιάζουσά ἐστι
φιλονεικία. οὐδὲ γὰρ πολυπραγμονήσας οἶδα τὰ
ἐγκλήματα, οἷς ἕκαστος ὑπεύθυνος ἢ ἔστιν ἢ
ὀνομάζεται. ὥστε οὕτως ὑμᾶς προσέχειν τῇ
ἡμετέρᾳ διανοίᾳ προσήκει, ὡς μηδὲν ἡμῶν δυναμένων ποιῆσαι κατὰ πρόσκλισιν,[8] μηδὲ προειλημ-
μένων εἰς τὴν κατά τινων διαβολήν. μόνον εἰ
εὐδοκία γένοιτο[9] τοῦ Κυρίου ἐκκλησιαστικῶς
πάντα καὶ ἀκολούθως πραχθῆναι.

Ἐλύπησε δὲ ἡμᾶς ὁ ποθεινότατος υἱὸς Δωρόθεος[10]
ὁ συνδιάκονος, ἀπαγγείλας περὶ τῆς εὐλαβείας
σου, ὅτι ὤκνησας μετασχεῖν αὐτῷ τῆς συνάξεως.

---

[1] μου E, Med.   [2] αἱ om. E.   [3] ἀδύνατοι E.
[4] σημῆναι tres MSS.   [5] ἀντεπενεγκεῖν E.

only because my body is worn out by long illness, but also because the passes over the Armenian mountains become a little later impassable even to those who are in the very vigour of youth. And I shall not hesitate to point this out to him in writing. However, I do not look for anything worth while to result from letters, judging from the man's strictness and the very nature of anything written; for the transmitted word is obviously by nature incapable of moving men. For there are many things to be said, many things to be heard from the other side, objections to be solved, one's own reasons to be advanced, none of which can be accomplished by the written word, inert and lifeless as it is, spread out upon the sheet of paper.

However, as I have said, I shall not refrain from writing. Be assured, however, in truth our most pious and beloved brother, that by God's grace I have no private quarrel with anyone at all. For I have not even had the curiosity to find out their charges to which the accused either are severally liable or are said to be liable. Consequently it is fitting that you should pay heed to our opinion, knowing that we are incapable of acting from bias and have not been prejudiced by the slander directed against any of the parties. Would only that the approval of the Lord might be granted, that everything be done in the Church's manner and in the proper form.

Our most beloved son Dorotheus, our deacon, caused us sorrow when he informed me about your Piety, that you refused to take part with him in

---

⁶ οὐδ' editi antiqi.   ⁷ ἡμῶν E.
⁸ πρόσκλησιν editi antiqi.   ⁹ γίγνοιτο editi antiqi.
¹⁰ Θεόδωρος unus ex Regiis.

389

καίτοι οὐ τοιαῦτα ἡμῖν ἦν τὰ ὠμιλημένα,[1] εἴ τι ἐγὼ
μέμνημαι. ἀποστεῖλαι μέντοι πρὸς τὴν δύσιν
ἐμοὶ μὲν παντελῶς ἐστιν ἀδύνατον, οὐδένα ἔχοντι
τῶν εἰς τὴν διακονίαν ταύτην ἐπιτηδείων. τῶν
δὲ αὐτόθεν ἀδελφῶν, ἐάν τις αἱρῆται τὸν ὑπὲρ τῶν
ἐκκλησιῶν κόπον ἀναδέξασθαι, οἶδε δηλονότι καὶ
πρὸς τίνας ὁρμήσει, καὶ ἐπὶ ποίῳ σκοπῷ, καὶ παρὰ
τίνων ἐφοδιασθῇ τοῖς γράμμασι, καὶ ποταποῖς
τούτοις. ἐγὼ μὲν γὰρ ἐν κύκλῳ περισκεψάμενος
ὁρῶ μεθ' ἑαυτοῦ οὐδένα. καὶ εὔχομαι μὲν τοῖς
ἑπτακισχιλίοις ἐναριθμηθῆναι τοῖς μὴ κάμψασι
γόνυ τῇ [2] Βάαλ. πλὴν ὅτι ζητοῦσι καὶ ἡμῶν τὴν
ψυχὴν οἱ πᾶσι τὰς ἑαυτῶν ἐπιβάλλοντες χεῖρας.
οὐ μέντοι τούτου γε ἕνεκεν ἐλλείψομέν τι τῆς
ὀφειλομένης σπουδῆς ταῖς τοῦ Θεοῦ ἐκκλησίαις.

CLVII

Ἀντιόχῳ

Πῶς οἴει βαρέως ἤνεγκα διαμαρτών σου τῆς
συντυχίας κατὰ τὸ θέρος; καίτοι οὐδὲ ἡ τῶν [3]
ἄλλων τοιαύτη γέγονεν, ὥστε μέχρι κόρου ἡμῖν
προελθεῖν· ἀλλ' οὖν καὶ ὄναρ ἰδεῖν τὰ ποθούμενα
φέρει τινὰ τοῖς ἀγαπῶσι παραμυθίαν. σὺ δὲ
οὐδὲ ἐπιστέλλεις, οὕτως ἀργὸς εἶ, ὥστε μηδὲ τὴν

---

[1] ὠμολογημένα editi antiqi.   [2] τῷ editi antiqi.
[3] ἡ τῶν] ἐτῶν E.

---

[1] Written in 373. Other letters to Antiochus, nephew
of Eusebius, are CXLVI, CLVIII, and CLXVIII. Letter
CCXXXIX makes reference to Antiochus. Since the present

his religious service. And yet such were not the
matters which were discussed by you and me, if I
recollect at all. To send a representative to the
West, however, is absolutely impossible for us, since
I have no one suitable for this mission. But if any
one of the brothers with you chooses to take upon
himself this task in behalf of the churches, he
knows, doubtless, to what person he shall proceed,
for what purpose, and by whom he shall be furnished
with letters, and by what sort of letters. For when
I look about me, I see in my own followers no one
at all. And I pray to be numbered amongst the
seven thousand who have not bent the knee to Baal.
I will only add that those who are laying their
hands on all are seeking our soul also. But not on
this account shall we be at all remiss in the zeal that
is due to the churches of God.

LETTER CLVII

To Antiochus [1]

You can imagine how disappointed I was at
failing to meet you during the summer! And yet
our meeting in other years was also not of such a
character as to reach the point of satiating us.
However, to see even in dreams the objects of one's
desire brings some little comfort to those who love.
But you do not even write, so slothful are you; con-

and the following letters are both couched in similar terms,
the Benedictine editors are inclined to believe that they are
really addressed to different people. Furthermore, the
slothfulness of which Basil complains would befit Eusebius
much better than Antiochus, who could not travel without
his uncle's permission.

COLLECTED LETTERS OF SAINT BASIL

ὑπόλειψιν[1] ἄλλῃ τινὶ αἰτίᾳ μᾶλλον ἢ τῷ ἀργῶς
ἔχειν πρὸς τὰς ὑπὲρ τῆς ἀγάπης ἀποδημίας λογίζεσθαι. ἀλλὰ τοῦτο μὲν πεπαύσθω ἡμῖν. εὔχου
δὲ ὑπὲρ ἡμῶν καὶ παρακάλει τὸν Κύριον μὴ
ἐγκαταλιπεῖν ἡμᾶς, ἀλλ' ὡς ἐκ τῶν ἐπελθόντων
παρήγαγεν ἡμᾶς πειρασμῶν, οὕτω καὶ ἐκ τῶν
προσδοκωμένων ῥύσασθαι εἰς δόξαν τοῦ ὀνόματος
αὐτοῦ, ἐφ' ᾧ ἠλπίσαμεν.

CLVIII

Ἀντιόχῳ

Ἐπειδὴ ἀντέστησάν μοι αἱ ἁμαρτίαι μου πρὸς
τὸ μὴ δυνηθῆναί με ἣν πάλαι εἶχον ἐπιθυμίαν
τῆς ὑμετέρας συντυχίας ἀγαγεῖν εἰς πέρας,
γράμμασι γοῦν παραμυθοῦμαι τὴν ἀπόλειψιν·
καὶ παρακαλοῦμεν[2] μὴ διαλιπεῖν[3] μεμνημένους
ἡμῶν ἐν ταῖς προσευχαῖς, ἵνα, ἐὰν ζῶμεν, καταξιωθῶμεν ὑμῶν ἀπολαῦσαι, εἰ δὲ μή, διὰ τῆς
βοηθείας τῶν προσευχῶν ὑμῶν μετὰ ἀγαθῆς
ἐλπίδος μεταναστεύσωμεν[4] ἀπὸ τοῦ κόσμου
τούτου. τὸν δὲ ἀδελφὸν τὸν ἐπὶ ταῖς καμήλοις[5]
παρατιθέμεθα ὑμῖν.

CLIX

Εὐπατερίῳ,[6] καὶ τῇ θυγατρί

Ὅσην εὐφροσύνην παρέσχε μοι τὸ γράμμα τῆς
κοσμιότητός σου εἰκάζεις πάντως αὐτοῖς[7] τοῖς

[1] ἀπόλειψιν E.   [2] ὑμᾶς add. editi antiqi.
[3] διαλείπειν editi antiqi.   [4] μεταναστῶμεν editi antiqi.
[5] ταῖς καμήλοις] τὰς καμήλους editi antiqi.
[6] Εὐπατρίῳ E, Med.   [7] αὐτός editi antiqi.

392

LETTER CLIX

sequently your failure to visit me is likewise to be
attributed to no other reason than that you are
slothful about undertaking journeys to gratify your
affection. However, let us say no more about this.
But pray for us and beg the Lord not to desert us,
but just as He has led us out of past trials, so to
deliver us also from those which are imminent, unto
the glory of His name wherein we have placed our
hope.

LETTER CLVIII

To Antiochus [1]

Since my sins have risen up against me, rendering
it impossible for me to realize the desire which I
have long had of visiting you, by letter at least I
can palliate my failure to appear; and we exhort
you not to leave off making mention of us in your
prayers, so that, if we live, we may be deemed
worthy of enjoying you, and if not, that by the aid
of your prayers we may pass on from this world with
good hope. And we put in your care the brother
who is in charge of the camels.

LETTER CLIX

To Eupaterius and his Daughter [2]

How much pleasure the letter of your Decorum
afforded me you certainly can infer from the very

[1] Written in 373. Cf. the previous letter with note.
[2] Written about 373, on the Nicene Creed and the Holy
Ghost. Eupaterius and his daughter are otherwise unknown.

ἐπεσταλμένοις. τί γὰρ ἂν ἥδιον γένοιτο ἀνθρώπῳ
εὐχὴν ποιουμένῳ φοβουμένοις Θεὸν ἀεὶ προσο-
μιλεῖν καὶ τοῦ παρ' αὐτῶν κέρδους μεταλαμβάνειν, γραμμάτων τοιούτων, δι' ὧν ἡ Θεοῦ γνῶσις
ἐπιζητεῖται; εἰ γὰρ τὸ ζῆν ἡμῖν Χριστός, ἀκολούθως καὶ ὁ λόγος ἡμῶν περὶ Χριστοῦ ὀφείλει
εἶναι, καὶ ἡ ἔννοια καὶ πᾶσα πρᾶξις τῶν ἐντολῶν
αὐτοῦ ἠρτῆσθαι, καὶ ἡ ψυχὴ ἡμῶν κατ' αὐτὸν
μεμορφῶσθαι. χαίρω τοίνυν περὶ τοιούτων ἐρω-
τώμενος καὶ συγχαίρω τοῖς ἐρωτῶσιν. ἡμῖν
τοίνυν ἑνὶ μὲν λόγῳ ἡ τῶν ἐν Νικαίᾳ συνελθόντων
πατέρων πίστις πασῶν τῶν ὕστερον ἐφευρε-
θεισῶν[1] προτετίμηται· ἐν ᾗ ὁμοούσιος ὁμολογεῖται ὁ Υἱὸς τῷ Πατρί, καὶ τῆς αὐτῆς ὑπάρχων
φύσεως ἧς ὁ γεννήσας. φῶς γὰρ ἐκ φωτός, καὶ
Θεὸν ἐκ Θεοῦ, καὶ ἀγαθὸν ἐξ ἀγαθοῦ, καὶ τὰ
τοιαῦτα πάντα, ὑπό τε τῶν ἁγίων ἐκείνων ὡμολο-
γήθη· καὶ ὑφ' ἡμῶν νῦν, τῶν εὐχομένων κατ'
ἴχνη βαίνειν ἐκείνοις, προσμαρτυρεῖται.

Ἐπειδὴ δὲ τὸ νῦν ἀνακύψαν παρὰ τῶν ἀεὶ[2]
καινοτομεῖν ἐπιχειρούντων ζήτημα, παρασιωπηθὲν
τοῖς πάλαι διὰ τὸ ἀναντίρρητον, ἀδιάρθρωτον κατε-
λείφθη (λέγω δὴ τὸ περὶ τοῦ ἁγίου Πνεύματος).
προστίθεμεν τὸν περὶ τούτου λόγον ἀκολούθως τῇ
τῆς Γραφῆς ἐννοίᾳ· ὅτι ὡς βαπτιζόμεθα, οὕτω
καὶ πιστεύομεν· ὡς πιστεύομεν, οὕτω καὶ δοξο-
λογοῦμεν. ἐπειδὴ οὖν βάπτισμα ἡμῖν δέδοται
παρὰ τοῦ Σωτῆρος εἰς ὄνομα Πατρὸς καὶ Υἱοῦ καὶ

---

[1] εὑρεθεισῶν E.   [2] τι add. editi antiqi.

[1] Cf. Phil. 1. 21: ἐμοὶ γὰρ τὸ ζῆν, Χριστός· καὶ τὸ ἀποθανεῖν κέρδος. "For me, to live is Christ : to die is gain."

394

tenor of your letter. For what could be sweeter to a man who prays that he may ever associate with God-fearing men and derive some of the profit such association yields than such letters as help us in our search for the knowledge of God? For if "to us, to live is Christ," [1] accordingly also our speech ought to be about Christ, and our thoughts and all our actions should depend upon His commands, and our souls should be moulded according to Him. I therefore rejoice when I am questioned about such matters and congratulate those who put the questions. As for us, then, to state it in a word, the creed of the Fathers who assembled at Nicaea has been honoured by us before all those formulated later, and in this the Son is confessed to be consubstantial with the Father, and to be of the same nature as the One who begot Him. For Light of Light, and God of God, and Good of Good (and all descriptions of this kind) has He been confessed to be by those holy men; and by us now, who pray that we may walk in their footsteps, witness to this is also borne.

But since the question which has now been brought up by those who are always attempting to make innovations, and which was passed over in silence by the men of former times because there was no dispute about it, has remained unexplained (I mean the question concerning the Holy Ghost), we are adding the explanation of this according to the sense of the Scriptures: namely, that as we are baptized, so also do we believe; as we believe, so also do we recite the doxology. Since, then, baptism has been given to us by our Saviour in the name of the Father and of the Son and of the Holy Spirit,

ἁγίου Πνεύματος, ἀκόλουθον τῷ βαπτίσματι τὴν
ὁμολογίαν τῆς πίστεως παρεχόμεθα, ἀκόλουθον
δὲ καὶ τὴν δοξολογίαν τῇ πίστει, συνδοξάζοντες
Πατρὶ καὶ Υἱῷ τὸ ἅγιον Πνεῦμα, τῷ πεπεῖσθαι
μὴ ἀλλότριον εἶναι τῆς θείας φύσεως. οὐ γὰρ ἂν
τῶν αὐτῶν μετέσχε τιμῶν τὸ ἀπεξενωμένον κατὰ
τὴν φύσιν. τοὺς δὲ κτίσμα λέγοντας τὸ Πνεῦμα
τὸ ἅγιον ἐλεοῦμεν, ὡς εἰς τὸ ἀσυγχώρητον πτῶμα [1]
τῆς εἰς αὐτὸ βλασφημίας διὰ τῆς τοιαύτης φωνῆς
καταπίπτοντας. ὅτι γὰρ διώρισται κτίσις θεότητος οὐδενὸς λόγου προσδεῖ τοῖς κατὰ μικρὸν [2] ταῖς
Γραφαῖς ἐγγεγυμνασμένοις. ἡ μὲν γὰρ κτίσις
δουλεύει, τὸ δὲ Πνεῦμα ἐλευθεροῖ· ἡ κτίσις ζωῆς
προσδεής ἐστι, τὸ Πνεῦμά ἐστι τὸ ζωοποιοῦν· ἡ
κτίσις διδασκαλίας προσδεῖται, τὸ Πνεῦμά ἐστι
τὸ δίδασκον· ἡ κτίσις ἁγιάζεται, τὸ Πνεῦμά ἐστι
τὸ ἁγιάζον. κἂν ἀγγέλους εἴπῃς, κἂν ἀρχαγ-
γέλους, κἂν πάσας τὰς ὑπερκοσμίους [3] δυνάμεις,
διὰ τοῦ Πνεύματος τὴν ἁγιωσύνην λαμβάνουσιν.
αὐτὸ δὲ τὸ Πνεῦμα φυσικὴν ἔχει τὴν ἁγιότητα,
οὐ κατὰ χάριν λαβόν, ἀλλὰ συνουσιωμένην αὐτῷ·
ὅθεν καὶ τῆς προσηγορίας τῆς τοῦ ἁγίου ἐξαιρέτως
τετύχηκεν. ὁ τοίνυν φύσει ἅγιον, ὡς φύσει ἅγιος

---

[1] πταῖσμα duo MSS.
[2] κατὰ μικρὸν] κἂν μικρὸν editi antiqi.
[3] ὑπερκοσμίας editi antiqi.

---

[1] Cf. Rom. 8. 2: ὁ γὰρ νόμος τοῦ πνεύματος τῆς ζωῆς ἐν
Χριστῷ Ἰησοῦ ἠλευθέρωσέ με ἀπὸ τοῦ νόμου τῆς ἁμαρτίας καὶ τοῦ
θανάτου. "For the law of the spirit of life, in Christ Jesus,
hath delivered me from the law of sin and death."
[2] John 6. 64.

we offer the confession of our faith in accordance with our baptism, and in accordance with our faith we also recite the doxology, glorifying the Holy Spirit along with the Father and the Son, because we are convinced that He is not foreign to the divine nature. For that which had been alienated by its nature could not have shared in the same honours. And we pity those who call the Spirit a creature, because they fall into the unpardonable error of blasphemy against Him by the use of such language. For the fact that any creature is distinct and separate from the Godhead needs no argument for those who are even a little versed in the Scriptures. For the creature is a slave, but the Spirit sets free;[1] the creature is in need of life, and " it is the Spirit that quickeneth ";[2] the creature needs teaching, and it is the Spirit that teaches;[3] the creature is sanctified, and it is the Spirit that sanctifies.[4] And if you name angels, and archangels, and all the heavenly powers, it is through the Holy Spirit that they receive their holiness. But the Spirit of Himself has natural sanctity, not receiving it by grace, but by being joined substantially to Him; whence also He has received the distinctive title of " holy." And He therefore is holy by nature, as the Father

---

[3] Cf. John 14. 26 : ὁ δὲ Παράκλητος, τὸ Πνεῦμα τὸ Ἅγιον, ὃ πέμψει ὁ Πατὴρ ἐν τῷ ὀνόματί μου, ἐκεῖνος ὑμᾶς διδάξει πάντα, καὶ ὑπομνήσει ὑμᾶς πάντα ἃ εἶπον ὑμῖν. " But the Paraclete, the Holy Ghost, whom the Father will send in My name, he will teach you all things, and bring all things to your mind, whatsoever I shall have said to you."

[4] Cf. Rom. 15. 16 : ἵνα γένηται ἡ προσφορὰ τῶν ἐθνῶν εὐπρόσδεκτος, ἡγιασμένη ἐν Πνεύματι Ἁγίῳ, " that the oblation of the Gentiles may be made acceptable and sanctified in the Holy Ghost."

397

ὁ Πατήρ, καὶ φύσει ἅγιος ὁ Υἱός, οὔτε αὐτοὶ τῆς θείας καὶ μακαρίας Τριάδος χωρίσαι καὶ διατεμεῖν ἀνεχόμεθα, οὔτε τοὺς εὐκόλως τῇ κτίσει συναριθμοῦντας ἀποδεχόμεθα.

Ταῦτα, ὥσπερ ἐν κεφαλαίῳ, ἀρκούντως τῇ εὐλαβείᾳ ὑμῶν εἰρήσθω. ἀπὸ γὰρ μικρῶν σπερμάτων γεωργήσετε τὸ πλεῖον τῆς εὐσεβείας, συνεργοῦντος ὑμῖν [1] τοῦ ἁγίου Πνεύματος. δίδου γὰρ σοφῷ ἀφορμήν, καὶ σοφώτερος ἔσται. τὴν δὲ τελειοτέραν διδασκαλίαν εἰς τὴν κατ' ὀφθαλμοὺς συντυχίαν ὑπερθησόμεθα, δι' ἧς καὶ τὰ ἀντικείμενα ἐπιλύσασθαι, καὶ πλατυτέρας τὰς ἐκ τῶν Γραφῶν παρασχέσθαι μαρτυρίας, καὶ πάντα τύπον τὸν ὑγιῆ τῆς πίστεως βεβαιώσασθαι δυνατόν. τὸ δὲ νῦν ἔχον συγγνώμην νείματε τῇ βραχύτητι. καὶ γὰρ οὐδ' ἂν ἐπέστειλα τὴν ἀρχήν, εἰ μὴ μείζονα ἡγούμην τὴν βλάβην ἀρνήσασθαι τὴν αἴτησιν παντελῶς, ἢ ἐλλιπῶς παρασχέσθαι.

CLX

Διοδώρῳ

Ἀφίκετο ἡμῖν γράμματα τὴν ἐπιγραφὴν ἔχοντα Διοδώρου, τὰ δὲ ἐφεξῆς ἄλλου τινὸς πρέπονται εἶναι μᾶλλον ἢ Διοδώρου. δοκεῖ γάρ μοί τις τῶν τεχνικῶν,[2] τὸ σὸν πρόσωπον ὑποδύς, οὕτως ἑαυτὸν ἀξιόπιστον ἐθελῆσαι ποιῆσαι τοῖς ἀκροωμένοις. ὅς γε, ἐρωτηθεὶς ὑπό τινος, εἰ θεμιτὸν

---

[1] ἡμῖν Harl.

[2] τις τῶν τεχνικῶν] τάχα τις τῶν βαναύσων τεχνιτῶν Harl.

is holy by nature, and the Son is holy by nature; and neither do we, for ourselves, tolerate the separation and severance of any member from the divine and blessed Trinity, nor do we receive those who are ready to reckon any member as a part of creation.

Let these statements, as a summary, be sufficient for your Piety. For from small seeds you will produce by cultivation the greater part of piety, the Holy Spirit co-operating in you. For "give an occasion to a wise man, and wisdom shall be added to him."[1] But we shall postpone a fuller explanation until we shall have a meeting face to face, which will enable us to resolve objections, and to furnish fuller testimony from the Scriptures, and to confirm every sound article of faith. But for the present grant pardon to my brevity. For I should not have written in the beginning, had I not thought it a greater harm to refuse the request altogether than to comply with it imperfectly.

LETTER CLX

To Diodorus [2]

A letter has come to us bearing the superscription of Diodorus, but all that follows is more appropriately to be ascribed to anyone rather than to Diodorus. For it seems to me that some cunning fellow, having put on the mask of your personality, wished in this way to make himself seem trustworthy to his hearers. This person, when asked by someone whether it was

[1] Prov. 9. 9.

[2] Written in 373 or 374, on marriage with a deceased wife's sister. Cf. Letter CXXXV and note.

αὐτῷ[1] πρὸς γάμον ἀγαγέσθαι τῆς γυναικὸς τελευτησάσης τὴν ἀδελφήν, οὐκ ἔφριξε τὴν ἐρώτησιν,
ἀλλὰ καὶ πράως ἤνεγκε τὴν ἀκοήν, καὶ τὸ ἀσελγὲς
ἐπιθύμημα πάνυ γενναίως[2] καὶ ἀγωνιστικῶς
συγκατέπραξεν. εἰ μὲν οὖν παρῆν μοι τὸ γράμμα,
αὐτὸ ἂν ἀπέστειλα καὶ ἐξήρκεις[3] σαυτῷ τε
ἀμῦναι καὶ τῇ ἀληθείᾳ. ἐπεὶ δὲ ὁ δείξας πάλιν
ἀφείλετο καὶ ὥσπερ τι τρόπαιον καθ᾽ ἡμῶν
περιέφερε, κεκωλυκότων τὸ ἐξ ἀρχῆς, ἔγγραφον
ἔχειν λέγων τὴν ἐξουσίαν, ἐπέστειλα νῦν σοι,
ὥστε διπλῇ τῇ χειρὶ ἡμᾶς ἐλθεῖν ἐπὶ τὸν νόθον
ἐκεῖνον λόγον καὶ μηδεμίαν αὐτῷ ἰσχὺν κατα-
λιπεῖν, ἵνα μὴ ἔχῃ βλάπτειν ῥᾳδίως τοὺς ἐντυγ-
χάνοντας.

Πρῶτον μὲν οὖν, ὃ μέγιστον ἐπὶ τῶν τοιούτων
ἐστί, τὸ παρ᾽ ἡμῖν ἔθος, ὃ ἔχομεν προβάλλειν,
νόμου δύναμιν ἔχον, διὰ τὸ ὑφ᾽ ἁγίων ἀνδρῶν τοὺς
θεσμοὺς ἡμῖν παραδοθῆναι. τοῦτο δὲ τοιοῦτόν
ἐστιν· ἐάν τις πάθει ἀκαθαρσίας ποτὲ κρατηθεὶς
ἐκπέσῃ πρὸς δυεῖν ἀδελφῶν ἄθεσμον κοινωνίαν,
μήτε γάμον ἡγεῖσθαι τοῦτον,[4] μηθ᾽ ὅλως εἰς
ἐκκλησίας πλήρωμα παραδέχεσθαι πρότερον ἢ
διαλῦσαι αὐτοὺς ἀπ᾽ ἀλλήλων. ὥστε, εἰ καὶ
μηδὲν ἕτερον εἰπεῖν ἦν, ἐξήρκει τὸ ἔθος πρὸς τὴν
τοῦ καλοῦ[5] φυλακήν. ἐπειδὴ δὲ ὁ τὴν ἐπιστολὴν
γράψας ἐπιχειρήματι κιβδήλῳ κακὸν τοσοῦτον
ἐπειράθη τῷ βίῳ ἐπαγαγεῖν, ἀνάγκη μηδὲ ἡμᾶς
τῆς ἐκ τῶν λογισμῶν βοηθείας ὑφέσθαι· καίτοι γε

---

[1] αὐτόν editi antiqi.   [2] αὐτῷ add. editi antiqi.
[3] ἐξήρκει editi antiqi.   [4] τοῦτο editi antiqi.
[5] κακοῦ E.

lawful for him to take in marriage the sister of his deceased wife, did not shudder in horror at the question, but, on the contrary, he even listened to it calmly, and quite gallantly and boldly gave his support to the licentious desire! Now, if the letter were actually at hand, I should have forwarded it to you, and you would be quite competent to defend both yourself and the truth. But since the person who showed me the letter took it away with him again and carried it about as a sort of trophy won from us who had forbidden this practice from the beginning, saying that he had a written permission, I am now writing to you that we may attack that spurious document with our combined strength and that we may leave it no validity, lest it should be the means of harming, as it easily might, those who chance to read it.

In the first place, then—a consideration that is very important in such matters—there is the custom observed among us, which we can cite in defence of our position, a custom having the force of a law, because our ordinances have been handed down to us by holy men. And this custom is as follows: If any man, overcome by a passion of impurity, shall fall into unlawful intercourse with two sisters, we do not consider this a marriage, nor do we receive them into the membership of the Church at all until they separate from one another. Therefore, even if nothing further were to be said, the custom is sufficient to safeguard what is right. But since the writer of the letter has attempted by his deceitful argumentation to introduce such an abomination into our lives, we on our part must not omit any argument that may be of assistance to us, although in

401

ἐπὶ τῶν σφόδρα ἐναργῶν μείζων ἐστὶ τοῦ λόγου ἡ παρ' ἑκάστου πρόληψις.

Γέγραπται,[1] φησίν, ἐν τῷ Λευιτικῷ· Γυναῖκα ἐπ' ἀδελφῇ αὐτῆς οὐ λήψῃ ἀντίζηλον, ἀποκαλύψαι τὴν ἀσχημοσύνην αὐτῆς ἐπ' αὐτῇ, ἔτι ζώσης αὐτῆς. δῆλον δὴ οὖν ἐκ τούτου εἶναί φησιν ὅτι συγχωρεῖται λαμβάνειν τελευτησάσης. πρὸς δὴ τοῦτο πρῶτον μὲν ἐκεῖνο ἐρῶ· ὅτι, ὅσα ὁ νόμος λέγει, τοῖς ἐν τῷ νόμῳ λαλεῖ· ἐπεὶ οὕτω γε καὶ περιτομῇ, καὶ Σαββάτῳ, καὶ ἀποχῇ βρωμάτων ὑποκεισόμεθα. οὐ γὰρ δή, ἐὰν μέν τι εὕρωμεν συντρέχον ἡμῶν ταῖς ἡδοναῖς, τῷ ζυγῷ τῆς δουλείας τοῦ νόμου ἑαυτοὺς ὑποθήσομεν, ἐὰν δέ τι φανῇ βαρὺ τῶν νομίμων, τότε πρὸς τὴν ἐν Χριστῷ ἐλευθερίαν ἀποδραμούμεθα. ἠρωτήθημεν εἰ γέγραπται λαμβάνειν γυναῖκα ἐπ' ἀδελφῇ. εἴπομεν, ὅπερ ἀσφαλὲς ἡμῖν καὶ ἀληθές, ὅτι οὐ γέγραπται. τὸ δ' ἐκ τῆς τοῦ ἀκολούθου ἐπιφορᾶς τὸ σιωπηθὲν συλλογίζεσθαι νομοθετοῦντός ἐστιν, οὐ τὰ τοῦ νόμου λέγοντος· ἐπεὶ οὕτω γε ἐξέσται τῷ βουλομένῳ κατατολμῆσαι καὶ ἔτι ζώσης τῆς γυναικὸς λαμβάνειν τὴν ἀδελφήν. τὸ γὰρ αὐτὸ τοῦτο σόφισμα καὶ ἐπ' ἐκείνου ἁρμόζει. γέγραπται γάρ, φησίν· οὐ λήψῃ ἀντίζηλον, ὡς[2] τήν γε ἔξω τοῦ ζήλου λαβεῖν οὐκ ἐκώλυσεν. ὁ δὴ συνηγορῶν τῷ πάθει ἀζηλότυπον εἶναι διοριεῖται τὸ

---

[1] γάρ add. E.   [2] ὥστε E.

---

[1] Lev. 18. 18.
[2] i.e. the Levitical law does not apply to Christians; if it did, they would have to practise circumcision, etc.

matters which are perfectly obvious the instinctive sentiment of the individual is of greater weight than formal reasoning.

It is written, he says, in Leviticus:[1] "Thou shalt not take thy wife's sister for a harlot, to rival her, neither shalt thou discover her nakedness while the wife is yet living." He therefore insists that it is evident from this passage that it is lawful to take her when the wife is deceased. In reply I have this to say in the first place: that whatever the law says, it says to those who are within the law;[2] since, if the law is interpreted in this way, we shall be subject to circumcision also, to the observance of the Sabbath, and to abstinence from meats. For surely it cannot be that, if we find anything in the law which fits in with our pleasures, we can subject ourselves to the yoke of servility to the law, but if any of the provisions of the law appears harsh, we can have recourse to the freedom which is in Christ! We were asked whether it is written that a man may take a woman as a wife after her sister. We said what in our opinion is incontestable and true—that it is not so written. But to reason out by the application of logical inference a point which has been passed over in silence in the law is a matter for the lawgiver and not for him who recites the provisions of the law; for in the latter event it will be possible for anyone who so wishes to presume to take the sister even while the wife is still living. For he applies this same sophism in the following argument also. For it is written, he says, "Thou shalt not take thy wife's sister for a harlot to rival her," so that the law did not prohibit taking the woman who is outside of rivalry. So the man who pleads for his passion will take the position

403

ἦθος τῶν ἀδελφῶν. ἀνηρημένης οὖν τῆς αἰτίας, δι᾽ ἣν ἀπηγόρευσε τὴν ἀμφοτέρων συνοίκησιν, τί τὸ κωλῦον ἔσται [1] λαμβάνειν τὰς ἀδελφάς; ἀλλ᾽ οὐ γέγραπται ταῦτα, φήσομεν. ἀλλ᾽ οὐδὲ ἐκεῖνα ὥρισται. ἡ δὲ ἔννοια τοῦ ἀκολούθου ὁμοίως ἀμφοτέραις [2] τὴν ἄδειαν δίδωσιν. ἔδει δέ, καὶ μικρὸν ἐπὶ τὰ κατόπιν τῆς νομοθεσίας ἐπαναδραμόντα, ἀπηλλάχθαι πραγμάτων.

Ἔοικε γὰρ οὐ πᾶν εἶδος ἁμαρτημάτων περιλαμβάνειν ὁ νομοθέτης, ἀλλ᾽ ἰδίως ἀπαγορεύειν τὰ τῶν Αἰγυπτίων, ὅθεν ἀπῆρεν ὁ Ἰσραήλ, καὶ τὰ τῶν Χαναναίων, πρὸς οὓς μεθίσταται. ἔχει γὰρ οὕτως ἡ λέξις. κατὰ τὰ ἐπιτηδεύματα γῆς Αἰγύπτου, ἐν ᾗ παρῳκήσατε ἐπ᾽ αὐτῆς, οὐ ποιήσετε· καὶ κατὰ τὰ ἐπιτηδεύματα γῆς Χαναάν, εἰς ἣν ἐγὼ εἰσάξω ὑμᾶς ἐκεῖ, οὐ ποιήσετε, καὶ ἐν τοῖς νομίμοις αὐτῶν οὐ πορεύσεσθε. ὥστε τοῦτο εἰκός [3] που τὸ εἶδος τῆς ἁμαρτίας μὴ ἐμπολιτεύεσθαι τότε παρὰ τοῖς ἔθνεσι· διὸ μηδὲ τῆς ἐπ᾽ αὐτῷ φυλακῆς προσδεηθῆναι τὸν νομοθέτην, ἀλλ᾽ ἀρκεσθῆναι τῷ ἀδιδάκτῳ ἔθει πρὸς τὴν τοῦ μύσους διαβολήν. πῶς οὖν, τὸ μεῖζον ἀπαγορεύσας, τὸ ἔλαττον ἐσιώπησεν; ὅτι ἐδόκει πολλοὺς [4] τῶν φιλοσάρκων, πρὸς τὸ ἔτι ζώσαις ἀδελφαῖς συνοικεῖν, τὸ ὑπόδειγμα βλάπτειν τοῦ πατριάρχου.

Ἡμᾶς δὲ τί χρὴ ποιεῖν; τὰ γεγραμμένα λέγειν, ἢ τὰ σιωπηθέντα προσεξεργάζεσθαι; αὐτίκα τὸ

---

[1] ἐστί editi antiqi.   [2] ἀμφοτέροις editi antiqi.
[3] εἰκός] εἰ καί editi antiqi.   [4] πολλοῖς editi antiqi.

---

[1] Lev. 18. 3.   [2] Probably Jacob; cf. Gen. 29 ff.

that the disposition of sisters precludes jealousy between them. Therefore, he will argue, if the cause is removed which led the law to forbid co-habitation with two women, what will there be to prohibit a man's taking the sisters? But we shall say, this is not what is written. But the former matter likewise is not defined. The logical inference, however, gives the permission to both sisters alike. But what we ought to do in order to get rid of the difficulty is to go back a little to the state of affairs preceding the promulgation of the law.

For the lawgiver does not seem to be covering all sorts of sin, but to be forbidding particularly the sins of the Egyptians, from whom Israel had gone forth, and those of the Canaanites, to whom Israel was migrating. The words read as follows: "You shall not do according to the custom of the land of Egypt, in which you dwelt: neither shall you act according to the manner of the country of Canaan, into which I will bring you, nor shall you walk in their ordinances." [1] Therefore it is likely that the form of sin here referred to was not at that time being practised among the Gentiles; and that, for this reason, it was not incumbent upon the lawgiver to provide against it, but that he was satisfied with the custom, which came from no instruction, for discrediting the abomination. How was it, then, that while forbidding the greater, he kept silent about the less? It was be-cause the example of the patriarch [2] seemed to harm many of those who were given over to the flesh, inducing them to cohabit with sisters still living.

But as for us, what ought we to do? To say what is written or to work out for ourselves such questions as are passed over in silence? For instance, it is not

μὴ δεῖν μιᾷ ἑταίρᾳ κεχρῆσθαι πατέρα καὶ υἱὸν ἐν
μὲν τοῖς νόμοις τούτοις οὐ γέγραπται, παρὰ δὲ τῷ
προφήτῃ μεγίστης κατηγορίας ἠξίωται. Υἱὸς
γάρ, φησί, καὶ πατὴρ πρὸς τὴν αὐτὴν παιδίσκην
εἰσεπορεύοντο. πόσα δὲ εἴδη ἄλλα τῶν ἀκα-
θάρτων παθῶν τὸ μὲν τῶν δαιμόνων διδασκαλεῖον
ἐξεῦρεν, ἡ δὲ θεία Γραφὴ ἀπεσιώπησε, τὸ σεμνὸν
ἑαυτῆς ταῖς τῶν αἰσχρῶν ὀνομασίαις καταρρυ-
παίνειν οὐχ αἱρουμένη, ἀλλὰ γενικοῖς ὀνόμασι τὰς
ἀκαθαρσίας διέβαλεν! ὡς καὶ ἀπόστολος Παῦλός
φησι· Πορνεία δὲ καὶ ἀκαθαρσία πᾶσα μηδὲ
ὀνομαζέσθω ἐν ὑμῖν, καθὼς πρέπει ἁγίοις, τῷ τῆς
ἀκαθαρσίας ὀνόματι τάς τε τῶν ἀρρένων ἀρρητο-
ποιίας καὶ τὰς τῶν θηλειῶν περιλαμβάνων. ὥστε
οὐ πάντως ἡ σιωπὴ ἄδειαν φέρει τοῖς φιληδόνοις.

Ἐγὼ δὲ οὐδὲ σεσιωπῆσθαι τὸ μέρος τοῦτό
φημι, ἀλλὰ καὶ πάνυ σφοδρῶς ἀπηγορευκέναι τὸν
νομοθέτην. τὸ γάρ, Οὐκ εἰσελεύσῃ πρὸς πάντα
οἰκεῖον σαρκός σου, ἀποκαλύψαι ἀσχημοσύνην
αὐτῶν, ἐμπεριεκτικόν ἐστι καὶ τούτου τοῦ εἴδους
τῆς οἰκειότητος. τί γὰρ ἂν γένοιτο οἰκειότερον
ἀνδρὶ τῆς ἑαυτοῦ γυναικός, μᾶλλον δὲ τῆς ἑαυτοῦ
σαρκός; οὐ γὰρ ἔτι εἰσὶ δύο, ἀλλὰ σὰρξ μία.
ὥστε διὰ τῆς γυναικὸς ἡ ἀδελφὴ πρὸς τὴν τοῦ
ἀνδρὸς οἰκειότητα μεταβαίνει. ὡς γὰρ μητέρα
γυναικὸς οὐ λήψεται, οὐδὲ θυγατέρα τῆς γυναικός,
διότι μηδὲ τὴν ἑαυτοῦ μητέρα, μηδὲ τὴν ἑαυτοῦ
θυγατέρα, οὕτως οὐδ' ἀδελφὴν γυναικός, διότι

---

[1] Amos 2. 7.
[2] Eph. 5. 3. Basil omits, after ἀκαθαρσία, ἢ πλεονεξία, "or
covetousness."
[3] Lev. 18. 6.

written, in these laws, that father and son may not
live with the same concubine, but in the prophet[1]
such a case is thought worthy of explicit mention.
"For the son and his father," he says, "have gone
to the same young woman." And how many other
forms of impure passions has the instruction of the
demons discovered, though the divine Scripture has
passed them over in silence, not choosing to sully its
dignity with the naming of shameful things, but,
instead, has censured impurities in general terms!
As the Apostle Paul[2] says : "But fornication and all
uncleanness, let it not so much as be named among
you, as becometh saints," thus comprehending under
the term "uncleanness" all abominable actions of
both males and females. Therefore silence does not
at all give licence to lovers of pleasure.

I assert, however, that this class of actions has not
been passed over in silence, but that the lawgiver
has forbidden them in very strong terms. That
passage:[3] "No man shall approach to her that is
near of kin to him, to uncover her nakedness," also
includes this form of relationship. For what could
be more closely related to a man than his wife, or
rather than his own flesh? For "they are not two,
but one flesh."[4] Therefore, through the wife the
sister passes into relationship with the husband. For
just as he will not take to himself his wife's mother,
nor his wife's daughter, because he does not take his
own mother nor his own daughter, so he will not
take his wife's sister, because he does not take his

[4] Cf. Matt. 19. 5 and 6: καὶ προσκολληθήσεται τῇ γυναικὶ
αὐτοῦ, καὶ ἔσονται οἱ δύο εἰς σάρκα μίαν· ὥστε οὐκέτι εἰσὶ δύο,
ἀλλὰ σάρξ μία. "And shall cleave to his wife, and they two
shall be in one flesh. Therefore now they are not two, but
one flesh."

μηδὲ ἀδελφὴν ἑαυτοῦ. καὶ τὸ ἀνάπαλιν, οὐδὲ τῇ
γυναικὶ ἐξέσται τοῖς οἰκείοις τοῦ ἀνδρὸς συνοικεῖν.
κοινὰ γὰρ ἐπ’ ἀμφοτέρων τῆς συγγενείας τὰ
δίκαια. ἐγὼ δὲ παντὶ τῷ περὶ γάμου βου-
λευομένῳ διαμαρτύρομαι, ὅτι παράγει τὸ σχῆμα
τοῦ κόσμου τούτου, καὶ ὁ καιρὸς συνεσταλμένος
ἐστίν, Ἵνα καὶ οἱ ἔχοντες γυναῖκας ὡς μὴ ἔχοντες
ὦσιν. ἐὰν δέ μοι παραναγινώσκῃ τὸ Αὐξάνεσθε
καὶ πληθύνεσθε, καταγελῶ τοῦ τῶν νομοθεσιῶν
τοὺς καιροὺς μὴ διακρίνοντος. πορνείας παραμυθία ὁ δεύτερος γάμος, οὐκ ἐφόδιον εἰς ἀσέλγειαν.
εἰ οὐκ ἐγκαρτερεύονται, γαμησάτωσαν, φησίν,
οὐχὶ δὲ [1] καὶ γαμοῦντες παρανομείτωσαν.

Οἱ δὲ οὐδὲ πρὸς τὴν φύσιν ἀποβλέπουσιν οἱ
τὴν ψυχὴν λημῶντες τῷ πάθει τῆς ἀτιμίας, πάλαι
διακρίνασαν τὰς τοῦ γένους προσηγορίας. ἐκ
ποίας γὰρ συγγενείας τοὺς γεννηθέντας προσαγο-
ρεύσουσιν ; [2] ἀδελφοὺς αὐτοὺς ἀλλήλων ἢ ἀνεψιοὺς
προσεροῦσιν ; ἀμφότερα γὰρ αὐτοῖς προσαρμόσει
διὰ τὴν σύγχυσιν. μὴ ποιήσῃς, ὦ ἄνθρωπε, τὴν
θείαν μητρυιὰν τῶν νηπίων· μηδὲ τὴν ἐν μητρὸς
τάξει θάλπειν ὀφείλουσαν, ταύτην ἐφοπλίσῃς ταῖς
ἀμειλίκτοις ζηλοτυπίαις. μόνον γὰρ τὸ γένος [3]
τῶν μητρυιῶν καὶ μετὰ θάνατον ἐλαύνει τὴν
ἔχθραν. μᾶλλον δὲ οἱ μὲν ἄλλως πολέμιοι τοῖς

δέ om. E.   [2] προσαγορεύουσιν E.

[3] μῖσος editi antiqi.

_____

[1] 1 Cor, 7, 31.

own sister. And, conversely, it will not be permitted
to the wife to cohabit with the relatives of her
husband. For the laws governing relationship are of
common application to both. But I earnestly declare
to everyone who is concerning himself about marriage, that "the fashion of this world passeth away" [1]
and that "the time is short"; and "that they also
who have wives, be as if they had none." [2] And if
he reads this passage to me: [3] "Increase and
multiply," I laugh at him, because he does not
distinguish the times of the promulgations of the
law. Second marriage is a relief from fornication,
not a means to lasciviousness. "But if they do not
contain themselves, let them marry," [4] he says, but
not "even though they are married let them break
the law."

But those whose souls are blinded by their infamous passion do not look even at nature, which
long ago distinguished the several titles of kinship.
Under what heading of relationship will those who
marry sisters name their sons? Will they call them
brothers or cousins of one another? For both names
will be appropriate to them on account of the confusion. Do not, sir, make the aunt the stepmother of
your little ones; do not arm with implacable jealousy
her who ought to cherish them in the place of their
mother. For it is the race of stepmothers alone
which carries its hatred even after death; or rather,
those who are in any other manner hostile to the

---

[2] Cf. 1 Cor. 7. 29 : τοῦτο δέ φημι, ἀδελφοί, ὁ καιρὸς συνεσταλ-
μένος· τὸ λοιπόν ἐστιν ἵνα καὶ οἱ ἔχοντες γυναῖκας, ὡς μὴ ἔχοντες
ὦσι. "This therefore I say, brethren, the time is short; it
remaineth, that they also who have wives, be as if they had
none."

[3] Gen. 1. 28.   [4] 1 Cor. 7. 9.

τεθνηκόσι σπένδονται, αἱ δὲ μητρυιαὶ τοῦ μίσους
μετὰ τὸν θάνατον ἄρχονται.

Κεφάλαιον δὲ τῶν εἰρημένων, εἰ μὲν νόμῳ τις
ὁρμᾶται πρὸς τὸν γάμον, ἤνοικται πᾶσα ἡ οἰκου-
μένη· εἰ δὲ ἐμπαθὴς αὐτῷ ἡ σπουδή, διὰ τοῦτο
καὶ πλέον ἀποκλεισθήτω, ῞Ινα μάθῃ τὸ ἑαυτοῦ
σκεῦος κτᾶσθαι ἐν ἁγιασμῷ καὶ τιμῇ, μὴ ἐν πάθει
ἐπιθυμίας. πλείονά με[1] λέγειν ὡρμημένον τὸ
μέτρον ἐπέχει[2] τῆς ἐπιστολῆς· εὔχομαι δὲ ἢ τὴν
παραίνεσιν ἡμῶν ἰσχυροτέραν τοῦ πάθους ἀποδειχθῆναι, ἢ μὴ ἐπιδημῆσαι τῇ ἡμετέρᾳ τὸ ἄγος
τοῦτο, ἀλλ᾽ ἐν οἷς ἂν ἐτολμήθη τόποις ἐναπο-
μεῖναι.

CLXI

᾿Αμφιλοχίῳ, χειροτονηθέντι ἐπισκόπῳ

Εὐλογητὸς ὁ Θεός, ὁ τοὺς καθ᾽ ἑκάστην γενεὰν
εὐαρεστοῦντας αὐτῷ ἐκλεγόμενος, καὶ γνωρίζων
τὰ σκεύη τῆς ἐκλογῆς, καὶ κεχρημένος αὐτοῖς
πρὸς τὴν λειτουργίαν τῶν ἁγίων· ὁ καὶ νῦν σε
φεύγοντα, ὡς αὐτὸς φής, οὐχ ἡμᾶς, ἀλλὰ τὴν
δι᾽ ἡμῶν προσδοκωμένην κλῆσιν, τοῖς ἀφύκτοις
δικτύοις τῆς χάριτος σαγηνεύσας, καὶ ἀγαγὼν
εἰς τὰ μέσα τῆς Πισιδίας, ὥστε ἀνθρώπους

[1] μοι E.   [2] ἐπέσχε editi antiqi.

[1] Cf. Herodotus 4, 154, and Euripides, *Alcestis* 309, where
stepmothers are said to be as dangerous to their predecessor's
children as vipers. In antiquity the unkindness of stepmothers was proverbial.

dead make their peace with them, but stepmothers begin their hatred after death.[1]

The summing up of what has been said is this: If anyone is bent upon lawful marriage, the whole world is opened to him; but if his haste is due to passion, let him be restrained all the more, "that every one of you should know how to possess his vessel in sanctification and honour, not in the passion of lust."[2] The limits of the letter forbid me, though eager, from speaking further. But I pray that either our exhortation may be proved stronger than passion, or that this abomination may not visit our district, but that it may be confined to the places where it has been ventured!

LETTER CLXI

To Amphilochius, on his Consecration as Bishop [3]

Blessed is God, who selects those in each generation who are pleasing to Him and makes known the vessels of His election,[4] and uses them for the ministry of the saints; He who even now has ensnared you with the inescapable nets of His grace, when, as you yourself admit, you are trying to escape, not us, but the expected call through us, and who has brought you into the midst of Pisidia, so that

[2] 1 Thess. 4. 4 and 5.

[3] Written in 374. Cf. Loofs, 46, note 5. For Amphilochius, cf. Letter CL and note.

[4] Cf. Acts 9. 15: εἶπε δὲ πρὸς αὐτὸν ὁ Κύριος, Πορεύου, ὅτι σκεῦος ἐκλογῆς μοί ἐστιν οὗτος, etc. "And the Lord said to him: Go thy way: for this man is to me a vessel of election," etc.

ζωγρεῖν τῷ Κυρίῳ καὶ ἕλκειν ἀπὸ τοῦ βυθοῦ
εἰς τὸ φῶς τοὺς ἐζωγρημένους ὑπὸ τοῦ διαβόλου
εἰς τὸ ἐκείνου θέλημα. λέγε οὖν καὶ σὺ τὰ τοῦ[1]
μακαρίου Δαβίδ· Ποῦ πορευθῶ ἀπὸ τοῦ πνεύματός σου; καὶ ἀπὸ τοῦ προσώπου σου, ποῦ
φύγω; τοιαῦτα γὰρ θαυματουργεῖ ὁ φιλάνθρωπος ἡμῶν Δεσπότης. ὄνοι[2] ἀπόλλυνται, ἵνα
βασιλεὺς Ἰσραὴλ γένηται. ἀλλ᾽ ἐκεῖνος μὲν
Ἰσραηλίτης ὢν τῷ Ἰσραὴλ ἐδόθη· σὲ δὲ ἡ
θρεψαμένη καὶ πρὸς τοσοῦτον ἀναβιβάσασα τῆς
ἀρετῆς ὕψος οὐκ ἔχει, ἀλλὰ τὴν γείτονα ὁρᾷ τῷ
ἰδίῳ κόσμῳ σεμνυνομένην. ἐπειδὴ δὲ εἷς λαὸς
πάντες οἱ εἰς Χριστὸν ἠλπικότες καὶ μία Ἐκκλησία νῦν οἱ Χριστοῦ, κἂν ἐκ διαφόρων τόπων
προσαγορεύηται, χαίρει καὶ ἡ πατρὶς καὶ εὐφραί-
νεται ταῖς τοῦ Κυρίου οἰκονομίαις, καὶ οὐχ ἡγεῖται
ἕνα ἄνδρα ἐζημιῶσθαι, ἀλλὰ δι᾽ ἑνὸς ἐκκλησίας
ὅλας προσειληφέναι. μόνον παράσχοι ὁ Κύριος
καὶ παρόντας ὁρᾶν ἡμᾶς[3] καὶ ἀπόντας ἀκούειν
τὴν προκοπήν σου τὴν ἐν τῷ εὐαγγελίῳ καὶ τὴν
εὐταξίαν τῶν ἐκκλησιῶν.

Ἀνδρίζου τοίνυν καὶ ἴσχυε, καὶ προπορεύου
τοῦ λαοῦ, ὃν ἐπίστευσε τῇ δεξιᾷ σου ὁ Ὕψιστος.
καὶ ὡς νοήμων κυβέρνησιν ποιησάμενος, πάσης
ζάλης ἀπὸ τῶν αἱρετικῶν πνευμάτων ἐγειρομένης

---

[1] τοῦ om. E.   [2] ἐχθροί editi antiqi.
[3] ὑμᾶς editi antiqi.

---

[1] Psal. 138. 7.
[2] Cf. 1 Kings 9. 3: καὶ ἀπώλοντο αἱ ὄνοι Κεὶς πατρὸς Σαούλ·
καὶ εἶπεν Κεὶς πρὸς Σαοὺλ τὸν υἱὸν αὐτοῦ Λάβε μετὰ σεαυτοῦ ἓν
τῶν παιδαρίων, καὶ ἀνάστητε καὶ πορεύθητε καὶ ζητήσατε τὰς

you may take men captive for the Lord and bring those who had already been taken captive by the devil from the depths into the light according to His will. Therefore you also may speak the words of the blessed David: " Whither shall I go from the spirit? or whither shall I flee from thy face?"[1] For such wonders does our kind-hearted Master work. "Asses are lost"[2] in order that a king may be given to Israel. But that man, being an Israelite, was given to Israel; yet the country which nurtured you and brought you up to such a height of virtue does not possess you, but beholds her neighbour priding herself upon her own ornament. But since all who have placed their hopes in Christ are one people and the followers of Christ are now one Church, even though He is called upon from divers places, your fatherland both rejoices and is made happy by the dispensations of the Lord, and she does not believe that she has lost one man, but that through one man she has acquired whole churches. May the Lord only grant that we being present may see, and also being absent may hear of, your progress in the Gospel and of the good discipline of your churches.

Play the man, then, and be strong, and go before the people whom the Most High has entrusted to your right hand. And like a wise helmsman who has assumed the command of a ship, rise superior in your resolution to every blast that is stirred up by

ὄνους. " And the asses of Cis, Saul's father, were lost : And Cis said to his son Saul : Take one of the servants with thee, and arise, go, and seek the asses." Basil may mean that the predecessors of Amphilochius in the see of Iconium, *i.e.* Faustinus and John, were not very wise bishops. Cf. Letter CXXXVIII.

ὑψηλότερος γενόμενος τῇ γνώμῃ, ἀβάπτιστον
τοῖς ἁλμυροῖς καὶ πικροῖς τῆς κακοδοξίας κύμασι
διαφύλασσε [1] τὴν ὁλκάδα, ἀναμένων τὴν γαλήνην,
ἣν ποιήσει ὁ Κύριος, ἐπειδὰν εὑρεθῇ φωνὴ ἀξία
τοῦ διαναστῆσαι αὐτὸν πρὸς τὴν ἐπιτίμησιν τῶν
πνευμάτων καὶ τῆς θαλάσσης. εἰ δὲ βούλει
ἡμᾶς λοιπὸν ὑπὸ τῆς μακρᾶς ἀρρωστίας ἐπειγο-
μένους [2] πρὸς τὴν ἀναγκαίαν ἔξοδον ἐπισκέψασθαι,
μήτε καιρὸν ἀναμείνῃς, μήτε τὸ παρ' ἡμῶν
σύνθημα, εἰδὼς ὅτι πατρικοῖς σπλάγχνοις πᾶσα
εὐκαιρία ἐστὶ περιπτύσσεσθαι τέκνον ἀγαπητὸν
καὶ λόγου παντὸς κρείττων ἡ κατὰ ψυχὴν
διάθεσις.

Βάρος δὲ ὑπερβαῖνον τὴν δύναμιν μὴ ὀδύρου.
εἰ μὲν γὰρ αὐτὸς ἦς ὁ μέλλων φέρειν τὸ βάσταγμα
τοῦτο, οὐδὲ οὕτως ἂν ἦν βαρύ, ἀλλ' ἀφορητὸν
παντελῶς. εἰ δὲ Κύριος ὁ συνδιαφέρων, Ἐπίρριψον ἐπὶ Κύριον τὴν μέριμνάν σου, καὶ αὐτὸς
ποιήσει. μόνον ἐκεῖνο παραφυλάσσειν ἐν πᾶσι
παρακλήθητι, μὴ αὐτὸς τοῖς μοχθηροῖς ἔθεσι
συμπεριφέρεσθαι, ἀλλὰ τὰ κακῶς προειλημμένα
διὰ τῆς δεδομένης σοι παρὰ Θεοῦ σοφίας μετα-
τιθέναι πρὸς τὸ χρήσιμον. καὶ γὰρ ἀπέστειλέ
σε Χριστὸς οὐχ ἑτέροις κατακολουθεῖν, ἀλλ'
αὐτὸν [3] καθηγεῖσθαι τῶν σωζομένων. καὶ παρακαλοῦμεν προσεύχεσθαι ὑπὲρ ἡμῶν, ἵνα, ἐὰν μὲν
ἔτι ὦμεν ἐπὶ τῆς ζωῆς ταύτης, ἰδεῖν σε μετὰ τῆς
ἐκκλησίας καταξιωθῶμεν· ἐὰν δὲ ἀπελθεῖν λοιπὸν
προσταχθῶμεν, ἐκεῖ ὑμᾶς ἴδωμεν παρὰ τῷ Κυρίῳ,

---

[1] διαφύλαξαι editi antiqi.   [2] ἀπαγομένους E.
[3] αὐτῶν E.

LETTER CLXI

the winds of heresy, and preserve your ship unsubmerged by the briny and bitter waves of error, awaiting the calm which the Lord will cause as soon as a voice is found worthy of rousing Him to rebuke the winds and the sea. And if you wish to visit us soon, driven on as we are by our long sickness towards the inevitable departure, do not await a suitable occasion nor the summons from us, knowing that to a father's heart every occasion is good for the embracing of a well-beloved child and that his soul's affection is a better summons than any spoken word.

Do not lament that the weight is beyond your strength. For if it were you alone that were to bear this burden, it would not be merely heavy but utterly unendurable. But if it is the Lord who helps you bear it, "cast thy care upon the Lord," [1] and He himself shall do it. Only, I beg you, be on your guard on every occasion against this—against being yourself carried away by wicked customs, but, through the wisdom granted you by God, transforming the evil customs which have hitherto had sway into something good. For Christ sent you forth, not to follow others, but yourself to guide those who are on the way to salvation. And we urge you to pray for us, in order that, if we are still in this life, we may be thought worthy of beholding you and your church; but if we are ordered soon to go hence, may we behold all of you there with the Lord, your church

---

[1] Cf. Psal. 55. 23: ἐπίρριψον ἐπὶ Κύριον τὴν μέριμνάν σου, καὶ αὐτός σε διαθρέψει· οὐ δώσει εἰς τὸν αἰῶνα σάλον τῷ δικαίῳ. "Cast thy care upon the Lord, and he shall sustain thee: he shall not suffer the just to waver for ever." Also 1 Peter 5. 7: πᾶσαν τὴν μέριμναν ὑμῶν ἐπιρρίψαντες ἐπ' αὐτόν, ὅτι αὐτῷ μέλει περὶ ὑμῶν. "Casting all your care upon him, for he hath care of you."

τὴν μὲν ὡς ἄμπελον εὐθηνοῦσαν ἐπ᾽ ἀγαθοῖς
ἔργοις, σὲ δέ, ὡς σοφὸν γεωργὸν καὶ ἀγαθὸν
δοῦλον ἐν καιρῷ διδόντα τοῖς ὁμοδούλοις τὸ
σιτομέτριον, πιστοῦ καὶ φρονίμου οἰκονόμου τὸν
μισθὸν κομιζόμενον.

Οἱ σὺν ἡμῖν πάντες ἀσπάζονταί σου τὴν
εὐλάβειαν. ἐρρωμένος καὶ εὔθυμος ἐν Κυρίῳ
εἴης· εὐδοκιμῶν ἐπὶ χαρίσμασι Πνεύματος καὶ
σοφίας φυλαχθείης.

CLXII

Εὐσεβίῳ, ἐπισκόπῳ Σαμοσάτων

Ἔοικέ μοι τοῦτο καὶ ὄκνον ἐμποιεῖν πρὸς τὸ
γράφειν καὶ ἀναγκαῖον αὐτὸ πάλιν ὑποδεικνύναι.
ὅταν μὲν γὰρ πρὸς τὸ τῆς ἐπιδημίας τῆς ἐμαυτοῦ
ἀπίδω[1] χρέος καὶ τὸ τῆς συντυχίας ὑπολογίσω-
μαι ὄφελος, πάνυ μοι[2] τῶν ἐπιστολῶν ὑπερορᾶν
ἔπεισιν ὡς οὐδὲ σκιᾶς λόγον ἐκπληροῦν δυναμένων
πρὸς τὴν ἀλήθειαν· ὅταν δὲ πάλιν λογίσωμαι,
ὅτι μόνη παραμυθία ἐστὶ τῶν μεγίστων καὶ
πρώτων διαμαρτόντα προσειπεῖν ἄνδρα τοσοῦτον,
καὶ ἱκετεῦσαι συνήθως[3] ὥστε μὴ ἐπιλανθάνεσθαι
ἡμῶν ἐπὶ τῶν προσευχῶν, οὐ μικρόν τί μοι κρίνειν
τὸ τῶν ἐπιστολῶν ἔπεισι. τὴν μὲν οὖν ἐλπίδα
τῆς παρουσίας οὔτε αὐτὸς ῥίψαι τῆς ψυχῆς
βούλομαι, οὔτε τὴν σὴν θεοσέβειαν ἀπογνῶναι.
αἰσχύνομαι γὰρ εἰ μὴ ταῖς σαῖς εὐχαῖς τοσοῦτον

---

[1] ἐπίδω editi antiqi. [2] με editi antiqi.
[3] τὰ συνήθη editi antiqi.

flourishing like a vine in good works, and you yourself, like a wise husbandman and a good servant who gives meat in due season to your fellow-servants, procuring the reward of a faithful and wise overseer.

All those who are with us send greetings to your Piety. May you be strong and cheerful in the Lord and enjoying good repute for the blessings of the Spirit and of wisdom, may you be preserved.

LETTER CLXII

To Eusebius, Bishop of Samosata [1]

THE following consideration, it seems to me, both induces hesitation as to writing and again indicates that writing is necessary. Whenever, that is, I contemplate my obligation to remain at home and then consider the advantage of a personal meeting, I am inclined to despise letters utterly as being incapable of amounting to even a shadow's worth as regards the truth ; but when, on the other hand, I consider that the only consolation for one who is deprived of the greatest and the foremost men is to address so great a man, and regularly to beg him not to forget us in his prayers, I am inclined to judge correspondence by letter to be of no small importance. I do not wish, however, either to banish from my mind all hope of a visit, or to give up my acquaintance with your Holiness. For I am ashamed of not seeming to be encouraged by your

---

[1] Written after Easter of 374. Cf. Loofs, 46, note 5. Basil is still hopeful of being able to visit Eusebius.

φανείην θαρσῶν, ὡς καὶ νέος ἐκ γέροντος ἔσεσθαι, εἰ τούτου γένοιτο χρεία,[1] οὐχ ὅπως ἐρρωμενέστερος μικρὸν ἐξ ἀσθενοῦς καὶ ἐξιτήλου παντάπασιν, ὁποῖος δὴ νῦν εἰμί.

Τοῦ δὲ μὴ ἤδη παρεῖναι τὰ αἴτια λόγῳ μὲν εἰπεῖν οὐ ῥᾴδιον, οὐ μόνον ὑπὸ τῆς παρούσης ἀσθενείας ἐξειργομένῳ, ἀλλ' οὐδὲ σχόντι[2] ποτὲ τοσαύτην τοῦ λόγου δύναμιν, ὥστε παντοδαπὴν καὶ ποικίλην νόσον ἐναργῶς ἐξαγγεῖλαι. πλὴν ὅτι ἀπὸ τῆς ἡμέρας τοῦ Πάσχα μέχρι[3] νῦν πυρετοὶ καὶ διάρροιαι, καὶ σπλάγχνων ἐπανα-στάσεις, ὥσπερ κύματά με[4] ἐπιβαπτίζοντα ὑπερσχεῖν οὐκ ἐᾷ. τὰ δὲ παρόντα οἷα καὶ τίνα ἦν, εἴποι ἂν καὶ ὁ ἀδελφὸς Βάραχος,[5] εἰ καὶ μὴ τῆς ἀληθείας ἀξίως, ἀλλ' ὅσον μαρτυρῆσαι τῇ αἰτίᾳ τῆς ὑπερθέσεως. πάνυ δὲ πέπεισμαι, εἰ γνησίως ἡμῖν συνεύξαιο, πάνθ' ἡμῖν λυθήσεσθαι[6] ῥᾳδίως τὰ δυσχερῆ.

CLXIII

Ἰοβίνῳ κόμητι

Εἶδόν σου τὴν ψυχὴν ἐν τοῖς γράμμασι. καὶ γὰρ τῷ ὄντι οὐδεὶς γραφεὺς χαρακτῆρα σώματος οὕτως ἀκριβῶς ἐκλαβεῖν δύναται ὡς λόγος ἐξεικονίσαι τῆς ψυχῆς τὰ ἀπόρρητα. τότε γὰρ τὸ[7] τοῦ ἤθους εὐσταθές, καὶ τὸ τῆς τιμῆς

---

[1] τούτου γένοιτο χρεία] καὶ τοῦτο γένοιτο χρεῖος editi antiqi.
[2] οὐδὲ σχόντι] οὐδ' ἔχοντι E.   [3] τοῦ add. E.
[4] τε E.   [5] Βάρουχος editi antiqi.
[6] λυθήσεται editi antiqi.   [7] τό om. E.

LETTER CLXIII

prayers to such an extent as even to expect to become young instead of old, if there should be need of that—to say nothing of becoming a little bit stronger instead of the weak and altogether powerless creature that I now am.

The reason why I am not already present with you is not easy to explain in words, not only because I am hampered by my present infirmity, but also because I never gained a command of language sufficient to enable me to describe clearly my varied and complex sickness. But the truth is that, from the day of Easter until now, fevers, dysenteries, and rebellions of my bowels, drenching me like recurring waves, have not permitted me to emerge. As for my present condition, our brother Barachus can tell you what it is in detail, if not adequately to the truth, at least sufficiently to attest the reason for my delay. But I am entirely convinced that, if you should really join your prayers to ours, we should easily be freed from all our troubles.

LETTER CLXIII

To Count Jovinus[1]

I saw your soul in your letter. For truly no painter can grasp so accurately the characteristics of the body as words can portray the secrets of the soul. For when I read your letter, its words adequately delineated to us the soundness of your

[1] Written after Easter of 374. Cf. Loofs, 46, note 5. Jovinus, a count of the Empire, appears from this letter to have been on intimate terms with Basil. Nothing more is known of him.

COLLECTED LETTERS OF SAINT BASIL

ἀληθινόν,¹ καὶ τὸ τῆς γνώμης ἐν πᾶσιν ἀκέραιον ²
ἱκανῶς ἡμῖν ὁ ἐν τοῖς γράμμασι λόγος ἐχα-
ρακτήρισεν· ὅθεν καὶ μεγάλην ἡμῖν παραμυθίαν
τῆς ἀπολείψεώς σου παρέσχετο. μὴ τοίνυν
διαλίπῃς τῇ ἀεὶ παραπιπτούσῃ προφάσει χρώ-
μενος πρὸς τὸ ἐπιστέλλειν καὶ τὴν διὰ μακροῦ
ταύτην ὁμιλίαν χαρίζεσθαι· ἐπειδὴ τῆς κατ'
ὀφθαλμοὺς συντυχίας ³ ἀπόγνωσιν ἡμῖν λοιπὸν
ἡ ἀσθένεια τοῦ σώματος ἐμποιεῖ. ἣν ὁπόσῃ
ἐστὶν ἐρεῖ σοι ὁ θεοφιλέστατος ἐπίσκοπος Ἀμφι-
λόχιος, ὁ καὶ γνωρίσας τῷ ἐπὶ πλεῖον συγγε-
γενῆσθαι ἡμῖν καὶ δυνατὸς ὢν λόγῳ παραστῆσαι
τὰ θεαθέντα. γνωρίζεσθαι δὲ βούλομαι τὰ
ἐμαυτοῦ δυσχερῆ οὐκ ἄλλου τινὸς ἕνεκεν ἢ τῆς
πρὸς τὸ ἐφεξῆς συγγνώμης, ὡς μὴ ῥαθυμίας ἔχειν
κατάγνωσιν ἐὰν ἄρα ἐλλίπωμεν ⁴ τὴν ἐπίσκεψιν
ὑμῶν. καίτοιγε οὐκ ἀπολογίας μᾶλλον ἢ παραμυθίας δεῖ πρὸς τὴν ζημίαν ταύτην. εἰ γὰρ ἦν
μοι δυνατὸν συνεῖναί σου τῇ σεμνότητι, πολλῷ
ἂν ἐγὼ τῶν παρ' ἄλλοις σπουδαζομένων ταύτην
ἐμαυτῷ προτιμοτέραν ἐθέμην.

CLXIV

Ἀσχολίῳ, ἐπισκόπῳ Θεσσαλονίκης

Ὅσης ἡμᾶς εὐφροσύνης ἐνέπλησε τὰ γράμματα
τῆς ὁσιότητός σου ἡμεῖς μὲν οὐκ ἂν ῥᾳδίως

¹ ἀληθές editi antiqi.   ² καίριον E, editi antiqi.
³ ὁμιλίας editi antiqi.   ⁴ ἐλλείπωμεν E.

¹ The visit of Amphilochius in 374 was probably the first
of a series of frequent visits. Basil was his spiritual father.
Amphilochius preferred to make his visits to Basil in the
420

character, the genuineness of your worth, and the integrity of your mind in everything; and so it brought to us great consolation for your absence. Therefore do not leave off availing yourself of any excuse that arises from time to time for writing me and for conferring on me the boon of this too long interrupted conversation; for our bodily weakness causes us now to despair of a personal interview. How serious an illness it is will be explained to you by our most God-beloved bishop Amphilochius,[1] who possesses both the knowledge by reason of having been much with us, and the ability to set forth in speech whatever he has seen. And I wish my difficulties to be known for no other object than your pardon in the future, that we may not be condemned for indifference if we do fail to pay you the visit. And yet there is not so much need of a defence as of some consolation to me for my loss therein. For if it had been possible for me to be with your August Reverence, I should have considered this as worth far more to me than the objects for which others earnestly strive.

LETTER CLXIV

To Ascholius, Bishop of Thessalonica[2]

How great was the joy with which the letter of your Holiness filled us we cannot easily describe,

autumn, because the anniversary of Basil's hospital was celebrated at that time. This hospital had a special interest for him, because it was here that he and Heracleidas had passed a solemn crisis in their lives. Cf. Letter CL.

[2] Written in 374. For this Ascholius, cf. Letter CLIV. The following letter is also addressed to him.

ἐνδείξασθαι δυνηθείημεν, ἀσθενοῦντος τοῦ λόγου
πρὸς τὴν ἐνάργειαν·[1] αὐτὸς δὲ καὶ παρὰ σεαυτῷ [2]
εἰκάζειν ὀφείλεις, τεκμαιρόμενος τῷ κάλλει τῶν
ἐπεσταλμένων. τί γὰρ οὐκ εἶχε τὰ γράμματα;
οὐ τὴν πρὸς Κύριον ἀγάπην; οὐ τὸ περὶ τοὺς
μάρτυρας θαῦμα, οὕτως ἐναργῶς τὸν τρόπον
τῆς ἀθλήσεως ὑπογράφοντα, ὥστε ὑπ᾽ ὄψιν
ἡμῖν [3] ἀγαγεῖν τὰ πράγματα; οὐ τὴν περὶ
ἡμᾶς αὐτοὺς τιμήν τε καὶ διάθεσιν; οὐχ ὅ τι ἂν
εἴποι τις τῶν καλλίστων; ὥστε, ὅτε εἰς χεῖρας
τὴν ἐπιστολὴν ἐδεξάμεθα, καὶ ἀνέγνωμεν αὐτὴν
πολλάκις, καὶ τὴν βρύουσαν ἐν αὐτῇ χάριν τοῦ
Πνεύματος κατεμάθομεν, νομίσαι ἡμᾶς ἐπὶ τῶν
ἀρχαίων καιρῶν γεγενῆσθαι, ἡνίκα ἤνθουν αἱ
ἐκκλησίαι τοῦ Θεοῦ, ἐρριζωμέναι τῇ πίστει,
ἡνωμέναι τῇ ἀγάπῃ, ὥσπερ ἐν ἑνὶ σώματι μιᾶς
συμπνοίας διαφόρων μελῶν ὑπαρχούσης· ὅτε
φανεροὶ μὲν οἱ διώκοντες, φανεροὶ δὲ οἱ διωκόμενοι·
πολεμούμενοι δὲ οἱ λαοὶ πλείους ἐγίνοντο, καὶ τὸ
αἷμα τῶν μαρτύρων ἄρδον τὰς ἐκκλησίας πολυ-
πλασίονας τοὺς ἀγωνιστὰς τῆς εὐσεβείας ἐξέτρεφε,
τῷ ζήλῳ τῶν προλαβόντων ἐπαποδυομένων τῶν
ἐφεξῆς. τότε Χριστιανοὶ μὲν πρὸς ἀλλήλους
εἰρήνην ἤγομεν,[4] εἰρήνην ἐκείνην, ἣν ὁ Κύριος
ἡμῖν κατέλιπεν, ἧς νῦν οὐδ᾽ ἴχνος ἡμῖν λοιπὸν
ὑπολέλειπται, οὕτως αὐτὴν ἀπηνῶς ἀπ᾽ ἀλλήλων
ἀπεδιώξαμεν. πλὴν ἀλλ᾽ ὅτι αἱ ψυχαὶ ἡμῶν
πρὸς τὴν παλαιὰν ἐκείνην μακαριότητα ἐπανῆλθον,
ἐπειδὴ γράμματα μὲν ἦλθεν ἐκ τῆς [5] μακρόθεν,
ἀνθοῦντα τῷ τῆς ἀγάπης κάλλει, μάρτυς δὲ ἡμῖν

---

[1] ἐνέργειαν E.   [2] σεαυτοῦ Harl.

words being too weak to set it clearly forth, but
you ought to be able to guess it by yourself,
deducing it from the beauty of what you wrote.
For what did the letter not contain? Did it not
contain love for the Lord? And admiration for the
martyrs, describing so clearly the manner of their
struggle that you brought the incidents before our
eyes? And respect and love for ourselves? Did it
not contain whatever one might mention of the most
noble attributes? Consequently, when we took the
letter in our hands, and read it again and again,
and perceived the grace of the Spirit that abounded
therein, we thought that we were back in the olden
times, when the churches of God flourished, taking
root in the faith, united by charity, there being,
as in a single body, a single harmony of the various
members; when the persecutors indeed were in
the open, but in the open were also the persecuted;
when the laity, though harassed, became more
numerous, and the blood of the martyrs watering
the churches nurtured many times as many champions of religion, later generations stripping themselves for combat in emulation of their predecessors.
Then we Christians had peace among ourselves,
that peace which the Lord left to us, of which
now not even a trace any longer remains to us, so
ruthlessly have we driven it away from one another.
But the fact is that our souls had already returned
to that old-time happiness when a letter came
from far away, blossoming with the beauty of
charity, and a witness had arrived among us from

---

3 ἡμῶν editi antiqi.   4 εἴχομεν editi antiqi.
5 γῆς E, Harl., Med., Reg. primus, Vat., Bigot. alter.

ἐπεδήμησεν ἐκ τῶν ἐπέκεινα Ἴστρου βαρβάρων,
δι᾽ ἑαυτοῦ κηρύσσων τῆς ἐκεῖ πολιτευομένης
πίστεως τὴν ἀκρίβειαν. τίς ἂν τὴν ἐπὶ τούτοις
εὐφροσύνην τῶν ψυχῶν ἡμῶν διηγήσαιτο ;[1] τίς
ἂν ἐπινοηθείη δύναμις λόγου ἐναργῶς ἐξαγγεῖλαι
τὴν ἐν τῷ κρυπτῷ τῆς καρδίας ἡμῶν διάθεσιν
δυναμένη ; ὅτε μέντοι εἴδομεν τὸν ἀθλητήν,
ἐμακαρίσαμεν αὐτοῦ τὸν ἀλείπτην, ὃς παρὰ τῷ
δικαίῳ κριτῇ τὸν τῆς δικαιοσύνης στέφανον καὶ
αὐτὸς ἀπολήψεται, πολλοὺς εἰς τὸν ὑπὲρ τῆς
εὐσεβείας ἐπιρρώσας ἀγῶνα.

Ἐπεὶ δὲ καὶ τοῦ μακαρίου ἀνδρὸς Εὐτυχοῦς
εἰς μνήμην ἡμᾶς ἤγαγες, καὶ ἐσέμνυνας ἡμῶν τὴν
πατρίδα ὡς αὐτὴν παρασχομένην τῆς εὐσεβείας
τὰ σπέρματα, εὔφρανας μὲν ἡμᾶς τῇ ὑπομνήσει
τῶν παλαιῶν, ἐλύπησας δὲ τῷ ἐλέγχῳ τῶν
ὁρωμένων. οὐδεὶς γὰρ ἡμῶν Εὐτυχεῖ τὴν ἀρετὴν
παραπλήσιος, οἵ γε τοσοῦτον ἀπέχομεν βαρβά-
ρους ἐξημερῶσαι τῇ δυνάμει τοῦ Πνεύματος καὶ
τῇ ἐνεργείᾳ τῶν παρ᾽ αὐτοῦ χαρισμάτων, ὥστε
καὶ τοὺς ἡμέρως ἔχοντας τῇ ὑπερβολῇ τῶν
ἁμαρτιῶν ἡμῶν ἐξηγριῶσθαι. ἑαυτοῖς γὰρ λογι-
ζόμεθα καὶ ταῖς ἡμετέραις ἁμαρτίαις τὴν αἰτίαν
τοῦ ἐπὶ τοσοῦτον χυθῆναι τὴν τῶν αἱρετικῶν
δυναστείαν. σχεδὸν γὰρ οὐδὲν μέρος[2] τῆς οἰκουμένης διαπέφευγε τὸν ἐκ τῆς αἱρέσεως ἐμπρησμόν.

---

[1] διηγήσηται Ε.　　　　[2] ἔτι add. editi antiqi.

the barbarians beyond the Danube,[1] proclaiming in person the strictness of the faith which is practised in that region. Who could describe the joy our souls felt at this? What power of speech could be devised that would be capable of announcing in clear terms the emotion hidden in our hearts? When, however, we saw the athlete, we blessed his trainer,[2] who will likewise receive at the hands of the just Judge the crown of righteousness, since he has strengthened many for the struggle in defence of our religion.

But since you have recalled to our minds the blessed man Eutyches,[3] and have exalted our fatherland for having by itself furnished the seeds of our religion, you cheered us indeed by calling up the past, but distressed us by exposing the conditions which we see to-day. For no one of us is comparable to Eutyches in virtue, since we are so far from having tamed the barbarians by the power of the Spirit and by the operation of His graces, that we have even by the enormity of our sins made savage those who were gentle. For we must impute to ourselves and to our sins the blame that the domination of the heretics has become so widespread. For almost no part of the world has escaped the conflagration of

---

[1] Basil regularly calls the Danube by the name Ister; cf. Letter XL.

[2] Ascholius is here called the trainer of the martyr Sabas; cf. the title of Letter CLV.

[3] A Christian of Cappadocia who was taken prisoner by the Goths in 260, and with some of his fellow-captives became a martyr for the faith, but only after he had already sown the seeds of the gospel in the land of his captivity. Cf. Philost. *H.E.* 2, 5.

τὰ δὲ σὰ διηγήματα, ἐνστάσεις ἀθλητικαί,[1] σώματα ὑπὲρ τῆς εὐσεβείας καταξαινόμενα, θυμὸς
βαρβαρικὸς ὑπὸ τῶν ἀκαταπλήκτων[2] τὴν καρδίαν
καταφρονούμενος, αἱ ποικίλαι βάσανοι τῶν διωκόντων, αἱ διὰ πάντων ἐνστάσεις τῶν ἀγωνιζομένων,
τὸ ξύλον, τὸ ὕδωρ, τὰ τελειωτικὰ τῶν μαρτύρων.
τὰ δὲ ἡμέτερα οἷα; ἀπέψυκται[3] ἡ ἀγάπη· πορθεῖ-
ται ἡ τῶν πατέρων διδασκαλία· ναυάγια περὶ τὴν
πίστιν πυκνά· σιγᾷ τῶν εὐσεβούντων τὰ στό-
ματα· λαοὶ τῶν εὐκτηρίων οἴκων ἐξελαθέντες ἐν
τῷ ὑπαίθρῳ πρὸς τὸν ἐν οὐρανοῖς Δεσπότην τὰς
χεῖρας αἴρουσι. καὶ αἱ μὲν θλίψεις βαρεῖαι,
μαρτύριον δὲ οὐδαμοῦ, διὰ τὸ τοὺς κακοῦντας
ἡμᾶς τὴν αὐτὴν ἡμῖν ἔχειν προσηγορίαν. ὑπὲρ
τούτων αὐτός τε δεήθητι τοῦ Κυρίου, καὶ πάντας
τοὺς γενναίους ἀθλητὰς τοῦ Χριστοῦ εἰς τὴν
ὑπὲρ τῶν ἐκκλησιῶν[4] προσευχὴν συμπαράλαβε,
ἵνα εἴπερ ἔτι χρόνοι τινὲς ὑπολείπονται τῇ
συστάσει τοῦ κόσμου, καὶ μὴ πρὸς τὴν ἐναντίαν
φορὰν συνελαύνεται τὰ πάντα, διαλλαγεὶς ὁ
Θεὸς ταῖς ἑαυτοῦ ἐκκλησίαις ἐπαναγάγῃ αὐτὰς
πρὸς τὴν ἀρχαίαν εἰρήνην.

---

[1] ἐνστάσεις ἀθλητικαί] ἔντασις ἀθλητική editi antiqi.
[2] ἀπλήκτων E.   [3] ἔψυκται E.
[4] τῶν ἐκκλησιῶν] τῆς Ἐκκλησίας E.

---

[1] *i.e.* the gladiatorial contests in which Christians were
made to fight.
[2] The following words from the Benedictine note, which
illustrate this mode of martyrdom, are from a letter of the
Gothic Church which was supposed to have been sent to the
Church of Caesarea along with the body of the martyr

heresy. But your story—contestants confronting each other,[1] bodies torn to pieces for religion's sake, barbarian rage treated with contempt by men undaunted of heart, the various tortures applied by the persecutors, the firm resistance of the contestants throughout, the beam, the water,[2]—these are the instruments for the perfecting of martyrs! But of what sort are ours? Charity has grown cold. The teaching of the Fathers is being destroyed; shipwrecks in the faith are frequent; the mouths of the pious are silent; the laity driven from the houses of prayer raise in the open their hands to the Master in heaven. And though grievous are our afflictions, yet nowhere is martyrdom, because those who harm us have the same appellation as ourselves. On behalf of these do you yourself beseech our Lord, and unite all the noble athletes of Christ in prayer on behalf of the churches, in order that, if there is still some time left for the existence of the world, and the universe is not being driven in the opposite direction,[3] God may become reconciled with His churches and lead them back to their ancient peace.

Sabas: τότε κατάγουσιν αὐτὸν εἰς τὸ ὕδωρ εὐχαριστοῦντα καὶ δοξάζοντα τὸν Θεόν . . . καὶ ῥίψαντες αὐτόν, καὶ ἐπιθέντες αὐτῷ ξύλον κατὰ τοῦ τραχήλου, ἐπίεζον εἰς τὸ βάθος. καὶ οὕτω τελεωθεὶς διὰ ξύλου καὶ ὕδατος, ἄχραντον ἐφύλαξεν τῆς σωτηρίας τὸ σύμβολον, ὢν ἐτῶν τριάκοντα ὀκτώ. "Then they bring him down to the water, as he gives thanks and glorifies God, . . . and having thrown him down, and placed a beam of wood upon his neck, they cast him into the deep. And so having met his end *by beam and water*, he kept the symbol of salvation undefiled, at the age of thirty-eight years." St. Sabas suffered martyrdom under Athanaricus, king of the Goths, towards the end of the fourth century.

[3] *i.e.* to destruction.

CLXV

Ἀσχολίῳ, ἐπισκόπῳ Θεσσαλονίκης

Παλαιὰν ἡμῖν εὐχὴν ὁ ἅγιος Θεὸς ἐξεπλήρωσε, καταξιώσας ἡμᾶς γράμμασι τῆς ἀληθινῆς σου θεοσεβείας ἐντυχεῖν. τὸ μὲν γὰρ μέγιστον καὶ τῆς μεγίστης σπουδῆς ἄξιον αὐτόν σε ἰδεῖν καὶ ὀφθῆναί σοι, καὶ τῶν ἐν σοὶ τοῦ Πνεύματος χαρισμάτων δι' ἑαυτῶν ἀπολαῦσαι· ἐπειδὴ δὲ τοῦτο ἥ τε τοῦ τόπου διάστασις ἀφαιρεῖται, καὶ αἱ ἰδίᾳ ἑκάτερον ἡμῶν κατέχουσαι περιστάσεις, δευτέρας εὐχῆς ἄξιον γράμμασι συνεχέσι τῆς ἐν Χριστῷ σου [1] ἀγάπης τρέφεσθαι τὴν ψυχήν. ὃ καὶ νῦν ἡμῖν ὑπῆρξεν, ὅτε ἐλάβομεν εἰς χεῖρας τὴν ἐπιστολὴν τῆς συνέσεώς σου· πλέον γὰρ ἢ διπλασίους ἐγενόμεθα τῇ ἀπολαύσει τῶν ἐπεσταλμένων. καὶ γὰρ ἦν τῷ ὄντι καὶ αὐτήν σου καθορᾶν τὴν ψυχήν, οἷον δι' ἐσόπτρου τινὸς τῶν λόγων διαφαινομένην. πολυπλασίονα δὲ ἡμῖν τὴν εὐφροσύνην ἐποίει οὐ μόνον τὸ τοιοῦτον εἶναί σε ὁποῖον ἡ πάντων μαρτυρία παρίστησιν, ἀλλ' ὅτι τὰ ἐν σοὶ καλὰ τῆς πατρίδος ἡμῶν ἐστὶ σεμνολογήματα. οἷον γὰρ εὐθαλής τις κλάδος ῥίζης γενναίας ἀφορμηθεὶς τῶν πνευματικῶν καρπῶν τὴν ὑπερορίαν ἐνέπλησας. ὥστε εἰκότως ἡ πατρὶς ἡμῶν τοῖς οἰκείοις βλαστήμασιν ἐπαγάλλεται. καὶ ἡνίκα τοὺς ὑπὲρ τῆς πίστεως ἀγῶνας διήθλεις,[2] ἐδόξαζε τὸν Θεόν,

---

[1] σου om. E. [2] διῆλθες editi antiqi.

---

[1] Written in 374. Cf. Letters CLIV and CLV with notes. According to the Benedictine edition this letter is

LETTER CLXV

To Ascholius, Bishop of Thessalonica [1]

THE holy God has fulfilled for us a prayer of long standing, having deemed us worthy to receive a letter from your true Holiness. For although the most important thing and worthy of our greatest zeal is to see you yourself and to be seen by you, and to enjoy at first hand the graces of the Spirit that are in you; yet since both distance in space and the preoccupations which detain each of us severally deprive us of this, it is worthy of a secondary prayer that our spirits may be nourished by frequent letters of your charity in Christ. And this is what has happened to us now, when we have taken into our hands the letter of your Sagacity; for our spirits have increased to more than double through the enjoyment of your communication. For it was possible actually to observe even your very soul reflected by your words as by a mirror. And our joy was increased many fold, not only by the fact that you are such a man as the testimony of all asserts, but also because the noble qualities in you are a source of pride to our own country. For like a vigorous branch sprung from a noble root you have filled with spiritual fruits the country beyond our own borders. Rightly, therefore, does our country glory in her own offshoot. And when you were struggling in the contests for the faith, she glorified

undoubtedly not addressed to Ascholius, but to Soranus, duke of Scythia. In Letter CLV Basil requested his relative Julius Soranus to send him relics of the Gothic martyrs. The present letter is an answer to Soranus for his prompt compliance in sending the relics of Saint Sabas.

ἀκούουσα τὴν τῶν πατέρων ἀγαθὴν κληρονομίαν
διαφυλαττομένην ἔν σοι.

Οἷα δέ σου[1] καὶ τὰ παρόντα ; μάρτυρι, νέον[2]
ἀθλήσαντι[3] ἐπὶ τῆς γείτονος ὑμῖν βαρβάρου, τὴν
ἐνεγκοῦσαν ἐτίμησας, οἷόν τις εὐγνώμων γεωργὸς
τοῖς παρασχομένοις τὰ σπέρματα τὰς ἀπαρχὰς
τῶν καρπῶν ἀποπέμπων. ὄντως[4] πρέποντα
ἀθλητῇ Χριστοῦ τὰ δῶρα· μάρτυς τῆς ἀληθείας
ἄρτι τὸν τῆς δικαιοσύνης ἀναδησάμενος στέφανον·
ὃν καὶ ὑπεδεξάμεθα χαίροντες, καὶ ἐδοξάσαμεν
τὸν Θεὸν τὸν ἐν πᾶσι τοῖς ἔθνεσι πληρώσαντα
λοιπὸν τὸ εὐαγγέλιον τοῦ Χριστοῦ αὐτοῦ. παρακέκλησο δὲ καὶ ἡμῶν τῶν ἀγαπώντων σε μεμνῆσθαι ἐν ταῖς προσευχαῖς, καὶ σπουδαίως ὑπὲρ τῶν
ψυχῶν ἡμῶν προσεύχεσθαι τῷ Κυρίῳ, ἵνα
καταξιωθῶμέν ποτε ἄρξασθαι καὶ αὐτοὶ δουλεύειν
τῷ Θεῷ[5] κατὰ τὴν ὁδὸν τῶν ἐντολῶν αὐτοῦ, ἃς
ἔδωκεν ἡμῖν εἰς σωτηρίαν.[6]

CLXVI

Εὐσεβίῳ, ἐπισκόπῳ Σαμοσάτων[7]

Τὰ πάντα τίμιος ὢν ἡμῖν καὶ τῶν φίλων ἐν
τοῖς γνησίοις ὁ αἰδεσιμώτατος ἀδελφὸς ἡμῶν

[1] σοι Med.
[2] μάρτυρι νέον] μαρτυρεῖ νέῳ editi antiqi.
[3] ἀνθήσαντι E.   [4] γάρ add. editi antiqi.
[5] Κυρίῳ E.   [6] αὐτοῦ add. E.
[7] πρεσβύτερος ὤν add. E, editi antiqi.

---

[1] Written in the late summer of 374. Cf. Loofs 46, note
5. For Eusebius, cf. previous letters addressed to him in
this volume. The present letter seems to be correctly
assigned to Gregory of Nazianzus by the Benedictine edition.
The style is quite unlike Basil's epistolary style, but very

God, having heard that the goodly heritage of the Fathers was being preserved in you.

But of what nature also are your present deeds! With a martyr, who but lately finished his struggle in the barbarian land neighbouring your own, you have honoured the land which bore you, sending, like a grateful husbandman, the first fruits back to those who supplied the seed. Truly worthy of Christ's athlete are the gifts; a martyr of the truth who has just been wreathed with the crown of righteousness; and we not only received him with joy, but also glorified the God who among all the Gentiles has already fulfilled the gospel of His Christ. But let me beg you to remember in your prayers us who love you, and for our souls' sake earnestly to pray to the Lord that we also may be thought worthy one day to begin to serve God according to the way of the commandments which He has given us unto salvation.

LETTER CLXVI

To Eusebius, Bishop of Samosata [1]

Though our most reverend brother Eupraxius [2] has been held in honour by us in every respect and counted among our true friends, he has been looked

similar to that of Gregory. Moreover, Eusebius had written to Gregory at the time assigned to this letter, and since Eupraxius was passing through Cappadocia on his way to Eusebius, it gave Gregory an opportunity to send his answer. Furthermore, the present letter is found in only four MSS. of Basil, Coislinianus 237, Vaticani 713 and 435, and Marcianus 79. This is a small proportion of the many extant MSS. of Basil, and no one of these four is included in the most ancient group.

[2] A disciple and intimate friend of Eusebius of Samosata.

Εὐπράξιος τιμιώτερος ὤφθη καὶ γνησιώτερος ἐκ
τῆς περὶ σὲ διαθέσεως· ὅς γε καὶ νῦν οὕτως
ὥρμησε πρὸς τὴν σὴν θεοσέβειαν (ἵν᾽ εἴπω τὸ τοῦ
Δαβίδ), ὡς ἔλαφος πολὺ δίψος καὶ οὐ φορητὸν
ποτίμῳ καὶ καθαρᾷ πηγῇ καταψύχουσα. καὶ
μακάριος ὅ σοι πλησιάζειν ἠξιωμένος.¹ καὶ
μακαριώτερος δὲ ὁ ὑπὲρ Χριστοῦ παθήμασι καὶ
τοῖς ὑπὲρ ἀληθείας ἱδρῶσι τοιαύτην ἐπιθεὶς
κορωνίδα, ἧς ὀλίγοι τῶν φοβουμένων τὸν Θεὸν
τετυχήκασιν. οὐ γὰρ ἀβασάνιστον ἐπεδείξω τὴν
ἀρετήν, οὐδὲ ἐν εὐδίας καιρῷ μόνον ὀρθῶς ἔπλευσας
καὶ τὰς τῶν ἄλλων ψυχὰς ἐκυβέρνησας, ἀλλ᾽ ἐν
ταῖς δυσχερείαις τῶν πειρασμῶν διεφάνης,² καὶ
τῶν διωκόντων γέγονας ὑψηλότερος τῷ γενναίως
μεταστῆναι τῆς ἐνεγκούσης.

Καὶ ἄλλοι μὲν τὸ πατρῷον ἔδαφος ἔχουσιν,
ἡμεῖς δὲ τὴν ἄνω πόλιν·³ ἄλλοι τὸν ἡμέτερον ἴσως
θρόνον, ἡμεῖς δὲ Χριστόν. ὦ τῆς πραγματείας
οἵων ὑπεριδόντες, οἷα κεκομίσμεθα· διήλθομεν
διὰ πυρὸς καὶ ὕδατος· πιστεύω δὲ ὅτι καὶ ἐξελευ-
σόμεθα εἰς ἀναψυχήν. οὐ γὰρ⁴ ἐγκαταλείψει
ἡμᾶς ὁ Θεὸς εἰς τέλος, οὐδὲ περιόψεται τὸν ὀρθὸν
λόγον δεδιωγμένον· ἀλλὰ κατὰ τὸ πλῆθος τῶν
ὀδυνῶν ἡμῶν αἱ παρακλήσεις αὐτοῦ εὐφρανοῦσιν
ἡμᾶς. τοῦτο μὲν οὖν καὶ πιστεύομεν καὶ εὐχόμεθα. σὺ δέ, παρακαλῶ, ὑπερεύχου τῆς ταπεινώ-

¹ καὶ μακάριος . . . ἠξιωμένος] om. E.

upon as more honoured and truer as the result of his
affection for you ; for he has now also hastened to
your Holiness in like manner, to use the words of
David,[1] as a hart which quenches a great and unendurable thirst at a sweet and a pure fountain.
And blessed is he who has been thought worthy to
associate with you. But even more blessed is he
who has crowned his sufferings for Christ's sake and
his labours for truth's sake with such a crown as few
of those who fear God have obtained. For the
virtue you have shown has not been untested, nor in
a time of calm only have you correctly sailed your
course and guided the souls of the others, but amid
the difficulties of your trials you have shone forth,
and you have risen superior to your persecutors by
nobly departing from the land which bore you.

And others indeed possess the land of their
fathers, but we the heavenly city ; others perhaps
have our throne, but we have Christ ! Oh, profitable
exchange ! For disdaining what things, what things
have we gained ! We have gone through fire and
water ; but I trust that we shall also come out into a
place of refreshment. For God will not forsake us
for ever, nor will He suffer the orthodox doctrine to
be persecuted ; nay, according to the multitude of
our pains His comforts shall gladden us. This at
any rate we both believe and pray. But do you, I
beseech you, pray for our humility, and as often as

---

[1] Cf. Psal. 41. 2 : ὃν τρόπον ἐπιποθεῖ ἡ ἔλαφος ἐπὶ τὰς πηγὰς
τῶν ὑδάτων, οὕτως ἐπιποθεῖ ἡ ψυχή μου πρὸς σέ, ὁ θεός. "As
the hart panteth after the fountains of water ; so my soul
panteth after thee, O God."

---

[2] ἀνεφάνης E.   [3] καί add. E.   [4] εἰς τέλος add. E.

σεως ἡμῶν, καὶ ὁσάκις ἂν ἐμπίπτῃ καιρός, εὐλογεῖν
ἡμᾶς διὰ γραμμάτων μὴ κατόκνει, καὶ εὐθυμοτέρους
ποιεῖν τὰ κατὰ σεαυτὸν δηλῶν, ὃ ποιῆσαι νῦν
κατηξίωσας.

CLXVII

Εὐσεβίῳ, ἐπισκόπῳ Σαμοσάτων

Καὶ γράφων καὶ μεμνημένος εὐφραίνεις ἡμᾶς,
καὶ τὸ τούτου μεῖζον, εὐλογῶν ἡμᾶς ἐν τοῖς γράμμασιν. ἡμεῖς δέ, εἰ μὲν [1] ἄξιοι τῶν σῶν παθημάτων καὶ τῆς ὑπὲρ Χριστοῦ ἀθλήσεως, κατηξιώθημεν ἂν καὶ μέχρι σου [2] γενόμενοι περιπτύξασθαί σου τὴν [3] θεοσέβειαν καὶ τύπον λαβεῖν
τῆς ἐν τοῖς παθήμασι καρτερίας. ἐπειδὴ δὲ
ἀνάξιοι τούτου τυγχάνομεν, πολλαῖς θλίψεσι καὶ
ἀσχολίαις ἐνεχόμενοι, ὃ δεύτερόν ἐστι ποιοῦμεν·
προσαγορεύομεν τὴν σὴν τελειότητα, καὶ ἀξιοῦμεν
μὴ κάμνειν σε μεμνημένον ἡμῶν. οὐ γὰρ ὠφέ-
λεια μόνον ἡμῖν τῶν σῶν καταξιοῦσθαι γραμμάτων, ἀλλὰ καὶ καύχημα πρὸς τοὺς πολλοὺς καὶ
καλλώπισμα, ὅτι λόγος ἡμῶν ἐστὶ παρὰ ἀνδρὶ
τοσούτῳ τὴν ἀρετὴν καὶ τοσαύτην ἔχοντι πρὸς
Θεὸν οἰκειότητα, ὥστε καὶ ἄλλους οἰκειοῦν
δύνασθαι καὶ λόγῳ καὶ ὑποδείγματι.

[1] εἰ μὲν] ἐσμέν editi antiqi.
[2] κατηξιώθημεν . . . σου] εὐχόμεθα ἰδεῖν E.
[3] σήν E.

---

[1] Written in the late summer of 374. Cf. Loofs 46, note
5. On Eusebius of Samosata see previous letters. The
Benedictine edition rightly assigns this letter to Gregory of

an occasion shall present itself, do not hesitate to bless us by letter and to make us more joyful by informing us of your own affairs, as you have just now deigned to do.

LETTER CLXVII

To Eusebius, Bishop of Samosata [1]

By writing and by being mindful of us you cause us pleasure, and, even more important than this, by blessing us in your letters. As for us, if we had been worthy of your sufferings and of your struggle for Christ's sake, we should have been permitted, coming to visit you, to embrace your Piety and to take you as a model of patience in sufferings. But since we are doubtless unworthy of this, being subject to many afflictions and cares, we are doing what is next best: we salute your Perfection, and we beg you not to become weary of remembering us. For not only is it a benefit to us to be thought worthy of your letters, but it is also a boast in the eyes of people at large and an ornament that some account is taken of us by a man so eminent in virtue, and who enjoys such intimacy with God that he is able to win others also over to Him by both word and example.

Nazianzus. Tillemont's objection that "afflictions and cares" fit Basil better than Gregory does not seem worthy. Gregory also had much to occupy him at this time. Furthermore, the fact that this letter is found regularly among the MSS. of Gregory, and in only Coislinianus 237, Vaticanus 713, Marcianus 79, and Mediceus IV. 14 of the MSS. of Basil, would in itself seem sufficient reason for assigning the letter to Gregory.

CLXVIII

Ἀντιόχῳ πρεσβυτέρῳ, ἀδελφιδῷ συνόντι ἐν τῇ
ἐξορίᾳ

Ὅσον ὀδύρομαι τὴν ἐκκλησίαν τὴν στερηθεῖσαν
τῆς τοῦ τοιούτου ποιμένος ἐπιστασίας, τοσοῦτον
μακαρίζω ὑμᾶς καταξιωθέντας ἐν τοιούτῳ καιρῷ
συνεῖναι ἀνδρὶ τὸν μέγαν ὑπὲρ τῆς εὐσεβείας[1]
διαθλοῦντι ἀγῶνα. πέπεισμαι γὰρ ὅτι ὁ Κύριος
καὶ ὑμᾶς τῆς αὐτῆς μερίδος καταξιώσει τοὺς
καλῶς ἀλείφοντας καὶ ἐπεγείροντας αὐτοῦ τὴν
προθυμίαν. ἡλίκον δὲ κέρδος ἐν ἡσυχίᾳ βαθείᾳ
ἀπολαύειν ἀνδρὸς τοσαῦτα μὲν ἐκ τῆς μαθήσεως
τοσαῦτα δὲ ἐκ τῆς πείρας τῶν πραγμάτων συνειλη-
χότος! ὥστε πέπεισμαι ὑμᾶς νῦν ἐγνωκέναι
τὸν ἄνδρα, ἡλίκος ἐστὶ τὴν σύνεσιν· διότι ἐν τῷ
παρελθόντι χρόνῳ καὶ αὐτὸς τὴν διάνοιαν εἶχεν
εἰς πολλὰ σχιζομένην καὶ ὑμεῖς οὐκ ἤγετε σχολὴν
ἀπὸ τῶν τοῦ βίου πραγμάτων, ὥστε ὅλοι προσ-
κεῖσθαι τῷ πνευματικῷ νάματι τῷ ἀπὸ καθαρᾶς
καρδίας τοῦ ἀνδρὸς προχεομένῳ. ἀλλὰ παράσχοι
ὁ Κύριος ὑμᾶς καὶ αὐτῷ παράκλησιν εἶναι καὶ
αὐτοὺς μὴ δεῖσθαι τῆς ἑτέρων παρηγορίας· ὅπερ
οὖν καὶ πέπεισμαι περὶ τῶν καρδιῶν ὑμῶν, τεκμαιρόμενος τῇ τε ἐμαυτοῦ πείρᾳ, ἣν πρὸς ὀλίγον
ὑμῶν ἐπειράθην, καὶ τῇ μεγάλῃ διδασκαλίᾳ τοῦ
καλοῦ καθηγητοῦ, οὗ μιᾶς ἡμέρας συνουσία αὐταρ-
κές ἐστιν ἐφόδιον πρὸς σωτηρίαν.

---

[1] ἐκκλησίας tres MSS. recentiores.

---

[1] Written in the late summer of 374. Cf. Loofs 46, note 5.

LETTER CLXVIII

LETTER CLXVIII

To the Presbyter Antiochus, Eusebius' Nephew, who was with him in Exile [1]

Much as I lament the Church's having been deprived of the care of such a shepherd,[2] equally do I congratulate you for having been accounted worthy at such a crisis to be present with a man who is fighting in the great contest in defence of our religion. For I am convinced that the Lord will account you also, who anoint him for the contest and stimulate his zeal, worthy of the same lot. But what an advantage it is to enjoy now in profound peace a man who has accumulated both so much from his learning and so much from his experience in affairs! I am therefore persuaded that you have now come to know the man, how great he is in wisdom; because in the past he on his own part kept his mind distracted on many things, and you on yours lacked the leisure from the affairs of life which would enable you to devote yourself wholly to the spiritual stream which flows from the pure heart of the man. But may the Lord grant that you may be a comfort to him in turn and may not yourself require consolation from others. And indeed I am convinced that this will be the case so far as the hearts of you both are concerned, judging not only from my experience, wherein I made trial of you both for a short time, but also by the great instruction of the Good Teacher, whose company for a single day is a sufficient viaticum for salvation.

Theodoret, IV. 12 and 13, describes the scene of Eusebius' forced departure into exile at the command of Valens.

[2] i.e. Eusebius.

437

COLLECTED LETTERS OF SAINT BASIL

CLXIX

Γρηγορίῳ Βασίλειος

Πρᾶγμα μὲν ὑπέστης ἐπιεικὲς καὶ[1] ἥμερον καὶ
φιλάνθρωπον τὴν τοῦ καταφρονητοῦ Γλυκερίου
(τέως γὰρ οὕτω γράφομεν) αἰχμαλωσίαν συναγα-
γών, καὶ τὴν κοινὴν ἀσχημοσύνην ἡμῶν, ὡς οἷόν
τε ἦν, συγκαλύψας. δεῖ δὲ[2] ὅμως τὴν σὴν εὐλάβειαν
μαθοῦσαν τὰ κατ᾽ αὐτὸν οὕτω λῦσαι τὴν ἀτιμίαν.

Οὗτος ὁ νῦν σοβαρὸς καὶ σεμνὸς ὑμῖν Γλυκέριος
ἐχειροτονήθη μὲν παρ᾽ ἡμῶν τῆς κατὰ Οὐήνεσαν[3]
ἐκκλησίας διάκονος, ὡς καὶ τῷ πρεσβυτέρῳ δια-
κονήσων καὶ τοῦ ἔργου τῆς ἐκκλησίας ἐπιμελησό-
μενος. καὶ γάρ ἐστιν, εἰ καὶ τὰ ἄλλα δύστροπος
ὁ ἀνήρ, ἀλλὰ τὰ ἐπίχειρα οὐκ ἀφυής. ἐπεὶ δὲ
κατέστη, τοῦ μὲν ἔργου ἠμέλησε τοσοῦτον ὅσον
οὐδὲ τὴν ἀρχὴν γεγονότος· παρθένους δὲ ἀθλίας
συναγαγὼν κατ᾽ ἰδίαν ἐξουσίαν καὶ αὐθεντίαν, τὰς
μὲν ἑκούσας προσδραμούσας αὐτῷ (οἶσθα δὲ τὸ
τῶν νέων περὶ τὰ τοιαῦτα πρόχειρον), τὰς δὲ
ἀκούσας ἀγελαρχεῖν ἐπεχείρησε, καὶ πατριαρχίας
ὄνομα ἑαυτῷ καὶ σχῆμα περιθείς, ἐξαίφνης
ἐσοβαρεύσατο, οὐκ ἔκ τινος ἀκολουθίας[4] καὶ
εὐσεβείας ἐπὶ τοῦτο ἐλθών, ἀλλ᾽ ἀφορμὴν βίου

---

[1] ἐπιεικὲς καὶ] ἐπιεικῶς Harl.
[2] συγκαλύψας. δεῖ δέ om. E.
[3] Σύννασαν Harl. [4] δικαίας add. editi antiqi.

---

[1] Written about 374. Letters CLXIX, CLXX, and
CLXXI treat of the strange doings of the deacon Glycerius.
Cf. W. M. Ramsay, *The Church in the Roman Empire before
A.D. 170*, 2nd ed., London, 1893, pp. 443–464.

LETTER CLXIX

Basil to Gregory [1]

You have, it is true, undertaken a kind, clement, and humane work in collecting the captive band of the contemptible Glycerius (for at the present time we must use this term) and in hiding our common shame as far as possible : but your Reverence ought, nevertheless, first to learn the facts about him and then to wipe out this dishonour.

This Glycerius, who is at present looked upon by you as merely an impetuous and swaggering fellow, was ordained by us as deacon of the church of Venesa,[2] with the idea that he should both serve the presbyter and look after the work of the church. For, however intractable the man is in other respects, yet he is not without natural talent as regards odd errands. But after he was appointed, he neglected his work as if it had not existed at all, but collecting some unfortunate virgins on his own authority and responsibility, some running to him willingly (and you know the tendency of young people in such matters) and others against their will, he undertook to be the leader of the company, and having invested himself with the name and apparel of a patriarch, he suddenly began to give himself airs, adopting this course, not from any motive of obedience or of piety, but because he preferred this source of livelihood,

---

The Gregory addressed is either of Nyssa or Nazianzus. Manuscript evidence favours Gregory of Nazianzus, but there are arguments in favour of Gregory of Nyssa. Cf. *Vita Basilii*, XXXI, 4.

[2] Other spellings are Veësa, Venata, and Synnasa.

ταύτην ὥσπερ ἄλλος τινὰ προστησάμενος· καὶ
μικροῦ τὴν ἐκκλησίαν πᾶσαν ἀνάστατον πεποίηκε,
περιφρονῶν μὲν τὸν ἑαυτοῦ πρεσβύτερον, ἄνδρα
καὶ πολιτείᾳ καὶ ἡλικίᾳ αἰδέσιμον, περιφρονῶν δὲ
τὸν χωρεπίσκοπον [1] καὶ ἡμᾶς ὡς οὐδενὸς ἀξίους,
θορύβων δὲ ἀεὶ καὶ ταραχῶν πληρῶν τὴν πόλιν
καὶ σύμπαν τὸ ἱερατεῖον.

Καὶ τέλος, ἵνα τι μὴ [2] λόγῳ ἐπιτιμηθῇ μικρὸν
παρ' ἡμῶν καὶ τοῦ χωρεπισκόπου πρὸς τὸ μὴ
καταφρονεῖν αὐτὸν (καὶ γὰρ καὶ τοὺς νέους
ἐγύμναζεν εἰς τὴν αὐτὴν ἀπόνοιαν), πρᾶγμα
διανοεῖται λίαν τολμηρὸν καὶ ἀπάνθρωπον.
συλήσας νῶν παρθένων ὅσας ἠδύνατο, καὶ νύκτα
τηρήσας, δραπέτης γίνεται. πάνυ σοι δεινὰ ταῦτα
φανεῖται.[3] σκόπει καὶ τὸν καιρόν. ἤγετο μὲν ἡ
ἐκεῖσε σύνοδος καὶ πολὺ πανταχόθεν, ὡς εἰκός,
ἐπέρρει τὸ πλῆθος. ὁ δὲ ἀντεξῆγε τὸν ἑαυτοῦ χορὸν
νέοις ἑπόμενον καὶ περιχορεύοντα, καὶ πολλὴν
μὲν κατήφειαν κινοῦντα τοῖς εὐλαβέσι, πολὺν δὲ
γέλωτα τοῖς ἀκρατέσι καὶ τὴν γλῶσσαν ἑτοιμο-
τέροις. καὶ οὐκ ἀρκεῖ ταῦτα, καίπερ τηλικαῦτα
ὄντα τὸ μέγεθος· ἀλλ' ἔτι καὶ τοὺς γονεῖς, ὡς
πυνθάνομαι, τῶν παρθένων τὴν ἀτεκνίαν οὐ
φέροντας, καὶ τὴν διασπορὰν ἐπαναγαγεῖν
βουλομένους, καὶ μετ' ὀδυρμῶν προσπίπτοντας,
ὡς εἰκός, ταῖς ἑαυτῶν θυγατράσι, περιυβρίζει καὶ
ἀτιμοῖ [4] ὁ θαυμαστὸς νεανίσκος μετὰ τοῦ ληστρι-
κοῦ συντάγματος.

Ταῦτα μὴ ἀνεκτὰ φανήτω τῇ σῇ εὐλαβείᾳ· καὶ

---

[1] ἐπίσκοπον E, Med.
[2] μή Combefisius, who would thus replace τι.
[3] φαίνεται Harl.

just as another man would choose one or another
occupation ; and he has all but overturned the whole
Church, scorning his own presbyter, a man who is
venerated for both his conduct and his age, and
scorning his chorepiscopus and ourselves as if
deserving no consideration at all, and continually
filling the city and the whole sanctuary with tumults
and disturbances.

And at last, in order to avoid receiving some slight
verbal rebuke from us and from his chorepiscopus so
that he should cease treating us with contempt (for
he proceeded to train the young men also to the
same folly), he is now planning an exceedingly daring
and abominable thing. Having stolen from us two
as many of the virgins as he could, and having
watched for a night, he has become a fugitive.
These things will seem quite dreadful to you. Consider also the occasion he chose. The local festival
was being held, and a great crowd from all sides, as
was natural, was gathering. And he led out his own
troop in turn, following young men and dancing
about them, and causing great shame to the pious,
but much laughter to the boisterous and the more
glib-tongued. And these acts are not enough,
although they are such in enormity, but he goes still
further, as I hear, when the parents of the virgins,
finding the loss of their children intolerable, wish to
bring home the scattered company and throw
themselves with tears, as is natural, at their daughters'
feet, this admirable young fellow and his predatory
band even insult and flout them.

Let not these things appear tolerable to your

---

⁴ ἀτιμάζει Harl.

γὰρ κοινὸς [1] πάντων ἡμῶν ὁ γέλως· ἀλλὰ μάλιστα
μὲν αὐτὸν κέλευσον μετὰ τῶν παρθένων ἐπανελ-
θεῖν· τύχοι γὰρ ἄν τινος φιλανθρωπίας εἰ μετὰ
σῶν ἐπανήκοι γραμμάτων· εἰ δὲ μή, τάς γε
παρθένους ἀπόπεμψον τῇ μητρὶ αὐτῶν τῇ ἐκκλησίᾳ. εἰ δὲ μή,[2] τάς γε βουλομένας τυραννεῖσθαι
μὴ συγχωρήσῃς, ἀλλ' ἐπανελθεῖν τύπωσον πρὸς
ἡμᾶς. ἢ μαρτυρόμεθά σοι [3] ὡς καὶ Θεῷ καὶ
ἀνθρώποις, ὅτι μὴ καλῶς ταῦτα γίνεται μηδὲ
θεσμοῖς ἐκκλησίας. Γλυκέριος δὲ εἰ μὲν ἐπανέλ-
θοι μετ' ἐπιστήμης καὶ τῆς πρεπούσης [4] εὐσταθείας, τοῦτο ἄριστον, εἰ δὲ μή, ἔστω πεπαυμένος
τῆς ὑπηρεσίας.

CLXX

Γλυκερίῳ

Μέχρι τίνος ἀπονοῇ, καὶ κακῶς μὲν [5] βουλεύῃ
περὶ σεαυτοῦ, κινεῖς δὲ [6] ἡμᾶς, αἰσχύνεις δὲ τὸ
κοινὸν τάγμα τῶν μοναστῶν; ἐπάνελθε οὖν τῷ
Θεῷ θαρρῶν καὶ ἡμῖν, οὗ τὴν φιλανθρωπίαν
μιμούμεθα. εἰ γὰρ καὶ πατρικῶς ἐπετιμήσαμεν,
ἀλλὰ καὶ συγγνωσόμεθα πατρικῶς.[7] ταῦτά σοι
παρ' ἡμῶν, ἐπειδὴ πολλοί τε ἱκετεύουσιν ἄλλοι,
καὶ πρὸ τῶν ἄλλων ὁ σὸς πρεσβύτερος, οὗ τὴν
πολιὰν αἰδούμεθα καὶ τὴν εὐσπλαγχνίαν. εἰ δὲ
μακρύνεις [8] ἀφ' ἡμῶν, τοῦ βαθμοῦ μὲν πάντως [9]

---

[1] κοινόν editi antiqi.   [2] τοῦτο add. editi antiqi.
[3] σοι] Θεὸν καὶ ἀνθρώπους Harl. ; σε E.
[4] παρούσης E, editi antiqi.   [5] μέν om. E.
[6] δὲ] μέν E, editi antiqi.
[7] πνευματικῶς apud Gregorium.

Reverence; for the ridicule affects us all in common; but if possible command him to return with the virgins; for he would meet with some consideration if he should come back with a letter from you; but if this cannot be, at least send back the virgins to their mother the Church. And if this is impossible, do not allow those at least who wish to return to be tyrannized over, but order them to come back to us. Otherwise we protest to you and also to God and men that these things are not done rightly nor in accord with the laws of the Church. Yet if Glycerius should return with understanding and with the becoming steadiness of mind, this would be best, but if not, let him be deposed from his ministry.

LETTER CLXX

To Glycerius[1]

How far will you go in your folly, and while acting unwisely concerning your own self, stir us to anger and put to shame the whole order of monks? Return, therefore, putting your confidence in God and in us who imitate His benevolence. For even though we have rebuked like a father, yet we shall also grant pardon like a father. This is the treatment you will receive at our hands, since many others are making pleas on your behalf and above the rest your own presbyter, whose grey hairs and kindness of heart we revere. But if you continue to hold aloof from us, then you have fallen

---

[1] For the date and content see the preceding letter.

---

[8] μακρύνοις Harl.   [9] παντός Reg. secundus.

ἐκπέπτωκας, ἐκπεσῇ δὲ καὶ τοῦ Θεοῦ μετὰ τῶν
μελῶν σου καὶ τῆς στολῆς, οἷς ἄγεις τὰς νέας,
οὐ πρὸς Θεόν, ἀλλ' εἰς βάραθρον.

CLXXI

Γρηγορίῳ [1]

Ἐπέσταλκά σοι καὶ πρώην περὶ Γλυκερίου καὶ
τῶν παρθένων. οἱ δὲ οὐδέπω καὶ τήμερον ἐπανή-
κασιν, ἀλλ' ἔτι μέλλουσιν, οὐκ οἶδα ὅθεν καὶ
ὅπως. οὐ γὰρ ἂν ἐκεῖνό σου καταγνοίην, ὡς ἐφ'
ἡμετέρᾳ διαβολῇ τοῦτο ποιεῖς, ἢ αὐτὸς πάσχων
τι πρὸς ἡμᾶς, ἢ ἄλλοις χαριζόμενος. ἡκέτωσαν
οὖν μηδὲν δεδοικότες· σὺ γενοῦ τούτου [2] ἐγγυητής.
καὶ γὰρ ἀλγοῦμεν τεμνομένων [3] τῶν μελῶν, εἰ καὶ
καλῶς [4] ἐτμήθησαν. εἰ δὲ ἀντιτείνοιεν, ἐπ' ἄλλους
τὸ βάρος, ἡμεῖς δὲ ἀποπλυνόμεθα.

CLXXII

Σωφρονίῳ ἐπισκόπῳ

Ὅπως ηὔφρανας ἡμᾶς τοῖς [5] γράμμασιν οὐδὲν
δεόμεθα γράφειν. εἰκάζεις γὰρ πάντως αὐτοῖς

[1] ἑταίρῳ add. E.
[2] σὺ γενοῦ τούτου] συγγένου τούτων editi antiqi. τούτων
apud Gregorium.
[3] τεμνομένων] τεμνόμενοι τῶν μελῶν apud Gregorium.
[4] κακῶς E, editi antiqi.   [5] τοῖς om. E.

[1] Cf. Tim. 3. 13 : οἱ γὰρ καλῶς διακονήσαντες, βαθμὸν ἑαυτοῖς
καλὸν περιποιοῦνται, καὶ πολλὴν παρρησίαν ἐν πίστει τῇ ἐν

LETTER CLXXII

entirely from your grade,[1] and you will also fall
from God with your songs and your finery, by which
you are leading the young women, not to God, but
to the pit.

LETTER CLXXI

To Gregory [2]

I HAVE written to you recently about Glycerius
and his virgins. And they have not yet to this
day returned, but are still delaying; why and how
I know not. For I could not lay the blame for this
matter against you and say that you are doing this
to discredit us, either because you have some
grievance against us yourself, or are doing it as a
favour for others. Therefore let them come, fearing
nothing; do you become surety for this. For we
are pained when our members are cut off, even if
they have been justly cut off. But if they resist, the
burden will rest upon others, and we are absolved.

LETTER CLXXII

To Sophronius, Bishop [3]

How you have pleased us by your letter we need
not write. For you can certainly surmise it from

Χριστῷ Ἰησοῦ. "For they that have ministered well shall
purchase to themselves a good degree, and much confidence
in the faith which is in Christ Jesus." The "degree" mentioned by Basil here is the diaconate.

[2] For date and content cf. Letter CLXIX and note.

[3] Written in 374. This Sophronius is distinguished by the
Benedictine edition from the Sophronius, *magister officiorum*,
to whom Letters XXXII, LXXVI, XCVI and others are
addressed. The present Sophronius is otherwise unknown.

445

COLLECTED LETTERS OF SAINT BASIL

οἷς ἐπέστειλας τοιούτοις οὖσι.[1] τὸν γὰρ πρῶτον
καρπὸν τοῦ Πνεύματος, τὴν ἀγάπην, ἔδειξας ἡμῖν
διὰ τοῦ γράμματος. τούτου δὲ τί ἂν γένοιτο
τιμιώτερον ἡμῖν ἐν τῇ παρούσῃ τῶν καιρῶν καταστάσει, ἡνίκα διὰ τὸ πληθυνθῆναι τὴν ἀνομίαν,
ἐψύγη τῶν πολλῶν ἡ ἀγάπη; οὐδὲν γὰρ οὕτω
σπάνιον νῦν ὡς ἀδελφοῦ συντυχία πνευματικοῦ,
καὶ ῥῆμα εἰρηνικόν, καὶ πνευματικὴ κοινωνία, ἣν
εὑρόντες ἐν τῇ σῇ τελειότητι ὑπερευχαριστήσαμεν
τῷ Κυρίῳ, δεόμενοι καὶ τῆς τελείας ἐπὶ σοὶ
μετασχεῖν εὐφροσύνης. εἰ γὰρ ἐπιστολαὶ τοιαῦται,
ὁποία ἡ συντυχία; καὶ εἰ πόρρωθεν οὕτως αἱρεῖς,
πόσου ἄξιος ἔσῃ ἐγγύθεν ἡμῖν ἐπιφανείς; εὖ δὲ
ἴσθι,[2] εἰ μὴ μυρίων ἀσχολιῶν περιεῖχε πλῆθος[3]
καὶ αἱ ἀπαραίτητοι αὗται ἀνάγκαι αἷς ἐνδεδέ-
μεθα, αὐτόν με ἐπειχθῆναι πρὸς τὴν σὴν τελειότητα.
καίτοιγε[4] μέγα μοι ἐμπόδιόν ἐστι πρὸς τὰς κινήσεις ἡ παλαιὰ αὕτη τοῦ σώματος ἀρρωστία, ἀλλ᾽
ὅμως οὐκ ἂν ὑπελογισάμην τοῦτο ἐμπόδιον τῆς
προσδοκωμένης ἕνεκεν ὠφελείας. τὸ γὰρ ἀνδρὶ τὰ
αὐτὰ φρονοῦντι καὶ τὴν τῶν πατέρων πρεσβεύον-
τι πίστιν, ὡς ὁ τῶν τιμίων ἀδελφῶν καὶ συμ-
πρεσβυτέρων λόγος,[5] καταξιωθῆναι περιτυχεῖν,
ὄντως ἐστὶν εἰς τὴν ἀρχαίαν μακαριότητα τῶν
ἐκκλησιῶν ἐπανελθεῖν, ὅτε ὀλίγοι μὲν ἦσαν οἱ
νοσοῦντες περὶ ζητήσεις, ἐν ἡσυχίᾳ δὲ ἦσαν
πάντες, ἐργάται ὄντες τῶν ἐντολῶν[6] ἀνεπαίσ-

---

[1] τοιούτοις οὖσι om. E.
[2] εὖ δὲ ἴσθι] ὥστε με E; ὥστε μοι Med.
[3] ἡμᾶς add. editi antiqi.   [4] καίτοι E.
[5] περὶ σοῦ add. editi antiqi.
[6] τοῦ Θεοῦ add. editi antiqi.

the very nature of the things you said in your letter. For you have shown us the first fruit of the Spirit, charity, through your letter. And what could be more precious to us than this in the present condition of the times, when, "because iniquity hath abounded, the charity of many hath grown cold"?[1] For nothing is so rare now as a meeting with a spiritual brother, and peaceful discourse, and spiritual communion; and since we have found this communion in your Perfection, we have rendered exceeding thanks to the Lord, beseeching also that we may share in the perfect joy that is in you. For if your letters are such, what would a meeting be! And if you can move me so from a distance, how estimable will you be when you appear to us from near at hand! But be assured that if we were not encompassed about by a multitude of countless preoccupations and by the present inexorable necessities by which we are constrained, I should have hastened to your Perfection in person. And yet a great obstacle to my moving about is this old infirmity of my body; but nevertheless I should have paid no heed to this obstacle for the sake of the anticipated profit. For to be thought worthy of meeting a man who holds the same opinions as myself and who reverences the faith of the Fathers, according to the account of our honoured brethren and fellow-presbyters, is in truth to return to the old-time blessedness of the churches, when those were few who suffered from the malady of inquiry, and all were in peace, being workmen fulfilling the com-

---

[1] Cf. Matt. 24. 12: καὶ διὰ τὸ πληθυνθῆναι τὴν ἀνομίαν, ψυγήσεται ἡ ἀγάπη τῶν πολλῶν. "And because iniquity hath abounded, the charity of many shall grow cold."

χυντοι, διὰ τῆς ἀπλῆς καὶ ἀπεριέργου ὁμολογίας
λατρεύοντες τῷ Κυρίῳ, καὶ[1] ἄσυλον τὴν πίστιν
καὶ ἀπερίεργον τὴν εἰς Πατέρα καὶ Υἱὸν καὶ
ἅγιον Πνεῦμα διαφυλάσσοντες.

CLXXIII

Πρὸς Θεοδώραν κανονικήν[2]

Ὀκνηροὺς ἡμᾶς ποιεῖ πρὸς τὸ γράφειν τὸ μὴ
πεπεῖσθαι τὰς ἐπιστολὰς ἡμῶν πάντως[3] ἐγχειρί-
ζεσθαι τῇ σῇ ἀγάπῃ ἀλλὰ κακίᾳ τῶν διακονούντων
μυρίους προεντυγχάνειν ἑτέρους· καὶ μάλιστα νῦν
οὕτω τεταραγμένων[4] τῶν κατὰ τὴν οἰκουμένην
πραγμάτων. διόπερ ἀναμένω[5] τρόπον τινὰ μεμφ-
θῆναι[6] καὶ[7] ἀπαιτηθῆναι βιαίως τὰς ἐπιστολάς,
ὥστε αὐτῷ τούτῳ τεκμηρίῳ χρήσασθαι τῆς ἀπο-
δόσεως. καὶ γράφοντες μὲν οὖν καὶ σιωπῶντες
ἓν ἔργον ἔχομεν ἐν ταῖς καρδίαις ἡμῶν, φυλάσσειν
τὴν μνήμην τῆς κοσμιότητός σου, καὶ προσεύχεσθαι τῷ Κυρίῳ δοῦναί σοι τελέσαι τὸν δρόμον
τῆς ἀγαθῆς πολιτείας καθὰ προείλου. τῷ ὄντι

---

[1] λατρεύοντες τῷ Κυρίῳ, καί om. E, Med.
[2] Θεοδώρᾳ κανονικῇ editi antiqi.; περὶ βίου κανονικοῦ add.
Harl.
[3] πάντας editi antiqi.   [4] τεταγμένων editi antiqi.
[5] ἀναμένομεν editi antiqi.   [6] πεμφθῆναι E.
[7] καί om. E.

---

[1] Cf. 2 Tim. 2. 15 : σπούδασον σεαυτὸν δόκιμον παραστῆσαι
τῷ Θεῷ, ἐργάτην ἀνεπαίσχυντον ὀρθοτομοῦντα τὸν λόγον τῆς
ἀληθείας. "Carefully study to present thyself approved

mandments and needing not to be ashamed,[1] serving
the Lord through a simple and not too elaborate
confession, and preserving inviolate and not too
elaborate their faith in the Father, Son, and Holy
Ghost.

LETTER CLXXIII

To Theodora, a Canoness [2]

We are rendered hesitant about writing by the
fact that we are not entirely assured that our letters
are placed in the hands of your Charity, but instead,
through the baseness of our messengers, innumerable
others read them first; and especially now when
throughout the world things are so disturbed.
Therefore I am waiting to be found fault with in
a measure and to have my letters forcefully demanded, so that I may treat this as itself a proof
of their delivery. However, both when writing and
when silent we keep in our hearts one duty—to
guard the memory of your Decorum and to pray
the Lord to grant that you may complete the course
of good conduct of life even as you have chosen.

unto God, a workman that needeth not to be ashamed, rightly
handling the word of truth."

[2] Written about the year 374. Canonicae were women
who devoted themselves to education, district visiting,
funerals, and various charitable works, and living in community apart from men. Cf. Socrates 1. 17 ; Sozomen 8. 23.
Rules were laid down for their guidance, as Basil here sets
forth, but St. Augustine in 423 drew up the first general
rules for such communities of women. They were distinguished from nuns in not being bound by vows, and from
deaconesses as not so distinctly discharging ministerial
duties.

449

γὰρ οὐ μικρὸς ἀγὼν ὁμολογοῦντι [1] τῆς ἐπαγγελίας
τὰ ἐφεξῆς ἐπάγειν. τὸ μὲν γὰρ προελέσθαι τὴν
κατὰ τὸ εὐαγγέλιον πολιτείαν παντός, τὸ δὲ καὶ
μέχρι τῶν μικροτάτων ἄγειν τὴν παρατήρησιν,
καὶ μηδὲν τῶν ἐκεῖ γεγραμμένων παρορᾶν, τοῦτο
πάνυ ὀλίγοις τῶν εἰς ἡμετέραν γνῶσιν ἡκόντων
κατώρθωται· ὥστε καὶ γλώσσῃ πεπεδημένῃ κεχρῆσθαι [2] καὶ ὀφθαλμῷ πεπαιδαγωγημένῳ κατὰ
τὸ βούλημα τοῦ εὐαγγελίου, καὶ χερσὶν ἐνεργεῖν
κατὰ τὸν σκοπὸν τῆς εὐαρεστήσεως τοῦ Θεοῦ,
καὶ πόδας κινεῖν καὶ ἑκάστῳ τῶν μελῶν οὕτω
κεχρῆσθαι ὡς ἐξ ἀρχῆς ὁ Δημιουργὸς ἡμῶν
ᾠκονόμησε· τὸ ἐν τῇ καταστολῇ κόσμιον, τὸ ἐν
ταῖς συντυχίαις τῶν ἀνδρῶν πεφυλαγμένον, τὸ
ἐν βρώμασιν αὔταρκες, τὸ ἐν τῇ κτήσει [3] τῶν
ἀναγκαίων ἀπέριττον. ταῦτα πάντα μικρὰ μὲν
ἁπλῶς οὕτω λεγόμενα, μεγάλου δὲ ἀγῶνος εἰς τὸ
κατορθωθῆναι χρήζοντα, ὡς ἐπ' αὐτῆς [4] τῆς ἀληθείας εὕρομεν. καὶ μὲν καὶ τὸ ἐν τῇ ταπεινο-
φροσύνῃ τέλειον, ὡς μήτε προγόνων περιφανείας
μεμνῆσθαι, μήτε, εἴ τι ὑπάρχει [5] ἡμῖν ἐκ [6] φύσεως
πλεονέκτημα ἢ κατὰ σῶμα ἢ κατὰ ψυχήν, τούτῳ
ἐπαίρεσθαι, μήτε τὰς ἔξωθεν περὶ ἡμῶν ὑπολήψεις
ἀφορμὴν ἐπάρσεώς τε καὶ φυσιώσεως ποιεῖσθαι,
ταῦτα τοῦ εὐαγγελικοῦ ἔχεται βίου. τὸ ἐν
ἐγκρατείᾳ εὔτονον, τὸ ἐν προσευχαῖς φιλόπονον,
τὸ ἐν φιλαδελφίᾳ συμπαθές, τὸ πρὸς τοὺς δεομένους κοινωνικόν, [7] τὸ τοῦ φρονήματος κατα-
βεβλημένον, ὁ συντριμμὸς τῆς καρδίας, [8] τὸ τῆς
πίστεως ὑγιές, τὸ ἐν σκυθρωπότητι ὁμαλόν, μηδέ-

---

[1] ὁμολογοῦντά τι editi antiqi.   [2] χρῆσθαι editi antiqi.

For truly it is no slight struggle for one who makes
a profession to carry out the consequences of his
promise. For choosing the evangelical life is in the
power of anyone, but carrying out its observance
even to the smallest details, and overlooking none
of the written rules—this has been accomplished
successfully by very few who have come to our
knowledge; as, for example, to keep the tongue
fettered and the eye disciplined according to the
intent of the Gospel, and to work with the hands
with a view to pleasing God, and to move the feet
and so to use each of the limbs as our Creator
ordained from the beginning; modesty in dress,
circumspection in the society of men, moderation in
food, simplicity in the acquisition of necessities.
All these things are small when thus simply mentioned, but require a great struggle to be observed
successfully, as in very truth we have discovered.
And, furthermore, perfection in humility, so that we
shall neither remember any distinction of ancestry,
nor, if we possess by nature any advantage whether
of body or of mind, be elated by this, nor to make
others' opinions of ourselves an occasion of exalta-
tion and pride—these things belong to the evangelical
life. Also constancy in self-control, assiduity in
prayer, sympathy in fraternal charity, generosity
toward the needy, subjection of pride, contrition
of heart, soundness of faith, equability in despond-

---

3 κτήσει E ; κυήσει editi.
4 ὡς ἐπ' αὐτῆς] εὑρήκαμεν editi antiqi.
5 ἐνυπάρχει editi antiqi.   6 ἐκ om. E.
7 τὸ πρὸς τοὺς δεομένους κοινωνικόν om. E.
8 τὸ πρὸς τοὺς δεομένους κοινωνικόν add. E.

ποτε τῆς ἐννοίας ἡμῶν λειπούσης τοῦ φοβεροῦ
καὶ ἀπαραιτήτου δικαστηρίου τὴν μνήμην πρὸς ὃ
ἐπειγόμεθα μὲν ἅπαντες, μέμνηνται δὲ αὐτοῦ καὶ
τὴν ἀπ' αὐτοῦ ἔκβασιν ἀγωνιῶσιν ἐλάχιστοι.

CLXXIV

Πρὸς ἐλευθέραν

Ἐγώ, καὶ πάνυ βουλόμενος συνεχῶς ἐπιστέλλειν τῇ εὐγενείᾳ ὑμῶν, ἐπέσχον[1] ἐμαυτὸν ἀεί,
μήπως δόξω τινὰς ὑμῖν πειρασμοὺς ἐπεγείρειν
διὰ τοὺς φιλέχθρως[2] πρὸς ἡμᾶς διακειμένους καί,
ὡς ἀκούω, μέχρι καὶ τούτων τὴν ἔχθραν ἐλαύ-
νοντας, ὥστε πολυπραγμονεῖν[3] εἴ πού τις καὶ
γράμμα ἡμέτερον δέχοιτο. ἐπειδὴ δὲ αὐτή, καλῶς
ποιοῦσα, κατῆρξας τοῦ γράμματος καὶ ἐπέστειλας
ἡμῖν ἃ[4] ἐχρῆν περὶ τῶν κατὰ τὴν[5] ψυχήν σου
πραγμάτων ἀνακοινουμένη, προετράπην εἰς τὸ
ἀντεπιστεῖλαι, ὁμοῦ μὲν τὰ ἐν τῷ παρελθόντι[6]
χρόνῳ ἐλλειφθέντα ἐπανορθούμενος, ὁμοῦ δὲ καὶ
πρὸς τὰ ἐπεσταλμένα παρὰ τῆς σῆς εὐγενείας
ἀποκρινόμενος.

Ὅτι μακαρία ἐστὶ[7] ψυχὴ ἡ νυκτὸς καὶ ἡμέρας
μηδεμίαν ἄλλην μέριμναν στρέφουσα ἢ πῶς ἐπὶ
τῆς μεγάλης ἡμέρας, καθ' ἣν πᾶσα ἡ κτίσις
περιστήσεται τὸν κριτὴν τὰς εὐθύνας τῶν πεπραγμένων ἀποδιδοῦσα, καὶ αὐτὴ δυνηθῇ κούφως ἀπο-

---

[1] ἀπέσχον editi antiqi.   [2] φιλεχθῶς editi antiqi.
[3] φιλοπραγμονεῖν E, Harl.

ency, never letting pass from our minds the remembrance of the awful and inexorable tribunal, towards
which we all indeed are hastening, though very few
are mindful of it or solicitous about what the issue
therefrom shall be.

LETTER CLXXIV

To a Widow[1]

I, ALTHOUGH wishing very much to write regularly
to your Nobility, have always checked myself, that
I may not seem to occasion you any trials on account
of those who are ill-disposed toward us, and, as I
hear, push their hatred so far that they make much
ado if anyone perchance receives even a letter from
us. But since you yourself, quite properly, have
taken the initiative in writing and in your letter
have communicated what you should as regards the
affairs of your soul, I have been moved to reply, at
one and the same time both rectifying my omissions
in the past, and replying to the present communications of your Nobility.

Take note that the soul is blessed which by night
and day revolves no other anxiety than how on the
great day, on which all creation shall stand about
the Judge and give an account of its deeds, it also
shall be able easily to discharge the reckoning of

---

[1] Written in 374.

---

4 ὡς E.　　　　　5 τήν om. E.
6 παρόντι E.　　　7 ἡ add. E.

θέσθαι τὸν λόγον τῶν βεβιωμένων. ὁ γὰρ ἐκείνην
τὴν ἡμέραν καὶ τὴν ὥραν πρὸ ὀφθαλμῶν τιθέμενος,
καὶ ἀεὶ μελετῶν τὴν ἐπὶ τοῦ ἀπαραλογίστου [1]
κριτηρίου ἀπολογίαν, ὁ τοιοῦτος ἢ οὐδὲν παντελῶς
ἢ ἐλάχιστα ἁμαρτήσεται, διότι [2] τὸ ἁμαρτάνειν
ἡμῖν κατὰ ἀπουσίαν τοῦ φόβου τοῦ Θεοῦ [3] γίνεται.
οἷς δ' ἂν ἐναργὴς παρῇ τῶν ἀπειλουμένων ἡ
προσδοκία, οὐδένα καιρὸν δώσει τοῖς τοιούτοις
ὁ σύνοικος φόβος εἰς ἀβουλήτους πράξεις ἢ
ἐνθυμήσεις ἐκπεσεῖν.

Καὶ μέμνησο τοίνυν τοῦ Θεοῦ, καὶ ἔχε τὸν
αὐτοῦ φόβον ἐν τῇ καρδίᾳ, καὶ πάντας εἰς τὴν
κοινωνίαν τῶν εὐχῶν παραλάμβανε. μεγάλη γὰρ
καὶ ἡ τῶν δυναμένων δυσωπεῖν τὸν Θεὸν βοήθεια.
καὶ μὴ διαλίπῃς ταῦτα ποιοῦσα. καὶ γὰρ καὶ
ζῶσιν ἡμῖν τὴν ἐν σαρκὶ ταύτῃ [4] ζωὴν ἀγαθὴ
ἔσται βοηθὸς ἡ προσευχή, καὶ ἀπερχομένοις
ἐντεῦθεν ἐφόδιον διαρκὲς πρὸς τὸν αἰῶνα τὸν
μέλλοντα. ὥσπερ δὲ ἡ φροντὶς πρᾶγμά ἐστιν
ἀγαθόν, οὕτω πάλιν ἡ ἀθυμία καὶ ἡ ἀπόγνωσις
καὶ τὸ δυσελπίστως ἔχειν πρὸς σωτηρίαν τῶν
βλαπτόντων ἐστὶ τὴν ψυχήν. ἐπέλπιζε τοίνυν
τῇ ἀγαθότητι τοῦ Θεοῦ, καὶ ἐκδέχου αὐτοῦ τὴν
ἀντίληψιν, γινώσκουσα ὅτι, ἐὰν καλῶς καὶ γνησίως
πρὸς αὐτὸν ἐπιστραφῶμεν, οὐ μόνον οὐκ ἀπορ-
ρίψει ἡμᾶς εἰς τὸ παντελές, ἀλλ' ἔτι λαλούντων
ἡμῶν τὰ ῥήματα τῆς προσευχῆς ἐρεῖ· Ἰδοὺ
πάρειμι.

---

[1] ἀπαραλογήτου editi antiqi.   [2] διόπερ E.

the life it has lived. For he who sets that day and hour before his eyes and ever meditates upon his defence before the tribunal which cannot be deceived, such a man will sin either not at all or very little, because sinning comes to pass in us through absence of the fear of God. But to whomsoever there is present the vivid expectation of the threatened punishments, the fear which dwells in such will give them no opportunity of falling into ill considered actions or thoughts.

Be mindful, then, of God, and keep the fear of Him in your heart, and invite all to communion in your prayers. For great is also the aid of those who are able to importune God. And do all these things without ceasing. For both while we live this life in the flesh will prayer be to us a goodly helper, and when we depart hence it will be a sufficient viaticum for the world to come. But just as anxious thought is a good thing, so again despondency, despair, and the attitude of misgiving as regards salvation are things that harm the soul. Hope, then, in the goodness of God, and expect His help, knowing that, if we turn to Him rightly and sincerely, not only will He not cast us off utterly, but will say even as we are uttering the words of our prayer : " Behold, I am with you."

---

[3] Κυρίου editi antiqi.   [4] ταύτην E.

CLXXV

Μαγνηνιανῷ [1] κόμητι

Πρώην ἐπέστελλέ μοι ἡ σεμνότης σου ἄλλα
τινὰ καὶ περὶ πίστεως γράψαι ἡμᾶς ἐναργῶς
προστάσσουσα. ἀλλ' ἐγὼ τὴν μὲν σὴν περὶ τὸ
πρᾶγμα ἄγαμαι σπουδήν,[2] καὶ εὔχομαι τῷ Θεῷ
ἀνενδότως σοι τῶν ἀγαθῶν τὴν αἵρεσιν ἐνυπάρχειν
καὶ ἀεί σε προκόπτοντα καὶ γνώσει καὶ ἔργοις
ἀγαθοῖς τελειοῦσθαι· διὰ δὲ τὸ μὴ βούλεσθαι
περὶ πίστεως σύνταγμα καταλιμπάνειν μηδὲ
γράφειν διαφόρους πίστεις, παρετηρησάμην μὴ [3]
ἀποστεῖλαι ἃ ἐπεζητήσατε.

Πλὴν δοκεῖτέ μοι περιηχεῖσθαι παρὰ τῶν
αὐτόθι, τῶν μηδὲν ἐργαζομένων, οἳ [4] ἐπὶ διαβολῇ
ἡμετέρᾳ λέγουσί τινα, ὡς ἐκ τούτου ἑαυτοὺς
συστήσοντες,[5] ἐὰν ἡμῶν τὰ αἴσχιστα καταψεύ-
σωνται. ἐκείνους μὲν γὰρ φανεροὶ ὁ παρελθὼν
χρόνος, καὶ προϊοῦσα ἡ πεῖρα φανερωτέρους
ποιήσει. ἡμεῖς δὲ παρακαλοῦμεν τοὺς ἠλπικότας
εἰς Χριστὸν μηδὲν παρὰ τὴν ἀρχαίαν περιεργά-
ζεσθαι πίστιν, ἀλλ' ὡς πιστεύομεν, οὕτω καὶ
βαπτίζεσθαι, ὡς δὲ βαπτιζόμεθα, οὕτω καὶ δοξο-
λογεῖν. ὀνόματα δὲ ἡμῖν ἀρκεῖ [6] ἐκεῖνα ὁμολογεῖν,

---

[1] Μαγνινιανῷ Med.   Μαγνημιανῷ editi antiqi.
[2] σπουδήν om. E.   [3] μή add. Capps.
[4] οἱ editi antiqi.   [5] συστήσαντες editi antiqi.
[6] ἀρκεῖν Med.

---

[1] Written about 374. This Magnenianus may be the one
mentioned in Letter CCCXXV, but he is otherwise unknown.
Another MS. reading is Magninianus.

LETTER CLXXV

To Count Magnenianus [1]

Just recently your Dignity wrote to me about certain other matters and explicitly commanding that we should write you concerning the faith. But while I admire your zeal regarding the matter, and pray God that you may adhere unswervingly to your choice of the good and that, always advancing in both knowledge and good works, you may become perfect; yet because I do not wish to leave behind me any work on the faith or to compose sundry creeds, I have kept to my resolution not to send what you have sought.[2]

However, you seem to me to be compassed by the din of men of that place,[3] who do no deed but say things in order to slander us, thinking to get credit for themselves from this, if they utter the most shameful lies about us. For the past reveals their characters and subsequent experience will reveal them even more clearly. But we exhort those who have put their hope in Christ not to concern themselves too much about any faith except the old, but, just as we believe, so also to be baptized, and just as we are baptized, so also to repeat the doxology.[4] And it is sufficient for us to confess those names which we

[2] A short time later Basil did this very thing for Amphilochius of Iconium, and wrote the treatise *De Spiritu Sancto*.

[3] The Benedictine edition (*Vita Basilii* XXX) thinks that the allusion is to Atarbius of Neocaesarea and some of his presbyters.

[4] Cf. Basil, *De Spiritu Sancto* 26.

457

ἃ παρελάβομεν παρὰ τῆς ἁγίας Γραφῆς καὶ τὴν
ἐπὶ τούτοις καινοτομίαν διαφεύγειν. οὐ γὰρ ἐν
τῇ ἐφευρέσει τῶν προσηγοριῶν ἡ σωτηρία ἡμῶν,
ἀλλ' ἐν τῇ ὑγιεῖ περὶ τῆς θεότητος εἰς ἣν πεπιστεύκαμεν ὁμολογίᾳ.

CLXXVI

Ἀμφιλοχίῳ, ἐπισκόπῳ Ἰκονίου

Παράσχοι ὁ ἅγιος Θεὸς ἐρρωμένῳ σοι τὸ σῶμα,
καὶ ἀπὸ πάσης ἀσχολίας ἀνειμένῳ, καὶ πάντα
πράττοντι κατὰ νοῦν, τὴν ἐπιστολὴν ἡμῶν ταύτην
εἰς χεῖρας ἐλθεῖν, ἵνα μὴ ἄπρακτος ἡμῶν ἡ
παράκλησις[1] γένηται, ἣν παρακαλοῦμεν νῦν
ἐπιφανῆναί σε ἡμῶν τῇ πόλει, ἐπὶ τῷ σεμνοτέραν
γενέσθαι τὴν πανήγυριν, ἣν δι' ἔτους ἄγειν ἐπὶ
τοῖς μάρτυσιν ἔθος ἐστὶν ἡμῶν τῇ ἐκκλησίᾳ.
πέπεισο γάρ, τιμιώτατέ μοι καὶ ποθεινότατε ὡς
ἀληθῶς, ὅτι πολλῶν εἰς πεῖραν ἐλθὼν ὁ παρ'
ἡμῖν[2] λαὸς τῆς οὐδενὸς οὕτως ἀντέχεται ἐπιτυχίας,
ὡς τῆς σῆς παρουσίας· τοιοῦτον κέντρον ἀγάπης
ἐκ τῆς μικρᾶς ἐκείνης συντυχίας ἐναφῆκας. ἵνα
οὖν καὶ ὁ Κύριος δοξασθῇ, καὶ λαοὶ εὐφρανθῶσι,
καὶ τιμηθῶσι μάρτυρες, καὶ ἡμεῖς οἱ γέροντες τῆς
ὀφειλομένης ἡμῖν παρὰ τέκνου γνησίου τύχωμεν
θεραπείας, καταξίωσον ἀόκνως μέχρις ἡμῶν
διαβῆναι, καὶ προλαβεῖν τὰς ἡμέρας τῆς συνόδου,
ὥστε ἐπὶ σχολῆς ἡμᾶς ἀλλήλοις συγγενέσθαι
καὶ[3] συμπαρακληθῆναι διὰ τῆς κοινωνίας τῶν

---

[1] παράκλητιν Ε.   [2] ἡμὼν editi antiqi.
[3] καί om. Ε.

LETTER CLXXVI

have received from the Holy Scripture and to shun
innovation in addition to them. For not in the
invention of appellations lies our salvation, but in the
sound confession of the Divinity in which we have
declared our faith.

LETTER CLXXVI

To Amphilochius, Bishop of Iconium [1]

May the holy God grant that this letter of ours
come into your hands, finding you strong in body,
free from all occupation, and faring in all respects
according to your wish, in order that our invitation
may not be in vain, which we now extend to you to
visit our city, for the purpose of rendering more
impressive the festival which it is the custom of our
church to celebrate annually in honour of the martyrs.[2]
For be assured, my most honoured and truly cherished
brother, that although our people have had experience of many visitors, they insist upon the visit
of no one so urgently as they do upon your coming;
so potent was the barb of love which you implanted
in them on the occasion of the former brief visit. In
order, therefore, that the Lord may be glorified, the
people made happy, the martyrs honoured, and we
old men receive the deference due to us from a true
son, deign to come to us without hesitation, and to
anticipate the days of the synod, so that we may
converse at leisure with each other and be mutually

[1] Written in 374. Basil invites Amphilochius to a festival
in honour of St. Eupsychius, and asks that he come three
days before the feast.
[2] *i.e.* Damas and Eupsychius. For Eupsychius, cf.
Letters, C, CLII, and CCLII.

πνευματικῶν χαρισμάτων. ἔστι δὲ ἡ ἡμέρα τῇ
πέμπτῃ τοῦ Σεπτεμβρίου. διὸ παρακαλοῦμεν
πρὸ τριῶν ἡμερῶν ἐπιστῆναι, ἵνα καὶ τοῦ
πτωχοτροφείου τὴν μνήμην μεγάλην ποιήσῃς τῇ
παρουσίᾳ. ἐρρωμένος καὶ εὔθυμος ἐν Κυρίῳ
ὑπερευχόμενός μου διαφυλαχθείης μοι καὶ τῇ τοῦ
Θεοῦ [1] ἐκκλησίᾳ χάριτι τοῦ Κυρίου.

CLXXVII

Σωφρονίῳ μαγίστρῳ

Καταλέγειν μὲν πάντας τοὺς δι' ἡμᾶς εὐερ-
γετηθέντας παρὰ τῆς σῆς μεγαλονοίας οὐ ῥάδιον·
οὕτω πολλοὺς μὲν [2] σύνισμεν ἑαυτοῖς εὐπεποιη-
κόσι διὰ τῆς μεγάλης σου χειρός, ἣν ὁ Κύριος
ἡμῖν σύμμαχον ἐπὶ τῶν μεγίστων καιρῶν ἐχαρίσατο. δικαιότατος δὲ πάντων καὶ ὁ νῦν προσαγόμενος διὰ τοῦ γράμματος ἡμῶν τυγχάνει,[3] ὁ
αἰδεσιμώτατος [4] ἀδελφὸς Εὐσέβιος, παραλόγῳ
συκοφαντίᾳ περιπεσών, ἣν ἀποσκεδάσαι μόνης
ἐστὶ τῆς σῆς ὀρθότητος. διὸ παρακαλοῦμεν, καὶ
τῷ δικαίῳ χαριζόμενον, καὶ πρὸς τὸ ἀνθρώπινον

---

[1] Χριστοῦ Ε.   [2] μέν om. E.
[3] τυγχάνειν editi antiqi.   [4] ἡμῶν add. editi antiqi.

---

[1] This date seems to be a mistake for the seventh, the day
of St. Eupsychius in the Greek calendar.

[2] By μνήμη the Benedictine edition understands the " mem-
orial " church or chapel erected by Basil in his hospital at
Caesarea, i.e. the church in the sense of a memorial. Cf.
Letter XCIV. For the use of μνήμη in this sense Du Cange

consoled through the communion of spiritual gifts. The day is the fifth of September.[1] Accordingly we urge you to arrive three days beforehand, in order that you may also make great by your presence the memorial chapel[2] of the house of the poor. In good health and joyful in the Lord, praying for me, may you be preserved to me and to the Church of God by the grace of the Lord.

LETTER CLXXVII

To Sophronius, Master[3]

To enumerate all those who for our sake have been benefited by your Magnanimity is not easy; to so many are we conscious of having done good through your mighty hand, which the Lord has graciously given to us as an ally in most critical times. But most worthy of all happens to be the one now being introduced to you through our letter, our most reverend brother Eusebius,[4] who has fallen under an absurd calumny, which it is in the power of your uprightness alone to repel. Therefore we urge you, favouring what is right, considering the

cites *Act. Conc. Chalced.* 1,144. He explains it as being equivalent to Latin *memoria*, i.e. *aedes sacra in qua extat sancti alicuius sepulcrum.* For such a use of *memoria*, cf. Augustine, *De Civ. Dei*, 22, 10: *Nos autem martyribus nostris non templa sicut diis sed memorias sicut hominibus mortuis fabricamus.*

[3] Written in 374. Sophronius, *magister officiorum*, was a fellow-student of Basil at Athens, and a friend of Gregory of Nazianzus. Other letters to this Sophronius are LXXVI, XCVI, CLXXVII, CLXXX, CXCII, and CCLXXII.

[4] Eusebius of Samosata. Cf. letters addressed to him.

461

ἀφορῶντα, καὶ ἡμῖν τὰς συνήθεις παρεχόμενον
χάριτας, ἀντὶ πάντων γενέσθαι τῷ ἀνδρί, καὶ
προστῆναι αὐτοῦ μετὰ τῆς[1] ἀληθείας. ἔχει γὰρ
οὐ μικρὰν συμμαχίαν τὴν ἀπὸ τοῦ δικαίου· ἣν
εἰ μὴ ὁ παρὼν καιρὸς καταβλάψειε, πάνυ ῥάδιον
σαφῶς καὶ ἀναντιρρήτως ἐπιδειχθήσεσθαι.[2]

CLXXVIII

Ἀβουργίῳ

Πολλοὺς οἶδα πολλάκις συστήσας τῇ τιμιότητί
σου καὶ γενόμενος ἐπὶ μεγίστων καιρῶν χρήσιμος
ἱκανῶς τοῖς καταπονουμένοις. οὐ μὴν τιμιώτερόν
γε ἐμοὶ οὐδ᾽ ὑπὲρ μειζόνων ἀγωνιζόμενον οἶδα
πρότερον παραπέμψας τῇ κοσμιότητί σου τοῦ
ποθεινοτάτου υἱοῦ Εὐσεβίου, τοῦ νῦν τὴν ἐπιστολὴν ταύτην ἐγχειρίζοντός σοι παρ᾽ ἡμῶν. ὃς
ποταπῷ μὲν συμπέπλεκται πράγματι αὐτός, ἂν
τύχοι τινὸς καιροῦ, διηγήσεταί σου τῇ σεμνότητι.
ἃ δὲ παρ᾽ ἡμῶν λεχθῆναι προσῆκε ταῦτά ἐστι·
μὴ παρασυρῆναι τὸν ἄνδρα, μηδὲ τῷ πολλοὺς
πεφηνέναι τοὺς ἐπὶ ταῖς χαλεπωτάταις πράξεσιν
ἑαλωκότας καὶ αὐτόν τι τῆς τῶν πολλῶν ὑπονοίας
παραπολαῦσαι· ἀλλὰ τυχεῖν δικαστηρίου, καὶ
εἰς ἐξέτασιν αὐτοῦ τὸν βίον ἀχθῆναι. ῥᾷστα
γὰρ οὕτω καὶ ἡ συκοφαντία φανερὰ γενήσεται,

---

[1] τῆς om. E.   [2] ἐπιδειχθῆναι editi antiqi.

lot of man, and conferring your customary favours upon us, to do your utmost for the man, and in company with the truth to defend him. For he has no mean alliance in having justice on his side, and unless the present crisis should interfere with this, it will be quite easy to give clear and irrefutable proof.

LETTER CLXXVIII

To Aburgius[1]

I know that I have often recommended many men to your Honour and that in the greatest crises I have proved sufficiently useful to those in affliction. But no man more honoured in my eyes or fighting for more important things have I ever before, I know, sent to your Decorum than our most beloved son Eusebius, who now places in your hands this letter from us. And in what sort of a difficulty he is involved he himself, if he should find an opportunity, will relate to your Dignity. But what is fitting that we ourselves should say is this : that the man should not be swept aside nor, because there are many who have clearly been caught in the most grievous acts, should he also in any degree incidentally derive disadvantage from the suspicion existing against the many ; on the contrary, he should obtain a trial, and his life should be subjected to examination. For in this way both will the calumny very easily become manifest, and this man, having

---

[1] Written in 374, on the same subject as the preceding. Previous letters addressed to Aburgius are XXXIII, LXXV, and CXLVII.

καὶ ὁ ἀνὴρ τυχὼν τῆς δικαιοτάτης προστασίας
κῆρυξ ἔσται διηνεκὴς τῶν ὑπηργμένων αὐτῷ
παρὰ τῆς σῆς ἡμερότητος.

CLXXIX

Ἀρινθαίῳ

Καὶ φιλελεύθερόν σε εἶναι καὶ φιλάνθρωπον τό
τε τῆς φύσεως εὐγενὲς καὶ τὸ πρὸς πάντας
κοινωνικὸν ἱκανῶς ἡμᾶς ἐκδιδάσκει. διὸ θαρροῦν-
τως [1] πρεσβεύομεν ὑπὲρ ἀνδρὸς λαμπροῦ μὲν
ἄνωθεν καὶ ἐκ προγόνων, πλείονος δὲ δι’ ἑαυτὸν
τιμῆς καὶ αἰδοῦς ἀξίου διὰ τὴν ἐνυπάρχουσαν
αὐτῷ τῶν τρόπων ἡμερότητα· ὥστε σε παρακληθέντα ὑφ’ ἡμῶν παραστῆναι αὐτῷ ἀγωνιζομένῳ
δίκην, τῆς μὲν ἀληθείας ἔνεκεν [2] εὐκαταφρόνητον,
ἐναγώνιον δὲ ἄλλως διὰ τὸ τῆς συκοφαντίας βαρύ.
μεγάλη γὰρ ἂν γένοιτο αὐτῷ ῥοπὴ πρὸς σωτηρίαν,
εἰ καταξιώσειάς τι ῥῆμα φιλάνθρωπον ὑπὲρ
αὐτοῦ προέσθαι, [3] προηγουμένως μὲν τῷ δικαίῳ
χαριζόμενος, ἔπειτα καὶ ἡμῖν τοῖς ἐξαιρέτοις
σου τὴν συνήθη τιμὴν καὶ χάριν καὶ ἐν τούτῳ
χαριζόμενος.

---

[1] θαρροῦντες tres recent. MSS.   [2] ἕνεκα editi antiqi.
[3] προίεσθαι editi antiqi.

---

[1] According to the Benedictine edition, the circumstances
referred to are Valens' cruelties upon those who were accused
of inquiring by divination as to who were to succeed him on
the throne. Cf. Amm. Marcell. 29, 1, 2.

received your most just protection, will be a perpetual herald of the benefits conferred upon him by
your Clemency.[1]

LETTER CLXXIX

To Arinthaeus [2]

THAT you are a lover both of freedom and of mankind the nobility of your nature and your accessibility
to all sufficiently informs us. Therefore with confidence do we address you in behalf of a man who is
indeed distinguished through long lineage and
through his ancestors, but worthy through his own
merit of greater honour and respect because of the
inherent gentleness of his character; so that at our
exhortation you may assist him in his fight against a
charge which, so far as the truth is concerned,
deserves nothing but contempt, but for the rest is
dangerous on account of the seriousness of the
calumny. For it would be of great influence towards
his safety if you would deign to say a kind word on
his behalf, since in the first place you would be
assisting justice, and secondly to us your chosen
friends you would be showing in this instance also
your accustomed honour and favour.

[2] Written in 374. Arinthaeus was an able general under
Valens. He was a friend of Basil and a staunch protector of
the Church, although, as was usual in that age, he deferred
baptism till his death-bed. Cf. Letter CCLXIX. He was
consul in 372, and must have died before Basil (379). If we
are to believe Theodoret (*Eccl. Hist.* 4, 30), he seconded the
general Trajan's rebuke of Valens in 378 ; so he must have
died but a few months before Basil. Cf. Tillemont, *Em-
pereurs*, 5, 100.

CLXXX

Σωφρονίῳ μαγίστρῳ, Εὐμαθίου ἕνεκεν

Ἀνδρὶ ἀξιολόγῳ περιτυχὼν περιστάσει οὐκ
ἀνεκτῇ κεχρημένῳ ἔπαθον τὴν ψυχήν. τί γὰρ
οὐκ ἔμελλον, ἄνθρωπος ὤν, ἀνθρώπῳ ἐλευθέρῳ
παρ᾽ ἀξίαν ἐμπεπλεγμένῳ πράγμασι συναλγεῖν;
καὶ βουλευσάμενος [1] πῶς ἂν γενοίμην αὐτῷ
χρήσιμος, μίαν εὗρον λύσιν τῆς κατεχούσης
αὐτὸν δυσχερείας, εἰ τῇ σῇ κοσμιότητι ποιήσαιμι
γνώριμον. σὸν οὖν τὸ ἐφεξῆς, τὴν σαυτοῦ σπουδήν,
ἣν εἰς πολλοὺς ἐφ᾽ [2] ἡμῖν μάρτυσιν [3] ἐπιδέδειξαι,
καὶ αὐτῷ παρασχέσθαι.

Τὸ δὲ πρᾶγμα γνωρίσει ἡ ἐπιδοθεῖσα παρ᾽
αὐτοῦ δέησις τοῖς βασιλεῦσιν, ἣν καὶ λαβεῖν εἰς
χεῖρας καὶ συμπρᾶξαι τῷ ἀνδρὶ τὰ δυνατὰ
παρακλήθητι. καὶ γὰρ Χριστιανῷ χαρίζῃ, [4] καὶ
εὐγενεῖ, καὶ ἀπὸ λόγου πολλοῦ τὸ αἰδέσιμον
ἐπαγομένῳ. ἐὰν δὲ προσθῶμεν, ὅτι καὶ ἡμεῖς
μεγάλην διὰ τῆς εἰς αὐτὸν εὐποιίας ὑποδεχόμεθα [5]
χάριν, πάντως, κἂν μικρὸν ᾖ ἄλλως τὸ ἡμέτερον,
ἀλλὰ τῆς σῆς σεμνότητος ἀεὶ ἐν λόγῳ ποιεῖσθαι
τὰ καθ᾽ ἡμᾶς ἀνεχομένης, οὐ μικρὸν φανεῖται τὸ
χαρισθὲν ἡμῖν.

---

[1] οὖν add. editi antiqi.   [2] ὑφ᾽ editi antiqi.
[3] μάρτυρας E.   [4] χαρίζει editi antiqi.
[5] ἀποδεχόμεθα E ; ἀποδεξόμεθα editi antiqi.

---

[1] Written in 374. Nothing is known about this Eumathius,
except for the present letter.

LETTER CLXXX

LETTER CLXXX

To Sophronius, the Master, in behalf of
Eumathius.[1]

On meeting an estimable man who found himself
in an unbearable situation I suffered in my soul.
For why, since I am man,[2] was I not to sympathize
with a free man involved in troubles beyond his
deserts? And in deliberating how I could be
helpful to him, I found but one solution of the
difficulty that besets him—if I should make him
known to your Decorum. The rest, therefore,
depends upon you—to place at his disposal also that
zeal of yours which on our testimony you have
shown to many.

The petition presented by him to the emperors
will inform you of the facts; and pray be kind
enough to take this into your hands and do all in
your power for the man. For you are doing a
favour to a Christian, to a man of noble birth, and to
one who wins respect through his great learning.
And if we add that we also shall receive a great
kindness through your good offices to him, assuredly,
even though our concerns are in general of small
importance to you, yet, since your August Reverence
always deigns to give consideration to our affairs, the
favour granted to us will not appear small.

---

[2] Cf. Menander, *Frag.* 602 K : οὐδείς ἐστί, μοι ἀλλότριος, ἂν
ᾖ χρηστός· ἡ φύσις μία πάντων, τὸ δ' οἰκεῖον συνίστησιν
τρόπος. "For me none is a foreigner if so be he is good.
One nature is in all and it is character that makes the tie of
kin." Cf. also Terence, *Heaut. Tim.* 77.

CLXXXI

Ὀτρηίῳ Μελητινης

Οἶδα ὅτι καὶ τῆς σῆς εὐλαβείας τοσοῦτον ἅπτεται ὁ χωρισμὸς τοῦ θεοφιλεστάτου ἐπισκόπου Εὐσεβίου ὅσον καὶ ἡμῶν αὐτῶν. ἐπεὶ οὖν ἀμφότεροι χρήζομεν παρακλήσεως, ἀλλήλοις γενώμεθα παραμυθία. καὶ σύ τε ἡμῖν ἐπίστελλε τὰ ἐκ Σαμοσάτων, ἡμεῖς τε ἅπερ ἂν μάθωμεν ἀπὸ τῆς Θράκης ἀπαγγελοῦμεν. φέρει γὰρ ἐμοὶ μὲν τὸ γινώσκειν τοῦ λαοῦ τὴν ἔνστασιν οὐ μικρὰν ῥᾳστώνην ἐκ τῶν παρόντων λυπηρῶν, τῇ δὲ σῇ χρηστότητι τὸ διδάσκεσθαι ἐν οἷς ἐστὶν ὁ κοινὸς ἡμῶν πατήρ. ἀμέλει καὶ νῦν οὐ γράμμασι σημαίνειν ἔχομεν· ἀλλ' αὐτὸν παρεστήσαμέν σοι τὸν ἀκριβῶς εἰδότα[1] καὶ ἀπαγγέλλοντα[2] ἐν οἷς αὐτὸν κατέλιπε, καὶ ὅπως καὶ φέροντα τὰ συμπίπτοντα. εὔχου τοίνυν καὶ ὑπὲρ αὐτοῦ καὶ ὑπὲρ ἡμῶν, ἵνα ὁ Κύριος ταχεῖαν ἀπαγάγῃ τῶν δεινῶν τούτων τὴν λύσιν.

CLXXXII

Τοῖς πρεσβυτέροις Σαμοσάτων[3]

Ὅσον λυπούμεθα ἐνθυμούμενοι τὴν ἐρημίαν τῆς ἐκκλησίας, τοσοῦτον μακαρίζομεν ὑμᾶς εἰς τοῦτο

---

[1] ἰδόντα E.

[2] ἀπαγγελοῦντα Coisl. secundus et Reg. secundus.

[3] Παυλίνῳ πρεσβυτέρῳ ἐν ἐξορίᾳ ὄντι Claromontanus. Παυλίνῳ πρεσβύτῃ editi antiqi.

LETTER CLXXXI

To Otreius of Meletine [1]

I know that the removal of the most God-beloved
bishop Eusebius touches your Reverence as much as
it does even ourselves.   Since, then, we both need
consolation, let us be a solace to each other.   And
do you write to us the news from Samosata, and we
shall report what we learn from Thrace.[2]   For to
me the knowledge of the steadfastness of your
people brings no small alleviation of our present
miseries, as does to your Uprightness information
regarding the condition of our common father.   To
be sure, even now we cannot inform you by letter ;
but   we   have   commended   to   you   one   who
accurately knows and reports in what state he left
him and how, moreover, he is bearing his afflictions.
Pray, therefore, both for him and for us, that the
Lord may bring a quick release from these troubles.

LETTER CLXXXII

To the Presbyters of Samosata [3]

As much as we grieve in considering the desola-
tion [4] of the Church, equally do we felicitate you on

---

[1] Written in 374.   Otreius, one of the leading orthodox
prelates of the fourth century, was at Tyana in 367, and at
Constantinople in 381.   Meletine, now Malatia, in Armenia
Minor.

[2] Eusebius was in exile there at this time.

[3] Written in 374.

[4] The reference is chiefly to the exile of Eusebius.

φθάσαντας τὸ μέτρον τῆς ἀθλήσεως, ὃ παράσχοι
ὑμῖν [1] ὁ Κύριος μακροθύμως παρελθεῖν, ἵνα καὶ
τῆς πιστῆς οἰκονομίας καὶ τῆς γενναίας ἐνστάσεως,
ἣν ὑπὲρ τοῦ ὀνόματος τοῦ Χριστοῦ ἐπεδείξασθε,
τὸν μέγαν μισθὸν ὑποδέξησθε.

CLXXXIII

Πολιτευομένοις Σαμοσάτων [2]

Ὅταν ἀπίδω ὅτι ὁ μὲν πειρασμὸς κατὰ πάσης
ἤδη κέχυται τῆς οἰκουμένης, καὶ αἱ μέγισται τῶν
ἐπὶ Συρίας πόλεων τῶν ἴσων ὑμῖν [3] πεπείρανται
παθημάτων, οὐ πανταχοῦ δὲ οὕτω δόκιμον καὶ
διαπρεπὲς ἐπ’ ἀγαθοῖς ἔργοις τὸ βουλευτήριον, ὡς
τὸ ὑμέτερον νῦν ἐπὶ τῇ σπουδῇ τῶν ἀγαθῶν
ἔργων διαβεβόηται, ἐγγύς εἰμι καὶ χάριν ἔχειν [4]
τοῖς οἰκονομηθεῖσιν. εἰ γὰρ μὴ ἐγεγόνει ἡ θλίψις
αὕτη, οὐκ ἂν ὑμῶν διεφάνη τὸ δόκιμον. ὥστε
ἔοικεν, ὅπερ ἐστὶ κάμινος χρυσῷ, τοῦτο εἶναι ἡ
ὑπὲρ τῆς εἰς Θεὸν ἐλπίδος θλίψις τοῖς ἀντι-
ποιουμένοις τινὸς ἀρετῆς.

Ἄγε οὖν, ὦ θαυμάσιοι, ὅπως τοῖς προπεπονη-
μένοις ἄξια ἐπαγάγητε τὰ ἑπόμενα, καὶ φανῆτε
μεγάλῃ κρηπῖδι ἀξιολογωτέραν ἐπιτιθέντες τὴν

[1] ἡμῖν E, Med.
[2] ἀγαπητικὴ προσφώνησις add. Reg. secundus, Coisl. secundus.
[3] ἡμῖν editi antiqi.
[4] ἐπί add. E.

[1] Written in 374, on Eusebius' exile.

your having already arrived at this limit of your struggle, through which may the Lord grant that you may pass patiently, in order that both for the faithful stewardship and for the noble steadfastness which you have shown for Christ's name, you may receive the great reward.

LETTER CLXXXIII

To the Senate of Samosata [1]

WHENEVER I observe that our trial has now become spread over the whole earth, and that the greatest cities of Syria have experienced sufferings the equal of your own, but that nowhere has the Senate shown itself so tested and distinguished in good works as yours has now been proclaimed because of its zeal for good works, I am almost even thankful for what has been ordained. For if this affliction had not come, neither would your probity have been made manifest. So it seems that what a furnace is to gold,[2] such is this affliction, endured on behalf of our hope in God, to those who lay claim to some degree of virtue.

Come then, O admirable men, see that to your labours already accomplished you add others to follow that are worthy of them, and that on the great foundation you are seen to place a capstone

---

[2] Cf. Prov. 17. 3 : ὥσπερ δοκιμάζεται ἐν καμίνῳ ἄργυρος καὶ χρυσός, οὕτως ἐκλεκταὶ καρδίαι παρὰ Κυρίῳ. "As silver is tried by fire, and gold in the furnace : so the Lord trieth the hearts." Cf. also Prov. 27. 21 : δοκίμιον ἀργύρῳ καὶ χρυσῷ πύρωσις, ἀνὴρ δὲ δοκιμάζεται διὰ στόματος ἐγκωμιαζόντων αὐτόν. "As silver is tried in the fining-pot and gold in the furnace : so a man is tried by the mouth of him that praiseth."

COLLECTED LETTERS OF SAINT BASIL

κορυφήν,¹ καὶ περίστητε μὲν τὸν ποιμένα τῆς
ἐκκλησίας, ὅταν δῷ ὁ Κύριος αὐτὸν ἐπὶ τῶν ἰδίων ²
φανῆναι θρόνων,³ ἄλλος ἄλλο τι τῶν ὑπὲρ τῆς
Ἐκκλησίας τοῦ Θεοῦ πεπολιτευμένων ἡμῖν ⁴
διηγούμενοι, ἐν δὲ τῇ μεγάλῃ τοῦ Κυρίου ἡμέρᾳ
ἕκαστος κατὰ τὴν ἀναλογίαν τῶν πεπονημένων
παρὰ τοῦ μεγαλοδώρου Θεοῦ δεχόμενοι τὴν ἀντίδοσιν. ἡμῶν δὲ μεμνημένοι καὶ ἐπιστέλλοντες
ὁσάκις ἂν ᾖ δυνατόν, δίκαιά τε ποιήσετε τοῖς
ἴσοις ἡμᾶς ἀμειβόμενοι, καὶ ἅμα οὐ μικρῶς ⁵ ἡμᾶς
εὐφρανεῖτε, τῆς ἡδίστης ἡμῖν φωνῆς ὑμῶν ἐναργῆ
σύμβολα διὰ τῶν γραμμάτων διαπεμπόμενοι.

CLXXXIV

Εὐσταθίῳ, ἐπισκόπῳ Ἱμμερίας ⁶

Οἶδα ὅτι στυγνοποιὸν πρᾶγμα ἡ ὀρφανία καὶ
πολυάσχολον, διὰ τὸ ἐρημίαν ἐπάγειν τῶν
προεστώτων. ὅθεν λογίζομαι καὶ τὴν σὴν εὐλάβειαν ἐπιστυγνάζουσαν τοῖς συμβεβηκόσι μὴ
ἐπιστέλλειν ἡμῖν, καὶ ὁμοῦ ἐν πλείονι εἶναι νῦν
ἀσχολίᾳ, περιτρέχειν ⁷ τὰ τοῦ Χριστοῦ ποίμνια
διὰ τὴν πανταχόθεν τῶν ἐχθρῶν ἐπανάστασιν.
ἀλλ' ἐπειδὴ πάσης λύπης παρηγορία ἡ πρὸς
τοὺς ὁμοψύχους ἐστὶν ὁμιλία, καταξίου ὁσάκις
ἂν δυνατόν σοι ἐπιστέλλειν ἡμῖν, καὶ αὐτός τε

¹ κορωνίδες Reg. secundus, Coisl. secundus, Paris.
² τῶν ἰδίων] τὸν ἴδιον Ε.   ³ θρόνον Ε.
⁴ ὑμῖν Ε.   ⁵ σμικρῶς Ε.
⁶ Ἐμμέρως Coisl. secundus, Reg. secundus.
⁷ περιέπειν Ε, Med.

more distinguished still, and that you may stand about the shepherd [1] of the Church, whenever the Lord grants him to appear on his proper throne, each one relating to us some different act performed on behalf of the Church of God, and on the great day of the Lord each one receiving from the bountiful God a reward proportionate to his labours.   But if you are mindful of us and write as often as is possible, you will do what is just by requiting us with like for like, and at the same time you will gladden us not a little by sending us through your letters vivid symbols of your voice which we find most sweet.

LETTER CLXXXIV

To Eustathius, Bishop of Himmeria [2]

I know that orphanhood brings sadness and causes much concern, because it occasions a loss of those who are placed over us.   Wherefore I consider that your Piety also, because he is saddened by what has come to pass, fails to write to us, and at the same time that he is at this moment still more preoccupied, in having to visit [3] the flocks of Christ because of the uprising of the enemy on every side. But since discourse between those of like minds is a consolation for every grief, deign as often as you can

---

[1] Eusebius, in exile at this time. Cf. the preceding letters.

[2] Written in 374.   Himmeria was in Osrhoene.   This Eustathius is otherwise unknown.

[3] The Benedictine edition suggests the reading περιτρέχειν τε, "and is visiting."

COLLECTED LETTERS OF SAINT BASIL

ἀναπαύεσθαι ἐν τῷ φθέγγεσθαι πρὸς ἡμᾶς, καὶ
ἡμᾶς παρηγορεῖν ἐν τῷ μεταδιδόναι ἡμῖν τῶν
σεαυτοῦ ῥημάτων. τοῦτο δὲ καὶ ἡμεῖς σπου-
δάσομεν ποιῆσαι ὁσάκις ἂν ἡμῖν ἐνδιδῷ τὰ πράγματα. εὔχου δὲ καὶ αὐτὸς καὶ πᾶσαν τὴν
ἀδελφότητα παρακάλεσον σπουδαίως δυσωπεῖν
τὸν Κύριον, ἵνα δείξῃ ποτὲ ἡμῖν λύσιν τῆς περιε-
χούσης ἡμᾶς κατηφείας.

CLXXXV

Θεοδότῳ, ἐπισκόπῳ Βεροίας

Οἶδα ὅτι, εἰ καὶ μὴ ἐπιστέλλεις ἡμῖν, ἀλλ᾽ ἐν
τῇ καρδίᾳ σου ὑπάρχει ἡ μνήμη ἡμῶν. καὶ τοῦτο
τεκμαίρομαι, οὐχ ὅτι αὐτὸς ἄξιός εἰμι μνήμης
τινὸς δεξιᾶς, ἀλλ᾽ ὅτι ἡ σὴ ψυχὴ πλουτεῖ ἐν τῇ
τῆς ἀγάπης περιουσίᾳ. πλὴν ἀλλ᾽ ὅσον δυνατόν
σοι ταῖς παρεμπιπτούσαις προφάσεσι κέχρησο
εἰς τὸ ἐπιστέλλειν ἡμῖν, ἵνα καὶ ἡμεῖς μᾶλλον
εὐψυχῶμεν μανθάνοντες τὰ περὶ ὑμῶν, καὶ
ἀφορμὴν λαμβάνωμεν εἰς τὸ καὶ αὐτοὶ σημαίνειν
ὑμῖν τὰ ἡμέτερα. οὗτος γάρ ἐστιν ὁ τρόπος τῆς
ὁμιλίας τοῖς τοσοῦτον διεζευγμένοις[1] τῷ σώματι,
ὁ δι᾽ ἐπιστολῶν, οὗ μὴ ἀποστερῶμεν ἀλλήλους,
καθόσον ἂν ἐνδιδῷ τὰ πράγματα. παράσχοι δὲ
ὁ Κύριος καὶ τὴν κατ᾽ ὀφθαλμοὺς ἡμῖν συντυχίαν,
ἵνα καὶ τὴν ἀγάπην αὐξήσωμεν καὶ τὴν εἰς τὸν
Δεσπότην ἡμῶν εὐχαριστίαν πλεονάσωμεν ἐπὶ
μείζοσι ταῖς παρ᾽ αὐτοῦ δωρεαῖς.

---

[1] διαζευγνυμένοις editi antiqi.

to write to us, and thus both to gain strength for yourself by speaking to us, and to console us by making us sharers of your words. And this too we also shall endeavour to do as often as circumstances permit us. And do you yourself pray, and exhort the whole brotherhood earnestly to importune the Lord, that He may one day show us release from the sorrow that surrounds us.

LETTER CLXXXV

To Theodotus, Bishop of Berrhoea [1]

I know that, even though you do not write to us, yet in your heart there exists the memory of us. And I judge this, not because I myself am worthy of any assurance of remembrance, but because your soul is rich in the abundance of charity. But nevertheless, in so far as it is possible for you, do make use of the opportunities that offer themselves to write to us, in order that we may be of better courage on learning of your affairs, and that we too may ourselves receive an opportunity of making ours known to you. For this is the means of conversation for those who are so widely separated in person, I mean correspondence by letter, and of this let us not deprive each other, in so far as circumstances may permit. And may the Lord grant us also a meeting face to face, in order that we may both increase our charity and multiply our thanksgiving to our Master for His still greater gifts.

[1] Written in 374. Theodotus was orthodox Bishop of Berrhoea in Syria under Valens. Nothing more is known about him.

INDEX OF PROPER NAMES

477

INDEX OF PROPER NAMES

INDEX OF PROPER NAMES

479

INDEX OF PROPER NAMES

PRINTED IN GREAT BRITAIN BY RICHARD CLAY & SONS, LIMITED,
BUNGAY, SUFFOLK.

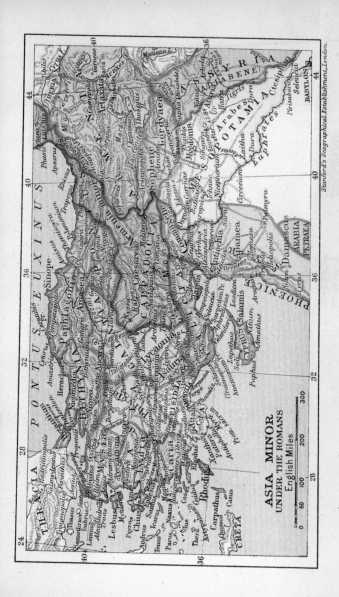

ASIA MINOR
UNDER THE ROMANS
English Miles

Stanford's Geographical Establishment, London.

THE LOEB CLASSICAL LIBRARY

VOLUMES ALREADY PUBLISHED

Latin Authors

APULEIUS. THE GOLDEN ASS (METAMORPHOSES).
W. Adlington (1566). Revised by S. Gaselee. (*4th Imp.*)

AULUS GELLIUS. J. C. Rolfe. 3 Vols.

AUSONIUS. H. G. Evelyn White. 2 Vols.

BOETHIUS: TRACTS AND DE CONSOLATIONE
PHILOSOPHIAE. Rev. H. F. Stewart and E. K. Rand.
(*2nd Imp.*)

CAESAR: CIVIL WARS. A. G. Peskett. (*2nd Imp.*)

CAESAR: GALLIC WAR. H. J. Edwards. (*4th Imp.*)

CATULLUS. F. W. Cornish; TIBULLUS. J. B. Postgate;
AND PERVIGILIUM VENERIS. J. W. Mackail. (*8th
Imp.*)

CICERO: DE FINIBUS. H. Rackham. (*2nd Imp.*)

CICERO: DE OFFICIIS. Walter Miller. (*2nd Imp.*)

CICERO: DE SENECTUTE, DE AMICITIA, DE
DIVINATIONE. W. A. Falconer. (*2nd Imp.*)

CICERO: DE REPUBLICA AND DE LEGIBUS. Clinton
Keyes.

CICERO: LETTERS TO ATTICUS. E. O. Winstedt.
3 Vols. (Vol. I. *4th Imp.*, Vols. II. and III. *2nd Imp.*)

CICERO: LETTERS TO HIS FRIENDS. W. Glynn
Williams. 3 Vols. Vol. I.

CICERO: PHILIPPICS. W. C. A. Ker.

CICERO: PRO ARCHIA, POST REDITUM, DE DOMO, ETC. N. H. Watts.

CICERO: TUSCULAN DISPUTATIONS. J. E. King.

CICERO: PRO CAECINA, PRO LEGE MANILIA, PRO CLUENTIO, PRO RABIRIO. H. Grose Hodge.

CLAUDIAN. M. Platnauer. 2 Vols.

CONFESSIONS OF ST. AUGUSTINE. W. Watts (1631). 2 Vols. (*3rd Imp.*)

FRONTINUS: STRATAGEMS AND AQUEDUCTS. C. E. Bennett.

FRONTO: CORRESPONDENCE. C. R. Haines. 2 Vols.

HORACE: ODES AND EPODES. C. E. Bennett. (*7th Imp.*)

HORACE: SATIRES, EPISTLES, ARS POETICA. H. R. Fairclough.

JUVENAL AND PERSIUS. G. G. Ramsay. (*4th Imp.*)

LIVY. B. O. Foster. 13 Vols. Vols. I.–IV. (Vol. I. *2nd Imp.*)

LUCRETIUS. W. H. D. Rouse. (*2nd Imp.*)

MARTIAL. W. C. A. Ker. 2 Vols. (*2nd Imp.*)

OVID: HEROIDES AND AMORES. Grant Showerman. (*2nd Imp.*)

OVID: METAMORPHOSES. F. J. Miller. 2 Vols. (Vol. I. *4th Imp.*, Vol. II. *3rd Imp.*)

OVID: TRISTIA AND EX PONTO. A. L. Wheeler.

PETRONIUS. M. Heseltine; SENECA: APOCOLO-CYNTOSIS. W. H. D. Rouse. (*5th Imp.*)

PLAUTUS. Paul Nixon. 5 Vols. Vols. I.-III. (Vol. I. *3rd Imp.*)

PLINY: LETTERS. Melmoth's Translation revised by W. M. L. Hutchinson. 2 Vols. (*3rd Imp.*)

PROPERTIUS. H. E. Butler. (*3rd Imp.*)

QUINTILIAN. H. E. Butler. 4 Vols.

SALLUST. J. C. Rolfe.

SCRIPTORES HISTORIAE AUGUSTAE. D. Magie
3 Vols. Vols. I. and II.

SENECA: EPISTULAE MORALES. R. M. Gummere.
3 Vols. (Vol. I. 2nd Imp.)

SENECA: MORAL ESSAYS. J. W. Basore. 3 Vols.
Vol. I.

SENECA: TRAGEDIES. F. J. Miller. 2 Vols. (2nd Imp.)

STATIUS. J. H. Mozley. 2 Vols.

SUETONIUS. J. C. Rolfe. 2 Vols. (3rd Imp.)

TACITUS: DIALOGUS. Sir Wm. Peterson and AGRI-
COLA AND GERMANIA. Maurice Hutton. (3rd Imp.)

TACITUS: HISTORIES. C. H. Moore. 2 Vols. Vol.

TERENCE. John Sargeaunt. 2 Vols. (5th Imp.)

VELLEIUS PATERCULUS AND RES GESTAE. F. W.
Shipley.

VIRGIL. H. R. Fairclough. 2 Vols. (Vol. I. 6th Imp.,
Vol. II. 3rd Imp.)

Greek Authors

ACHILLES TATIUS. S. Gaselee.

AENEAS TACTICUS: ASCLEPIODOTUS AND ONA-SANDER. The Illinois Greek Club.

AESCHINES. C. D. Adams.

AESCHYLUS. H. Weir Smyth. 2 Vols. (Vol. I. *2nd Imp.*)

APOLLODORUS. Sir James G. Frazer. 2 Vols.

APOLLONIUS RHODIUS. R. C. Seaton. (*3rd Imp.*)

THE APOSTOLIC FATHERS. Kirsopp Lake. 2 Vols. (Vol. I. *4th Imp.*, Vol. II. *3rd Imp.*)

APPIAN'S ROMAN HISTORY. Horace White. 4 Vols. (Vol. IV. *2nd Imp.*)

ARISTOPHANES. Benjamin Bickley Rogers. 3 Vols. (*2nd Imp.*) Verse trans.

ARISTOTLE: THE "ART" OF RHETORIC. J. H. Freese.

ARISTOTLE: THE NICOMACHEAN ETHICS. H. Rackham.

ARISTOTLE: POETICS AND LONGINUS. W. Hamilton Fyfe; DEMETRIUS ON STYLE. W. Rhys Roberts.

ATHENAEUS: DEIPNOSOPHISTAE. C. B. Gulick. 7 Vols. Vols. I and II.

CALLIMACHUS AND LYCOPHRON. A. W. Mair; ARATUS. G. R. Mair.

CLEMENT OF ALEXANDRIA. Rev. G. W. Butterworth.

DAPHNIS AND CHLOE. Thornley's Translation revised by J. M. Edmonds; AND PARTHENIUS. S. Gaselee. (*2nd Imp.*)

DEMOSTHENES, DE CORONA AND DE FALSA LEGATIONE. C. A. Vince and J. H. Vince.

DIO CASSIUS: ROMAN HISTORY. E. Cary. 9 Vols.

DIOGENES LAERTIUS. R. D. Hicks. 2 Vols.

EPICTETUS. W. A. Oldfather. 2 Vols. Vol. I.

EURIPIDES. A. S. Way. 4 Vols. (Vol. I. *3rd Imp.*, Vols. II. and IV. *4th Imp.*, Vol. III. *2nd Imp.*) Verse trans.

EUSEBIUS: ECCLESIASTICAL HISTORY. Kirsopp Lake. 2 Vols. Vol. I.

GALEN: ON THE NATURAL FACULTIES. A. J. Brock. (2nd Imp.)

THE GREEK ANTHOLOGY. W. R. Paton. 5 Vols. (Vol. I. 3rd Imp., Vol. II. 2nd Imp.)

THE GREEK BUCOLIC POETS (THEOCRITUS, BION, MOSCHUS). J. M. Edmonds. (5th Imp.)

HERODOTUS. A. D. Godley. 4 Vols. (Vols. I.-III. 2nd Imp.)

HESIOD AND THE HOMERIC HYMNS. H. G. Evelyn White. (3rd Imp.)

HIPPOCRATES. W. H. S. Jones and E. T. Withington. 4 Vols. Vols. I.-III.

HOMER: ILIAD. A. T. Murray. 2 Vols. (Vol. I. 2nd Imp.)

HOMER: ODYSSEY. A. T. Murray. 2 Vols. (Vol. I. 4th Imp., Vol. II. 2nd Imp.)

ISAEUS. E. W. Forster.

ISOCRATES. G. B. Norlin. 3 Vols. Vol. I.

JOSEPHUS: H. St. J. Thackeray. 8 Vols. Vols. I.-III.

JULIAN. Wilmer Cave Wright. 3 Vols.

LUCIAN. A. M. Harmon. 8 Vols. Vols. I.-IV. (Vol. I. 3rd Imp., Vol. II. 2nd Imp.)

LYRA GRAECA. J. M. Edmonds. 3 Vols. (Vol. I. 2nd Ed.)

MARCUS AURELIUS. C. R. Haines. (2nd Imp.)

MENANDER. F. G. Allinson.

OPPIAN, COLLUTHUS, TRYPHIODORUS, A. W. Mair.

PAUSANIAS: DESCRIPTION OF GREECE. W. H. S. Jones. 5 Vols. and Companion Vol. Vols. I. and II.

PHILOSTRATUS: THE LIFE OF APOLLONIUS OF TYANA. F. C. Conybeare. 2 Vols. (Vol. I. 3rd Imp., Vol. II. 2nd Imp.)

PHILOSTRATUS AND EUNAPIUS: LIVES OF THE SOPHISTS. Wilmer Cave Wright.

PINDAR. Sir J. E. Sandys. (4th Imp.)

PLATO: CHARMIDES, ALCIBIADES, HIPPARCHUS, THE LOVERS, THEAGES, MINOS AND EPINOMIS. W. R. M. Lamb.

PLATO: CRATYLUS, PARMENIDES, GREATER HIP-
PIAS, LESSER HIPPIAS. H. N. Fowler.

PLATO: EUTHYPHRO, APOLOGY, CRITO, PHAEDO,
PHAEDRUS. H. N. Fowler. (5th Imp.)

PLATO: LACHES, PROTAGORAS, MENO, EUTHY-
DEMUS. W. R. M. Lamb.

PLATO: LAWS. Rev. R. G. Bury. 2 Vols.

PLATO: LYSIS, SYMPOSIUM, GORGIAS. W. R. M.
Lamb.

PLATO: STATESMAN, PHILEBUS. H. N. Fowler;
ION. W. R. M. Lamb.

PLATO: THEAETETUS AND SOPHIST. H. N. Fowler.

PLUTARCH: MORALIA. F. C. Babbitt. 14 Vols. Vol. I.

PLUTARCH: THE PARALLEL LIVES. B. Perrin. 11
Vols. (Vols. I., II. and VII. 2nd Imp.)

POLYBIUS. W. R. Paton. 6 Vols.

PROCOPIUS: HISTORY OF THE WARS. H. B.
Dewing. 7 Vols. I.-IV.

QUINTUS SMYRNAEUS. A. S. Way. Verse trans.

SOPHOCLES. F. Storr. 2 Vols. (Vol. I. 5th Imp., Vol.
II. 3rd Imp.) Verse trans.

ST. BASIL: LETTERS. R. J. Deferrari. 4 Vols. Vols. I.
and II.

ST. JOHN DAMASCENE: BARLAAM AND IOASAPH.
Rev. G. R. Woodward and Harold Mattingly.

STRABO: GEOGRAPHY. Horace L. Jones. 8 Vols.
Vols. I.-V.

THEOPHRASTUS: ENQUIRY INTO PLANTS. Sir
Arthur Hort, Bart. 2 Vols.

THUCYDIDES. C. F. Smith. 4 Vols. (Vol. I. 2nd Imp.)

XENOPHON: CYROPAEDIA. Walter Miller. 2 Vols.
(Vol. I. 2nd Imp.)

XENOPHON: HELLENICA, ANABASIS, APOLOGY
AND SYMPOSIUM. C. L. Brownson and O. J. Todd.
3 Vols.

XENOPHON: MEMORABILIA AND OECONOMICUS.
E. C. Marchant.

XENOPHON: SCRIPTA MINORA. E. C. Marchant.

Greek Authors

ARISTOTLE, OECONOMICA, etc., G. C. Armstrong.

ARISTOTLE, ORGANON, W. M. L. Hutchinson.

ARISTOTLE, PHYSICS, Rev. P. Wicksteed.

ARISTOTLE, POLITICS AND ATHENIAN CONSTI-
TUTION, Edward Capps.

ARRIAN, HIST. OF ALEXANDER AND INDICA, Rev.
E. Iliffe Robson. 2 Vols.

DEMOSTHENES, OLYNTHIACS, PHILIPPICS, LEP-
TINES AND MINOR SPEECHES, J. H. Vince.

DEMOSTHENES, MEIDIAS, ANDROTION, ARISTO-
CRATES, TIMOCRATES, J. H. Vince.

DEMOSTHENES, PRIVATE ORATIONS, G. M. Calhoun.

DIO CHRYSOSTOM, W. E. Waters.

GREEK IAMBIC AND ELEGIAC POETS, J. M. Edmonds.

LYSIAS, W. R. M. Lamb.

PAPYRI, A. S. Hunt.

PHILO, F. M. Colson and Rev. G. H. Whitaker.

PHILOSTRATUS, IMAGINES, Arthur Fairbanks.

PLATO, REPUBLIC, Paul Shorey.

PLATO, TIMAEUS, CRITIAS, CLITIPHO, MENEXE-
NUS, EPISTULAE, Rev. R. G. Bury.

SEXTUS EMPIRICUS, Rev. R. G. Bury.

THEOPHRASTUS, CHARACTERS, J. M. Edmonds;
HERODES; CHOLIAMBIC FRAGMENTS, etc., A. D.
Knox.

Latin Authors

BEDE, ECCLESIASTICAL HISTORY.

CICERO, IN CATILINAM, PRO MURENA, PRO SULLA, B. L. Ullmann.

CICERO, DE NATURA DEORUM, H. Rackham.

CICERO, DE ORATORE, ORATOR, BRUTUS, Charles Stuttaford.

CICERO, IN PISONEM, PRO SCAURO, PRO FONTEIO, PRO MILONE, etc., N. H. Watts.

CICERO, PRO SEXTIO, IN VATINIUM, PRO CAELIO, PRO PROVINCIIS CONSULARIBUS, PRO BALBO, D. Morrah.

CICERO, VERRINE ORATIONS, L. H. G. Greenwood.

CORNELIUS NEPOS, J. C. Rolfe.

ENNIUS, LUCILIUS and other specimens of Old Latin, E. H. Warmington.

FLORUS, E. S. Forster.

LUCAN, J. D. Duff.

OVID: ARS AMATORIA, REMEDIA, AMORIS, etc. J. H. Mozley.

OVID, FASTI, Sir J. G. Frazer.

PLINY, NATURAL HISTORY, W. H. S. Jones and L. F. Newman.

ST. AUGUSTINE, MINOR WORKS.

SIDONIUS, LETTERS. E. V. Arnold and W. B. Anderson.

TACITUS, ANNALS, John Jackson.

VALERIUS FLACCUS, A. F. Scholfield.

VITRUVIUS, DE ARCHITECTURA, F. Granger.

DESCRIPTIVE PROSPECTUS ON APPLICATION

London - - WILLIAM HEINEMANN
New York - - - G. PUTNAM'S SONS